No Half Measures

ALAN "DOGS" JONES

By ANITA HUGHES

ACKNOWLEDGMENTS

I would like to dedicate this book to Susan, Amanda, Lisa and Neil Jones. I would also like to thank Neil Hughes and Kayleigh Taylor for their help in creating this book.

1 NAKED PUNISHMENT

August 1978 Los Rosales Prison, Ceuta, North Africa.

'Well Alan you have surprised yourself now. You've managed to get some kip in this hellhole. Well fucking done!'

Lifting the top half of my naked body to a ninety degree angle my broken ribs crunched and sent shooting pains through my body. I looked down to my balls; thank Christ the swelling had gone down. I had a gentle feel of my enlarged testicles and the dull ache from the kicking and rifle butts had all but gone. Well that's one good thing. After inspecting the bruising on the rest of my body a shot of positivity poured through my veins. I am healing. However my mental state was far beyond repair. I couldn't shake my guilt. Poor fucking Danny! Shot and killed because of my plans to escape.

I slapped the side of my face hard. Come on Alan! Danny wanted it like the rest of us. We had to try. We had to. It's not our fault he succumbed to having the epitaph to die trying. Come on Alan, remain positive! You need to keep you head! Sanity is the only fucking thing these Spics can't take away from you now. Come on, live for Danny!

'The poor blond French bastard!' I shouted out loud as a tear rolled down my cheek.

As I got up from the cold dark flagstones that carpeted my cell I tried not to yelp out loud just in case one of the Spanish guards was outside to hear. They had heard plenty of my screaming several days ago. Bastards! I hated the fact I had to scream but as John McGlaughlin said they would have killed me if I didn't. They would have never have stopped the beating. I owed John my life. Without him shouting to me I would have been another dead prisoner, forgotten and swallowed by the Spanish judicial system.

I had a flashback of the night my injuries were caused and carefully dissected the actions of each guard. I imagined myself executing unspeakable violence and cruelty to each one of them. Above all, one would pay the most. That was the director's son. The image of him whipping me with the thick metal chain and huge fuck off padlock would never leave my mind. It sickened me to remember his manic eyes shining in the night as he lashed and lashed my ribs with zeal and pleasure. I thought he would never stop.

There were two reasons why I despised the director's son the most. Firstly was because of his age. I was in my mid-thirties and he was barely twenty. Being beaten by someone still wet behind the ears was a huge dent to my ego. Even though I knew I would have easily beaten the weedy bugger if we had fought mano y mano. The other reason was because he found his weapon of choice resting unused on a prison door. It was not enough to strike me with a club or rifle butt like the other guards used. Oh no, this little prick wanted to be inventive and find something that would really crush some bones. Each time he struck me with the solid padlock I could feel my ribs crack. The pain was sickening.

I bet after the savage beating he ran to tell Daddy how he and four other guards hit the fuck out of me. Sad really as that venom I have for him still remains to this day. I really should let my bitterness subside and replace it with another more pleasurable experience. Such as my time in Oslo with Bo and two other prostitutes. But that's another story.

Before I allowed myself to think about how long I was to spend in my solitary punishment cell I decided I needed something to do. I had already spent four days in here, but they were consumed with writhing in agony and clinging onto consciousness. But fuck me there was not a lot to do when the only furniture that adorned my cell was stones. I did not have a sink, a bed or even bedding. My toilet was just a stinking hole in the floor. I had nothing!

However I was not going to allow myself to dwell, that was the sure road to madness, if I was going to spend the next few years in here I was going to try and retain my sanity. I was not going to mark on the walls the days I had spent in here; that would be far too depressing. Although this was common in the many British prisons I had been too, I never saw the point. By marking down the days spent in prison till release would surely only prolong the agony?

Mind you I never saw one marked wall or calendar in Los Rosales prison. That was probably because the people in this prison, either like me didn't actually know how long their sentence was to be, or that it would be a time consuming hobby as I had heard the majority of Spanish prisoners faced sentences between thirty to one hundred years. Now that would take a lot of wall to write on.

So stones it was to play with. I marked out a grid that consisted of sixty four squares with eight rows and columns. I neatly shaded the alternate squares. Well I could afford to do it properly there was sod all else to do. I rounded up all the stones and placed them on the squares a row in from the side on both sides. I then with foil molded crude shapes resembling to me two kings, two queens, four rooks, four bishops and four knights. The foil was from used cigarettes packets. I had collected the foil yesterday when I was allowed my one hour solitary exercise in the normally communal patio. A patio is what the Spanish referred to as a prison exercise yard.

After several hours work I stood back and admired my chess board. My satisfaction lasted only a few seconds as my shining moment was disturbed by the jangle of keys rapping the door and two short sharp thuds.

'Senor Cohones!' a gruff voice shouted from behind the door.

The door sharply opened and two Spanish guards entered my pit. They looked at me like scum naked, bruised and dirty. Whilst they stood there clean in starched pressed uniforms, their turquoise blue shirts free from filth and their shiny buttons glistening in the sun. The blond guard was tapping his baton into his open hand whilst the shorter fatter more Spanish looking guard was carrying a bucket of water. I stood up, closed my eyes and held my breath so my ribs wouldn't be shocked. I knew what was coming next. I heard the familiar whoosh as the guard threw the bucket of ice cold water onto me. I don't know why they did this. Maybe it was my crude form of a shower as there were no washing facilities in my cell. Possibly it was to add to my punishment. But I would have preferred to have gone without. Standing naked in front of the two guards as they doused with me with water was a bit too homoerotic for my liking. Although I would catch them staring at my cock, they seemed to prefer looking at their trophy of bruises on my chest. With that I shuddered and shook myself like a dog; wiping with my hands the drips of water that were tickling my skin. I had no towel to dry myself off. I just had to dry through the heat of the Moroccan sun coming through the bars of my pit.

Then after the bucket wash my breakfast was brought in. It's soup. Thank god it is soup. Soup was the one of the least disgusting meals you could have in this place. I especially liked the black crunchy things the soup contained. They did taste quite salty but they were very flavoursome. They must have been a local herb or some kind of weird Moroccan pepper. The other meals you could have would be paella or grey slop, each containing ungutted fish or pig trotters.

The guard with the soup and bottle of water walked towards me. His thumb firmly gripped on the bowl causing him to make contact with my food. I tried not to think about his fingers and his grubby blooded hands contaminating my already probable health hazard of a meal. He carefully lowered it gently to the direction of the ground. Right at the very last minute he smacked down the bowl allowing most of the contents to go over me, on the floor and on my neatly crafted chessboard. Thankfully it was lukewarm so it didn't scold against my naked skin, but he did piss me off dirtying my chessboard. However I wasn't going to give him the satisfaction of knowing he'd upset me. I contained the venom that flowed through my veins by gulping hard and sinking it into the pit of my stomach.

'Gracias,' I said grinning wildly.

My sarcasm did not translate to the thick bastard as he seemed annoyed and confused at my gratitude whilst strutting back to the door. The other taller blond guard stared at me for a while, still tapping his baton in his open hand a few times more. Eventually he turned away and sauntered with arrogance out of the cell, his keys smashing his thigh with every stride. After several seconds the door was slammed shut with a bang, the echo from this crashing noise would ricochet around the room making my whole body jolt. Every time they would go to shut the door it seemed to take longer and longer, prolonging my anticipation of the clamour.

I waited until their footsteps faded away and all I could hear was my own white noise again. It felt sweet relief when I knew they were far away. I settled myself and sat cross legged on the floor and ate my soup, crunching hard on the black bits and slurping down the other unknown lumps. The water went down in one as I was so thirsty. The last four days was a haze so maybe my liquid intake wasn't so good. Putting my bottle and bowl to the side of the room, my stomach gurgled and groaned and my throat felt scratched and dry. I was still hungry and thirsty.

Right, where was I? Oh yes playing chess. Right so as I am playing chess with myself I will have to remember who went last. I mean which side I played on last. Maybe I should call myself two names. Oh fuck! Maybe playing chess against myself wasn't a good way to stop the onset of madness. I am not even into a game yet and I am already planting the seed for a split personality. Oh well at least I will have someone to talk to.

I sat on the side I called Alan 1, very original I know but I was excited to have something to do so sod the labelling. Right what to do? I moved the small stone / pawn that was in front of my king one square. I then moved over to the Alan 2's side. I pondered for a moment and moved my pawn that was in front of the castle. That is interesting. Now what is he thinking there. That was a bit of a strange move. Then Alan 1 moved the bishop on the side of the king three squares going diagonally. I scurried round to Alan 2's side and moved the rook into a ninety degree L shape. As I played and played I started not to notice myself moving from side to side but genuinely believing I was playing as a disembodied self. It was hypnotic and consuming constantly thinking and thinking on ways to out think myself.

Then a loud bang came from above. My reality and consciousness flooded back into my body. For a few milliseconds after the jolt I could feel myself looking around the room as if I had been outside it. In some strange way I had as the chessboard had engorged me into its world.

I jumped up to try and look through the bars of my cell window to understand what the bang was. Had someone got on the roof? Had someone jumped off? Were they pushed to their death? The bang came again but it was definitely from above so there was no point in wasting my energy trying to look out the window. I stood still and arched my head to one side directing my ear in line with the sounds. After several minutes listening and concentrating, there was nothing but silence.

Annoyed at being awakened from my game I shook my head in dismay and returned back to the game and sat back down. Right where was I? Oh yes it was the turn of Alan 1. I looked at my pieces and then over to Alan 2's. What could I do now? How could I trap him?

I held in my index finger and thumb a pawn that took my interest and flitted back and fore with glances to my side and to Alan 2's. Whilst staring at my piece below I could see in my peripheral vision one of my chess pieces moving. Oh fuck Alan you have gone mad. Frightened to look, I paused for breath. I closed my eyes and told myself I was mistaken. With a flash of bravery I stared hard back at the stone. There was no movement thank fuck. Then a few moments later the stone turned around and I could see a face. If I had enough stomach contents I think they would have been in my mouth at this point. With more courage I got up and moved in to have a closer look in the dim light of my cell. On closer inspection I could see the stone was in fact a rat. I was very glad I wasn't hallucinating but I fucking hated rats. But in that moment I was thankful for the germ infested rodent, at least it was something different than a stone to look at.

The rat looked back at me, his whiskers going ten to the dozen with his beady eyes gentle and glazed. I looked around my cell trying to work out where the little bastard had come from. Then the rat came in closer.

'Hi little fella. You come to visit another dirty rat?'

I stayed still not to frighten the little mite, although quite frightened myself. However my curiosity triumphed as I kept my nerve and stayed still revelling in the fact that I had never seen a rat so close up. I was amazed at how fast his whiskers oscillated.

He then shuffled over to my bowl. He turned back to look at me. I did not move. He then started licking my bowl. With every few licks bobbing his head up to see what I was doing. I sat rigid and let the little bugger lick my soup bowl clean, I had finished it anyway. I was fascinated by the rat, his every action left me mesmerised. He looked round again and stared into my bewildered eyes. Then slowly and lightly he scuttled closer and closer towards me whilst sniffing in the air. Without warning he ran up my leg. He stopped again carefully watching my face and body for any signs of imminent movement. Once he saw all was calm he proceeded to shuffle up towards my thigh.

Although it was only a rat, it felt nice to be in the presence of another living creature. It was a comfort not to be alone. Although I had regular visits from the guards I did not look at them as possessing life, rather the takers of life, sometimes in its literal sense. Like Danny.

As the rat travelled up my leg I started to feel a little anxious being naked. The guards had stripped me of my filthy clothes and left them outside the door as a sort of added extra to my solitary confinement. Personally I think the beating, the stark loneliness in this solitary confinement cell and no bed was enough, but oh you have to hand it to them they punish properly.

The rat stopped at my kneecap and raised his two front claws, moving his head from side to side whist sniffing in the air. I cupped my genitalia to avoid tempting the rat with my dangly offerings. If he had tried to nibble them I would have had no hesitation in throwing him across the room. This would have upset me as I would hate to cause harm to any animal.

The rat went back down on to four claws and travelled half way up my thigh. Once he reached my hip bone it felt too close for comfort. I slapped my thigh sending shockwaves through my skin. The rat stopped in his tracks, turned round and scarpered off a hundred miles an hour into the darkened corner of the cell. I shuffled onto my feet as quick as I could; I darted my gaze into the shadows but I still couldn't fathom the little buggers entrance. I have since learned that rats can get into holes that are only a half an inch wide.

'That's right ratty. I had enough problems coping with the men in here wanting to explore my gonads never mind you 'n' all. You can fuck right off!'

'You lost it English bastard. You gone Ceuta mad!' shouted a disembodied voice from above.'

'Hey man! Who is that? Where are you?'

'It's Chino man. My cell's above you.'

'Nice to hear you…….. Oh and I am not English I am Welsh. And I am not mad I was talking to a rat.'

That statement sounded better in my head. After several seconds the words caught up with Chino, and he began to bellow with laughter. His chuckles and snorts brought a glow in my heart and made me break a smile on my dirty face. I had missed his broken English and strange accent that incorporated both Chinese and Moroccan twangs. I wish I could have seen his friendly face as he had such an infectious smile. Out of all the lads in the prison Chino's smile seemed to beam the most, but this could have been down to the fact he was constantly stoned. Being one of Ceuta prison's main drug dealers he could afford too as he always had a constant supply.

'You okay down there,' asked Chino.

'Yeah I'm alright.'

'The boys were worried……they thought………'

'I'm alright it will take more than a good beating to keep me down,' I quickly replied filling in the silence.

'Hey Alan you want Bob?'

'Who the hell is Bob?'

'The one and only Bob man.'

What the bloody hell was that supposed to mean? Had Chino turned the other cheek, literally? Then my thoughts about Chino being gay subsided as the mellow tones of Bob Dylan blared out loudly from above travelling down the concrete wall softening them a little and bringing light into the darkness of my cell.

After a few verses of Mr Tambourine man the music screeched to halt.

'Oi you I was enjoying that!' I screamed

'Alan I want your help to tell me what he says.'

'What?'

'I want you to tell me what he is singing about. I don't get it.'

'Oh I see……………..Err……..get me a joint and I shall tell you.'

Several minutes went by. The silence killed me. I thought I could cope alone in here for god knows how long. But having the conversation with Chino, Bob's music and the thought of hashish made me feel depressed. This distraction had made me realise I missed my compadres in the communal cells. It's funny that I craved to be in my own cell rather than be in the cells when I was in the main prison of Ceuta. Now I have the opportunity to be on my own I realised this is not what I wanted, especially under these conditions. It was laughable that I thought the main prison was bad. I also wanted to ask him about Danny but I couldn't pluck up the courage. I wanted to hold out hope he was still alive and didn't want it to be confirmed he was dead.

'Hey Alan look outside your window,' shouted down Chino.

I looked outside the barred window to see what Chino was on about. I could not believe my eyes, as I saw on a fashioned rope dangling the best present in the world. She was beautiful. A big fat juicy rolled up joint full of the Moroccan best, lit up in all her glory. Like a kid on Christmas morning I stared at my present marvelling in the moment before enjoying its splendid properties.

'Can I drop the rope yet?'

'Not yet man. Hang on! Hang on!'

I woke up from my dream and scampered to the window. It took me several attempts to jump up and catch the dangling string with joint in tow. I stretched my arm and body to grab her, straining my broken ribs and making my bruised body throb. Once I held her in my hand the pain in my body and mind melted away for an instant. As I held her to my lips I paused for a second before drawing in the biggest toke of my life. My lungs hated me with every second as the air reverberated on my battered ribs. It was worth it though. This was the best joint of my life.

'How's that man?'

'It's alright,' I said nonchalantly.

I really wanted to kiss his dirty filthy feet for this present, but I would never tell him that. He wanted my help with Bob so I had to make him think that he needed me more than I needed the blow and this conversation.

'So we have a deal, you gonna tell me about Bob?'

'Yeah you got a deal but...'

'But...what?'

'But I will only start on my second joint.'

'Alan you push your luck, but deal,' Chino said laughing.

With that, he played the song all the way once and then as promised he lowered down a second joint. I again clamoured to the window to retrieve my prize but this time with less vigour. As I grabbed the joint I could see she was extinguished from all her glory.

'Oi Chino it's not lit!'

'What?'

'I need fire.'

'Oh I'll send matches down. God Alan you are really hard work.'

Again he kept his word as a bundle of matches was promptly sent down. I retrieved them from the high window and lit the end of the joint until it was the colour of amber. I then lay down on my bed of flagstones ready to enjoy being stoned and the understated beauty of Bob Dylan's songs.

'Are you ready now Alan?'

'Yes. What do you want to know?'

'Why is he talking about a guy with a tambourine?'

'Well let me see.........he is talking in the song about a guy playing the tambourine as a song......... However a guy with a tambourine can't really play a song can he................. So maybe the tambourine doesn't represent a musician but rather someone or something that inspired or influenced Bob Dylan.................. A person maybe .... Or it could be drugs.'

'Drugs! It's about drugs!' shouted Chino above excitedly.'

'Really?'

'Maybe.............I mean when he says 'plays a song for me' is he really asking for drugs? Also when he says 'I am sleepy and there's no place I am going to'. It's like us man were stuck in here bored off our tits........ So what are we to do?'

'Get high!' said Chino excitedly.

'Damn right!'

Chino laughed and then remained quiet for several minutes. Although I could not see him I imagined his face smiling and connecting with Bob on a deeper plane more than just with the tuneful music.

'So what drugs Alan?'

'Well............ he says 'jingle jangle mornings'. To me that sounds like a hangover so alcohol and possibly hash as it sounds a bit spacey.'

'Also he talks about the 'magic swirling ship'. So that's sounds a bit trippy to me maybe…….maybe he likes the old LSD. '

'Really?'

'Hey Chino, you and Dylan would have got on great you love Hash and a bit of Californian sunshine'

'He does sound pretty cool Alan.'

'Time for another one?'

The second song he played by Bob Dylan was Señor (Tales Of Yankee Power).

Señor (Tales Of Yankee Power)

Senor, senor, can you tell me where we're headin?
Lincoln County Road or Armageddon?
Seems like I been down this way before
Is there any truth in that, senor?

Senor, senor, do you know where she is hidin'?
How long are we gonna be riding?
How long must I keep my eyes glued to the door?
Will there be any comfort there senor?

The music cut out and Chino stopped talking. I could tell something was wrong.

Maybe something was going down upstairs. Fight? Rape? Who knows? Well I couldn't get involved so I shrugged my shoulders. Still stoned and infused with inspiration by Dylan's music I flailed around the room like a mad man. Singing at the top of my voice and dancing to a melodic beat that only I could hear. Over and over I repeated the words from the last song he played 'How long must I keep my eyes glued to the door? Will there be any comfort there senor?'

Then there was a rap at the door. It was the guards coming to give me my evening meal of fish gut slosh probably. I didn't care that they were coming in I was free and happy so I carried on singing and flailing. Once they opened the door and looked at me they then looked at each other confused. I decided to strut around the room once more in the style of Mick Jagger. I was happy and in my stoned mind thought maybe I could get a laugh out of these guys. With that I continued dancing until I stopped in the middle of the room and wailed at the top of my lungs 'Senor! Senor!' whilst smiling and giggling. As I looked back, I noticed the blond guard shaking his head. Whilst the shorter stockier more authentic looking Spanish guard charged towards me.

I stood still as he launched onto me. He grabbed my left shoulder in a vice like grip and swung with all his might a right hook across my chin which sent shockwaves through my cheekbone. Shocked more than anything, I did not wince in pain and clutched my jaw in confusion. Then not looking satisfied with his first punch he hit me again, this time in the shoulder. I was angry now and decided to stand my ground I wasn't been knocked down easily. Stupid I know as this was not a fair fight but I continued to take the beating and remain standing. However after a dig in my exposed bruised ribs I went down like a sack of shit. The pain was agonising. I couldn't bear to breathe. Coming round from the shock I could see the guard looking down at me on the floor. With a smile on his face and a nod he seemed to accept this was enough brutality for the day. And thank god too. With that he beckoned to the other guard that they should leave.

The taller blond guard smiled at the abuse I received and swiftly turned around to leave the cell. They probably left feeling all warm and fuzzy inside from a nice days beating.

I remained on the floor clutching my aching ribs until their footsteps had trailed into nothing. I was bemused for several minutes as to what had just happened. I mean there was no reason for it. How the fuck can they justify beating me up for doing a bit of dancing! Unless they thought I was taking the piss by shouting 'Señor Señor'? But still! Can't they fucking handle a bit of banter! Actually what the fuck was I saying! I knew in my two months in Los Rosales that the guards hated happy prisoners and shunned any conversation, let alone banter. Their only means of communication seemed to be via their fists. But it didn't matter how much they beat me I wasn't going to shut up. They could break my body but they couldn't break my spirit. I was determined to find a way out of Los Rosales.

I looked down at my naked and battered body crouched on all fours like a dog. Two months ago I could never have imagined in wildest nightmares to have been in this situation. My life two months ago was all about wearing sharp suits, travelling the world and meeting the most glamorous of women. If it wasn't for being caught smuggling cannabis across North Africa on what was to be my last ever trip this place would have never entered my head. The trip that was to set me up for life ended up to be my downfall. Right now I should have been with my working girl Bo travelling Europe pondering on legitimate business ventures after making £90,000. In today's money £90,000 is just shy of half a million pounds.

I wonder if things would have panned out differently if my associates had accepted the offer from Howard Marks, instead of us three going it alone.

2 MY CRIMINAL C.V. AND LIFE OF PISS STORIES

My name is Alan Jones and I was born 19th of April 1942. I was not born in a hospital or house like most. I was born in a pub called the Llewellyn Arms Hotel, in the town of Pentre deep in the Rhondda Valleys, South Wales. Maybe this unusual birthplace contributed to my decision in choosing the alternative lifestyle of a criminal. It could also be the reason why I feel such a close bond to drinking establishments; as whenever I walk past a pub or club I feel drawn to it and have to dive inside. My fascination could also be explained by my love of drink and meeting crazy alcoholics.

One of my first crimes was dodging the train fare when I was 15 on the journey from Ton Pentre railway station to Paddington Station. Ton Pentre being in South Wales and Paddington of course is just outside of London. For over four hours on a journey just under 200 miles I had to hide from the ticket collector and any people I thought would be a jobs worth and dob me in. I hid in the toilets, the luggage compartments and under chairs. It was really hard work.

I was going to London as I was running away from home. I was sick and tired of the arguments and fights between me and my father. Things had got particularly worse at this age as I had decided to leave school and not take my exams. He was livid. I think he thought by constantly being on my case about my education I would continue, but in the end it just made me further defiant to not even try and leave. But not wanting to take my exams wasn't just about apathy; naturally I wasn't that bright and found it hard to concentrate for long periods of time. I also hated the claustrophobia of a class room. I would rather be outside running around with my mates. I didn't want to passively listen whilst the teacher spouted knowledge in a dusty classroom. I did however enjoy playing sports. I loved the rush of endorphins from doing any physical exercise and with sports I felt in charge. I was doing something. I wasn't controlled. It did not matter what sport I was taught in school I would master it with ease and conviction.

It wasn't just his pushiness that would annoy me it was his whole attitude to life. I could not understand at all where he was coming from. He was so strict and regimented. This probably stemmed from years and years of serving in the army. I on the other hand was more relaxed with life and liked to push the boundaries instead of conforming to the norm. I hated routine. I liked things that were out of ordinary, new and exciting.

Even at 11 years of age I was defiant against my father's wishes for education as I point blank refused to sit the 11 plus examination. If you achieved well in the 11 plus you went to grammar school and if you didn't you were sent to secondary modern. I thought by going to secondary modern and being labelled a thicky my father would give up. I probably wouldn't have passed my 11 plus anyways but I eliminated all chances. However my plan did not work even by going to secondary modern he still did not ease up.

Despite being hundreds of miles from home and only 15 I was elated when I stepped off the train onto Paddington station. Part of this elation was that I did not have to hide anymore. I stretched my body which ached slightly. It felt great that I could walk around freely. I did not have my father breathing down my neck. No one here knew me or could not tell my parents what trouble I had got in to. I was completely alone. I had peace.

As I walked as part of a large crowd I was amazed at how everyone around me was walking so fast. Also despite my curious stares nobody looked back at me. Instead with a blinkered look they strode forward fast as if they had a divine purpose which had a time limit. It was so strange. In the Rhondda where I was from everyone walked at a much slower pace and would make a point of looking at everyone who passed. We would even in the Rhondda be courteous and say hello to complete strangers.

There was a story I heard which I would like to think is true about Katherine Jenkins. Apparently when she first went around London she would say hello to people she did not know on the streets as she was used to in her small Welsh town and then was stunned by the glares she received back. This stuns me too as who would refuse saying hello back to such a gorgeous woman. Well now due to her fame I bet she doesn't have that problem anymore.

After hours and hours of wandering around, the buzz of London wore off as the reality set in, I did not have any money, food or a place to stay. I decided the best option was to stay at my Auntie Iris's who lived in a basement flat in Hans place, Knightsbridge. It was only two miles or so away from Paddington station.

When I turned up on my Auntie's doorstep her face was a picture. She looked around and around for my mother, her sister and my father. Once the penny dropped I was alone, her mouth dropped more with shock. I explained to her that I had run away. I told her about how me and dad were at each other's throats and I could not stick it anymore. I told her I was sick of him constantly trying to bully me. After she got over the initial shock of seeing me she said I could stay, as long as it was okay with Mam. I begged and begged her not to ring as I did not want anyone to know where I was. However deep down I was glad she did. My Mam would have worried greatly. I wanted to punish my father but not her. My Mam had done no wrong. She loved me for who I was and never pushed me towards anything I didn't want to. Unlike him.

Whilst in London my Auntie showed me her boss's luxury penthouse flat in Mayfair. She was the PA to the managing director of ICI so she had access to the keys and she knew he would not be there on the weekend. I remember being so excited going into such a posh looking building I counted the steps to the flat. There were 97. How messed up is that, I can still remember this and yet struggle with the missus's birthday.

Anyways, once in the flat I was not disappointed. It was gorgeous. It was so modern and different to the living rooms of the terraced houses in the Rhondda I was used to. Also the best thing about the flat was the view. You could see the whole of London from up high. It was awe-inspiring. I loved looking out at the city. I felt like a king. This flat is what I wanted in the future. I wanted to be like my aunties boss. I wanted to be rich, powerful and have a penthouse suite. This was fantastic.

Unfortunately my stay had to end. On the 15th day my auntie turned to me and told me I had to go home. It hurt as she piped on about how she did want me to stay but that I had to go back as my mother missed me. She also said she could not keep me as by law I had to stay in my parents care till I was 16. She told me to chase my dreams of making enough money to live in a penthouse flat like her boss. I smiled at her encouragement but knew that would not be my destiny. Without an education and being a local Rhondda boy, the only options left for me was to work in a factory or down a coal mine. Dejected I travelled back home and stayed with my parents.

My next offence was more serious. At the age of 16 I broke into several solicitors' offices in Pontypridd. Pontypridd incidentally being the birthplace of Tom Jones. I was not alone and did it together with my school friends Vernon Gwyer and Dai John (better known as Dai Cave). From the solicitor's offices we stole petty cash and alcohol. It was Dai's idea. After a day of bunking off school he told us how he had seen well-dressed solicitors sipping fine wine and whiskey celebrating with clients through the window of their offices. He also told us about the box of money they pulled out of their desk drawers intermittently throughout the day. Both Vernon and I were up for the mischief but for Dai the stealing was more for survival. He needed the money as his mother didn't work and his father had buggered off years ago. Plus any money his mother could get hold of would be spent on alcohol and be pissed up the wall. The reason why we called him Dai Cave was because his mother never looked after him and he was always in shabby clothes and had a stinking house. He did actually look like he could have lived in a cave.

Although I did not need the money like Dai, I wanted easy money. I also wanted the free supply of alcohol so I could enjoy it with my mates. I think this was the turning point in my life, when I started to realise maybe crime does pay. Maybe I didn't need an education to chase my dream of being rich.

However it was Vernon who had the least to gain from breaking into the solicitors. His father was the manager of Gelli colliery so he never wanted for anything. He always had pocket money and was well dressed. He was also quite intelligent and did very well in school so he had options. The only motive for him would be to do it for face. He always wanted to appear the hard man. Which on some accounts was rightly so as he was a gutsy fighter when we got in to scraps.

It took several months before the police eventually caught us. We did have a good run though; with money in our back pockets and a constant supply of alcohol. If only the solicitors saw the way we downed bottle after bottle of their fine malt whiskies in the back lanes. They probably would have thought that was more criminal than the stealing of their petty cash.

All three of us were arrested by the police and later sent to the Courts of Quarter Sessions in Cardiff to account for our charges of burglary. The quarter sessions were as their name suggests held four times a year and presided over by a Justice of the Peace. They were court sessions where small and petty crimes were normally heard.

Despite being arrested, sent to court and having a right bollocking off by my parents; I didn't care. Even in the seriousness of the court I was not worried about what I had done, what people thought of me or even what was to happen next. In court I did not take a blind bit of notice as to what was going on. Instead I fidgeted with my hands in my pockets and looked all around the room. I even walked out of the court several times. Sometimes I told them I needed the toilet and other times I just wandered out. My only motivation to do this was because I was bored and I wanted to show off to Vern and Dai that I didn't give a toss. They too followed my lead and played around.

The seriousness of my situation only dawned on me when I was sentenced. We were all given 9 months to 3 years in Borstal. The length of the sentence would depend on our behaviour.

After being sentenced we were whisked away by uniformed police officers and taken to Cardiff prison. Despite the prison being for adults and housing very dangerous criminals, we were sent there until they decided which borstal to despatch us to. The first shock was the strip search by the prison officers. Then as further humiliation they took our civilian clothes and handed out the prison uniform to dress in. We even had prison issued underwear which consisted of greyish white itchy y fronts which were slightly too loose for my slim teenage frame.

Once dressed we were all taken to our cell. Luckily, it was only us three in the cell. We did not have to worry about sharing it with an unwelcomed guest.

On the first night we all played fuck jumping around the bunk beds and then on to the floor. We ran around the room like we didn't have a care in the world whilst exploring the basic room we were provided. Really, inside I did care and I was a little disconcerted but I wouldn't let Vern and Dai know. I could see in their eyes they were doing the same. Putting on a brave face. It was more evident when the lights went out and the cell door slammed. We were all deathly quiet. Never in our history of friendship did we have a quiet moment. We were all probably doing the same; processing the events of the day and what lay ahead for us whilst being in prison. That night I felt so trapped.

At first prison was quite exciting not knowing what was going to happen next. Mingling in and around big dangerous looking men who had violent exciting stories to tell. However after a few days it became boring as I soon got used to the same regime. Each day we would get up at the same time, have breakfast at the same time, be set to work at the same time, have dinner and other breaks at the same time. Then lights out at the same time. Plus the work we had to do for the majority of the day was mind numbing and tedious. The jobs consisted of sorting out screws by putting them in their correct compartments, hour after hour.

I remember after two weeks my head went whilst I was doing the job of sorting screws. The monotony got to me and I needed a break. In order to have some peace I stuck my hand up and asked a screw if I could go to the toilet. Once in the corridor I shuffled around procrastinating, enjoying a few moments peace from the screws in both senses of the word. Shortly after a prisoner officer walked past. In order to waste a bit more time, I headed towards the urinal for a place to hide so I didn't get shoved back into work if the same officer came past again. Plus by this time I did actually need to pee. Once at the urinal I sighed and flopped out my Mr Happy and proceeded to have a piss. As I let out an ahh of relief the door softly opened and shut as someone entered the room. I turned my head whilst still directing the stream in the urinal and looked as the tall guy walked in the room. It was strange, I was sure I had seen his face somewhere before, but I couldn't think where. Not wanting to stare I looked back at my yellow fountain. Whilst keeping my head forward I sneakily looked again, as the prisoner stood next to me. Where did I recognise him from? Several seconds went by and the familiar stranger did not make any signs of getting his dick out to have a piss. I looked to his face again and was disturbed by his soulless eyes and sunken cheeks. I felt so uncomfortable that the hairs on the back of my neck were standing up. This did not feel right. Why wasn't he flopping out his knob and watering the bowl. In my head I was shouting at my bladder to hurry up and empty as I wanted to be ready if this guy was going to try something. Then I heard the door go again and hurried steps. Before I could turn around I was grabbed and dragged out of the toilets. My line of piss shot up the wall, on the mystery guy and onto me. There was piss flying everywhere. Once dragged outside I was slammed half-heartedly into the corridor wall. Angrily I raised my fists and with courage I turned to see what bastard had covered me in my own piss. As I turned around about to strike a hefty blow I could see it was a screw so I retreated my fist. A little on edge he pointed me to do up my fly. Once, I was decent and more composed the screw explained why he dragged me out. He said he did it as the guy standing next to me was John Straffen.

John Straffen was a serial killer and paedophile. He strangled and bludgeoned to death three little girls; two five year olds and a nine year old. His victims were Cicely Batstone, Brenda Goddard and Linda Bowyer. Linda Bowyer was murdered when Straffen escaped from Broadmoor high security hospital. He only went missing for a few hours but managed to murder the defenseless five year old. Despite his M.O. being for little girls they were worried he would target me. Although a boy, I was young, slim and had a baby face making me look considerably younger than 16.

Despite the prison officer looking out for me, I did not appreciate his help at the time. I felt strong and invincible in the naivety of youth that if he took me on I could have beaten him. To this day I don't know whether Straffen would have tried anything but it still makes me wonder.

After a month Vern was moved from Cardiff Prison to his borstal but me and Dai stayed. Our new prison roommate was Michael Loveridge. He was in his mid-twenties and had thick wavy black hair. He had a muscular frame and dark eyes. In the same prison was his brother Nigel. They were thick as thieves if you pardon the pun. Always up to something; always in trouble. It was probably the reason why the screws split them up and put one in with us. Outside of prison Michael and Nigel Loveridge were very well known gangsters in the Cardiff area.

On the first night when Michael came into our cell it felt really awkward. He was really quiet and quite tense in his body. It was as if he was primed at any moment to attack. After a few hours Dai and I ignored the fact we had a new cell mate and played fuck. Laughing and taking the piss out of each other as we would normally do. We also punched each other in arms and mucked about play fighting. Whilst doing this Michael gave out a big huff at our childish games as he laid on his bed. As I turned around to Michael I was faced with a scowl. It felt like a warning to stop. Dai eventually looked over. He obviously felt the same threat as his demeanour shrank and he stopped giving me a dead arm. I decided to go on the top bunk and get ready for bed. Dai did the same and got under his covers on the lower bunk. After a few minutes of silence Dai and I started to quietly chat. I decided in a moment of madness to scare the fuck out of Dai by jumping off the bunk straight on to the floor. I tried not to laugh as I imagined how much of a big girl he would sound screaming when I did this. After an internal count to three I leapt off the bunk. As I hit the floor the front part of my right foot caught the piss pot. The painted green metal piss pot brimming with piss flew up in air rotated and splashed everywhere. Most of it went on Michael. I gasped as I gawped at Michael's face streaming with yellow piss. He spat on the floor as he got off the bed clenching his fists and growling. First of all I looked to either side for a way to run or hide. There was nowhere. Then as he stood up from the bed I realised I would have to just stand and fight. I stood firm as he leapt onto me and grabbed my biceps shaking my body ferociously. With his right fist he went to take a swing but luckily Dai stopped him by jumping up and grabbing round his neck. Dai hung on and didn't let go. Angered further, Michael turned around and around to try and shake Dai off. Eventually he did. Then for several minutes all three of us wrestled and scrapped.

Out of breath Michael pulled to one side and put his arm out declaring no more. With adrenalin still pumping in our bodies me and Dai stood firm with serious faces awaiting the next blow. Michael put his hands on his knees still breathing heavily whist staring at us. After an uncomfortable silence he smiled and then started to uncontrollably laugh. Not knowing how to respond we did the same. Well, it was fucking funny covering someone with piss. Once he had his breath back he walked over and put his arms around us.

'Fair play boys! You don't give up. You're like me and my brother,' he said half chuckling.

'I will forget what you did this time. But listen to me. Never ever do that again!'

Shocked at how I came off so lightly by covering a gangster full of piss I nodded ferociously.

'Agreed!'

Another set of brothers in Cardiff prison were the Boucher brothers. Like with the Loveridges they were very close and not people to mess with. It was the Boucher brothers who showed me my first prison riot. During one of our relentless work sessions sorting out screws and bolts the Boucher brothers revolted by climbing up the inner metal frame that encased the room and stirring up other prisons by shouting and ranting. As they shouted and ranted it was like a fucking bar room brawl everyone started fighting. Screws with prisoners. Prisoners with prisoners. It was chaos. I loved it! It was like I was starring in my own western watching people being knocked out and thrown over tables. However me and Dai couldn't enjoy the show for too long as we were the first to be grabbed by the screws and taken to the safety of our cell.

After two months me and Dai were eventually released from Cardiff prison and sent to HMP Latchmere House in Richmond, Surrey. Latchmere house was a resettlement prison. It was a youth prison where delinquent young people were sent in order to be assessed so they could be sent to the appropriate Borstal. Borstal was another youth prison institution but it would be where you would spend the majority of your sentence.

The main aim of Latchmere was to teach you how to behave before you were sent to your chosen borstal. At Latchmere they were strict and disciplined boys by adopting military style regimes. A boot camp if you will. For instance you had to make your beds every day, everywhere had to be spotlessly clean, your belongings had to be tidied away neatly, clothes folded and most importantly your piss pot had to be gleaming.

We would also be assigned jobs in the day. I worked in the kitchens and as a labourer cutting the sugar beet on the farm. Ironically, scruffy Dai Cave was set to work as a cleaner.

If you did not comply with the tasks set or behaved badly; the punishment would be no recreation time. The first two weeks there I was punished every day and experienced no recreation time. Although not a lover of people telling me what to do, I did everything they asked and god damn it I did it well. The only thing I would be penalised on every time would be my fucking piss pot. On inspection they expected it to be clean and gleaming. Well mine was fucking clean but it did not gleam. It was scruffy looking and the metal was tarnished with green and brown paint marks.

After two weeks of being punished for this I was livid. Listening to the other boys playing records, laughing and messing about wound me up further. I decided enough was enough. I needed to knick someone else's piss pot to get recreation.

The next morning I emptied my scruffy fucking painted piss pot in the shower and plonked it outside. I looked to either side as a few other boys were doing the same, having a shower with their piss pots outside. Perfect. I quickly jumped in the shower, soaped a little and then jumped out drying myself as fast as I could with a towel.

A few cubicles past me I saw the most beautiful piss pot I had ever seen. I could hear its owner singing away in the shower. I looked in either direction to make sure I wasn't been watched and quickly snatched it leaving behind mine in its place. With stolen piss pot in hand I legged it back to my room.

I smiled to myself as I admired my new piss pot. This time I will get my recreation. As I did up my last button on my shirt getting dressed a very tall ginger monster entered my cell. With my piss pot in his gigantic hands he slammed it on the floor whilst he scowled at his piss pot laying at my feet. Of all the fucking people to upset, I upset him. He was the biggest in the

Borstal. He was also the daddy, meaning that he was in charge and someone who everyone looked up to. Why couldn't it have been a weedy kid?

'You! You little bugger have something that belongs to me!'

'No I don't!' I retorted defiantly.

'Yes you do,' he hissed.

'Now give me back my piss pot.'

'This piss pot is mine now!'

'Give me back my piss pot or else!'

'Else what?'

My words ignited a rage. The tall stocky red faced boy lunged towards me. With shock I picked up the piss pot and hit him square in the face. After the hit he stumbled backwards and had a very shocked expression on his face. Then little cuts appeared on his lips and cheeks which immediately gushed with blood. His face seemed to drop. What the fuck had I done! With his hands he mopped up some of the gushing blood and then looked back at his red palms. Faced with his blood stained hands his eyebrows widened in shock. I looked back at the piss pot to work out what I had done. I hadn't hit him that hard. Before I could make any sense of it screws were sent in and we were separated. I was taken to a punishment cell and the ginger monster presumably to the hospital for a fair amount of stitches.

After several hours I was taken out of the punishment cell and brought in front of the governor. As I walked into his office I was still in shock as to what had happened. I was also pissed off as this would probably mean I will never ever get recreation now. More importantly I would probably have to do the full three year sentence after a stunt like this.

The governor motioned me to sit down and feeling dejected I slumped in the chair as he stared at me inquisitively. In front of me lying on the governors table was the piss pot I had stolen.

'Alan........ Why did you steal this chamber pot?'

'Because I did not get recreation sir.'

'What do you mean?'

'With the piss pot you gave me, I could not make it gleam. No matter what I tried. It was stained with paint.'

'Why did you pick this one Alan?'

'Well because it was so clean,' I said as I pointed to the piss pot on the table.

'Hmmmmm. So you only took it to get recreation.'

'Yes. I just wanted to have recreation. What else would I take it for?'

'Look I am really sorry...................... I did everything else you asked. I made the bed. I worked real hard in the fields. I…. I….'

'Okay Alan.'

'And I only hit him because he came flying at me. I would have given it back.'

'Okay Alan, calm down.'

'So what happens now? I bet I will never get recreation,' I said sulking with arms crossed.

'Not necessarily Alan.'

'What?'

'Feel the edge of that piss pot.'

'What?............... Why?'

'Just feel the edge.'

Taken a back I did as he said and with my right index finger I stroked the texture of the edge of the piss pot. As I stroked around the bowl it felt very sharp and quite painful to touch.

'Ouch! That's quite sharp.'

'Indeed Alan.'

'But why are you telling me this.'

'For a few months we know the boy you attacked was bullying other boys. We would see them with nasty cuts and bruises on their shins and arms. Well what we didn't know is how he did it. But thanks to this awful situation we now know he sharpened his pot to make a weapon'

'You mean he was cutting people with it.'

'Yes.'

'Wow! No wonder his face opened up when I hit him.'

'Now Alan, if we issue another chamber pot which you can get clean are you going to stay out of trouble.'

'Yes. Yes of course.'

'Well behave and keep your nose clean and I will see to it you get recreation.'

'Thank you. That will be great.'

'Now leave Alan and see to it I don't see your face again.'

The governor was true to his word, I did get a new piss pot and recreation for when I behaved. Mind you, I did not hold up my end of the bargain. I got into a few more scraps and several times I had to stand before the governor explaining my actions. But boys will be boys.

After a few months I was reallocated to Hollesley Bay Borstal in Woodbridge, Suffolk. I felt relieved finally getting to Borstal. I now knew that this would be my last port of call before I finished my sentence.

At the Borstal were so many different boys from different walks of life. They came from all parts of the UK and there were also boys of different races. Edwin Bush being one such boy. He was known as Eurasian as his mother and father were of different ethnicities, one was of European descent and the other from Asian descent. I had never seen an Asian boy in my predominately white world of the Rhondda so seeing someone of mixed race was even more incredible. Amazed by his darker skin tone I got to know Edwin and befriended him. He was a nice lad but did have a quick temper on him.

I was friends with Edwin for over a year. He was released before me and sent back home. After several months of being released he committed murder. On 3rd March 1961 he murdered Mrs Elsie May Batten, an assistant in Louis Meier's antique shop in London's West End. He killed her by stabbing her with an antique dagger in the chest and neck. In his defence he said she had greatly upset him by saying "You niggers are all the same. You come in and never buy anything.' I couldn't believe it how someone I knew could have killed someone, especially an innocent woman, albeit a nasty venomous racist woman. Why did he do it! I can only think he did it out of panic as he probably wanted to knick the dagger. I would never have thought he was capable of murder though.

Edwin was caught through the identikit system. The identikit system is when the police build up a likeness of a person sought for a crime when matching from strips showing facial features with witness descriptions. Edwin Bush's case is notable in the history of British justice as he was the first man to be caught by the identikit system. In May 1961 he was sentenced to death by hanging. Before he was set to be hanged he was given the right to request a specific prison officer he liked to take him to the gallows. He requested Hobo Brand, one of the Borstal officers, to take him. His real name wasn't Hobo, but we used to call him this as he dressed quite scruffy. I remember Brand's grave face when he left to see Edwin and his even graver face when he returned. He told us how Bush took it like a man and went quietly. Edwin was the second to last man in London to be hanged. He was only 21. What a fucking stupid thing he did and such a waste of a life.

I stayed in Borstal for a year and a half. When I was released and sent back home to the valleys, I led a relatively crime free life for many years. My main income was from manual labouring jobs I picked up here and there.

I did not commit my next crime until my late twenties. As per usual it was not my idea but a few mates putting the idea on the table. The job entailed stealing a 1970 Cortina Mark 1 2000E from Lockyer and Peacy garage in Ferndale, stripping it and selling on the parts. I did the job mainly for the easy money but also for the thrill. It also seemed like such a tight plan and a crime where we would never be caught.

When we carried out the job greed took hold and we ended up stealing two cars and the safe. We would have got away with it too as the police suspected the heist was by a London or Cardiff gang. Their suspicions were so strong they even closed lanes of the M4 motorway directly after the raid. Little did they realise the criminals were myself and associates who lived on their doorstep only a few miles away.

We all for a while thought that we had gotten away with it and that the local police weren't interested in the case. We thought maybe paperwork was sent down to Cardiff and that they still believed it was criminals out of the area. Alas that wasn't the case, for me anyways. I was caught for my role.

My undoing was when a mate asked if he could have one of the car doors before we dumped them over the Rhigos Mountain. I told him he could have it as long he had the door repainted before he fitted it. Did he? Oh no he put the striking aubergine coloured door straight onto his gold Cortina. As he lived on the main road, it wasn't long till a nosey plod caught up with him and I was fingered. Sent down for four years because of a fucking door!

I served part of my time in Shepton Mallet. As my sentence was four years I was entitled to my own personal cell and I had to share a landing with offenders who also had sentences of four years or more. My neighbours in the cells next to me were Hill, one of the Birmingham Six and Mad Frankie Fraser. I never involved myself with Hill nobody did, as they were disgusted at what we thought he had done. Knowing now he was innocent makes me feel bad at the vicious bullying he received at the hands of the other prisoners. I can still hear his screams from when they used to tip boiling hot tea over him. I only spoke a few words to Frankie. I could not get close to him as he was always escorted everywhere by two screws. This was not surprising with his history as he was always heavily involved with gangs in prison and had a large record of violence to the screws. When I was allowed a chance to speak to him he seemed okay and would always be polite and make a point of saying hello.

When I was released I spent a year or so living it up in London. Shagging around, having the odd joint, generally having a good time. I funded my lifestyle by working on building sites. However the fun did not continue as a girl I went out with ran out on me and took a shit load of my money with her. Feeling shafted, sick of London and alone I decided to go back home for a while and with all the money she took, I couldn't afford to stay.

I went back to live with my parents in their small home town called Ton Pentre in the Rhondda. Once I was back in South Wales I remember looking up at my familiar beautiful mountains and feeling secure. I even pondered on whether I should go straight. Where had a life of crime got me? Prison! No money! No prospects! That's where it had got me. Where were my fancy cars and penthouse suites? Where was my power?

I wanted my independence back but I couldn't afford my own place. As a compromise I lived with my brother in Dinas, a few miles down the road from Ton Pentre. I made a completely honest living for a change as a taxi driver.

It was great at first working the taxis; the excitement of not knowing who was going to enter my taxi cab, using different routes in and around the valleys. The girls dressed in miniskirts and low cut tops. The groups of lads going out for a laugh in Cardiff. The eccentric old dears who would regale me with stories of the past as I took them to the shops.

After several months the initial excitement wore off. All the faces moulded into one. I started to feel constricted like I couldn't breathe taking the same routes and the same people around and around. But, I had to be grateful I had a job. I was an ex-con after all.

However little did I know that one Sunday afternoon would bring about a question that would change my life forever. Where I would have to choose between my safe boring life in the Rhondda or opt for a more dangerous ride involving masses of money and adventure. However the latter would also mean going back to crime and the possibility of prison.

The Saturday afternoon before the event I decided after my taxiing shift I would go down to my Mams. I wanted to see her but there also was an ulterior motive. I wanted to crash at her house so I could go round with my mates in Treherbert, only a few miles down the road. Plus by being at Mams I would have the added benefit of a delicious Sunday lunch the next day, albeit with the rest of my family round the table. This was one of the very few occasions I would grace my father with my presence.

I liked going to Treherbert for a drink especially to the Baglan Hotel. It was my release and one of the few things I looked forward to. Oh that and the smoking cannabis and shagging. Yep they were my top three. The Baglan Hotel in the 70's was fantastic. Once through those doors it was a buzz as you didn't know what was going to happen next with so many characters adding to the mix. One of the regulars of the pub was a horse.

I especially loved it when new people came to the pub. It would make me realise this place was special, as sometimes I would look upon the craziness as normal. The most shocked visitors we had were two Londoners. I can see faces their now as they stood at the door motionless mouths wide open looking on at our hive of activity. I don't know what shocked them the most. It could have been the horse. It could have been our sheer rowdiness. Or it could have been because my mate, the landlord's son, Jeff riding his motorbike through the thronging crowd. I just don't know.

With the Baglan pub in my mind and a smile on my face I drove down the main road through the Rhondda Valleys. I felt on auto pilot. I had been up and down here thousands of times. Everything was the same. As I looked around I could see people happily walking around chatting getting on with their everyday lives. I wanted to be happy too but I didn't want to settle for this. I dreamed of more. I wanted money! I wanted adventure!

I arrived at my mother's house and parked up. I paused as I got out of the car to take a look round in my familiar surroundings. With a sigh I looked at the picturesque mountains admiring their magnificence but fearing their imprisonment. I yearned to see the world. I despised myself for not embracing the awesome backdrop I had on my doorstep, and instead looking on them as if I was there captive.

As I entered the house Mam was already waiting for me at the door. She must have seen my car.

'Hi Mam.'

'Where have you been Alan? I thought you would have been down earlier,' she said in worried tones whilst looking out the window as if to check no-one was watching.

'With my brother.'

'Are you okay mam?'

I could see by the look on her face that it wasn't her fussing as per usual but something had startled her. She looked at the floor and paused. I didn't question her as I knew if I gave her a few moments, she would collect her thoughts and say what she had to. I knew no matter what it was, she would still say it softly and with love as she always did.

Despite all the trouble I got into she would always be enchanted by me and pour on love the way only a mother can. I was her first born and although a black sheep, she never gave up on me. More fool her, but I loved her for this.

'Are you in trouble Alan?'

'What are you on about Mam? I have not being out of prison long. Even if I wanted to I haven't had much time to create another sentence.'

She ignored my flippant comment and looked to the floor shaking her head.

'Look Mam I haven't done anything.'

Still shoulders slumped I put my arm around her and looked her deep in the eyes. I think she could tell I was telling the truth. This time! She knew that I genuinely wanted to go straight. My life was as I had portrayed to her a taxi driver by day and socialite in the pubs by night. The only extracurricular activity I hid from her was my many one night stands. However bless my Mother how was she to believe me. I was a bugger for lying. Even when caught red handed I would shout till I was blue in the face I was innocent of my crimes.

'It's just two men came down and they were looking for you. They were both dressed very smart...... I thought they might have been detectives but....... I don't know. ....They didn't seem like the police. They were very well spoken.'

Fuck me. Who the hell was that? Had I upset someone?

'The younger one of the two said they would come back again tomorrow .... Err around 1pm.'

'What were their names?'

'They didn't say!' she shrieked.

'Don't worry about it Mam. I'm not. It's probably nothing.'

It was true that I wasn't worried but I was excited and intrigued. That night with the lads in the Baglan Hotel pub went quickly in a haze of cigarettes and alcohol. I wasn't involved with much of the banter that night as although my body was present my mind was far away. I was too busy thinking about my impending visitors.

'Right Alan you'd better piss off its closing time,' Jeff shouted.

'Eh?'

'Look you dopey sod time to go home. You've been on another planet tonight.'

'Okay okay. Just knackered that's all.'

As I got into bed that night my thoughts raced. I was searching my memory banks to guess who and why someone wanted to see me so urgently. Although tanked up with alcohol my mind could not be numbed.

Who were they? Police? Nah it couldn't be. They locked me up and I haven't done anything since the robbery…..The other stuff in the past. Nah got away with that……..Was it over a woman? Had I bedded someone married?…….Nah I remembered the girls and they were definitely single. I knew this as the Rhondda is a very local place where everybody knows everybody! Mind you, had I bedded someone I forgot about and they were married? Nah still not very probable. Was it to do with kidnapping the kids? It can't be that. Can it? That was such a long time ago.

Enough was enough and my excitement had got the better of me. I had tossed and turned too much. There was no point in trying to sleep. I needed to get up. When I rose out of bed and looked at my clock it was 5 am.

Quietly in the dark of the early morning I paced around the kitchen grabbing tit bits of meat from the fridge. As I chewed I racked my brains further. It would have been far simpler if my Mam had said it was two women. Then I could have made a list.

Then my thoughts switched to Monday. I was back on the taxis. My excitement and giddiness plummeted and my thoughts were again sluggish. Back on the leash and back on the mapped routes. However, I had to console myself, it could have been worse. I could have working down the coal mines or in a factory. I wouldn't have minded the physicality of both these jobs as I loved keeping myself in good condition, but I never liked to be caged up in one place. At least with the taxis I had freedom, although this was restricted.

If only I had done as my Dad and Auntie had said. Done well in school, I could have been in a high flying job. I could be the boss and making decisions. Mind you, this was a silly thing to think as I was not bright and it would have taken serious application from myself to achieve anything. I was a boy who was just good at sports.

Saying this there was one subject I was okay at, Geography. I did remember quite a few things on what I was taught and I did used to like learning about different cultures. It fascinated me how people elsewhere in the world could be so different. A particular favourite was when I studied the Mongolians. I especially loved the way they celebrated the Nadaam festival, or Eriyn Gurvan Nadaam, which is the biggest festival of the year for Mongolians. In this festival they would put on two horse races. The horses of two years old would race for 10 miles and the seventeen year old horses would race for 17 miles. Up to 1,000 horses would compete on the cross country races. Also the jockeys that would be chosen would be children between 5 to 13 years of age. Mongolians chose children so young as they believed the race should be more about the skill of the horse than its rider. When I was taught this at 9 years old I thought this was amazing; I would be more than eligible to enter a horse race. Also the winning jockey is praised with the title Tumny Ekh or "leader of ten thousand" and the five winning horses are talked about and revered in poetry and music.

I think I also liked Geography as it was different to my reality. Talking about different cultures was like talking about aliens, as in the valleys in my youth it was predominantly white and Welsh in population. I had never heard of anyone venturing abroad. Not like it is today. In my era of the fifty's and sixty's the furthest people in the valleys would venture would be places like Barry Island, Porthcawl and Tenby. Always at the same time on the allotted Miners fortnight holiday at the start of July. How fucking boring! Only in Geography via my imagination could I travel to these exotic countries.

At last the Sunday morning dredged into the afternoon and 1pm finally came, announced by the grandfather clock that rang loud and proud in the hallway. However the fanfare was in vain. There was no knock at the door. I looked out of the lace windows over and over but nothing. The street was desolate. It got to 1.30pm and I was furious. I had churned myself up all last night and today for this and nobody was here. I put back the curtain and walked away in rage.

My Mam entered the room wearing a flowery frilly pinny and a worried expression. She could see me boiling over with unease.

'Do you want a cup of tea love?'

'No I don't I'm off to the pub.'

'But what about those guys............... Plus. Plus dinner will be ready in an hour.'

'It's half one now I am not waiting around. I have wasted enough time. And I'll make it a swift half.'

'Aye swift Half!' she snorted with laughter.

'Alan it may be important,' she said reverting back to her anxious composure.

How true she was. With that our conversation was broken as the knocker on the door gently tapped twice. Both my Mam and I gasped as we looked in the direction of the door. I marched over with annoyance and swung back the door full force nearly hitting myself in the face. As I faced my mysterious visitors my anger instantly dissipated as it was none other than Troy and Mort, my old cell mates. I had met them in HMP Bristol Prison where I served part of my sentence for stealing the cars until I was later sent to Shepton

How different they looked from when I met them in HMP Bristol. Their jeans and t-shirts replaced by a suit. Their beards replaced by perfectly shaven skin. They both looked very handsome and affluent. It was obvious they had done well for themselves after prison.

After the initial shock I went over and firmly embraced my friends of a few months porridge.

'Hi Troy. Hi Mort. Well what a nice surprise. Come in. Come in.'

'So what have you been doing with yourself?'

'Oh you know keeping out of trouble. Doing a bit of taxiing.'

'How about you?'

Troy didn't answer but instead smiled and looked in the direction of my Mother politely. I swung myself round to follow his gaze and I could see my Mam motionless in the corner looking at the three of us from afar. From the bewilderment on her face I could see she was thinking how myself, Troy and Mort were acquainted. How was I, the ex-con comparatively scruff bag, friends with these well-dressed men. Before I let her thoughts race into worry I beckoned her over. She promptly and gently stood up grabbing nervously her collar of her blouse with one hand. She let her other arm dangle to the side as if she didn't know what to do with herself.

I had to think quickly on my feet as I didn't want to tell her where we really met. I didn't want her to worry. Then as my mouth started moving my brain kicked in. I shocked myself as the lies poured out.

'Mam meet Troy. He works importing and exporting cars. I helped to sell a few cars a while back when I was in London.'

Her anxiety melted as she smiled. I had convinced her. I could see relief in her eyes. She nodded at them both in a shy attempt to say hello and then promptly left to leave us catch up. She went off to carry on with her usual Sunday house work duties that she would occupy herself with whilst the ingredients of the Sunday dinner were cooking. I was glad I had convinced her. I didn't like to worry her.

Both mine and Troy's eyes followed my mother's back as she walked out of the room and in sync with each other waited scores of seconds before talking. Mort watched on.

'Jesus Christ you two. What's with the visit? Are you in any trouble? Do you need help?'

'Not in trouble as such but I do require your services. However we cannot talk here,' said Troy in hushed tones.

'Let's go to the pub then.'

'No I had something different in mind,' Troy said playfully.

'Okay....'

'Have your Sunday lunch which I can smell on the go and we will be back to tell you the deal. I will take you for a ride in my new car and spoil you this evening.'

'You cannot keep me hanging like this. What's the deal man?'

'Patience Alan. Just dress smart casual. I have a few people you need to meet before you decide.'

'Decide what?'

My question fell on deaf ears as I watched them both smiling as if leaving me out of a joke. I hated being in the dark but I could see they were not ready to tell me their plans.

'Okay I will see you later. But when?'

'Will two hours be enough?' said Mort

'Yeah that's fine.'

I sat down as I usually did with my family on a Sunday afternoon. Around the table were my Mother, Father and two Brothers, Norman and Philip. Normally out of my brothers I would be the one to take time with my food as with most things in life I would like to savour the moment. Not this day. I was too excited and wanted to get ready to go, so I shovelled down each mouthful fast. The last time I felt this excited was when I burned rubber in the Cortina after the robbery.

'Who were your visitors then Alan?' questioned my brother Norman.

'Just some people I kinda know.'

'What do they want?'

'They might be able to give me a job selling cars.'

'Where did you meet them?'

'Look Norman..........I met them in London after my release. I sold a few in the past for them but they had to lay me off so I had to come back down here to see your ugly mug.'

'It's a bit strange. To come all the way from London,' Philip asked looking bemused.

'Just quit it you two, I haven't got all the details yet myself.'

I turned my gaze from my brothers to avoid any more probing questions and shovelled down the food in bigger bites.

'Slow down Alan. What's the rush?' gently asked my Mam.

'Oh Troy and Mort are coming back to tell me more about the job in a few hours.'

As soon as I had finished the contents of my plate I whizzed off to the bathroom. It took me just under an hour to get ready. I had never paid so much attention on preening myself before, even when on an impending date. My hair combed to perfection. My beard trimmed and tidied. I put on my smartest clothes and polished my shoes till they gleamed. As I stood in the mirror and looked at my groomed reflection I felt a little nervous. I felt like I was preparing for a job interview, but with the greatest disadvantage of not actually knowing what the job was or entailed.

Feeling clean and fresh I waited on the doorstep in the bracing wind for my ride. I was half an hour early on the door than agreed but I wanted to show my enthusiasm and commitment to whatever they were putting on the table. Ahh the unknown, I hadn't felt such a buzz for a while. My stomach knotted each time a car went past.

The front door banged behind me. It was my brother Norman leaving the house. I quickly turned my head and looked to the floor. In the brief moment I caught eyes with him I knew he was going to grill me further.

'Stood you up have they?'

'Shut up. I am just early.'

'Selling cars? I don't think so. You're up to something dodgy. You always are.'

Before I could retort and get into sibling bickering, a gentle beeping broke my train of thought. We both looked round and saw Troy in his car. I say car but to me that day it looked more like a piece of art. It was a beautiful 1970's Mercedes-Benz 280SE coupe in silver. Although there was no sun that day this magnificent car beamed in all her glory. It stuck out like a sore thumb outside the terraced houses of this working class town. People round here thought to themselves they were lucky to even be able to buy a car let alone own one like this.

'See look at his car. Now you can see he is a car salesman. Well you have a nice time down the pub Norm. I am off for a ride in a Merc.'

When I left, Norman still hadn't closed his mouth from the spectacle of this beautiful machine, but he did manage to wave at us like a very slow robot in shock as we whizzed off.

I sat in the brown leather front passenger seat and gawped at its luxurious interior. I was so in awe, I was oblivious to the valleys disappearing behind. I also was unintentionally ignoring Troy and Mort as the car held my captivation.

'Alan. Alan!' bellowed Troy.

'Yes sorry Troy.'

'Beautiful isn't she?'

'Damn right!'

'Help us with our deal and you too could own one of these and much more.'

'I am listening.'

'Right Alan to cut to the chase the deal is with drugs.'

'Drugs?'

'What sort of drugs?'

'Not heavy drugs only cannabis. We want you to help us smuggle them from Morocco to Europe.'

My mind raced I had not been prepared for this. The only thing I could retain in my memory banks from this conversation was the words Morocco, Europe and Cannabis. The other details could not be processed and stored as I was jarred by shock. I remember Troy mainly did all the talking and I watched his lips moving as I nodded, but the whole conversation was a blur. Morocco, Europe and Cannabis. What the fuck?

Looking at my watch I realised we had been in the car for several hours but it felt like minutes to my brain. The Mercedes then came to a sudden but smooth halt as we stopped outside a big Victorian Mansion, which I could only place somewhere in the middle of Berkshire. I had not been paying much attention to where we were. I was still consumed with the words spoken by Troy.

'Alan now we play,' smiled Troy

'Where are we?'

'Mort tell him where we are.'

'This used to be Rod Stewart's house.'

'You bought this off Rod Stewart?'

'No!' he laughed.

'This is Joe Brown's house.'

'Ahh I see….. What?......... The real Joe Brown?'

'Yeah he's an old mate of mine and he is having a house party,' said Mort.

I could not believe it. I was to attend Joe Brown's party. Although not so much in the limelight today he dominated the charts and British TV in the seventies. He was one of my idols. One of the original Rock & Roll Stars to come out of the UK and one of the first UK session men. He had played guitar with Gene Vincent, Eddie Cochran, Johnny Cash and other US stars when they came over to Europe to tour. Joe even had The Beatles to open his shows for him. He was such an amazing musician!

Once inside I was taken aback again it was such a beautiful house and kitted out with everything modern. It was magnificent. Time again went quickly as my head was dizzy with excitement. My dizziness extenuated from downing glass after glass of champagne. I pointed Joe out to Troy as he wanted to introduce me to him. With that he took my arm dragged me over to Joe's direction. As we approached Troy and Mort instantly took up a dialect. Watching them conversing I could see from their body language they were relaxed and had known each other for years. He wasn't just an acquaintance. I didn't say much and just stood there smiling following the conversation. I remained quiet as I was a little too drunk and star struck to reply.

As my eyes averted from looking at Joe, I looked around at the other guests in the room. From glancing around I noticed that there were considerably more women than men and each one of the women were in their own right stunning and dripping in the latest fashion. They all looked like models or actresses, which they probably were and probably here to ride on Joe's fame. My head was swimming in decadence. Life was good. This was the dream. Maybe I should take up the guitar like Joe. Maybe I could have a house like this and make loads of money too.

Ahh, this party was a complete dream for me! If heaven was a party it would be this one. Only a few hours ago I was looking forward to a nice Sunday lunch! And here I was at Joe Brown's party. Me! A working class valley boy who grew up in a terraced house, here rubbing shoulders with a celebrity and models. In the setting of this beautiful mansion after being chauffeur driven in a luxurious Merc. If the job with Troy and Mort means getting money like Joe had. I was in.

Then sobriety kicked in as my thoughts turned back to reality. Back to the deal. Why did Troy and Mort pick me and how the hell did they locate my address? I don't ever remember writing my address down when I met them in Bristol prison. Mind you, looking at where I was, it seemed these boys had their fingers in many pies, so maybe it was best not to ask how they got to me.

As for picking me that was still a shock. The only thing that sticks in my mind was because of our closeness in Bristol prison. Troy, Mort, a guy from Merthyr who I can't remember his name and myself were the only Welsh people in one of the wings of Bristol prison. The rest of the prisoners were predominately English and although I didn't care it was just an unwritten rule we would be separate and have a sort of rivalry. So us four bonded together in our isolated minority.

I don't know to this day what Troy and Mort were sent down for. It is just something you never ask in prison and plus they never divulged. I think it was to do with money. I was down for the burglary at the garage and the guy from Merthyr, was done for grand theft auto of a bus. He told us after a night on the piss he decided to steal a bus and drive home. When he tried to park the bus a few streets from where he lived he crashed it into the front of a house. He must have been going quite fast as the bonnet of the bus went straight into their living room. When he looked up straight after the crash he told me how he could see an elderly couple looking half scared to death sitting on the sofa watching TV with their plates of dinner on their laps. They were okay and unhurt, but however missing the front part of their house. He did try to leg it after the crash but the walls wedged his doors shut. He tried and tried but he couldn't get out and run. He had to wait there until the police could free him from the car whilst the old couple stared on.

Unlike us three me, Troy and Mort, the Merthyr guy was a bit of a mental case and could be very violent. I mean I have been in many fights don't get me wrong but this guy was something else. He would beat other prisoners to within an inch of their life only stopping once they had dropped to the floor in a pool of blood. He would almost always be the instigator of the fights. He actively skulked round the prison to find his prey and had a set of rules on how he chose his victims. At the top of the list were paedophiles (or as we called them nonces), child killers and rapists.

I felt a sense of pride Mort and Troy chose me for the job. Although downright dangerous it felt good they chose me. I don't remember what I did to impress them and plus I didn't stay long with them in Bristol. I spent most of my sentence in Shepton Mallet. Oh boy if they had seen me there they would have been more impressed at my ingenuity. There I beat the system. I didn't let the buggers grind me down! The biggest stink I made there was when I told the parole board to stick their release papers up their arse.

I first divulged to my prison mates in Shepton Mallet I was going to deny parole when we were at dinner in the canteen. I remember as usual I sat down with my group of friends on our table. As usual we didn't speak for a few moments all too busy noisily eating our food to the tune of background noise of the other prisoners. Then Jack broke the silence by resting his knife down on the table and with his fork, he pointed it in my direction.

'Hey Al why aren't you excited? I have heard you are due for parole. Two and half years for a four year stint.............. Not bad,' he said whilst till chewing on his sausage and mash.

'Yeah, I know.'

'So why have you got a face like a smacked arse?' piped up Pete.

'You look like a man who's only started his sentence and not a bugger who is going to get released in a few weeks,' Jack chimed in again.

'Whose saying I want to be released...........In fact don't be too sure I am going...........I am gonna tell them to stick it.'

Everyone around the table simultaneously put their knives and fork down and stared towards me in bewilderment. All searching my eyes for answers and asking why I would forgo my freedom. I smiled back. I knew what I was doing. Well I thought I did.

'Alan you're pissing mad,' said Jack

'Ahh you going to miss us,' Pete said taking the piss whilst puckering his lips and making kissing sounds.

'Sod off Pete. I have my reasons for not accepting my parole. And that's that.'

'You're winding us up Alan. No-one in their right mind would refuse getting out of this dump,' said Jack laughing again, regaining his jaunty composure and tucking back into his dinner.

'I mean. What do you have to gain?' Joe added.

'I am deadly serious. You just watch me boy. I will say no.'

The conversation about my parole meeting dominated the dinner time. They probed and probed but I was not going to tell them my reasons. It was none of their business. They eventually relented asking but resolved the conversation by making up a wager. They betted their snout as to whether I would or wouldn't be stupid enough to deny bail. Snout was a prison term for tobacco. Each prisoner had an average tobacco allowance of ¾ of an ounce to an ounce per week, but many prisoners saved tobacco for transactions or wagers. Non-smokers in prisons had a great advantage. For this bet I had eight ounces riding on me to accept my freedom. Only I bet on me to refuse. These ounces were mine for the taking. I wasn't going to back down.

As I left the canteen I went alone to my cell and sat on my thin mattress. I waited for the screw to take me to my parole hearing. Only 1% of doubt niggled in my mind to say yes to parole. The other 99% was strong and defiant to say no. Even if it meant I was to serve my full four years which would have meant another year and half in prison. It didn't fucking matter. I was not going to accept. I gulped hard at this impending prospect.

However the lump in my throat dispersed as I heard the jangling keys and the heavy footsteps of the impending screw. My frame was rigid and the adrenalin flowed readily through my veins ready for the disdain of the governor.

'Come on Alan. Off to your parole board.'

The screw escorted me to the room via a passage of barred gates staying behind me at all times. I entered the governor's office with clenched hands holding on to my defiance. I watched as the screw closed the door behind me and stood in a respectful sentry position blocking the doorway. I walked over and stood on the designated matt in front of the governor who sat behind a great wooden desk. We said our hellos and it was off with the proceedings. I wasn't really involved at first as he just reeled off from a piece of paper about my crime, my behaviour and the grounds for which I was allowed parole. I was just about to drift my attention when he stopped and eyeballed me for a reaction.

'So Alan how do you feel? You will be released from here in a few weeks. ....Great news isn't it?'

He stretched over to pass me the release papers and a pen, intending me to sign and be gone. I didn't move. Confused he stretched over again with the papers. Again I remained rigid and did not make any attempt to take the papers or his pen.

'Here are the papers, Alan. All you have to do is sign them and you are free to go.'

His confused glances turned to annoyance as I further made no attempt to accept the paper in my hands. He eventually accepted defeat and slammed them on the table in front of him. I paused and looked down at the floor. I allowed a few moments to go by so I could compose myself and to make sure he was actually concentrating on me. It seemed before he was just going through the motions.

'If I was to accept parole………Only if………… Where would I have to go?'

Taken a back the governor lifted his head up in shock. I could see in his eyes he was puzzled as to my question and at my calm composure.

'Er er with your family of course. We have contacted them and they are quite happy for you to stay down there for the time being,' he said smiling.

'Well I am sorry I am not happy about that. So I would like to refuse parole please.'

'Alan……..err………What? You are refusing………..parole?'

'Yes!'

'In all my time….. In all my time I have never heard a single prisoner refuse…… Don't you know how lucky you are to be granted this?'

An uncomfortable silence ensued for several seconds. He looked at me in anger whilst I stared back in quiet confidence.

'Sit down Alan.' he ordered whilst pointing to a chair in front of him.

With respect I obeyed and sat down.

'What are you reasons Alan?'

'Look I apologise. I have my reasons as to why ……but they are personal…..I don't wish to discuss them here…………. I'm very sorry.'

'This is serious now Alan. You are denying parole. It could be a long time in the future when we would give you another opportunity. If at all!'

'So be it. But I just can't accept.'

The prison governor was stunned. When I turned to look at the prison officer he too looked taken aback.

The governor probed and probed a while further as to my reasons but I did not let up anything. Eventually out of annoyance he ordered me to leave and the prison officer took me back to the main prison where he ceased being my shadow. I looked upwards towards the landing where the cells were. I could see my lads resting their arms on the metal rails above. All looking down smoking and awaiting the outcome of my parole hearing. That's it smoke up lads!

With arrogance I sauntered up the steps grinning like a Cheshire cat. All eyes and ears focused on me and what I had to say.

'Look at him……………. he said yes. He wouldn't be grinning so if he had to spend another year and half in here……………. Come on then

Alan hand over your bacco,' said Pete smugly.

'Not so fast Pete. I did say no.'

Again I had stunned silence.

'Bollocks. You wouldn't be so fucking stupid. Would you?' said Peter again.

Peter threw down his cigarette and raced down the steps. He went off to confirm my story. He did have a lot to lose mind as he bet three ounces.

Pete came back dragging his feet. It had been confirmed I had said no and he painfully handed over the snout as did the other lads.

All the other lads went on exercise several hours later. I refused and stayed in my cell alone with my thoughts whilst pawing my prizes of packets and packets of snout. Although nice, the snout was not equivalent to the price of freedom. What have I fucking done! Another year and a half!

Calm down Alan, it's the only way. I told myself. You're doing the right thing. You needed to refuse as there was no way you were going back home to the Rhondda. It was London where you were needed. For the kids! I didn't want to be constrained to the Rhondda seeing a fucking parole officer every week. I had work to do!

A few days went by. They seemed to drag longer than they had before. The lads noticed my quietness and my withdrawal from banter, but they still took the piss about denying parole. But I had the last laugh as I smoked to oblivion in front of them with their precious bacco.

'Alan!' shouted a screw in my direction.

'Get down here your parole officer wants to speak with you!'

Angus MacGoughy was my parole officer. As I approached him I could see he was majorly pissed off. He pulled my t-shirt sleeve and dragged me to his empty quiet office. He began berating me as to why I refused. Telling me the great lengths he went to in order to get my parole. I nodded as he spoke but didn't speak back.

'Now Alan why is it you refused parole. You have said to me you're not institutionalised.'

I responded to his question with a shrug.

'Well, it must be a bloody good reason. So let's have it!'

'Look I'm sorry I cannot say. But I will say…….'

'Spit it out then!'

'I don't want to go home!'

'What?'

'I don't want to go to the Rhondda.'

'I would like to go to London.'

'Why?'

'Look as I said it is for personal reasons…………But if you plan to send me to the Rhondda I will refuse parole as many times as you give it.'

Making my point I look backed at the floor tightly closing my lips. To gain eye contact MacGoughy shook me by the shoulders pushing his face close into mine.

'Look Alan you can't very well choose where you would want to go. Or else we'd be having requests left, right and centre to Acapulco…. I mean why not the Rhondda. Your family is there for god's sake!'

'Well if that is the case, I'm sorry I still say no.'

MacGoughy drew in a big breath sighing deeply. He scowled at me for several seconds but realised he was wasting his time. I was not going to feel guilty and I was sure to hell not going to change my mind. After a few seconds of uncomfortable eyeballing he turned his head and shook it gently.

'Okay Alan so where in sodding London do you want to go?' he asked sarcastically.

'Anywhere near Hayes end would be great.'

'Hayes end?'

'Yes near Cowley.'

'Cowley, Oxford?'

'No near Uxbridge.'

With that he shook his head again half smiling and half grimacing.

'Christ sake Alan………Right……….That's all. You may go.'

That night I couldn't sleep. Mulling over in my mind the events of the parole meeting and the visit from MacGoughy. Had I gone too far? I didn't much care for the governor but I liked MacGoughy. He had done a lot for me in here and now I was making life difficult for him. Spitting back in his face all the help and support. It was through him I had the chance of parole.

However, I comforted myself as I knew it wasn't my fault. I had to ask for this. It was the actions of my second wife, Pauline. If she hadn't visited me several weeks ago and told me what she had done I wouldn't be in this mess and would have happily gone straight back to the Rhondda. Mind I was glad she told me. And now I needed to sort it out.

Although Pauline and I weren't together she still came to visits taking along our two beautiful boys, Lee and Dale. She had given me the Dear John letter months and months ago. She was now shacked up with Jim and residing somewhere near Hayes end, near to Uxbridge. This was all fine. I was slightly annoyed at her at first but it didn't take long for me to bounce back. I was in prison for Christ sake, I understood. Plus on my way out I knew there were plenty of fish left in the pet shop for me.

On her last visit was to be the most upsetting though. I knew something was wrong as soon as she walked into the visiting room. Her face was drawn and her eyes sheepish. I firstly asked about the kids as they weren't with her and questioned how they were getting on in school. She didn't reply. As I stared hard at her she seemed frozen in fear and holding back on the conversation. I continued talking by myself asking and asking why she was not talking to me and why she looked so god damn scared. Eventually after my incessant questioning it came pouring out. She ranted on and on about how she couldn't cope with the kids and how her life was a mess. I nodded and nodded listening sympathetically as I knew this was leading somewhere. When she talked it was hard to comprehend what she was saying as she was so frantic with tears and catching her breath uttering each word. She eventually calmed herself down. It was then she told me quietly so the screws could not hear what she had done. She had put our two little boys into care. I was speechless and chilled to my core. I couldn't even shout, speak or do anything. I just felt numb. I didn't know what to say and felt powerless as there was nothing I could do. Plus I didn't want to get angry. I was so embarrassed and didn't want anyone else to hear what she allowed to happen to our beautiful boys. The shame of it! If only I was not in fucking prison and was there for her. I could have talked her round. I could have looked after the kids myself. But I couldn't. I was here. Looking into Pauline's eyes I wanted to scream and shout but nothing would come out. I lost myself in her eyes as I connected with her and could see she was feeling the same. Pure guilt. I did not tell anyone about what happened, not even MacGoughy who I think would have understood. I was just too proud. I did not want anyone to know my kids had been put into care. I was ashamed and embarrassed. Plus I knew that if I was released on parole I would be sent to South Wales. Every morning I would have to report to a police station in the Rhondda. I wouldn't be able to go to London and look for my boys. Hence the reason why I had to deny bail. The night after her visit I prayed for my boys Lee and Dale. I was not religious but I felt powerless and couldn't do much else.

Luckily my prayers were answered MacGoughy had managed to appeal for me to reside near to Cowley where I wanted. I take homage here to MacGoughy as I didn't even benefit him with any answer as to why I wanted to go and he still did it.

I was told that I was to reside in a hostel in Cowley and report to the police station each day. As I left the prison, I felt elated that I had beaten the system, but more importantly I could help get my kids back. So with my train ticket in my hand courtesy of her majesty I headed straight to Paddington station where I got off and made my way.

Once in Cowley I located the police station and hostel with ease. The hostel was a right dump just as I expected but I didn't care I was near enough to Pauline, who could tell me where the kids were. All I knew about where she lived was that it was in Hayes end a few miles from Uxbridge. I didn't have an address or even know where she lived but I knew she worked at the Nestle chocolate factory. All I needed to do was find that factory.

After a few days I managed to get a job working on a building site. I wanted to have my own money so I could fund my travels in trying to locate Pauline. I also wanted my own place as I couldn't stick being in the hostel. It was dire. It was filthy and depressing. I also had to share a room full of youngsters all ex-cons being in trouble for thieving or drugs, sometimes both.

It was due to their crimes that I would be awoken in the early hours of the morning by the police coming in and doing a raid. I wasn't worried when they searched me as I hadn't nicked anything. It just pissed me off not getting a good night sleep for work the next morning. However it was no wonder they did it as the raids were almost always fruitful. On every raid, one or two of the gobshites were taken away and nicked for carrying stolen goods or drugs.

Although I was a thief and an ex-con too. I was not like them. They stole from family, friends and the man on the street. I only ever stole from businesses. They even didn't think twice at robbing each other's stuff. In the hostel there was an endless cycle of things going missing and the kids fighting amongst themselves as they blamed each other. It was due to this I couldn't store food in the communal fridge as when I came home from a hard days slog on the building site some bugger would have nicked it.

However I just put up with it and kept a low profile. In the day I would work and in the late afternoon I would have a scout about asking everybody and anybody if they knew where the factory was. No fucking google in those days.

After about a week my investigations pulled off and I had the address for Nestles in Hayes. I took a day off work and travelled there by bus. When I got to the building I headed straight to the reception area and marched up to the secretary demanding she put a call out for Pauline. I explained that Pauline was my wife and that it was of grave importance I had to speak to her. I managed to get through and she nodded at my request so I waited for Pauline to turn up outside.

Eventually she came out of one of the side doors of this vast building. I could see she hadn't seen me yet as she looked around in all directions. Once Pauline caught my gaze she gasped. She was wearing the same frightened and worn expression as on her last visit. I grabbed her gently by the arm and walked her into town. As we walked I demanded she tell me where the children were. I also told her she had no choice but to come with me to take them back. As we walked and walked she kept putting up an argument at how she couldn't get them back. How she couldn't cope. I tried to stay calm at first and listen as I needed her help. However as she droned on and on, my patience wore thin. I screamed that it was not her or me she had to think of. It was the kids. As I said the names Dale and Lee her chin started to quiver and her eyes welled up. Each time she blinked lines of tears exploded down her face. I had broken through.

'Oh Alan. What have I done?'

'I know I know,' I said as I consoled her in my arms

'Now Pauline, where are the kids?' I said gently.

'Bridgend,' she said spitting salvia from the corner of her mouth.

I shook my head in dismay. Fucking Bridgend I thought. I couldn't believe it. Bridgend is in South Wales. If I had known this I could have gone straight home to the Rhondda as it was only just over 10 miles away from where my mother lived. From Hayes where I was now, Bridgend was over 150 miles away. All that flaming trouble to get my parole changed. Bloody typical! I decided not to get annoyed with Pauline as she had told me what I wanted. It wouldn't have helped matters. She was hurting enough.

'Thank you Pauline.'

'Now you understand we sort this out now and get them.'

'Now? Err… I have work.'

'No! Now Pauline.'

With that she took herself out of my arms and wiped her tears. She composed herself and nodded emphatically.

Thankfully she kept her word and the next day we travelled to Bridgend. We arrived in Bridgend around 1pm. As it was midweek and in the afternoon we knew they wouldn't be in the care home but in school. Luckily Pauline knew where the school was so we headed straight there.

Once at the school we marched around the building looking into each classroom looking for our babies. Pauline lagged behind. Eventually I found their classroom. Although the boys were different in age they were in the same classroom together. It warmed my heart to see them and I was glad they were together. Although abandoned by Pauline and myself. They had each other. Not for much longer they had Mammy and Daddy too.

I could have stayed at the window for hours gazing at their angelic little faces. However I had to snap myself out of this and get into action to take them back. With that I barged straight into the school and stormed down the corridor to the classroom I had seen them in. I gently opened the door and smiled warmly at the teacher.

Although I approached quietly and calmly the teacher was still shocked and aghast at mine and Pauline's surprise visit. Before I could say anything both Dale and Lee came running towards us. The classroom echoed as they screamed and shouted Mammy and Daddy over and over. It was hard not to cry as they grabbed tightly around my legs. The teacher did try to make us leave and asked us to return when school was finished. Luckily I managed to persuade her we needed to take them now. On the spot I made a fuss at how the social should have told them we now had custody. How we had tickets for the train and we were already running late. I could see she wasn't buying it. Our only saviour was when she looked at the kids.

They did not let go of us for a second. Eventually she relented and nodded in agreement we could take them away.

That was one of the best moments in my life scooping my kids in my arms and taking them out of that school. I had kidnapped my own kids. Luckily I had no reprisals from the social for this. Even if I did I wouldn't have cared. It was for the greater good. I wasn't going to allow my kids to grow up in care. Thankfully they remained with Pauline and never went back. I did have to leave my poor boys again but at least I left them with their mother.

'Alan! Alan!' shouted Troy.

'Err sorry away with the fairies this champagne is strong.'

'Good isn't it! So you in with us on the deal.'

'Yes. I have decided. I'll do it,' I whispered to Troy and Mort. I said it quietly so as not to alert anyone's attention at Joe's party. Not that it mattered as everyone was suitably inebriated.

'We'll meet again over the next few weeks and I can give you more details on the plan.

3 NAÏVE BEGINNINGS

1975 – Europe & North Africa

Looking out from the ferry I could see we were about to dock at Calais Port. This was the first time I had left the British Isles and had travelled abroad. I was excited at venturing into the unknown, meeting different people from different cultures and experiencing their world. This was also the first time I embarked on a drug smuggling mission.

The tannoy echoed and crackled in the background informing us to board our vehicles. I threw my half-finished fag into the troubled waters of the English Channel and went to locate my ride. She was a turquoise Bedford carvanette and to be my only companion on this epic journey.

I revved her up and prepared to leave the ferry in the queue amongst the other cars, buses and lorries packed with workers, travel makers and business men. A rush of adrenalin and excitement pulsed round my veins as I slowly edged my way further and further to the front, nearing the entry into France. It took only thirty minutes for me to leave the queue and pass through passport control, but this still was too long for me. I was ready. I wanted to be on the open roads now!

When eventually freed I took out my excitement by driving fast down the E15 Rocade E road down along to the E15 les autoroutes whilst also enjoying the exhilaration of driving on the wrong side of the road. I wanted to pass quickly through France and Spain; it was Morocco where I wanted to be. That was where the action was going to happen, that's when the fun would start.

After travelling thirty miles or so down the E15 les auto routes I pulled into the first service station in my path and decided to assess my situation. From my pocket I took out my neatly hand written map and gently unfolded it. This fingered my journey through France. I decided in that moment that I needed to be vigilant with my maps and keep them close, my caravanette would be my only witness. Although they only contained routes, I deemed it too much information. I pawed the journey and repeated in my mind the plans of the next few weeks. I rehearsed and rehearsed what I needed to do, my confidence and excitement grew.

My journey was going to take me through ten countries in all France,

Spain, Morocco, Algeria, Tunis, Sicily, Italy, Germany, Denmark and eventually my final destination of Norway. It worked out to be around 5000 miles of driving. The hashish powder would be sought from Morocco and then I would have to smuggle it through the remaining six countries to take it to Norway. Although the journey was mammoth and the risks were high smuggling through so many countries, it was worth it. You would earn three times more selling cannabis in Norway than in the UK. In the UK we were looking at earning £30,000 in total for the job, not excluding travel expenses etc. In Norway we could sell it for £90,000, three times the amount, three times the hassle but three times the pleasure. In today's money £90,000 is worth just shy of half a million pound.

I delved into my bag and checked I still had my two passports. Unlike Howard Marks I did not fake my passports and use different aliases. I would go to the passport offices in the UK and said I had lost my passport, in order to gain copies. I would have one passport which I referred to as the dirty passport used only when I was going through countries associated with drug smuggling. My clean passport would only contain stamps from going through European countries. This was so I wouldn't have much problems going through passport control travelling up from Italy to Norway on my last leg of the journey. I had a lot of fun getting new passports, as I would make up each time a new job I was doing. However I did like to put down salesman, as this would suggest to the passport controls that I was travelling for my job. Well technically that was true. I was travelling and selling a commodity in demand.

Like Howard Marks I believe that deep thought should go into legalising cannabis. I personally feel alcohol and tobacco is far more harmful. I mean you can get a prescription for cannabis on the NHS but not for a few pints and a packet of fags. Look at our booze Britain and cases of yob attacks. Give yobs cannabis they would be too busy sitting in their living room laughing their tits off and munching their face off. Mind if it were to be legalised would that take some of the fun out of it?

Incidentally I had met Howard Marks when Troy, Mort and myself had our final meeting tightening up the details of this trip. He arrived unannounced with an American friend at Troy's place of business. He came in as he wanted to buy equipment from Troy which Mort had designed. Mort was our technical guy in charge of engineering vehicles so we could conceal the cargo as well as other forms of transportation.

I remember in our impromptu meeting Howard being quietly spoken and very respectful in his attitude. He seemed a genuinely nice guy but when I saw him I still felt uneasy, as I didn't know him or of him. I could see mysterious depths of which I couldn't fathom. Paranoid at whether he could be friend or foe, or even a copper, I kept my guard up.

The American he brought with him was the showman and did most of the talking. I wasn't fussed on him either as he was a bit too cocky. You could see it in his face the confidence oozing out of every pore. I wondered at the time if this was false confidence and was overcompensating for nerves.

Whilst we all conversed the American produced a pack of playing cards. With the cards he demonstrated a great sleight of hand and performed tricks. Although not fond of his attitude his card skills impressed me greatly. So much so I asked him whether he would show how to do them. With that he went quiet. Although I wasn't long in his company I would have bet money that this was a rare moment when his mouth didn't move. The absence from his noise led to an unease. I remember him looking over to Howard with shifty eyes. Howard nodded back at him as if they telepathically just had a conversation and had reached an agreement. The American then asked if we would go on a deal with them. It was a bit of a shock. We had just planned to do our own and here we were discussing another one.

Troy, Mort and I took ourselves away to a quiet corner and discussed privately the offer these strangers had made. Before we talked I could see Troy and Mort had a flicker of interest but like me they weren't wholly comfortable with the idea of bringing more people in. I was the most disinterested. At the time I felt we had enough things going on with the trip we planned. Plus with more people would mean more people knowing leading to risks that information would get out. But more importantly more people would mean less money. After only a few minutes of deliberations we decided it was no and broke the news. The American tried to push a little more as he said he would show me how he did the tricks if I came on the deal We still said no. Jesus Christ I wasn't 5 years old knowing magic tricks wouldn't have persuaded me. Howard just nodded at us and accepted it. We did say that we would be in touch. However this didn't happen.

In hindsight this could have been a great deal and we could have achieved more success but how were we to know at the time what was lurking behind Howard's great smile. C'est la vie. Maybe it would have been different if we weren't so close at setting out on our deal. Well Howard went his way and I went mine.

I had settled my nerves by studying the maps. I refuelled at the pumps of the service station and then went inside to the cafeteria to refresh myself with coffee and a cake. Feeling calm and relaxed now I ploughed on through the first leg of my journey through France. I was going well. In all it took about three and half hours from Calais to Saint Dennis which was just on the outskirts of Paris. I did not get lost once and was sufficiently sure of my way. That was until I approached Paris. I had previously been warned of the dangers of driving in this city so my plan was to avoid the centre and follow the south route (sud) around Paris and pick up the road at Fontaine Blauau, on my way to Spain. Well that was my well intentioned plan but instead I got lost and Paris drew me in.

My hand written map was not welcome here in Paris. I needed to understand her roads and get myself out. Her roads were a patchwork of old and new, with different textures of cobbles and tarmac. On top of that they were consumed with thick and heavy traffic. However I was determined to understand Paris, use her roads and leave her like a one night stand but I knew she was not going to make it easy for me.

I passed through some medieval parts of the city. Again the streets were thick with cars. There was also much shouting in French from the drivers around me, profanities I should imagine. This was accompanied by the constant tune of tooting horns.

If the noise wasn't distracting enough I had to take care of the other people on the road. In amongst the traffic jams any movement would cause immense panic. As soon as there was bit of road to manoeuvre there were many cars changing lanes at short notice. I lost count the amount of times I and people around were nearly embroiled in an accident. I could not let this happen I had to hone my senses there was no way I was having an accident. No way. I wanted to retain my anonymity. It is no wonder the tourist board in France suggests that if you should sample this intense driving experience it is best to have a navigator or guide.

My head spun as I danced and danced around the roads of Paris. I was getting nowhere fast. I decided my best option was to get my bearings. I needed to get off the road, park my van and assess the situation. However as I looked around still concentrating on the cars in front I couldn't see any car parking spaces. Even the streets were choked with parked cars. The roads seemed endless and chaotic which proved difficult to focus on the buildings and landmarks I had passed. So I could have been going around in circles for all I knew. It's no wonder many Parisian households do not possess a car.

I looked at my watch as I was in a still bit of traffic. I had been dancing the afternoon away with her for an hour. This was no good. This was my first trip and I wanted to make a good impression. I needed to leave Paris's grasp. But what to do?

The cars in front then started moving and I got in the excitement of putting down my pedals. This was short-lived as I had to break sharply for a pedestrian and cyclist dangerously and fearlessly jaywalking past my vehicle and across heavy traffic. Annoyance filled my head as I knew that the pedestrian and cyclist's behaviour was not allowed, however if I was to have hit them I would have been prosecuted as French law would take it up with me and say I should have been in control of my car. My anger quickly subsided as this near miss gave me an idea and my adrenalin pumped up. I knew what I had to do. I needed to speak to a Parisian who could tell me the path I should take.

Finally after another thirty minutes of dancing around the roads in a sea of chaos I spotted a place on the corner of the road and parked up with glee. With my hands still on the wheel I closed my eyes and nodded my head forward taking a break from the immense concentration I had just endured. After a deep breath I pulled myself back into the situation and looked around. I could see several yards away leaning on the wall of a building three Parisians conversing. They looked like students. There was a tall dark haired boy and two other dark haired pretty girls all in their early twenties. They were laughing and having a chat as they puffed on cigarettes. I rolled down my window and decided to play the lost tourist card. Being a man this was a big blow to my ego to ask for directions, but it needed to be done.

'Excusez-moi.' I shouted in a mock French accent.

'Allo!' The boy retorted.

'Je ne parle pas français. Parlez-vous anglais?

'Oui. I speak English'

'I am lost I need to go to Spain. Espanol? Via the E15 to Auxerre'

'Ah oui. You need to leave on the main roads. Er er how you say the doors. You need to find the doors. Er er theeze are the main part of the city. Follow theeze doors and look for the sud.'

'Doors?'

'Doors oui. Right I have to go now sorry. Au revoir. Bon voyage'

Dumbfounded I fell silent as the three students slipped away into the throng of the crowds. I wanted to question them more but obviously they had a prior engagement. Look for the sud he said. I knew that meant south but I hadn't seen any signs for the south. Also doors! What the fuck does he mean? As I ventured along the Paris streets I was still lost as ever, but this time I was looking at the doors of everything in my path. The doors on buildings. The doors of houses. The doors of ornate churches I passed.

What a fucking load of bollocks. Stupid French git he was winding me up. That was it I decided I needed take another break. So luckily I found another tight parking space for my caravanette and walked down the street scouting out the nearest telephone exchange and a café for some grub. I found the telephone exchange quite easily and contacted Troy to say I was in France and everything was okay. Didn't tell him I was lost as I didn't want to worry him. Plus I didn't want to admit being lost in the first country.

I found a café easily enough and bought a coffee once again, but I decided to have something more substantial for food and so had a delicious baguette filled with chicken and brie. I savoured each bite in order to procrastinate from driving. Once it was finished I ambled back to my van with dread at taking the wheel again and joining the circus back on the road, but I needed to get out of here. I stopped before I put the keys in the van and looked along the busy street. Ahead of me was a great arch and on it was a sign which said the sud. It then dawned on me I had passed quite a few of these large arches in and around the city. However as I looked at the arch more closely I noticed they had doors on them. Mind in my defence I wouldn't have noticed them that easily when driving, as the doors were open. Jesus Christ Almighty! So that's what he fucking meant. He was on about these great arches with these big medieval doors that were open. I laughed to myself and was empowered by a moment of epiphany. If I had the time of day I would have felt bad about slagging the guy off in my head but I was far too busy for that. But I will take homage here. Thanks Frenchie.

With my new found knowledge I paid attention to the arches some saying sud some saying du nord. So I avoided the nord and kept with the sud. I eventually came across the E50 this was not the road I had wanted but the road was taking me away from the city. I was thankful for that at least. Then the road turned into the E15. This was the right road however I could not be sure I was on the right path still, as the names of the places passing me by I had not noted. Pertles, Villabe, Lisses. I nervously ploughed on driving along the French motorway called L'autoroute du soleil. This was to be apt as this road was to be my ray of sunshine and sure enough after 10 miles there it was. A signpost saying Fontainebleau. Ahhh thank god I recognise this place from the maps. I was back on track.

After the kerfuffle in Paris I decided I wanted to make headway even though I was exhausted. I had already been driving on and off for over 6 hours and Paris had zapped me of strength. However I ignored my body and carried on driving. I wanted to at least on my first day try and drive through the majority of France. I managed to do a solid 5 hours but eventually retreated at Valence at nine o'clock at night. My mind wanted to do more but my eyes were not a willing. I did originally want to get to Perpignan which is snug to the Spanish border but that was still too far away. It was 375 miles and over 7 and a half hours of driving too far away. Mind one great thing about being in a caravanette was that I could just park it up and go to bed. There was no hassle in having to find a hotel.

I awoke the next day refreshed but still weary in mind from the day before. Hopefully no surprises today, but I am ready for them if there is. Bring them on. Luckily the second day went great as I went on the right roads as planned travelling miles and miles around the French coast line. It took just shy of eight hours of driving to Perpignan. Passing through Nimes, Montpellier and Narbonne. Everything felt perfect on this stretch of driving. I didn't get lost, the sun was out and warm enough to heat my soul but the sea breezes cool enough so my bollocks didn't stick to my legs.

After having a forty minute break in Perpignan I was ready to go back on the open road again. In this time I did well I managed to find a telephone exchange and inform Troy my position, have food and a very satisfying shit. I was ready to venture into a new country now, that of Spain. After twenty miles of leaving Perpignan I was at La Jonquera the border passport control to Spain. I passed through with flying colours and was waved into the country. Once I entered Spain I drove off to the side of a quiet road and took out my French map. I no longer needed this so I burned it and discarded to the side of an empty road, leaving a trail of ash. I wanted to forget Paris. Whilst I closed my door I could feel my body overheating. This was due to the temperature rising as I went deeper and deeper into Spain and coupled with the feverish excitement I had at nearing Morocco. Although hot and tired I managed to drive for another five hours and ended up in Tortosa. Again I found somewhere to park up and settled for the night.

My third day of travelling was to be my most successful I had managed to do 13 hours ending up in Algeciras. I did feel a bit gutted though as I was too late to catch a ferry from Algeciras to Morocco, but at least I would be fresh for her tomorrow.

Although I haven't really acknowledged Spain on this journey in this chapter I will make up for this in years to come. And I can promise Spain will be more of a bitch to me than Paris ever was.

I woke up at 6.30am. Despite being early I was very excited. I could have stayed in bed longer as the ferry was at nine and the journey there was only a twenty minute or so drive. So I killed an hour and half drinking coffee and reading Time magazines. I loved reading these magazines as I found them entertaining and useful. It was in these magazines I would learn about the countries I was entering and more importantly about their stability. There was no way I was doing a drug smuggling mission in the middle of a civil war. Can you imagine, excuse me mate can you point your big guns that way and let me pass through with my huge quantities of dope. Ain't happening.

I looked at my watch and it was ten to eight in the morning. I had waited long enough; I decided it was time to drive to the ferry. Driving towards Algeciras Port it suddenly dawned on me not only was I travelling to a different country today, Morocco, I would also be entering a new continent. With excitement I drove fast to the ferry.

Once the ferry from Algeciras to Tangier started to move I felt relaxed. I much preferred travelling in this fashion than nearly killing myself with long stints of driving. In the distance I could see straight ahead Gibraltar in all its glory and Europa point separating the land from the sea. The sun shone over Gibraltar and highlighted its magnificent backdrop of the limestone rocks. This was the only sight I remembered as we sailed around the tip of Spain. For the rest of my journey I sat on a seat folded my arms and closed my eyes half in a dream as I allowed the thoughts and feelings of the past three days wash over me. My thoughts drifted from the green green grass of home, to the white cliffs of Dover, to the farms of France, to the sand of Spain and now to the dust of Morocco. I felt at peace as we bobbed gently to the next destination. Although early morning I could feel the temperature rising. Spain had been hot but this heat was unbearable.

The noise from the people on the ferry shouting and walking around awoke me from my dream. This was a sure sign the ferry was nearing land. This was confirmed when I opened my eyes and could see the new land I had to conquer. It was littered with white buildings and greenery here and there. The place glistened as the sun beat down hard upon it. It did look beautiful. I agreed with John Gunther who said 'For anybody inclined to be a crook, Tangier offers a setting almost too perfect to be believed.'

It seemed to take forever to unload the ferry. It was not as swift as the Dover to Calais crossing. However I did not care today. My day should be pretty straight forward. I was in the place Tangier where I needed to be and I was meeting Ahmed after 7pm and Troy should be in the airport at around 8pm. As it was only 11am I had plenty of time to kill and so I sat back and let them take as long as they wanted. Which they did.

When I finally left the Ferry and changed my money at the bureau du change into Moroccan dirhams a shudder went down my spine having to drive again but at least it was only for a short while. As I bobbled along in my caravanette into this unknown new country I felt like an alien.

The climate was nothing like I was used to. So dry and hot! And it was only morning. This was the first time I had ever seen Moroccan people and their Muslim attire. I found it hard to concentrate on the road as I felt myself getting lost in looking at their strange clothing. I was shocked at how little skin they displayed. Especially the women, as I could only see their eyes and hands. On some of the burkas the women even wore a black transparent veil that went over the eye slit, obscuring their eyes even more. Although their attire was generic I noted various different styles, shapes, patterns and colours. Some wore ornate and beautiful materials obviously denoting wealth where as some just wore plain black material which looked more rag like, obviously the poorer of society.

I came to a section in the road where I had a set of three choices of direction. Either to remain on the Rue Dar El Baroud, or I could go down the Rue De La Marine or there was also the Rue Med Torres. After seconds of deliberation I picked the Rue Med Torres. I picked this as I thought it would take me on the coast road so I could have a nose at the sights of the Mediterranean and then come back down to the new town which is where I had been told to get a hotel.

The roads were shocking when I came off the ferry but they started to get particularly worse as I ventured down this road. The atmosphere seemed to change to, from a tourist friendly place to rather a local's place. It also went from a smoothish road to one that was paved in cobbles and housed small dingy shops. As I travelled down further and further, I could see in the eyes of the people I was not welcome here. Had I taken the wrong turning? I trudged on hoping that I could quickly bypass this place. Before I knew it there were swarms and swarms of Moroccans walking around my van as if I didn't exist. Some purposely were in front of my van walking at a crawling pace. Some stood and chatted pretending not to realise I was there. I wanted to get out of my van and say 'Oi' but I did not know what reception I would get. It got to the point where my caravanette could not move as the bodies increased and increased. I felt choked. I now couldn't move in any direction. I looked around and could not see another car in sight. Is this why? Are cars not supposed to go down here? My ponderings were short lived and I was pulled back to reality by short sharp thuds. The thuds were coming from people hitting my caravanette with large pieces of wood. I was under attack. Without thinking I beeped my horn angrily. Fuck should I be doing this? Will this make it worse? What the hell have you done Alan? In the country for only twenty minutes and already you have a baying mob for your blood. The bangs got louder and louder as they hit my beautiful caravette with increasing ferocity. Oh shit!

As I looked at the crowd I could see a young boy of say 14 or 15 years struggling to make a path through the swarm. He managed to get through and stood at the side of my passenger door looking through the window at me sympathetically. He knocked on my window politely and was shouting something. I could barely hear him as he was drowned out from the others shouting and banging. He shouted again but I still could not hear but from reading his lips I am sure he said 'I can help you'. He spoke English? Did I just imagine that? I pondered a while as to whether to let him in. Will this boy make the situation worse? Has he a knife? Is he going to rob me? Also I found it strange he was speaking in my native tongue. Well I threw caution to the wind and thought with my current situation I hadn't anything to loose. I opened the door only a few inches and he got in slamming the door whilst skillfully not allowing anyone else to get in.

'Hi, I am Said. I can be your guide for the day.'

'What?'

What the fuck? I am here under attack and this little shit wants to guide me around. A tour of historic churches was far from my mind. One thing I will give him is he spoke good English and oddly with an English accent.

'Look I can help you. I will get you out of here safely'

'Ok…'

As I nodded to him to accept his services he opened the door and started shouting in Arabic and pushing people. It took a while but slowly the human traffic parted and I managed to drive my van out of the Medina

Once away from the baying mob I zipped along to the new town. Ahh this was nice, I could breathe again. On the roads in the new town there were only cars no crowds. Also this part of Tangier seemed more tourist friendly with its pleasant large hotels and sparkling white shops. No wonder Troy said to stay here. He also said that the Medina was open to tourists but only up to 10pm after that without a guide it was a very dangerous place indeed. I looked across to my guide who was smiling awaiting his money. I decided to give him a fiver. Which was a hell of a lot but he was worth every penny. The young boy went off back in the direction of the Medina. I bet that night him and his family had a good laugh at me and celebrated their good fortune of an easy fiver. However I was thankful.

I looked around the new town and went scouting for a hotel. Although I had the caravanette I felt I would be much safer in a hotel especially after the stick mob adventure. I came across the Hotel Paris. It wasn't the best in Morocco but I liked its location. It was near to the street so I could view my caravanette from my hotel window. As I went into the clean no frills basic hotel room I opened the curtain to observe my caravanette. I was still unhappy. I did not feel my transport was safe. So I wandered off outside the hotel looking for another guide. Sure enough another young guy gained my attention and realised I needed services he could offer. This boy was a bit older, in his mid-twenties I would have guessed. Also I could see he was stocky as the material he wore clung to his muscles. He would be perfect enough to be my caravanette bodyguard.

'Er excuse me'

'Hi. What can I do for you?'

'This is mine.' I said pointing to the caravanette.

'I want you to watch over her. I will pay good money'

'Certainly'

In an instant he sat down cross legged on the pavement staring hard at the caravanette. He didn't even ask how long he would have to stay there for or how much I would give him. Well job done I thought and left him to it as I went back to the hotel bedroom. I sat down on the hard wooden chair next to the bed and pulled out the address of Ahmed who was to be our supplier of the hashish powder. This part was going to be a bit tricky. I had an address but not much of a map to go on. Also I did not want to ask anyone directions as I didn't want to raise suspicions. It wouldn't take much of a genius to realise why a westerner would have connections with a Moroccan farmer. Another problem I found was that the address said the Medina. This sent shudders through my mind as this was the place where my caravanette was beaten. I wonder what sort of reception I will receive when I go by foot. I know Troy said tourists could go there in the day but I proved that wrong.

Before I walked to the Medina I had to go through the New town. I decided to have a little nosey around as I had plenty of time to kill or be killed. I was also raring myself up for the people with sticks. Maybe I should take a plank of wood too.

In the New town I perused through the windows of the quaint shops and boutiques noting the wealth in this part of town. As I walked on and on towards the direction of the Medina I could feel the atmosphere changing again from free and laid back to poverty and fear. However when I walked down the same roads where my caravanette was beaten, it was okay as a pedestrian I was left alone. People just walked by. I could see some would pretend they hadn't seen me. Even though that was pretty unlikely as I stuck out like a sore thumb, a white man in a sea of darker skin. Some looked at me curiously but then stopped their gaze when my eyes connected with theirs. As I looked around at the shops I noted they were far smaller and dustier than in the shiny modern new town. As I looked into the windows it seemed there wasn't a theme they seemed to sell a random selection of products, a kind of bric-a-brac if you will.

I passed a place called the Petit Socco. This was apparently once famous for male prostitutes and boy brothels, but now thankfully it was a quiet square containing winding alleys, cafes and many shops. A butchers shop caught my attention, as the meat in the window looked diseased and was swarming with flies. Nice!

Along the streets were strewn with beggars, mainly young children. A few of the children had no legs from the knee down. They got themselves around by sitting their stumps on a kind of skateboard and pushed themselves along the streets with their dirty hands. It was heartbreaking to see. I had never witnessed poverty on such a scale. I paid a lot of money to those children as I walked by. Mind you my money was probably a drop in the ocean for them but I felt I needed to give something. Plus they were the only people to acknowledge me.

I also passed a young woman sat on the side of street begging. Although I could only see her eyes I could tell she was beautiful. She was clutching a new born baby in her arms who was wrapped in rags. She seemed different to the other beggars she was alone where she was and her attitude was not as persistent in begging. It was as if she didn't care whether I gave her money or not. The others were more forceful especially the children who would grab at my ankles pleading. However when I gave her a handful of Dirhams I could tell she was smiling as her eyes twinkled. I looked at her and then pointed at the baby and then to my mouth. I was asking her please feed the baby. Her eye twinkled again as she nodded at my instructions. As I walked off I felt strange and emotional at meeting this community. However I had to shake myself out of this and get my mindset back on the job. There was no room for getting sentimental in this business.

With my mind back on track for locating Ahmed's shop I paced up and down the streets. I did not get my address out just yet. This map and address was so important I daren't risk it in the open. So I plodded along. I ventured into cafes and decided on which one had the nicest smell coming from it. They all mainly did but after a while I chose my café and went in. I had a drink of mint tea for the very first time and sampled a harira. The harira was a rich soup of meat and chick peas it was unusual and delicious, and very filling. The Mint tea was also very refreshing on the taste buds. Once I had finished the soup my stomach gurgled. I hope the meat wasn't from the butchers I had just seen. Oh well in Rome. Well Morocco but you know what I mean.

I decided I seemed close enough so I pulled out my neatly folded paper with Ahmed's shop address. I was right to do so as I found it as I passed five shops. It was a lot smaller than I imagined. I looked around and tried to take a picture in my mind of its location. I wasn't going to go in yet as I was far too early. It was now three o'clock and I had been told to specifically meet after 7pm not before. So I walked away quietly. On the way back through the Medina I ignored the beggars, the crowd and activities going on. I was concentrating on the roads and noting land marks I had passed. I was memorising my route for when I was to venture back that night. Once back to my hotel I decided to have a bit of a lie down before the big meet tonight.

Time flew fast lying on my bed in the Hotel Paris. I nearly fell asleep a few times but I fortunately managed to jolt myself back to consciousness. It was now 6 o'clock time was getting ready to amble to the Medina. I looked outside the hotel sure enough there he was my guide sat down cross legged on the pavement in the same spot protecting my beloved Caravanette. Fair play to the guy.

I put my jacket on as the air grew a bit colder and ambled slowly along to the Medina. The beggars had gone now and the streets were practically empty. I found the shop easily again but this time I could venture in. On my clock said 7.00pm. Bang on time. As I went into the shop I shut the door quietly. I looked around in this tiny shop at the bric-a-brac they sold like the other shops. It was shocking that he had not much there to sell. I also thought it odd that this tiny shop with nothing much in it was to be the hub for a million pound weed operation. I couldn't believe it. As I approached the humble wooden make shift counter, there was guy in his forties standing proudly behind with his hands behind his back. I could see this was not Ahmed, as I was informed he was much older than this. He stared at me never leaving my gaze. This is weird on the streets they treated me like a leper and in here I could feel his eyes burning into my soul.

'Hi my name is Alan. I am looking for Ahmed.'

'One moment I will see if he is here'

I turned my back as he disappeared off in the back room to find Ahmed and I again surveyed this humble shop. Only seconds went by when a guy in his sixties with grey hair whizzed into the room. His clothing was plain but from the tailoring I could tell it was expensive.

'Hi Alan. I am Ahmed.' He shouted magnanimously

Ahmed extended his right arm out and shook my hand. Once we had shaken he put his right hand immediately onto his chest. This took me by surprise as I had never seen a greeting like this before. However I have since learned that in Muslim culture if someone puts their hand on their heart after a handshake it means they respect you. It is a sign of showing honour.

'Hello nice to meet you Ahmed'

'How was your trip down here?'

'Yeah okay its lovely round here'

'I hope you had no trouble?'

'No not at all. Everything was fine'

The way Ahmed asked the question seemed like he knew something. Nah I am just being paranoid. I did not tell Ahmed what had happened with the stick mob I thought it best to keep it to myself. This and getting lost in Paris. I wanted to look professional. Plus the problems were behind me now there was no need to divulge my skirmishes.

'What time is Troy coming?'

'He told me to pick him up outside the airport around 8pm'

'Do you know how to get to the airport?'

'Yes isn't it off the Rue D'Angleterre onto Avenue Christophe Columb'

'Yes that's right'

It felt a little bit awkward talking to Ahmed for the very first time. I was very cautious as I did not want to make a mistake by saying something or doing something that may disrespect him in regards to his beliefs or culture. I had little knowledge on the Muslim religious faith. I felt very susceptible to putting my foot in my mouth. However luckily in our conversations he seemed contented and not upset. He smiled throughout.

It made it so much easier that he could converse with me in fluent English. He mainly talked to me about avoiding some areas. He was telling me I was okay in the Medina up until 10pm without a guide but that I should stay away from the Port especially at night. I wasn't really taking in what he was saying as I couldn't get over the fact he said that I was okay in the Medina. In my head I was saying er just a few hours ago mate in your safe Medina I was being attacked by the locals.

'Right Ahmed I better go and get Troy'

'Okay but it is only a few miles down the road and you still have twenty minutes before his flight comes in'

'I like to be early'

'Okay well if Troy is not too tired. Come back and have a sebsi'

I nodded and left. On the journey to the airport I was trying to fathom what the hell a sebsi was. Is it a special kind of mint tea? Well it definitely sounds like something you drink. Maybe an alcohol of some kind? Actually scrap that I did know that Muslims do not drink alcohol and Ahmed seemed a proud man he wouldn't allow that. Well I hope if Troy doesn't want to go to see him tonight he offers me another one so I know what the bloody hell it is.

As Ahmed said I was way early for Troy but I didn't mind. I preferred waiting rather than meeting all red and aggravated. It doesn't give a good impression. In the ten minutes or some I slowly rolled a fag and puffed on it feeling relaxed. It felt nice I was to have a companion for the next few days. I would not be alone and the only white boy in town. I drifted off into a day dream. Again my mind was replaying the events of the last few days. My mind was accommodating and catching up with my body that had driven for 1000's of miles.

Two loud knocks came from the window. Shocked half to death I darted my gaze to the window. It was Troy. Quickly I opened the door and let him in. I was a bit shocked he managed to see me first but I suppose my caravanette outside the airport did stick out.

'Well Alan you made it this far.'

'Yes indeed.'

'Did you enjoy the driving? I mean you haven't seen France, Spain and Morocco before have you?'

'Well to be honest Troy I didn't really have time to look I just wanted to concentrate on getting myself here.'

'Well at least your here Alan so let's have a bit of fun while Ahmed sorts the powder.'

'What do you mean?'

'Well as I said before it could take four days to a week and a half for Ahmed to get the hashish.'

'Yeah you said the Moroccans do not really run their life by time'

'Mind you it's not only that. The stuff has to come by donkey. As in Ketama where it is farmed there are police outposts so they put it on the donkeys and make them go up the mountains and on treacherous terrain.'

'How long are you staying Troy?'

'Three days. I will sort out the business with Ahmed and spend a little time with you and off I go.'

'Right come on Alan let's get a shift on.'

'Okay.'

'Oh and I am going to be staying at the hotel Villa de France.'

'Where did you book into Alan?'

'The Hotel Paris'

'Ahh that's good my hotel is only a bit further down than yours.'

Troy gave me directions to the hotel but it was pretty straight forward as all I had to do as he said was head for my hotel and his was a bit further on to the right. I hadn't been this far South so I looked at his hotel with fresh eyes. It was much nicer than mine. It was more of a four star hotel. On the door there was even security in the shape of two large burly men dressed up smart with red Fez's on their head. Also the hotel had a carpark out the back. I did not feel jealous. Well maybe slightly envious but I stopped myself. Troy and Mort were my backers there part in the job was the money and connections. So I was privileged to work with them. There was no way I could fund such a stunt. But what I lacked in money I made up with courage.

'Right I will check in and unpack my stuff you wait here and we shall go back to Ahmed's.'

'Yeah okay'

Waiting for Troy felt like an age. Mind I didn't care there was not much going down tonight. Only I was to have a sebsi for the first time. I hope I liked it. Eventually Troy got back in the van and I whizzed up the road a few yards down and parked the caravanette outside my hotel. Easily I found another guide to look after my van and off me and Troy headed on foot to the Medina. As it grew darker I felt on guard as we ventured down to the Medina. Although a little unnerving I found the adrenalin rushing through my veins exhilarating. Plus the dingy dark alleys were the most exotic I had ever walked through.

We rolled into Ahmed's to have some fun. Around him was a group of older gentleman. I could not pin their ages but they could have been in their 70's perhaps 80's. They all sat in a circle of chairs. There were two extra chairs presumably for Troy and I. We did not sit straight away. We waited respectfully until Ahmed beckoned us.

'Hi Troy very nice to see you.'

As Ahmed did so with me he shook Troy's hand and then gently banged his palm on his heart. Troy did the same. I need to remember to do this I thought.

'How was your flight?'

'Yeah fine Ahmed.'

'Well Alan you take a seat and join us in a sebsi.'

'Troy do you fancy any?'

'Nah I am fine. I will just have a mint tea'

Troy took his chair slightly out of the circle to show he wasn't partaking in this ritual. I was a bit concerned but also very excited. Why had Troy take himself out? Is it really foul and disgusting? Should I have asked or maybe watched before doing this. Well it was time. I loved the excitement of new things. I noticed all the guys had pouches of some kind of tobacco. Only it didn't smell like tobacco. It smelt like kif. When I saw him take the stuff out of the pouch my suspicions were right, it was indeed kif. With the kif in his hand he squashed it into a pipe and smoked it. A ha! It was similar to me in the UK sitting with a few mates passing a spliff. The rules must be same everywhere as they too passed it to the left. It went round and round quite a few times. I carefully watched on noting the way they refilled the pipe so I could do exactly the same. I did try to avoid refilling the pipe by taking only a few puffs and passing it on, but the guy next to me elbowed me to smoke more. The last of the sebsis really hurt my lungs. Once the sebsi was extinguished all eyes were on me to perform the ritual. To my relief I did it with perfection and the others just carried on as normal. Which I took as a compliment at least they did not show disappointment. Once the bags were all gone and we were all sufficiently stoned it was time for another cup of mint tea. As I sat back the sebsi started really kicking in. However I did managed to pull it together and look relatively normal even though I felt stoned within an inch of my life. The other seventy and eighty year old men seemed fine.

Trying to keep my eyes focused and stopping them from rolling around in my head I sipped on mint tea. In the background I could hear Troy's voice rise as he was talking to Ahmed. Interested I honed in listening to their conversation.

'Can you guarantee Alan's safety?'

'Yes don't worry in the New town he is fine. In the Medina he is fine. He just needs to stay away from the docks at night. That is where I cannot guarantee his safety.'

As he said these words he stared over to me reemphasising the point even though he had already told me this once before.

'Right Alan it's getting late shall we go home?'

'Yes I am tired its being a long day. Thanks Ahmed for everything.'

'Call in tomorrow again after 7pm if you want. You're always welcome.'

Ahmed also sent a young man in his mid-twenties to chaperone us home. I did try to refuse but Ahmed would have none of it.

As we closed the door we headed through the Medina.

'Hey fancy the docks Troy?'

'Alan that is not even funny.'

'Look Troy I will be fine. I am good with surprises.'

'Look Alan I know this is business but I do want to make sure you are safe too.'

'Trust me Troy I am good at getting out of scrapes.'

'Please do not venture to the docks.'

'Don't worry.'

For the next two days with Troy there it felt like it was a holiday. I was with my friend drinking and eating the day and night away. We also toured around in the caravanette looking at the sights and buying postcards every place we visited. The strangest sight to me was that of a Roman Catholic Church in the New town of Tangier. I thought everybody was Muslim here, well perhaps not. In the evenings we would also go down to see Ahmed and I would smoke myself into oblivion. Oh what a life!

The last day of Troy's stay arrived too quickly for me. The day zipped along as he took me yet another great place to eat. This time it was grilled fish. It was stunning as you could tell it was so fresh. Probably caught from the Mediterranean Sea that day. Then by the time we knew it, it was after 7pm. Time to wander down to Ahmed's again for tea and a sebsi.

As I had visited Ahmed's shop for a few days now I started to feel confident and comfortable when talking to Ahmed and decided I wanted to find out more about his people.

'Ahmed?'

'Yes Alan.'

'Where are the parents of the children who beg on the street? And why are there so many?'

'They are probably begging or working too.'

'So work here can be begging.'

'Also why do the children with no legs do it?'

'Shouldn't they be at home?'

'Look Alan...... Some of those children don't have a home. Plus the parents will get more money for their children if they are without limbs.'

I could feel a lump in my throat. I was disgusted by the thought that a parent would allow their children to beg, especially the even more vulnerable ones with disabilities. But what Ahmed had to say next shocked me to bone and still continues to send shivers down my spine.

'Also because they are poor some of the parents will cause their children to be disabled by tying their legs when they are very young to the railway track and have an oncoming train to take them off. Then they would cauterize them with tar,' he said coldly and rather matter of fact.

My head went numb and I could feel the blood drain from my face. On the one hand I wanted to attack everyone in the shop apart from Troy for allowing such atrocities to go on. On the other I was in the middle of a pretty heavy cannabis deal so I needed to keep my cool. Stoned and confused my eyes spun round as I tried to fathom how to deal with this. Troy could see I was upset and caught me by the arm. He took me over to the other side of the room out of earshot of Ahmed.

'Look Alan. Keep cool. I know it is horrendous what he has just said but we can't do anything. But in a weird way we are helping.'

'How?'

'Us and the other drug smugglers are bringing money here. Now Ahmed is a good man he funds his family and other relatives foremost from his deals but he does also distribute and use the services of many and I mean many local people.'

'Now are you okay?'

'Yes Troy I am fine just taken a back that's all.'

Ahmed could see we had finished and approached us.

'Is everything okay gentleman?'

'Yes Ahmed. I think I am tired and need to go to bed.'

On the way back Troy and I didn't speak much. It was a shame the last night he was in Morocco ended on a bit of downer. But reality can be a cruel bitch. Especially for the poorest here. Those poor kids.

The next day I took Troy to the airport. He told me to spend the rest of my stay in the Hotel Ville de France. He said the reason was so the caravanette would be safer in the car park but I knew it was a gesture to try and make me feel better. I agreed to move hotels and waved him back off to the UK. I had been in Morocco for four days now and started to tire. I did not want to walk past the poor anymore. It would make me so angry. However I still did. I also put double the money down knowing what the poor sods had been through. Maybe I should stick to the New town more, so I could focus on the job. But anyways I needed to go in the Medina to see Ahmed and to see whether the powder was ready. That was also slightly annoying me the fact he couldn't tell me a time. But again I had to keep my cool and be patient. Remember Alan think about the donkeys.

It was six o'clock and I was pottering round the Medina and the new town yet again. On my travels I met a policeman. He was standing in the middle of the road directing the traffic. Although busy doing his job he managed to hold my gaze for a few seconds. When he did so he smiled at me. This really unnerved me. Why was he smiling? No stranger from Morocco had smiled at me before. Did he know something? I didn't particularly want him of all people keeping tabs on me. So I tried to avoid his glances but once I met his gaze I could see him staring hard. Not to seem suspicious I raised half a smile back whilst lowering my head to look like a shy tourist. As he turned away avoiding my gaze I looked at him again I was so sure I had seen him before. Feeling a bit paranoid I looked away and continued ambling around the Medina until 7 ish when I would be allowed in Ahmed's. A devilish thought had crossed my mind and I thought about being a sod. What would happen if I went now to Ahmed's I thought? Before the allotted time. God forbid. I smiled to myself and only entertained the possibility. I shouldn't really be thinking this. I needed to respect Ahmed. Plus he probably chose 7pm as the Medina would be closed down and there would be few if none on the streets. He probably did this to make me safe, but where was he when I was attacked by sticks.

Before I went to Ahmed I saw the young woman again holding the babe in her arms. I put the money in the bowl and did the same actions as I always did to ask her to feed the baby. Each time I did she smiled more as if it was an intimate private joke we had. I started to walk away but stopped after an uncontrollable urge to see her face. So I plucked up the courage and walked back. I asked her could she pull back the mouth piece on her veil and I did the actions to portray the act. Although she never spoke back I think she knew what I said before I did the actions but I could not be sure. I think she could speak English as she seemed to understand, but she never uttered a word. It was very common in Morocco that people could speak four or more languages, the common ones being Arabic, French, Spanish and English. It was especially common in young boys in their teens to their thirties to speak numerous languages as they would use this as a trade in being a guide. I came across many boys who would offer their services as guides. When they first spoke to me they did so in an American twang but after I spoke they would revert to an English accent. However I never encountered any to do so in a Welsh accent. Maybe on my next trip if I was to make it that far, I would try to teach them.

After I asked her to remove her veil she looked to the floor as she was pondering what to do. I didn't want to make her feel uncomfortable so I waved my hand as if to say fair enough and was about to walk away. With that she waved her hand back at me and nodded. So I waited as she unpinned the mouth piece. I was right she was beautiful. I smiled at her appreciating her beauty and pointed to put back her mouthpiece and I went on my merry way. What a beautiful girl? What a waste?

It was 7.00pm and I edged my way to Ahmed's shop. I was bit anxious as I did make a faux pas yesterday by showing a little emotion. I had to make sure that I was more business like today. So I entered the shop confidently and conversed with Ahmed and his friends. It was amicable for a while as we had the sebsi and mint tea but then the conversation stopped and Ahmed looked hard at me.

'Alan can we request something of you?'

'Certainly. What is it?'

'Please can you stop giving the woman on the streets money?'

'What woman?'

'Oh you mean the young girl with a baby.'

'Yes.'

'Why?'

'She is on the street with her baby as she has disgraced her family and has been outcasted from the community. You are not to give her any more money. If you don't stop I fear for your safety.'

'I understand.'

I didn't understand but I didn't know how to react. I tried to keep cool and not display emotion. I made sure my body language was in agreement and my face was calm and not aggressive. However inside I was reeling. I wanted to ask more of her crime but I feared this would antagonise. I feared also her crime would not warrant starvation of a young girl and her baby. I mean what fucking would! After the serious discussion the conversation went back to normal everyone seemed happy and stoned. I pretended also to be happy. It was hard to keep up the pretence. Every fibre in my being wanted to shout 'why?'

I made sure I said goodbye to Ahmed fondly to show I had no hard feelings for him stopping me giving money to the girl. In reality I was consumed with rage. I needed to keep my cool though and think of the deal. That night was the first time the sebsi did not make me feel stoned. But I had to remind myself this was a different world to mine, I had to understand that but I would never respect it.

The next day I decided to drive around and go sightseeing. I avoided going on the streets of the Medina. I did it to avoid the girl. Again I saw on my travels the local policeman. He was young approximately in his late twenties early thirties. As I went passed he seemed to favour my caravanette before the rest by letting me through early. Although this was a nice gesture I received it with grave caution. I decided to take back my van to the hotel and hide out in my hotel room away from the gaze of the local copper. I read a book and had a few naps. In the moments I was conscious I felt paranoid the police were on to me.

I looked at my clock and it was 6.30. Time enough to amble down to Ahmed's to see if the hashish was ready. Before I got there I forgot to avoid the street where she was, it was too late now I had to go past. She spotted me, as she smiled and looked up to greet me. I did not move towards her. I looked at her and then looked to the floor with my hands in the air shaking my head. She nodded. It was strange in that nod I could tell she knew. She knew I had been warned off and that I couldn't give her any more money. She looked away and avoided my gaze. Feeling saddened and angry I turned around and went on to Ahmed's. Again I had another night of amicable conversation. When really I wanted to say what the fuck are you doing letting a young mother and baby starve. Again I left Ahmed's smiling and happy and shaking his hand in all that respectful crap. I did leave earlier than usual so I could refuse his guides services. He still offered them but I assured him I would go straight to the hotel. It was a fat lie though as I didn't want to go straight back, I needed to walk off my anger and frustration. So for a while after I roamed the streets kicking around in the dirt whilst cursing under my breath. Then in a moment of madness I decided to venture off to the Docks. Sod Ahmed! Sod Morocco! He may have warned me to stop giving that woman money but he can't fucking tell me where to go. With purpose I waltzed off down to the docks. As I entered near to the sea the atmosphere felt creepy. It was so dark. It was worse than the first time I entered the Medina. This may have not been such a good idea. However my nerve held up and my excitement got the better of me as I ventured on into the forbidden parts.

I roamed around looking at the sea glistening and the waves lapping in the dark. It wasn't long until I decided I had seen enough. There was not much down here and it was far too quiet for my liking. So I turned around and headed back to the hotel so I could sleep off my resentment. As I left the docks I could see a flight of stone steps which was leading in the direction of the new town. So with enthusiasm I climbed up them happy to go home and rest my weary feet.

Once I trundled half way up the steps I was surrounded by three teenage boys shrouded in black material each carrying a big carving knife. There hoods were up and they wore dark scarves obscuring their mouths all I could see were their dark brown eyes. As I looked at each one of them I knew they meant business. Oh fuck! To show I was unarmed I held up my hands. The tallest boy stepped forward and pointed to my pockets. I took out slowly my wallet and held it out towards him. With his knife glistening in the moonlight he pointed the wallet to the floor. So as instructed I tossed it carefully to his feet. The boys still surrounding me waited for a response. They had my wallet what more did they want. With that the boy pointed to my trousers holding his knife inches from my nose. Confused I shrugged with my hands still held in the air. A boy to his right did the action of taking off his trousers.

'Oh . . . . . . You want me to take off my trousers.'

All the boys nodded. I was a bit taken aback but as instructed I took off my trousers and threw them to the floor. The boy with the knife then pointed to take off my other clothing but stopped once I was left only wearing a pair of white y fronts. Thankfully the pointing ceased but they held my gaze staring hard at me for several seconds. What are they fucking doing now! They have my money. They have literally the clothes off my back. Is it my life they want? Is it! And just as quickly as it started it was over. One of the boys picked up my clothes, the tallest held my wallet and the other carried my shoes. Then they ran full pelt disappearing into the dark. I waited a while to get over the shock. Then I realised I needed to get the fuck out of here. So I started running in the direction of the New Town. I caused a stir when I ran past the post which had the late night telephone exchange. I don't think they expected to see a white boy in his pants running past. I could see them with telephones in hand gasping and laughing. This was not a good day.

I stepped up a gear as I could feel my face redden with embarrassment as I passed other tourists. I felt a sigh of relief when I could see the hotel in the distance. The two Fez wearing guards saw me as I approached, laughing a little. Which I thought was bit mean and unprofessional. But I forgot this when one of them kindly took me by the arm and quickly ushered me to my room. Thankfully as it was late none of the other guests saw.

That night I didn't sleep much through all the stress, excitement and worry of my mugging. Ahmed was right. The docks were not the place to be. I learned that the hard way.

Twenty to seven the next night I left the hotel as I did to amble along to Ahmed's. I tried to avoid being noticed by the Fez wearing guards, but they saw me. As I looked towards them I could see them smiling. Bastards.

I carried on and again was outside Ahmed's shop. This time I was going to keep my wits about me when I left and I would not go through the docks. No way sir. As I went into the shop I noticed it was only me and Ahmed that was a bit strange. Where were the old fellas who would already be here chugging away on a sebsis. Ahmed stood solemnly by the door.

'Hi Alan.'

It got even weirder as he did not pat his chest and shake my right hand. What was going on? Why was he upset with me?

'Hi Ahmed.'

'Are you okay Alan?'

'Yeah fine just waiting for the powder to be ready.'

'Anything you want to tell me?'

'Er no.'

'You sure?'

'No everything is fine.'

With that he nodded and took me to the side of the shop pointing on a chair that had a pile of neatly folded fresh clean clothes with an empty wallet on the top of it. They were my clothes and my empty wallet. What the!

'Look Alan I am sorry I could not get your money back but all your clothes are there and your shoes.'

I was speechless. He had somehow retrieved my clothes and shoes for me. How the fuck did he manage that! I couldn't think of anything to say but I had to say something.

'Er that's fine Ahmed err …….. Thanks for getting my clothes back for me.'

'There is one other thing.'

'Yes.'

He beckoned with his hand in the backroom for someone to come in. As I watched on three teenaged boys entered the room.

'Now Alan these are to be your body guards from now on. It would be safer if you went around with these boys. Plus they can take you places where tourists daren't go. As I can see you have an eye for adventure.'

Again I was speechless. Bodyguards? And I couldn't be sure as it was so dark last night but I had an inkling these were the very three boys who had robbed me. I didn't know what to do. But I thought best not ask questions and just accept Ahmed's offer. It would be strange to go round with bodyguards, especially if these were the three who left me to run through Tangiers in my pants.

'Thanks Ahmed.'

Then as I looked to the floor the group of men that I was used to being there entered the room for sebsi time. They must have been in the backroom. At least Ahmed didn't embarrass me in front of his friends. Mind you I bet they knew what was going on.

I sat down and joined them. It was sebsi time again. For the most of the night I did not join in the conversation much. I was still too stunned at what just happened. I was also a little embarrassed as Ahmed would have known I defied him and went to the docks last night. However that was incredibly nice of him to give me body guards. It was nice also as he could probably see I was bit of bugger who when I wanted to do something I would. So the safest way for me to see unsafe places would be logically to have bodyguards. Although quiet I did smile, laugh and respond appropriately to the conversations that took place.

Thinking about it now years on I am a little paranoid as to whether Ahmed set me up in that mugging and it had served as a warning. As it all seemed a bit odd. However I don't care as whether instigated or by chance it worked I realised the dangers of Morocco without paying my life. There were many cases I had heard about where tourists were stripped and killed after they were mugged.

It was around 9 o'clock and then there was a rap at the door. This wasn't uncommon there were always street kids trying their luck and wanting to come in to join the bigger boys. However it wasn't this time as I could see Ahmed welcoming the person in. I turned my head to see who it was as I leaned back on the chair. A young gentleman in his late twenties entered. I had a feeling of déjàvous. I was sure I had seen him before. Before he could greet all the other men he caught my gaze.

'Hello Alan. Do you recognise me now?'

'Er sorry no……no I don't.'

'It's probably because I am not wearing my uniform.'

I turned to Ahmed and he nodded as if to say this guy was okay and I looked back. It then dawned on me he was the smiley local bobby. Now I get it I shouldn't had feared him Ahmed had him in his pocket.

'Ah yes I know you now.'

'Hi Alan nice to meet you.'

The next day I felt energised. I didn't feel so paranoid today. It was comforting to think that Ahmed knew so many people so he could keep an eye on me. I felt he was like an omnipotent being that shone through others in and around Morocco.

The next morning as I left the hotel I waved at the security fez men and held my head up high. I didn't care about what happened the night before last, that was gone. I am alive and so didn't care. As I jauntily walked across I could see three teenage boys sat cross legged on the pavement. As I drew nearer they stood up as if out respect. It was the boys from last night in Ahmed's shop. My bodyguards.

'Right boys where do you want to take me today?'

'Where would you like me to go Alan?'

'Where tourists like me shouldn't go,' I said smiling and feeling happy with the world.'

For the next three days the boys took me around here there and everywhere. This time it wasn't the usual touristy sightseeing. This time it was in the back and beyond and I loved it. They took me to a football game and they also took me to the local cinema. Which was the smallest cinema I had ever been in. It was more like a shack with a projector but it was interesting. Inside it did not hold many people only around 20 or 30 or so. On the screen was Charlie Chaplin in black and white. I was amazed at looking at the faces on the children and adults in that theatre as they relished this outdated film. I had seen it before but as apart of a documentary about old films. They were watching it with fresh eyes. I must admit I did enjoy and laugh along soaking up the positivity in the atmosphere. Mind the laughing was also helped by the joints that were passed around.

By this point I had been in Morocco for ten days. Nearly a week and a half had passed. Mind you I started to soak up the culture and did not care if I had to stay another week especially with my new body guards. I relished their youth and their insights into the true Morocco. However it was not to be that I would stay another week as when I went up to Ahmed's at 7pm as unusual we then had the nod that the powder was finally ready. There was no sebsi and mint tea that night. It was now time for business. As instructed I went back to my hotel to have a good night's kip before tomorrow's ride to Ahmed's farm.

The next morning one of Ahmed's trusted guides met me outside the hotel. I would have said he was about 19 years old. He was also very serious in his nature for a young boy. Which I liked as this was serious business. As strangers we both piled into my caravanette. He instructed me where to go and directed me to Ketama. After forty miles or so I looked at my fuel gage and realised I needed more petrol. I turned to my guide and informed him. He seemed annoyed at this but instructed me where to go for fuel. We pulled off towards the side of the road, I say roads but they were more like dirt tracks. We had been travelling for over an hour and it was around 9 o'clock at night. I was a bit shocked when I looked up to where we parked next to, the petrol station he took me too looked more like a shack sort of café place rather than a petrol station. As we entered inside I could see the makeshift petrol station was filled with men ranging from their teens to eighties. People were sitting down in different fashions and chatting quite happily. I noticed each man had a gun next to them of varying shapes and sizes, mostly they were rifles. Some had then propped against the wall, some had them slung over their shoulder by a strap and others had them just by their side ready for use. Then as they noticed me enter the room a silence dawned. All eyes were on me. Oh shit. However my guide stepped in front of me with his hands in the air and conversed with them in Arabic. What he seemed to say was smoothing these guys over. Thank God! I was not a threat or prey to them. My guide turned round and smiled. It was a bit disconcerting as he too looked relieved.

'It's okay Alan. Everything is fine.'

'Did you tell them I was your father?'

The boy did not laugh but smiled. In the shack I bought a few beers and supped away. We refuelled the caravanette and then politely left.

Feeling glad we were out of there I got back on the open road again being directed to the back of beyond with my stranger for a guide. The last part of the journey felt like an incredibly long road. This road was called the Route de l'Unite. It was bumpy and dangerous and went through mountains. Also every now again we would see people by the side of the road. My guide would inform me to stop. He would converse in Arabic with them and then they would leave and everything was fine. Looking back on it now I was very naïve. I did not realise the people on the side of the road were armed and dangerous bandits. I had to give credit to my guide. He was so good at his job at appeasing people and explaining our path that I was not even aware of any dangers.

As we got to Ahmed's house the boy breathed a sigh of relief. I now know why. I was just thankful I wasn't driving anymore. So what's next I thought? As I got out of the caravanette Ahmed came to greet us. It was so dark but I could make out his gentle smile.

'Right Alan. Are you ready? Or do you want anything to drink or eat.'

'No thanks. Let's get to it!'

Ahmed's associates brought out bags and bags of cannabis powder as he watched on. They laid them on the floor for me to transfer. The powder was to go into the empty gas bottles I had brought. What I hoped is that when I went through customs if they found these they would assume it was gas. One of the bottles was to be attached to the cooker and another put in an underground floor compartment specifically designed for it to be stored. I hoped only people who had owned a caravanette would know this compartment existed and maybe customs wouldn't. Probably unlikely but I enjoyed thinking this was true.

It took hours and hours to pour the powder in. If this wasn't stressful enough Ahmed and his associates were eyeballing me, so I daren't drop any of their precious powder. Also I was trying to get as much of the powder in the bottles as possible. I used a stick plunger to poke down and compact in as much as I could. This didn't seem to please Ahmed and Co, but I didn't care more cannabis powder more money as far as I was concerned. The work was exhausting and took just under an hour of careful filling for both bottles. Once I was finished and was satisfied I had a sufficient amount I put one in the under floor compartment and the other I attached to the cooker. The guide then directed me out of Ketama. On the way back we did not seem to get stopped as much as before on the Route de L'Unite. Mind you it was very late at night. I was thankful as I wanted to get back.

When I eventually arrived at my hotel I wanted to collapse but I remained composed in front of my guide.

'You need protection for your vehicle.'

'No its okay I will get someone.'

'No, no it's okay I have sorted it for you. Your vehicle will be safe.'

'Okay thanks a lot for that.'

'Good bye.'

As I stepped out of the van it was just getting light. God knows what time it was I couldn't remember. As I approached the doors lazy legged I could see concern on the Fez security men. One approached me and then looked around before he grabbed me firmly by the arm. What the fuck? Is he police? Is this a set up? I struggled a bit but his grip was too tight. The security guard then frog marched me up the steps of the hotel looking around as to make sure no one was looking. He pushed me down my corridor and quickly opened my room. He forced me into the bathroom. I was now getting very concerned. Maybe he wasn't the police and wanted to try some funny business.

'What's going on? What's wrong man?' I shouted.

With that he put his finger on his lips making shushing sounds for me to keep quiet. He then pointed to my face and then to the mirror. What the!

'Look in the mirror,' he said gritting his teeth.

As I looked in the mirror I could see what the panic was about. My light brown hair was now ginger from all the cannabis powder. The powder had also formed like a beard around my face. I looked back at the guard. I had been caught out. When I looked back he could see me searching his eyes to see what happens next. With that he smiled. He then belly laughed and shook his head.

'Have a wash. I will see you tomorrow.'

Thankfully he left the room and continued to chuckle away. I think he is okay. He would have called the police if he was going to shop me. Mind you I better get out of Morocco fast. I could not believe it. I didn't realise I was covered in cannabis powder. It's a good bloody job I didn't walk down the street like that and only the Fez men saw. Well I had a laugh to myself and decided I needed to catch up on my sleep before my mega drive over the next few days.

As I pulled off in the caravanette the next morning, leaving behind in my rear view window Tangier I felt a sadness that I had to leave this weird and wonderful place. I also felt very tightly wound as I had kilos and kilos of powder on board and seven more countries to smuggle into. However I just had to keep my wits about me at border and passport controls. It will be fine.

I plodded again on my journey. I had done around 170 miles from Tangier to Fes via Meknes. It would have been quicker if you look at a map to go from Tangier on the road that goes past Tetouan and Nador in order to get to the Oujda border but it would not have been safer. This would involve going through Ketama and as I explained earlier it would involve fighting off bandits. Also Ahmed and Troy informed me not to go this way so I heeded their advice this time. I had learnt my lesson. I don't particularly like running around in my Y-fronts.

As I looked down at my petrol gauge I realised she was running low. Great got to fill her up again! I could not let her run too low in Morocco as I did not know where the nearest service stations were. Plus in between the towns were miles of unpopulated areas where I didn't want to get stuck with no petrol.

I passed a plain building and a man was walking out of it on the main road. I flagged him down to ask for directions to the nearest petrol station of sorts. Oh shit! As he turned round and caught my attention I could see he was a policeman. And the plain building must have been a police station. However as I flagged him down and he had spotted me I had to wait as he ventured over. It's okay it doesn't matter he's a policeman just play the lost tourist card. It's fine! You don't have I'm a drug smuggler tattooed to your head. Or any cannabis dust in your hair now. It's fine.

'Hi do you know where the nearest petrol station is?'

'Yes I do… Can I grab a lift and I'll direct you there.'

'Er are you sure you can take me there. I don't want to stop you from working.'

'Oh no it's okay I just finished my shift and I would be grateful of the lift.'

'Er okay. Yeah jump in. I suppose.'

Perfect! Only just loaded my vehicle with narcotics and I concoct a situation where I have a fucking copper in my car. Keep calm Alan. He doesn't know he just thinks you're a tourist. Why would he suspect? Take him to the petrol station and then go.

The journey in the van took only five or ten minutes but it felt like forever. I relaxed a little when he pointed to pull over. Yet again the petrol station was disguised as a shack by the side of the road. Mind you I looked again and realised it looked more like someone's house. The policeman promptly jumped out of the van and told me to stay here a minute. I was so tempted to burn rubber but I wouldn't have got very far if I did leave him there. I don't think he was on to me anyway. Well I was 85% convinced.

As paranoid thoughts flowed in my mind I watched intently as he knocked on the door to the house. A man and a woman in plain black material answered the door. Then they both disappeared back into the house and the policeman looked at me nodded and smiled. After an agonising five minutes went by three little boys came running out heading straight for my caravanette. The police man continued to talk with the man and woman, who I would assume were the parents of these three young boys. I then turned to the kids as they pointed to drive to a pump. I obeyed and drove to the pump. They stood in a row whilst they waited for me to park. Once I had stopped they then ran to the pump lined in height order the smallest first. The littlest one who only looked about five started pumping in the petrol. Although young he showed good strength. It wasn't like the pumps we have now in the UK. These pumps were old fashioned and seemed hard to use. I wanted to help them as they seemed to struggle after a while. Mind I daren't as the parents were watching on. After the first child was out of puff the next in the queue started and so on. Although it seemed hard work for them they were really enjoying it. Smiling as they pumped and pumped with great determination. It took ages for them to fill my van. It was an agonising wait as I was still not too sure of the policeman.

Eventually the van was filled up. The father and the police man came over and I paid for the petrol. I gave a bit more and told the father I was proud of the kid's hard work. He shook my hands warmly and then stood with his family. As we left the petrol station the family waved us on. I felt a bit of relief. Mind you I still had an off duty policeman by my side. I didn't ask how long until his stop I waited for him to say. Thankfully it was only several miles down the road. As he got out of the van and I could see him waving in my rear view mirror, I was at peace again. Thank fuck.

I continued on from Oujda into Algeria, across Algeria into Tunis. Everything went to plan and I was making real headway. I was waved through all the passport control points and border controls. They did check my van but not extensively. They opened the doors of the caravanette and had a scout around. I made sure I left post cards of places I had been to, tourist trinkets and travel guides. Making them feel like I was just a traveller and not a person to distrust. I felt exhausted when I got to Tunis. I had driven over a 1000 miles across North Africa in three days on roads that weren't worthy to be called a road. When I got to Tunis I was happy in the knowledge that my travelling that day would be by ferry. No hard work for me I could have a break. However I was still worried I still had to use my dirty passport through two more countries, that of Sicily and Italy.

As I boarded the Ferry I decided to get some air and go on the top deck. Inside the ferry was too busy I just wanted to keep a low profile. I passed the time looking at the waves crashing about as we made our way to Sicily. As I looked in the waters I could see something rippling in the waves. In order to get a closer look I went to the rail on the side. There was also a woman next to me looking down at the moving creatures.

'Can you see them?' the woman said excitedly in an American accent.

I looked again and could make out the creatures had long smooth snouts. They were dolphins.

'Yeah I can. I have never seen a dolphin before.'

'You know what they say don't you. About dolphins coming to greet people on boats.'

'No.'

'That it's a sign of luck.'

'Really?'

'Yes.'

'Well that's good to know.'

I smiled at the American and waved as I wandered off. I walked away from her as I had to hold my emotion back. I wanted to snog her brains out for saying that. As although not a superstitious man I found it very comforting. Thank you very much. I needed all the luck I could get.

She was right everything did work out. I was fine with my dirty passport in Italy. Now I could relax a little I could use my clean passport only documenting European countries shaking the suspicion of my travels in North Africa. I tried to pass through Italy as quickly as I could and did not go into a hotel. Troy had warned me that in certain areas of Italy it is rife with car theft. Not on my watch So I protected her and slept inside. The only annoying thing was I couldn't have a coffee or a cup of tea now as I had no gas to heat up the water on the cooker. The gas bottles were occupied.

It took another four days to travel through Italy through Germany and then to Denmark. Again I got tired and was looking forward to another Ferry journey. This time taking me from Denmark to Norway. When I got into Hirtshals in Denmark it was late to catch a ferry so I stayed the night. Although it was only eight o'clock at night I went to bed as I was completely shattered. I decided to treat myself and stay in a motel. It was called Hirtshals cross. I wanted to have some comfort. Plus I wanted to look my best meeting Troy, Mort and our customers. I fell to sleep straight away and stayed comatose till 6 am in the morning. When I woke I felt refreshed and like I had slept for a week. I couldn't sleep anymore so I stretched myself and wandered around the room. For a few hours I was just pacing getting the blood flowing back into my legs from all the driving and pondering about what was next to happen. At around 7am I decided to get ready and head downstairs to the dining room and have some breakfast.

Once I finished my breakfast I felt ready for the last leg of the journey, Oslo. I felt I could almost touch its soil. As I left my table and wiped my gob with a serviette I headed down the winding corridor towards the bathroom for a piss. As I ventured down the corridor I could hear a muffled commotion. As I pricked my ears up to listen I distinguished the sounds as drunken laughing, singing and music playing. What the hell was going on at 8am in the morning? After a slash I was curious and decided to head in the direction of the party. As I followed the corridor the noises grew louder and drunker. My heart quickened. As I went further down the corridor the noise intensified and I arrived at the door where the sounds were emanating from. I paused for a moment to gain courage and then with valour in my heart I opened the door. As I entered the back room of the motel I was now in the epicentre of the commotion. The room was full of men wearing thick black boots, and thick woollen jumpers. Strewn on the floor were bulky bright yellow fisherman coats all dripping wet. All the men were red in the face and very merry. It felt like Christmas Eve.

To the side was a man playing the piano although his ability was hindered by alcohol consumption as he tripped some keys. The rest tunefully sang. When the occupants of the room acknowledged my presence, one by one they went quiet with the pianist being the last to stop his noise. Oh shit! Here we go again me the only foreigner in the room where I shouldn't have been. Well at least unlike in Morocco they weren't carrying guns.

'What's happening I said playfully?'

'We are celebrating a day's fishing,' he slurred in a Danish accent

'It's looks fun. May I join you?'

With that they all looked at each other and eventually nodded. Then there was an almighty cheer of yes's and the commotion continued but this time much louder. Two of the fishermen put their arms round me and passed me a drink. I had never had a drink so early before. It felt very liberating. I also had never drunk with a complete bunch of strangers. These guys were great and completely mental. Mind you I suppose you had to have a strong mindset to do what these guys did in working on the open seas. They have one of the dangerous jobs in the world. And no wonder they celebrated so. They had fish, they were alive, they were happy. I joined in privately celebrating to myself on my journey. One more country and I am there! Cheers lads. I drank with the fisherman till 11 am in the morning.

I changed my plans again and decided it was best if I went midafternoon by Ferry to Norway. I needed a few hours to sleep, sober up and become presentable. So after the session with the fisherman I went back to bed for a few hours.

When I woke again for the second time that day I felt sluggish. I had overslept and over drank, but I had to put that to the back of mind and get on the ferry. I had a shower and freshened up. I looked in the mirror and made faces to try and convince myself I looked at my peak. But in reality I looked fucked.

On the ferry to Norway was bracing although it was the start of August. I had been through so many humid countries, my body was in shock. However it did feel nice not being sweaty for a change. The briskness of the air made me come to my senses again but I was still far away from complete sobriety.

I informed Troy I was coming the day before. He sounded excited. He was also probably relieved that it worked. I managed to smuggle my way through. The ferry left around left around 3pm and took just over four hours. I arrived in Oslo after 7pm and I booked myself into the hotel Troy had informed me to go to. Once there I was relieved and put a call out for him at reception as he was staying in the same hotel. I waited for him at reception to come and meet me.

I slumped on the corner of the reception desk much to the dismay of the receptionist as this was a posh establishment. It was nearly over. With that I heard footsteps behind. As I turned Troy was stood there smiling.

'Hey Alan it's great to see you!'

'Likewise.'

'How was the trip?'

'Interesting.'

That night we dined in the luxurious restaurant part of the hotel. Everywhere was lined with solid oak. It was the full silver service with waiters and waitresses waiting to the side of room ready to run and pander to any whim from the high class cliental.

Troy ordered steak I decided to follow suit. It was the best cooked steak I had ever eaten. It was the perfect meal. I ate it slowly and savoured each bite. This was a nice change after eating crap from service stations or exotic foods which I couldn't be sure on its contents. Troy then ordered red wine which went with the steak perfectly. This is why I went through hell travelling. This is why. Oh what a life.

After the meal we went into another room. The room was like a very small night club. There was music playing, people dancing on the tiny dance floor and people sitting around chatting having fun. It wasn't a big room and there must have only been thirty people in there at tops. Mind you the expense of the place I could see why. Troy and I chatted again laughing at what we had done. Toasting ourselves and downing the wine by the bottle load.

In the corner of my eye three ladies caught my attention. They were all very beautiful. One of the girls was about five foot two with blond hair the other two were slightly taller and brunette.

'Hey Alan are you looking at those there?'

'Yes I am. They're gorgeous,' I slurred

'Shall we go over?'

'Definitely'

As we walked over the girls caught our attention and smiled. They welcomed us to the table. We all sat there chatting and having a good time. I was telling the girls I was a professional footballer who had just gone into retirement and I was living the high life. Troy didn't stray so flamboyantly from the truth as he informed them he was a businessman. After a while Troy started to look restless. I wasn't I was having the time of my life and these girls were soaking it up.

'Alan I am going to go my room now. You don't mind.'

'No not at all. I am quite happy here.'

The girls all giggled at my comment and I smiled back with a wide grin. I bought the girls drinks all night and made sure they never spent a penny. I also kept the conversation up and tried to amuse them. However no matter what I said they were lapping me up. God I am good.

'Another drink girls.'

There was a chorus of 'yes please' from all three as I went over to the small overpriced bar.

As I wandered back with a tray of glasses and wine, the girls were giggling to themselves. Something had amused them. Was it me? Did they think I was a prat and could see through my lies? Nah I don't think so I could have been a footballer I was fighting fit even though in my mid-thirties. I put the tray down slighter harder on the table than needed to grab their attention. Bo the blond then turned to my gaze she could tell I was curious at their conversation. With that she looked around to make sure no one else in the room was watching and with her finger beckoned me close. I am in here she wants a kiss.

'Alan,' she whispered softly, her sweet breath blowing on my skin.

'Do you know what we are?'

'No but I am sure you are going to tell me.'

'We are prostitutes.'

Well after that comment I was glad I put the tray down I probably would have dropped it otherwise. Smashing the most expensive round I had paid for in my life. They looked far from what I imagined prostitutes to be. They looked like models and had a sophisticated manner. I was shocked. I paused in thought for a minute at what to say, however then it hit me.

'Well that makes it more exciting.'

The girls giggled in unison. Nothing else was said on the matter and the night carried on with drinking, dancing and laughing.

The room started to empty and the girls looked to the door. With that they stood and said they were leaving. I escorted them to the front of the hotel and opened their taxi doors as they piled in. I was about to close the door when Bo put her hand on the door to stop me.

'Alan. Would you like to come back with us?'

Well with that I wanted to jump straight in but trying to hold back my excitement I casually glided into the back of the taxi trying to be cool. We all shuffled round so I was in the middle with a girl either side and one in the front. The brunette in the front had her body turned round to look at me and she was fawning all over me. A threesome I thought. Could my night get any better?

Halfway through the journey Bo turned to me and was whispering to me in hush tones so as not for the driver to hear.

'Alan?'

'Yes.'

'So which one of us do you want?'

Oh shit! Threesome idea has gone out the window. Part of me did want to say all three but I stopped myself as I wanted to keep up the pretence of the chivalrous retired footballer.

'May I go home with you Bo?'

'I hoped you say that.'

That night I went to Bo's house and it was straight to bed. No night cap or coffee straight down to business so to speak. That night we had sex twice and then later again in the early hours of the morning. What a release after so many days travelling.

The next day dawned. I woke up with a smile on my face but I was feeling a bit fuzzy and hung over. As I looked around I remembered I hadn't gone back to my hotel room. Where the hell was I? My memories of last night then flooded back. Right I came back with Bo but I don't remember where the taxi took us. All I knew was that I was in Oslo. I panicked a little and jolted upright awake. I looked next to me and Bo was not there. I dived on the floor and pawed my jeans for my wallet but it was not there. However when I looked around I found my wallet on the other side of the room. I paused before I looked inside as I had a bad feeling. However this went when I saw all my money was there. My keys were also in my pocket jangling quite happily. Thank god she didn't fleece me. But where the hell was she? Where the hell am I? I quickly got dressed to survey my surroundings. When I looked around her flat I was amazed. It was so beautifully clean and everything was top notch. I ended my search of Bo in the kitchen. Again I was taken aback she must have been good at her job. The wall was covered in ornate tiles and every appliance was new.

On the coffee peculator I could see a note suck to it. It read 'Alan I have put some coffee on for you. Sorry had to go out. I will be back soon.'. It was signed with Bo and an x. I relaxed on her luxurious comfortable sofa with a mug of coffee in my hand awaiting Bo.

To her word she came back with shopping. Before she had time to put it away I grabbed her hand in the kitchen and turned my head pointing to the bedroom. Bo smiled and nodded as she swiftly dropped the shopping and also her knickers. Then again we had sex but this time I was sober and I could revel in the moment as she lay next to me.

When I left her flat we kissed on the door. I said to her I would come again. I kept true to my word, as every time I finished my travelling I would celebrate with Bo. In the journeys to come I would when I got to the hotel in Oslo give her call and tell her to cancel all appointments as Alan was here. What a girl?

I got in the taxi which Bo had arranged for me and headed back to the hotel. I am glad the driver never attempted to speak to me as I wanted to revel in the moment. I didn't want this decadence to end.

Once back to the hotel I called on Troy. It was back again down to business. We took the powder to be mixed and pressed to make bars. Troy even made the three feathers part of the mould to show this was made by Welsh hands. These bars were then taken to our customers Sevine and Karl. Sevine and Karl were younger than me, both around their late twenties. They were both friends who had met in University and remained friends ever since.

Once we had supplied the pair we had to wait for them to distribute it before we could have all the money. So it meant spending a few days in Oslo. Well if needs must I suppose. They did give us a fraction of the money upfront as insurance. I didn't like not being paid in full. However Troy seemed okay with it so I followed suit. It was his money he was losing anyway.

That night Troy had said he wanted to take me to a restaurant he liked. I was game. So off we went in his hired Jaguar and headed off to the restaurant. We had a good laugh in the car about last night's events and I filled him in on how I filled in Bo. He laughed and seemed happy for me. We travelled on and on. I didn't take much notice of what was happening around the car I just enjoyed the ride and Troy's conversation. Suddenly Troy stopped the car and in front was a light and like an entrance to a cave. It glowed green so we passed through. Troy looked over to my seatbelt and smiled I had it on. He then turned back to the road.

'Alan are you ready?'

'For what?'

'Just hang on to your seat.'

Well before I could question him he pushed down the accelerator till it was flat to the floor and sped through the tunnel. Holding on to the sides of the chair I looked outside the window and realised we were going up a road that spiralled up a mountain. I clung to my seat shouting crazy fucker in my head as we flew up. As we got half way up I relaxed a little as I realised it was hollowed in such angle that it was likely we were going to fly off the road and die. Probably still possible though

Once at the top he slowed down and then broke hard. I breathed out and steadied my dizzy head.

'You crazy bastard.'

Troy couldn't stop laughing, but when he did he explained he had been a few times before and that someone had also done that to him. He also explained it was fine to do which I gathered as the way the spirals are set out. Still fucking scary mind. Shaking my head we went in the restaurant and enjoyed another stunningly decadent meal.

Troy only had a few more days left to go in Oslo as he had already booked his ticket. However the money still wasn't there. We both decided to scout them out. Finding Sevine was easy. He seemed the more sensible one of the two. Once we cornered him he promptly took us two to his main two customers. He directed us in the car and we went off. We arrived at a picturesque snow mapped chalet in the middle of nowhere. Once inside its interior looked as beautiful as its surroundings. A bit flamboyant but nice. Once in the house I met the occupants. Sevine had told me they were a gay couple. I had never met anyone who was gay. I was bit nervous at first but they soon made me feel at ease by giving me a glass of fine wine. I don't know why I felt nervous as they were too busy putting their arms round each other to notice me. They were a good bunch. Once we asked for money he smiled at me and said very camply not to worry and how could I say such a thing.

He took me to his safe and opened it. As I peered inside I could not believe my eyes inside was masses and masses of money all neatly piled and bound. There were also gold bars. He pointed to the middle shelf saying that was ours. We collected it and left. Sevine was done. The money was right and nicely packed.

However when it came to Karl it wasn't so easy. We had to track him as he wasn't at home. Sevine did give us the tipoff that he was doing a gig that night supporting a local rock band in a local club. On our way we saw him on a side street. Obviously he was just making his way down. Annoyed and pissed off I turned to Troy and said I was going to have him.

In the hired Merc we had this time I mounted the pavement and wedged him to the building. He stood still in fear at nearly being run over and being pinned by my car. However, he did look relieved when he saw it was us. He promptly sat in the car and questioned us what was the matter whilst also still whimpering in fear.

'Money Karl,' I said sternly.

'Okay okay.'

Well I had never seen anything like it he was pulling crumpled notes for every pocket. It was like confetti. After several minutes of counting his crumpled notes he stopped and put it in the holdall as we asked.

'Now Karl me and Troy are going to count this. It better be right.'

'Don't worry it is. I am sure.'

'Oh another thing there is one other dealer you need to get money off.'

'What?'

'Yeah a mate of Sevine's. Ask Sevine he will show you where he lives.'

'Okay thanks.'

With that he got out the car and carried on his merry way in a slightly stoned stupor. We headed back to Sevine's.

'Karl said you owe us more money. Apparently you have another guy involved.'

'Aahh yes he still hasn't give me the money.'

'Well Sevine we want it by tonight. It's going to take all day tomorrow as it is counting Karl's crumpled notes.'

'What do you want us to do? Show him where he lives?'

'Yes.'

Back in the Merc we go. I was driving again. Sevine directed us through the city of Oslo for his friend's house. Once there we knocked on the door, it was 12 at night. We could see the lights were on but there was no answer. I tried and I tried and still no signs of life. Luckily the door was ajar so we let ourselves in. We all searched around the entire house but couldn't find him. We called and called his name but no answer. I was just about to shrug my shoulders when Sevine pointed to a string dangling from a trap door placed in the ceiling. I pulled the string and a row of stairs came down. It was quite nifty. He pointed upwards and said he might be up there.

Once I walked up the stairs I was greeted with a messy room reminding me that of a student's. Clothes strewn everywhere. The haze of pot smoke hanging in the air. On the bed was our guy asleep in a drunken and stoned stupor. I walked over to the bed and leaned over his face. He was sleeping fast. I put my hands on the scruff off his collar and shouted very loudly 'Money' in his face. The bloke woke up and with fright in his eyes and screamed at the top of his voice. I startled him as he didn't know who the fuck I was and why I was grabbing his collar in his own bedroom. He carried on screaming for quite a while. I didn't know what to do. This wasn't good. We didn't want other people to hear this. I didn't know whether to slap him or what. He even frightened me with his screaming. I could hear Sevine and Troy shouting from below asking me what the hell I was doing and whether I was trying to kill him. Luckily he calmed down when he heard Sevine below. Once he stopped screaming I beckoned him down the trap door steps and he lead us to the kitchen. We all had a laugh about it. He gave us some bottle of beers to drink whilst he went to hunt out his money.

Again like Karl he gave us reams and reams of crumpled notes but we were satisfied.

That next day at the hotel we counted the money. We made sure we locked the hotel room door and between us straighten out the crumpled money and put them neatly into piles. The money was correct. That was a relief it was all right we didn't have to do anything else except enjoy the rest of the holiday and get ready to go back to the UK. I did not catch a flight like Troy as I had to take the caravanette back for the next trip.

Despite getting lost, having my caravanette pelted by stones and being mugged and stripped by a Moroccan gang this by far was my least eventful trip. The trips to come would prove to test my nerve and cunning. Smuggling was not for the fainthearted.

4 HOB KNOB

In the middle of the night I found myself once again in Ketama scrabbling around in the dark on Ahmed's farm. Ahmed and his associates were in a huddle talking in Arabic whilst I was busy listening and watching out for any sign of movement in the dark distance. I felt paranoid we were being watched. Although I couldn't see anything or hear any noise I imagined we were surrounded by bandits pointing at us with their gun muzzles. Looking back to Ahmed and his men I could see one of them looking at me with suspicion. I think he could see the panic in my eyes. I quickly changed my demeanour to calm and shone him a full toothed smile. I don't understand why I was worrying; Ahmed has had a farm in Ketama for years and years and he knew practically everyone, probably all the bandits too. No one would try and cross him. I think I had watched too many action movies where the bad guys would try and take over. Actually wait, technically in a film we would be classed as the bad guys too.

I darted my gaze back to the task in hand and turned my attention back to getting the two gas containers level in the hard uneven ground. After turning them around and around I managed to corkscrew them into the dirt so they were sturdy enough to support themselves. I beckoned Ahmed over to pass the hashish oil. He then signalled to one of his men to go over and get it. It was the man with the suspicious eyes that came across. Although quite lean, his height and solemn dark face gave him an imposing presence. He put the bucket of hashish oil on the floor and a funnel on top of the canister. Then to my dismay he picked up the bucket and started to cock it at an angle towards the top of the canister.

'No stop!' I shouted.

Ahmed's brow furrowed in confusion.

'I want to pour it in myself,' I said firmly.

Ahmed smiled and nodded. In Arabic he called to his aide to put down the bucket, whilst pointing to the floor. As instructed he laid it back on the ground and went back to where he was standing. He grunted under his breath as if annoyed at being told what to do.

I did feel a bit of a prick for demanding I poured in the oil but I did it because I didn't want them to short change me. I knew if I let them they would try and pour in as little as possible, whereas I would make sure I crammed in as much as I could get away with. I mean I wouldn't really blame them for doing that as I would have done the same in their sandals.

I smiled and proceeded to pour in the oil. I felt a little unnerved pouring in the gooey brown liquid as everyone stared hard. They were obviously watching to see if I would spill any, but I was determined not too. Although the bucket wasn't heavy it was a bit of an art keeping my arm and shoulder still to provide a steady stream. After the first one was filled with no spills I felt at ease pouring the oil into the second. I think my calmness was also helped by the slight intoxication I was feeling from the sweet warm delightful fumes from the oil.

I put the bucket down with a smile and admired my handy work. I was going to have to persuade Mort and Troy to look at getting hashish oil again. It was so much easier than scooping in the powder over and over. Pour in the oil and away to go, no mess or hassle at all. Plus the oil is worth triple than that of the powder, due to its higher potency, so I don't think it would have taken them much persuasion to change.

The only tricky part of the operation, like with the powder, was screwing the top back on the gas canister. Unlike today the gas ganisters around in the 70's had to be screwed down. Mort made me practice over and over before I went on any trips, as he warned I had to make sure like a screw going into a bolt I met the bite. If I didn't align it properly I could knacker the thread and the top would be loose or even worse would not tighten up at all. If that happened it would have been dire. The smell would have stunk out my caravanette and I would be surely pulled over by customs and the police. Luckily like with last time it was all okay and I managed to screw the top down.

Also like the last time I put one of the canisters in a secret underground compartment and the other was hooked up to the gas stove. I smiled imagining customs officers searching my van and walking past the stove. They will never notice that. The only bum side to doing this was that I wouldn't be able to have a fresh cup of coffee in the morning. But it was a small price to pay.

With the canisters secure in the caravanette my guide and I returned back to Tangier from Ketama. Free from bandit country. It felt such a relief. The guide cleared his throat loudly, which I took as a great hint he wanted paying and to fuck off. With a smile I gave him over the agreed money and a tip as I was feeling generous. I watched on as he ran off into the darkness. I didn't even get so much as a thank you or even a wave goodbye. That boy really wanted to get home. Well I suppose it was the early hours of the morning. It had been a long night.

I took a moment to breathe comfortably again. I had survived another trip from Ketama. I looked into the mirror as my dark ringed eyes stared back. God I was tired I needed some sleep. I continued to look in the mirror to inspect my face for any dirt or hash oil. To my delight my face was relatively clean. I had no ginger hashish beard this time. I began laughing as I remembered the mess I was in last year coupled with the overzealous Fez security man. It took a while to stop laughing; I think I was a little hyper from being so tired and possibly a touch stoned from the hash fumes. I eventually composed myself and beckoned over a guy in the shadows who I had arranged to watch over the caravanette.

Despite enlisting the services of a local to watch over my van I still felt uneasy at leaving the oil in my van. I couldn't help worrying about it being nicked or ransacked. I did get a few hours' sleep but I intermittently woke up checking my van was still there through the hotel window.

When I got up I felt even more tired than the night before. I decided I couldn't go on like this, if I wanted peace of mind and sleep I needed to stay inside the van. So after breakfast I checked out. But I didn't really want to leave Tangier as I had only been here for five days. There was no way I could make my way to the Algerian border and appear like an easy going traveller. But on the other hand I wanted to make a move as I had the hash now. I felt stuck. As a compromise I came to the decision to leave Tangier and go on my way to Algeria but whilst making many stops along the way, so the days would pass by quickly. I needed to be in Morocco for at least a week or more so as not to raise suspicion.

I planned to set off in the late afternoon so I couldn't make much progress on my journey so I wasted time pottering around Tangier; looking at the markets and having a bit of food. I even had a few hours' kip in the van outside the hotel.

When I did eventually set off from Tangier it was at 5 o'clock. I regretted the kip though as when I set off I felt really groggy. But feeling this weary did in a way help me to get into a laid back mindset as I couldn't envisage going fast like I usually did. Small progress was the name of the game today.

As I left the hotel car park I waved good bye to the Fez men in my rear view mirror that I could see standing proudly at the hotel entrance. Good bye fellas! Looking at my watch I thought about taking it off and really embracing the Moroccan laissez-faire attitude, of where time has no relevance. But in the end I couldn't bring myself to do it. I liked knowing the time and on a superficial note I didn't want to show off my line of pasty white skin.

After a few slow moving hours on the road I stopped to look at the map. Getting tired I decided that I would end my journey in Rabat which was only shy of 150 miles from Tangier. I could have made it to Meknes, but I fancied settling down in Rabat so that I could explore it the next day. Meknes can wait for tomorrow.

Continuing to chug along at a relaxed pace I travelled with ease through

Asilah, Larache and passed swiftly through Kenitra. From being so slow I ended up in Rabat at quarter to ten at night. I really didn't know where the time had gone. With the darkness closing in I quickly set about finding a place to park up for the night. But from travelling around the streets I couldn't see anywhere secluded enough. Every street seemed filled with pockets of young Moroccan men. Ploughing on I eventually stumbled on a desolate road devoid of buildings and activity. There were places to the side of the road where it would be easy for me to just pull off, but again I felt too much in view. The sun was now a distant memory and it was near to pitch black with a few street lights dotted here and there. Luckily before all hope was lost and from one nosey turning to the right I stumbled on a nice big car park just off to the side of the main road. It was empty of cars and life, in the middle of what appeared to be nowhere. It was perfect. Just to make sure I was definitely alone I drove around and around the massive empty space. Looking around in the beam of my headlights I couldn't pick out any buildings in the distance either. This seemed strange that such a big car park had no obvious reason for it. No buildings or factories were nearby. Just nothing. Maybe they used it for a market? After circling the car park for a third time I decided enough was enough. I was now satisfied I was just in the company of just me.

I picked a space right at the back in the corner of the car park to park up, so if anyone poked their car through the entrance I couldn't be easily spotted. I wanted to be out of the view of any gangs or even worse police. With extreme glee I switched off the engine and allowed my eyes to close. I was now ready for a good night's kip. My weary body was so tired I instantly relaxed in the driver's chair. I could have dropped off there and then but I pushed myself to get out and stay in the back of the caravanette. For a start the bed would have been comfier and secondly I wouldn't be on view. Plus, being in the front I think I would have been spooked out by any noises or animals roaming around in the night.

Once in the back of the van I quickly undressed and lay down. I don't remember anything after that so I must have felt straight to sleep. Not surprising with all the excitement and lack of sleep I had the night before. I had been waiting for this.

The next morning I was disturbed from a deep slumber by several bangs on the door to the back of the caravanette. The bangs were so ferocious it made my van shake. What the fuck was going on? My heart pounded hard as I looked around in a dazed panic trying to imagine who was outside. Was I at the epicentre of an earthquake? Quickly I ran around the room picking up my t-shirt, pair of shorts and sandals. In the midst of dressing the banging stopped and I could hear several voices speaking in Arabic. Shit! Shit! Shit! I bet that's the fucking police. Just as I finished making myself decent the rapping started up again. Whoever was outside sounded really pissed off!

Picking up my watch I was further disturbed to find it was only quarter past seven in the morning. Of all the times to be under attack it would have to be now. As I ambled to the doors, the rapping grew louder and more forceful; whoever was doing it was getting more and more pissed off by the lack of response.

Feeling threatened I hid an iron bar which I took for protection and put it within reach behind the door. Then with a deep breath and a smile I gently turned the handle and revealed slowly my mysterious early morning audience.

Behind the door I was met with three stern looking Moroccans wearing military style uniforms pointing black powerful looking rifles towards my face. I had not expected this! What had I done to earn such a serious response? I had only being in Rabat for a night. Maybe this car park was a part of a military base. Or were they police who tracked me from Tangier? One thing I knew for certain was that I needed more than an iron bar to fight myself out of this one.

Putting my hands in the air facing upwards I gulped hard shaking my head in confusion. As I looked into the eyes of each of the men I could see them sizing me up, looking for an excuse to unload their weapons.

'Is there a problem?' I said politely and as calmly as I could with three gun muzzles pointing at me face.

'Why are you here?' barked one of the men in a direct and angry tone.

'You shouldn't be here!' he snapped.

'Er............I am a traveler.' I said pointing to my caravanette and British licence plate.

'English yes. But why you stay here!' he said pointing to the ground with force.

'Er.......er........I stayed here the night as I saw it was empty and because I was tired from driving.'

The guard within arms reach and at point blank range eased his grip on the rifle but continued staring hard into my eyes. The other two guards kept their guns cocked towards me but turned their heads slightly to engage in a conversation. They spoke in hushed Arabic whilst flitting their eyes back and for as if waiting for any sudden movement on my behalf. There was no fucking chance of that. Once they all finished their deliberations they all nodded in agreement and turned back to face me providing their full undivided attention.

'Where do you plan to go now?'

'Er I am just travelling around Morocco for a few days and then I plan to go back to Europe.'

The guard looked towards his two friends and again spoke quietly in Arabic as if to ascertain whether he had believed my story. After eyeing up my vehicle and what seemed an eternity of silence they turned the attention back on to me.

'Do you know where you are?'

'Er….. Rabat?'

The guards smiled and looked at each other. I could sense they were on the verge of laughing.

'Am I not in Rabat?'

'Yes but do you know what this car park is for?'

'No sorry I don't. The local market?'

'This is the car park to the palace of King Hassan II,' he said thumping his fist on his heart.

'The King!...............Really....................I am really sorry I didn't know.'

Oh shit this was worse than I thought! I wasn't only trespassing on private land which I was thought was owned by the military, I was in the royal grounds of the King of Morocco. Amazed and shocked I continued shaking my head plus appearing apologetic at my intrusiveness. All three relaxed their guns and had a conversation, again which was inaudible. I don't know why they bothered I couldn't understand a word. Unless they thought I was a spy. Oh god I hope not that would mean both an intensive search and an interrogation.

One of the men broke a smile again whilst pointing at me and shaking his head. They all then paused looking at each other as if they were pondering on a question. The question was probably 'What are we going to do with this knob?' The silence was then broken by one of them pointing to the exit, the other two nodded. It seemed they had resolved the problem. I dreaded what was in store and gulped hard. The taller more senior guard walked towards me. He reached into his pocket. Oh god! Please no handcuffs. Oh god! Only inches away he stared hard into my face.

'You must go now!' he said stern pointing to the exit.

'I can go............Oh yes thank you ……..I will and sorry about being here and………thank you.'

'Please do not stay here again,' the guard said smiling.

'No never again!'

'So I can go and drive off now?'

'Yes you must leave now,' he ordered with a sinister grin.

Before they could change their mind I quickly dove out of the back of the van, closed her back doors, jumped into the driver's seat and sped off. Never had I felt such a rush of adrenalin in the early hours of the morning. In my rear few mirror I could see the three men shaking their heads. I had such a lucky escape.

I drove for miles in shock. When I did eventually calm down I pulled over to the side of a quiet road and began to process the events that had just happened. I then began to laugh uncontrollably.

Of all the fucking places! Of all the fucking places to sleep for the night I had to pick there. Having a laugh made me feel such relief and the stress of the morning seemed to just melt away. I was amazed at how lightly I had got off. From that situation I could have been interviewed and searched. Then I really would have been in the shit!

I have since learned the car park was for visitors of the palace. I wasn't really anywhere near the palace grounds as it was quite far in the distance. However judging on the guard's reaction I was still too close for comfort to their beloved King.

Bright and alert after my early morning scare I headed off to look around Rabat. I spent the majority of the day walking around the medina there looking at the spectacular 17th century architecture and looking at the locals stalls seeing what different foods they had on offer. They mainly just offered lumpy soups and rice concoctions of which I didn't know the names of. They all looked wonderfully exotic though and smelt like they contained an abundance of spice. As and when I got hungry I did sample a few. I made sure with any food I had was piping hot so as to decrease the risk of having food poisoning.

In the afternoon I drove to Meknes. Whilst it was still light I found a quiet street to park on. I decided never to park in a desolate car park again and to always find rest stops early whilst it was still light. I wasn't going to make the mistake of trespassing on private property again, especially property owned by the King. Although it was early evening I decided to just chill out in my van and read some magazines before I went off to sleep. I didn't want to go out and get caught up in any more excitement.

The next morning I travelled on foot around Meknes. There I saw the Bab Mansour El-Aleuj, which is said to be the finest gateway in North Africa. It was indeed impressive and ornate in design. Although I wouldn't have been able to say if this was indeed most impressive, this being the only gateway I had seen. I also ambled along admiring the mosques and especially at the grand mosque. So different in design from our architecture, it felt like I was in an Alien land. I too also felt like a bit of alien as I did not come across any other western tourists. I was the only white guy in the crowds and crowds of Moroccans. I was the only person bearing skin amidst the locals shrouded in material. Like with Tangier no one stared back at me. I could see them looking out of the sides of their eyes at me but no one would exchange my glances.

When it reached evening I grew restless. I was hot from the humidity and my feet were sore from the hours of walking around. I also felt tetchy as I was bored now of wasting time. I mean it was great to be a visitor to such places as Meknes and Rabat but I was now itching for adventure back on the open road. I had Oslo in my sights again. As it was early evening it was far too late to start travelling. So I had to spend one more night in Meknes. It was also too early for bed so I decided to replenish my energy levels by having mint tea and cous cous in a local restaurant that night. It was delicious and just what I needed to fill me.

The next morning I woke up at ten o'clock. For the first time after Ketama I had managed to get a lie in. This was good as I needed this rest for the long stint of driving I had ahead of me. Although ambitious I had planned to go from Meknes to the border of Morocco and then on to Oran. Through speed and determination my plans were going well as I arrived to the border just before five o'clock as planned.

At the border control as last time I was subjected to checks. They asked me to open all my doors and wait by the side of my vehicle as the two passport control officers did a search inside. I did panic a little as one of them called me over. Thankfully he only ushered me over to point out my duty free half bottles of whiskey and pouches of tobacco. I explained they were mine and gifts for people at home. Although there was no dialogue he didn't ask me to leave but made sure I was aware of his shifty eyes concentrating on my gifts. I think I knew exactly what he wanted me to do but I waited just to make sure. A few seconds went by as he pawed my goods looking back and fore at me. He picked up one of the whiskey bottles nodding to himself as if he was in agreement of the brand I had bought was good. It wasn't really as it was the cheapest I could find. Then when his eyeballing hints were almost too rude I poised myself as I was almost positive I was on his wavelength. So to start the act I shook my head reluctantly pointing at my legal drugs and then back at the passport officers.

'Er......would you like some?' I said with a huff of annoyance.

There was no answer but he shone me a great smile. I was relieved he didn't get cross at my offer of a bribe.

'Oh go on then take a few................. I have enough.'

Within seconds he reached out like a fat kid in a sweet shop and grabbed three pouches and two half bottles. He turned to me waiting for some acceptance of his takings, I retorted with a shallow nod. Then as quick as you like the search was over and I was free to go. Cheap gifts for them and a quicker search for me! Great stuff! This was a really good set up. I decided I would do this every time I smuggled.

Feeling positive at getting through customs with ease I whizzed through into Algeria and by nightfall managed to reach Oran. I parked up on the street of a nice looking housing estate and five minutes from a local police station. Algeria was not a safe place and by being near to the police would mean less chance of people wanting to break into my caravan. It was a risky move to put myself under their nose but it was even more dangerous to isolate myself. I did run the risk of a nosey policeman but I would only be here for a night, so hopefully not long enough for them to get too suspicious.

The next morning I felt again both refreshed and assertive. I was ready again for some long hours behind the wheel. Today's target was getting all the way through Algeria and being nearby or in Tunis by evening. On paper this was completely achievable. So with hope in my heart I started up the van and away I went. But after only travelling a few miles I realised I wasn't going to make the progress I wanted. My caravanette didn't drive as well as she normally did, she kept stalling and seemed sluggish. Then as I approached Achaacha I switched on my wipers to wipe off a load of dust that hit my windscreen only to find they didn't work. So I stopped the car and wiped the screen down. Then to my dismay after further investigation I found that none of my lights or indicators was working either. My electrics appeared shot.

I put the problems to the back of my mind and chugged on further along to Tenes, Cherchell and then just inside El-Jazair. The further I got the more I was hesitant to continue. I mean I knew it wasn't too much of a problem not having indicators and lights, as the roads I travelled on were not heavily laden with traffic, so there weren't too many instances where I had to signal where I was going. Also I could just travel in the day and therefore this would override my need for lights. But it wasn't just the lights that were gone, the van was struggling to rev up properly and I had stalled now on six separate occasions. This didn't look good.

In El-Jazair I got out of the car and frantically checked the electrics again, only to confirm they were still dead. Scratching my head for several minutes I had to assess the situation. Do I or don't I carry onto Tunis? I had over 300 miles to go. It was possible I could make it.

I looked under the bonnet at the battery. I knew this was a waste of time but I still looked in a vain attempt to find a solution. It dawned on me this could be a part of a bigger problem. The electrics for minor things such as windscreen wipers were fine. Not much chance of rain. However it worried me that it could eventually lead to my battery dying, and then I would be screwed. There was no way I wanted to break down. I did not want that at all, especially in Algeria. It would have been far easier if I had these problems in Europe I would have been able to find a mechanic more easily and plus in Europe they were more likely to have the necessary parts. Here would have been much trickier as garages were few and far between. I was in half a mind to carry on but I knew this was dangerous. I was driving through such desolate areas I could have got stuck in the middle of nowhere. Also I was worried about the police finding me broken down and checking my vehicle over. They would surely want to pin something on me rather than guide me to my destination of Tunis. It would be easier for them and they wouldn't have to look very far. All they would have to do is find my canisters of cannabis oil.

Getting caught in Algeria was by far my worst fear as Troy had told me stories of the prisons there. He said that he had heard of labour camps where prisoners were forced to work long hours in extreme heats in the dessert. Also more worryingly he said if caught the Algerian authorities may neglect in informing the UK authorities, so it was gravely possible I would have no contact with the outside world. I would just be lost and forgotten. I don't know whether this was true but I was damned if I was going to find out. I was happy for that regime whether true or false to remain a mystery.

After much pondering and chain smoking at the side of the road I eventually made my mind up. I decided my best option was to halt my journey now. This meant the only plausible route I could take would be a ferry from El-Jazair port to Marseilles. Then once in Marseille hopefully, I could get my van fixed and it would be merry sailing to Oslo. The only flaw with this plan was going to be getting through Marseilles customs undetected. I knew for a fact my vehicle would have been more scrutinised than with the North African customs. However this was the risk I would have to take. So with the thought of being caught firmly tucked away in the back of my mind I headed off in search of travel agents in El-Jazair. Thankfully it didn't take long to find one and I managed to procure my tickets to board the Hobart ferry the next day. I only had to spend one more day in Algeria.

In the morning I boarded the ferry with the other cars, vans and buses. It was such a doddle getting on as there were no searches, I as the rest of the people around me seemed to be whizzed inside ready for the long crossing. Parking up the caravanette and leaving it in the car park on the ferry felt strange though. Normally I would guard her with my life with dope in tow and here I was leaving her on her own for over 24 hours. But I knew she would be safe. In fact I did start to feel some relief not to be burdened with her for a good few hours as it meant I could wander free without having to worry about her or the oil's safety.

In the beginning of the journey I drank coffee wanting to keep my wits about me. But then after discovering a bar it wasn't long till I succumbed to having a bit of a tipple. Well, I did have a day to enjoy myself with no responsibilities. Plus if the Marseille customs was to get me it would be the last good drink I'd have for a while. I paced myself at first sipping a couple of pints of ciders. But then the pints were soon chased down when I struck up conversation with a British lorry driver who was from up north and the Algerian purser of the boat. They were gulping them back like it was water, so I followed suit. When in Rome! Rome being the Mediterranean sea at this point in time. I don't remember much of our drunken conversations but I knew I had fun. In fact the only bit I did recollect was selling my Omega watch for thirty quid to the lorry driver, it was worth about fifty but I didn't care as he seemed to want it more than me.

The morning after the night before drew in and the ferry docked in Marseille. My honeymoon period was now over. It was time for me to be privy to my first passport control European style. The situation I was to face was to be gravely daunting. It would be a minor miracle if I wasn't searched after issuing my passport littered with Moroccan stamps. However the seriousness evaded me when I off got the ferry and I drove up the winding road up to the passport check point, as all I could concentrate on was my stinking hang over. With every bump in the road my head pounded whilst vomit rose up in my throat. It was then I really began to regret getting drunk.

When I arrived at the top of the hill my mind was made dizzy with the choice of several lanes ahead filled with cars and small vans queuing to get through customs. Getting my bearings I decided to join one of the central queues, hoping to hide in amidst the crowd of cars and blend in with the rest of the holiday makers. Towards the back I couldn't see much as there were scores of Moroccans in cars who had suitcases upon suitcases stacked high on top of their roofs. Some could have quite easily been the same height as a truck.

Slowly I ebbed further and further into the queue until I was nearing the front. I could now see by sticking my head all the way out of the window that at the end of each lane were bollards with barriers manually operated by the passport control officers. I could see the passport officers checking the drivers and passengers passports. As I looked round everyone so far had no problems, once their passports were checked, with ease the barriers were lifted and they were free to enter Marseille. I hope to god they to do the same with me.

I was now four cars behind the leader of the queue so I rested my pounding head in my hands on the steering wheel. I massaged my temples and tried to summon the strength from within to pull off looking innocent. I didn't fear the officers seeing me doing this as my caravanette was obscured by a Moroccan's family car in front which had seven suitcases piled high on top.

After several minutes went by I now was at the head of the queue. I drove over to the officer and put on a big smile whilst I pulled down my window all the way to the bottom. The custom's officer then stuck his head through the window and retrieved the passport in my open hand. As he did so he grimaced. I think he must have smelt my eggy alcoholic burp I had done only moments ago. This wasn't a good start.

The officer inhaled in a deep breath and then started to look through the pages of my passport. Just as I had feared he seemed to study all the Moroccan stamps. I just kept looking at him full in the face as if I was expecting to be let through. He only looked up once and then pointed towards an office on the side of the road.

'What's wrong?'

In French he said something and pointed again towards the office. I shrugged my shoulders pretending I didn't understand. Once more he pointed in the direction and scowled. I decided to obey his instructions as I don't think pissing him off wasting his time would have helped.

Reluctantly I drove over to the little island with an office and parked up. Within seconds a friendly looking female customs officer came across. Now this looked promising. She looked amicable enough to persuade with a story. But no sooner as I said this to myself two stern looking male customs officers arrived on the scene. Great reinforcements! I could see from their dark eyes and thick moustaches they meant business.

The taller male officer with the bushiest moustache thumped on my passenger door and signalled me to get out. I instantly took a dislike to him which I hid behind a concerned smile. Once out I was asked to show my passport for a second time. The two men shook their heads and stared at me with vitriol. I retorted by opening my hands and looking confused. They ignored my body language and strode off leaving me in the company of the awkward petite brunette female officer. The two men soon returned carrying big flimsy metal sticks which they proceeded to poke into the cavities of my caravan. It wasn't enough my van was feeling poorly she now had rigorously probed by two Frenchmen. However I was happy to see them poking in the completely wrong places. Carry on boys you will find nothing tucked away there. After minutes of excessive jabbing they seemed annoyed at not finding anything. But not giving up they turned their attention to the inside of the caravanette. Excitedly they ripped her apart overturning my belongings inside for the pursuit of anything illegal. From the van I could hear their heavy footsteps stomping around and angry growls in French. Turning my back from the caravan I desperately had a look around for anywhere to escape if the proverbial was to hit the fan. However after scanning the area I became distracted as I could see the passengers and drivers in the other cars gasping and gossiping to one another at my vehicle being raided. Being on show I felt quite embarrassed and annoyed.

Returning back to my situation I stared at the female customs officer. I could feel her unease as she would only make eye contact for milliseconds. I don't know whether she was shy or it was because she could sense my annoyance. One thing was for certain she seemed more sympathetic than the other two. Conscious of her presence I purposely fixed my stare to complete horror. There was a part of me that actually was disgusted at the treatment of my ride but I embellished this to air my confused innocent tourist act. Then when I felt the moment was right I put my arms in the air and scratched my head in bewilderment. I stared at the young girl and shook my head. She looked at me with suspicious eyes at first but then looked at the floor as if embarrassed at my discomfort.

'Parlez-vous anglais?' I said to the woman

'Oui.'

'What are they doing? What are they looking for?'

'Zey are lukin for drugsa.'

'Drugs!' I said disgusted.

'Why?'

One of the macho male officers heard us talking and came out of the van over to me and stared hard into my face.

'Drugga! Drugga! Drugga!' he spat.

'Drugs!' I said retaliation, raising my voice in anger. My head hurting from the loudness of my voice.

'I do none of that. I am a retired rugby player.'

As I said this I mimed just in case the lady officer couldn't understand me speaking the action of injecting myself and then crossing my hands as if to say no way. I mimed the act of injecting as well to try to instil in them that those were the only types of drugs I knew about. This was to put them off the scent for looking for cannabis. I continued huffing and puffing whilst shaking my head in anger. Trying to show them how offended and disgraced I was at such an accusation. What a natural born liar I was. Well even though my play acting was good this didn't deter the men from going back inside to ransack my caravanette further. The female officer remained outside with me. She kept looking at me with an awkward smile. I think she was falling for my act but it was a shame she could not share these feelings with her overzealous colleagues. As she looked in her twenties I was guessing she was new to the job and wanted to give me the benefit of the doubt. Whereas the two older men were obviously a bit more experienced and could see exactly what I was about. Well, unless they just mistrusted everyone?

The caravanette continued to shake. Watching on as the Bedford swayed from side to side I wondered how innocent tourists felt about their rides being ripped apart when they genuinely had nothing to hide. How annoying must that be? And embarrassing as everyone watches.

Then one of the men from inside called to the female customs officer. She in turn beckoned me inside the caravanette.

To my dismay the male officer that annoyed me the most was pointing at the gas canister filled with oil in the opened cupboard under the oven hobs. On his face shone a wicked smile causing his moustache to curl at the ends. Oh shit!

'What's in here sir?' he said tapping the bottle spitting with each word.

'Gas!' I hissed with sarcasm tapping at the label.

The officer closed his eyes further in a nasty looking squint. I retaliated to his scowl by putting my hands on my hips and looking at him defiantly.

We both stared at each other for a while as if squaring up for a fight. The other male officer left the caravanette and went outside.

After several uncomfortable moments the female officer stood between us and faced the male officer whilst having her back to me. Then in a sweet French accent she spoke to the officer. He moved his head so he could still scowl at me over the petite French woman's shoulder. I continued to stare back. The woman then put her arm on the male officer's shoulder and pointed to the gas. He nodded and backed away as if to let her handle the situation. That's it mate leave it to someone with some decorum.

'Right Monsieur Jones please put on the gas.'

'What?'

'Well if it is gas we would like you to show us,' she said politely

'You want me to turn it on?' I said gulping down hard.

'Yes please,' she smiled.

Oh fuck! I thought she was on my side. She seemed taken in by my ex-rugby player story. Why is she making me do this? Why couldn't they just believe me and leave it be? I will have to show my hobs don't emit gas. I will have to show them my secret passenger.

I walked over to the gas bottle slowly and put my hands on the top. As I unscrewed the top I looked up to see her gentle smile. I think she did believe after all and that was why she was making me do this. It seemed she really did think that there would only be gas emitting from the bottle. In comparison I could see the other male officer thought different. He had a smug grin beaming across his face as if he knew that gas wouldn't come out of the canister and that I had something to hide.

To buy me a few seconds to think of a way out I fumbled around with the nozzle. Think Alan think!

5 BURIED SECRETS

Whilst pretending to struggle untwisting the screw I had a quick look towards the back of the caravanette and could see the other male officer standing in the doorway. The bastard was blocking my escape route. There was no way I could quickly leg it out of the port now. I was surrounded. To make me feel more claustrophobic he walked over. I turned my attention back to what I was doing but I still could feel his heavy footsteps drawing nearer from behind. I continued to play act the screw was really tight. Then to my complete surprise the officer from behind grabbed my arm and went to turn the nozzle. I managed to push him away.

'No!' I shouted.

'This is my caravanette. I will put on the gas,' I said firmly.

The male officer then shook his head and began shouting at the female officer in French whilst pointing in my direction. Now I had really pissed him off. After he finished berating the female officer tentatively walked over.

'Er Mr Jones my friends say that if you don't manage to unscrew it in the next few er er seconds they will be forced to release zee gas.'

'Sorry I know.........It's just that it is a little tight.'

She nodded and returned back to standing a few paces away, allowing me to have some personal space and being able to breathe.

I pondered on continuing to pretend struggle but there was no point. I had run out of time. I had no way out. I only had two options left open for me. Either I would show them I had no gas in the bottle or they would find out themselves. It didn't matter which option I chose, both would result in spending a night in a French police cell and then years in a French prison. Well that's if they further explored what was inside. Hey that's it! Maybe they won't look. Maybe the oil won't be discovered after all. I could tell them that the gas bottle was empty. But then again I would have to explain why the empty gas bottle smelt like cannabis oil. Nope I was still fucked. Only a miracle could save me now.

Taking a deep breath I switched on the gas and turned the knob on the hob. After a nervous few seconds the hob hissed and the smell of gas smell filled the air. I was dumbfounded. It made me question as to whether I had filled it after all with cannabis oil. What was going on?

Coming back to reality I quickly switched of the gas hob and screwed the gas back down. I didn't want the smell of the cannabis oil to leak out for the officers to smell. I didn't know where the fuck the gas had come from but I wasn't allowing them to smell my dark passenger.

'This is dangerous making me release gas in such a small space,' I said wafting in the air and coughing as if getting rid of the smell of gas.

'Happy now?' I said sarcastically.

The female customs officers smiled and turned to reveal her big white teeth to the other two male customs officer. The male officers shook their head and continued to look at me with suspicion.

'So?' I said with anger.

'Thank you Mr Jones you are free to go,' said the female officer politely.

'Good! I have been held up for long enough!' I bellowed.

Confidently I strutted out of the caranvette and into the driver's seat. I shone a stony look at the officers as they lifted the barriers. I wanted to make a quick exit and hold my head up high in the air with disdain, but my caravanette didn't allow this. Instead she sickly spluttered and failed to start up twice. I felt quite embarrassed. Thankfully on the third time she managed to rev up. I couldn't think of anything worse than spending more company with these three stooges and then maybe having to ask for a tow.

I whizzed off down the empty roads of the Port. All the other passengers had long been and gone. I was the last person out to be allowed into Marseille. I didn't care though! I was just thankful to leave with my freedom.

Whilst aimlessly driving around Marseille in shock I pondered on how there was still gas in the canister. I mean I had emptied it and filled it with cannabis oil in Ketama. After racking my brain the only solution I could come up with was that maybe there was still some gas left in the canister and it had risen to the top. I mean I am no scientist but it seemed the only rational explanation and gas is obviously lighter than oil. Whatever the hell had happened I was glad it did. No prison for me with the frogs.

When I eventually got over the shock of my close encounter with French customs my hangover kicked back in like a bitch. My head throbbed and my brain felt tight as if I had gone several rounds in a vice. To make me feel better I stopped off at the nearest café for coffee and a baguette. I then plodded back on driving but soon had to stop to vomit up my food at the side of the road. Although I was sick I did feel a bit better for it. To wash away the chunks in my mouth I swilled them down with a bottle of water I bought in the café. After only a few minutes back on the road I felt I couldn't continue. I was just so tired and drained. I decided I needed to have a lay down so I pulled off to the side of the nearest quiet road.

After waking up from a few hours' sleep I felt so much better. I felt human again. Thinking more clearly I decided I now needed to take action.

I needed to tell Troy what had happened and to ask his advice about a local mechanic.

It took over half an hour to find the local telephone exchange. I had to go to many shops on the high street and sift through the locals who could speak English or a reasonable amount of it. Then I had to listen carefully to their instructions. All of which made my head throb again. But the hassle was worth it as I eventually found one.

It took a while before it was my time to use the phone. I was glad about this as it gave me time to think of what to say to Troy. I decided my first words were going to be 'Don't panic.'

In my head I repeated over and over what I was going to say and how I was going to say it. But I needn't have bothered as when I started talking to Troy I instantly forgot everything I had planned. I think it was his constant interjections that didn't help. His panicked yelling also made me want to laugh. When he eventually calmed down enough for me to tell him the full story he was totally taken aback. He also couldn't seem to process the fact I was in France and at how I managed to elude the French customs to gain entry. Over and over he kept saying 'But you should be in Tunis'. I think he must have thought if he kept saying it he could transport me there. In a kind of Dorothy, Wizard of Oz sort of fashion.

Once the penny had dropped Troy managed to compose himself and changed from being a concerned friend to a calm business partner. He instructed me to go to the nearest mechanic and then to ring him again in a few hours so he could impart his flight details. Troy had made the decision he wanted to travel with me through Europe and onto Oslo. I think he wanted to take back some control. I think I unnerved him with the catastrophic changes I made to his preset plans. But as far as I was concerned there was nothing else I could have done. I mean the caravanette was fucked.

It annoyed me that Troy felt he had to make that decision to come and accompany me but it didn't bother me he wanted to tag along. In fact I relished the idea of seeing him and having a bit of company on the road. I just wished he would have chosen to come and didn't feel like he had too.

When he arrived the next day I laughed again at his face when I imparted exactly what had happened. He still couldn't get to grips with it. Thankfully in the night we eventually lay the French customs chapter to rest and began discussing other topics. At first on the agenda of conversation was business but then after a few bottles of red wine it turned into the debauched and we had a great laugh.

We spent a few days in Marseilles as it took a while for the caravanette to be fixed. This was because the parts had to be sought especially. Not being a French made car he didn't have the bits to hand. As the mechanic spoke in French we didn't know exactly what he had done. But after he had fixed it I did have a little look in the engine. I could see the battery was replaced and parts of the engine looked a little cleaner. This was good enough for me.

Well whatever he had done he had managed to improve the performance as she felt a lot better to drive and the electrics kicked back in. So with optimism again I set off again, this time with Troy. As I predicted the journey was a lot more fun with Troy than on my own as we had such a laugh talking about days in prison, past relationships and what we planned to do in Oslo. He knew I had Bo at the top of my agenda. Oh and of course joint top of the list was collecting the lovely money from our customers.

We had a relatively smooth journey to Oslo but we did have to endure a few arse clenching moments along the way. In a way I was glad we encountered problems as it perfectly demonstrated to Troy the stuff I had to put up with and that it didn't matter how tight he made a plan, anything could happen at any moment when smuggling. This is when the ability to think on your feet needed to kick in.

Our first setback happened in Germany when we encountered an overzealous customs officer who openly accused of us of transporting drugs and ordered for us get out so he could do a search. Normally I would look shocked and appalled and let them get on with it but for some reason having Troy in the car made me feel I could go a step further. So in retort to his blatant rudeness and open accusations, although true, I shouted at him saying how disgusted I was at him at making such cruel accusations. I told him how I played football professionally and the mere thought of touching drugs sickened me. I ended my rant with telling him he could do all the searches he wanted but that he would just end up wasting time and looking like a fool. The customs officer didn't say anything back and instead walked away. In the mirror I could see him skulking around the caravanette and inspecting her. Troy stared at me with a mix of anger and terror. Whilst making sure my Kraut friend wasn't looking I quietly told Troy I knew I was doing and shone him a confident smile. But my confident words or calm demeanour didn't seem to pacify him. In fact I think my self-assurance disturbed him further.

The Kraut eventually popped up on Troy's side of the caravanette. With menace he tapped on the window which Troy obediently and promptly pulled down. Before the officer could say anything I asked him again if he wanted to waste time and for us to get out of the vehicle. He didn't say anything and just stared back. To further poke the bear I said 'Well' and folded my arms.

Then to my complete surprise the Kraut dipped his head and waved us through. He told us we didn't need to have a search. Filled with happiness and adrenalin it was hard not to laugh or smile. I had to fix my upset face and drive off.

After a mile of driving I still couldn't speak or look at Troy. I was gob smacked. Never had my disgruntled tourist play act worked so well. Never had I managed to go through a customs point after being accused of smuggling without having a search. I was getting better at my job. Troy was quiet too.

The silence was only lifted when I let out a big sigh. I think I must have been stunting my breathing as it felt nice to let out a big exhale. The exhale then turned to a massive laugh. It must have been an infectious one as Troy seemed to involuntarily let out a few bellows too.

Then when the laughter dissipated Troy hit me hard in the arm and began shouting at me for the stunt I just pulled. I just smiled and concentrated on the road ahead whilst driving. On and on he berated me. When he eventually calmed down and took a moment to pause I told him the reasons why I had done it. I told him that if a person has something to hide they either stay quiet or run away. But if someone feels hard done by or are accused of something they haven't done then it is only natural they are going to react with anger and upset, hence the reason why I was so rude to the Kraut. After I said this he went quiet and gently nodded as if he agreed with the theory.

I also told him that at every moment I knew what the customs officer was thinking and that I had complete control. This was an out and out lie. I was bricking it all the way along. I even thought that I gone too far and my rudeness would only serve to make him do a more extensive search than normal, which could then have led to him finding our oil. But I didn't want Troy to know that. I wanted to instil into him that I was competent and knew exactly what I was doing at all times. I did this so that maybe in the future it would make him worry less about deviations from the plan and that he would cut me some slack if things went slightly off route.

The other set back was that the electrics in the caravanette went again. The fat fucking French mechanic had not completely fixed it. But then again he may have tried to tell us that as I do remember him wittering on about something in French when he gave the van back but obviously neither Troy or I understood. We just nodded and then fucked off. Maybe in that mysterious conversation he was trying to tell us it was only a temporary fix.

Well without the electrics it was fine in the sunny countries going across Europe but going through Norway and driving on roads of snow on the tops of mountains when even in the day the light isn't great was very scary indeed. Especially when the snow was coming down heavy and I hadn't got the use of windscreen wipers too. Poor Troy had to hang out of the window and scoop up the snow with the useless blades so I could see where I was going. I really don't know how we didn't die on that journey.

Or how Troy didn't get hyperthermia or frost bite.

When we reached our final destination at the heart of Oslo we were both were extremely relived. The Bedford although not fully functional had managed to get us there. She had done her job, but despite this success we decided she should now retire. Even if she could have been fixed I don't think I could have trusted her again, especially not on another 5000 mile trip. I didn't even trust her to take me home. When I told Troy this he agreed with me. So we decided to lay to her to rest in the car park of the airport in Oslo.

I still today wonder what happened to her. I would like to think she is still there at the airport waiting for me but I know it wouldn't be the case. I know she would have since been long gone. I just hoped that she hadn't been scrapped. Maybe someone bought her and then lovingly restored her to her former glorious self. Maybe she still is cruising the roads today.

On the next trip we decided I would take a Grenada car instead of a caravanette. So instead of hiding the hashish in gas canisters, Mort had now cleverly engineered the petrol tank to hide my illegal cargo. Another difference with using the Grenada was that instead of smuggling oil or powder I was now going to be concealing hashish bars. From the money of the other trips Troy invested it in buying a generator and a machine to press the hashish into bars. This meant everything could be done in-house at Ahmed's farm. We didn't have to mess about in Oslo making the bars.

In the Grenada I blitzed my way travelling through France and Spain. I could really get up speed; unlike with the caravanette where I was halted by the sheer weight. Driving in the car was also a hell of a lot quieter. I didn't have to contend with things bouncing around making noise or having great thumping noises transcending from my back end whenever I went over the slightest bump. Having the car was by far the easiest. Getting to Morocco was a cinch.

After loading the cannabis into the petrol tank I left Tangier after only a few days of visiting. This time I didn't care about wasting time and looking like a tourist. I felt cocky and untouchable. I felt that no customs officer would ever find my dark passenger. Especially the customs officers across North Africa, as I knew for a fact none of them had garage pits. In fact out of every search I had across North Africa not one of them included looking underneath. They seemed only concerned with the contents inside. Oh that and my free booze and tobacco.

But like with my last trip it wasn't the customs that I needed to worry about, instead my problem was again the health of my vehicle. And again the vehicle failed in Algeria. It was as if Algeria was my Bermuda triangle for broken vehicles. What made it more gutting was the Grenada was relatively new and had only managed under half of the trip. At least with the caravanette it had done two. The mechanical problems were also more severe as the problems this time wasn't with the electrics but with the engine. It seemed that after every fifty miles or so it would overheat and produce clouds of steam, even though it was filled with plenty of water. I could only ascertain it was the humid conditions. But despite the hot weather this car wasn't old, it should have been alright.

After the third time she overheated I pulled the Grenada over to the side of a lonely coastal road overlooking the Mediterranean Sea. I stared out of the side window, and ahead of me was a beautiful scene. The sky was blue and the sea looked magnificent as its high waves crashed and rippled. I didn't absorb the beauty though, as my mind was else where. My concerns were for my car. My view out of the windscreen in front was obscured as there were clouds of steam coming from my bonnet. I felt encased.

'Shit Shit Shit,' I hissed to myself whilst slamming the steering wheel hard with the palm of my hand.

I got out the car and looked under the bonnet wafting away the prevailing steam. Like with the caravanette I didn't know why I had a look. I mean I was no mechanic I wouldn't have been able to spot the problem let alone fix it. Although one thing I knew was that it definitely would haven't made it across Tunis. Without electrics was iffy but with a faulty engine was a definite no no.

Why couldn't I have broken down in Europe? It could have been anywhere in Europe. I could have gone to a mechanic and even maybe have sought an English speaking one and then it could have possibly been fixed. But no it had to be here, again.

Feeling a bit stressed I pulled out a fag from my pocket and stared out along the coast of El Jazier in Algers, Algeria. After lighting up my smoke I took a big inhale and allowed my mind to escape for a second or two from the enormity of my situation into the cool blue waters ahead. Watching the waves lapping away in the distance I wished that they would carry me away to Europe, away from the suspicion of North Africa.

In the distance I could seeing something moving in the water. It was so far out I couldn't tell whether it was a ferry or rowing boat. I wondered whether it was the Hobart I had been on. I pondered on whether I should take another trip across to Marseille. I mean I got away with it last time. Maybe I could do the same again. But the thought of being searched by French customs made me fill up with dread. Also I knew for fact that in the Marseille customs they had garage pits as I saw them on my last visit. Another thing I was also infinitely aware of was that they were deeply suspicious of anyone who had Moroccan stamps in their passports. Of which I had plenty. It also didn't help that it was only a year on since I had been to the port. It would be just my luck that I would have had the same three stooges looking at my car and despite the passing of time I think they would have still recognised me as I don't think many white Brits make that journey. So sticking out like a sore thumb and doing two trips in two years across Morocco would not have looked good. They would definitely cast me as smuggler and not a tourist.

I knocked on the head the idea of getting a ferry and then thought about buying a new car. But there were three major problems with this plan. The first was that if I had bought a car I wouldn't have had enough money to continue with my trip e.g. having enough money for hotels, food and petrol. The second problem was that I would have had to hide the cannabis inside my car. This would have meant that it could have easily been found in a search by any of the customs officer across North Africa. Finally if I bought a car how was I to find out if it was a dud. With the language barrier and having no mechanic skills I could have bought a car which wouldn't have lasted. So with these major problems I decided getting a new car wasn't the way to go either.

I continued looking at the unsettled water of the Med. I was in ore of the way the waves would thrash around with greater and greater intensity until they found themselves smashing against the low lying rocks. It was this sight that inspired my epiphany. I now knew what I should do next. Feeling so empowered made goose bumps shoot down my exposed arms. That and the fact the temperature was dropping too.

With my plan set in my mind I wanted to whizz off into the distance but I knew I couldn't. I needed to let my engine cool enough so it would be okay to be able to drive. To pass the time away I went for a walk and read a few pages of a magazine.

When I decided the car was okay to move I could see on my watch it was 8 o'clock. This was quite bad as I needed to put my plan into action before it got too dark. I needed light to locate the perfect spot. With gusto I reversed the car and pointed her back along the coast road. Although I was retracing my steps I felt empowered and alive as I now knew what I had to do. My stomach painfully churned and cramped, partly through excitement and partly due to hunger. I hadn't eaten anything since noon.

As I cruised along the empty coastal road the car gurgled and spluttered. It was not long now, she was soon going die. Trying to ignore the noises and steam rising from the sides of the bonnet I kept looking out for higher and higher terrain. I passed walls and walls of rocks that overlooked the sea but they weren't big enough. They also didn't look accessible for me to drive up. I continued to ignore the steam. But surely enough the steam was too much and again had to give her another break. My car was making me more worried now as she was steaming up only after 10 miles. I knew this meant she was getting sicker and sicker.

My head felt heavy in my hands as my mind became plagued with doubts. Come on Alan. Come on car. Not long now I promise just give me a few more miles of driving. That's all I ask.

'Come on Alan. Priorities. Fucking Priorities. Get the hash and yourself out of the fucking country,' I shouted to myself.

'Think about getting to Oslo. Think of Bo. Think about the money.'

When the steam died down I started up the car again. This time I didn't wait for her to cool. I was pumped up ready to go. I was pumped up ready for action. After several miles of zooming down the coastal road I began to lose hope again. I still couldn't find what I was looking for and wisps of steam were again rising. But just as my despair had sunk to its lowest I whipped around a sharp corner only to find my faith in hope was restored again. Finally I had found what I had been searching for as in front of me was a magnificent cliff that looked mostly accessible mostly by road.

I paused for a moment to prepare myself for taking the car up such a steep road. I stroked the steering wheel and willed in my mind for my car to do one last bit of driving. With courage in my heart I put the accelerator flat to the floor. The car growled as if in pain and struggled up the steep incline. It took a while but she managed to get up there. Once on top of the road I looked at the view of the sea down below. I felt triumphant but this was also bittersweet as I knew this would be where she would meet the end. I slowly drove two or three feet clear to the end of the cliff gently caressing the steering wheel in my tired hands for one last time.

I got out of the car and cased the area. Even on the coast in Algeria under the cover of darkness on a secluded cliff I was still paranoid of being caught. However it was not long before I assured myself I was alone and there were no prying eyes. I then decided to set to work.

On my back I shuffled under the car with a wrench in my hand to set free my dark passenger. I unscrewed the tow bar and tossed it to the side. The car shook a little and I worried about the handbrake being not on. Whilst wedged under the car I went through my motions hesitantly. It was through recalling back I had remembered I had put the handbrake on. I didn't have to worry about being compacted in Algerian soil by my own car. I suppose that's one way to go.

I carried on unscrewing parts of the engine underneath until I got to the petrol tank. Gently I unclipped the tank and placed it carefully on the floor. I then shuffled from underneath the car and dragged the tank into open view. Then using more tools I unscrewed the compartment at the bottom of the tank and opened it to reveal the beautiful bars and bars of hashish. I had a smegal moment with my 'precious' hash as I stroked and was mesmerised by her volume. Then a noisy gull from above quickly brought me back to reality, and made me realise I should be obscuring her from view.

Quickly and with care I placed all the bars in the bottom of a holdall, and then tossed a few articles on top including a few personal possessions, clothes, fags and passport.

With the holdall on my back I opened the car door, stroking the edges with affection. Bye my good friend. Trying not to get upset I put the car into drive as it was an automatic and lifted the handbrake. With speed I edged away from the Grenada and watched her as she glided over the cliff and smashed into the waves.

It was amazing how little time it took for a vehicle to be submerged by the dominance of the sea. But at that particular time it felt like hours had passed as my eyes darted round again watching for any figures in the dark witnessing this event

After I watched my companion fall and crash into the sea I felt both liberated and alone to the elements. I clutched onto the relief of getting rid of the car was good and tried to forget about the heavier burden of carrying a holdall bursting with hash. I looked in the distance out towards the lit up city of El-Jazair from where I came and worked out it must be about 15 miles away. Right Alan I thought to myself. You have the hash and you have got ridden of the car. Now what do we do. There is too much here to take on a plane. This would be a guaranteed prison sentence. What to do? What to fucking do?

I carefully trundled down the rough terrain to get to the road below where I could travel along and think of what to do next. I walked a few miles on the solitary road comforted by the sounds of the sea. In the distance I could see a little town and further still were tree lined mountains. The mountains reminded me of home, in the Rhondda. Feeling homesick and tired I headed towards them in a vain attempt they would bring me comfort and inspiration.

On reaching the town my senses were heightened. I was relaxed on the coast as it would be very unlikely I would bump into any soul here. However now I was nearing the town I would not have this luxury. The evidence of hotels and shops showed this area would be frequently populated and I could be prey to thieves and muggers. I would have to be on guard. I didn't have the luxury of Ahmed's protection here. I tried to stay in the shadows and away from the little light that came from the shop fronts and houses. I wished I had brought my fucking djellaba. This would have hidden my tourist clothes and I could have blended a bit more into the background.

I practically ran through the town whilst constantly on the lookout for any unwelcome shadowy figures. I felt a sigh of relief as the houses and shops started to dwindle. I was now heading in the direction of another lonely road leading me to the tree lined mountains. With each step I could feel the adrenalin subside. I now felt calm again.

Then suddenly in the other direction I could see a dark figure walking towards me. Who the fuck is this now? Please just be a young kid ambling through the roads at night. Please just be another European smuggler in the same predicament. Please don't be a mugger. Not again. I carried on walking. I tensed my muscles in my arms and awaited the possibility of a fight. For that moment I had forgotten the agony of the strap from my holdall digging a hole into my right shoulder. After a few yards I could tell that it was a man. Great! Just fucking great! The possibility was now 50/50 as to whether they were just a local bastard or mugger bastard. Well whoever he was, if he was going to try and steal my hash I wasn't going down without a fight. I didn't even care if he had a weapon. I wasn't losing my hash! When the shadowy figure came closer I realised it was far worse than I could ever have imagined.

The man that appeared before me was none other than an Algerian police man. Fucking Brilliant! Just what I needed!

On his face was a mix of bewilderment and suspicion. You could see the questions he wanted to ask. Why is a white guy here walking around late at night? Why are you going in the direction of the mountains? What is in the bag?

Right Alan here we go. Let's do what you are good at. Let's act it up.

'Hi there. Hi there,' I shouted to the policeman.

I waved and beckoned him close. I thought if I initiated contact, it would add the air of illusion that I didn't care that he was looking at me, and I had nothing to hide. My only trump card to play was being a lost tourist.

'Airport? Aiporto?' I shouted.

The policeman didn't move but exchanged another puzzled glance. Obviously he couldn't understand English. So I did the gesture of an aeroplane and pointed to my bag.

'Ahh,' replied the policeman.

Fucking hell. Now he is in the story great. The policeman retorted in French but soon realised from my shaking head I didn't understand. He then pointed to the airport near El-Jazair. I knew that was where the airport was and it was quite obvious as even from our distance you could see the runway lights all lit up, but luckily he looked as if he believed I was lost. He then drew in the air with his finger how to get back on to the coast road and then on to the airport. I pretended as if I was puzzled at the beginning with a bewildered glance. Then I put my hand on my chin and looked down and back up again.

'Ahh,' I replied.

Although I connected with the policeman this story I was still was paranoid that he was suspicious at my wanderings towards the mountains. He must have been thinking why was I not in a car? Why was I not in a taxi? Why was I walking to the middle of nowhere?

Whilst thinking this he smiled and pointed to the airport and gestured for me to follow him. Well that's a polite chap taking me to the airport.

Mind you this did not seem logical the airport was at least ten to fifteen miles away, but I lived in hope.

As I trundled behind I thought to myself about Troy and Mort, if only they could see me now carrying pounds of hashish in the middle of fucking Algeria with a policeman as a guide. That's hopefully if I get the chance to tell them.

In the distance I could see a little hut. I looked at it more closely. Now it didn't look like conventional one but I had hunch what it was. When I entered it with the policeman a feeling of horror washed over me as my instincts were right. This was the local police station. It looked very poorly resourced though as the table looked handmade and was held up with barrels.

Sat behind the flimsy table was another police man. When we walked in he was busy looking through paperwork. But when he saw my ugly mug his attention was swiftly diverted. After seconds of eyeballing me up and down he then looked to his friend.

My chaperone then went behind the counter and started talking to his colleague in Arabic. He spoke French to me but Arabic to his mate. I think he did so to conceal the conversation from me as I was more likely to know French being a European. However he really didn't have too as I knew neither well. As they conversed I noticed the other policeman never took his eyes off me. Probably because I was the only white man in the village, probably because his mate was telling him in Arabic how I was skulking about in the middle of the night or maybe he fancied me. Well whatever the reason he unnerved me, but I tried not to show this and plastered a dopey smile on my face.

To get more comfortable I put my case on the floor. Although it was very heavy I put it down as if it was quite light. I wanted to press it into their minds it was full of clothes and that I was just a traveller.

I stretched my arms and looked to the door towards the back of the hut. Although I couldn't see them I guessed through there were some makeshift cells. This worried me. There was no way I was going in there.

'Er excusez moi,' I said to the policeman.

I pointed at my watch and then yawned.

'Hotel?' I questioned.

They both looked at me blankly as they clearly did not understand. They jabbered in French again and I put my hands in the air communicating I couldn't understand. It was too my advantage I couldn't understand as at least I didn't have to explain what I was doing and they couldn't interrogate me.

I tried again to ask them for a hotel. But this time I put my hands together under my chin and tilted my head to gesture sleep. Still no penny was a dropping.

'Hotel? Look time no aiporto,' I asked again whilst pointing to my watch and doing aeroplane impressions.

The second time I gestured sleep. They got it. My charades exploits had worked. Smiles dawned on their faces as they connected. I thought by asking for a hotel they would think I wasn't dodgy as I wanted to stay and wasn't going to run. Thus by not running would have meant I had nothing to hide. Despite the fact running was all I could think of.

By suggesting a hotel would mean they wouldn't have the hassle of banging me up and making an extra breakfast for my white ugly mug in the morning. Well that's if they even gave breakfast to their detainees.

They continued to talk again in Arabic to each other. I smiled gently whilst politely waiting as they conversed.

The policeman who escorted me seemed to ask a question to the other as he put his palm facing up and pointed towards him. The guy at the desk retorted with a shrug. They both then looked at me. Then the policeman who escorted me came round from the desk and stood over me. I smiled but my hands tensed ready to push him and run if he tried to grab me. Mind this probably would not have been a good idea as I wouldn't have got very far as I could see on his belt was a loaded pistol and although I couldn't see it I was betting the other guy was tooled up too. But I didn't care. If there was chance I could run and be free I was going to take it.

Thankfully to my great relief he put his hand on my shoulder and pointed to the door. Hallelujah. Great stuff we are out of here. I picked up my holdall and off we went. Presumably he was taking me to hotel. From the police station we walked a few steps down the road until he beckoned me to wait.

He knocked on the door of an old, dusty and dirty looking house. An elderly man who I guessed was in his eighties answered the door. From looking at his pallor he looked only days away from death.

The policeman and the hotelier conversed in Arabic for a few minutes until they both turned to me and beckoned me in. The policeman smiled but the hotelier grimaced as if my visit was of great annoyance. The feeling was mutual. But instead of showing him rudeness I smiled at him politely.

As I entered the house they continued to talk more which left me chance to survey this 'hotel'. After a quick look round I decided it was the pits. It was dark, dingy and filthy. I couldn't make out the corners of the room which made me feel there were some weird and wonderful creatures lurking. Looking in the middle of the floor a cockroach lay dead. Even an insect that could withstand a nuclear explosion couldn't survive here.

Then the hotelier and the policeman simultaneously stopped talking and looked at me. I retorted with a smile and a wave. The policeman then turned back to the elderly man and shook his hand. As he walked out of the door he gave me a gentle nod whilst shouting in Arabic to the hotelier.

It was now just me and the old man. He walked over and started grunting at me in Arabic. I didn't have a clue what he was on about until he kept opening his hands like a book, doing impressions of stamping and then aeroplane noises. It became obvious he wanted my passport. I don't know whether he wanted to have a look or take it from me. But that was not going to happen. There was no way I was showing it to him and god forbid was I going to give it to him. No way. I would never get myself out of this country. So I kept up the pretence I didn't have a clue. Aggressively he grunted more and was doing the same actions over and over again. I could see he was getting annoyed. I wanted to laugh as he got more animated with anger as I carried on pretending I hadn't got a clue what he was on about. Once I thought I couldn't stretch his charades exploits anymore I then nodded and pointed my finger in the air conveying I had just twigged. He breathed a sigh of relief as I pointed to my bag telling him I was going to find the passport he wanted to see. He nodded at me and waited. I knew exactly where my passport was but didn't want to show him that and so I rummaged around the several pockets I had pretending I couldn't find it. I made sure several minutes went by as I wanted to be sure Mr Algerian plod was back at his desk before I did anything. The old man grew tired of me searching through my bag and sat down in a chair. I looked at my watch again and timed ten minutes had passed. This was my chance it should be time enough for me to escape. So I quickly zipped up my case and legged it out of the house. I ran and ran in the direction of the mountains and didn't look back. After a sprint of a couple miles I eventually turned round. I felt relieved to see no one was following me but I kept on running as far as my legs would take me. I only let up when I got near to the woods that hugged the bottom of the mountain. I looked at my watch and over twenty minutes had now lapsed. I decided to take a breather. What a relief too. In the pitch black in the middle of the dirt track I put down my holdall and breathed in deeply preparing myself for the second part of the plan. My lungs were sore and my throat was burning but I decided I had to put the pain at the back of mind, I had to carry on. I walked along at a very slow place. I had to fight my mind which wanted to lie on the floor and collapse. I hit my chest and pumped myself up again and started walking a bit faster in the direction of the mountains. When I got to the foot of the mountains I could see they were encased by boundary walls. This was not a problem, although several metres high I manage to scale them. Once on top I walked along on the wall and luckily the drop on the other side of the wall wasn't that great due to the steep gradient of the mountain. As I fell to the ground I noticed it grew much darker as it was thicker with trees. This didn't worry me. In fact it made me feel better as I would be unnoticeable. Happily I trudged up the mountain up through the trees. Every time there was a clearing the moon would light my way but for the majority of the journey I was shrouded in darkness.

When I got half way up the mountain I came across another clearing. As I looked around two trees stood out from the rest. This was it; this was where I decided to bury the hash. I marked the trees crudely so it wasn't obvious but it would be easy for me to locate again. Then with my feet I measured the distance from both trees. Once I counted the steps I halved them and marked out the middle scuffing the ground with my shoe. Luckily the soil was soft enough for me to dig it out with a nearby rock. Once the hole was deep enough I placed the bars and bars of cannabis in and with relief started the process of covering it back up again. I patted with my shoes and bare hands. I tried to make the soil as compacted as I could and not like it had been freshly unearthed. To further hide my burial I scattered layers and layers of leaves. This was sufficient I was happy. As I stood where the hash was I looked through the clearing of the trees at the view in front trying to store the image in my mind. As I looked out ahead I could see some large buildings and lights two to three miles to the right. To hazard a guess I would have said they looked like oil refineries.

Funnily enough this place came to my mind years later after reading an Andy McNab book. In it he described these surroundings as being part of an Algerian prince's palace. Well I would like to think it was this place as it would be fitting. I don't like to do things by halves.

I also thought it was a perfect spot as I noticed in the distance a light house straight ahead. This would be a good key to help me find my hash on a return journey back.

All muddy and exhausted I headed back to Algiers, Algeria. I avoided the town where I had run from the hotelier and trudged on into the darkness. I kept my money close too I was still worried about the threat of mugging. However at least now I was free from the hash. It took hours to walk the five miles or so to Algiers. My weariness and dehydration impeded my ability to walk but I dug deep and carried on with weak legs.

Once I got into Algiers it was early morning and I went into the first hotel I came across. Normally I would scout around for the best looking one but after my night I didn't care. The hotel I came across was the worst one I had ever stayed in. I would have even said it was worse than the old guys I had just been to hours before. But being absolutely knackered I was just thankful for a bed.

I woke up at ten in the morning. I was still fully dressed. I must haven't have had the energy to take them off. My shoes were still on my feet too. But looking around the hotel room I was glad I didn't take anything off. I was glad to have a barrier to the filth.

But despite the room I felt happy. I had managed to hide the hash without being caught. All I needed to do now was get a flight home and tell Troy and then come back again with another car. Easy.

When I stood up I realised I needed to freshen myself up. I also needed to buy a new top as the only clothes I had in my bag was a fresh pair of trousers and Y-fronts. I couldn't get on the plane with my muddied T-shirt. I would be asking to get questioned not to mention it would be embarrassing.

With a big stretch I headed out of my room in search for the washing and toilet facilities. Stiffly I walked around until I had found it. I was very shocked to find the toilet was a hole in the floor. Now I was really fucking roughing it. Relieving myself peeing in the stinking hole I shuffled my feet around. Then to my horror I could see an army of cockroaches crawling over my pumps and trying to climb up my leg. Swiftly I finished peeing and started kicking off roaches from my pumps and ankles.

When I calmed myself down from being angry I went back in the cockroach infested room for a wash. Looking at the sink further pissed me off as it was stinking and more importantly it had no taps. In the holes where they should have been taps was rolled up toilet paper.

Great! How was I supposed to fucking wash? Seething I put on last night's dirty clothes and headed downstairs. I shouted at the Hotelier if you could have called him that and warned him that if he didn't get fresh bottles of water for me to wash with I would refuse to pay him. I then went off to find a local market where I bought a new top. After scouring around in the heat I managed to find a smart thin black turtle neck top. It was the wrong colour to wear in a hot country but I didn't plan to be in Algeria for very much longer. It would however be good to wear as it would cover the scratches on my arms and the immense sunburn I had on my neck and chest from all the walking around for hours and hours I did yesterday in the sun. It would also do the main job I wanted it to do which was to look presentable.

After buying the top I also went to a café and stuffed my face with exotic food and downed cup after cup of mint tea. I had never been so hungry and thirsty in my life.

With a full belly and my new top I went back to the hotel. To my relief the hotelier had kept his word and bought a few bottles of water. I promptly went upstairs and washed myself as best I could with the water. I also pulled my beard scissors out and tried to trim and tidy my beard as much as could. Once clean and sort of fresh faced I put on my clean clothes. I now felt okay again and not so much of a scruff bag. I was a little embarrassed with my fingernails though as they were stinking. I did try to scoop out the dirt with the sharp edge of my fingernails but I couldn't lift up all the dirt. But it was enough for me. As long as I didn't show off my fingernails I did look presentable. It also didn't matter about my sunburnt face as I bet a lot of European passengers over the years had worn this look.

I got to the airport early in the afternoon and managed to book a flight the same day. I only had to wait around for a few hours so I passed the time away reading a book I had bought at a stand in the airport. When I could hear the boarding calls for my plane I waited for a large group of people to stand up. Once the queue had grown pretty long I wandered over making sure I was one of the last. I don't know why I did this as I needn't have felt worried. I had no hash on me. As far as I was concerned there was nothing they could pin on me. But despite this I still pressed it in my mind to be as late as I could so they would not have time to probe me.

I ended up being the last but one to join the boarding queue. Behind me there was a guy dressed in a smart grey pin stripe suit. Because of the heat he had his top two buttons open and his tie loosened. He also looked very flustered and annoyed as I noticed he looked at his watch every few minutes and fidgeted around clicking his fingers.

The queue eventually dwindled down until it was my turn. I was calm and all smiles. I tried to hide my weariness of last night. I didn't want to give him any clues of last night's antics. I pushed the passport with one hand over the desk to him and then quickly hid my dirty fingernails under the desk. The passport officer looked at my passport and then looked at me with suspicion, but I wasn't nervous. It was his job to look this way. Plus I was now used to being looked at with contempt and suspicion. I didn't need to panic. This was normal.

A further three times he looked up at me and then back at my picture. Again I felt no twinges of alarm. Maybe he was double checking my face. I did look pretty different now with my burnt face. But it was okay if he wanted additional proof I had other means of identification and cards. He then started pawing through the pages of my passport and seemed to analyse each stamp with great detail. In my peripheral vision I could see greater movement from the guy behind. It seemed he was getting even more fidgety. Boy he really wanted to leave this country more than me. After a few seconds I turned around and caught his gaze. He then stood still and smiled back. It was nice to see a friendly face for a change.

As I turned back around my passport was thrust back into my face by the passport officer and he had his finger on the car symbol printed in my passport. At first I didn't know what he was on about. But then I got the gist. He could see from the stamp that I had taken a car to Algeria. Obviously now he wanted me to explain where the car was and why I wasn't still travelling in it? Although it seemed like a trivial matter I knew it was in fact quite a serious matter as I knew from what Troy had told me that many Europeans made big business by driving Mercs to Algeria so they can be sold for huge profits. We had discussed doing something similar. But like with smuggling hash smuggling in cars was also highly illegal and carried a hefty prison sentence too. From looking at my stamp this was clearly what he thought I had done.

Trying not to panic I looked back at the passport officer with confusion and naivety. He kept shouting 'car, car, car, where is it?' whilst jabbing the picture of the stamped car with his long skinny finger.

Several seconds passed and I was fucking stumped. I was normally a good actor in these high intense situations and usually came up with a solution, but this time I drew a complete blank. I think my brain was just too tired to conjure up anything. I was screwed.

Then the man from behind could see the commotion and asked what was wrong and why it was taking so long for me to go through. The passport control officer did not respond to the man from behind but instead shouted again 'car, car, car where's your car'. The man behind then prodded me hard in the shoulder

'Tell them what happened.'

'What?'

'Tell them how their lot nicked your car.'

Fucking brilliant idea! That man I thank for with my life. Yes that is what I was to do show them my car was nicked.

This then gave me the confidence and I shouted blue murder about how his people nicked my car and left me in this predicament where I had to get a plane. I went on the defensive. To reiterate my point I gestured with my hands the Arab symbol for stealing which is palm down and a quick swiping action in an anticlockwise direction. Incidentally the Italian stealing gesture is a slowed down version as crooks are stereotyped as to being more meticulous and not as quick.

Anyway this worked as the passport officer seemed slightly embarrassed. The wind in his arrogant sails had diminished as I informed symbolically that one of his countrymen dishonoured himself. However he did still look pensive and was thinking as to whether to explore the matter of the missing car further. But luckily for me the man behind piped up again pointing to his watch emphasising any action now would mean he would be late too and it could be for nothing

Several anxious moments went by for all three of us. I was thinking shit I am in trouble. The guy behind was probably thinking shit he will miss his plane too. The passport officer was thinking shit he could be creating a fuss over nothing. Luckily for me and the guy behind I was let through.

I walked away from the passport officer and waited for the other guy to pass though. He was waved on instantly by the officer. When he caught up with me I nudged into his arm.

'Thanks!' I said beaming with a smile.

'That's okay. Come on lets go. We have a plane to catch.'

When we got to the bus terminal we were greeted by annoyed passengers as they had been waiting for us. But they soon stopped staring when the bus sped off onto the runway. Once it stopped everyone dived off including the man who had helped me. I watched on as they all plodded up to the steps and onto the plane with their hand luggage. I decided to have a fag to calm my nerves before enduring the long flight back to the UK. When the last person disappeared through the hatch of the plane I continue to puff my cigarette as I stepped onto the bottom of the steps heading up to the plane. The beautiful stewardess was standing at the top and was looking down at me and smiling. She was wearing a green and blue beautiful kilt which was apart of her Air Caledonia Uniform. I wished for a gust of wind to reveal her undergarments. I imagined she was wearing lacy knickers and stockings.

I looked around standing on the steps and surveyed the surroundings. I was glad to leave this place. I had a few too many close shaves here but it was okay I was almost home and dry. All I needed to do now was get on the plane.

After smoking two thirds of my fag I was nearing my last few drags when I could hear a car screeching towards me on the runway. Puzzled I looked on as the car stopped short of the steps and three armed airport policeman came spilling out. They shouted to me to come off the steps. I pretended I could not hear.

The men obviously wanted to interrogate me further about the missing car. Then this would raise more questions like why I didn't report it to the police. But it didn't matter whether I was innocent or not, according to Troy the Algerian authorities would throw people into jail just merely on suspicion alone. I hoped to god he was wrong. Well, I was soon going to find out.

6 NONE SHALL PASS

At the bottom of the plane steps at Algeria's main airport I couldn't think of what to do. I mean this was a crazy situation. I had three policeman drawing guns on me and I didn't even have anything on me. I mean I don't care if Troy said anything goes with the police in Algeria, this wasn't right. But it would have just been my luck to get sent down for something I hadn't done. Then again I did have a car stamp on my passport but no car. Maybe this could have been enough to put me away. I mean I didn't report it as missing to any authorities. Also I wonder if they would find out about me running away from a local police station the night before. Now that really wouldn't have looked good.

Looking annoyed that I wasn't moving one of the uniformed men slowly approached me. Shit! Here we go!

'Sir please come down from the steps. We have more questions.'

I didn't move. I was frozen to the spot racking my brain on how to get out of this. Whatever this was?

'No,' shouted the stewardess loudly from the top of the steps.

I looked up and she was waving her hands wildly. What the hell was she up too? With speed she trotted down the plane steps in a set of blue high heels. She then hung over the side and shouted in French at the guards. Although I didn't know what she was saying I could tell it was aggressive as she had one hand on her hip whilst she frantically shook her finger in the air. A bit taken back I watched on.

She then turned to me and told me to board the plane.

'Er.........Okay...........Thank you,' I said surprised.

With no time to spare I hurried up the steps as fast I could. I didn't need telling twice. Whilst bombing up to the top full throttle I could still hear her shouting. That's my girl! You tell them that this flight is leaving now with me on it.

Once onboard I breathed a sigh of relief, but I knew it was still too soon to really relax. Only when this baby was up in the sky could I truly settle.

Walking down the middle aisle of the plane looking for my seat I sensed a tense atmosphere. Everyone stared at me with angry eyes again. I had no fans here. Well I couldn't blame them really. I'd be pissed off if someone held me up twice too.

I tried to ignore their stares and looked around for my row.

'You can sit here if you want,' said a friendly male voice from behind me.

When I looked up I could see it came from the well-dressed fellow who had helped me in the passport queue. To reiterate the point he patted the seat next to him hard.

'Don't mind if I do,' I said warmly

It was nice to see a friendly face.

Nervously I watched the door of the plane. I wondered who won with the slanging match. I hope to god it was the hostess. But then again could she really stop the police from taking me? Could she really assert more authority?

'I didn't catch your name before,' said the man.

'It's Alan,' I said distracted still looking towards the door.

'Charmed,' he said laughing. 'Well I won't ask what you have been doing in Algeria.'

I turned and could see he was eyeing up my dirty fingernails. I quickly hid my hands and just smiled.

To my relief my angel entered the plane and shut the hatch. There's my woman. Then the other stewardess instructed us to put on our seatbelts over the tanoy. I gladly did. Then the captain introduced himself and to my sweet relief we had lift off. That's nice! Now I can breathe again. I closed my eyes and smiled. It was all over.

The hostess came over to me and apologised. She explained that the policemen shouldn't have asked me to get off the plane, as being on the plane I was technically on British soil. It was very naughty of them to try and coax me off. If they wanted to speak to me they should have done it before I boarded the plane. God I loved this woman. In that moment I could have married her making her wife number three.

She asked me about my car and I explained about how it was stolen. Her light blue eyes twinkled as she looked on at me with sympathy.

To my annoyance a man across the way vied for her attention and she promptly left. I turned back to my new friend and shook him by the hand and thanked him. He scrunched up his eyes trying to work me out and gave another suspicious look to my dirty finger nails.

I slouched into the back of the chair and rested my eyes. I had such an eventful night and day I just wanted to get some sleep. But my new friend next to me had other plans. He wanted to talk and talk. Thankfully though he didn't pry about my reasons for being in Algeria and quite happily babbled on about himself. I did give him a bit of waffle that I was here on business but I didn't have to go into detail on what or with whom.

I found out from him he was a solicitor carrying out some work on behalf of a big firm in Algeria. It wasn't the most interesting of conversations I admit, but at that time I didn't care. I was just glad to be free.

'So Alan you obviously have done a bit of business in Algeria from what you said, so maybe you could help me out.'

'I will try,' I said with intrigue.

'I want to know,' he said leaning in as if he was going to impart a secret.

'How do you get the Arabs to stick to their meeting times?'

I couldn't help but laugh at his question.

'What's so funny?' he said with a serious demeanour.

'You can't.'

'But why?'

'They are different to you and me. They are not governed by time. Time means nothing to them. Trust me no matter what you do you won't rush them. You have to be patient.'

'I see,' he sighed.

It was obvious my answer didn't please him as he stared with annoyance at the floor. I think he thought I would part with some magical advice that could help him out.

In the background I could hear the jingle and chinking of the drinks trolley being pushed around the plane. I looked over in delight. I could just do with some beer and food. I was famished. My jeans felt very loose too. The travelling and last night's fun had made me lose quite a considerable bit of weight in a short space of time. I needed to sort that out.

'Hey Alan. Have you tried the Algerian wine?'

'Er….No…..Why'

'Oh Alan it is fabulous,' he said enthusiastically. 'That is one thing the Algerians can get right. The wine they produce is simply amazing.'

'Well that's sorted then.'

I caught hold of the hostess and asked for two bottles of red Algerian wine. The solicitor went to put his hands in his pockets and I stopped him.

'No no my friend I will pay. I owe you for the airport.'

'Oh okay. Thank you.'

Despite only having little cups to pour them in the wine went down quickly. He was right the wine was very tasty. I don't remember much after drinking the first bottle but somewhere in my psyche I know that this was the best ever flight I had ever taken.

I did go back out to Algeria and recover the hash. Troy also came with me. We managed to get to Oslo relatively unscathed too.

When Troy asked if I was up for yet another trip he was amazed to find out I was. He couldn't believe that after so many near misses with the law it didn't shake my confidence. Although nerve racking the fact I was nearly caught out only served to make me feel stronger and in some ways invincible. I felt that there no situation too hot or heavy for me to handle and even get out of. Especially the trip when I was diverted to Marscille, I still can't believe now how I am not rotting in a French prison. Now that really should have been a certain don't pass go and go straight to jail job. But I am glad my good luck prevailed.

I did however decide the next trip was to be my last trip, as I worked out I had enough money to live off if I invested it wisely. I didn't quite know what to do with it yet but I had a few ideas. One such plan was to stay in Wales and to invest in property in Cardiff, such as with student housing. The other idea was to live with Bo in Oslo and start a business. I didn't quite know what in but Bo had quite a few clever little ideas mainly regarding fashion. Maybe I could have been her pimp and invested in her. But then again she was far too independent for that. Well in her whoring business that was.

On what was to be my last ever trip I again used a Grenada car and again smuggled bars and bars of hashish by concealing them in the petrol tank. Again everything seemed to be plain sailing from travelling from Dover to Morocco as I ripped through Spain and France. Even Ahmed was on the ball when I got to Morocco as it only took three days for the bars. This was the quickest he had ever been. It meant that it was also possible that on my fourth day in North Africa I could have been in Algeria. This sounded crazy when I thought about my first trip which took me just under two weeks in Tangiers alone.

So with the Algerian border on my mind I left Tangier at eight in the morning and swiftly whizzed through Larache, Rabat and Fes. I then caught a drink and a bite to eat just outside of Fes and carried on again. I was astonished at how the journey was going. In fact it was going a little too well for my liking as every time something was hunky dory something on my vehicle would bloody fail. Feeling paranoid on this trip I would have trouble again I regularly stopped and checked the car for smoke, its electrics and whether the water was topped up. To my astonishment all seemed fine.

Nearing Oujda, Morocco I looked at my map and judged I was only a few miles away from the border into Algeria. Needing a break as I had been driving for a few hours I looked out for a place to pull over. I wanted to collect my thoughts together before going through border control. Although I felt safer with the cargo hidden underneath I still liked to hone my senses and be ready to play act to the guards just in case any unforeseen circumstances were to occur.

Looking at my watch I had plenty of time anyway as it was only just past four o'clock in the afternoon. I always aimed to pass through border controls around half four in the hope that like the British shift system the border guards would finish at five o'clock to swap over. So if this was true and they were close to the end of their shift they would be less likely to do an intensive search of my car as surely they would want to go home instead.

Well that is what I always hoped anyways.

I pulled over by a bridge that overlooked the Oued Isly stream that ran through Morocco. It was nice to get out of the car and have a good old stretch. Then to cure my nicotine cravings I lit up a fag, leaned against the bridge and closed my eyes. Covering my eyes into darkness felt nice, as for so many hours I had to concentrate on the road squinting hard through the blinding light of the North African sun. Feeling relaxed I loosened my arms and leaned them over the side of the bridge allowing my mind to wander. I reflected on how lucky I was that Mort and Troy had found me. How fantastic it was to work and play in such exotic climbs and how I would be sad that this would be the last time. Maybe I could do just one more trip.

Time went quick as when I glanced at my watch again it was now twenty past four. It was time now to set off again. I quickly tossed my lit cigarette over the side and watched with glee as it plopped into the water below. The stream slowly carried it away in its gentle waters. Feeling refreshed I got back in the car again for another long stint of driving.

On arrival at the border there were crowds of people. This was strange as I didn't remember seeing any people on any of my other trips, unless I hadn't noticed them. Nah I would have noticed them, surely. They were pretty hard to miss. Maybe their bus hadn't turned up or had broken down, as I remember Ahmed saying there was only one bus that would go from Morocco to Algeria. Now I thought the transport in rural Wales was bad.

When I crawled past in my car and looked around it did look like they had been there for a while, as the majority were sat or lying down on the dirt floor trying to make themselves as comfortable as possible, in the profuse heat. On each person's face was a pained expression and masses of sweat. Poor buggers.

Before getting to the uniformed and armed guards I decided to beckon a few people to get into my car and take them through the border to the biggest Algerian city I would pass. I thought to myself if I do this I may be able to go through customs more quickly as maybe the guards would appreciate me cutting down the crowds. I also did it out of pity as it was such a scorching hot day, despite being late in the afternoon.

With my window wound down, a smile and a hand gesture, a man and three women wearing djellabas approached my car. Opening my passenger door I again waved them in. The man sat next to me in the front and the three women shuffled into the back. The man I would say was in his mid-thirties and the women in the back were of three generations. It looked like he was with his wife, mother in law and his wife's grandma. Poor sod! I was only speculating but I recognised his aggrieved expression and believed that look could transcend many languages. But then again it could have been his three wives. He might have liked a selection of age and experience.

I said hello to everyone in the car but no one responded. Great none of them could speak English. Feeling uncomfortable at the lack of response I turned my head back round and concentrated on the road ahead. This was going to be a tense drive. By not being able to speak to them I felt apprehensive about my stranger's intentions. Did they just want a lift? Or were they taking the opportunity to mug me. Looking at the man next to me and the women in my rear view mirror, they also looked unsure of me. Maybe I didn't need to worry, as they seemed just as concerned about my intentions as I did about theirs.

I decided to try again conveying friendliness by smiling to the man next to me and the three women behind, but all of them greeted me with suspicious glances. The cheeky sods! They could have smiled. I was giving them a lift after all. A little appreciation wouldn't have gone a miss.

I began to become a little unnerved when I noticed all the arms of my passengers were obscured. It looked like they all had their arms folded and had tucked them into the folded material of their djellabas. Why did they conceal their hands so? What were they trying to hide? Weapons? To comfort myself I stroked my heel on a big metal bar that I kept hidden just under my seat. If they were going to pull something out, so was I.

It was possible that they were also carrying weapons for safety. I mean I had a metal bar to protect myself. Looking again at their concealed arms I fantasised about what weapons they could have had. Did they have guns? Knives? A chain maybe?

I thought about it so much it made me want to create a situation where I knew they would bring out their weapons. If indeed they did have any. I dallied with pulling out my metal bar to see what reaction I would get and if they produced anything. It would be like a sort of rock, paper, and scissors game but with instruments of pain. By applying reason I decided not to do that as I knew it would only serve to antagonise the situation. I had enough to deal with carrying the hash without pulling weapons out on people. Come on Alan back to the task in hand! Get through customs first!

I drove my car slowly to border control. The uniformed armed guard waved for me to stop. Time for a new country I thought. I jumped out the car and gestured my passengers to follow suit. The man sat next to me struggled to help the oldest woman out. Here we go they will open all my doors, have a scout inside, look at me as if I am a terrorist, find nothing and send me through. I had been through this rigmarole so many times. Each time they searched it seemed to take longer as I knew what was coming.

So once out of the car I smiled at my passengers. Again they did not smile back. Ungrateful bastards! The uniformed guard came over and put his hand on my shoulder and pointed me to go back in the car. What? Wait a minute. This wasn't right?

'No search we can just go through,' I asked the guard whilst pointing to the direction of Algeria.

The guard laughed. I knew that no search at a border through Morocco was as likely as Keith Richards becoming an activist against drugs, but I always tried to stay optimistic.

'I am sorry sir you cannot pass through.'

'Why?'

'There is a war on. So there is no entry through here today,' the guard said somberly.

'A war?'

'Yes.'

'For how long?'

My response was returned with silence and a nonchalant shrug. I stared at the guard and he looked back awaiting me to return to my car and go back. I stood for several minutes just looking at him and trying to comprehend what he had said and what it meant to my travels. I became lost in my own thoughts. But I was soon brought back to reality when I could see the nice border guard putting his hand on the pistol that was secured on his belt. So without a further question or hesitation I got back into the car with my unwanted guests and dropped them in the exact same position as where they had started.

It felt so painful retracing my steps. All that travelling was for no reason. I had basically just wasted hours and hours of my life. I wondered about taking another break but I was too wound up for that. I decided to carry on driving and take my frustration out on the road. Not knowing what I was going to do next I decided to just head back towards Tangier.

After driving through Oujda once again I came to a split in the road where in the one direction was Taourirt which lead to Fes or the other direction which lead to Ahfir onto Hoceima through to Ketama. On paper the latter option would have been the quickest to get to Tangier but then on the other hand it would have also been the most dangerous. From doing my nightly drug run up to Ahmed's farms I knew it was bandit country, I had seen the scores of dangerous eyes waiting on the road ready to thieve and kill. It used to shit me up going through with a guide and Ahmed's blessing. I think on my own I would have been eaten alive. Despite the danger I was still very tempted, but in the end reason prevailed and I pointed the Grenada back along to Taourirt. I had already had enough excitement I could cope with for one day.

After a few hours on the road I began to flag again. I decided I had worked out enough of my frustration on the road and now needed to find a place to stay the night. A good sleep was what was called for. The prayers to my weary eyes were soon answered in Fes where I stumbled upon a decent looking place which most importantly had a secure car park.

When I parked up my vehicle my stomach groaned with hunger, but I couldn't be bothered to go and search for food whether it be from a local restaurant or from trying to find out if the hotel did food. Instead I stuffed my mouth with a soggy warm chocolate which I remembered putting in my glove compartment a few days ago and went to reception. As soon as I had my keys I went straight to my room and collapsed on the bed. My express intention was to get some sleep or rest, but instead I just ended up thinking out the day and wallowing.

Right I can't go through Algeria which means my only option to leave North Africa is via leaving a Moroccan port on a ferry to Spain. I mean it wouldn't be suspicious at all leaving Morocco the hashish highway of North Africa back into Spain.

Oh god! Even Troy and Ahmed told me that leaving via Moroccan ports was a complete no no, as the customs offices on the Spanish side are strict and hell bent on finding smugglers.

I did think about trying to enter through another border of Algeria too, but I decided that was probably pointless, if one border was closed then presumably the rest were. I mean it wouldn't have made much sense to close one and not the others, especially with a war on.

I decided driving around Algeria wasn't an option either as it would have added an extra 2500 miles to my journey. Plus I would have had to go through Libya, a country I hadn't familiarised myself with. I would have also had to travel blind as my handwritten maps didn't include that way around Algeria. Which noted would have been very fun and exciting, but would be equally as stupid and reckless. I just had to suck it up and go back through Europe via Morocco.

I took my time in the morning getting back to Tangier. I decided to waste a few more days until I had been in Morocco for a week to look like I was a traveller. It was quite boring hanging around especially as I didn't go and see Ahmed, or anyone else I knew. I did this as I didn't want him to know I was back. I was worried that if I told him about going from Ceuta to Algeciras he would only tell Troy and this was what I didn't want. Only I wanted to tell Troy about this, and after the event. There was no way I was speaking to him before as I knew he would freak. I also didn't want his negative vibes to dent my confidence. I couldn't have done with that. I needed all the balls I could muster.

Finally the seventh day in Morocco came and I queued up with the other travellers to board the ferry onto Southern Spain. Like them I littered my car with, whiskey, tobacco, trinkets and postcards. Like them I wore a sunburnt smile and relaxed clothes as if I'd had the holiday of my life. Like them I waited patiently in the small queue.

In the car in front I could see a man reading the Time Out magazine. Seeing this made my blood boil I realised I should have bought that before I went on my trip as in there it sometimes said about the rising tensions between countries. I might have foreseen the border closure. I mean I usually did buy this magazine but it slipped my mind this time and boy would I fucking pay for it. Feeling pissed off I kicked the bottom of the car.

Since doing this book I have found no reference to a war at this time or as to why the borders were closed that day. The only possible reason I have found was that the Polisario Front were active at this time. The Polisario front was a "Popular Front for the Liberation of Saguia el-Hamra and Río de Oro" and who were working for the Sahrawi rebel movement working for the independence of Western Sahara from Morocco. Their express intention was by militarily forcing an end to Spanish colonization. At this time their army used to inflict severe damage through guerrilla-style hit-and-run attacks against enemy forces in Western Sahara and in Morocco and Mauritania. Maybe it was this. Maybe there was a threat of violence so they had to close. However I cannot entirely be sure.

Well whatever the hell it was, it really put me in the shit. But despite this drawback I chalked it up to experience and carried on regardless. It was just another thing to set my pulse racing. Just another adventure for me to endure and inform Troy and Mort of.

Nearing the end of the small queue in front I could now see the ferry in full view. I could also see in front customs officers leaning into people's cars and asking for their passports. The officers seemed happy enough with their passports and directed them straight through. I showed my passport to the Morrocan passport control officers and everything was good. They had a little glance at the pages and with a smile let me through. My heart rate rocketed as I tried to contain my elation. With sweaty hands I nervously smiled and nodded as I tentatively edged forward behind the small queue ahead.

In front now I could see the Spanish passport control officers. They took a little longer looking at the passports of the few people ahead but still no one was pulled to the side. My heart felt like it was pounding out of my chest as I watched on, but on the outside I tried to exude cool and calm.

It was now my turn. I didn't feel ready it was all too quick. Where were the queues to shield me? But as requested I handed my passport over. They seemed preoccupied by my Moroccan stamps. After a few seconds of flicking through the pages he pointed over to a road just off to the side which lead to a bricked building with no windows. I exchanged a confused glance but with more vitriol he pointed to the road again.

I shrugged with annoyance but obeyed his command. When I pulled up three men in mechanic overalls came over and opened up the roller door on the outside of the building. As I drove through I went over a kind of pit. Once I was stationary the guards pulled the sliding garage doors shut leaving a gap of a few inches allowing a bit of sun light to stream through. This was okay I thought, all they wanted to do was some random searches. That's fine. Just don't think about the pits below. I mean they would have to be deeply suspicious to look underneath. It will be okay.

All three customs officers beckoned me out of the car which I did so happily and promptly. I got out of their way and leaned against the cool brick wall. I smiled to give an air of a man on holiday just having a minor delay with a search. The officers then opened the doors and looked inside. They dug through my bags, fags, bottles of whiskey and postcards which I purposely left strewn across the back seat. They picked up my camera which I strategically placed on the passenger seat along with a filled in post card wedged underneath it.

Satisfied with the search in the car they paid attention to my boot and had a good old root in my suitcase. Then they went back to looking inside the car by taking off panels and panels to see if I had anything stuffed down the sides. Jesus these boys were going to town! I didn't know half the panels they took off even existed.

I watched on getting annoyed as it was taking far longer than I liked. But I couldn't do anything about it apart from wait. Once satisfied they all looked back at me. I shone back a blank look whilst also looking at my watch, trying to encourage them to hurry.

Then one of the officers went into the pit to take a look underneath the car. He beckoned in Spanish to the other officer to have a look too. As I looked over I could see they were interested in the metal tow bar underneath. Why are they looking at that? Dear god please stop!

The officer who noticed the tail bar looked over to me. It was as if he was trying to assess my eyes for guilt. I retorted to his glance with a bewildered expression. I tried to communicate to him that I didn't know what the hell they were looking for. He looked swiftly away. Had I convinced him?

The officer looked back at the tail bar and the other two other officers came around to assess the situation. They were pulling it and pushing it but it didn't move. Oh please let them tire of this. Please let them think this is more hassle than it is worth. After a while they all stood up and went to the corner of the room whilst still keeping a watchful eye on me. They seemed to be discussing whether to take off the tail bar or not. This went on for far too long for my liking. The ferry was meant to be leaving in just under half an hour. I hope to god they don't make me miss my ferry. I couldn't go through this rigmarole again tomorrow.

They all then came back and to my horror one was holding a bag of tools. Fuck! Two of the officers dropped down into the pit underneath my Grenada, whilst one stayed on the ground above watching me. I watched the two men underneath as they struggled for ages trying to get the damn thing off. I would have laughed if I had nothing to conceal, as they were making a real meal of it. Maybe I will be okay, it does look normal under the car. They may not unscrew the petrol tank.

After minutes of struggling they eventually freed the tail bar and plonked it on the floor. I couldn't see now what they were doing as they tinkered underneath the workings of the car. My heart beating faster each time they clonked with spanners

Then the metallic sound was drowned out by them shouting in Spanish. What have they found now? If I am going get caught just please for god sake get it over with I screamed in my head! However I emptied my mind again. Keep your cool Alan. You have been in worse situations. They were lifting parts and parts off my car from the pit onto the floor of the garage.

Then to my utmost horror I could see them lifting the petrol tank up from the pit. Oh shit!

7 NO NO SENIOR!

All three customs officers gathered round the petrol tank as if it was the Holy Grail. They fucking knew. Come on Alan stay calm. It is not over yet! You have been in worst scrapes than this. I crossed my fingers behind my back hoping for some luck of a miracle. Maybe they won't find the secret compartment filled with hash.

Well, even if I was caught there was nothing else I could have done. I had play acted to the best of my abilities, but the tourist card was just not good enough for these bastards.

I watched on as they all gathered around the petrol tank, I felt jealous as they pawed her. Come on Alan keep cool. They eventually set to work opening her up with screwdrivers and other tools. Once opened they wiggled inside of her a big bendy stick causing the petrol juices to lap.

After probing her for a few seconds they eventually all nodded as if in agreement of something and then discarded the bendy stick dripping with petrol on the floor. What were they doing now? Was everything cool? Was it time to put it back? Please let it be so! I hope they are quick as now I had only had 20 minutes before the ferry left.

Then I watched with horror as one of the men started to pour the contents of the petrol tank into a bucket. That was it! I was fucked! They did intend to probe deeper. There was no way now I wasn't going to be caught. Once emptied they were sure to find the secret compartment. Nothing could save me. The only way out now was to escape.

Trying not to draw attention to myself I shiftily had a look around the dark dingy bricked hut of a garage. Right how was I going to escape these three armed guards? Think Alan think! The noise of the petrol glugging made it hard to concentrate on my thoughts. Plus the smell didn't help, as it made me feel quite nauseous.

Come on Alan. Man up! Think! Looking around the only escape route I had was through the metal sliding door. I needed to get passed the officers and through there to have a chance of legging it. I was grateful it was slightly open which gave me more time than if it wasn't open at all. However the gap of the open door was only about 20 inches or so wide, but with a push I reckoned I could fit through. It would be a tight squeeze but it was doable. But the only problem was avoiding being shot in the process as I could see all of them carried pistols.

I looked back at the petrol. It wouldn't be long now till it stopped flowing and they would make the discovery. God I could do with a fag! I stroked the pocket of my jeans and could feel my Zippo lighter. That's it! That's fucking it!

Pretending I was going to smoke I pulled out my cigarettes and a lighter. I didn't need to pretend as the two officers in front were still immersed in watching the petrol pour into the bucket. Right here I go! The plan in my head was that I would flick my Zippo lighter as if to light a fag. But instead I would toss it into the bucket of petrol and then run in the commotion of an explosion. I had heard about American soldiers using Zippos and that these lighters can be slid across the floor and would still remain lit in order to ignite something flammable, such as lines of petrol. Hopefully an explosion would distract the guards enough so they wouldn't fire at me with their pistols. But then again would the Zippo lighter be suffocated too much with the large amount of petrol and not catch fire? I just didn't know.

With adrenalin pumping I flicked the lid of the Zippo. Right here we go. But before I could turn the wheel of the lighter with my thumb I felt a cool metal object jab into my neck.

'No no senior,' said the officer behind.

I turned my head slightly to look and could see the object was a gun.

I couldn't believe it. I had forgotten about the customs officer behind me. It is funny though to this day I don't know whether he realised my intentions or it was because I was planning on smoking with petrol around. I had the sneaking suspicion he knew what I was up too. On reflection I was thankful I didn't cause an explosion. I would have hated being responsible for killing or burning three innocent men. Even if they were going to put me in the shit. Plus in all likelihood it would have probably gone wrong and I would have been shot, or even set on fire too.

'Give the lighter to me,' he ordered.

'Okay okay I will give you the lighter. I will have a fag later,' I said apologetically. 'I will have a fag after you have searched my vehicle.'

Carefully I passed back the lighter to the customs officer. Despite giving him the lighter he still continued sticking the gun into my neck

'Erm......... Can you put the gun away?'

I was still pushing my luck playing the tourist card. Well, they hadn't found the hash yet. The guard however never responded. He did however ease up with the gun. I could still feel it resting on my neck but it didn't seem to jab as much into my skin.

That was it! Plan b was fucked as well. All I could do now was stare ahead. I felt sick as I was forced to watch as the last drips of petrol dropped into the bucket. The men looked at each other and shook their heads at the amount of petrol in the bucket. It was obvious he knew that there should have been more petrol in there. Well then the inevitable happened and they set about dissecting the petrol tank and my secret compartment was found. Once open my beautiful hashish bars were exposed. I had never seen anyone look as happier as these three bastards when they found them. Shit!

The customs officer laid the hashish bars in front of me and stared at my reaction.

'What the hell is that?'

All the three men stayed silent and continued staring into my eyes.

'How did that get in there?'

Still I was greeted with silence.

'Is no one going to answer me? What is it?' I protested in agitation.

Despite my best efforts all my remarks fell on deaf ears. They smiled and grinned as if they didn't care. All they were concerned about was finding the hash. My innocence wasn't up for discussion. God I felt sorry for the poor bastards who had stuff planted. It appeared it didn't matter.

I was then escorted by the gun happy guard outside and into a building full of small offices where I was swiftly hand cuffed and ordered to sit and wait for the British consulate. In the time I waited I concocted a story in my head about how the hashish got there and how I was innocent. With my story straight I went about trying to use my body language to communicate to the customs officers around me I was innocent. I did this by shaking my head and looking to the sky as if I did not know was happening. I shouldn't have bothered as none of them gave me a second glance.

After a few hours I could hear chattering in English at the door. Looking through the glass at the top of the door I could see a tall, British looking man in his thirties wearing a suit. That must be the consulate.

'Hi! It's Alan isn't it?' he said extending his arm.

'Yes,' I said shaking his hand firmly.

'I am Biggy. The British consulate for this area.'

I instantly hated him. He was far too smarmy. Plus I thought it was a bit stupid checking I was Alan; he knew it was as the bastards probably showed them my passport which they confiscated.

'Right well anyway. I am here to tell you what happens next.'

'What happens next?' I said disgusted.

'This shouldn't be happening at all. That stuff they found isn't mine.'

'I see,' he said smiling as if not listening to word I was saying.

'The only thing I can think of is that I lent my car to two Londoners the other day in Morocco. I mean they were in a bind so me being nice I lent it to them.'

'Right,'

'Yes right! So I can only think it was them that put the stuff on me.'

'I mean what was it anyway?'

'Look Alan I am really sorry but I won't be able to help you with the details. But you will have a chance to say this to the police in an interview and at your hearing. The only thing I can advise you about now is what happens next.'

I shouted and argued for a while protesting my innocence, but this didn't work. Biggy, although he pretended to be was not interested at all. All he wanted was for me to shut up and listen.

Eventually I relented and allowed him to tell me his itinerary of proceedings. Nothing sank in though when he talked. I was too busy fretting and trying to get over the fact that I was caught. Plus I think I blocked him out as his voice played on my nerves. He reminded me of a fucking car salesman.

'Well Alan this is all that I can tell you at the moment. I will hopefully see you again.'

I shook his hand politely and smiled as if I was trying to be brave about my situation. In reality I wanted to strangle the bastard and demand he would get me out of here.

8 A SWAP OF CUSTODY

Once the consulate was gone I could see a bit more action happening in the office. Before it seemed they were all procrastinating as I watched them wandering around chatting, sitting on their arses and drinking coffee. Now they were shuffling around, had paperwork in hand and looking like they had a set purpose. I didn't like this one bit.

I watched through the window as two customs officers went outside. I could see they were getting my things out the car and proceeding to shove them in the back of another car. Once all the doors were shut they disappeared past the window and reappeared at the door. The two men entered the room and grunted in Spanish with my two captors. Who in turn grunted back in agreement and excused my bellboys.

Without warning the taller of the two customs officers grabbed my left bicep and with the palm of his other hand pushed in the middle of my shoulder blade. The other custom officer joined in not wanting to miss the fun. I don't know what was the point of this shoving? I would have moved and cooperated. They could have just asked or signalled me to move. The pushing and shoving continued until we got to the car. Then as one of nice men opened the car door, I was launched without warning head first in the back. Which is great when you are wearing handcuffs. Luckily I didn't bang my head but it did hurt a little as my face scraped the back seat of the car. I literally did a nose dive. After a few seconds of shock I got myself up and removed my arse away from sticking out of the car. Then literally a second later the door slammed. I wonder if he brilliantly timed this or that he didn't care if it hit me. As soon as I hauled myself up to an upright position my captors had got in the front and we pulled away from Ceuta Port.

It took several minutes to adopt a comfortable position. Once I did I relaxed my muscles and body, and took my attention to the scenery passing by, but as I stared out of the window thoughts started flooding in my mind about what was to happen next.

I hope to god I get a proper interview with the police than I did with my good for nothing consulate. Maybe I could convince them I was innocent? But then again would they care? They had all the evidence they needed?

I racked my brain to think about what Troy and Ahmed had told me about Moroccan justice and couldn't think of anything they had said that would help. I mean they probably didn't think they needed too as I always promised to go through Algeria with the hash, but with the war, Morocco was my only option. I hope to god Morocco was not as strict as Algeria.

My thoughts subsided as the car screeched and grounded to an emergency stop. My stomach felt like it had done a 180 degrees flip as I tensed from the sudden halt. When I looked outside the window I could see there was no reason for the emergency breaking. I think he did it to piss me off as I could see him smirking in the driver's mirror. Prick!

Just as my stomach returned to its natural position one my captors opened the door and wrenched me out of the car. The other customs officer felt like he hadn't had his fair share and he joined in shoving me along. I felt annoyed and embarrassed being pulled and pushed about like some naughty school kid on the public streets. However the feeling subsided when I faced my nemesis which I tried to avoid for so many years. It wasn't a conventional one I would have known in Britain, but it was what it was, a police station. My senses ignored the pushing and shoving, and I absorbed all my efforts in being blinkered to what was happening ahead. As we entered the building the two custom officers went straight to the desk that welcomed us. The custom officers grunted with the police officers behind the desk in Spanish whilst pointing at me intermittently. The not knowing was killing me. Why wouldn't they speak to me in English? Why were they talking in Spanish and not Arabic? And even if they couldn't speak English they could have tried to talk to me and make me understand what the fuck was going on. The conversation of grunts ceased when one of my captors nodded and started to walk away. The other captor held my arm as one of the police officers came around. As my freedom was traded to police custody the two customs officers smiled and waved farewell.

Now I had someone new to shove me about. However the Moroccan police officer was much gentler, he didn't pull my arm but merely guided it. As I looked at his face I could see no emotion. His eyes were dark and seemed dead inside. As he walked me through corridor after corridor it seemed like he was in a trance, as if he was just going through the motions. Turning my attention from the officer I looked ahead and could see no more corridors. What I could see was a big police cell. Oh fucking hell.

I could see inside the cell as it wasn't a room but a sort of giant metal bird cage. I had stayed in my fair share of cells but nothing like that before. It was like something out of a western movie. I didn't know these buggers still existed in real life. Inside the cage were about twenty to thirty men; a mix of Spanish and Moroccans. They all looked downright dirty and dangerous. I don't think my white arse in there would have added to the mood. As we drew closer and closer my mind raced. There was no way I was going in there. No way. I would get killed. I had to think now. I could have taken the guard out and run. But this wasn't such a clever idea, he was armed and his police friends were armed. Plus where would I run. Think Alan think! With my body I tensed and gave resistance to the gentle shoves of the police officer. To my surprise the police officer did not put up a fight and merely carried on with the same strength. Oh fuck! Oh fuck! Oh fuck!

Once outside the cell I could see I had the attention from all the inmates inside. Some smiled evilly whilst others scowled with vengeance. Fucking hell I was going to be their white bait! Those guys weren't going to play nice. As I looked at their faces I could tell I would be in for some nasty surprises. Whether that was by being mugged, beaten, raped or killed. Or even maybe all of the above.

The guard kept one hand on my shoulder whilst he unclipped the big heavy metal keys which were secured on his belt. As he did so I turned my back to the cell and shouted 'No!' I caught his attention from shouting. He looked puzzled but continued to search through the keys for the right one for the cell. Again I defiantly shouted No! The guard half shrugged. He went to look down to ignore me but I stamped my feet and jerked my body violently from his grip.

'No I am not going in there!' I bawled.

Over and over I shouted no and jerked. The police officer face lit up with annoyance as I continued to put him off finding the right key. Then to my delight I could see other cells next door.

'In there!' I said softly pointing to the solitary cells next door.

'In there!' I said again slightly louder.

I stood my ground outside the cell. I couldn't believe what I was doing. Challenging a police man in a foreign country. He looked at me with anger and glanced over to the cells next door. He shook his head and let loose his grip on the heavy keys until they crashed on his thigh. The noise in the cell behind grew quiet. It felt like an age whilst exchanging glances with the police officer, but I stood defiantly looking hard into his eyes. My heart pounded fast. I could feel my adrenalin bubbling and tickling under the surface of my skin.

Without warning he pulled my shirt sleeve and pushed me in the direction of the cells next door. He then proceeded to open them with another set of keys on his belt. He flung open the cell door and pointed inside. He then took off my handcuffs, pushed me inside and slammed the door shut. I felt a sigh of relief. I was alone. I was still in the shit, but at least I didn't have to engage in battle with the men next door. I had won one victory but I knew the war wasn't over. I now had to think of a way out of here.

The cells next door comprised of brick walls, a bucket to shit and piss in and a hard bench. I had no distractions from myself. I sat on the bench and inhaled deeply. I sat down trying to make sense of the day's event. I couldn't believe I was caught on my last fucking trip. My last trip to set me up for life and here I was.

No Alan. Come on. Don't lose hope. You're the player. You'll think of way out of here.

But it didn't matter how hard I tried. I had nothing. My mind was blank.

I reached into my pocket and took out my possessions. This consisted of a novel and a wad of notes. I threw them on the bench and continued looking at the floor. Again nothing came to mind. Oh dear I wonder what Troy and Mort will say when they find out. I glanced back over at the money and then at the novel and it suddenly dawned on me. What the fuck! I am in a police station and I have been put in a cell. And I have my possessions. They didn't take these from me. No searches? Why? Also they haven't taken any details or asked me anything. I haven't had a picture to pose for and no stained fingers to mark. Was I really in a police station? This is absurd. Plus where was my fucking one phone call. What sort of justice is this? I would be really fucking pissed off if I was an innocent. One thing I had to be grateful for was that I still had my cash. The animals next door didn't have an opportunity to take it. I was carrying just shy of six grand; to those fuckers next door I was a millionaire. Mind, would this cash be of any worth here, and how long was I going to be in here for?

I decided to calm myself down as I picked up the novel from the bench. Reading the novel helped me to keep my mind off the enormity of the situation. Funny enough the novel was an exciting and dangerous novel. God knows why I brought this novel on my journey as I didn't need it. And I certainly did need the book now. I had already had all the excitement and danger a person could bear. However it did spur me on. I had fire in my belly for the next chapter of events.

In the morning the guards rapped the hatch on the cell and woke me up. Two guards then ripped open the door and entered the room with strength and vigour. Bleary eyed I saw them stride over. Without warning one guard nudged me in the arm and grunted in Spanish. With the only word I could recognise being senior. I sat up with my hands firmly gripping onto the bench. The other quieter guard brought out a pair of hand cuffs and passed them to the leading guard whilst staring at me and smiling. I put my hands out ready. I knew if I wasn't quick enough they would have wrenched my arms in place. I didn't want to satisfy their impatient aggressive needs. I had learned from yesterday. Come on fucking give it to me then I screamed in my head.

Hand cuffed and bound the two guards grabbed a fore arm each and whisked me down the corridors. They took me outside into the brilliant sunshine. Unable to cover my eyes I squinted whilst also trying to look at the ground and avoiding my feet to trip on anything in my way. Blinded by the light I was pushed forward to the side of a police car. Whilst being held by one guard the other wrenched open the door and flung me in whilst slamming the door with force behind me. Where the fuck was I going now?

The car ride was a bumpy one. I felt fully awake now to appreciate the anxiety of my impending destination. But as it was so overwhelming it also didn't feel real. I felt like I was in a dream or watching a film of this happening to someone else. But it wasn't a dream. It was reality and I just had to live with it. Also it made me laugh as I didn't even know where I was going. I had a pretty good idea it was a prison, but I didn't know what to expect. In Britain I knew the places and the name of the prisons as I had frequented a few. Here they could have been taking me any fucking where. I looked outside the window and embraced my view. This might be the last time I see the outside world for a while.

9 ROSES WITH THORNS

Well my ignorance was broken as my carriage arrived at a large set of prison gates. On a big sign it stated this was Los Rosales, Ceuta. The literal meaning for Los Rosales in Spanish is The Roses. What a nice name for a prison. But I could bet that was the only nicest thing about it. A few minutes went by until two guards dressed in prison uniform opened the gates. Their large rifles slung over their shoulders got in the way as they opened the big hefty doors. They had a brief chat with my two captors until they all paused and looked at me. In a cheeky moment I wanted to wave and smile but I thought from their hostility I was best being quiet. We were then waved through and made our way to the main prison building. I turned my head to watch the two guards shut the big entrance doors. That was it. I was now shut away from the rest of the world and entering my new domain. What have I done? Then the car stopped again. I looked ahead and I could see another set of large wooden doors. This was the entrance to my new fortress. I could see all around the perimeter of the building guards patrolling. Their guns glinted in the warm Moroccan sun as they proudly carried them around. Although their uniforms were similar to military dress their behaviour did not appear regimented or ordered. They all seemed quite arrogant and relaxed as they strutted around whilst smoking on cigarettes. This looked a completely different set up to the one I was used to in Britain.

Without warning I was wrenched out of the car in hand cuffs by one of the policeman and taken to a small door on the edge of the main doors. The other policeman carried my suitcase. A prison guard opened the door and I was shoved inside. The policemen and the prison guards then had a brief chat until my handcuffs were ripped off. I gripped and stroked my red wrists gaining a bit of relief from their tight bind. I listened to the conversation intensely as they spoke in Spanish, but understood nothing. I longed to understand what was going on.

But the only thing that was apparent was my custody was been exchanged again. The police officers gave me one more disdainful look and then left through the small door. I smiled at the prison guard and put my hands in the air and asked him what was next. The prison guard retorted with a scowl. For a few minutes he wittered in Spanish and pointed at my suitcase. I shook my head. His face grew more annoyed as he pointed to me and then kicked my bag. Okay okay jobsworth! I will pick up my fucking bag. I picked up my bag and stood still. With his hand he pointed forward. I waited for him to start walking but then with a huff he shoved me and pointed forward again. Fine I will start walking. As I walked and walked in the big open space I noticed the ornate tiles on the floor. I hope the inside of the prison is going to be as nice as this. After a few yards he led me to a hexagonal office which had no walls only windows. It was such a strange shape but intelligent in design for a prison as you could see what was happening all around you.

I waited at the door. The guard pointed again, from his cue I opened it and walked through. The guard quickly followed and the door behind banged shut. Inside the office I was greeted by several prison guards. There were all milling around, smoking, laughing and drinking coffee. The desks were all littered with papers and coffee stains. I could see no tidy spaces or any sort of order. On one of the desks were several packs of cards and dominos. Then too my surprise I could also see bottles and bottles of whiskey and vodka in open view under some of the desks. These surely must have been the stashes they found from the inmates.

Their jovial attitude and banter of the prison guards ceased as they turned to look at me their new inmate. I could see the annoyance in the eyes of the guards as I walked through. I was glad when I left the office to the other side of the building; I couldn't stand the hostility that was all around me. I turned and watched the guard closing the door. As he did so one of the guards beckoned him back and chattered in Spanish.

Whilst the guard babbled on I took the opportunity to look around at my new home. On this side of the office there were no tiles on the floor like with the entrance and everywhere looked grimy. The only thing that gleamed was the windows around the guard's office. Also around the office was a sort of metal scaffolding which was decorated with a sort of chicken mesh. The metal mesh looked like a recent addition. Which begs the question what were they protecting themselves from? This bird was not going to be fun.

The guard could see I was taking too much of an interest and poked me to hurry quickly past. As I turned to look at his hand shoving me I noticed on the belt of his uniform hung a big black heavy truncheon. I bet that hurts to be beaten with.

Carrying my heavy suitcase he shoved me from corridor after corridor of the prison. Each corridor smelled the same, burnt, with the added flavour of urine and rubbish. I also noticed along each corridor there was considerable fire damage on the walls and ceilings. This looked like it had happened recently.

I was then taken to the bottom of a concrete stairwell which had a heavy gate at the bottom which hung open. I could hear a patter of hurried steps behind. As I turned to look I could see a prisoner. To my surprise he had the key. What the fuck was a prisoner doing with a key to part of the prison? This place was weird. With that the prisoner scampered up the steps in a hurried fashion. Although he held a key to a part of the prison the prisoner seemed like a trained dog to the guard and was very nervous of his master. The guard poked me in the back to follow suit like his subordinate and rush along. I did not fucking rush though. I took my time. I was not going to be his bitch.

At the top of the stairwell there was another heavy gate. This time it was locked. The key the prisoner had opened this part. Once opened I realised we were stepping up to the roof of the prison. On the roof was a sort of concrete room which looked like it had been plonked on. A prisoner with the key to the roof! Now this was fucking nuts!

The room was filled with cases and bags. The guard pointed at my case and then to a section of the room. I took my case and dropped it where he pointed. I was about to leave when he pointed back at the case and grumbled in Spanish. I didn't understand a word he said but I went back to my case and opened it looking at the guard for assurance and acceptance my actions were correct. The prisoner then piped up and told me in broken English quietly to take out the things I wanted. I looked in my case. What was I going to need? I decided quickly to take a set of clothes out. I had some good stuff in there such a gorgeous black pin striped tailored suit. I would normally wear this when I was in Oslo. However I decided I didn't need this here. The only things I took out were a white t-shirt, jeans and shorts. I was not going to be a target in this prison so I took the plainest clothes as to hide my wealth. When I had the stuff I wanted the prison guard barked and nodded his head to leave the room.

With my little bundle of clothes the prison guard shoved me through the corridors once more. As we walked down I noticed prisoners littered everywhere. Although I didn't know the precise time I knew it was mid-morning. Why was everyone just standing about chatting. Where there no timetables of activities or jobs in here? It all seemed much disorganised. Looking into the eyes of each inmate I could see them trying to weigh me up as I walked past. The guard then finally stopped and opened a cell door and pointed me inside. The guard promptly disappeared before I could ask him any questions. Well I take it this is my cell then! Not even so much as a goodbye.

I hung around outside the door in shock as again as I had no details taken off me, no finger prints taken and no inspection. Where also was my interview to tell my side of the fucking story? This was absolutely ludicrous.

But on the flip side I had to look at the positives, I still had a fuck load of cash on me and I didn't get poked around in any delicate places. I just fucking hope Interpol knew where I was, as there was no other record as to my existence here. However I patted my jeans pocket adorned with cash and felt a little happier.

I gulped as I stepped inside the cell. Looking around I could see it was approximately 5 metres by 5 metres decorated with pale green paint and grime. The cell had a bunk by the window and a bed to the right of the door. There was also a toilet. Well I say a toilet, but really it was a hole in the floor to the side and a grimy small sink. The smells emanating from both were absolutely rank. On the bunks were two men who looked in their late twenties and European. Great this time I had to share. Mind you if I was right and they were European we would at least have some common ground. They also didn't look mean like the inhabitants of the metal cage in the police station. Their faces seemed warm and absent from malice. But time would tell if this was true.

I pointed at the empty bed and they nodded. I then carried my clothes over and decided to investigate my sleeping arrangements. I pulled back the flimsy sheets to a sight which made me sick to the stomach. The mattress was covered in a variety of different stains of which I couldn't or even probably wouldn't have wanted to identify. But one thing was for sure it stunk of piss. Mind you that seemed to be the general aroma around this whole fucking place, so I will probably have to get used to that for a while. I put down my small bundle clothes on the floor. This seemed cleaner than putting it on the bed. Plus there was no furniture to store clothes. Being hopeful I took off the sheets and proceeded to turn the filthy mattress over to see if the over side was any better. As I twisted the mattress and exposed the flimsy metal frame I disturbed crumbs of rust which littered the floor. This must have been caused by the piss soaking through to the frame and rusting it. Nice! As I looked at the other side I realised this was even worse. This side was browner. I convinced myself this was only rust and decided to turn the mattress back to its original better side. Lost in shock I sat down and looked around the room at the squalor. Oh my god how long would I have to stay here. Then a voice shouted out and broke my disturbed thoughts.

'Hi I am Joseph,' said the stranger in a gentle French accent.

'And this is my friend,' he said pointing to the other cell mate.

As I looked up I could see Joseph looking at me with half pity and half empathy.

'Oh Hi… Hi I am Alan.'

'First things first. We can't use the sink or the toilet in the cell,' he said as if he had rattled this off many times before.

'What?…………Why?'

'Look they don't work. There is no water.'

'What!'

'Yeah I know it's bad. But they don't work.'

'Have you told the guards about it?'

Both the boys laughed and only stopped when they noticed the confusion on my face was turning to anger.

'They won't listen Alan.'

'Do you want me to show you around the prison?' asked Joseph as if to change the subject.

'Nah man I am okay. I will get round by myself.'

I felt a little awkward refusing Joseph's help, but I preferred to be alone in venturing my new surroundings. Joseph did seem like an okay bloke and on first impressions a sound guy but I couldn't be sure of that yet. I would need a little time to figure him out. His friend also seemed harmless to, almost too timid for prison, but again I needed his measure. Plus I thought by being on my own I could think more clearly without their distractions. It was comforting though that they could speak English and were seemingly approachable.

'Well no time like the present Joe. Is Joe okay to call you by?' I said playfully.

'No! Only Joseph please.'

'Okay well see you later I am off for a wander.'

I was thankful to leave the room I couldn't be bothered with conversation at this point. I wanted action. Only actions could help me now to get out of here. However I needed to first get my bearings on this place and find out how it functioned. So I went off to explore.

I walked along the corridor lined with cells; the smell of burnt ash hit my nose. I was thankful for this as it masked the aroma of piss. I made sure I carefully looked at each prisoner that lined the corridors and cells whilst not engaging in a threatening stare but making them aware I was ready and watchful. Reaching the end of the landing I scuttled down the steps on to the ground floor and passed more prisoners. Why was everyone standing around chatting? Later Alan. Just case the joint first.

I carried on making sure I was noting my route so I knew how to get back to my cell and my piss soaked bed for the night. As I walked along the ground floor I passed more cells. These were of no use to me so I carried on. Then a set of steps caught my eye. They were similar to the ones that lead up to the luggage room but this time there was no gate at the bottom. I looked around and checked no-one was watching just in case this was forbidden and headed upwards. I carefully climbed the steep concrete steps. As I reached the top I had two choices of doors to go into. The left was open so I decided this to be my first choice. I carefully opened the door. As it creaked open I could see no one inside and decided to proceed. The room was empty apart from a large ping pong table that stood shattered and worn in the centre of the room. There was nothing going on in here so

I headed to the next room. As I opened the second door, again this room was empty of life. However this was adorned with furniture of a religious nature. There were hymn books and other religious paraphernalia scattered around. It looked like a sort of mock Catholic Church. There was a lecture stand for where I would imagine the priest would stand and worn wooden benches for the congregation. I imagined for a second the masses that took place in here and the benches lined with sinners flocking to repent there misdeeds. This room as with the majority of the prison was blackened by the fire. Even the sanctity of this mock Church was not spared destruction. As I walked around on the wooden floor with only my footsteps echoing I felt a bit tentative like I shouldn't have been in here. I wasn't a religious man as such and certainly not a Catholic but my curiosity won over as I scouted a round a little more. The fire really took its toll in here, there were ash piles littered everywhere. Each bible was singed. I wanted to meet the guys who had done this. If I couldn't get out of here with the courts or a good lawyer I'd join with them to escape. Satisfied I had seen enough I headed back towards the door. Before I left I realised there was something not right about this room. As I turned round it dawned on me that one thing at least hadn't been ravaged by the fire and stuck out like a sore thumb. Chilled to the bone I went over to inspect. Set in the back wall stood majestically a five foot or so statue of the Virgin Mary. What the! She had not been touched. How could everything in this room be burned to cinders and blackened but this stand majestic and tall. The colours on the statue were perfect in blue and gold. I stared for a few moments at the apparition in amazement. This then turned to unease as I couldn't explain it. I didn't have time for this so I put it to the back of my mind and left the church.

After scouting around more I found the kitchens and the room for washing clothes. I didn't go into the kitchen as this was busy with people in there but I had a nose through the hatch. The kitchen was filthy. There were residue of food everywhere on the walls, floors and surfaces. Nowhere was clean. I decided not to look closely as I had to eat something whilst in here so I might as well not look. The hatch had a counter on it; this too was encrusted with food residue. The hatch was presumably where the food was placed for prisoners to collect. What I couldn't fathom was where the dining hall was. Where the fuck do you eat your food?

In the washing room there were no washing machines or dryers. There were just lines for clothes to be hung. There were two prisoners in there frantically scrubbing a pair of kecks on a concrete slab which he used as a scrubbing board. One of the men stopped to look and was about to engage conversation but I put a stop to it by nodding and walking away quickly. I wasn't ready yet to mingle. I wanted to know the layout of the prison first.

Right I had the majority of the inside of the prison down after several hours roaming around, now I decided to head outside. It would be good to get some air as it was quite stuffy in the prison. Inside had a sort of greenhouse effect from the sun blasting down in the heat of the African summer. As I passed through I came across a step going upwards to a concrete yard which was encased by three walls made out of blocks of cement. I felt a bit more on guard out here as there were crowds and crowds of people. I felt very vulnerable as I wandered through the throng of individuals and small groups that gathered out in the baking sun. Again as with the theme of the prison there wasn't much furniture. Outside were only four wooden chairs that looked like they would break if a gnat sat on them and one long table that was scratched and chewed from abuse. I felt eyes watching my every move. I didn't fucking care though I had been in prison before. Shunning their evil looks I stalked the grounds for several minutes nosing at what little it had to offer. As several minutes passed my radar for impending danger shut down. I decided to stand in the corner of two adjourning concrete walls to have a bit of a rest. In the corner a shadow was cast sheltering a little for the unyielding Moroccan Sun. I leaned back into the wall and went into my own internal dialogue. Taking in what I had seen of the prison. Thinking of a way out.

Just a fucking minute. I had found the church big deal. I knew where the ping pong table that's fine for when I get bored. I had found the kitchen and where they laundered the clothes too. But where the fuck where the toilets and showers? There must have a toilet somewhere if I couldn't have a fucking shit in my own cell.

Then the other strange thing was that the large majority of prisoners I had seen out here were Spanish. Even the guards were Spanish. I found this very strange being in Morocco, Where were the Moroccans? Why wasn't anyone wearing djellabas? As I looked around and around I eventually saw the Moroccan community. They were in an exercise yard that lay side by side with this one but separated by a stone wall and a gate.

I was about to wander over to look at the Moroccan yard when a group of five Spanish walked by. I stood slowly upright not to make them aware I was ready if they attempted to fight. However this was fine they were just passing by to talk to another group of prisoners who were in my path. When they passed I felt sick to my stomach. They smelt as if they had bathed in their own sweat for a month. Their clothes were also torn. When I looked more closely at their clothes I realised they were not mottled with patterns but with stains; only finger tip spots remained of what the fabric should have looked like. Oh please to fucking god there is a shower in this place or a means to clean. I am not going round like that. As the ammonia smell dispersed a little I again relaxed and looked to the floor deep in thought. I drifted off thinking about Oslo, where I should have been.

Then all of a sudden I was jolted back to reality as I saw two pairs of sandals standing stationary in front of me only inches away. I pushed away my hands from the wall and stood tall. Looking up to the faces of the sandal owners I felt more at ease. It was my two cell mates.

'Hi Alan.'

'Hi.'

'Had a good look round the patio?'

'Patio?'

'Yeah out here we call this the patio.'

'Yeah not much here is there.'

'No.'

'One thing though. Where are the toilets and showers?'

'The toilet and the showers are over there,' he said pointing to the back of the patio.

'Outside?'

'Yeah. Why?'

'Cheers I shall go and have a look.'

Joseph smiled back at me as I walked by him seeming curious at my reluctance to engage him or his friend again. As I walked on I realised he said toilet instead of toilets. It must have been a French to English translation mishap.

As I strode towards the corner a slight whiff of shit and piss hit my nose. This increased with ferocity as I headed further and further to the back of the patio. My nose unwilling headed to the eight foot breeze block wall that sectioned off a part of the patio. The stench of human waste became unbearable as I walked around the corner but I continued to trudge on. I walked through the opening and then was faced with the toilet. There wasn't even a door for privacy. Also this wasn't like a toilet I was used to in the UK. This was a simple fucking hole in the ground job. Of which there was one. Joseph didn't get it wrong there was indeed only one toilet. All around the hole was shit splatter. I could also see turds floating at the bottom in the shallow water. It looked like this didn't work properly either. One toilet to sixty odd prisoners and it didn't seem to work. There is no way I am using that. I am getting out of here right now. I will save a dump for when I see my lawyer. I left the toilet and welled up with anger. This prison was disgusting. I decided to check out the showers which were adjoining. The showers too were basic as it was a simple pipe with a make shift tap. There were only two showers but looking at the majority of the prisoners I doubted there would be a fucking queue. Two fucking showers and one toilet. It beggars belief. Walking away from the showers I looked back at the toilet towards the side. It then dawned on me. Not only was the toilet open for anyone round the corner to see you there was also a good vantage point from the showers. Jesus Christ! So you could see someone showering when you were having a full on shit.

Annoyed and disgusted I headed back to the patio. I strided across back over to Joseph and his friend.

'I cannot believe this place. One fucking toilet Joe! One!'

'It's Joseph.'

'Sorry!'

'Alan you are just going to have to get used to it like the rest of us have.'

'No way am I going to get used to this. This is not right!'

'Alan what can we do?'

'We can complain to the guards, the director any fucker I am not staying in these conditions.'

'I shouldn't be here I am innocent.'

'Look Alan the guards won't listen.'

'Well it's worth a try. I will make them listen. You will see.'

Joseph seemed mixed in his body language. His face was smiling but his shoulders tensed. I sensed he thought I was mad to ask the guards to improve conditions and was wary of my determination and anger. What were they so scared of? I will guess I have to find out for myself.

'So how can we speak to the guards?'

'There is no speaking to them,' Joseph's friend piped up.

'Well it's worth a fucking try. Where do they congregate then?'

'In the Centro.'

'What's the Centro?'

'The office you passed through on your way in here.'

I turned to march off to the glass office which I remembered from my premature tour by the prison guard. With that Joseph grabbed my fore arm. Shocked I stared at him and clenched my fist ready. Joseph sensed my outrage and sharply withdrew his grab.

'Alan look they won't listen to you now,' he said calmly.

'Why?'

'Look Alan its four o'clock now. The guards are winding down. Talk to them in the morning. They will be more likely to hear you out. But seriously you have a hard task to get through to them my friend. Also tea is nearly ready. If you are not there to get your grub they will just chuck it out.'

I paused for a moment or two reflecting on what Joseph had said. Maybe he was right. I was all guns blazing. They would be less likely to take notice of me. By getting angry in an argument you lose half the battle. But I still need to be angry to act as an innocent man. I was going to have to think seriously about my approach.

'Okay but I will go straight down there tomorrow.'

'Right Alan we will see you in a few hours when we get locked up we just got to dish up food as we work in the kitchens.'

'Okay see you later.'

I resumed back to my original position and leaned against the wall and watched the prison community wander by. I observed each man's behaviour in order to gauge who would be helpful and who would be a hindrance. I felt a little relieved to see a score of Europeans dotted around. I wasn't alone and hopefully like Joseph and his mate they could speak English. Compared with the Spanish who huddled together in tight groups the other Europeans seem to adopt more personal space around their persons and spoke in only groups of two to three. This annoyed me as I could not count without being obvious how many Europeans there were. Then without warning everyone turned and walked the same way back towards the main prison.

As people from either side walked passed me I joined in the queue at the tail end. It must have been time for food. Thank god I was starving. Altogether as cons we walked in the shape of a v dispersing through the small door. I kept my hand in my pocket clutching on to my wads of notes as I didn't want to picket pocketed. The queue was slow and arduous. Once I got to three deep in the queue I looked around the people ahead at what lay in store. On the hatch counter one of the 'cooks' ladled out a sort of stew onto a flimsy plate. The slop was slimy and uninviting. When it was my turn I saw the slop first hand and it looked even more disgusting. I looked at the guy dishing it up with a grimace. He then plopped a brown bottle to the side. Is that beer? I hope to god it was! I needed a drink. Once he had finished serving me he grunted at me and pointed in the other direction. I took my bowl of crap and bottle like a zombie transfixed as I stared at this so called food.

I then followed a throng of people wondering where to eat this monstrosity. As I followed some went off into their cells whilst other congregated outside. What a surprise this place had no designated eating area. I decided to go to my cell; at least there would be far fewer flies inside. Plus the smell of the inhabitants and the toilet facilities would not have added to my appetite.

Once in the cell I sat on the floor propped my back up against the wall and stared at the contents of my food. As I swished around the stew with my flimsy spoon I examined it. It looked like a hundred men had spat in it. Then something hard connected with my spoon. What the fuck is that? I scooped out a large gristly object, as the stew gunk ran off it became clear what it was. It was a pig's trotter. Disgusted I plopped it back in the stew and turned away.

I sampled a few more bites avoiding the trotter wading in my bowl. I was so hungry. I hadn't eaten for over twenty hours. However after the third mouthful I couldn't stomach it. My taste buds and vision won over my hunger. I could not eat this.

I twisted the bottle cap and took a sip. It was what I thought, this was beer. So they have to serve alcohol to make you eat this crap then.

As I swigged the last drops of the sweet tasting alcohol Joseph and his friend entered the room.

'Hi Alan.'

'Hi.'

'Enjoy your food?'

'Yum spit and pig trotters. My fucking favourite.'

'Hey if you suck the pig trotter they are tasty you know.'

'I will pass thanks.'

I didn't want to say too much more as he worked in the kitchens but he could see by the fullness of the bowl there were no compliments to the chef.

'If you don't like the food there is the econumato.'

'What's that?'

'It a little shop that sell tins and other stuff.'

'Yeah I might have a look at that tomorrow.'

Both Joseph and his friend sat on the bottom bunk. I did not stare but fleetingly watched in the corner of my eye at what they were up to. From the brief glances I could see they had papers, tobacco and a block of weed. They proceeded to roll up a few joints. I tried to avoid looking at them and instead watched a cockroach crawl the length of the room. As I watched it go under the bunk bed I noticed a few bottles of beer were hoarded underneath. I counted about six bottles of beer. Party in the cells tonight then boys is it. My ears pricked up as I could hear heavy footsteps and loud bellows in Spanish. This was then preceded by bangs and bangs of gates.

'Are they shutting us up for the night?'

'Yeah it's just after seven so they are locking us up now.'

'Do the cell doors not get shut?'

'No that's far too much trouble for them.'

'They just shout to us to close the gates at the end of each cell block.'

'Lazy bastards!'

'Yes they are.'

Joseph continued to lick and roll a stockpile of spliffs.

'So all the prisoners can go into each other's cells now?'

'Yeah but we close our door we are not bothered. It's less hassle if you know what I mean.'

I didn't but I agreed anyway.

On the bed lay ten neatly rolled joints. The two boys then packed away the papers, block of resin and tobacco. They both looked at me. I turned away as obviously they were hiding it and didn't want me to see.

Then Joseph's friend lit the first joint and lay back on the bed taking a few puffs. He then passed it onto Joseph who also took a few puffs. I looked over curious but tried to not to look like I was gasping. I would have kissed his feet for a drag, but there was no fucking way I was going to be begging him. With that he turned and smiled.

'Alan.'

'Yes.'

'Do you want to join us in a spliff?'

'Yes okay.'

I thought to myself yes this is a nice gesture but surely enough he will sting me some time to buy hash soon. Mind I don't care I have the money, but I won't reveal to him that yet. I went over and sat on the floor next to the bottom bunk. I wasn't ready to sit with them yet. I still kept a little distance.

After we inhaled the first joint my mind went hazy and felt like cotton wool. It was such a nice feeling. If I closed my eyes for a few seconds I could forget I was here but I could not keep my eyes closed forever.

As we smoked and had a laugh the stumpy bottles of beer came out.

'Er Joseph can I have a few bottles.'

'It will cost.'

'Yes that's okay'

'10 pesetas.'

'Nah it's okay.'

There was a pause until Joseph lowered the price. I agreed and enjoyed taking a sip.

What the hell was going on? I was in prison drinking and being stoned. I was using the very fucking thing that I was incarcerated for smuggling. Double standards or what. You can smoke it but don't smuggle it. One thing at least I could enjoy my time here a little by being wasted. But I don't plan to stay here for long. The more and more stoned I got the more it felt like I was in a university dorm than a prison cell. I could hear happy commotion from the adjoining cells. Presumably they were getting up to same shit. Then we could hear bottles clinking loudly reverberating around the corridors. This sounded so loud. Joseph and his friend seemed quieter. Then in a distance I could hear maniacal laughter echoing the halls.

'Somebody's having a big party,' I said jovially,

'Yeah probably the guards,' Joseph said solemnly

'What the guards drink on duty?'

'You have a lot to learn my friend.'

Intrigued I froze my body concentrating on hearing the noises from outside. The laughter had ceased now and there was silence. After a few minutes I was about to grab another bottle when a loud bang reverberated around the room. It sounded like something metal had been struck with some force. My ears pricked up but no-one else in the room batted an eyelid. I looked around confused at how a noise that loud did not shake them. It doesn't matter how stoned and drunk they were that was fucking loud. Then there were noises of chains being smashed again and again against something. The smashing was constant. It was like a sort of whipping noise. This lasted several minutes until I heard screams. The screams only lasted seconds but they were piercing. What the hell is going on?

With a joint in one hand I bolted upright from leaning on the wall. I was about to get up and go to the door, when Joseph stretched over and put a hand on my shoulder.

'Leave it Alan. There is nothing you can do,' he slurred.

I had so many questions. But did I really want the answers? Who was being tortured? Prisoner against prisoner? Guard against prisoner? What place had I been resigned to?

'What's going on?'

'Alan leave it….. There is nothing we can do.'

The banter and conversation ceased between me, Joseph and the other boy. I was bemused looking at the floor and Joseph and his friend seemed perplexed to. It seemed they were used to screams but by me questioning them I had awakened their minds to the reality again. They looked like they had grown used to ignoring. The atmosphere felt very awkward. Being selfish I ignored the screams too. I will find out more in the morning, right now I wanted to get off my face so maybe I could get some sleep.

After a few minutes or so the conversation went back to banter. Although trying to brave my situation and fearing the unknown screams I tried to be light hearted. Until I wore myself out.

'Right I'm off to bed.'

I don't know why I told them that. They would have realised that if I had just walked over to my bed, but I thought I would be polite.

I went to bed in my clothes. Well I had no pyjamas and I was a bit cold with my thin sheet. Plus I wanted to keep my money close. I lay there looking through the bars to the night time sky above. How long do I have to endure this? Who was screaming and why? It's either court or escape but I don't care which. I am getting out of here.

I was just about ready to doze off into a slumber when I was disturbed by howling. What the hell is that now? Do we have wild animals in the prison too? Was it a prisoner gone mad? Either prospect wasn't a pleasant thought. I looked over to Joseph and his friend they were too in bed now but did not flinch at the howls. This howling must be commonplace too. It continued several seconds more. Then there was shouting and laughing at the howling. What is this place?

10 NETWORKING

Even in the few semi-conscious moments of coming out of sleep I could not pretend I was elsewhere, as the stench from my body heat coupled with the urine soaked sheets brought me straight back to reality. The smell magnified as I arose to a complete conscious state from my slumber. As I sat up on the bed I felt dirty and nauseous. I also had a slight headache and felt fuzzy from last night's session of alcohol and hashish.

With a sigh I looked over to the bunks squinting at the sunlight pouring through the window. The bunks were empty. Where the fuck were they? Oh well at least I didn't have to make small talk. I much preferred being on my own.

I sat on the bed with my head in my hands thinking about the events of the last two days. Gutted was the main emotion. As I let out a slight cough my throat felt like it was on fire. The soreness was probably caused by smoking, drinking and from being greatly dehydrated. My stomach then started to gurgle angrily at only having stomach acid to dissolve.

Not wanting to face another day in here I looked up at the ceiling. I wanted to let my mind wander to a peaceful place with no concerns, but this was impossible. I had so many questions. The annoyance of not knowing welled up inside. I needed some answers for what the hell was going to happen to me. How many years would they give me for smuggling? Could I blag my way out by a lawyer? Which begs the question how do I even get a lawyer?

I breathed in deeply with only adrenalin causing activity. That's it I need answers. With that I jumped up out of bed and got dressed, which constituted a pair of flip flops and shorts. It was North Africa in the middle of summer and I was in a prison, nothing else was required. Right Alan the plan for today was to befriend anyone I can. Strength in numbers. Plus to talk to the guards and protest my innocence.

With determination I decided to make my way to the patio. From scouting around yesterday that seemed to be where the most prisoners congregated, so this is where I could pick out the people I needed to talk to. As I walked through the corridors I was still being stared at as the new boy. Hopefully I will always remain the new boy and they will never get used to my ugly mug. I wanted to be out of here. I just engaged their stares again fleetingly and walked past with confidence and ease. As I went out to the patio there seemed to be more prisoners than yesterday. It was early morning so maybe they were taking advantage of the cooler temperatures before it really kicked in like a bitch in the middle of the day.

When I approached the open air toilets there was a queue. Great! I danced around with the rest awaiting my turn. When second in the queue I peered towards the toilet and could not believe my eyes. In front of me were two Spaniards being quite economical as one was squatting over having a shit whilst the other was spraying his piss towards the side. What fucking savages! Eventually it was my turn. I turned to the Spaniard behind with a scowl. Warning him there is no fucking way I am looking at his tanned arse while I relieve myself for my morning constitutional. He backed his eyes away quickly. I had won the game of stares. At last my turn! I had warmed to the stench in the queue but this was heightened as I stood over the shitty hole and pulled my dick out of my shorts. I directed my piss in the direction of the hole and then looked upwards to avoid looking at the turds floating in the water below. It took a few seconds to perform the act of urination as I was not used to having such a queue of men watching me before. I think I had a bit of stage fright. But surely enough it came and it felt good to relieve myself.

After shaking my drippers I hid away my bits. I did not want anyone to get excited at catching a glimpse. I knew from my travels some of the Spanish were a fruity lot as I had been hit on a few times. With my bladder feeling much lighter now I could concentrate on getting things done and headed outside.

Before I could make one circuit of the patio I noticed the throng of people outside were diminishing. What's happening here? I felt a glimmer of excitement as I joined the crowd to see what was occurring. I ambled along with the other inmates and made sure I had my right hand in my pocket clutching on to my notes. As I walked out of the patio into the building it dawned on me it must be breakfast as I could smell something cooking. Oh great I wonder what fucking delight Joseph has cooked for me today.

As I waited in the queue I could smell fish. Ah great cooked fish just what you want first thing in the morning in a hot country after stinking of piss from a manky mattress. Great stuff! Oh well. I will give it a try. When I was at the beginning of the queue I saw Joseph serving.

'Hi Joe.'

Joseph did not say anything but shook his head and scowled back.

'Oh sorry I said Joe again didn't I. I will start again. Hi Joseph.'

'Hi Alan,' Joseph said shaking his head and with a slight smile as if forgiving my faux pas.

'What have we got here?'

'Sardines, a roll and coffee,' he said excitedly.

As I looked down at the plate I was horrified. The sardines had been fried whole and not even gutted. The damn thing still had its head on. Shocked I stared at the plate as the fish stared back.

'Alan. Are you okay? What's wrong with your fish?'

'Erm erm nothing…..nothing….. cheers for the food mate.'

I smiled and walked away swallowing my disgust at his offering.

Dumbfounded I headed to the patio. I wasn't eating this in the cell. It would stink. Most of the prisoners had the same idea as the patio was pretty full. I looked over to the four chairs and table, this was also full. So I squatted in the corner with the plate on my lap looking at my breakfast. I wouldn't sit down on the ground as it was stinking. It was a carpet of phlegm, fag butts and rotten food. For Dutch courage I swigged a mouthful of coffee and then tried the fish. To my surprise it tasted quite good, but I was still put off digging in its flesh to avoid its slushy insides. As I looked around almost everyone had finished their breakfast. Obviously they were accustomed to this and needed nutrition. Some still had their bread rolls and as I looked around I could see them dunking them in the coffee. That's weird dipping bread into a drink. I joined in with the dunking. The novelty of doing this made me have some enjoyment. Plus the bread was quite hard so softening made it nicer to swallow. Once finished I took my plate back to the kitchen and returned to the patio. I stroked my stomach as it groaned. I wasn't full but I did feel a little bit more energised after my meagre food.

Right come on Alan let's find me a useful friend. I looked around the courtyard for potential people and eyed up their body language and tried to predict what nationality they were and if they could speak English.

As I looked around and around, out of nowhere appeared one of the prison guards. I watched on as he strode through the crowd confidently. Each prisoner that he passed stepped back as if out of fear to give way. In his clean starched uniform I watched on as he strided to the gate on the far side of the patio and stood guard. What is he up to? Intrigued I went over to the other side of the wall to have a look. Also I could kill two birds with one stone as not only could I feed my curiosity I could also plead my innocence.

As I walked over I could see he was guarding the gate between the Moroccan patio and our mixed European patio. I wondered for a few seconds again as to why they would segregate but then controlled my mind back on the task in hand. I can think about that later.

He did not notice me at first walking towards him, so I beamed my gaze at him and stared deep into his eyes. Eventually he spotted me when I was only yards away. At first he looked puzzled but as I got nearer and nearer this altered to concern. He stood up from a relaxed slouched position from the wall and proceeded to lift his rib cage and straighten his back. It was if he wanted to demonstrate his full height. I think he saw me as a threat and was ready for my challenge. I carried on walking, but I relaxed my pace in order not to appear aggressive. I wanted his help. Once I was near enough I made sure I allowed for plenty of personal space.

'Hi I am Alan,' I said in a friendly calm voice.

The guard didn't reply and simply looked through me.

'Er...... I wish to complain as I am not happy about being here.'

Still no response was gained. Although he was both rigid physically and facially I was sure I could see a slight annoyance growing in his eyes at my attempt to engage in conversation.

'I er.......... not happy here .... should not be here .... policer made mistake ....innocent..........'

As I talked and talked I could see he didn't understand English so I talked slowly like a British tourist abroad trying to get my point across. But like a British tourist I got nowhere, even with trying to use my hands.

After a few minutes the guard reacted and pointed in the other direction to go and grunted a few words in Spanish. Although I did not know what he said I bet it was along the lines of fuck off over there. I carried on talking pretending I didn't know what he was angling at. Mid-sentence he again grunted but this time louder and hung his arm in the air longer as he pointed to where the rest of the prisoners were. With that I could hear laughing in the corner. I looked to the side and I could see a lone prisoner standing in the full heat of the sun watching and tittering at my conversation. When I looked back at the guard he lightly touched with his right hand the baton on his belt and tilted his head to one side. This was not a good sign. I decided I wasn't getting anywhere. I also didn't fancy being on the receiving end of his big black stick so I turned around and headed off. Fine I will fucking go away.

As I walked away from the guard, the laughing from the lone prisoner continued but this time louder. I tried to fleetingly exchange a glance his way, and each time I met his eyes staring hard into mine. Although pissed off at being the butt of his joke I was also intrigued so I went over to introduce myself.

'Hi I am Alan,' I said lifting my hand up and then putting them behind my back.

'Hi Alan my name's John. John MacGoughlin,' he said in a broad Liverpuddlin accent.'

'Taffy hey?' he giggled

'Yup!'

'So you're a long way from home too.'

'Yup.'

Looking at him I would never have guessed he was of British origin. He looked more of Spanish origin with his dark brown hair and skin. Boy he had a suntan. How fucking long had he been here to get like that?

'Look mate I really wouldn't bother pleading your innocence in here.'

'If you haven't already noticed, they don't fucking care. I mean look at this place.'

After each sentence he spoke he laughed. This pissed me off as the way he was talking to me was in a cocky mocking tone. He acted like he was rule of the roost. I ignored this and shone him fake smiles as I watched his lips move as he babbled on. I let his conversation pass over me until he really started to rattle me and I had to make an outburst.

'Well I am going to make them listen John. I am innocent and I want out of here. I shouldn't be here,' I growled whilst stabbing the air imagining I was pointing my finger straight through him.

'Yeah yeah innocent mate. Good luck with that!'

He laughed again. Listening to his laughs made me have an instant urge to beat him in the head over and over with a blunt object. I tried not to show my anger and nodded intently as he talked on and on again. I didn't want to get involved in a fight. I needed to keep on track. I couldn't distract myself from my main aims of the day. As he continued prattling on about himself I felt a tap on my shoulder. Unnerved I turned around with a clenched fist and scowled. As soon as I saw it was Joseph I retreated my fist and smiled. Joseph was greatly shocked and muttered in French as if a little frightened by my instant aggression. This was the second time I had threatened a punch.

'You don't like surprises then Alan,' Joseph said trying to gain back his calm composure.

'No sorry I don't Joseph.................Hey look I remembered this time.'

My mood instantly changed to a happy one when I saw Joseph's gentle smile. We both laughed at me remembering his name. As I turned around I could see John now looked serious. He had a puzzled expression as to what I had remembered. He seemed annoyed at not being part of the joke. Then as Joseph and I talked more he wandered off, probably feeling a little left out of our conversation. We both watched on as he swaggered to the other end of the patio. I was so glad he was gone. His arrogance annoyed me.

'Did you enjoy your breakfast?'

'Yeah it was okay.'

'You know you can get food at the economato.'

'The econo what o.'

'It's Spanish for shop.'

'Oh yeah you did say last night.'

'Have you been to the Centro yet Alan?'

'No I went over to that git over there,' I said pointing to the guard outside the gate.

'He was of no help.'

'Well good luck in trying to get the other guards in the Centro to listen.'

'Thanks.'

'Before I do can you point me out a few people in here who I can talk with good English like you? Not like John.'

With that Joseph laughed. He didn't admit it but I think he felt the same way about John's confident bombastic attitude. He then continued to point carefully at people in the courtyard and provided me with little sketches such as where they were from, their names and also their reasons for being here. I felt a pang of guilt having to ask this. I mean how fucking ignorant was I, they could understand my language but I couldn't understand there's. I mean I can't even speak my own native language of Welsh.

He also told me a few interesting things about the prison on how to get alcohol and hashish. The alcohol was fine as you would get one or two a day to go with your food at mealtimes. So people who did not drink would sell theirs. Which was how Joseph had a lot of bottles under his bed. Also god knows why someone would sell their beers, I mean drinking beats being sober in this place every time. Mind it was probably out of a need for money or to trade it for something else. Then Joseph went silent as if he had exhausted all he had to say.

'Joseph,' I said breaking the silence.

'Yes Alan.'

'What the fuck is going on here?'

'What do you mean?'

'Why is the prison run by the Spanish?'

He explained that Ceuta despite being in North Africa was a part of Spain and was run by the Spanish authorities. This explained a lot. In that moment I wished I was caught in Tangier and sent to a Moroccan run prison. Maybe I could have gained freedom by using Ahmed's name. I knew he had contacts with the police so maybe he could have helped me.

Also with the Moroccans they also understood English, so I could have found out what was going on and how to get a lawyer. It seemed none of the Spanish knew English. They were just as ignorant as me.

'The other thing Joseph. There was no finger printing or paperwork taken when I came here. Nothing is organised. And who was the poor sod screaming last night.'

Joseph was smiling until I said my last sentence about the screaming man. He turned his back and looked to the floor.

'That was Dominic.'

'What was happening to him?'

'Have you noticed the prison is burnt a little?'

'Slightly! It's fucking black everywhere.'

Joseph laughed again but his face still turned back to unease

'Well Dominic went mad several days ago and tried to burn the place to the ground. He caused much panic. The econumato was also raided. Even the Centro was raided. I don't know whether he had planned it as a riot or not.'

'That is why they have railings and wire now around the Centro.'

'I thought it looked new when I entered the prison.'

'That night was such madness. The guards even ran when Dominic and a few others smashed the windows of the Centro and went on a rampage. They even stole the guard's beers, smoked their cigarettes and ate their food.'

'Oh my god!' I exclaimed laughing at the outrageousness of it all.

'That's another thing I can't get my head round the fact that the prison guards drink on duty.'

'Oh Alan you make me laugh. Yes they drink, hit, and smoke.'

'Well after the fire the guards took Dominic away and every night we can hear him scream. And there is nothing we can do for him.'

'Why did only he get punished?'

'He was the leader.'

My head was swimming. It was too much information to take in. Prison riot with fire. Drunken and tortuous guards.

I carried on laughing and shaking my head out of shock when all of a sudden Joseph elbowed me in the ribs as if to say shut up. I was a little pissed off but took my cues off him as something had given him a fright. As I looked ahead I could see a man with very dark hair and an olive sun tan making a beeline towards us. He was quite a good looking man the sort you wouldn't want to take out when you are trying to the pull the ladies yourself. However his looks were jaded by a frown and a drained expression.

Joseph waved and nodded. The other man flippantly waved and nodded whilst showing a brief smile. As I watched on at the non-verbal conversation between the dark skinned man and Joseph I could tell there was a big fucking white elephant in the room. To break the unease I held out my hand to shake and introduced myself. The dark stranger shook my right hand with his and with the other put his hand on his chest and told me in a broad Italian accent his name was Enio. After the introductions silence dawned again. Joseph was about to say something when Enio interrupted by muttering in Italian. He pointed to the prison building and waved goodbye. Even though I could not understand his Italian words it was obvious he was awkward about something and wanted to make a quick exit.

'Bloody hell Joseph he was bit of miserable.'

'He was a very good friend of Dominic's.'

'Oh I see.'

Joseph nodded as he continued to stare at Enio walking towards the main prison building and disappearing into the crowd.

Joseph and I chatted for several hours after in the blazing heat. Despite both being from different parts of the world we seemed to understand each other quite well and could at ease drift off talking on a wide spectrum of subjects. I lost myself talking to him so much that I even forgot where I was when we were walking around and around in a circle stretching our legs around the patio. This was the first time I felt comfortable. Joseph to talk to was so relaxed and positive. Then I felt angry. I shouldn't be getting used to this dump I needed to get out of here. I shouldn't be fucking nesting. My arms tensed and my adrenalin flowed again. I had my information from Joseph and now I was wasting my time chatting about crap. I now needed action. So I made my excuses and left Joseph. My second port of call was going to see Franc in the laundry. He was useful on two counts. Firstly he was the man who would wash my clothes for a small fee. Secondly after speaking to Joseph I was told he spoke very good English and Spanish so he would be able to tell me things of interest.

As I headed towards the laundry room I slapped my head in my hands with annoyance as I forgot to ask him about the howling. But then that could wait. I don't think knowing the perpetrator of the howling was going to help me find a way out of here.

I stepped into the prison and felt a bit of relief from the overbearing sun. But I couldn't escape the warmth as inside were drafts of heat everywhere. It was so stuffy. But at least it was only waves of heat and not a continuous beam. I hung outside the laundry observing first before wading straight into conversation. I watched a while as the two fairly large French men were busy in their work. One was scrubbing and scrubbing clothes, his hands looking red raw as if he had been doing this job for a while. The other taller man was wringing out the excess water from the clothes that had being washed and scrubbed. After a few seconds both men clocked my surveillance and both edged towards me.

'Hi my name is Alan and Joseph my roommate tells me you're the guys who I see about cleaning my clothes. Which one is Franc?'

'Hi Alan. Yeah come on in. I am Franc. We are the ones, who wash clothes,' the man wringing the water answered.

'So what do you need washing Alan?'

'Well nothing yet I am only on my second day. I am just laying down the groundwork. Maybe tomorrow'

'Well it costs 10 pesetas per item. If you want them ironed it's an extra 5 pesetas.'

'Nah it's okay on the ironing.'

I nearly died of laughter at his serious comment on ironing. Ironing in this fucking place! What for? But I kept serious as I did not want to offend him

'Well I have seen some of the stains on the prisoner's clothes you must have your work cut out?'

'Oh no we don't wash everyone's. Some are just just....... far too much. We only do clothes for the Europeans.'

'Fair enough.'

'Yes we do not do any of the Spanish prisoner's clothes. They can just walk around in their own filth.'

'But then again none of the Spanish have every asked,' he said laughing.

I found it very weird how he excluded the Spanish from the term European. He classed them as a completely different race. Maybe this was because the prison was under Spanish control.

He was right about the Spanish. Every single one I came across was stinking. That's not to say the Spanish people as a whole were disgusting as travelling through Spain I never met anyone who looked like them. It just looked like the Spanish in this prison were poor and the dregs of their society.

I continued chatting for a while. Then I realised I should be going to the Centro. I remembered from yesterday Joseph saying I had more of a chance when I spoke to them at the start of their shift. I then said a rushed goodbye and told the brothers I was going to the Centro. They did not laugh like MacGoughlin or look concerned like Joseph. They just both looked shell shocked at such an idea. Fuck me! Has no one got any balls in this place to change the system!

I marched off to the Centro. I was determined to make them listen. I walked slowly to the weirdly shaped hexagonal office nodding my head up and down and looking from side to side as I was racking my brain on what I needed to say. I paused before reaching the office door until I was certain. With a nod to myself and a deep breath I knocked on the door.

As I looked through the glass the three guards inside looked puzzled. The guard nearest to the door flung it open.

'Qué?'

'Hi I am Alan Jones.'

'Alan?'

The officer went back inside and scrabbled on his disorganised desk for something. He then yelped in joy as he picked up a piece of paper. With paper in his hand he rounded up the other guards and then returned back to the door. As he wafted it in front of their eyes they all gathered round to have a look. They all looked down fleetingly at the paper whilst glancing sporadically at me. He then pointed at the paper and said 'Cohones cohones'. With that laughter spilled around the room. What the fuck? What were they laughing at? As they all turned back to give me attention I smiled to join in with the joke, even if it was probably aimed at me. When they heard me laughing they all simultaneously stopped and stared hard. This felt a perfect atmosphere for tumble weed to go by. Gees, fucking hell! From one extreme to the other; intense moments of hilarity to instant condemnation!

Well okay they look pissed off but at least I had their attention. I again gave a spiel like I did with the guard in the courtyard. Saying about how I was innocent and how I should not be here. Unlike the guard outside they did at least exchange eye contact. However, again I felt no connection with them but at least they were looking so I carried on. After a few minutes the guy with the sheet of paper raised and lowered his right hand and mumbled in Spanish. I ceased my talking and tried to listen hard. I watched his lips as he spoke but it was useless. I did not understand. After he finished his unknown utterances in Spanish he pointed to the direction I came. Great! Again I am getting told to fuck off. Obviously no guards spoke English here.

I put my hands in the air and walked away. Bastards. I know they didn't understand my English but there are ways and means. Right time for plan b I need to find a prisoner who can translate for me.

I decided to go back to the courtyard and pick out who I could get to go with me to the Centro. Mind I didn't need to rush as I would have to wait for a change in shifts and try the next lot of guards. This would mean another stinking night in here and talking to the guards tomorrow on the dayshift.

Outside in the courtyard there was a different guard protecting the gate between the Spanish and Moroccan patios. I decided to investigate further the forbidden Moroccan patio. Not to draw attention I first did a lap of the patio. I didn't want to stride straight across to him as maybe he too would have a penchant of stroking his truncheon. After completing a lap I veered to the side and walked over to the wall. He had spotted me but I avoided his glances and made him aware I was not going to talk to him. I cautiously walked over to the wall by the gate so I could peek through and see what he was guarding. I lent on the wall and closed my eyes to convey to him I was resting. After a few minutes I looked over to the guard, he had stopped looking at me now. He had now found interest in smoking a fag.

I went a little closer and looked through the gate. Through the patio I could see a sea of Moroccan prisoners all wearing different types of djellabas. It was like a parallel world. I was transfixed. As I watched on I again thought to myself as to why they had been segregated. After several deliberations I finally decided it was probably because tensions with Spanish inmates could have flared up as Ceuta was an enclave of Spain. The Moroccans may have shown hostility to the Spanish and regarded them as their oppressors. Also many of the Spanish in turn would have not wanted to walk with the Moroccans as I knew many could be racist. Also they would have probably feared the Moroccans as they were larger in population.

Looking into their secret world I noticed major differences to the conditions of their patio. For a start their patio was spotlessly clean. No fag butts, phlegm or food covered their floor. The air also smelt delicious. There were wafts of exotic food cooking smells drifting over into my stinking world. On closer inspection I could see they were coming from a guy cooking something like rice in a tin. It smelt so nice. As I watched them mill around and looked back at my European patio it seemed to be more civilised. They were a prouder dressed and tidier bunch compared with the majority of stinkers in my patio. I wonder if I could get a djellaba from somewhere and join with them.

I then felt eyes burning into my chest. As I looked across I could see the guard was staring hard at me with a look of annoyance and suspicion at my interest. I decided it would be best to leave. Ignorant git! I was just having a look.

After looking at the Moroccans I felt unclean myself and headed to the outside showers. Thankfully there was no one else around not even anyone squatting over the shitty bog. It was nice to have solitude and no prying eyes. I stripped off and put my clothes within reach on the driest and clearest bit of concrete floor I could find. I then went under the shower and turned the tap. It took a few seconds before the water came through but surely it did with drips of ice cold water. Jesus Christ. I did a little high pitched scream from the shock of the coldness, but I stopped myself quickly as I did not want anyone to hear my girlish screams.

With concentration and holding my breath I acclimatised after a few minutes. Until I enjoyed being cooler after sweating so much in the sun. As the cool water dripped down my body I felt a little anxious about what Joseph had said about the guards. I needed to tread carefully with them. But I was still determined to make them listen. It was strange having a shower in the outside. A bit too liberating for my liking but I loved washing away the repression. I swirled my bits clean as best I could without soap.

After several minutes went by my solitude was broken by the sound of footsteps in the distance. I decided that was my cue to leave. I shook the drips of ice cold water off like a dog and put my clothes straight on. This felt so alien. Mind I would dry soon enough as the sun had flared to up maximum velocity. In wet shorts I headed to the yard and walked round to dry off. This only took an uncomfortable half hour.

As I walked around I saw John MacGoughlin. He smiled and I nodded back at him, but he carried on walking the opposite direction. I'm glad he did as I didn't want to engage in conversation as he was of no use to me as it was clear he thought my plan was a waste of time. I didn't want to soak up anymore of his pessimism. I will show him, hopefully.

As I walked round I noticed only one of the seats by the long table was occupied. This seemed strange normally all the seats would be made use of, but yet this guy sat alone. Also it was odd that he seemed Moroccan in skin tone but that can't be right as surely he should be in the other yard. He wasn't wearing Muslim dress either, so maybe I was wrong about his ethnicity. I mean I was wrong with John. Isolated I watched him looking into the sky at the moon casting a shadow. I decided to walk closer by on my path around the patio as he took my interest. I could see he was wearing a very rustic goatskin. It wasn't even a custom made goatskin jacket. It looked like it had been stripped off the goat just yesterday. I wonder if he had killed it and was wearing it as a trophy. Plus what the fuck is he mental in this heat wearing that. The other prisoners either were like me going bear chest or sporting a flimsy light t-shirt. He did have shorts on though accompanied by Jesus sandals. As I neared towards him I caught a glimpse of his eyes. They seemed very animalistic and uneasy. On first impressions he looked like a complete nutter. He then must have felt my eyes staring as he stopped looking at the sky and glanced over to me. I smiled gently and nodded. He smiled back through his beard and long straggly hair. His eyes were wide and manic. Engaging in a stare I could now confirm he was indeed a mentalist. Luckily for me he stared back at the sky. There was someone who I really did not want to exchange eye contact with. I really wouldn't want to know what he was capable of in a fight. But despite his crazy exterior I was intrigued. He would have been fun to talk to. I would have tried to avoid any sharp pointy things being in his reach if I did though.

I decided to go back into the prison to shelter a bit from the heat. I also decided to have a look at the economato Joseph had mentioned about earlier. After several minutes of roaming around inside I eventually found the prison shop Joseph spoke about. Although I wouldn't have describe it as shop or even tuck shop at that. It was just a few shelves with very little choice.

However despite the lack of options it was still nice to be able to have some kind of selection. Also it was nice to think it hadn't been made in the fly and rat infested kitchen of the prison.

On the shelves in the shop there were just tins and tins of stuff, also cheese, biscuits and bottles of water. I decided to buy a few tins, but this felt like a lottery as I couldn't read what was in it. Also the guy who ran the economato could not speak a word of English, so I just pointed to the tins at random and hoped for the best. Oh well at least it will make tea interesting in a good way. I also bought some biscuits.

These will be useful for the munchies tonight. Well that's if I can score some weed off Joseph again. I opened the biscuits and tried one. They were nice and actually tasted edible.

Right back to business I need someone to help with me with the guards. I went outside and I continued to munch on the biscuits as I thought about who could help. It then dawned on me about Franc and his brother. Joseph had told me he was pretty good at speaking Spanish as well as English. However I decided to leave it till tomorrow to speak to them. It was getting late in the day and nearing locking up time. Plus they would be more likely to listen in the morning rather than after a long day of scrubbing and scrubbing.

That night ended like the last one did in a haze of hash, but this time there was no booze. Joseph and his friend hadn't managed to barter with anyone for alcohol today. Also the screams came and went but this was fine, I was ready for them now. But now I could also put a name to them. Poor fucking Dominic. Then just as I was drifting to sleep yet again I was awoken by howling and a shouting commotion. However the howling and shouts were short lived and sleep for me did eventually ensue.

11 IGNORANCE IS BLISS

Although it was only my third morning at Los Rosales prison it felt like ground hog day. Yet again I felt sick at the smells emanating from my bed. Yet again I was blinded by bright sunshine cascading through the window. Yet again the bunks of Joseph and his mate were empty. Mind their empty beds were no longer a mystery. I had clocked on now this was probably because they were in the kitchens making some delightful breakfast for me and the rest of the scum in here.

Another fucking day in this shithole! Despite my circumstances I did feel a bit more positive. At least I had a few acquaintances now. The way I looked at it was the more people I knew the more information I could get on a way out of here. Also I think my upbeat attitude was because I felt less hungry than in the last few days. The biscuits I had bought from the economato served as a filling snack throughout the night.

Feeling a little peckish as I acclimatised my eyes to the light in the room I reached down under my bed to grab the biscuits. I had wrapped them tightly up in a pair of jeans. I did this so the roaches did not have a free meal on me. I unravelled my treats and I nibbled on a couple. After the second biscuit I couldn't eat any more as the rancid ammonia smell put me off and won out over the calls from my stomach. I wrapped the biscuits back up again tightly and then jumped out of bed. I also made sure I hid them out of sight. I did this so that they weren't on display for someone else to steal. Then a wave of anger washed over me as I imagined if I were to catch someone nicking my biscuits. I would have pummelled them over and over with my fists. They would have had a few punches to the nose and several digs to the guts. When my rage died down I realised how pathetic my thoughts had become. I was now willing to inflict willful damage and risk injury to myself for a packet of biscuits? What had I become? Only a few weeks ago I was a travelling business man albeit buying and selling an illegal substance. But I never harmed others and at worst I inspired a bit of fun and here I was now, reduced to thinking like an animal. Over food!

Today I decided to wear a t-shirt with my shorts, as I wanted to cover up my skin that got slightly sun burnt from the many hours I spent outside with Joseph. Well that's one positive from being in here, I suppose I will get a great tan. Mind I didn't want one as quite as severe as John

MacGloughlin's.

My groin ached as I was desperate for a pee. Feeling like I was going to burst I walked quickly to the patio outside and towards the revolting open air toilets. Like yesterday there was a queue. Being a man I never thought I would experience the queuing system at a toilet before especially under these conditions. Although it was only about ten minutes or so in reality the waiting to my bladder felt like hours had gone by. However once it was my turn and I dangled my hose over the shit filled hole and felt a much needed release. A little less shy I closed my eyes and smiled intensively whilst letting out the biggest sigh of relief in my life. It was wonderful to piss.

After I had finished I opened my eyes and scowled back at the Spaniards all staring back at me. None of them were probably gay and even if they were probably did not fancy me. But just in case I was letting everyone know I was not that sort of boy and that if they tried I would have smacked them one.

Once fully relieved I headed back to my cell to retrieve my dirty clothes of the last few days and then went to pay a visit to Franc and his brother in the laundry. With crumpled filthy clothes covered in dust under my arm, I hanged outside the laundry and knocked on the outside wall. As I did so Franc and his brother both popped their heads round inquisitively. Franc beckoned me with his finger into their makeshift cleaning room.

'Hi you two!'

'Hi Alan.'

'So you have some clothes for me to wash?'

'Yes if you don't mind. It was 5 pesetas you said per item.'

'Er no it was 10,' Franc corrected.

'Well okay I will pay 10.'

'Er..........One............. thing about the clothes. They do smell a bit of piss. I can assure you it's not me. But the mattress I am sleeping on is absolutely filthy. It's disgusting.'

Both Franc and his brother looked up with their heads slightly tilted downwards and nodded as if out of empathy. It looked like they too had experienced the delights of sleeping on a minging mattress.

'It's okay Alan we know..........Now if you just put your clothes over there with the rest,' Franc said whilst pointing to the corner of the room where there were a few bundles of clothes.

I walked over and put my clothes with the rest ready to be scrubbed, cleaned and dried by the French brothers.

'Oh Alan keep yours separate from the rest,' Franc shouted over.

'Yeah I have done that.'

Once I left my clothes and paid my money the brothers both smiled and then carried on with their duties. Franc was scrubbing frantically a pair of Y-fronts whilst his brother was hanging out various T-shirts and shorts to dry. Although it was my cue to leave I hovered around the room awkwardly. My awkwardness was then broken when Franc opened up conversation again

'So how did you get on at the Centro with the guards?' Franc asked.

'Well they didn't understand me?'

'Ah yes very few of the guards can speak English.'

'Yeah………which is a problem really,' I sighed

I paused for a moment. Then Franc looked at me fleetingly and hurriedly went to the sink to rinse the freshly scrubbed pants. Before I asked anything I could feel by his demeanour he had instantly clicked as to what I was about to say next.

'Franc?'

'Yes Alan,' he groaned with a sigh.

'Joseph said you could speak Spanish quite well.'

'Er…..er…..only a little,' Franc stated with reluctance.

'Do you fancy having some fun with me and coming to talk with the guards?'

Franc looked over to his brother. His brother didn't reply and looked to the floor

'Er well….. I am little busy Alan.'

'Come on Franc it's not only to plead my innocence. We could complain about the conditions and maybe make some changes around here.'

Franc leaned on a makeshift table with his head in his hands shaking his head slightly.

'Come on Franc you've seen this place. What's the harm in asking? Come on! I mean you don't want to let a customer down. Do you?'

Franc could see I was not going to give up easily and eventually with a lot of reluctance agreed. I think the only reason why he did it was because I had paid for his services and I think he knew I would be a good customer. But whatever the reason was I didn't care I was just happy I could now make the guards understand what I am saying. Even though getting them to listen would be a different matter.

'Well Franc I will go now but I will back right after breakfast.'

'Okay Alan,' he groaned.

Before breakfast I was going to have a shower but when I got to the outside shower and bog facilities there were too many men around for my liking. I was now used to pissing in front of a crowd but I wasn't ready to shower in front of one. It's not that I am not averse to showing my body in a public changing room but in a prison with frustrated men there is always a worry.

Today's breakfast was soup of all things with bread and a drink of coffee. I don't know if I was getting used to the slop served to me but all things considered the soup wasn't bad. It also contained very flavoursome hard crunchy things. It was the first meal I had where I ate it whole. Even Joseph was surprised when I returned back to him my empty tray through the kitchen hatch. As I looked around everyone else had left the black bits in their bowls. That's strange they seemed so tasty to me.

Feeling rejuvenated from food I decided to have a wander round the patio with the rest of the men in the mid-morning sun. It was a nice time of day. The sun wasn't too hot. Also today there was a gentle breeze. This cool wind was probably coming off the Mediterranean Sea which was only a few miles away. Such a nice change from feeling hot and sticky.

After two laps of the patio at an ambling place orbiting the stationary Spic guarding the gate, I crossed paths with John.

Oh here we fucking go. How is the Liverpuddlian bastard going to annoy me today? I was in a good mood all things considering and now I had to lay eyes on him. I bet he is going to spoil the day now. I put my head down in an attempt to ignore him but out of the corner of my eye I could see him making a beeline straight towards me.

'Hi Alan.'

'Hi John, nearly didn't see you there.'

'So how did you get on with pleading with your innocence like?'

'They told me to come back tomorrow.'

John laughed. As he laughed I felt the compulsion to sock him in the mouth. This was an odd feeling to have as very few people got under my skin. Come on Alan proactive not reactive. Save the fighting for the guards. I was about to make my excuses and leave but I couldn't get a word in edge ways as he jabbered on and on. Fucking hells bells! I nodded politely as if I was taking in his conversation but I was biding my time to think of a way to escape. Why the fuck did the only Brit in here have to be such a cocky sod?

'Look Alan you're wasting your breath. You might as well enjoy the sunshine mate than wasting your fucking time with those fucking dicks.'

'Anyways the only people that will listen to yous, is the consulate and lawyer.'

My ears pricked up. For once he had caught my attention. For once I could gain some vital information here.

'When do they visit?' I excitedly asked.

'Tomorrow actually.'

'That's really good to know. Thanks John.'

'But Al I am afraid their useless as well. But one thing at least they will pretend to fucking listen and can speak English.'

'What are they called?'

'Well the consulate is Biggy and he also comes with a lawyer Malero.'

The name Biggy sounded familiar but I couldn't think why. I was also too excited to rack my brains and buzzing on the fact I would get to talk to legal representation. Maybe they could get me off. Oh god a lawyer! I felt at least with half a chance now on being able to leave. Right tomorrow is my big performance on my innocence.

'Great stuff. I shall have a nice chat with them tomorrow.'

'Again look Alan don't get your hopes up. Seriously mate don't.'

'Where there is a will John there is always a way.'

'Well all the luck to you mate.'

Again I was annoyed with his pessimism but this time he sounded more like he was being genuine and not taking the piss. It sounded like he did want me to succeed and wanted to share my hope. I think he had been in the prison for too long. He had just resigned himself to being here.

There was no way I was going to lose hope. It didn't matter how long I was in prison for I vowed never to give up. I had a chomp between my teeth which I was going to grind through. All the way! No fucking half measures! Whether it was through legal or illegal means I was going to find a way out.

We carried on walking around the patio. As we did so I noticed the Spanish prisoners just stood and slouched on the sides of the walls spitting every now and again, adding to the patch work of phlegm on the floor. It seemed mostly the Europeans who would walk round. This was probably because the Spanish were used to the heat and could stand in one place whilst the sun beamed down whilst on its incineration setting. We Europeans needed some air to breathe in the heat. So we had to create it artificially by walking around.

As we walked John rambled on about what he missed about being home in the UK. I did not say anything back as I didn't want to go down that road. In fact I wanted to escape from his conversation and go and see Franc but I felt obliged to listen. It seemed he needed to talk and get a lot of things off his chest. I don't think he had many friends if any as he was always on his own. I think he was a bit of a loner, either that or people avoided him because of his crap people skills.

I was grateful for him telling me about the lawyer and consulate so I repaid his information with time and companionship. As he continued chattering I noticed a glint in his eye as if he really enjoyed my company. He probably did feel close to me being a fellow Brit. Maybe John wasn't so bad after all.

Then mid-sentence I stopped John as I suddenly remembered I wanted to ask him about the howling. He looked at me stunned and patiently waited at to what I had to say. I paused for a moment before I said anything. I felt a little paranoid that maybe the howling I had heard wasn't real. Maybe the spliffs Joseph gave me were laced with something that would make you hallucinate? I decided to bite the bullet and ask. I really hope I hadn't imagined it as John would really take the piss.

'Er John what the hell is that howling in the nights?'

John started laughing which really wound me up. It seemed everything in this place was one fucking joke after another I had to drag out. Well I never found anything funny.

'Oh that is the wolf man.'

'Wolf man?' I said unconvinced.

'Yeah'

John looked around the patio until he found what he was looking for. He clicked his fingers and pointed carefully in the direction of the corner.

'See the guy over there?' he said in hushed tones as if scared the man in question would hear.

'Where?'

'Next to the wall over there.'

'You can't miss him. He is the only fucker wearing the sheep skin.'

'Oh him. Yeah saw him yesterday. I think its goat's skin though'

'Well whatever fucking animal. That guy there is the wolf man.'

'What?'

The wolf man was dressed exactly like he was yesterday and again was staring dead ahead unflinching, luckily though not in our direction. Although he was stationary in expression and body, you could see there was a hive of activity and unease inside of him. A ticking time bomb of emotions.

'It's him that howls.'

'Fucking right weirdo.'

'Why does he do it?'

'Don't fucking know? But when that moon is out and full he loves it.' Yup my instincts were right that guy was a mentalist. Mind it didn't take much deduction from the fact he was wearing a goatskin in the middle of summer

'Yeah he really pisses everyone off. It's funny really. I think the boys like it when he does it though as we get to shout out like.'

'Yeah I suppose,' I said as I chuckled

'He has a cell on his own. Been told he won't share. Even the guards won't put anyone with him.'

'Also all the weeks I have been in here I have never seen him speak to anyone really. And obviously no one wants to speak to him. Also he never parts with his goat jacket. Never once have I seen him not wearing it. Even when it's fucking cooking man.'

Internally I disagreed with John. I wanted to talk to him. Odd characters are the best people to talk to as you never know what they are going to do or say. Mind I will leave it for today as I have other things on my mind. Plus I wanted a little bit of a measure on him before I would converse. John then said goodbye and headed to the bogs. I decided it was now time to get Franc and plead my case with the guards.

Feeling confident I breezed into the laundry and stood in front of Franc.

'Hey Franc you haven't forget our date today.'

'I know Alan,' he moaned.

Francs brother in the corner looked up and shook his head but smiled as we left the room.

As we approached the office the colour in Franc's face seemed to drain away. His slightly tanned red cheeks now looked white with a tinge of green. I tried to take his mind off his nerves by telling him exactly what I wanted him to say. Although he nodded in agreement as if he was listening I could see he was distracted by fear at the guards ahead.

I knocked on the door. There were four guards this time. All new faces. From my instruction I pointed Franc to get closer to the door.

Then a few moments later a guard came to the door whilst the other three hung behind him waiting what I had to say.

'Hola! Hola!' shouted the guard furthest away.

'Que,' said the guard nearest to the door.

'Franc tell them I wish to speak to them using you as my interpreter.'

Franc looked at me pensive but sure enough voiced a sentence in Spanish to the guard. The guard look puzzled and retorted.

'What did he say franc?'

'He wants to know what about.'

'Tell him I am innocent and that I am angry that I haven't had an interview with the police so I can verify this.'

'Veri what …. I don't know this word?'

'Tell him I can show him I am innocent.'

With that Franc paused but sure enough he spoke to him in Spanish. Hopefully he translated literally what I had said.

Once he finished the guards started laughing and looked on at me and smiled. He then as the other guard did the other day went inside and scrabbled for paperwork. Obviously paperwork about my crime. He brought back the scrappy piece of paper and then like the other guard pointed at it and laughed. He showed the other guards they too laughed in return. And shouted 'Cohones!'.

'What are they saying?'

'Sorry Alan I can't quite hear.'

'They are saying cohones. What does this mean?'

Slightly angered I stared at Franc for answers.

He shook his head and didn't reply

'It doesn't matter Alan. What do you want me to say next?'

'Tell him that it is serious that I am here and that the British government will fight for my release.'

He reluctantly relayed the message. I could tell by the tone of his voice he was expressing my words gently and not with the full force I would have. But what was I to do as I couldn't speak Spic. Plus I wasn't wholly convinced he was saying exactly what I wanted to say.

With that the nearest guard waved a goodbye sign at Franc

'Mañana! Mañana!' he shouted as he shooed us away.

He then looked at me whilst smiling and also waved goodbye at my direction. I watched on as he shut the door. It didn't take the guards long to settle back into their conversation, coffees and fags.

'Come on Alan lets go. We tried.'

'What did he say?'

'To come back to tomorrow.'

I watched inside for a few seconds but I had no second glances back from the guards, just a closed door. I wanted to break down the door and make them listen but that would have been no use. I calmed myself by looking at the scaffolding and metal mesh around the office. I didn't want to end up like Dominic. Don't go mental or you will be tortured too. From surveying the scaffolding I could see blood marks splattered here and there, it was probably Dominic's. This must be where they would beat him night after night. In a sick way I bet the guards find it fitting. Feeling disgusted and angry I turned around and followed Franc back into the laundry.

Once back his brother stopped scrubbing a pair of jeans and came over to hear the fall out of our conversation.

'So tell me now Franc. What does cohones mean?' I said sternly.

With that Franc's brother burst into spontaneous laughter.

More laughing! This was really playing on my tits. Now what was the fucking joke about! I stared at Franc hard awaiting an answer.

'What is cohones?' I spat in anger.

'Er Alan your second name is Jones.'

'Yes so what's so fucking funny about that?'

'Well in Spanish cohones means cock.'

'Yeah so!' I blurted impatiently.

'Well Jones the way it is said is similar to cohones.'

I could feel a glaze of red mist descend over my eyes and adrenalin surging around my boiling blood.

'So you mean those pricks out there have been calling me a cock.'

With anger I slammed my fist in the wall. When I looked back at Franc and his brother they both looked nervous at my reaction. Until it was like a switch flipped in my brain and it dawned on me it was fucking funny my name was similar to cock. I then burst into laughter too. The laughter spilt over to Franc and his brother until we all fell about in hysterics.

'What bastards! Cock indeed! Well if that's what they want to call me I will make sure I am the biggest cock to them. Their jobs aren't going to be fucking so easy with me around,' I said trying to gain my calm composure back.

Franc and his brother laughed again.

'Also what does many many ana mean?'

'Oh you mean mañana,' said Franc. 'Basically it just means tomorrow.'

'Well that is sorted then!' I chuckled.

'What is?' asked Franc confused.

'Tomorrow me and you Franc we shall speak to the guards again.'

Franc went quiet but before I could let him answer I said my goodbyes and left. I felt a little bit of shit for assuming and not asking him outright to come tomorrow but I needed to force his hand a little in order to help me. I think if I'd have let him he would have tried to wriggle out of it.

As I left the laundry I could smell dinner was up so I headed to the filthy hatch to see what grub was up. It was fish. Again it was served whole and not gutted. I also had bread to go with it and a dumpy bottle of beer. Well after some of the shit I have eaten in here I suppose this was not the worst. At least I could tell what it was. Also the taste wouldn't matter as my palette could always be cleansed by beer.

With food and beer in hand a blond thickset prisoner walked in front, catching my eye. Hey another European. I followed him from a distance out to the patio. I watched as he crouched in the far right hand corner. Pretending to be nonchalant I walked over and lowered myself down next to him. As I chewed my food I remembered Joseph had pointed him out yesterday and told me he was German and named Karl.

'Hi! It's Karl isn't it?'

Karl glanced at me in contempt and then stared straight back to his plate. Although only the head and guts remained he still poked around for anything edible. With a long pause and a gentle sigh he nodded at my question.

After a few questions I did eventually get Karl to talk but it was quite painful as he was one of the most miserable bastards I had ever spoken to. There was no emotion to him and when he answered he always appeared very direct. This could have been in part due to a language barrier I suppose. But his face also resembled a smacked arse too. However one thing was for certain I was feeling quite positive before and this depressing git was bringing me right down.

'So how you finding it in here?' I asked.

'Hell on Earth,' Karl groaned.

I wanted to give up on the conversation there and then but I persevered. It seemed like Karl was no longer a man but now an empty husk. Which was useful to me as he would give me answers to questions without idle chit chat or for a fee. He just simply didn't care.

'Look Karl why are you so down?'

'Because I have been sentenced to eight years in here. Well that is of course if they don't put me somewhere equally as disgusting,' he said whistling on his fs.

'Eight years…….. Wow!'

'What did you do?'

'I smuggled eight kilos of hash.'

'What?'

Alarm bells rang in my mind. I had smuggled nearly triple that.

'Fuck!'

'Yes eight years.'

'Er Karl. Can you tell me what sort of stretch I am looking at if I am to be found guilty?'

'How much?'

'How much of what?'

'How much did you smuggle?' he said with annoyance at my misunderstanding.

'Twenty six kilos.'

'Twenty six,' he repeated.

'Yes.'

'Well if you smuggle about five kilos you are looking at five or six years.'

'Okay.'

'But you know the thing with five kilos which I wish I knew now is you can get a fine and get out of prison.'

'After five kilos it is only prison.'

'Because I was over by three kilos I have to stay here!'

'Wow Karl that is really bad luck,' I said pandering to his whines.

'So in my case what would it be?'

'So if it is twenty six kilos you are looking at a minimum of twenty six years,' he said staring deep into my eyes without any emotion.

'What!' I yelled.

'Yes I would say about that.'

'Oh right.'

With that I walked away. I did not even say goodbye to Karl, not that he would have cared as he seemed contented in his own misery. The fish I had just eaten gained new life as it was doing rotations in my stomach. I fought hard with my stomach not to wretch at this discovery. Fear and anxiety hit, as my brain throbbed. No fucking way! Twenty six years. No fucking way!

I went to sit in the opposite corner of the patio away from everyone and on my own. I sat motionless in the corner with the blistering heat of the midday sun pouring down. I couldn't feel the heat. I was too numb.

Maybe he was joking. Maybe he was winding me up. I looked over to Karl at his miserable face. Don't be silly Alan he's German. He wouldn't joke. Well if he was I would soon find out the truth tomorrow from the lawyer.

After my shock subsided a little I could feel the heat piercing through my skin like knives. To cool myself down and to wash off the stench of Ceuta I headed to the showers.

The day went quickly as I spent most of time formulating my defence for the impending visit from the consulate and lawyer.

I did relax a little in the night after a session of smoking. Also finding out the contents of one of the tins I bought at the economato brought a little excitement too. Once opened with the help of Joseph stealing a tin opener from the kitchen I was not disappointed. It was a tin of peaches in juice. I liked tinned fruit. It felt like just the comfort food I needed to spark a little enjoyment in this hell. Mind a bit of cream wouldn't have gone a miss.

That night I must have nodded straight off as I didn't even remember getting into bed. I was glad of this as I did not get to hear the screams or howls.

12 NO HELP FROM THE EMBASSY

In the morning I awoke restless and tired. The number twenty six echoed the walls of my mind over and over in a mantra. Twenty six years! But I had to forget that and think about my speech with the consulate and lawyer. At least they will listen. What good it will do I don't know. But I will have to try.

When I went to the patio for my morning constitutional there seemed to be a hub of excitement in the air. Everyone looked less scruffy too. Even the Spanish! This was probably because they were either excited to have a visit from the consulate and lawyer. Or they had loved ones and family members down for a visit too.

I suppose I should make an effort and have a shower. I had not seen a mirror for a few days but from stroking my ragged facial hair it was apparent I needed a trim. I was just about to find Joseph to see if he had a pair of scissors when I stopped myself. I didn't want to look groomed for my visit. That would send the wrong message. I didn't want to look like I was settling in well. I wanted to look like a man who was innocent and couldn't deal with prison. I needed to smell and look the dirtiest, to show I was a man not used to surviving in such squalor.

Around mid-morning I was called up for my visit. It appeared I was one of the first. I wondered if they did this as I was new. As I entered the room I ran through my speech in my head. Come on Alan twenty six years is a long time to rot in this place. Think innocence.

As I sat down I was flummoxed. The speech I repeated in a mantra was forgotten and my mood was dampened, as in front of me was the guy who visited me straight after my arrest. I stared at him and he stared back confused. I had forgotten I had met the consulate before. I just didn't think. I knew I had heard of the name Biggy. Mind you I had probably forgotten as I had more pressing things on my mind. As I stared at him I could feel my temper rising. He was a useless git at my arrest. I doubted he was going to make any waves for me now. Probably feeling uncomfortable at my direct gaze Biggy stared at the floor. Yeah look to the floor. You can't look me in the eye can you at what you have done to me. I tried to calm myself down as I sat on the chair. I decided to concentrate on Malero's face. Could he be my ray of light? He is a lawyer after all. Maybe he can make the shit I am in smell like roses?

'Hi Alan,' said Malero.

'This is not right!' I shouted. 'I am innocent and should not be here.'

'Look Alan as I said at your arrest you were caught in possession,' said Biggy calmly.

'To the Moroccan authorities you were caught with it on you. Whether you put it there or not does not matter. You have to pay for it,' continued Biggy.

'That does not make it right!' I shouted as I slammed down the palm of my hand hard on the table making Biggy jump.

I wanted to jump out of my seat and grab him. How dare he say I have to pay for it! Cock! Calm down Alan. I breathed in and sat back down.

'So I rot in here while those two Londoners roam free?'

'Er well Alan.'

'So you Biggy can watch as a fellow Brit who is innocent rots here? With the conditions like they are! I mean I wouldn't even keep an animal in here.'

'Where is your loyalty to me? Surely you have influence. Can't you request an investigation or something?'

Biggy gulped hard. I had pulled on his heart strings. He paused to reflect on how to answer, but luckily for him he didn't have to as Malero piped in

'I am afraid he can't help. His role is to look after your welfare.'

With that I burst out laughing but this was spiked with rage. As I stood up from the chair I paced up and down.

'Welfare! Welfare! I am sleeping on a piss soaked mattress. I have not eaten food or drunk properly for days. What is served up isn't fit for human consumption. I am listening to screams off prisoners in the night having a beating off the guards and wondering when it my time for my punishment. And for what Biggy. For what! Lending my van to two scoundrels!'

Again Biggy fell quiet and looked to the floor. I was making him suffer. I was making him realise the position he had as a consulate was serious. Not just some jolly jaunt where he could parade about in the sun. It appeared I had convinced him or at least put a shred of doubt in his mind that I was innocent. Maybe this was enough. Maybe he will fight for me. When I looked over to Malero his expression did not change. He looked mostly serious, maybe with a tinge of compassion or it could have been wind. I could also see in his eyes he didn't believe me. Either that or he just didn't fucking care. His expression reminded me that of Karl the German, albeit not as dismal.

'Alan let's get back to the matter in hand. You only have twenty more minutes to speak to us,' said Malero calmly.

'Okay well I want to know what my sentence will be if I plead not guilty but if the court as you said finds me guilty.'

'In my opinion taking into account the amount of cannabis you had you are looking at about twenty one years.'

I didn't know how to react. Should I have been angry at the Kraut for adding five years? Should have I been happy it was a lesser sentence than I thought? I was mixed and confused. But one thing was sure one day was too long to stay in this place let alone twenty one years. That was practically a lifetime!

'Does this have to go to trial? Can't we appeal against the arrest?'

'No Alan what's done is done. Your case I am afraid will go to trial.'

'Can't we build a case around the two Londoners?'

'I am sorry Alan, you were caught with it so you get punished. We can mention the Londoners but I really don't think they will take it into consideration.'

In that moment I was glad I was guilty. If I had been planted with the cannabis I would have had uncontrollable rage. However I imagined I was innocent and tried to keep up the pretence in front of Biggy and Malero. I did this by having a pained expression as I paced up and down the room anxiously.

'If as you say it doesn't matter whether I am innocent and I will still be found guilty. Is there no way to reduce my sentence?'

'Yes there is,' said Malero smiling. 'You can possibly reduce your sentence with financier.'

'What's that?'

'You can finance my services as a lawyer and I can consult with the judge on your behalf to reduce your sentence.'

'So let me get this straight I can pay you to get my sentence reduced?'

'Yes sort of.'

'But will it be guaranteed?'

'I can't guarantee no.'

'What so I can pay you for nothing.'

'There are no guarantees but almost every time I have spoken to a judge on behalf of a client I have managed to reduce their sentence by a year.'

'How much is this service?'

Malero waffled on about what he did, the charges and all about the legalities. However the figure that he arrived at was the equivalent of £1000 per consult. I could not believe it! This was outrageous!

Although I did have money on me and some money stored away at home I did not want to tell the consulate and the lawyer just yet. So if I wanted to be free I would have to pay £21000. But Malero did explain I wouldn't be able to just hand it over in full and be let go. I would have to serve a good few years. I couldn't just completely buy my way out.

'So you mean to say although I am innocent I won't be proven not guilty. But it's okay for you guys to let me buy years off my sentence?'

'I am afraid Alan it's your only chance of getting out of here sooner,' said Biggy actually sounding like he gave a damn.

'It's also a racket.'

'Well whatever you think Alan you will need to let us know quickly if you want Malero to get to work and meet up with the judge.'

'Let me think about it.'

I didn't want to hand over money just yet or provide any bank details as I wanted to find out if this was legitimate. I wanted to ask a few other prisoners to see if they were doing the same and if it actually worked.

I waffled on about how unfair my imprisonment was because of my innocence until my half an hour was up. I think when the guard stepped forward to collect me they both look relieved. I was shocked at actually seeing a guard performing a duty. This was a rare fucking sight indeed! But they probably had to keep up some sort of pretence in front of the consulate. Although I bet even Biggy knew what little the guards did.

'Well I will be back to see you in another few days.'

'Yeah whatever good that will do.'

As I left I hoped Biggy was rattled by me. I day dreamed he was sticking his finger in many pies trying to pull strings for me. However I knew in my hearts of hearts this was unlikely.

In the patio everyone seemed to be buzzing. They were not like the drones I was used too from the past few days. Everyone seemed to walk around as if they had purpose. I think the visits from the consults, family and friends had stirred everyone up and I could feel it too. There was more chatter as each relayed the new things they heard from the outside world of which we were all forbidden from. As I stood in the middle of the patio I opened my ears to hear all the conversations that were going on all around. Spanish, French, Italian jabbering all merging into one. I liked the fact I could hear no English. For a few minutes I pretended I knew what they were saying and made conversations up in my head.

In the distance I could see John MacGoughlin making a beeline for me across the patio. My heart sank. Oh shit not him. I know what he wants. He wants to gloat about Biggy and Malero. Again he was right. Cocky bastard!

'Hi Alan.'

'How did it go with the consulate?'

'Well one thing I have learned is you can pay your way out of here.'

'What?'

'Financier?'

'Oh yeah I know. Crazy isn't it?'

'I got to him though John,' I said smiling through gritted teeth

'What do you mean?'

'He does think I am innocent. I don't know what much good that will do. But at least he should fight for me at least.'

'Well I wouldn't waste your breath.'

'Well I will sleep better tonight knowing that he won't.'

'Alan you wicked bastard.'

'Actually fuck what I am saying. Nice one!'

We both laughed. I was surprised today he hadn't annoyed me yet. Maybe I got him wrong. Maybe he was bearable. At least I could have a laugh with him as he got my humour.

With that I could heard a commotion in Spanish to the corner of the patio. When I turned around I saw just over a score of Spanish inmates sit on the floor in a circle. They were laughing and jabbering, despite sitting on the skanky floor. Then all went quiet from the group when a guy near the middle of the circle pulled out a simple acoustic guitar. What the fuck? He then started strumming and braying the strings. Producing only what I can describe as a Spanish flavoured tune. The men then in the circle started clapping. It was a bit of spectacle but luckily I managed not to laugh through the shock of how spontaneously it had occurred. Plus the clapping was incredible. I hadn't heard anything like this before. Mesmerised I watched the entertainment. John looked over at me and smiled, enjoying my reactions to this new event, of which he was probably used to. I tried to copy their clapping. I hoped if anyone Spanish were watching they could see I was trying to imitate and wasn't taking the piss. I must have looked quite silly though as I couldn't do it and wasn't as skilled enough as they were. Although it was only clapping it was pretty hard the way they did it so rhythmically.

'What the fuck are you doing Alan? Said John whilst laughing hysterically.

'Don't fucking start losing it now!' John shouted again laughing at my pathetic attempts.

I carried on for a bit making John laugh more and more until he was holding his stomach. After a while I ceased clapping as I started to become frustrated at not being able to do it right.

I sat back and watched the entertainment. Boy the Spanish were good at this. Also the clapping was grippingly melodic. Almost tribal even. It was nice to see everyone around smiling. This was one of the nicest times I had spent in the yard. Everyone fed off each other's happiness and the music added to the atmosphere. It felt like we were all one community and not just a bunch of filthy bastard crims from all parts of Europe.

That night Joseph, his mate and I smoked hash through to the early hours of the morning. We didn't chatter much. I think we had all enjoyed the day and just reflected internally with our own dialogues.

In the corner of the room I could see a fly buzzing around. When I went closer to investigate I could see it wasn't a fly. It was a fucking mosquito. Great I am going to be bitten tonight. Due to the swarms of mosquitoes we would normally close the window in the night after we had pissed them off with our smoking. But this one was a bugger. It was like me. It wanted to be where it shouldn't. I called Joseph and his friend over to my bed to watch the mosquito. Being stoned it did not take much persuasion.

Mesmerised we all sat toking on joints watching the mosquito whizz around the room cutting through the lines of smoke. After several rotations of the room I noticed the mosquito's flying was slowing down and becoming erratic. I was going to let it out of the window, but I was too relaxed. I just could not be bothered to open the window. The hash was flowing through my veins sending messages around my body to not move. Again and again I watched it. It was definitely making smaller loops and going slower.

'Hey Joseph look.'

'Yeah man I am looking.'

'No look at the way its flying.'

'What Alan? What am I meant to be looking at?'

'At the mosquito.'

'I am looking at it.'

'Well look again.'

Joseph bent forward closer to the mosquito's flight path and tried in his stoned state to watch closer. After a few minutes the rotations stopped and the mosquito glided slower to the floor.

'Oh my god we killed the mosquito with our smoke,' said Joseph.

'No do you know what I think Joseph. That mosquito my friend is stoned.'

With that we all fell in hysterics for about half an hour. My stomach ached at the amount I laughed. After this we had both decided we couldn't top the day and went to bed. For the first time I smiled as I lay in bed. So it's not that bad twenty one years instead of twenty six years. Plus I can pay to get a few years off. Mind I will leave that for a while as I wasn't paying just yet. A grand at a time was a lot of money. I wanted Biggy to stew and I will see if over the next few days he can sort an interview or anything with the police or courts first. I think I was holding my breath but I did not want to drain thousands of pounds out of my money if I didn't need to.

Then my eyes grew heavy and I looked at the stars in the night sky shrouded in the blackness of the cell. Again the wolf man howled. However no one told him to shut up today he was allowed peace to communicate to his moon god.

Another day I thought as my eyes closed and was ready to drift. Images flooded to mind as I was in the early stages of sleep. And then a thought came and I jolted upright fully awake. Wait this is not right! There were no bangs, crashes or screams. They must have eased up on Dominic. Maybe they too were infected by the positivity of today. Maybe no beating tonight.

I only entertained this possibility for a second until a darker thought flooded to mind. Did they go too far with the beating? Could he be dead? That night I fell asleep thinking about the pain on Enio's face of worry and I conjured an image of what Dominic looked like and what he must have went through. They shouldn't be able to get away with this. Biggy should be fighting this!

13 THE INNOCENT GAY

'Alan… Alan.' I could hear Joseph whisper as he gently shook the back of my left arm.

I woke up blearily eyed. I tried to force my eyes fully open but the tiredness and the blinding light from the sun prevented me. Squinting I looked ahead to see Joseph excitedly hovering around my bed. I wriggled around trying to jolt my jangled brain into consciousness as I grunted and groaned from an uncomfortable nights sleep.

'What?' I said annoyed through a yawn.

'I have heard we are having a new cell mate today.'

'What? Really? What happened to your mate?' I asked feeling more awake at such a surprise.

'He was released and now we have a new one.'

This pissed me off having someone adding to the mix. I had just gotten used to Joseph and his mate in the room. Fucking guards!

After coming round a little I wondered who would be put in here with us. Feeling tense I ran through the worst people. I just hoped he wouldn't be a nutter or a stinking Spic. Or even a right cocky bastard.

I started writhing around in bed trying to get myself to a fully awake state. I shook my head and with all my might sat upright with my back against the filthy wall. Joseph jumped onto his top bunk looking satisfied I was awake and ready to share the arrival of our new cell mate. We both went quiet for a while. I expect he was doing the same as me, running through the possibilities of who would cast a shadow at our door

'You sure Joseph we're having someone new?'

'Yeah I heard the guards talking.'

'Do you know who he is? What he has done?'

'No they didn't say anything about that. We have to find that part out for ourselves.'

'Great!' I groaned.

Joseph seemed very nervous. I think it is because he knew he was prey if an aggressive bully was put with us. He was a mild mannered soul and looked the type at backing down at any sign of trouble. Not someone who would put up a fight.

However he had done well so far fitting in prison. He shielded himself away from any potential trouble by working in the kitchen and by only associating himself with people he could trust. Although not confrontational I did see he had great strength inside of him. Maybe he would cope. As they always say you have to watch out for the quiet ones.

If the guy was a dick and bullied Joseph I wouldn't have stood for that. I liked Joseph as he was very useful to me as he had a good inside knowledge on the prison and a regular supply of hash. Also after the many days I had spent with him I was starting to see him as a friend too.

Me I didn't care. If an aggressive guy did come in and wanted to fight, fight I shall. I would have tried to avoid any violence though by using humour or cunning, but if there was no way out I wouldn't cower down. The bigger the fuckers the harder they fall I say. Even if that means great injury to myself.

Oh god why do I have to been thinking about this shit! I should be making my way up to Oslo by now. Not here. I admired Joseph and the way he stomached the foulness of this prison. I couldn't. I would never resign myself to being here. It would be like I accepted the downright rank conditions. Also I promised myself to never give up on freedom. No matter what I faced. I could and would not allow myself to be hollow like Karl the German. The guards can take every fucking thing away from me but not my fight!

'Hey Joseph.'

Joseph didn't respond. He looked deep in thought as he hugged his knees whilst staring to the floor as several roaches scuttled by.

'Oi Joe,' I shouted.

'Huh.'

'Hey Alan you called me Joe again. For the last time its Joseph. That is the name I was christened with!'

'Well you weren't fucking listening were you! I wanted your attention,' I said whilst I chuckled at his sensitive nature at being called Joe.

'Sorry Alan,' he said smiling. 'What were you saying?'

'Did you notice last night there was no screaming or banging?'

'What do you mean?'

'You know from Dominic.'

Joseph's instantly went quiet and his expression turned to confusion. Looking up he cocked his head pointing the pupils of his eyes to the left. I could see a metaphorical clock ticking away as he racked his brain about last night's events and as to whether I was right. After several seconds he then stared straight ahead and beamed at me a great smile. However once he exchanged glances with me he could see I was not smiling but looked greatly worried. I shook my head and it then hit him like a bullet as he gasped.

'Oh Alan no. You don't think….'

'Look we don't know Joseph. The guards probably had enough. They can't get away with murder.'

'Oh they could.'

'Well I hope not for Dominic's sake.'

As we both stared out into the distance weighing up the possibility of whether Dominic was dead or not the door burst open. Standing at the door was a thick set prison guard who tossed in our new cell mate. Just like with me the stranger walked in alone sporting an annoyed and confused reaction. Our new cell mate was quite tall and quite stout but with a bit of belly. He smelled nicely of aftershave and was quite well turned out. Well it's not going to be long once the scum sticks to him in this place.

He looked as if he was in his late twenties and had nicely cut long hair. He also looked European in his nature. Right that's half the battle. A European. I can live with that. Also he smelt alright so he didn't look like he was going to be a stinker either. Now all I needed to know is what his game plan was in here. Will he be a bully? Will he steal? How was he going to play it?

I watched on as he went over to his bed. He looked shocked at the filth on his bed and around the room. It was nice to see he looked more horrified than me. He shuddered and stood away from the bed looking like he was frightened that something might jump out. Which was quite a high possibility as the prison was infested with a fantastic array of insects and bed bugs.

He then started muttering to himself. I listened closely and it sounded like German. Yes he's definitely a European.

Joseph hung over the bed and popped his head down to view the new cell mate.

'Hi I am Joseph. That's Alan over there.'

'Yes. Yes. Very nice to meet you,' the stranger shrieked whilst his arms quivered.

'You okay?' I asked.

'No I am not! I shouldn't be here! I haven't done anything wrong!'

'Yeah right! You're just as bad as Alan over there. He's innocent too!'

Joseph and I laughed but the German seemed incensed.

'It's true!' he screeched whilst stamping his feet on the floor.

'I didn't! I didn't! I didn't!'

Then out of nowhere he started crying and rocking back and fore on the bed.

What the fuck? Both Joseph and I looked at each other. I was worried we would get a nutter or a stinker. I never saw the possibility of a crier. Both being men and unsure on what to do we stared blankly at each other with our hands in the air. I had never come across a crier in prison. I have seen the odd man cry when I have caught him on his own. I too have cried in prison but in the privacy of my own cell. Never openly in front of anyone, especially the way he was blubbering. Then thankfully Joseph jumped off his bed and sat next to him. He put his hand on his shoulder and patted him. He did so in a firm manner as if to still exert masculinity despite the emotional situation.

'What is your name?'

'Ernst,' he said catching his breath through the tears.

'Ernst okay well you tell us what happened and in English if you can.'

He then started to calm down and blub a lot less. As I watched him sniffing and catching his breath I realised Ernst was very fucking lucky to come in our room. I don't think any of the other prisoners would have been so understanding. If he thinks this cell is an eye opener he is going to have a real shock when he sees what the rest of the prison has to offer. For his sake he will need to toughen up and fast.

'Well I was driving back from Morocco to Spain and I was in a queue to board the ferry at Ceuta. Well in the queue was some Moroccan boy. He asked for a lift and I was feeling generous that day so I said okay. Well just before we got through customs. He says he has to go to the toilet.'

'Oh how could I have been so stupid?' he wailed whilst blubbering again.

Joseph looked over to me with raised eyebrows. I wanted to laugh but kept my emotions under check. Ernst breathed in deeply and composed himself again.

'Well…. when they searched my vehicle he put five kilos of hashish in a bag in my car.'

'Why did you let him in your car?' asked Joseph.

'I know. I know I shouldn't. I am too friendly for my own good. My mother has always said that I am too soft.'

Joseph and I looked at each other again. I flapped my hand in a limp wristed fashion. Joseph nodded. He had also read between the lines of what Ernst had said and ascertained that he did not give the lift out of generosity but rather he wanted gay favours. He thought he was going to have a Moroccan boy freebie for helping him out in a tight spot so he could get into his tight spot.

'So …….' said Joseph not knowing what to say.

'Yes,' Ernst smiled.

'Why were you going to Morocco?' I asked trying to fill in the silence.

'Oh you know. Just for a holiday,' Ernst said shiftily.

Morocco for a holiday indeed. I knew and I could tell Joseph knew exactly why he went there so he could have a teenage boy or two.

'It's great for the culture and the people I find,' Ernst said looking at the floor.

'Mind I don't feel that anymore.'

'Well no you wouldn't after having to come to this shit hole.'

'Where are you actually from?' enquired Joseph.

'Switzerland.'

'So like us a long way from home'

'Ya.'

'Look I have to go now Ernst. I am sure I will see you around.'

'Oh no. Where are you going?'

'I work in the kitchens so I am afraid I will have to go.'

'Oh right. I see. Well thank you for talking to me and being nice.'

'See you Alan,' Joseph said grinning like a Cheshire cat as he left the room.

Oh great Joseph. Dump the new boy on me. The new possibly gay crying boy. When Joseph vanished through the door I lied back down on the bed. I was still not ready to get out of my pit just yet. I still needed to come round a bit more. Every now and again I glanced over at Ernst. He too was lying down. He adopted the fetal position and continually shook his head muttering to himself.

'Look Ernst. I would wipe your tears and stop crying. It's not going to get you anywhere in here.'

'But Alan it's all…..it's all such a mess,' he gasped.

'Look Ernst whether you like it not you're stuck here and crying like that is not going to help. They will crucify you.'

'I know…..I know,' he whimpered.

'Look Ernst I am off to the laundry. If you want to come with me that's fine but for heaven's sake stop crying and wipe your eyes.'

'It's okay Alan. I would rather just stay here.'

'Well I will see you later.'

I went to the laundry with the sheet off my bed. I had decided maybe if that were clean it would smell less when my sweat mixed with the stains on the mattress. It probably wouldn't make much difference but hopefully the smell might dull a little.

As I entered the laundry Franc was sorting out a pile of clothes whilst his brother was finishing up after having a wash down in the sink.

'Hi Franc.'

'Hi Alan.'

'You ready for more mañana?'

It was nice to see that Franc was now well up for our jaunts to the office. I think he liked my resolve. I think my fight and passion had lit something inside of him too. Either that or it was one way to pass the time and wind up the guards.

'Yup I also need my sheet washing.'

'No problems. Hand it over.'

'Also another thing.'

'What now Alan?'

'Whilst I am here can I use the sink to wash?'

Franc and his brother looked at each other. I was such a cheeky bastard but I didn't care.

'Oh come on! I hate watching the spics having a shit whilst I wash myself.'

'Plus I reckon they piss in them.'

'I don't know,' said Franc with a smile.

'Come on I am a good customer.'

'Oh go on then.'

Franc's brother also gave me some soap. It felt amazing to wash myself with soap. I actually started to feel clean. My body will have a little break from being sweaty and smelly. For allowing me this privilege I bunged them a few extra pesetas. It was worth it. Also by paying I thought this would make them feel obliged to let me do this again.

I walked out into the patio and felt great and refreshed. It's amazing what a bit of soap can do to your outlook. As I approached the milling yard I could see John was out already. For once he didn't see me and I headed straight towards him. I wanted to see what the miserable git had to say for himself today.

'Hi John!'

'Hi.'

'Hey we have a new guy in our cell.'

'Oh yeah. Is he alright?'

'He's not taking it well though.'

'Does anybody?'

'Yeah but he's innocent.'

'Ahhhh He's innocent like you. Don't make me laugh Alan,' he tittered.

'No John. I think he is telling the truth.'

'Well there will be two of yous protesting your innocence to the guards now,' he smiled.

I told John the story and my suspicions on him being gay. John was not sympathetic at all but weak with laughter.

'What a poor sod. But that is fucking funny.'

'I know. Bless him.'

'Also watch your arsehole tonight.'

'Yeah I know.'

'Nah I think is he okay. He is too soft to try anything on like that I think.'

'Well he may get frustrated and wound up you know.'

'Well if he does try anything he is getting some of that,' I said to John showing him a clench fist.

With that Ernst appeared outside. He looked like a sheep to the wolves as he tentatively skulked around the patio. You could see with great fear he eyed up all the men around. He then spotted me and headed over.

'Alan, Alan.'

'You okay?'

'No!'

'What now?'

'I have just being robbed.'

'What?'

'They took my watch and some money.'

Both John and I roared with laughter at the unfortunate soul. He looked horrified at our reactions. But he has to realise there is no sympathy in this place.

'Well I don't think it's funny.'

'How would you like it?'

'Like I told you before. You are going to have to toughen up. Also keep your money and things out of sight and as close to you as possible.'

With that he huffed and looked to the floor in annoyance. I think he wanted sympathy.

'You had your breakfast yet Ernst?'

'Er no.'

'Well hurry quick inside or they will chuck it out.'

I gave him directions and off he scampered inside. John and I tittered again to ourselves about Ernst's bad luck.

After several minutes Ernst returned back. He did not come over to see John and me. He was probably embarrassed or pissed off at our reactions to him being mugged. I watched on as he headed into the corner of the patio. The look of horror on his face was immense as he stared down at the slop he was served. I was glad I had met Ernst. He made me feel better. There is always somebody worse off than you. And the fact he does appear innocent made him all the more pitiful.

Despite Ernst's great upset we did manage that night in the cell to have a laugh with him. This was also helped by giving him a few joints and beers.

Also I was glad Dominic's screaming had stopped. I don't think Ernst could have handled hearing that. There was also no howling. The moon tonight was occluded by clouds so the wolf man was denied his nightly ritual.

14 BOMB MAKING 101

After being in Los Rosales prison for a week now I was used to the routine of the place. However I still did not feel at ease. I could not be in this stinking prison for a moment longer. I didn't fucking care how. I was getting out.

It had sunk in now after two meetings with Biggy and Malero my sentence would not be quashed. I had played the innocence card over and over but it didn't matter. This would not wash. I knew now going through the legal route I was not getting out of here soon. It was obvious I was not going to be taken seriously. However I decided to still maintain my innocence to everyone I met just in case. I would say it to the guards, prisoners, Biggy and Malero. Well actually to any fucker that would listen.

The only thing Biggy and Malero could do or should I say was willing to do was reduce my sentence. But this had the added sting of taking a hefty blow to my bank balance. A grand each time Malero had tea with the judge. Cheating swindling fuckers! Or another option would be I could escape. The latter was becoming more and more appealing. It meant I would be out of prison quickly and not shafted in monetary terms. The only slight drawback was that it was highly dangerous. Especially as around the perimeter of the prison there were heavily armed guards. I bet they were just itching to have a bit of shooting practice.

I decided to entertain the possibility of escape so I scouted around the prison at any weaknesses in the security. I found plenty but after several days of weighing it up the easiest route I saw was via the luggage room on top of the roof. The luggage room was perfect as a) not many prisoners congregated there and b) I never ever saw a guard hanging around. Actually tell a lie you may see them early morning in the week if they had prisoners coming in, but apart from that, that was it. Also the luggage room was on the roof and the guards were all on ground level. Being on the roof I hope it would mean I was less spottable. Thank god there were no turrets with guards in this prison.

From the patio I could just about see the roof and where it adjoined to the boundary walls. It looked like there was a gap of about three meters from the inside wall to the outside boundary wall. I reckoned I could jump that. Yes there was a large possibility I could fall to the ground and break my back or even injure my legs, but I tried not to think about that. And also even if I got there I ran the risk of being shot. But hey ho I was a willing to try. All or nothing! No half measures!

Over the next few days I started to become quite serious in my intent on escape. I also kept annoying the trusted prisoner who could get the key to the luggage room asking him once a day if I could go to get things out of my suitcase. This was okay to do as many prisoners would be allowed to go up there but probably not as many times as I did. Every time I went up I had a sly look around on the roof. Also whilst up there I would try to talk to trusted prisoner in order to befriend him. However he never entertained my conversation. Each time he took me up there he just seemed nervous and impatient. Also he rarely made eye contact. He always seemed more concerned at looking at the stairs as if he was afraid someone would come bounding up. I really needed him to talk to me as a large chink of my plan involved getting him onside.

With escape on my mind I stood alone smoking a fag outside in the patio. Fleetingly staring up onto the roof until Joseph crossed my path.

'Alan… Alan I need a 1000 pesetas to buy half an ounce,' he said whilst shiftily looking around.

'You would have your money back and some blow of course.'

I knew it. There was no such thing as a free lunch in prison. I knew this time would come where he would ask me for money. But fair dos I had helped him smoke his stash of hash. Plus I was thankful to Joseph for his overall help. However with him asking for money I decided to use it to my advantage.

'Yeah fine but on one condition.'

'What Alan?'

'Get me in the kitchens.'

'What? You want to work in the kitchens?'

'Yup.'

'Yeah okay. I will see what I can do.'

'It's a deal then,' he said walking away.

'Oh Alan.'

'What?'

'You know you don't get paid for working in the kitchens,' he shouted back.

'I should hope not looking at the state of the food you serve.'

He laughed and left hurriedly on the plight of the hashish. I didn't care that I wouldn't get paid in the kitchen there would be other ways I could use it to my own advantage. Plus it would be nice to control what I could eat. I needed my strength if I was to escape and be on the run. It was also near to the luggage room so I could plan further the finer details of my escape.

For the first part of the week I decided to socialise with as many people as I could to give an air to the guards I was finally adjusting. I also had stopped my daily jaunts with Franc on shouting off my innocence to the guards. I even took advantage of the ping pong table. I was pretty good at beating people. That was until I started playing with a young Spic. He was fantastic. Each time we played there would a bit of a crowd from the Spics cheering on the boy and on my side were a few of the Europeans. God the boy was good. He was so good I would lose my head. I would out of frustration slam the ball about and then bang my bat on the floor. The Spanish loved it and laughed at my frustration. However I later found out the boy was a junior state champion for the sport. I didn't feel as bad for loosing after learning that. No wonder he was so good. I also started to play chess with my new roommate Ernst. He taught me the basics and how the pieces moved but he would never teach me any strategies. He said I should develop this myself. I played around thirty games that week but not once did I win. The bastard! Mind I was glad Ernst had this skill. At least he could feel top dog at something.

Also when I played Ernst I could never concentrate. He would always make me laugh when telling me what else he had stolen that day. He would never learn. I told him not to flash his stuff about. When he had only been in the prison four days he had his watch, money and radio stolen. Probably from the Spanish they were excellent pick pockets and probably had distracted him to gain the larger items.

After scoring the hash Joseph came hurriedly back.

'Where is it? Let's look at the goods,' I said excitedly.

'Oh they are in the room. I didn't want the guards to spot it. I know they don't care. But still if they saw it they could take it off us.'

'Fair enough.'

'Oh Alan. Another thing just being speaking to John and he has asked if he can move in with us.'

'He can't we haven't got a free bed in our cell.'

'Well apparently Ernst has found a cell with somebody.'

'Oh right I see.'

'So what do you think?'

'Well its better than the guards springing a new one we don't know on us.'

'That is true. And John isn't that bad.'

'But still Joseph I will have to think about it.'

I suppose I got John wrong. Maybe he wasn't a loner. Although I did not like him straight up I had warmed up to him considerably. However I was still cautious I knew us together in a room could cause trouble as we were both fit with our mouths and like me I think he was fit with his fists too. Which would be a little annoying as this could detract me from my plans of escape.

As I thought about whether to have John in the cell the temperatures outside started to soar. My skin was reddening and sweat was pouring. I decided to go in the showers and wet my face. The sun was so unbearably hot today. As I approached the toilets and showers the putrid smell invited me in. Yuck it seemed to get worse not better.

Before I stepped round the corner I heard whispering and splashing. I did not have a good feeling about this but yet I plunged on towards the showers. Once in the mock toilet come shower room I was shocked and horrified. Under the showers stood Ernst and some young Moroccan boy. They were kissing in a naked embrace.

Quickly I left and went back to the patio. My head was jangled and I was out of breath. I was in that much shock. Well I was right then Ernst was a homosexual. Also trust Ernst to find one of the very few Moroccan boys in the Spanish quarters. Also I bet he probably paid him. I wonder if the boy will fleece him too.

It took a while for me to register what I had just seen. I had heard about gay acts but never met anyone gay or seen them at first hand. This was the late seventies. Also I could never imagine kissing another man, especially in this filthy stinking place. Oh dear god. I could see in the corner some space for me to stand where there was a bit of shade from the sun. Just as I got myself in a comfortable position John approached

'You okay?' asked John out of concern

'Errrrr yes. Yes I am fine.'

'Anyways has Joseph told you?' he asked excitedly

'Er….Yes……..Yes he did.'

'So am I in or what?'

'Errrrr yes. Yes definitely yes you can share our cell.'

'Ahhh thanks mate.'

'No problems.'

'Right I am just off for a piss and then I shall move me stuff.'

'Go ahead.'

With that John beamed a massive smile and happily walked towards the toilets. Maybe I should warn him.

'John! John!'

'Yeah Al,' he shouted in the distance.

'Er nothing. It was nothing.'

'Okay see you later,' he replied looking a little perplexed.

Nah I will let him have a shock too! I chuckled to myself as he swaggered to the toilets. With that only seconds went by and he was back. Ernst mustn't have finished. It was obvious John had a pee as he frantically was doing up his zip as he came back from the bogs. Like lighting he strode back over to me. His darkened face was white with shock and his eyes filled with annoyance.

'That was quick,' I said trying to contain my chuckling.

'You bastard! You knew they were in there!'

I could not answer John's question as his annoyance made me laugh more.

'No wonder you want me in your cell so badly.'

'Well it's not for your personality and looks you ugly bastard,' I tittered

John saw the funny side too as he laughed and patted me on the shoulder as if to say fair play I'd had him on a joke.

That week my plans came together. I was more and more gaining the trust of the prisoner who had access to the key as I bantered with him in the luggage room. I also managed to gain a position in the kitchens as one of the staff had been taken to another prison. The kitchen was just how I imagined and much more. Everywhere was littered with bits of rotting food. On the counters, on the floor and curiously on the ceiling. Also dotted everywhere were cockroaches and piles and piles of rat droppings. The stench and heat in the room was stifling.

However I had to look at the positive side. I could prepare my own food at least. Instead of having the slop the rest of the prisoners had I could use the ingredients to make something I fancied. One of which was melted cheese on toast. Although I did have to buy the cheese from the econamato. It was worth it though and it felt comforting to eat as it reminded me of home. It was also nice to be able to gut the fish too before I put it in the fryer to cook. The only thing I didn't learn to cook was the soup. Joseph seemed to have the monopoly on this. However I didn't care as I liked the way he made it.

In the kitchen were all Europeans. This was strange as the majority of the prisoners were Spanish. When asked I was told that the guards and the Europeans did not like them working in the kitchen. And thank god too as most of them didn't wash. The hygiene and conditions of the kitchen were bad enough without adding their filthy hands to it. Plus apparently none of the Spanish had ever expressed an interest in working in the kitchen anyway.

It was good to work in the kitchen with the other Europeans. I did not feel I had to be always on guard as I did when in the patio. I was in a small group and more or less I could trust everyone. There was always a happy and busy atmosphere going on. Also the smells in the kitchen of cooking used to lift me. This also encouraged my appetite and made me feel more energised as I was eating more food and food which I chose to eat. However I was still rapidly losing weight and diminishing day by the day. I think this was through concern and sweating in the incredible heat.

The other benefit in the kitchen was that they had their own toilet. This was by far nicer and smelt less than the toilet in the patio. It was kept very clean as everyone in the kitchen would have a turn at cleaning it using detergents. It was so nice to not use the outside toilets. No more catching a glimpse of Ernst having bum fun.

The only major snag of working in the kitchen was the unbearable heat. It was cooking outside with high temperatures but coupled with cookers and fryers on, it was oppressive.

My fourth day of working in the kitchen was a Sunday. It felt as every other day. Everyone was assigned to different jobs of cutting and cooking. However today we were to make paella. I had never cooked this so I was intrigued at how to make it and how it would have tasted. I also got excited when I heard we were given alcohol to put into it in the shape of two bottles of red wine. This shall be very different to Sunday dinners which I am used too. I busied myself cutting peppers and mushrooms until I noticed most of the boys had gone. I turned around to see Joseph about to do the same as he was tidying stuff away. Before he disappeared through the door I called out to him.

'Where you off?'

'Oh we are going to Church.'

'Oh okay.'

'Yes we are all going to mass.'

'Fair enough.'

'Do you want to come?'

'Nah it's okay. I will stay.'

As Joseph left the kitchen the head chef Columbo walked by my station. He looked as if he was puzzled as to why I was still here.

'You not going to church Alan?'

'Nah.'

'Well that makes a change. I will have company for once,' he said smiling.

'Yup.'

I felt a little annoyed when I thought about the boys in church. I was here slaving away. Maybe I should have gone up to the service to see what it was about. I had never been to a Catholic mass before. I chopped up very roughly the vegetables. Normally I would chop them to the best of my ability with the blunt knife I had but I decided not to make the effort. Why should I when the rest of the kitchen boys were up there sat on their arses repenting their sins. We are all going to hell boys. I also didn't peel some of the vegetables properly. Well nobody did it for me so I wasn't go to do it for them. Although Columbo was around too he appeared to do very little.

'What now boss?' I said encouraging him to do some work.

'As it's Sunday and we are making paella we shall make it outside on the patio.'

'Outside?'

'Yes on the kitchen patio.'

'Yeah,' he said whilst beckoning me outside

On the patio I could see logs burning and on top of the logs were four hot plates and on top of this was the biggest pan I had ever seen in my life. Well I suppose this was to feed the sixty or so prisoners. In the pan was stock bubbling away. He then took all the chopped vegetables that I had done and which some of the other boys had done and stuck it in the pan.

'Now Alan you stir I have things to do in the office.'

'Yes okay.'

I looked around and around and could not see an office. What the fuck was Columbo on about?

'Right Alan before I go can you tell me when you think it is thick enough so I can put in the wine.'

'How will I know?'

'You will know.'

Oh well let's have a go I thought. I sat next to the bubbling Paella stirring and stirring. It was hard work with a pan that size. Also the heat from the Paella coupled with the heat of the sun made me feel dizzy, but I wasn't going to stop. I had a job to do. When I looked round at Columbo's quote unquote office it was a small bricked room which had hole for a window but no glass. Rather like that of a store cupboard. There was only enough room for a chair where Columbo could park his lazy fat arse. Office I said to myself and laughed. I had been stirring for ages and ages. After a while I noticed the liquid was starting to thicken giving resistance to my stirrings.

'Columbo come and have a look! I think it needs wine now!'

'No I am not ready to put it in. It isn't ready yet anyway?'

'You sure? I think it is getting thicker.'

'No no I am not ready. Do not rush me Alan. Do not rush me.'

When I looked round at Columbo in his office I could see he was glugging away at the red wine straight from the bottle. The other bottle of wine was clinking as it rolled round on the floor empty. What a liar. He had drunk the wine. Well that's one thing for sure there wasn't going to be any vino in this paella. Columbo had seen to that. I didn't say a word about the wine and carried on stirring. Would wine make fish heads and guts taste better anyway? Probably not! When I looked at my watch fifteen minutes had passed by but it felt like seconds. The stirring was hypnotic.

'Alan how you doing with the paella?'

'It's really starting to thicken up now.'

'Okay okay I will add in the wine now. I think the vino is ready.'

'What you talking about you crazy bastard you drank the wine?'

'Ah ha there shall be wine Alan,' he slurred whilst in mid hiccup.

With that Columbo smiled and stood by the edge of the pan. He then turned to me with a wild grin.

'Alan they want fucking vino. They get fucking vino,' he said in hysterics.

Columbo then proceeded to undo the button on his trousers and unzip his fly. Then to my shock and horror he pissed in the paella. He flapped his old boy around making patterns into the bubbling food. I stood back in amazement but when I caught his smile I couldn't help but laugh.

Now what was I going to eat? I certainly wasn't going to get my chops around that, knowing its special ingredient. I began to feel sick about how I enjoyed last week's paella. Oh fuck me what a special place this is.

'Right Alan I think it is done.'

'Oh yes I would agree with you there.'

Columbo continued to giggle and then stumbled a little towards me and patted me on the shoulder.

'I am fucking starving man. This looked nice as well,' I groaned

'Don't worry Alan I have some paella for us in the kitchen. Promise there is no vino in that as I will be eating that too,' he slurred in my ear hole.

'Our secret. Yeah?' Columbo whispered.

Thank Christ for that I thought. I had pee free paella. When everyone came back from church it felt pretty horrific to watch them eating the piss paella. Columbo stared at me from a distance smiling. I didn't know whether to laugh, cry or be sick.

From that day Columbo and I started to banter and talk more. As we were alone when the other boys were in Church, it was nice to have a one to one and converse without an audience. I found out Columbo was from Columbia hence the nickname and that he was caught for smuggling cocaine. His business wasn't all cocaine as he dabbled in diamonds too. In his trade he mainly consorted with barristers and lawyers. This scared me a little as if Columbo dealt with barristers and lawyers and he couldn't get out. What chance had I? Mind mine was a lesser offence as it was cannabis. But still.

The third week passed by quickly now that I was cooking in the kitchen. However any free moments I had were still consumed with plans of escape. Despite my improved conditions I still couldn't handle thinking of doing a twenty one year stretch in here. No way!

Sunday morning came quickly again. It dawned on me that I didn't think of Troy and Mort and my family. I had been concentrating so much on how to get out of here I had forgotten about the outside world. Maybe I needed to resign myself to the fact I was here and not getting out soon. Maybe I should think about contacting them. Mort and Troy would have known something was wrong as I had not been in touch. Maybe they would have thought I have done a runner with the blow and cash. As this trip was to be my last and set me up for life. Maybe they will think I got greedy. I will need to get in touch and set them straight. Mind my family would probably be none the wiser as I would regularly disappear for a few weeks on end, even months and then return out of the blue. Oh shit what is my Mam going to think when she finds out? Oh I would do anything for her not to find out. She doesn't even know about the smuggling.

When eleven o'clock came I found myself still in bed looking at the floor feeling a bit melancholy. Twenty one years ringing in my mind. As I looked up Joseph rushed into the room and sat next to me. His body was jittery and his eyes bright. I could tell he was bursting to tell me something.

'Hi,' I said solemnly

'Alan Alan. Columbo's not well.'

'What's wrong?'

'Just a bit rough I think. Nothing to worry about.'

'Do you want me to see if someone can cover for him with you tonight?'

'Nah I will be fine. Columbo is only there really to add the wine,' I said smirking

'Eh?'

'Oh nothing just saying I do most of the work and that he is lazy.'

'Oh okay.'

'You coming to the kitchen now?'

'Er yes yes you go on ahead. I will catch you up.'

I headed to Francs for a wash. After wiping myself down it then dawned on me that I would be on my own in the kitchen for a few hours, whilst everyone was in Church. This was the perfect opportunity to escape. Before I headed off to the kitchens I tracked down the trusted prisoner with a key. He smiled at me as he took me on yet another daily jaunt to the luggage room. He quickly opened the gate and now was keener in eye contact when I gathered my things. I made sure I let him go first down the steps. I waited behind as he was locking the gate. I put my arm on his shoulder and he turned to me with a confused expression on his face.

'Leave it open,' I said softly but with stern undertones.

Confused at my English he squinted and pouted.

'Leave it open,' I repeated.

As I said this I mimed him not to lock the gate he understood and shook his head gravely.

'Leave it open and I will give you a 1000 pesetas,' I said pulling a wad from my pockets to show him.

This was a lot of money to give but I needed him to be onside. The only way he would do it would be through great temptation. He looked blankly at the wads of money.

He still shook his head but he did seem tempted as he bit his lip. Not taking no for an answer I thrust the money in his hands and looked stern and aggressive. Eventually he gently nodded and left the gate unlocked.

Serious in thought I headed to the kitchens. To settle my nerves I busied myself chopping vegetables. This also was good in not rousing any suspicion. As far as they knew I was just getting things ready for the paella.

Although it only took a few minutes for the boys to leave for Church it felt like hours. I nervously looked around as each one left.

'See you lads. Have a good one. Pray for me now won't you,' I shouted after them.

Once I was sure they were all gone I peeped outside to see if the coast was clear. It was. I was on my own and could set to work.

First thing was first I needed to create a distraction for when I was escaping. After a quick look around I decided to make a self-made bomb. My materials were two gas canisters and cooker rings. I unrigged two gas bottles from one of the cookers and then put them on rings of another cooker. I then lit the rings underneath. My plan was to blow up the gas bottles and cause a distraction so I could jump across to the boundary walls and away. My only fear was that I didn't know how big an explosion it would be as I had never blown up gas bottles before. The Church was upstairs where all the sinners would congregate. Would I kill anyone by doing this? But I was so desperate to escape and get away I didn't care. I also didn't know if the gas canisters would shoot up into the ceiling and I would feel the blast and get killed or injure myself. Oh well it was a risk I had to take.

I stood by the door with my hand on the wall watching the flame burning and burning away. How long was this going to take? Could the bottles blow up straight away? Could it take hours? All these thoughts raced through my mind as I watched on. My heart was beating faster and the adrenalin pumping ready to propel me to leg it. I decided to wait only a few minutes and then run to the roof and await a bang so the outside guards would go in the prison and hopefully leave me to escape.

'Come on… come on,' I whispered as I watched the flames lick the canisters.

Then out of nowhere I felt a strong hand on my arm and a club wedged into my shoulder blades. This was followed by the words, 'No no senior' in a Spanish accent. Fuck me this was the second time I was stopped making an explosion and the same words were said to me then. I turned around and just as I had assumed it was one of the guards.

Then another guard rushed in and turned off the hobs. I watched on as he took the gas bottles off the rings with tea towels so as not to burn his fingers. After the bomb was defused all three guard's attention was on me. With me in the middle they closed in two tapping clubs in their open palms. As expected I was given a swift beating. One used fists the other two used the clubs from their belts. I protected myself as much as could from their kicks, punches and hits. After the reprimand I was left alone. That was weird. Why hadn't they put me in solitary? Why hadn't they tortured me like Dominic? Mind I suppose Dominic actually caused damage and plus the guards were probably touchy about their beer being raided. Oh well, chalk that up to experience Alan.

On the walk back to my cell I pondered the day's events and I was thankful. Really doing that I could have killed someone. Of those people could have been Joseph, and that would have really hurt me. Maybe it was fate. I couldn't have lived knowing that my actions could have killed.

I realised who my snitch was. It must have been the fucking trusted Spic with the key to the storage. He was the only one privy to part of my plan, even though I didn't tell him fuck all else. Mind I suppose he must have known I was escaping. I decided to leave him alone as I couldn't prove it. Plus I couldn't be bothered with the trouble. I wanted to concentrate on other escape plans instead.

I sat on my bed getting ready for lock down assessing the minimal damage the guards had caused. I had several bruises on my torso, arms and legs. They hadn't caused any damage to my face or fore arms. This was probably to hide it from the consulate and lawyer. Not that they would have bothered anyway. But I was happy it wasn't on my face just in case I had a hearing soon. I wanted to look my best. As I prodded some of my bruises John and Joseph entered the room.

'Gees! What have you been up?' asked John.

'I tried to escape.'

'What?' gasped Joseph.

'Haven't you learned from Dominic?'

'I know but I don't care Joseph! All I want is out of here.'

Joseph seemed dumbfounded and confused at my blasé attitude to being caught and beaten.

'So how?' asked John intrigued.

'I was going to set off the gas bottles in the kitchen and cause a diversion and leg it

'Leg it where.'

'Up on the roof. I had the guy who has access to the key to the luggage room leave open the door.'

'What went wrong?'

'The guards caught me.'

'Probably the guy with the key.'

'Yup you are probably right John.'

'Well Alan you are very lucky they only did that to you man.'

'Very lucky!' said Joseph sounding very angry.

'Look Joseph I don't fucking care! The guards can do what they like but they won't break my spirit.'

'I hear that Alan,' shouted John.

'Thanks John.'

'Only Alan next time let me know about it. I will come with yous to escape like.'

15 FORBIDDEN MOROCCO

I had been in Los Rosales for about a month now. I couldn't believe how time had flown. The last few weeks went especially quick. This was largely due to working in the kitchen and being busied by jobs and having a set routine. Also the boys in the kitchen were such a laugh. Conversation and banter made working feel like minutes rather than hours.

Now time stood still. I did not have much to do as I was banned from the kitchens by the guards. Not surprising seen as I nearly blew the place to smithereens. I was now forced to be bored and hot walking around aimlessly with the rest of the prisoners. My only comfort was having John to talk to whilst we circled the patio over and over. I also played games of ping pong and chess with Ernst. However I didn't get much pleasure out of these activities and played only out of sheer boredom. I think my enjoyment was dulled further as I could not win at either game. Stupid fucking Spanish junior state champion. Stupid fucking Ernst and his reluctance to teach me strategy in chess. Not that I was a bad loser or anything.

Also without the kitchen job I gave up my rights on preparing my own food. No more could I control the ingredients and flavour. However I did tell Joseph I expected preferential treatment now. I wanted clean food. Also the other stipulation was that any fish had to be gutted. Which fair play to him he did. To hide the special treatment from the other prisoners he snuck dinners to me after everyone else had collected theirs. I am glad he agreed to the clean food and I didn't have to bully him into it. I think he knew he would have an easier life if he didn't put up a protest. Also I think he did it to encourage me to eat as he always seemed concerned about my weight. He was right to be. As each day as I stared down at my body I could see I was becoming more and more painfully thin. I was starting to look like a holocaust victim. When I stroked hard my straggly bearded chin I could also feel my face becoming gaunt. Although I didn't have scales I reckoned I had lost over a stone, possibly even two. Despite the rapid weight loss I didn't feel my strength had gone. A little of my energy maybe but not my strength. On a practical level I was so glad my shorts were elasticated and held up. Here was one place I didn't want them falling down.

The failed escape attempt did knock me for six mentally. I think the adrenalin that surged on that Sunday afternoon had drained me a little. Plus the little beating I had afterwards did not help my mood. The little pain from the bruises I didn't care about. That was nothing. What hurt was my pride. Firstly I felt bad for not being successful in my attempt and secondly because the way the guards punished me like a school boy. I was a man in my late thirties. How did I get reduced to this?

Luckily when Biggy and Malero came down they did not ask me about the escape. That's one good thing; the guards hadn't said anything about that. I don't think it would have helped my case. I wonder if they could add to your sentence for bad behaviour. They probably could as it seems with the Spanish judicial system anything goes.

Malero and Biggy seemed confused at my quietness. Normally each time I saw them I would passionately tell them of my innocence and annoyance at being here. Today I just asked more about financier and listened. Nodding and making noises where appropriate to show I understood and was paying attention. Although I could tell they knew I was a bit down neither Biggy nor Malero reproached me about this. Probably thought better not ask as it would open another can of worms. And heaven forbid they'd have to listen or at least look like they cared. I could forgive Malero for his callousness as he was a lawyer, it goes with the job, but Biggy I could not. He was a consulate. An authority figure connected to my welfare and rights. Well all I can say he was very shit at his job! Plus I did not really want to unload any of my concerns with these guys. They couldn't help me! There would have been no point.

As Malero waffled legal mumbo jumbo Biggy nodded along looking like a well-acted politician. My mind drifted as I fixated about the money. Right so I needed to give him the equivalent in pesetas of a grand at a time. I mean I had just fewer than five grand on me in crumpled notes. However I was not handing that over. Firstly, it was handy in prison. Money talked. I could buy stuff I needed and use it to keep people on side. Also secondly I did not want to give cash as I wanted to do this officially. Financier sounded fucking dodgy enough without handing over unaccounted for cash. Plus it would not look good on my part having so much money on me. I much preferred to send it via a solicitor in a cheque to create a paper trail. So if the bastards did rip me off I could track it. The only problem was my money was tied up with Troy and Mort so I would need to get a message to them first. Also I needed to do it without alerting the guards or anyone here about them as they may rightly connect them as my business partners. It made it worse that there was no phone in the prison. That would have made life far easier. One simple phone call and away you go.

After Malero finished talking I asked him about how I could get the money to him. Biggy stepped in and told me I could send money via a cheque or through a solicitor. However he did warn me that the mail service was not reliable. He also subtly implied stuff was posted or went missing due to the laziness and neglectful attitude of the guards. Well that didn't surprise me in the least. I mentioned I was not a very wealthy man and that I would have to get the money off my family. I did this to see if I could pull any heart strings but both of them stared at me blankly. Oh well worth a try I thought. I was hoping they may reduce the amount but oh no they did not have anything to say about that. To cease the silence I put on an act that I would see what I could do. Malero resumed talking about all the formalities right until the end of visiting time.

After my visit I went straight to the econumato and bought paper, pens two stamps and two envelopes. Behind me in the queue was Cheno one of the drug dealers in Los Rosales who was mine and Joseph's supplier of hashish. He too had several envelopes in his hands and writing materials. I hadn't really spoken to him much but I knew him to nod too in the patio. Again here I did not say anything just smiled with a slight nod. He grinned wildly back. Before I could leave Cheno shouted my name.

'Yeah Cheno?'

'You sending post?'

'Yes,' I said a bit bluntly after such a stupid question. I mean it was quite obvious I was.

'Who you sending too? Family? Friends?'

What a nosey git! Mind I better talk to him as he does give us good quality hashish which aids me to chill out in this unbearable place.

'Yeah family. They don't know I am here yet.'

'Really? But you have been here for weeks,' he said confused.

'Yeah just over a month.'

'And only now you tell them?'

'Yup.'

'Wow.'

A silence dawned as he took in the fact I hadn't told my family. He then looked to the floor. Obviously he had gone in his own world. I waited until he was back in the room as it was obvious he stopped for another reason rather than idle chit chat. Come on Cheno back to the point. I stared on smiling consciously trying to stop myself from looking annoyed.

'Oh sorry Alan. Was away then,' he said laughing away.

'Er why don't you come to my cell for a smoke.'

'Why?'

'I have an idea that I would like to run by you.'

I pondered a while on his question. I looked into his smiling eyes to try and detect his reasons. Well I wasn't getting any vibes he wanted me. It seemed to me he needed me for something. I hope to god it was business related though. I was almost sure it was.

'Okay I will see you there just let me write and send these.'

'Okay,' retorted Cheno obviously a little annoyed I didn't jump to his demands straight away.

With that I walked away deep in thought about what to say in my letters and about Cheno. I wondered what he was up to. I wonder how his plans involved me. Oh well I will guess I will find out sooner or later.

In the privacy of my cell I was back on track thinking about writing my letters. Sod Cheno's plans. Reducing my sentence was way more important. Right so I needed to send a letter to someone who I could trust to impart a message to Troy and Mort. Also someone who I could trust to deliver the message and get things done. I did not want a family member involved as I did not want them to suspect any misdeeds. I didn't want any more worry for them. They were going to be in bits after hearing about my imprisonment anyway. I couldn't add any more pressure on. Plus I would be worried they may tell the police about Mort and Troy to try and get me free. I needed someone who was impartial. After racking my brain I decided to send a letter through to Phillip Llewellyn. Yeah I trusted him. He would do this for me. Mind it was still too dangerous to send with the guards. I could write the letter subtly. Maybe if I did some kind of code he could crack it and then do what I needed. I thought over and over about how I could this. So I needed to tell him to go to Mort and Troy to ask for the money. Then the money needed to be given to the solicitors Peter Price. However the dealings with the solicitor had to be done all through Phillip Llewellyn. No links could be made.

Before I could think of a code I became paranoid again. If I did it in code that would look even more suspicious. More heat would be thrown on Phillip Llewellyn. Then he may crack and tell the authorities about Mort and Troy. Oh god! Whilst I sat on the bed ferociously tapping the pen on the empty clean paper my head started to throb. Oh a headache was not useful right now! I rubbed my forehead gently with my finger tips in attempt to ease the pain. My head felt quite warm and clammy. Oh please god I can't be getting ill. I won't allow it. My neck also started to become itchy and as I scratched I could feel a raised rash occurring.

Annoyed I hid the pen, paper and envelopes under the bed. I couldn't even start the letter. As I rubbed my forehead out of annoyance my warm hands felt burned from the heat emanating from it. I can' be ill. I won't allow this! Investigating the rash further by touch I could feel rings forming on my neck. With my index finger I traced the rash. I had about four rings going around. What the hell!

I put to the back of mind my rash and also tried to ignore that I was feeling unwell. I needed to keep my mind occupied on getting a message to Troy and Mort for money. Being ill was not part of my plan. I headed off to the patio to aid my distraction from feeling sick. Maybe the sun will help.

Once at the patio I saw John in the distance dawdling around with his hands behind his back. Every now again he was kicking fag butts on the floor. Obviously incredibly bored just doing it for doing sake.

'Hey John!' I shouted disturbing his bored thoughts.

'Oh hi Alan.'

'What you been up to then?'

'Just bought some stuff to write a letter home.'

'Oh right.'

'Yeah I think it's time to tell them where I am.'

'What the fuck Alan? You haven't even told your family yet?'

'No,' I chuckled at his flabbergasted expression.

'Gees!'

'Well I was hoping I didn't have to tell them and that I would be free by now.'

'Oh Alan.'

We walked around and around the patio. John did most of the talking. I half listened out of politeness but the rest of my brain was thinking about how to get a message to Phillip Llewellyn. After a while I couldn't walk anymore. I was hot, sticky and getting weary from walking. I persuaded John we needed to stop and take respite in the little shade the patio offered. Also the spot was a good vantage point to watch the Moroccans. I liked watching them. I wondered if they watched us lot in here too. They probably did and looked on at us like we were monkeys. Squatting on the floor in our filth whilst shouting at one another. With the majority of Spanish dirtily dressed and demonstrating disgraceful manners. Some of the dirty bastards also pissed in the patio rather than in the bogs. Animals! There was no decorum or grace here not like with the Moroccans.

'Hey Alan!' John shouted jabbing me in the arm with his sharp elbow.

'What the fuck John?'

'Your obsessed with those Arabs in there man.'

'So?' I said annoyed. 'I like watching them. There is fuck all else to do.'

'I can see that…. I just don't know why you find them so interesting. I mean it's not like you'll ever go and talk to em.'

'What do you mean?'

'Well there in there. We are in ere. Never the twain shall meet n' all that shit.'

'Funny you should say that John as I was thinking about going in there for a visit.'

John laughed.

'Why do you want to go in there Alan?'

'Just to see what it was like.'

'You're fucking bonkers to want to go in there.'

'Why? They are people just like us.'

'Yeah but you are different. You is white. They is not.'

'Plus they believe in different religions and stuff.'

'I bet you they would welcome me John.'

'I would like to see that.'

'Well first things first you have to get in there.'

'The gate to the Arab world is always guarded. Plus I have never seen another European go in there. So this can only ever be a hypothetical situation.'

'That's really odd. They are only prisoners for Christ sakes. Why can't I visit them?'

'Oh Alan!' John giggled.

That was it now John had challenged me. It didn't annoy me he didn't believe I could do it. Not like when he taunted me about getting free. I mean technically he was winning on that point. But hey the battle may be lost but the war wasn't over yet. His doubts this time helped to spur me on. I needed his disbelief to encourage me to do it. With fire in my belly I could forget about the heat from my fever. Also there may be other benefits from getting friendly with my Arab neighbours, besides getting one over John and feeding my curiosity. I didn't know what yet but I am sure there would be something to exploit. There was also the great possibility I would get my head kicked in by the Arabs if I went in there but well C'est la vie!

Both John and I fell quiet whilst still crouching in the shade. I carried on observing the other patio. Every now and again I would look up to check if any of the other prisoners on our side of the fence were uncomfortably close or looking dodgy. When I intermittently checked everything seemed good. I would also look across to John. He too seemed in his own world.

Our peace was broken by Enio and Joseph chatting and walking towards us. Joseph seemed his usual happy bright self and Enio looked like he had the weight of the world on his shoulders. Probably still worrying about poor Dominic. As Enio approached further I could see his good looks had been tainted as all on his face were angry red bites. Looking at his legs and arms I could see these too were plastered in irritated pustules. Poor sod! Enio didn't hang around long with us and made a quick exit after a few minutes. He probably felt uncomfortable as John and I couldn't really communicate with him. He couldn't speak English and we couldn't speak a language he could. Plus it looked like he wanted to stew about things on his own.

'Hey Joseph. Those are some nasty looking bites on Enio.'

'I know I told him to shut the windows in his cell. Mosquitoes have bitten him all through the night.'

'Jesus Christ there must have been a plague of them to do that.'

'Or he could do what we do and make the fuckers stoned.'

Joseph and I laughed as we remembered about the stray mosquito we made stoned. John looked on confused. You could see he was a bit upset at being left out but he did not ask as to what we were talking about. Joseph looked uncomfortable when looking at John's stern face and swiftly changed the conversation.

'Anyway I told him to go to the medico.'

'Medico?' I questioned.

'Yeah there is a prison doctor.'

Oh I've heard it all now. A prison fucking doctor! Never would I have a thought a prison with such poor sanitation, food not fit for human consumption and dire living conditions would have an in-house doctor. I wonder what he was like. I bet unsympathetic and probably barbaric. God I shuddered to think what tools he would use in examining people. Mind it was good to know. I could be wrong. Maybe I could see him about my rash.

'Oh Alan I think you may need to go to the doctors too.'

'I'm fine.'

'You have a rash going around your neck.'

'I know.'

'It doesn't look good.'

'Don't fuss its nothing.'

I could see John was even more upset now about Joseph noticing about the rash. Obviously he hadn't noticed. In a way I was glad. I didn't like other men noticing things on my body and pointing out stuff.

'Tell him John. He needs to go to the medico.'

'Joseph is right. We are in Africa man. Every disease is potentially deadly.'

'Thanks John ever the fucking ray of sunshine.'

'John is right Alan. You could die,' he said in high pitched anxious voice.

'Look I will think about it. Just leave it.'

Before Joseph and I could argue anymore Cheno joined the group. Joseph and John were a little taken aback. They clearly didn't see him coming this way. Plus Cheno didn't really hang around with us so the fact he approached was probably a little weird.

'Hi guys.'

In unison John, Joseph and I grumbled back a hello.

A silence descended as nobody knew what to say. Joseph broke it briefly by saying goodbye and leaving to the kitchens. Cheno stared at John with a smile. Although nothing was said John knew that it was his cue for him to leave. John received the message loud and clear as he went off saying he needed a shower.

'So Alan are you ready for that smoke now?'

'Yes. Yes I am.'

I was glad Cheno had come along. He stopped the nagging from Joseph and also I needed something to take my mind of my throbbing head and achy joints.

We ambled along the corridors across to Cheno's cell. Once inside I was quite jealous. In Ceuta terms this was quite plush. Firstly he did not share with anyone he had the cell to himself. Lucky bastard! Also his bed looked cleaner and a hell of lot sturdier than mine. To the side of his bed was a bedside table with cassettes and a cassette player come radio. Wow! Without asking I rifled through his collection of cassettes. They were all mainly Bob Dylan tracks. Remembering I hadn't asked I looked up to the reaction of Cheno. Luckily he wasn't pissed off. Instead he smiled seeming to appreciate my enthusiastic reaction to his collection.

'You want me to put one on?'

'Oh yes,' I said like a five year old kid.

'A bit of Bob Dylan whilst having a spliff?'

'Hell fucking yeah!'

He put on Mr Tambourine man and sat down on the bed. From his draw he pulled out tobacco and two sheets of tobacco paper. Neatly he opened the two papers on the side table and rolled out gently in a sausage shape tobacco. Next he heated up the block of honey coloured resin and then sprinkled it over the tobacco like a gourmet chef finishing off a dish with herbs. Once his index fingers and thumbs were all most clean from hashish bits he picked up the paper rolled, licked and then sealed. Once the ends were twisted he passed one to me whilst he had put the other in his mouth.

With matches in his hand he shuffled up the bed and put his back against the wall. He lifted up his knees and lit the spliff. He looked very comfortable. I beckoned for the matches and lit up my free spliff too. Well I doubted it was totally free. I think Cheno would make me pay for this but I wondered how. With lit spliff in hand I stayed sat upright with feet on the floor ready to hear what he had to say. I slouched my body to convey I was relaxed in order to put Cheno at ease.

At first he just made idle chit chat. He broke the ice by asking me questions on where I was from and how I came to be here. I told him I was from Wales. Straight away this stumped him. He hadn't heard of Wales before. In order to ease his confusion I explained how it was near England. I also lied to him and told him how I was innocent and planted with drugs. He skillfully strayed away from this subject. I could tell he rightly didn't believe me. Plus I think he thought if encouraged I would dominate this conversation about my innocence. He obviously really didn't care what I had to say it seemed he just wanted me to like him enough in order to make me do something for him. Can't blame him really. I liked his style. It's exactly how I would play things.

Once I was sick of answering his questions. I decided to turn the questions on him. He felt less comfortable answering than being the questioner. Too fucking shay!

I found out he was of mixed race as he had Moroccan mother and Chinese father. That would explain his unusual features. I thought he didn't look wholly like a Moroccan. I wondered where the American music influence came from though. He also explained he was in Ceuta for carrying cannabis. He skated around his conviction. Obviously he was not totally happy about talking about it. His demeanour changed to being serious and he looked pained in expression whilst staring into space. I decided to change the mood of the conversation by enquiring as to why I was here.

'So what did you want to talk about?'

With that he took in a huge toke from the joint and smiled. He eyes half twinkled as if he was trying to come back to his normal jaunty composure.

'Well when I saw you in the econumato you gave me an idea.'

'I knew from what you bought you were writing back home.'

'It got me to thinking about smuggling drugs into prison.'

'What?'

'Yes I reckon it's possible to get in drugs by post,' he retorted excitedly making the wrinkles at the side of his eyes crinkle as he smiled.

'Where do I fit in?'

'Well being English the guards would be less inclined to go to the effort of translating it.'

'I am Welsh.'

'You know what I mean.'

'All we need is for someone you know to find and buy LSD tabs. Then post them back. We could make loads of money in here.'

I did consider his proposition only momentarily but thinking about it in my head this was going to be a resounding no. There were so many things wrong with doing this. First of all who would I trust to give money to buy these and send them? What would happen if they got into trouble? Plus would they even get posted to me. There was a chance they could get found in the mail en route. They might even get lost in the mail. The guards may intercept. This was a highly risky situation. Plus I never wanted to get in on LSD drugs. These were too hard. I had tried them and had a good trip. But they were not my cup of tea. Cannabis was my limit now with using and selling. And after being in here cannabis was now my limit in selling. Fair play to Cheno though I loved the way he conveyed the idea as so simple.

Cheno stayed quiet. He hunched his head down making it look like he had a nonexistent neck. With a still expression he smiled at me with eyebrows raised waiting for an answer. I looked down and wondered how to let him down gently. I decided not to say no or yes, but to give the impression I was entertaining the idea.

'It's a bit risky.'

'I know Alan but I reckon it would be good.'

'I take it you like a bit of the old Californian sunshine Cheno.'

'Oh yes.'

'Well I will write a few more letters and check the situation out. But seriously it's risky.'

We tussled a bit more on the issue. Cheno dumbed down the fact it was dangerous whilst I concentrated on what would happen if the guards found it and how it wouldn't look good on my case or his. Luckily for me a punter knocked on the door wanting a fix from Cheno. I used this as an excuse to leave. Cheno gestured with his hand for me to stop but then nodded his head allowing me to leave. Oh shit! I bet he won't let this drop. I am going to have to avoid him for a while or find a way out of here. That's going to be hard in such confined circumstances.

'Alan,' he shouted after me.

'Yeah,' I said nonchalantly whist turning my head back.

'Think about what I said yeah.'

'Will do!'

Feeling stoned I headed back to the patio to John. I told him about Cheno's plans. He too thought it was too high risk and not really worth the hassle. After my brief input to the conversation John did as he always did and took over with what he wanted to say. I listened on being polite albeit slightly annoyed. I should in some way feel honoured as I think I was the only one he could ever talk to like this. I never saw him properly chatting to anyone else. He must have bottled up so much when he first was here.

Then peace and quiet eventually dawned. As I looked across I could see John had closed his eyes and was smiling pointing his face towards the sun. He looked lighter as if a burden had lifted. I could also see he had exhausted all what he had to say. At first I was appreciative of the silence with only the humming of other people's conversation appearing at the fringes of my hearing. But once the lack of noise seeped into my brain my inner thoughts increased their buzzing volume. A queasy and uneasy feeling then sloshed around in my stomach. Oh shit! I am going to have to write home. I am going to have to tell my Mam, family and friends what had happened. I don't know why but thinking about them made me feel worse than actually being here myself. Somehow by admitting it to others it made it real where I was and what was happening. To calm myself down I decided to forget about writing home for the minute. I rationalised that I needed to hear from Phillip Llewellyn or Peter Price before I could make contact with them. Then I would have something to say to them. If they knew I was sorting things out it wouldn't be so bad. Really I knew in my heart of hearts I was just putting things off but I liked the immediate relief of pushing the worry back to the pit of my stomach.

To further distract myself from feeling anxious and unwell I decided to put my plan into action of getting into the Moroccan patio. Without warning to anyone I stood up from my crouched position and marched over to the fence separating the two prison populations. The guard leaning on the gate looked suspicious and annoyed. Turning my face away from his gaze I looked dead ahead at a group of Moroccan boys and started shouting. I shouted words and phrases I had picked up from Ahmed. I said hello, thank you and my name over and over again in Arabic. At first I created interest as almost all the Moroccans stared at me looking stern and shocked. They all craned their heads upwards like Meer Kats. There angry faces turned to confusion as they listened carefully to what I was saying. At first they probably thought I was taking the piss. But when they heard I was saying respectful words in their native language it was if they didn't know what to make of it. However after several minutes their interest died as everyone averted their gaze. As I looked around they pretended very convincingly they could not hear me. Despite their ignorance I carried on ranting the phrases getting louder and louder. My throat hating me after each shout as it was becoming more and more sore and dry.

'Oi Alan!' I could hear John shout from behind.

'What!' I shouted without turning back.

With that I could feel a finger dig in my back. I turned around to John half smirking.

'What the fuck are you doing?'

'I told you I am going to get in that patio.'

'The only thing you're going to get is a hiding from the guards if you are not careful.'

'Nah they can't do that I am not harming anyone.'

'Oh Alan you are fucking nuts.'

'Nah I am not nuts. Just a little different,' I said laughing excitedly.

'I mean if you do get in there. Aren't you worried they'll string you up?'

'It's the risk I take.'

I looked into John's eyes and I could see he feared me a little. Not because of my size or presence as he was far bigger in height and build. Neither in aggression too as he seemed way more hostile. I think it was my unpredictability. He was obviously a little taken aback at my outbursts to the Moroccans. I liked this. Acting the potential nutter could make my life so much easier in here. I could be like the wolf man feared because people don't know what I am going to do next. I wonder if the wolf man acted like that as a ploy. I then flashbacked to the image of his eyes. Nah his eyes were wild and immersed in madness. I would put money on the fact he was definitely a fruit loop.

In the night I kept out of conversation and let John and Joseph talk. It was nice to see John conversing with someone else enthusiastically for a change. This would be useful in giving me a break. Whilst they talked I disappeared to my own thoughts about what I would write in a letter to my

Mam and family. About how to get a message to Mort and Troy via Phillip. I also thought about ways to penetrate the Arab patio. Then all these different thoughts that raced around in my mind merged into one brilliant idea. I could write a letter to Phillip and give it to one of the Arabs to post. They could give it to their family when they visited and post it out. Then there would be no trace to the guards or any authorities about me mentioning my colleagues. Plus I could probably trust the Arabs more than the guards to post it. Only problem was I needed to make contact in order to give them my letter. Putting this problem to one side I penned a letter to Phillip. It didn't take long and the words poured out. I knew exactly what to write as I had thought about it for so many days. Once finished I folded it up and put it under my pillow safe. Contented I rested my head.

I must have fallen asleep early that night as my last memory was of John and Joseph talking. Probably a good thing as I needed rest. Plus Joseph would have just kept nagging on about the doctors again.

The next few days went quickly in a haze. Partly this was due to me feeling like utter crap the other half was because I busied my days shouting and shouting across to the Moroccans. I had a purpose again!

On the third day of shouting across to the Moroccans I grew bored. Even the guard didn't notice me anymore. What the fuck am I doing! Ranting and raving and not getting anyway. I hope this comes to something or else I will just look like an annoying dick. I wondered if they did eventually listen they will agree to send my letter. Oh I give up! Angry I stormed over to Joseph and John chatting away as they circled the patio.

'Finally given up have we?' John mocked.

'No just finished for the day.'

'That rash is looking worse Alan.'

'Oh sod off Joseph!'

Joseph bowed his head down and bit his lip. His normally happy go lucky expression was transformed into a grumpy frown.

'Look sorry Joseph not feeling myself. When is the flaming doctor coming then?'

'I know you won't go Alan,' mumbled Joseph

'I will. I will. If it means you stop acting like a woman.'

Joseph was right. There was a high possibility I wouldn't have gone.

'Look if you go to the doctor I maybe able to help you get in the Moroccan side.'

'What? Tell me now.'

'No.'

'Oh Joseph come on tell me.'

'Look the doctor is in today. You go and I will give you a possible way in.'

As promised that day I went to the doctors. I saw Enio coming out of the medico as I approached. He didn't see me even though he walked straight past, so I didn't bother saying hello. He looked preoccupied with the two pills he had in his hand as he stumbled past. Well that's a good sign I suppose he does prescribe tablets. They are not still using leaches then. With a deep breath I knocked on the door. When I heard a voice from the other side I walked in.

I was greeted by a humourless Moroccan looking doctor. Well despite my reservations he looked the part. He had a white coat on, serious expression and glasses. His balding black hair, slight chubbiness and age of late forties also added to the impression he was qualified. I promptly sat down and watched on as his eyes looked up to me and then down to the paper he had in front of him.

'What's wrong with you?' he said in an irritated tone.

What the fuck! Not even a hello or an address of name. How rude.

'Hi doctor I am Alan,' I said in a friendly tone. This statement was only greeted with silence. I didn't manage to melt his cold stare one iota.

'Well doctor I have this rash here,' I said pointing to my neck.

He moved his spectacles to the end of his nose and craned his head across the table for a closer look. He looked at my neck with great concentration for a whole two seconds and then scribbled something down on a piece of paper.

'Ah yes that is fine and easily treatable.'

With that he picked up some tablets from the door and slammed them in front of me.'

'You may go now,' he said shooing me out of the room like a stray cat.

'Er doctor what have I got?'

'Ring worm.'

'Worms?'

'Yes.'

'Are you sure? Don't you need to run any tests?'

'No quite sure. You may go,' he said admiring the paperwork in front of him.

I wonder what he put in his little write up about our consultation, with great emphasis on the little. This job was probably a nice little earner for him. Also he didn't have to care. We were only a bunch of low, dirty crims. Didn't matter if we lived or died really.

As I left the doctors I imagined my face doing the exact same gobsmacked expression as Enio. I too also look preoccupied with the 2 tablets he thrust in my hands. I couldn't believe how he didn't examine me or even ask about symptoms. I mean I could be misjudging him. It is not outside the realms of possibility that he was a super doctor and could see exactly what was wrong. But what the hell!

That night I told Joseph about the pills and seeing the doctor. He was so happy I did go and that my diagnosis was something curable. I didn't tell him the doctor's methods or lack of as that would have worried him. When John heard my news he looked relieved but verbally took the piss. He taunted me saying I was like a fucking dog. I suppose worms were a bit of an embarrassing ailment to have. It would have been a bit more macho if I had a disease or something potentially life threatening. Mind I wasn't so keen on having a deadly disease, so worms was good enough for me.

As promised Joseph imparted his gem of wisdom about how I could penetrate the formidable Arab patio. He said I should speak to the wolf man. I could have kicked myself. Of course! He looked Moroccan he may have a clue on how I could get in. Plus he could teach me a few new phrases as the ones I knew were getting very repetitive and boring to say.

'Yes Alan so you talk to Lobo.'

'Loco.'

'No no no Alan Lobo.'

'Lobo.'

'Yes yes it is very important you say Lobo.'

'Why's that?'

'Well Lobo means wolf and Loco means crazy.'

'He doesn't seem to mind the nick name wolf but I would hate to think what he would do if you called him Loco.'

John was laughing in the background at me repeating the word lobo over and over and Joseph correcting me. I carried on but felt distracted by him. I bet he was imagining me going over to Wolfie and accidentally calling him a nutter. Then Wolfie giving me a good pasting. I was having this thought but did not find the prospect hilarious. I just hope if I do fuck up he hasn't got a knife or a self-made pointy thing to stick in me. Oh well you live and learn.

The next day came swiftly. I could feel the anticipation of Joseph and John as I strode over to the Wolf Man. Here goes. I decided instead of engaging him straight on I would do a circuit first. After doing one complete circuit I looked back to Joseph and John. John was grinning whilst Joseph shook his head in concern. Both of them squinted and had their hands in a salute to avoid the blinding light from the sun.

I turned back and looked at the Wolf Man. Here it goes. Calmly and slowly I walked towards him. Once only a yard away he said hello to me. I was taken aback. Obviously he was more alert and conscious than I would give him credit for. Taken by surprise I stayed in the place where he greeted and came no further.

'Hi er Lobo.'

'Hi Alan.'

'What the hell! He knew my name too.'

'That rash around your neck looks bad.'

'Yeah being to the doctors and got some pills.'

'You don't need those.'

Without warning he stood up and quickly stomped up close with keen attention to my neck. With his hand he put it on my face and roughly turned my neck to a 90 degree angle to his right.

'What do you think it is?' I asked. Trying to calm my voice and show I didn't care that his unhinged wolf hands were wrapped around my neck.

'It's worms,' he said as he let go of my neck and went back to sit down.

'That's what the doctor said.'

'Well it is easy to see.'

'I wouldn't take the pills though.'

'Why?'

'It would be easier if the body cures it.'

'What do you mean?'

I will show you. With the index finger on his right hand he stuck it in his gob and sucked on it. With great concentration I watched on as he sucked. As he sucked his serious expression turned to a manic grin. Oh fuck what was he up too! Hope he wasn't trying to fucking seduce me. After a few seconds he pulled out his moist finger and lightly touched it with his index finger as if he was checking if it was sufficiently wet. Then with his damp finger he drew circles on his neck. What the hell was this guy doing?

'Come on Alan do it with me.'

To show willing to the crazy fucker I repeated what he had just done. On the first part of putting my finger in my mouth he shouted in Arabic at me. It was obvious I was doing it wrong.

'No! Like this,' he said whilst really fingering the inside of his gums.

'You need to get the spit in your mouth from here,' he said lifting up his lips and pointing to his gums.

On my second try he nodded and smiled appearing pleased I had correctly copied him. What the hell was I doing?

'How will this kill the worms?'

'When you have worms your body fights it. And it fights it most in the spit in your mouth. Creating an acid.'

'Once this is put on the worm it will die.'

'Thanks Lobo good to know,' I said totally taken aback and forgetting my original purpose.

'Also Alan always start from where the ring begins and follow it around.'

'Yeah okay.'

'Everyday!' he shouted loudly.

'Yes Lobo every day.'

'Everyday,' he repeated but with much less vigour.

I didn't know whether this was an old wives tale or scientific fact or something that just popped into his crazy little mind at that moment in time but I decided to keep it as plan b if the tablets didn't work.

Lobo went quiet. He looked down at the ground slightly swaying as he sweated profusely in his homemade goat jacket. How uncomfortable must he be wearing that. Best not comment out loud about his jacket. He obviously loved wearing the thing. I mean why else would he wear it every day.

'Er Lobo,' I said gaining courage to talk to him again.

'Yes,' he said shining me an unnerving stare.

'Can I also ask your help with getting into the Arab patio?'

'Why would you want to go there?' he said a little angered.

'Only because I want to see if they can get a message to my friend I know in Morocco.'

'I have seen you.'

'Pardon,' I replied confused.

'I have seen you talking to them,' he said as if they were aliens from another world.

'Er...Yes..... I was shouting to them to see if they would invite me over.'

'You can only get an invite from one man.'

'Oh who?'

'Palermo.'

'Pal... ere r er.'

'Mo.'

'Palermo,' he shouted as if annoyed at my crap verbatim skills.

'Palermo that's his name,' I repeated.

'No of course not!'

'Oh!'

'Palermo is what he is known as.'

'Oh.'

'It means Dove.'

'Who is he?'

'He is their leader. A sort of elder.'

'So you reckon I should say take me to your leader,' I said laughing.

'No you should say Palermo,' Lobo answered deadpan. He either didn't get it or did not appreciate my humour.

'Everything is decided with him,' he hissed.

'Oh thanks Loco I mean Lobo.'

Thankfully the Wolf Man didn't react and just walked away. He did not say a good bye or any hint of parting words when he wandered off. A few seconds later he laughed manically which made me feel uneasy. I wondered if he heard me say Loco. Oh well he seemed okay. So Palermo I needed to shout meaning Dove. Meaning the leader. Right!

I walked back to John and Joseph at ease and smiling. I tried to convey that I wasn't scared at all after my clipped conversation with Wolfie. Well mostly I wasn't. Both John and Joseph seemed impressed that I came back intact and also managed to gain sense out of him. John was still pessimistic about my chances of getting access to the Arab world but I think he laid on thick the negativity to spur me on. I think he liked the sort of double act thing we had going on. He would say no and I would say yes. Secretly I think he wanted me to be successful though. If only to watch me get a battering.

With the name of Palermo I had new found enthusiasm in shouting across to the Moroccans. After shouting his name a few times nearly everyone at different instances turned around and looked at me. I have their attention again. Brilliant! I smiled and continued. However after ten or more times shouting his name the eye contact again stopped. They all carried on their business and ignored me. Fuck! Fuck! Fuck! Come on Alan don't stop until they let you in.

Two days passed and still I was being ignored. It didn't matter that I said Palermo. Also my mood was worsened by the worms. The tablets didn't appear to be doing anything and the chain links on my neck seemed longer and more prominent by touch. On a break from shouting the Wolf Man appeared from out of nowhere in front of me. It was probably because I was in my own world and not paying attention but his immediate apparition still spooked me.

'Alan!' he shouted.

'Yes Lobo.'

'Remember to rub,' he said whilst rubbing his neck in a circular motion.

'Yes Lobo. I will thanks.'

'Oh and I think they are listening,' he said grinning widely

'Who are listening?'

'They are,' he said pointing to the Moroccan patio.

'Okay.'

Despite feeling unnerved by his speech, eyes and mannerisms I gained confidence in what he said. I hope he was right. Before I could confirm it he ended the conversation like last time by walking away and not looking back but this time there was no crazy laughter. Well let's see if he's right then. With determination I went back over to the gate and shouted. This time with more volume and zeal than I had ever done before. I felt at ease at being so loud as the guard wasn't nearby as instead of guarding the gate he was having a heated discussion with a group of Spics. Mid shout I was shushed by a young Moroccan boy in his mid-twenties. I could see from his face he was extremely pissed off by my distraction as his brow furrowed and his head shook.

'Please I need to get a message,' I said quietly.

With a huff he approached the gate. He looked gutted at engaging with me. He probably hated the fact he was the first to crack under my tirade of shouting.

'What message?'

'Please tell Palermo I would like to speak to him.'

'What about?'

'I want to know if he has the same friend as me.'

'What?'

'Please I need to send an urgent message.'

'I can pay money.'

The Moroccan boy sighed and scratched his head. He looked into my eyes for an uncomfortable few seconds as if he was assessing my sincerity. I simply stared back with a slight smile.

'Wait here. I will see if he wants to speak with you.'

I watched on as the boy weaved in and out of the groups of men wearing djellabas through the Arab patio until he had completely disappeared into the thronging crowd. To pass the time of waiting I wondered what Palermo looked like. From the meaning Dove didn't provide me with any initial hints. Also what was with that? It's not really a good name for a prison leader. To me Dove signifies peace and beauty. A leader's name should be more aggressive or denoting bravery. Like Mad Dai or Fearless Mike.

I awoke from my reverie as the young boy returned. He was accompanied by a man I would say was in his late seventies to early nineties. I couldn't quite be sure. All I knew was that he was pretty dam old as his hair was white and stripped of any colour. He also had wrinkles on his wrinkles.

I couldn't really make out his frame as his djellaba was black and hid his body well. I imagined though it was thin and frail as the features on his face denoted. Despite looking weather beaten and fragile I could see in his eyes a balance of wisdom and fire. Just from his presence I felt immediate respect for him and I could see also how despite his age he was a strong authority figure. He also had a magical Gandalf quality about him.

'Hello, I am Palermo. You wish to speak with me.'

'Oh yes. Yes I do,' I said whilst putting my right hand on my heart and extending my right arm for a hand shake.

Palermo looked taken aback by my greeting. Being western I bet he was surprised at how I knew to greet a Muslim with respect. He responded by shaking my hand but he did not put his hand to his heart. Well that's fair enough he did not know me yet. Plus maybe he was showing his minions his respect had to be earned before rewarding. Or maybe he didn't because I was white and not Arab. Who knows?

'Er thank you for seeing me Palermo. I know you are a very important man. The reason why I want to talk is to see if you know Ahmed.'

'Ahmed?'

'Yes Ahmed is a very good friend of mine who owns a shop in Tangier.'

'I was just wondering if you could help me in getting a message across.'

'Why don't you mail it?'

'I don't trust the guards. I fear they are too lazy,' I said whilst checking the guard was still busy.

Palermo nodded in agreement at my comment and smiled breathing out a slight laugh.

'Oh please Palermo if I could get this message across it will help my case.'

Palermo paused but I think could see in my eyes I wasn't going to give up until he helped me. I would have yelled day and night, especially now from this interaction. I had now cracked them.

The gate guard strutted back over. He looked uneasy at seeing me converse with Palermo through the gate.

'Well we will see what we can do.'

'What is your name?'

'Alan.'

'Alan you know you will have to pay.'

'Not a problem.'

With that Palermo walked over and spoke to the guard. I don't know what was being said as it was all in Spanish. Palermo had the palm of his hand on show and pointed to me. The guard put his hands up in the air and shook his head. He also smiled slightly. It looked like Palermo was asking for my passage but the lazy guard could not be arsed to open the gate and contemplated trouble if he did. I joined in then on the commotion by walking towards the guard and smiling I pointed to the Arab patio and shouted 'Por favour', meaning please in Spanish over and over.

As the commotion of Palermo and I talking was going on I noticed groups of young Moroccan boys straightening up their stances and looking serious. Slowly the groups became closer and closer to Palermo and the guard. I think the guard noticed this as his smile turned sour and slightly worried over the tense faces looming around him. After staring for several seconds he huffed and then turned to me and ushered me through the gate. Easy as you like. Yes that's it Spic open up the gate. You do anything for an easier life. You don't want a riot on your hands.

I walked tentatively through the gate to the Arab patio. Fucking hell what have you done Alan? You have gone into a world where you have no friends or allies. You could be mugged, raped or killed. Possibly all three. Oh well here goes. I tried to hide my nervous excitement by walking in a positive stride. After days and days of shouting I was here. Now I hope they help me with my letter. Or at least let me leave intact of life, limbs, tight bum hole and belongings.

I walked next to but slightly behind Palermo. He walked in a graceful manner with hands behind his back. Although he was a leader in the prison world he reminded me more of a religious figure. So at ease. So respectful and wise in appearance. As I looked around I could see a few men walking with us and loosely surrounding us. They were obviously Palermo's body guards. Protecting him just in case I was a threat. I smiled and tried to seem as calm as possible to portray no threats. I always had my hands on show to convey no weapons. Walking through the patio I had a little look around just in case this was to be my one and only opportunity to have a look. Dotted here and there on the floor were men with the tins I had seen before from a far. On closer inspection I could see they were cooking cous cous. The smell up close was even more tantalising and delicious. I needed to show Joseph this so he could cook food that smelt this beautiful and tasty. He needed a cookery lesson from these guys.

Walking through I felt uneasy. So many eyes stared at me. I could feel from their stares they had many questions they wanted to ask as to why I was here.

Eventually Palermo stopped when we neared a set of chairs and a table. He turned around and invited me to sit down. So I did. He then too sat down with a slight smile on his face. Although annoyed at first at my constant tirade of questions I think he was warming up to me. I think he enjoyed this new circumstance. Although not obviously on show I could still feel the eyes and close contact from the body guards. I dared with the idea to grab Palermo's jacket to see the fast reaction times from his men but then decided that would be a completely idiotic thing to do.

Palermo got proceedings under way as he grilled me on everything. He asked about where I was from, why I was here and mostly about Ahmed. I told him everything I knew. It was funny in the Spanish and Europe side of the prison I began with a lie of innocence and maintained it for weeks and weeks. I met Palermo for a few seconds and spilled all about the truth. Mind I needed to. It would be quite a hard story to construct as to how I knew Ahmed without divulging about the cannabis smuggling. It was the only way to try and get him onside. From telling him about my illegal antics he could see why I couldn't go through the proper channels of mailing it.

Palermo soon grew tired of listening. I too was waning about things I could say about Ahmed.

'Alan I think I know of the man you speak about.'

'He is quite a powerful man and a good friend of mine.'

'Oh that he is Palermo.'

'He has helped me in a few scrapes,' I smiled remembering about the Y-front mugging incident.

'Scrapes what do you mean?'

'Er unforeseen problems.'

'Oh.'

'Do you have the letter on you that you want to send?'

'Er yes. Yes I do,' I said scrabbling around under my clothing as I tucked it in my jeans.

'Here it is.'

'Okay Alan I will speak to the others on sending this.'

'Oh thank you Palermo that would be fantastic.'

'Well Alan they still will have to agree.'

'Well thank you for trying.'

'But we do expect money in return if we do send it.'

'Yes that is fine with me.'

'I think they will agree with me to send it though.'

'When will I know a decision?'

'We shall give you a signal tomorrow across the patio.'

'Couldn't you tell me when I visit tomorrow?'

'Er..' Palermo said surprised.

'Can I come over tomorrow and you can tell me the decision.'

My question was greeted by silence. I could see Palermo's mind working over time as to whether to let me in again tomorrow. His eyes squinting as he weighed up the possibility.

'Please it would be nice to get away from that dirty lot. I much prefer it in here.'

'What do you mean?'

'They are so filthy in there. Here is lovely and clean. Where I am they act like a bunch of animals.'

'Please let me visit.'

Again I was greeted by silence. Palermo stroked his beard with his index finger still pained with weighing up the option of inviting me or not.

'Oh come on Palermo.'

'I bet today we have really annoyed the guards with this visit.'

'Let's worry them a bit more.'

Palermo smiled at my mischievous comment. I think I had cracked through with this comment. Despite our many differences I bet my life he and his people hated the guards as much as I did. With hope I looked into his wise eyes. He shook his head whilst grinning more.

'Well I will speak to the others and see what I can do.'

'Thanks Palermo for inviting me in.'

'If you can help me and I can visit I would be extremely grateful.'

'Well we will see.'

Palermo and his body guards escorted me back to my patio. I walked slowly savouring this strange and exciting experience just in case I wasn't allowed back in again. After one last look around I shook Palermo's hand and touched my heart again. He shook my hands smiled and nodded. I was a little gutted he didn't touch his heart after our conversation but still understood that he had to think about pleasing everyone and not just me. I think he did genuinely like me though as his smiles seemed honest and not fake. With one last wave I signalled to the guard I wanted to return back into my world. The guard did not look happy opening the gate for me. I don't know whether it was because he thought the Europeans were joining forces with the Arabs. Or it was because he had to open the gate instead of standing there and doing nothing. I just don't know but I felt pleased I had pissed him off.

Grinning like a man on acid I walked over to Joseph, John and Enio. All had stunned expressions and smiles.

'Told you John I would do it.'

'I will give you that one Alan. I will give you that.'

'Are you okay? They didn't hurt you or threaten you?' said Joseph anxiously.

'No no they were very nice.'

'What was Palermo like?' probed John.

The questions about my visit went on all day, mainly by Joseph but when the word spread around Franc and his brother too came in on the action. John tired very quickly talking about my visit as I think he was slightly miffed as I had managed it and was bored of the attention I was getting. Apparently after asking everyone I was the first European to ever be invited across. I mean admittedly maybe nobody had ever tried. I mean why would they? But nonetheless it felt nice I had made history. A sort of crim ambassador bridging two nations. My reputation of being a bit of an unpredictable wild man was nicely developing.

That night as I settled down to go to sleep all that was on my mind was the letter to Phillip. It was a pretty big risk giving it to Palermo and the others. They were strangers. There was a possibility they would not send it or give the letter to the guards. Oh well! Before I sunk into depressive thoughts I convinced myself they wouldn't do that. Plus there was nothing now I could do about it anyway. I would just have to wait and see what fate had dealt.

16 SPANISH EYES

I decided not to take the prescribed pills anymore for the worms, as none of my symptoms were alleviated. I still felt feverish and shit. The rash around my neck seemed more inflamed and by touch I was convinced another ring was starting. It was possible I hadn't given them chance to kick in as I had only taken them for a few days but I discounted this.

I wondered as to why they weren't working which evoked a flurry of paranoid thoughts. Maybe the pills had nothing to do with curing my worms. I began to fantasize about what the pills could have been for. Were they sedatives instructed by the guards to give me in order to keep me calm and too drowsy for any trouble? If so Joseph could have been in on it. He was keen for me to go to the doctors. Nah he wouldn't do that! Maybe the guards were slowly trying to kill me with poison. Or it was possible the tablets were nothing, just a placebo in order to look like they were medicating me but really were saving money on their prison budget. The latter was probably the most plausible by the evidence that nothing in the prison looked bought or new. It wouldn't have surprised me if all the furniture in here was acquired by the local dump or just found. The food as well was probably the slops that butchers and fisherman would normally chuck out.

Well looks like time for plan b to come into action. If the pills won't cure let's take the advice of Mr Wolf. Before I spat on my neck I made sure no one was watching as I would have been embarrassed if someone had caught me. Luckily I was alone inside the cell as John and Joseph weren't around. I also had a quick look outside the door onto the corridor to make sure they weren't outside or that there weren't any other prying eyes.

Once I felt secure I was alone I lay on the bed. I sucked on my index finger and rubbed ferociously around my gums and then applied the spittle onto the rings. I hope this works. I can't believe I am choosing the words of a mad man, instead of taking medication from an educated and experienced doctor. Oh well Wolfie's ritual wouldn't hurt me but the pills could. As I lubed up my rough neck I felt instant relief as it cooled the heat. I had a pang of uneasiness as I wondered at whether I was going mad myself. Was the hashish making me paranoid and too suspicious? Or was I just being too cautious in such a hostile prison? There was always the possibility I was right to be worried. Then my thoughts drifted off at what my family were up too. What they must have thought about my disappearance. That's if they noticed, as it was normal for me to go weeks and weeks without getting into contact. Before I could dwell too deeply a loud noise from the corridor jolted me. It sounded like someone had dropped something. My moment of solitude was broken and I quickly rubbed in the spit until my neck felt dry. Feeling ashamed I headed with quick pace to the patio.

I angled my neck to the sun drying off any spit I had on it. I didn't want to have to explain my wet neck to any of the guys. Looking through the crowds of Spanish prisoners I managed to spot John in the corner. He was playing chess with Ernst. Go on Ernst beat the cocky fucker I thought as I smiled to myself. I then noticed Enio talking amicably with a Spaniard whilst being shown goods he could buy. On sale today was a few watches which were painful to look at as they glinted in the sun. Enio looked more at peace today, as if he was getting on with things and not mourning so much the absence of his friend Dominic. Good for you Enio! At the end of the day you can only count on yourself in here.

I then had an eerie feeling someone was watching me. As I turned around I was indeed right. A young man in his early twenties from the Moroccan patio was looking dead at me whilst beckoning me over with his hand. They must have reached a decision about the letter. In excitement I trotted over to the gate and asked the Spanish guard to let me in. The night before Joseph had taught me how to say it. But he didn't make a move. The young Moroccan boy in the other patio began shouting across. The guard turned around to see what he was saying. The guard's eyes darted around. He seemed to notice the scores of Arabs looking his way and slowly making their way over. His cheeks looked drawn as he chewed on the inside of his mouth. Then just like yesterday he huffed and opened the gate.

Once in I was taken by the boy to Palermo. When I reached him I decided to raise my hand in a western hi instead of extending a formal handshake. I didn't want him to feel uncomfortable and decide whether to touch his heart or not. Plus I was not going to give him something without nothing in return.

'Hey Palermo the guards are really suspicious of us.'

'Suspicious? What do you mean?'

'They don't like our meetings,' I said smiling leaning close in to Palermo.

'I think you are right Alan.'

'So are you going to post the letter?'

'Yes we have decided we will but only for money.'

I stared hard at Palermo awaiting a fee to be named but silence was only returned. This reminded me of being in Morocco with my minders and guides. As with them no fee or ball park figure would be mentioned and it was always up to me to suggest about how much to give. I hated that. I would feel a scum bag if I offered lower than what I thought was worthy. But then again I would feel bad at offering just enough. So, like with the guides I gave slightly over what I was comfortable with for their discreet mail service. Oh well this was an investment. I was in with the Moroccans.

After the transaction was over the proceedings were less business like and Palermo seemed more relaxed which in turn allowed me to chill out too. We talked and talked about Ahmed, Morocco and the guards. Palermo became so at ease in my company he even allowed me to join in having a sebsis with a few of his pals. This could also have been because I told him how I enjoyed having a sebsis with Ahmed. Maybe he thought I was hinting. Oh well I didn't care I liked free kif. Well this time it technically wasn't so free as I did give him a generous amount of money.

The sebsis knocked me for six as the kif was so strong. The strength made the hash Cheno got us for joints seem like normal cigarettes. Palermo noticed I wasn't handling the kif as well as the rest. He seemed concerned and commented on the greenness of my face. Although embarrassed I told him it was because of the strength and as I was not feeling very well. Not wanting to sound ungrateful at the free sebsis session I complimented him on the strength and complained at how Cheno's hash was obviously from inferior yields. To my surprise Palermo offered to supply me with hash. I was shocked but at the same time happy with forming an arrangement. He then talked about the different forms of hashish he could get hold of. I told him I wanted it as a block of resin and to be strong. He laughed and joked on whether I and the other Europeans could handle it. I told him we would soon get used to it. Then we talked about prices which seemed strange. The prices quoted by Palermo were a lot higher than Cheno's. After a lively discussion I did manage to knock him down a few pesetas but it was still higher than what Cheno charged. I told myself it would be worth it. I mean the stuff would be higher in quality and strength. Also by forging such a relationship I had allies all around the prison. This could prove useful. Maybe I should also befriend the Spanish too. That really would get the guard's backs up and give them something to worry about.

Once the conversation had dried and Palermo seemed to get fidgety I decided it was time to leave. We had both got what we wanted out of the meeting. I was promised my letter being delivered with the added bonus of gaining a new drug supplier. Whilst Palermo had the satisfaction of fleecing me of a bit of money and happy in the knowledge the guards were terrified of our union.

The next few days after this visit I felt so much at peace. There was nothing I could do now but just sit back and relax awaiting Troy and Mort's answer. That's assuming they will. Oh shut up Alan they will! They were probably highly worried at my disappearance.

Physically I was relieved too as no longer did I feel unwell. My temperature seemed normal and my aches less. The rash on my neck had shrunk and the last ring and a half of the link was almost gone. Maybe there was something in what Wolfie had said. Or possibly I had convinced my body to cure itself and had tricked it into getting better. Whatever the reason I was happy. The hashish Palermo had supplied made me feel better too. Having a joint on his stuff really made my body feel lighter and my head fuzzy allowing it to escape from dark depressive thoughts and pain.

When a few of the Europeans had heard I got resin from the Arabs they all asked to buy bits off me. I agreed to this but made them pay in order to try it. It was expensive stuff. They all noticed the difference between the Moroccans grade of quality with Cheno's. It was just unfortunate I could not make a profit due to the price. It felt good as to their compliments on the hashish though. They also marvelled at how I was welcomed by the Arabs and how I managed to convince the guards to allow me to cross the divide. I think like me they loved the fact the Spanish guards didn't know what to make of it and appeared worried each time I visited.

Feeling a little happier despite being in Los Rosales prison I floated around the prison day dreaming and letting my mind wander. I walked through the corridors past the lines of cells. I walked to the Centro and around the large empty space outside it. Then to the laundry, up to the ping room, onto the mock Catholic Church and then to the patio.

Back in the patio my mood dampened as I heard shouting from a score of Spanish prisoners. I could feel in the air an aggressive atmosphere as I looked at the arguing men. There faces were filled with resentment as they barked and pointed at one another. What the hell? The other prisoners watched on like me seeming just as curious and confused. Looking down at the hands of a few I could see they were clutching bags and bedding. Then just as the commotion started the men with the belongings disappeared out of the patio.

'Alan! Alan!' shouted Joseph as he excitedly jogged across the patio.

'Where's the fire?'

'What fire? Where?' he said shocked looking around in all directions for a fire.

'Sorry Joseph it's just an expression.'

'A what?' spluttered Joseph. 'Did Enio start it this time?'

'Look forget it Joseph. What's wrong? You were about to tell me something?'

'Yes I was but there is no time you have to come quick.'

'Why?' I said as Joseph grabbed my arm and pulled, encouraging me to follow.

I decided not to resist and caught up with his pace trotting alongside. Feeling on show I tried to convey my jog as stiffly and manly as I could. I did not want to appear worried but just in a rush. I looked ahead at Joseph and hated how camp he could look. He too like Ernst needed lessons in how to appear more street wise in regards to body language.

Joseph took me to our cell where I was greeted by John frantically running around and putting stuff into the centre of his sheet on the bed.

'What's a matter with you guys?'

'Alan the guards are moving us into a dormitory,' barked John.

'What with other guys?'

'Er yes with other guys,' retorted John sarcastically.

'Yup it looks like they are moving some us Europeans to the Spanish dormitory,' Joseph yelped.

'Spanish dormitory,' I said stumped. 'Oh man!'

'Yeah I know it sucks but come on Alan pack your things like me and Joseph. Cos' if you don't the guards will. And if they find any drugs or money they will keep it.'

With that I jumped to it doing exactly the same as Joseph and John. There was no way they were getting my lumps of hash off me or my money. I was surprised we didn't bump into each once as we ran around the room picking up our own stuff. It took only a few minutes for me to bundle my stuff in the sheet and roll it up. We all didn't really have much in the way of belongings anyway. John and Joseph finished too and sat by their crumpled sheets looking concerned. A silence dawned as we awaited the guards.

'Are you sure Joseph they are moving us too?'

'Yeah one of the boys told me your name was mentioned so presumably they also want me and John too.'

'Well if they don't want us we could always trade beds with some of the Spanish to join you.'

'Awwww Joseph you don't want to be separated from me,' I said jokingly trying to lighten the mood.

'Shut up Alan!' Joseph snapped

'Make it noted I only stick with you for your money and hash,' said John

I didn't take his comment to heart as I knew it wasn't the whole truth. Sure I knew John and Joseph did like the fact I had a bit of money and a constant supply hash but I also knew they both liked me too. Plus they probably liked me as in this place you had to have a better the devil you know philosophy. Especially as the Europeans were a minority in this mainly Spanish hell hole.

Then after a few minutes of silence two uniformed men stormed into the room. We all immediately stood to attention gripping tight out sheets filled with our meagre belongings. The bigger taller Spic guard with very dark brown hair and eyes scowled at us. He looked very annoyed. Probably at the fact he didn't get to drag us out of bed or scatter our stuff on the floor. He did though get some enjoyment as he overturned each of our beds and chucked the mattresses on the floor. With his baton he prodded and poked my bed frame and the frame for the bunks as if he was looking for something. Once he was satisfied there was nothing to be found but dust and crumbs of rust, he looked at each one of us with another scowl. Although a little unnerved about what he was planning I stared back concentrating on trying to fix a nonchalant stare. I wasn't showing any emotion to this fucker! He seemed annoyed at my face and turned his attention to Joseph. Joseph displayed a wide eyed shocked expression which seemed to please him as his eyes narrowed and a grin appeared.

Then without warning he grunted in Spanish and pulled Joseph's arm flinging him to the door way encouraging him to drag his sheet along the floor. Then the other guard looked at John and me, with his hands he jerked them back and fore signalling to leave immediately. We both promptly obeyed and with bulging sheets followed him outside to the corridor where other Europeans had been herded up. The guards pushed through to the front of the crowd and then beckoned us to follow, which we did so like sheep. They took us to a dormitory, which they referred to as brigada, on the first floor. When I got to the room I was amazed at the size after sharing such a tiny cell. However there was not much free space as around thirty or so beds littered the room. After looking around I could see over half the beds were already occupied by Spanish bodies. They stared on at the eleven of us Europeans as we looked around dumbfounded at our new surroundings. Out of confusion I just blankly looked around wondering what to do. Looking at the ten others they did the same. We were all shell shocked.

I was the first of the Europeans to walk around the room. I looked back and still none of the rest had moved. I decided to seize my opportunity and check out the best bed. I examined a few but as I did the other Europeans cottoned on to what I was doing and also made a move to find a bed. Feeling pressured I picked the best bed out of the four I had examined.

I say best bed but what I meant was the bed which frame had the least rust and the mattress which had the fewest stains. With my new bed chosen I lay in it breaking it in and starting the foundation of my body groove. The pillow was quite thin and lumpy so I put my arms under my head with one hand on top of another. I stared at the ceiling alone with my thoughts. I was still conscious of the others in the room as I could hear a slight hum as the Europeans were now talking. They were probably questioning about the change of circumstance. I kept out of conversation as I couldn't be arsed to talk or listen. I was too pissed off. Being in a cell with two guys was crap but now with around thirty would be especially crap. Why couldn't I be on my own! Why did they put me in here? Then as I looked around a possible answer dawned on me. The guards could have put us in here because of what Dominic and I had done. Did they think all of us Europeans would cause trouble sooner rather than later and thought it would be better to keep us cooped up in one room? Did they want to localise 'us' the problem. Maybe that's why they kept some Spanish in there so they could keep an eye on us. The Spanish were infamous for snitching. The other Europeans used to joke they found dobbing on people easier than breathing, if it meant a comfortable life for them with the guards. They would even grass on each other.

After the first initial awkwardness the atmosphere then changed to a sort of party vibe amongst the Europeans. I liked this! Instead of going down in the dumps we fucking decided to make the most of it. Feeling sociable I decided to get to know each of the Europeans I was sharing with, well at least their names and country of origin. In the room we had two French men Joseph Toquec and Gert Twingelstein, two Germans, Bernard Michel and Volker Wabmann, two Swiss guys, one Yugoslavian Omahen Miso and one Dain Lennard Nielson. Now all I had to do was remember their names. I wonder if I could get a diary to write stuff like this down. It then dawned on me I could ask my Mam in a letter to send one.

The Spanish huddled content chatting whilst we laughed and joked sharing out bottles of beer and spliffs. The atmosphere was so lively every now and again I would forget I was in prison, but rather in a strange party full of dirty looking men with a variety of foreign accents. Maybe it wouldn't be so bad sharing with so many men. Despite having less or no moments to myself the conversation would never be dry. Plus I could bow out of conversation a little more with Joseph and John as they had more people to blag now.

The party atmosphere carried on until the early hours of the morning. I don't think the Spanish were so keen on our late night rowdiness though as we could hear them grumbling under their sheets. Then when we really started to take the piss as a few started to get argumentative and shouted. We then decided to call it a day and go to sleep. I amazed myself at how quickly and soundly I went off to sleep, despite being in a strange room with so many other men. I think the alcohol and blow definitely helped.

The morning brought a large headache which was exacerbated by the immense light that shone through the cell window. My throat also felt dry and sore. I had just got myself better from being ill and now I inflict this on myself. I looked at my watch and it was 10 o'clock. Dangling my feet over the bed onto the cold floor I held my head my hands caressing my temples. With a deep sigh I lifted my hung over body off the bed and went to the economato to buy some much needed water.

With a deep breath I downed two bottles of water in extreme thirst. The water felt so nice in my mouth as it hydrated my rough tongue but it angered my sickly stomach as it sloshed around. I stood still a while in order to keep the water down as I felt a bit nauseous. Then I was struck by tirade of hiccups. With both hands I covered my mouth hating each time my sternum jolted. Before I could indulge in self-pity a guard came along and called me to the office. Trying to hold my breath I walked with him to the Centro. I was asked to wait outside as he searched for something in the office.

In order to take my mind off my hiccups and queasiness I looked around the big open space in front of the Centro. It was such a waste of a room. This could have been utilised for something. I examined the walls and noticed three lines were marked out along it. I had never noticed these before. Screwing my eyes up I looked deeper at the lines pondering as to what they were for. I wonder if they were used for some sort of game.

Then my attention was brought back to the guard who had returned back with a piece of paper in one hand and a pen in the other. With the paper he thrust it in my face. Confused I grabbed the sheet and had a look. It was all in Spanish but luckily I had seen this type of slip before. I knew it was something to do with the visits. With my finger I scanned each line of Spanish on the sheet hoping to see a word I recognised. The concentration from doing this made my headache feel ten times as worse but I soldiered on. About mid-way down I finally stumbled across three names I recognised. Oh my god! The names on the visit slip were that of Ahmed, Mort and Troy.

I looked up to the guard who returned a bored look whilst slapping a pen into my hand. Then with a huff he pointed to a line where I had to sign. Immediately I scribbled away and signed for the visit to take place. With nervous excitement I hurried back to my cell and lay on the bed. In that moment I instantly forgot I had a raging hang over John was in the next bed reading a book I had given him to read.

I put my head in my hands rubbing my face up and down trying to take in the fact that Mort and Troy would visit. I thought Ahmed might have visited being local but I never envisaged Mort and Troy to come. Oh that would be fantastic to see them again and explain. Then my excitement was squashed as the ramification of the visit seeped in.

I can't see them. What if the guards or authorities link me to them? They could end up in here too. I mean Ahmed is alright he probably could get off with his contacts but Mort and Troy. What's to say they won't get them in here and throw away the key? I can't allow that. Oh god! Feeling stressed I chewed my thumb nail on my left hand.

'Alan you okay,' John said quietly as if to stop the Spaniards from being able to hear. Even though it didn't matter as none could probably speak English.

'Ermm I have a visit.'

'That's strange the consulate and lawyer have only just been.'

'No no. I have a visit from friends.'

'You have friends in Morocco,' he said surprised.

'Er yeah…. I mean… er no.'

'Well that's good isn't it?' he said examining my eyes in bewilderment.

'Er yeah….well…'

'What's the problem?'

'Well what if the guards connect us?'

'What do you mean?'

'Well they put me in here without much questions asked. What's to say they won't do the same with them?'

'Well that's not strictly true Alan. You did have kilos upon kilos of hashish on you too.'

'Yeah I know but you know what I mean.'

'Well turn them away.'

'I can't! Two of them have come from London.'

'Wow they are coming all the way from London,' he shouted. 'Who are they?'

'Just friends,' I whispered.

'I mean. I can't not see them after they have travelled all that way. Plus I need to convince them to give me money in order to reduce my sentence.'

'Oh I see friends hey,' said John. I imagined pound signs flashing in his eyes as he looked at me. I mean he knew I had a bit of money but this little tit bit of information also informed him I have important wealthy friends too.

'I knew it,' John shouted.

'What?'

'I knew you weren't innocent,' he said slapping the book shut in his hands.

'I am innocent,' I said playfully

'Yeah yeah.'

'John I am innocent and that's the story I am sticking too.'

John averted his eye contact and fumbled through the pages to get back to where he was in the book. He shook his head whilst smiling to himself. He was obviously infected by my exciting news of visitors and by the revelation that I wasn't innocent. I didn't care he knew. All I was worried about was Troy and Mort. Then as I stared at John an idea materialised. I need not have to turn away my friends. More importantly I also need not visit them myself.

'John?' I said as if asking a question.

'Yes,' he said elongating the word as if worried about my question but whilst not taking his eyes from my book.

'Can you do me a favour?'

'Depends.'

'Depends on what?'

'What it is and what I get in return.'

'Were mates aren't we?'

'Forget it Alan if there is nothing in it for me I am not doing it.'

'Can you go on the visit for me?'

'What?' John shrieked as he lifted his attention from the book and stared on at me.

'Can you see my friends for me and pass on a message?'

'You sort me with a few bottles of beer and I will think about it.'

'I ain't fucking buying you any beers unless you say yes and do it.'

'I want eight beers.'

'I will give you four'

'Six.'

'Five.'

'Done!' I said shaking his hand.

'So what's the message?'

'Right.'

I went on to explain about what I wanted him to say. I told him to tell them that I was okay and that I had told the authorities I was innocent. I wanted him to state to them I was protecting them by sending him on the visit. I wanted them to know I didn't want them linked with me just in case they pulled them in for questioning. Or like me just simply dumped into a cell. I also told him to ask about the money I needed and that they needed to give it to Peter Price via Phillip Llewellyn.

As I explained about the visit John smiled. Although he didn't say I could tell by the sparkle in his eyes he was excited to go on a visit with my friends the next day. I suppose it would be nice to have visitors. I mean we did get to see Biggy and Malero but I didn't consider these visitors. They didn't give me a taste of the outside world or alleviate any worries. They simply just depressed me and informed me on ways of how they could shaft me. After our conversation John went back to reading my book.

I suppose now I needed to keep the promise with myself and write a letter to Mam and the family. I now knew Troy and Mort wanted contact and hopefully wanted to help me financially. So I could give her some positive information and say we were looking at a way to getting my sentence reduced. Unlike the letter to Phillip the letter to my Mam didn't flow easily. I found it hard to put into words what had happened to me and where I was. With determination I trudged on and completed it within a few hours. In the letter I told her I was innocent. I thought it would be best as then the police wouldn't be banging her door wanting to question her.

I managed to complete the letter in a few hours. I hid the letter under my mattress as I was still not ready to give it to the guards. I just wanted confirmation from Troy and Mort first that they would help and provide the money before I sent it. Again I was procrastinating as I was not ready to send it off.

That night I couldn't sleep as I screwed myself up in stress after knowing that Ahmed, Troy and Mort would be in the same fucking building as me but I couldn't see them. I so wished to see a familiar friendly face. Out of anger I punched the bed and sighed.

Luckily everyone else was asleep and my actions weren't questioned. That was one thing in here. So much as a fucking sneeze and people were asking why you did it. Especially Joseph he was one of the worst for that. Always fussing.

The next day dragged on until we had the signal the visits were on. Outside the corridor I looked on at John and smiled as I shook his hands.

'You sure mate you don't want to see your friends yourself?'

'I want to John. I really do. But I can't. It might not be safe for them.'

'Ok well here goes. Just hope they don't fucking shoot the messenger.'

'Nah they won't. They're all nice guys.'

'Have fun!' I called out.

Whilst watching John walk off I imagined myself yanking his arm back and me going back instead. I put my arms behind my back and with my right arm grabbed tightly around my wrist as if to restrain myself just in case my body listened to my runaway thoughts. When John disappeared out of sight I went back to the patio and walked around in the sun kicking a stone around and around trying to take my mind off things. I didn't have to feel on guard or look around much as there weren't many people outside today. Most of them were on visits. Plus I didn't care as I felt a little down. One of the select few in the patio was old Wolfy. I felt better when I looked at him. It could have been worse. I could have lost my mind, have no friends and be visited by no-one. Mind there is time for that to happen. I wonder what crazy fucked up clothing I will wear if I lose it in this place.

The hour of visiting time dragged on so slow. I couldn't wait for it to be over and for John to inform me of how they all were and more importantly if they would help. I looked at my watch and finally it was time for John to be back. However as I waited and waited I couldn't see him. Fucking hell come on John!

Then eventually John came into view. I watched on as he sauntered towards me with a massive smile. Oh I could have swung for the bastard. Despite the fact it was my idea for him to go on the visit I still blamed him for taking my place. I knew I was being irrational but I hated him for having fun with my friends. I shook my head trying to gain composure and create an artificial breeze in the humid air. Come on Alan cool it.

John with his index finger signalled me to leave the patio. I nodded and walked over. In hushed tones John told me to walk with him back to the dormitory where there were less people to hear. Thankfully in the dormitory there were no Europeans around just a few Spaniards having siestas on their beds.

'So how did it go?'

'Yeah Alan all's good. They want to help you and are willing to give you the money as and when.'

'Ahhh good,' I said relieved.

'You told them how to send it?'

'Yeah yeah. They already knew that anyways from your letter.'

'So how did they seem? Were they okay?'

'Yeah well they were shocked at first when they saw my ugly mug instead of yours,' John chuckled.

'They looked really gutted.'

'You told them why I couldn't go.'

'Yeah, yeah I did.........I think they really respected yous for that.'

'Oh that's good,' I said with a big sigh of relief.

My angry feelings towards John subsided. What he departed about the conversation was music to my ears. Anything else I could find out was just a bonus. I was so glad they would give me the money. Although I was even more strangely made up by the fact they were appreciative I was protecting them. I mean I could have shopped them but I didn't. I didn't think it was fair as it wasn't their fault I was here. I chose to do the smuggling and I got caught. So I get punished. That's the way it is. Plus what's the point in dragging them into it. It wouldn't have helped my position here.

'Were they angry about me getting caught?'

'No man they weren't. If anything they seemed worried and a bit guilty yous' were taking all the flack like.'

I could have kissed John. His words made me feel so much better. I am glad Troy and Mort didn't see me as an idiot or a screw up.

After I had exhausted all possible questions I kept my promise to John and gave him the bottles of beer he asked for. I kept also the promise to myself and gave the guards my stamped letter for home. I walked slowly and hesitantly to the Centro and it took a while to knock on the door but I am glad I did. I felt so liberated handing over the letter to the guard. My family would now know in a few days. It would be out in the open. That's it. I hoped they hadn't realised I was missing and weren't worried.

17 REMOVED HIGHS

The morning air felt cooler on my face as I awoke. I don't know whether the temperature had really dropped or I was getting used to the heat of Morocco. I felt I could breathe better too, as if today the air wasn't as humid. It was still warm though as my body was a bath of sweat. My pants as per usual were glued to my crotch area and my balls uncomfortably stuck to my thigh. In fact the whole of my body felt moist causing my filthy stained sheet to stick to my torso and shins. I hated mornings, especially in this place.

I looked at my watch and it was only quarter to seven. I had to wait fifteen minutes for the guards to open up. Well in theory fifteen minutes. The guards greatly varied on their opening up times but one thing was for sure they never opened up early. I didn't mind waiting. I wasn't feeling energetic enough to get out of bed anyway. I wanted to lie in my pit a little longer. I would just have to forget about the pain in my football sized bladder.

To get comfortable I released my balls from my thigh allowing them freedom to swing and peeled the sheet from my wet body. As I wriggled around getting comfy, drips of sweat on the back of my neck were disturbed causing them to slide down my spine. This made the skin on the back of my neck feel incredibly itchy. Quickly with blunt nails I ferociously scratched and scratched numbing my tickling skin. To make sure the itching was under control I rubbed my back several times from side to side on the sheet.

Annoyed with feeling itchy and completely awake I sat up in bed and surveyed the room. All the Europeans and the majority of the Spanish were soundly asleep. The room would have been in complete silence if it wasn't for the orchestra of heavy breathers and snorers. Actually orchestra was not the right word as the noises were in no way tuneful. I wondered if I snored. I suppose I will never find out in here. It's not the sort of question you ask another bloke.

The couple of Spanish that were awake both wore the same miserable expression. One sat cross legged rocking slightly back and fore with his head in his hands. The other sat up but with arms folded. God glum looking sods! Things could be worse! I wonder what was going through their minds.

Before I could ponder as to what they were thinking, my thoughts were disturbed by shouts from the guards below. I then could hear the tinkling sound of keys and clanking as they opened of the gate at the top of the stairwell. Every morning it used to make me chuckle that they only locked this gate and not the door at the bottom of the steps. I suppose it was too much for them to unlock two gates every morning. What a bunch of lazy gits!

Well here we go! Time to get up! I hopped out of bed and jumped into a pair of shorts and slotted on my flip flops. Once dressed I suddenly realised that I was the first out of bed this morning. This had never happened before. Normally I was always one of the last to rise as I liked to lie in. Embracing this new experience I zipped out of the dormitory becoming also the first person out of the door.

I hot footed it to the patio to try and be the first out there too. When I got there I wasn't as there were already a few people milling about. Despite not being the first it felt nice still being one of only a few. Wolfy was one of the few already up and about before me. I couldn't help but stare at him with curious eyes at his beast like nature. He stood out even more today without the crowds around him. His eyes connected with mine before I could avert my gaze. I tried to pretend I was merely browsing around but this didn't work as he made a beeline towards me. I wonder what words of wisdom he has got to tell me today. Both excited and unnerved I stood still as he skulked across. I said hello but he did not return any words. Instead he looked at my neck, nodded and smiled. He seemed very pleased that my rash had gone. I thanked him for his advice but he still didn't talk. I repeated my thanks just in case he didn't hear the first time but again he didn't acknowledge what I had said. Instead he just looked up to the sky and walked away. If he was of sound mind I would have considered that as fucking rude but seen as its old Wolfy I let it go. He obviously didn't want to talk today.

After I completed a few circuits the patio became swarmed with people. The majority of the prison population had now woken up. I looked around for my ten European roommates. After a brief scan I saw a few dotted around here and there. I didn't go and chat to any of them. I couldn't be bothered too. I had done enough chatting and mucking about last night. In fact that is all we did every night since we were all moved in a week and a half ago. The constant partying never grew tiresome though as each one of the boys were characters in their own way and very interesting to talk to. I genuinely liked each and every one of them. There was not one bad egg I could see. Everyone else got on well with each other too which resulted in us becoming a tight group of friends.

Within this group there was a sort of division though. Bernard,

Omahen, Lennard, Gert and Daniel would mainly chat amongst themselves. Whilst I normally kept close to Ernst, John and Joseph as I already knew them and I was also started to get really pally with French Danny. He was such a nice guy to get on with. In stature he was quite imposing as he was tall and stocky, but this didn't match his gentle nature. He was not cocky or arrogant. He also loved the women. Towards the end of the night when he was drunk he would always talk about his conquests and sex. I knew he wasn't lying as just by his looks alone I reckon he could pull the girls. He was a blond muscular Adonis. Lucky fucker! I would never have gone out with him on the pull. I mean I was sandy blond in hair and muscular but not like his model status. I was shorter and a lot more of a rougher man to his gentle features.

I think the guards worried about how close we were all becoming as they started to pay keen attention to us if we huddled in large groups around the prison. The most obvious in their surveillance was the guard who protected the gate across the two patios as he would stare right through us if we talked. Before we moved into the dormitory he only appeared to watch the Moroccans, now it seemed we were the new subject of his gaze. The guards who we would shit up the most by being in large groups were the Centro guards too. It was by accident one morning we found this out when a group of five of us decided to all go together to check if there was any post. As we approached we noticed their eyes widen and were shocked by their instant presence at the door. When I had been to the office door on my own or with two or three others the guards were slow to react and would make us wait for their attention. But with five or more of us they were there straight away with our post. Again on my own or in a smaller group this would not happen and the guards could fumble about for ages. Once we noticed this we only went to the Centro in larger groups. I think they were worried we would start a riot when we congregated in higher numbers. Dominic really must have shaken them up.

It was funny really as the guards needn't have worried. None of the Europeans spoke of any plans to escape or form a riot. We never even brainstormed any ideas. The Europeans on the whole just tolerated now the shit hole that was Los Rosales. All eleven of us had been there for over a month and whether we liked it or not we were slowly getting used to the abysmal conditions. We now just got on with things the best we could.

Even on the fore front of my mind was not escape. I did have a few ideas floating around about how too but even I was busied by other things. Such as awaiting a letter from my family and awaiting the progress of Malero after giving him several thousand pounds. Even though it sickened me to say it I too like the other Europeans was also starting to tolerate life here. I always vowed in the beginning I would not stick for the disgusting conditions and the guard's insolence but what could I do. I think in a way it was healthy for me to just go with the flow. I don't think I could have carried on protesting. It would have been too tiring to keep on fighting everything. Now I decided to choose my battles carefully with the guards and battles which I could win.

After breakfast I decided to pay a visit to the Arab patio. I hadn't seen Palermo for a while but more importantly I was running low on hash. When I approached the gate the guard opened it up with no questions asked. Well this makes a change they normally make me wait a while and have to square it with someone in the patio. He also smiled in a strange way, as if he had gained the upper hand in some way. I ignored it and passed through.

Palermo seemed happy to see me and even happier when I ordered of an ounce of his Moroccan finest. Straight away he sorted me out and relieved me of a wad of notes. I put the honey block of resin in my pocket and stroked it affectionately against my thigh. My sweet saviour! Like last time Palermo asked me if I wanted to join him and his mates on a sebsis session. I replied with an enthusiastic yes as I was not one to turn down good quality kif, but this time I wasn't going to allow myself to go green. Concentrating hard and breathing deeply I managed to evade throwing a whitey. I felt pleased with myself. Even Palermo made a comment about how I looked better this time. I said that it was because I wasn't feeling ill anymore and my worms had gone. He nodded and smiled.

When conversation ran out and I felt I had outstayed my welcome I stood up to leave. Palermo patted my back out of warmth and smiled. I was just about to walk off when I felt pressure on my bladder and the instant urge to pee. I think I had smoked and chatted so much my bodily functions didn't have time to register, the kif had addled my brain

'Er Palermo before I go could I possibly go to your toilet?'

'Our toilet?' Palermo replied stunned.

'Er sorry Alan I don't think you can.'

'Please,' I begged jumping up and down in an animated fashion.

With a huff he replied. 'Let me see what I can do.'

I could have made it to my own patio toilet as I wasn't that desperate. I decided to put on such an act as I wanted to see what the fuss was about. Why were they preventing me from going? As with everything with life, if someone told me I can't do something or go somewhere, I would strive with everything in my power to do the opposite. The word can't simply wasn't in my vocabulary.

I watched on as they huddled in a group to talk about whether I could or could not use their toilet. I held my breath and danced around a little more stooping my body in order to evoke sympathy. They all just looked on with serious eyes and scratched their chins.

After a few minutes passed and when I was actually nearing the verge of peeing myself they eventually came across to give me the verdict. Thankfully they agreed for me to go but on the condition I would wash my hands before and after. Palmero said there was a bucket to the side which I needed to fill with water. Once I had finished the water should be put down the toilet and the bucket rinsed out. I realised then why they had made so much fuss. This clean attitude was because most of the Moroccans were Muslims, and to be a good Muslim you had to adhere to good personal hygiene and washing rituals. I nodded respectfully agreeing to their terms.

I then legged it with desperation across to their toilets. I quickly filled a bucket full of water and put it next to me. When I saw the toilet I looked at it in ore. The water was so clean. I could even see my own reflection in it. It was the same type of toilet we had, a simple hole in the floor job, but as holes in the floor go it was fucking marvellous. Not a piece of shit in sight and beautifully clean inside and out. It also smelled nice as if they put some sort of cleaning product in the water too. No wonder they didn't want me to see this. This was the Mecca of all toilets, well in Los Rosales prison anyway. How could I go to another toilet now after seeing this one? With great happiness I relieved myself. I even forced out a shit as I had to take advantage of such facilities. Another great thing was I could relax. I didn't have to worry about any other fucker walking in on me as the Arabs would wait for the person to come out first before going to the toilet. Also the same was with showering. They did this as Muslims as a part of their religion were private about showing parts of their body to one another. That was it, I needed to buy a djellaba and convert. This was such a better way of life.

When I came from the toilet, I thanked them for such an honour and touched my heart as I said so. I also told them I did exactly what they said in regards to cleaning myself and the bucket. I wanted them to know whilst in there I had been respectful. I also complimented them on the cleanliness of the toilets and explained how I wished the Spanish in my patio would do the same. They smiled and seemed to take pleasure out of my compliments. I can't fucking believe I am saying how much I loved their bog! Los Rosales prison has a lot to answer for.

Feeling happily relieved and lighter I headed back to my dirty world. My good fortune continued as the Centro guards finally had mail to give me today. This was my tenth consecutive visit in a row. When the guard handed me the letter I am sure he and all the other Centro guards breathed a sigh of relief knowing I would finally leave them alone for a few days.

I recognised the handwriting of the address as my Mams. I gulped hard and hesitated a little before I opened it. I was afraid at what the family had to say. Maybe they didn't believe I was innocent which was rightly so. Was the letter just going to be about how disappointed they were? I quickly opened it in a bid to stop my depressive thoughts. I need not have stammered as the letter was just what I needed. It was written by Mam and mainly asked about how I was and if I was coping in prison. She also said she believed in my innocence and said she was going to fight to help get me out. It astonished me she thought I wasn't guilty. All the times I had lied before. The fact I was lying now. I always appreciated the faith she had in me despite the fact she was wrong too. I never saw her as a fool for this but just a doting mother always wanting to believe the best in her son. God I was a bastard! In the envelope was also a seven year diary. This made me laugh. I couldn't believe she had given me something to highlight the possible years I would face. Only my Mam could be so unconsciously thoughtless. It was a good diary though. It was small enough to carry around with me but had a lot of pages for me to write in it.

That night I felt at peace. Everything was now out of my hands. My family knew and was protesting my innocence. Malero was having meetings with the judge trying to bargain on how many years they should sentence me. Well that's what he said he was doing, but I had to have a leap of faith on that one as I never saw any paperwork to verify this. But if this was just a con I would make it my life's work after prison to track the bastard down for the money. If I had no years taken off and I had wasted 1000's of pounds to that fucker he would have had a lot to worry about when I came out.

That night we had a party in the brigada, with a session of hash and alcohol. The hash was supplied by me which would gain a big cheer from all the lads. This made me feel like the big man and a sort of leader. Well I was the most rich and the eldest, so it was only fitting I should be. The alcohol was pooled together and we shared it out. It was a good night and I fell asleep in a drunken stoned slumber.

Before my head could wake up my arm was grabbed and a familiar voice whispered to me to get up whilst there was shouting in Spanish in the background. I could also hear furniture being dragged and people stomping around. So much noise going on! My head was groggy and my eyes were reluctant to open. I knew two things in this semi-conscious state; one that it was early in the fucking morning and two that I was going to have a stinker of a headache. I was then physically shaken. This greatly pissed me off. I quickly opened my eyes and then grabbed the perpetrator around the neck and squeezed.

It took a few seconds to recognise that the person who I about to strangle was Danny. He stared back in shock. I quickly retracted my hands from around his muscular neck and asked what the fuck was going on. Before he could explain a guard came over and shouted whilst pointing to the wall. I followed Danny to the wall and watched what he did as I didn't know what the guard had asked. I walked over to the wall and watched as he stood with feet and legs stretched. As I looked around the room nearly everyone was standing facing the wall. I stood there gob smacked still trying to fathom in my jangled brain as to what was going on. A guard then shouted in my direction. Okay Okay Pedro calm the fuck down I will stand at the wall like the rest.

With arms and leg stretched facing the dirty wall I listened to the guards turning everything over in the room. What the fuck are they looking for? I turned my head to the side to see what they were doing. I then went white as I saw then picking up my lovely hash from my pillow case and putting them into bags. This was a fucking drugs raid. Then about ten men down the line I could see a guard coming across doing a body search. Remembering I had a little lump of hash down my pants I looked around at all the guards. Picking a time when none of the guard's eyes were on me I quickly retrieved the lump and put it in my mouth under my tongue. The guards mustn't have seen as I had heard no shouting in my direction. Then it came to me to be frisked! He patted me down from the back and then turned me around to touch me up from the front. The guards hands reaching around my privates made me feel sick and angry. I wanted to break everyone bone in his body. Thankfully it didn't take too long and it wasn't invasive. Then once all of us were searched the guards called and everyone stepped away from the wall which I did too. I watched on as the last guard left the room with several bags. It disheartened me to see blocks and blocks of hash just swiped. Worryingly in another bag the guard carried was sharp knives and sticks. I know us Europeans didn't carry any weapons so these fucking must have come from the Spanish. Right that's one thing sorted I am definitely not having a fucking argument with them. I wasn't having one of those things stuck in me.

I couldn't believe the time when I looked at my watch. It was now only 6 am in the morning. I searched in my pillow case and couldn't find the rest of my ounce. My nicely fresh hash bought only yesterday had gone. I wonder if that fucking guard at the gate knew what I was doing and that is why he smiled at me. Well at least I had a little block left. I will just have to go and see the Moroccans for some more.

'Can you believe that?' Danny shouted.

'I know,' added John.

'Has anyone being left with any?'

All ten of the Europeans answered no in a low and somber voice.

'What nothing?'

Again there was a chorus of no's but this time not so enthusiastic.

John and Danny came over to sit on my bed. I spat out the little block I manage to salvage and show it them. I put my fingers to my lips and made a shush noise to halt them from shouting it out. I didn't want many people to know I had the last bit of hash. They smiled and looked happy I managed to hide it from the guards.

When I looked around everyone was glum. Heads were down and morale was low. The guards had beaten us down again. I can't believe they took our hash. What the fuck! I mean we were happy not harming anyone. This was our release to help us relax and fucking deal with the dire conditions and the way the guards treated us. Now they had taken our only means of escape. I wasn't having this. This is fucking not on! Exploding with hate I jumped up on the bed and called out to everyone.

'Look guys don't let those fucking guards win.'

'We shouldn't just take this lying down.'

'We need to go right now to the Centro and protest about this!'

'We can't they won't listen,' Joseph shouted

I stared at Joseph with impassioned eyes.

'Well we have to fucking try!'

I waited for support but no one piped up. Even my closest friends Danny and John didn't utter a word and instead just stared out into the distance.

'Fine! Well I am going to go myself!'

With that I quickly got dressed and picked up my bottle of water which had been strewn across the floor. Not looking behind I with purpose strutted out of the door down the steps and across the prison to the Centro. Once at the office I looked behind and could see I had a few followers in the shape of Joseph, John, and Danny. They didn't stand directly behind me but watched from a distance.

I knocked loudly on the door of the Centro and beamed a big friendly smile. Right the first fucking approach I will try is being Mr Nice. Probably won't fucking work but it was worth a try. The guards as usual took their time in answering the door. Knowing I couldn't speak Spanish the guard who answered the door didn't say a word and instead concentrated a disdainful look my way as he slurped on a hot cup of coffee.

'Er hi. Can I talk to you about hashish?' I said pointing table behind him.

He moved aside and pointed to the hash as if verifying I meant this. I answered him with a nod. He too nodded back. On the table were three piles. I recognised two of the piles. One of them was the Spanish's contribution of a few bits and blocks. In another pile was our stash and in the last pile, the biggest pile, there was quite a few kilos. I needed to find the owner of the third pile, he must have had fucking loads. I wondered if that was Cheno's stockpile. Before I could contemplate further the owner of the third pile the guard cleared his throat as if to hurry me.

'Er can I have some?' I said pointing to me and the hashish.

The guard looked astounded and then laughed.

'No no senior.'

'Er I need this to sleep. Please please. Just a little,' I pointed to the hashish and put my hands together begging. I then with my thumb and index finger closed them together leaving a little gap in a bid to show him I wanted a little piece and then mimicked the action for sleep.

The guard waved his free hand and shook his head. I kept asking and asking but each time I was greeted with a verbal no and a shake of the head. Then when he had enough of me he barked at me and slammed the door shut in my face. The door was only inches away from my nose. Feeling annoyed by his sheer rudeness I stood and stared at the guards scowling. Out of temper I kicked and punched the wall outside. I didn't look back to see the guards reaction. I didn't fucking care.

I walked past John, Joseph and Danny and didn't acknowledge them. I couldn't speak to them yet as I was consumed with so much rage. I heard them call me to come over and talk, but I carried on walking with fists clenched off to the patio. Once outside I walked a few circuits in order to make sense of what had just happened and to try and calm down. I really thought there was an unwritten rule with the guards that as long as we kept the hash out of sight, didn't smoke it in front of them and kept out of trouble we would be fine. Then they pull a fucking drug raid on us. I mean surely it was in their best interest for us to be chilled out rather than angry and in a mood to start a fucking riot. I don't know why I was shocked nothing in here made sense. I don't know why I even bothered trying to talk to them. They didn't fucking care. They probably enjoyed our misery.

Walking round didn't help as the heat of the sun increased the fiery rage contained within my blood. I could feel the veins bulging in my neck as I tensed my shoulders and calves. I bet the guards are fucking laughing at me and happy at pissing me off. I imagined the guards clutching their stomachs laughing whilst drinking coffee in the Centro. I could fucking kill every last fucking one of them. I then imagined myself smashing up the Centro and punching a few of the guards.

I hot footed it to the showers in order to calm down. I knew if I continued to wind myself up I would have gone to the Centro and started fighting. I took my T-shirt off but stayed in my shorts and switched on the icy cold water. Trying to stop my body for shivering took my mind off my violent thoughts. A riot or hitting out a prison guard was not going to solve anything. True it would make me feel better in the short term, but in the long run things would have been worse.

When my anger had subsided to safe levels where I wasn't about to do anything stupid I put back on my T-shirt and went for a walk around the patio again. My wet skin felt nice drying in the burning sun.

When I felt almost all dry I headed over to the Moroccan patio to score some more hashish. Like yesterday the guard smiled and let me in straight away. I could have fucking ripped out his eyes and shoved them down his throat. I felt sick to the stomach passing his greasy face.

The Arab world was like a mirror image of my boys this morning all glum and defeated. Even Palermo did not greet me with a smile when I sat next to him and said hi.

'What's wrong with everyone?'

'The guards came last night and took away our hashish and kif.'

'You too!'

It then dawned on me that the third pile must have been from the Moroccans. I figured they would have a few kilos.

'Well that's a shame I was going to ask if I can buy some more.'

I looked ahead feeling down. I wonder if I could sleep without it. I had smoked nearly every night. Would my body naturally allow me to lose consciousness of a few hours? I couldn't face not having sleep in here. Dreaming and not thinking was a pleasure I didn't want to live without.

'Alan!' snapped Palermo.

'Sorry yes,' I mumbled back after being distracted with my thoughts.

'I have a plan to get back our hash or at least some.'

'What's that?'

'Come back in a few days and you will see.'

'Well I hope you have more success than me. I tried to get some back from the guards today.'

'How?'

'I said I wanted some to help me sleep. Try and persuade them we would be rowdy in the nights if we didn't have any back. But they didn't listen.'

'I mean Palermo the truth is I think it does help me sleep so god knows how I will get through the next few days with this drought.'

'As I said come back in a few days hopefully I will have some for you.'

'What are you going to do?'

That night with a clear head I lay on my bed thinking whilst the other Europeans talked quietly. It felt so strange being so quiet. I missed the raised voices and laughter. With my middle finger on my right hand I stroked the little block of hash I had under the pillow. I wasn't going to have it tonight. I would savour it. This was now a precious commodity in here. I wasn't just going to squander it. As I rubbed it and then smelt its glorious smell I felt a bit ashamed of giving it so much power over me. Why were we acting so downtrodden! Hash and alcohol was not the only thing that united us. We also had common ground in hating the guards and taking the piss out of them and more importantly a strong group spirit. Feeling empowered after a moment of epiphany I called over Danny, John and Yan. They agreed with me that we shouldn't have let the guards win so easily. I also told them to truly be free of them and win we needed to escape. This part of my conversation didn't go down too well as everyone shrugged or spouted on why it was a bad idea. I hushed their concerns and told them that in a few days I was going to leave this place with them or without them. They probed me on the plan which I happily divulged. That night I did manage to sleep but it took much longer to drop. Throughout the night I was also disturbed several times from really loud snores.

The next day I felt really tired and walked around like a zombie for the most of it. My body being so limp and lifeless did provide a good cover for when I looked around to go through my escape plan. I couldn't see how the plan could go wrong as we only had one obstacle in our way from getting us out and that was the barred gate at the top of the steps leading to our dormitory. I mean thanks to the laziness of the guards we didn't have to think about the bottom gate as this was always left open. Plus the bars on the locked gate could be easily bent using wet towels or sheets. Then once these were bent we could get out to the patio, onto the wall and then hop over the boundary wall. Then the only other problem was the armed perimeter guards. But I am sure with luck and timing we could evade them. I mean we had to be thankful this prison didn't have towers too as we didn't have to think about guards seeing or shooting us from above

In the night John, Joseph, and Danny came over and said they would come on the escape with me. I was glad. On a practical level it meant I would have help in bending the bars as that would be a long laborious process. Taking it in turns to bend would make it quicker for us to create a hole and more time to run away once through. Plus it would be nice to have a bit of company with my life on the run.

I told them to tell the rest of the Europeans that in three nights we were gone so they could to think about coming. I also stressed that the plan of escape was not to leave the brigada walls. The Spanish were also to be avoided when discussing plans. I did not want them catching wind of this.

The next two days went quickly as I felt incredibly happy thinking about the escape. I couldn't see how we would fail. I was soon to be free.

Joseph, John, Danny and I over the next few days discussed what to do after running away. We all agreed to head to Algeria as they wouldn't go looking for us there. Once in Algeria I would ring Mort, Troy and Ahmed as I was sure between the three of them they could come up with a way out. I was thinking having false passports would be a good idea. Everyone agreed going to Algeria was our best option. Danny suggested we should try to swim as the police would probably assume we would escape on foot. I thought this was an excellent idea and agreed. I didn't like to tell him I was a very poor swimmer. I was rubbish at swimming in a shallow calm pool; god knows what I would be like in the sea and over a distance of around twenty miles or so. I suppose I would be swimming for my life so adrenalin hopefully would help me out there.

Tomorrow will be our last day here. Feeling nostalgic I decided to hop across to the Arab patio. I should go and see Palermo before I leave. I also wondered at what he did in order protest against the drug raid. When I met up with Palermo I was shocked to find him injured and in pain. I was even more stunned to find the reason was because he had been beaten up by the guards. Even Palermo a man in his eighties was not exempt from their fists.

Palermo had wound up the guards as he gave them an ultimatum. He told them if they did not give the hash back they would go on hunger strike. Obviously the guards said they wouldn't make a deal so the Arabs started the protest. Two days in they probably realised the seriousness of this as if any of the Moroccans had died from the strike the prison would have been in the papers. Possibly also causing a backlash with the Arab community in Ceuta against the Spanish. So in order to stop it they then brought Palermo to the office and beat the shit out of him. Palermo still urged his men to carry on the strike after his beating but the boys did not want any more harm to come to him.

I told Palermo not to lose heart and to continue fighting, but maybe in another way. I congratulated him on his idea of a hunger strike and told him he must have wound up the guards with what they did to him. He seemed very appreciative of my kind words as he smiled through his pain. I wanted so much to thank him and tell him this was our last goodbye but I wanted as few people to know about our escape as possible.

That night I divulged more about the plan of escape to the other six Europeans. I received a stunned silence when I told them. When I asked if they wanted to join us there was no answer? I told them if they stayed they were to keep our plans secret and not talk about it front of anyone else. I also asked if they were to stay behind tomorrow night that they'd keep the Spanish from immediately shouting for the guards. They nodded at this. I then returned back to sitting with John, Joseph and Danny.

That night whilst asleep I was gently nudged and felt a hand over my mouth. Shocked I instantly opened my eyes to find Bernard sat on my bed with his finger on his lips. I looked around at everyone sleep.

'Alan just to let you know all us Europeans are in for tomorrow,' he said with a smile.

'Good to know.'

18 OVER THE WALL

It was to be tonight we would put the escape plans into action. After speaking to all the ten boys that day in the patio each one was in on the escape. What courage they had to follow me especially after each one of them had heard the screams off Dominic. They had heard the horrific penalties the Spanish guards could inflict if we were to be caught. I was not going to let that happen though. We were going to be successful! My lads and I were going to be free of Los Rosales!

I was glad all ten lads were in. I didn't have to feel suspicious that any would grass me to the guards. Even if a few did bow out I don't think they would have told. Not like the Spic on my first escape. Even after I gave him all that fucking money! Oh well that was history now. Now for the future on the run.

The day dragged on as I paced and paced around with only the escape on my mind. To busy myself I stuffed myself with bits and bobs I had bought from the economato. I had biscuits, a tin of peaches and a few bottles of water. After tonight I didn't know where my next meal was coming from, so I ate and ate to store up energy. I even polished off all the three meals that were given to us courtesy of the prison kitchens. Despite the meals being especially rank today. So much for Joseph and his clean meals!

Feeling constantly paranoid everyone knew my plans I toured the whole prison eyeing up the guards and the Spanish prisoners. Thankfully they didn't look back with suspicious eyes. They all looked at me the same way they always had; very briefly and with contempt. I liked this. Obviously they weren't aware of what was going down which felt a real comfort.

To retain my energy after my last meal for the day I stood still for a while in the patio. To pass time I stared across to the Moroccans. Each one of them looked dejected which saddened me. They were obviously still mourning the loss of their hash and still upset at the brutal treatment Palermo suffered. Who could have guessed a frail old man was not exempt from the guard's violence. Dotted on the floor were a few men keeping busy cooking cous cous and other stuff in tins. I wished they had kept on with their hunger strike even after Palermo was beaten. Or at least thought of another way to aggravate the guards or bargain to get their hash back. It pained me to see how they just accepted the punishment from the guards. Come on guys fight back! I took courage in looking at my fellow men dotted around. Although they did not smile they all had their heads held high with hope. They could see through the concrete walls to the ocean again. Come on boys feel the freedom.

Finally I took great relief when my watch displayed six o'clock. We could now get things underway. I went around the Europeans telling them that one by one they should go up to the dormitory. I warned them they had to come alone or in small groups as we didn't want to make a mass exodus together. This would have alerted the guards or at least have got the Spanish prisoners sniffing.

Before I went up I made sure I collected the wet sheets from Franc and his brother. They did look a little confused as to why I didn't want them drying but thankfully they left me alone and did not question. They probably assumed I would hang them in my cell. Or did not give another thought as they were near to finishing for the day. I was going to miss those guys. I dallied with telling them but decided the less people who knew the better.

With rolled up wet sheets I came back into the dormitory. Already waiting in there were Danny and John. I dumped the sheets on the bed and folded them up as if I was laying them there ready to make my bed. I did this to disguise the fact the sheets were wet. I didn't want the Spanish to notice just yet and scupper our plans.

I sat on my bed avoiding the wet sheets. John and Danny came over and sat next to me. Slowly but surely after fifteen minutes had passed all eleven of us were in the dormitory. As I requested they either came in alone or in small groups. The only problem was that we were all in the dormitory with three quarters of an hour away from lock up time. This may look suss as normally almost everyone would stay outside as long as they could. Oh fuck it! Come on Alan it's okay the guards won't have noticed they would just herd us in and then fuck off. The Spanish may have noticed but I doubt they will have put two and two together.

We took advantage of the time alone before the Spanish arrived finalising the plan. It didn't really matter if we talked about the plan in front of the Spanish as I very much doubted they spoke any of our languages of English, French, Dutch and German but just to be on the safe side we didn't.

In our brief run over the plan I realised we hadn't talked about after getting over the wall. As we were a big group of eleven now, escaping meant that if we stuck together we would have been spotted more easily than if we split up on our own or in small groups. I quickly divulged this to the group. Luckily everyone agreed with me and thankfully we managed quickly to sort out groups. People mainly paired up by the countries they came from or who were geographically closer to. So Daniel was to go with Joseph and Gert as they were all French. Ernst was to go with the other Swiss guy. Omahen paired with Lennard as Yugoslavia and Denmark were the furthest countries away. In my group was to be Danny and John. Despite Danny coming from France he wanted to stick close to me. John grumbled that Danny should have joined the French group. Danny said he wanted to stick with me because of my contacts in Morocco. Before they got into an argument I divulged I couldn't swim and said to John I needed Danny in order to help me. Danny smiled appreciative of my support and was a little astounded as I only told him now that I wasn't a good swimmer.

Then the second thing we had to get out of the way was who was going to be the first man on the wall. Only Danny and I volunteered. It was not surprising other people didn't put their hands up as the first guy had the huge responsibility of securing the sheets and scouting out the armed perimeter guards, emphasis being on the armed part. After the coin flip it was decided the first guy was to be Danny. I wasn't relieved as I wouldn't have cared if it was me. My only concern was getting the fuck out of here. I think it was better for Danny to be the first on a practical level as he was much taller than I. He could have scaled up the wall far more easily and jumped off the other side with a lesser likelihood of injury.

Eventually lock up time dawned and our Spanish cell mates came in. As I turned to see them spill into the room I could see a few disconcerted faces. They were obviously taken aback at how we were all here, quiet and laying on our beds deep in thought. However when I looked around again a few moments later I received no stares and they were all busy chatting to one another. Great stuff!

When the Spanish had settled down we started to talk again.

'So what time do you reckon we start?' asked Danny.

'Not yet. We need to allow the Centro guards a bit of time to get drunk and take their mind off their jobs.'

'That should be about now,' laughed John.

'I reckon we should start in an hour as it will take a while to the bend the bars.'

'Then it should be about nine o'clock.'

'The only big thing we needed to worry about is whether the perimeter guards have their eyes off the ball too,' retorted John.

'Let's pray they do,' said Danny with a grave expression.

After an hour and half we heard the guards laughing and clinking bottles. They were in the party mood. Each one of us looked at each other and nodded. We were all thinking the same. Now was the time to start. I handed the wet towels to Danny and slapped him on the shoulder signalling to go downstairs. Once all the Europeans left the room I pointed at all the Spanish. I ushered a shush whilst putting my index finger to my lips. Then with my index finger I stroked it quickly across my neck imitating a knife. I then growled in English and swung fists in the air a few times. I hoped they got the point. They looked annoyed but did not utter a word as they continued with their conversation whilst tucked up in their beds.

As I stared at my fellow Spanish cell mates a little while longer I couldn't believe how they didn't want in. Didn't they want to escape the horrendous conditions too? Danny told me it was because in their society they expected it. Unlike us Europeans we chose to get into smuggling and from that we earned big money. The majority of the Spanish here was poor and committed their crimes more out of survival than to make masses of money. They were an uneducated under class who were given no support by the government and hidden away in the bad areas of Spain. To live and eat they needed to steal. It was even possible this stinking prison was even better than their homes back in Spain. Poor bastards if that was true.

After quietly trotting down the stairs I could see the boys had got to work bending the bars. Good stuff! These bars were the only thing blocking us from getting out.

Like I explained they had wrapped them around and wound and wound the wet sheets. We had sourced a chair leg which we also wrapped up in the wet sheets. We used the leg as a sort of lever. Everyone took turns and with zest kept winding and pulling. At first it was disheartening as it didn't look as if the bars with bending. Each time somebody took the reigns they twisted and twisted with all their might but nothing was noticeably happening. Another frustrating part of the twisting was that we could not make any noises. I found it especially hard to hold my breath and suppress the groans I wanted to make exuding the effort I was putting in. Thankfully after half an hour or so the fruits of our labour were starting to become noticeable as on the left bar a bend occurred for us to exploit. Then after a few minutes a bend occurred on the right bar we wrapped with sheets. Despite the progress the winding seemed never ending.

Nervously I looked at my watch which said ten o'clock. We were an hour behind schedule. However it didn't matter if we went through around eleven. We still would have around eight hours on the run until the guards realised we were missing. That's if one of the Spanish prisoners didn't squeal on us before morning. I dallied on tying them all to the bed and putting gags on their mouths, but this would have taken too much time. Plus it may not have worked as there were more of them than us, they may have overpowered us.

At a quarter to eleven Bernard poked me in the arm and pointed at the bars. I looked and I could see we were on our way to making a big enough hole. He smiled, put his thumbs up and nodded suggesting the hole was big enough.

'You sure it's big enough,' I whispered.

'Yeah I think is.'

I wasn't so sure. I was probably one of the most slimmest and shortest guys in here and even I was looking at it as an obstacle. God knows what the bigger guys must have been feeling. Danny alone was around six foot and forty inches wide in the chest area.

After speaking to the other boys they all agreed it was wide enough. So without another thought I jumped up and squeezed myself through. It wasn't easy but I did manage to get through without being stuck. A few of the smaller boys followed me and they too found it just manageable. Then the larger lads were left behind. Before each one approached the opening they looked as if they were psyching themselves up and imagining the hole to be bigger. Each one struggled painfully and slowly through. If it wasn't such a tense moment I would have laughed heartily at all the larger men squeezing through with pained expressions as they tried to invert their stomachs by breathing in.

Thankfully though every one of the boys managed to contort their body in order to get through. Then in a line we all lightly ran towards the patio, conscious of making as little sound as possible from our footsteps. In the patio we looked around and then ran to the wall and lined up. Danny was the first in line and I was second. I watched as he looked on in the dark patio and waited for him to make a move. He then cocked his head in the air as if listening out for any noise. All was silent.

I nudged Danny he looked back and nodded. Breathing in deeply I pointed upwards to give the signal all was well. Danny received it loud and clear as he nervously smiled and signalled for a bunk up. John and I grabbed Danny's muscular legs and pushed him up. He clambered a little scuffing his shoes on the dusty wall but then regained his footing and got up. Everyone froze and all cocked their heads to the sides listening for any sounds. Thankfully there was none. We hadn't disturbed the guards.

Once up Danny crouched low grabbing onto the side of the wall nearest us. He smiled widely as if disbelieving at where he was and what he was doing. I beamed a supportive grin back. Seeing Danny up there made me so happy. The journey was nearly over. I could forget Morocco and Los Rosales. I would be free soon. I wondered what life on the run would be like.

Danny then shuffled around on his knees and looked at what was over the other side of the wall. He was obviously looking out for the armed perimeter guards. From below I stared at the back of his head waiting for him to turn and signal for the fashioned rope we had made out of sheets. Come on Danny I can't stay in this place a moment longer. To dampen down my impatience I looked at my sheet and visualised over and over how I was going to swing it up and get it to him in one throw. I flicked my stare up to Danny and back to the sheet over and over. Eventually Danny turned back shuffling on his knees again and smiled with thumbs up. He then pushed up with his ankles and crouched so his elbows were at the same height as his knees getting ready to catch the twisted up sheets. I looked down at the twisted sheets and swung it back and fore a few times gaining courage to throw. Come on Alan you can do this!

I swung back the twisted sheets for the last time but before I could swing it upwards I was disturbed by the sound of gun shots being fired. In shock I dropped our fashioned rope. I looked around and listened to try and find out where the shots were coming from. I realised then the bullets were aimed at the wall. It sounded like a machine gun. I couldn't believe at how so many bullets were being sprayed about. Scared I whipped my head back up at Danny. His face turned to horror as a deluge of bullets poured down on him. I watched as he fell to his knees and turned in every direction like a trapped animal. Some of the bullets bounced off the wall and caused dust to spew out from different sections of the wall. Then in amidst the firing Danny yelled something inaudible and fell out of sight.

'Danny,' I whispered.

'Danny,' I whispered a bit louder.

I stood up on tip toes trying to look to see if he was still up there on the wall. But I couldn't see him. He must have fallen off as he was shot. Poor Danny!

As I looked around at the nine other Europeans each stood still in fear. Some hyperventilated a little; others put their hands behind their necks as if they were stumped at what to do next. John after only a few seconds of deliberating was the first to react and ran full speed back towards the dormitory. Not long after everyone followed. I was the last to leave. I hung around a few seconds more as I felt compelled to stare at the wall. My stomach tensed hard as I wished with all my might Danny would stand back up and jump back down on our side of the wall. But he didn't. Then I took my cue to leave when I heard voices from the other side. It sounded like the guards. I imagined them assessing the damage to Danny as he lay in a pool of blood. I hope to god he was alive. I hope they will do the decent thing and take him to hospital if it's bad. Oh god I hope he's alright. Even if he didn't get shot it was a pretty big fall to the floor as the wall was at least sixteen foot in height, possibly more.

Once back at the stretched barred gate I caught up with a few of the bigger boys going through. Unlike last time the boys flew through making mincemeat of the bars despite the small opening. What took us a good half an hour before getting through now only took a few minutes. On my turn it was the same. I glided straight through. My body didn't even touch the sides. Full of adrenalin I ran towards the brigade, I nearly tripped over my own feet going so fast. Without slowing down I launched myself into the air and onto my bed. I lay on the bed searching for a sheet to cover me up with. It then dawned on me my sheet was downstairs and wound as rope for escaping. Oh shit! All I could do was lay there and await the fury.

Seconds later we could hear the guards stomping up the stairs. I looked around at all the Europeans. All had closed their eyes and were pretending to be asleep. I then did the same. As the guards entered the room I could smell the alcohol on their breath and hear there huffs from running upstairs. I tried to calm my heavy breathing from all the running and scrunched up my eyes.

'Levantarse!' screamed a guard as I heard him strike his baton against the wall.

What the fuck does that mean! I was guessing it meant wake up but I decided to stay put until I could hear the others moving.

'Levantarse!' he shouted again.

I then heard yelps from some of the Spanish prisoners. When I opened my eyes and turned I could see the guards were going around the Spanish violently ripping off the sheets and dragging them out of their beds. I saw one of the prisoners being squeezed around the biceps and then flung across the room. Boy he flew. A Spanish guy a few beds down from me got out willingly and folded his arms looking down to the floor. He stroked his arms in a bid to get warm as he was only standing there in a pair of off white Y-fronts.

Quickly the guards were making progress towards the European part of the room. I watched on as our guys were flung out of bed too. It was obvious we were the escapees as all of us were fully dressed. Most of us including me still had shoes on as we didn't have enough time to fling them off. A guard pointed to Danny's empty bed. Before the guards got to me I decided to get out of bed on my own accord. I lifted my head up high and put my hands in the air. Despite showing cooperation a guard still grabbed me around my waist and flung me towards the direction of the door. Not wanting to fall I tensed my body and pushed down my weight to my feet to steady myself. Then the guard ushered me outside along with the rest of the prisoners.

'Patio!' exclaimed one of the guards as he banged his baton on the wall a second time.

As I passed the barred gate I felt the stretched bars and sighed. We were so close. A guard saw me do this and clubbed me in the kidneys to move. I looked back and scowled but proceeded forward.

On the way down the steps there was quite a bit of pushing and shoving from the guards. My heart thudded with each step. Once outside I could see the guards had already started punishing. The Spanish were the first to get it. I saw groups and groups of them being hit over and over by the guards as they shivered in just their pants. I walked past a group of three being hit by the same guard. From the force of the hits made one of the Spanish prisoners fall into my path and with leg raised I accidentally tripped him up. I looked down and was shocked by the fear on his face. Then all of sudden he started screeching in Spanish as he sat cross legged on the floor at my feet. Obviously he was begging them to stop. The guard smiled as he bent over to look at the snivelling pitiful man. I shook my head as I rushed past. Then in that split second the man flashed his eyes when he saw me and stood bolt upright. With his lips still trembling he pointed at me and started shouting in Spanish. Due to the shouting the guards stopped dragging him and pushed me in front of the man. Again he pointed and shouted. I could feel his impassioned spit as he sprayed it over my face. Then the other Spanish cell mates joined in making a commotion. Bastards! It was obvious they were ratting me out. I also heard some of them say 'cappo' over and over. I knew what that meant. That meant leader. What a bunch of snitches!

I was then dragged over to an open bit of space on the patio. The guard who dragged me pulled his baton out and smiled. He then also signalled two other guards with his free hand to join him. The guard with the baton moved towards me lifting it in the air ready to strike. I put my hands in the air and moved away but as I did another guard moved in. Again I moved from the second guard until a third came and blocked my way. They had edged in from all directions. I felt completely surrounded. Breathing in deeply I kept turning around and around in circles looking for a way out but there was none. As I turned around and around I noticed each had a weapon and were poised to use them. Two had batons and one had a rifle turned the opposite way. Then without warning the first hit came in and someone had struck me hard on the back. Then I felt another hit to my bicep. Then I watched as the guard with the rifle butt came in and cracked me in the ribs. After that I couldn't decipher where the hits were coming from as they rained upon me one after the other. Over and over. Time moved slowly as my body went into shock. I tried to stay standing but eventually the hits and punches made me dizzy and unbalanced. Then one of the guards shoved me to the ground. A little dazed and numb I was about to get up when I heard snarling in my left ear. Getting into the fetal position I turned my head around to look at where the noise was coming from. Looking up I could see there was a salivating Alsatian dog only inches away from my face. I could smell its fishy dog breath as he panted and growled. The dog pulled and pulled trying to free himself from the tight reign of the guard. In fright I looked up at the dog and then to the guards who all stared down and smiled. They must have brought the dog in order to keep me still whilst they pounded me. I must have been far too wriggly for their liking. I wasn't going to just take it like the Spanish did!

They looked down at me for a while. Why have they stopped? What the fuck is going on? Come on you fuckers what are you waiting for? Then in the distance I could hear the clank of a heavy chain being dragged. The clanking got louder until I could see where it was coming from. Standing in front of me was a guard with a huge metal chain. I recognised the guard as the director's son. Cheno had pointed him out to me once before. I also recognised the chain too. It was the chain they put on the big prison doors to lock them up. Dangling at the end was a huge fuck off padlock. When I looked at the director's son's face as he swung the chain it sent shivers down my spine. He looked more unhinged than the Wolf Man. He was pure evil in human form.

Then without warning the beating started up again. However this time they had a new weapon of a chain which they could whip me with. The padlock smashing me in the ribs over and over was the worst pain I had ever experienced. My lungs and ribs felt crushed. I wanted to be sick but all I could do was cover my arms over where they struck in a bid to protect. Each part of my body throbbed as it was pummelled and pummelled. I could hear the guards groaning after exerting themselves swinging in and swinging in.

My mouth filled with blood as I bit my lip from one of the hits. When will it stop! I couldn't take anymore. In the distance I could hear the yelps of the other prisoners who were being beaten at the same time as me. I could also hear muffled shouting. Then the shouting became clearer and I could tell it was coming from John. I concentrated mid hit at what he had to say.

'Alan scream. Scream Alan they won't stop. Scream Alan or they will kill you!'

After his shouts I could hear groans as if he had being hit badly. He was probably being hit harder for shouting. Then I heard him scream and decided to follow suit. At first I couldn't as I found it hard to catch my breath amidst the hits. I tried over and over to summon up a noise but nothing would come out. It was only when I received another blow by the padlock to my shattered ribs my vocal chords woke up and sprang into action. I screamed and screamed. Thankfully John was right the hits decreased and eventually the beating did stop. I wonder what they would have done if I hadn't screamed. I wondered how long they would they have carried on for.

Free from the hits my pain receptors kicked in at full force as my whole body felt like one throb. I wished for my numbness to return. After the guards caught their breath, two of them grabbed me by the wrists and yanked me up. I groaned in pain but made sure I stayed standing. The director's son smiled manically seeming pleased he had spilt my blood. I wanted so much to nut him in the face the cocky little prick.

I tried to catch my breath but it felt like knives were piercing my lung with each breath. Each time my ribcage lifted I could feel and hear the bones cracking. I looked around and most of the prisoners had gone.

Ahead I could see a few of the Europeans being ushered out of the patio. I was to be the last man out.

Once out of the patio I was pushed along until I was in the space outside the Centro. All around were the rest of prisoners from my dormitory. Before I could look around and check on my fellow Europeans a guard shoved me to the wall. Once there he pointed. I stood still looking at the wall. Then I could hear him growl with annoyance as he kicked my legs inches apart and grabbed my arms to touch the wall. I looked back at the guard to see if I was doing it right. The guard scowled really screwing up his eyes and his mouth. With his baton he whacked the wall in anger. I looked at where he whacked and could see a line marked out on the wall. I quickly with my fingertips touched the line. Thankfully I did it right as the guard took a few steps back and stood at ease watching me. I breathed a shallow sigh of relief as I watched him hitting the baton in his open hands. The guard although Spanish did not look like the rest. He had striking gingery blonde hair and blue eyes but despite his looks his attitude was of a Spanish guard through and through. Bastard! I stared back at the lines I was touching. Well now I knew what these were for.

Behind me I could hear the guards shouting and rushed footsteps. I turned round my head slyly to see what was going on. I could see they were sending people back to the dormitory. I managed to pick out Jan and John. Thankfully they both looked okay as they skulked away. Then out of nowhere I felt a strike to my bollocks. It must have been the blond Spic from behind. He really clubbed me hard. In blinding pain I fell to the floor clutching my balls. I bit the side of mouth in order feel pain there instead. As I looked to the side I could see the guard smiling. With his stick he pointed at the wall and then to his eyes. Obviously he wanted me to keep my eyes forward. I fucking learnt the hard way. Thankfully he didn't grab me and he allowed me to clamber back myself and touch the line. I felt sick as vomit rose up from stomach into my mouth. When I got up with arms stretched on the wall he pointed upwards to another line. The fucker made me stretch further. The pain in my chest, my head, in fact my whole body was immense. I swallowed back down the vomit trying not to think about the sour acidic taste on my tongue.

After the strike to the balls I stayed with my head facing forward. With all my might I tried to keep my hands up in the air and not move my legs. I didn't want another strike there. I didn't want more pain. The stretching was hard though. All I wanted to do was drop to the floor in a heap. I wanted to escape my pain. I closed my eyes wishing they would take me somewhere so I could fall asleep or unconscious. If only I could have a joint now. That would have eased me. Not having to feel my body.

I stood concentrating my eyes forward trying not swoon. I could hear the guards taking the prisoners away one by one. Slowly the room became quiet as it was bereft of Spanish and European prisoners. Although I could not turn around to confirm this I sensed I was on my own as the room grew quiet. The only sound was of the guards talking. Oh fuck what are they planning? Oh god please not another kicking! I've had enough. Am I now going to be like Dominic? The new whipping boy the guards can have fun with every night. I wonder where they will put me.

I must have lost consciousness for a split second as my arms slid down the wall and my knees wobbled. Once I came back around I tried to clamber back up the wall. The blond guard hit me in the balls again. I clutched my groin blowing air through my gritted teeth. Oh the dull ache was unbearable. In my back I could feel the baton from the guard prodding me. Trying to stay calm I struggled back up stretching my arms and legs whilst looking forward.

The waiting of what was to happen next was agonising physically and mentally. I wished for fuck sake they'd get it over with. Maybe I should get my head in the way of one of their strikes. Being unconscious would have been so much bliss right now. Oh god what are they waiting for?

Then my thoughts were silenced by the sound of evil laughter. I could hear the guards talking and saying 'Cohones'. I wished they would get the punishment over and done with. More talking in Spanish ensued but I could not decipher any words. Oh fuck here we go.

To the side of my head I felt the greasy hands of the blond Spic from behind. He yanked my head to look left. He then grabbed my dirty hair and pushed it forward.

'Mirar a su amigo,' he cackled.

When I looked I could not believe my eyes. It was Danny. He wanted me to watch as two guards dragged his lifeless body along the corridor. A lump caught in my throat as I looked at Danny's closed eyes and flailing body. The guard at the front of him was dragging him by the hair whilst the guard behind him loosely grabbed his ankles allowing his stomach to scrape the floor. Oh Danny! I wanted to feel angry about the way they were carrying him but all I could feel was sorrow and guilt. Following behind his body was a trail of blood. Oh sweet Jesus! Please pull through! I hoped to god they take you to a hospital. That's if… That's if he wasn't already dead. I hoped he was just unconscious. The pain in my body disappeared as I watched him pass. I shook my head as I couldn't believe what I was seeing. Oh god! The vomit from my stomach returned as my head felt light and dizzy. Then two guards grabbed an arm each and dragged me along another corridor. I didn't care and went with it as I wasn't in pain anymore. I felt numb and in a dreamlike state. It didn't feel real. I didn't want it to be real. Oh fuck what have I done! That should have been me. If I hadn't loss the toss that would have been me!

I was taken down steps I never knew existed before. It went to an underground level and to the bowels of Ceuta prison. The steps led to the outside and I was taken through a sort of courtyard, similar to the patio but a lot smaller. Then at the end of the small patio stood a room made of concrete blocks with a solid looking wooden door. The guards opened up the door and pointed inside. As I walked in the guards pulled at my clothes. I looked confused. The guards again tugged at my clothes ferociously and pointed to the floor. I looked at my clothes knowing full well he wanted me to strip. When he took out his baton I started to strip. Seeing the guards looking impatient I tried to undress as quickly as I could but it was hard as my injuries plagued me with pain as I twisted and moved. Also the blood from the deep cuts and tears in my skin had dripped and dried onto my clothing. I felt searing pain as I had to peel away the clothes causing my wounds to reopen and bleed again. It stung to separate skin from material. Once naked I stood cowering with my hands protecting my balls. Without taking his eyes off me the guard retrieved the pile of my clothes. He then withdrew his look as he prodded the pocket of my trousers. Oh shit! After a bit of rummaging he found my stash of cash. He waved the cash in my direction and smiled. The other guard then ushered me inside my new cell and then banged the door behind.

Feeling tired I explored around the dark room for a bed. Carefully I shuffled across the room to find a wall. Then I went around the room. After one complete circuit around the walls the only thing I found was a toilet or should I say hole in the floor. But I didn't need to feel that out as I could work out where it was from the almighty smell of shit. Then I went into the middle and walked around in circles. After I completed a few circles I was then back to touching a wall again. That's strange nothing got in my way. I then with my hands walked around the room waving my arm around in front. It then dawned on me I wasn't bumping into anything at all. That could mean only one thing, that there was nothing in here. No bed, no sink, no furniture. Just fuck all!

I breathed a shallow sigh clutching my ribs as I did so. Tired and aching I slowly bent down to sit on the floor. I nestled my naked bruised backside on the rough flag stoned floor and stretched out my crunchy bruised and battered legs. To ease the pain from my swollen throbbing testicles I opened my legs several inches apart. After examining my bollocks they felt twice the size as normal. I yelped in pain as I laid them back down. With my hand I reached out to the wall and then gently scooted over so I could lean my back onto it. Once I settled into position I breathed a sigh of relief as I could now relax. I was not going to move from this position until morning. Hopefully I will pass out from the pain soon.

Oh god poor Danny! Oh god! In anger I yelled out in frustration as loud as I could. This was returned by silence. Then as I remembered Danny's limp body I sobbed ferociously, as I cried so many strong emotions rushed through me. Amongst them I felt pain, sorrow, fear, loneliness and anger. I shook my head as I wiped away my wet eyes. Oh god! After the tears stopped I stared ahead not actually looking at anything and felt numb. My mind went blank. It was like as if someone had hollowed out my personality and thoughts just leaving an empty shell. Being disconnected from thinking my body went limp. I felt broken.

19 EMPTY DREAMS

Startled my eyes bolted open and I felt instantly awake. My diaphragm contracted as I gasped for breath. My body jolted as if I had been given an electric shock. I wasn't ready for this instant consciousness. Then with the click of a finger the pain of last night's injuries flooded back through my body and made me feel sick. Every part of my body felt bruised and stiff. The worst of the pain came from my smashed up ribs.

'Fuck! Fuck! Fuck!' I shouted in agony tensing my stomach.

To ease the pain in my chest I gently rested the palms on each side of my ribs and concentrated on taking slow shallow breaths. After relaxing my breathing the pain did subside but only served to draw attention to the pain in my back and ball sack. Both of which throbbed and felt swollen too.

When I touched my forehead it felt warm and clammy. The sun rays must have been beaming down on me for a while through the barred window. It wasn't that hot though, so it must have been early morning. Gauging the temperature and the position of the Sun, I would have guessed it had only just set which meant it was sometime before seven o'clock.

The illumination of light allowed me to have a proper look around my cell. It was how I imagined it from feeling around in the pitch black last night. Dark and completely fucking empty. Even the brightness of the North African sun could not make this room glow. The only thing the room did contain was stones. The uneven floor was littered with them of varying shapes and sizes.

I looked at the patch of floor next to me in order to size up where I needed to put my hand in order to lift my body to a standing position. I gritted my teeth and closed my eyes trying to push out thoughts of how painful it would be getting up.

Come on Alan you need to get up and start the old blood pumping around your body. This was true in particular to my arse cheeks and legs as they were completely dead. Not surprising after being in the same position for so long.

With a deep breath I put my right hand down on the floor and bent my left leg so my ankle was in line with my knee. On an internal count of three I leaned my body on my right hand and lifted my arse cheek off the floor. I only managed to lift myself an inch high until I dropped back down in sheer agony. The pain was unbearable. I thought breathing hurt. Fuck me moving around really fucking stung. My lips trembled as I recovered from the pain.

Come on Alan stop being a big wuss and get up. Suck it up!

Looking to the floor again I decided I would try a new approach. A better option would be to get on all fours and walk up the walls. That might help stop my rib cage from being twisted and moved around so much. So I lifted up my right knee to join my left in a bent position. I placed down my left hand onto the floor. Staring hard at the wall in front of me I did another internal count of three. I pushed down on my right hand and right foot and swung my body so I was on all fours.

'Ahhhhh! Fuck me! Fuck me! That bastard hurt! Ahhhhh! Jesus fucking Christ!' I yelled.

Come on Alan half way there. You can fucking do it! I scowled at the wall as if it was my nemesis. I then lifted my knees up and shuffled forward so my whole weight was on my ankles. I growled in order to concentrate on something other than the pain as I walked up the wall with my hands trying to keep my rib cage steady as I moved. Once standing I allowed my arms to be loose and rested my face on the wall trying to concentrate on keeping my breathing shallow.

'Phew! Come on Alan you have done it!' I said panting.

As the blood managed to flow again freely in my legs and bottom I was attacked by extreme case of pins and needles. Keeping my torso and hips still I wobbled my thighs and calves in order to encourage the circulation back. From moving around made my legs feel like they had been replaced with an oscillating group of pins that pricked intermittently and randomly at the surface of my skin. The pins and needles were uncomfortable but it was nothing compared with the pain from my injuries. In fact I almost welcomed it as aiding a bit of relief. This rush of feeling made my body feel alive and not broken.

Pushing my arms away from the wall I slowly straightened my body to a standing position and looked around the room. I then surveyed the damage to my body. I was shocked at the bruising. From the top of my chest all the way down to my balls was almost completely black. There were some small patches of my natural skin colour left but even these were interspersed with mottled dark purple marks. Jesus Christ! They had kicked, punched and whipped me into one bruise. No wonder all my ribs felt broken. It was because they probably were. My upper arms and thighs too were speckled with bruises but they really went to town on my torso. It looked like they had specifically targeted my ribs too. Looking at my hands, past my elbow and knees there were again very few bruises. From feeling my face this too felt pain free and untouched by clubs, chains, kicks and rifle butts. Sneaky bastards! They had purposely targeted parts of my body that were covered when I wore clothes. They didn't want my injuries where they could be seen. God knows why they fucking cared about this. I was in solitary confinement and in prison. Who the fuck did I have to show? Who was going to see into my window?

I walked over to the barred windows to see what view I had if any. Looking out I wasn't surprised. All I could see was a wall. The window was also quite high so I couldn't even see the ground. Just a fucking wall. In that moment I felt very claustrophobic and isolated.

The first two days in my solitary confinement cell dragged by. My waking hours were consumed with immense pain and boredom. The only distraction I had were when the guards came to see me. Each day they visited me four times. When the sun rose they would come to throw water over me and give me breakfast. In the midday sun when it was hottest they would bring my lunch. Then a little while after that they would come and take me to the Spanish patio for an hour to wander round. There was never anyone else in the patio though. They must have locked up the other boys for an hour whilst they let me have exercise. The Moroccans too in their patio were nowhere to be seen. Being outside was also the only time I was permitted to wear clothes. Each time they brought me back to my cell I was forced to remove them and leave them outside. God knows what fucking for. Possibly as punishment? Maybe they wanted to marvel at their patchwork of pain? Maybe they thought I would hang myself? Or possibly did they think I would make a weapon and try to conceal it? The latter was probably the most plausible answer behind the nakedness, considering how many people in this prison carried homemade weapons, especially the Spanish. Then on the last visit they would bring me my tea.

I also noticed with the guards visits they would always come in pairs. Fucking yellow bellied bastards! They must have feared I would attack them if they came on their own! Despite the fact I was naked, broken and battered. This really made me laugh. Though thinking about it they were probably right to have worried. I possibly would have fancied my chances with the one guard.

The third day started to pan out like the rest. Bucket wash, breakfast, and dinner. However on solitary exercise the atmosphere from the guards seemed different. I could sense they were apprehensive about something. Normally they would both relentlessly stare at me with a smug and relaxed expression whilst they chatted. Today though they seemed distracted and caught up with talking. They intermittently every few minutes would look at their watch. I decided to take advantage of them being distracted and went around collecting the shiny foil paper from the fag packets strewn on the floor. I pretended I was picking up the fag packets in a bid to find cigarettes. I didn't want them to see me just in case they took them off me. I wanted the shiny paper in order to make chess pieces with. I thought by playing chess with myself I could take my mind off things and not be so fucking bored. Maybe I could come up with some strategies to beat Ernst when I am later released back in the mainstream prison. That's if I am ever allowed to go back. Or not disposed of like Dominic.

When I was outside I would hear voices coming from inside the prison. I could never distinguish the voices but I would still listen hard to see if I could hear my lads. I never did though. What I would have given to talk to them again! What I would have given to see Danny!

Then out of nowhere another screw appeared. He yelled in Spanish to the other two guards. They nodded and walked over to me. They both hooked their arms around my biceps, locking my elbows. I was then dragged to the direction of the gate. I tried to walk at the same speed as the guards whilst trying not to move my torso in a bid to avoid twisting or contorting my body and causing pain. It didn't work my ribs were moved around causing them to throb and ache. Although in agony I bit my lip in order to suppress any groans. I wasn't going to fucking give them the pleasure of knowing I was in pain.

Instead of taking me back to the underground cell they took through the Centro office and along the corridor to the other offices based at the front of the prison. Then once past these I was taken to the visiting room and shoved inside. I stumbled forward holding onto my ribs. I gritted my teeth and sucked in air in a bid to suppress a groan. Come on Alan don't you fucking yell. Keep the fucker in. I turned around and stared angrily at the guard. He just looked right through me as he crossed his arms and leant on the door preventing access.

I turned back around and looked at my visitor. I couldn't believe it. It was fucking Biggy. There was no Malero with him though, which was a bit odd. So this was obviously not a visit to chat about my case or getting money off me.

Catching my breath I sat down on a chair flashing Biggy an unimpressed look, whilst shrugging my shoulders. Biggy's face looked sour with anger. This was weird Biggy was normally all smiles. What the fuck is going on? I emphasised my look of confusion by putting my hands in the air. What the fuck did Biggy have to be angry for? How had I pissed him off?

'Hi Alan,' he said with gritted teeth.

I didn't reply to his stern greeting. I wasn't having this! He was my consulate he should speak to me with respect. Trying to ignore him I looked to the ceiling. After a few seconds I flicked my stare back to Biggy. He looked even angrier now as a hint of red started to sear through his bronzed cheeks. Noisily he drummed with his fingers on the desk. When an uncomfortable score of seconds went by Biggy shook his head and breathed out a huff.

This was weird. I never knew him to be quiet for so long. Where had the smarmy happy go lucky talker gone? Why the fuck did he look so pissed?

He wasn't fucking beaten, put into solitary confinement with fuck all and forced to be naked for twenty three hours a day.

'I was informed of your escape Alan,' he blurted.

I still didn't respond. Why did he think I gave a flying fuck at whether he knew or not.

'Why did you do it?'

I couldn't help but laugh in his face. I then shook my head and looked to the floor as I folded my arms. I still refused to answer. This jumped up toffee nosed git was asking me why I was doing it. I hoped in his lifetime he would get in trouble and spend time here. Maybe when I get out I will plant something on him so he can know what it feels like. Then he wouldn't ask such stupid fucking questions. Why the fuck did I do it? Every sodding week I would complain about this place. Was he for real or what?

'Do you know because of you I have been sacked from my position here?'

'I have to go and work in the mainland of Spain now, because of you,' he said pointing his finger as if he wanted it to poke straight through me.

Feeling really angry I laughed again and looked to the floor. Oh I get it now because he couldn't control me he had been sacked. Good enough for him, he was a crap consulate anyway. What really made me laugh was the fact that he wanted sympathy from me. The cheeky sod! He did not give me sympathy or give a shit about my wellbeing. All he gave a toss about was lining his pockets with money and having a cushy lifestyle.

'Come on man, speak up. What have you got to say for yourself Alan?'

'What have I got to say?' I said sticking my finger in my bruised breastbone.

'Two words…. Fuck you!'

'Is that all!' hissed Biggy.

'I can't fucking believe this,' I said shaking my head.

'You expect me to feel sorry for you. I should feel guilty. What the fuck for Biggy? What the fuck for?'

'Maybe if you did your job properly in the first place I wouldn't have had to escape and poor fucking you would still have your cushy little job.'

Biggy breathed in sharply and screwed up his lips which resembled a dog's arse.

'I told you I was innocent. I told you how bad the conditions were in here.'

'And what did you do,' I said nodding. 'Fuck all!'

'I….. I!' I said vehemently. 'Wouldn't have had to escape if you had helped me,' I said pointing my finger dead centre between his eyes.

I could feel myself welling up from being so angry and in pain, but I somehow managed to stop any tears leaking down my face.

'Obviously Alan there is no talking to you. Well this will be the last time

I see you and the last time I will visit here.'

'Good!'

'Well I will be off. I would think very carefully about what you have done.'

'My conscience is clear Biggy. What about yours?'

'Goodbye Alan.'

'Good riddance Biggy.'

Then from the visiting room I was sent back down to my underground hell and given my tea. I would now be left alone from the guards till around seven in the morning the next day. For twelve hours I was bored and alone. I would have loved to have gone straight to sleep but with the pain it was near to impossible. I would pass out rather than sleep. Time tonight went even slower. I was still reeling over my visit with Biggy. I just couldn't get over the fact he wanted me to feel sorry for him. Okay my injuries weren't on show but he fucking must have seen the way I carried myself. He would have known they would have been heavy with me. He wasn't fucking stupid! But yet he wanted me to feel sorry for him. Plus there wasn't that much to feel sorry for. He had not lost his job entirely. He could still work on the Spanish mainland. I say using the word work very loosely.

My anger eventually subsided and I grew bored. I decided like I did the other two nights to go into my conscious dream world, in a bid to escape the pain and depressive thoughts. I would imagine being far away from Ceuta. I would lift my soul out of my body and imagine it floating above through the bars of the cell. I would go up into the sky and fly across the waters of the Mediterranean Sea along the straits of Gibraltar. Then I would float over Spain and around the Bay of Biscay. I would hover across France and over the English Channel to the UK mainland. From the South of England I would be carried across by the wind to Wales and imagine I could see the mountains of the South Wales valleys below. Like a satellite zooming down I would see images of my mother and brothers. I imagined my children of varying ages and what they were doing. I imagined looking in the Baglan hotel and seeing my friends wiling away the hours drinking and gossiping in a plume of cigarette smoke. I also would make a visit to Oslo and see Bo drinking coffee wearing a beautiful negligee. I enjoyed these moments. Although not real they felt like it. It was nice to escape. My body wouldn't allow me to stray for long though. It would always eventually drag me back to reality with a bang and the pain would be back.

20 FRIENDS REUNITED

I stayed in solitary confinement in total for two long weeks. It was quite bad being alone with naff all in my cell but I suppose it could have been worse. The guards could have kept beating me every night like they did with Dominic. They could have starved me or even worse killed me. The only thing I found hard to bear was not having a bed. It was so painful sleeping on the floor with broken ribs and extensive bruising. Thankfully Cheno realised I was below his cell and gave me the odd reprieve with joints for pain relief. It would have made it worse having nothing. Plus his company and my pet rat helped me not to feel so alone. This and also my dream world where I would visit family, friends and old lovers.

On my 15th morning in solitary confinement I knew something was up as the guards hadn't brought me my breakfast like they usually did. Plus they did not give me my bucket wash. When I stood naked in the doorway squinting my eyes awaiting the whoosh of water I felt only clothes being chucked at me. Confused I looked down at my stinking clothes and then back to the guards. I had managed to catch in my hands my T-shirt and shorts but my stained Y-fronts had fallen on the dirty floor.

One of the guards yelled in Spanish and pointed to my clothes. I did not understand a word but guessed he wanted me to put my clothes on. It was a bit early for clothes; normally I would wear these after dinner. I could see they were impatient as they both fidgeted about, so to piss them off, I dressed very slowly. I liked my small victories.

When putting on my clothes I started to feel weird. I was naked for 23 hours a day for 14 days so it felt strange having cloth against my skin. Plus I much preferred not wearing my clothes as they didn't feel or smell nice to wear. They hadn't been washed properly in weeks and were still covered in dirt and blood from the night of the escape. I did try and wash them by showering in then but when they dried they felt stiff and crunchy. My underpants felt the most gross to wear as I had alternated them so many times.

When I finally dressed each guard took an arm and marched me out of the patio and up to the steps to the Centro. Where the fuck was they taking me now and more importantly where's my bastard breakfast? Was I to meet with Biggy again? Or Biggy's replacement? Maybe the governor wanted a chat. Oh I would fuck love to have a chat with him alone. I wouldn't have minded having a baseball bat too, and one with metal spikes coming out of it.

I was taken in the prison and to the bottom of the steps of the Spanish brigada. I was shocked. It felt so long since I had been in the main part of the prison. Was I going to see my lads again? I tried not to smile or look happy just in case they were bringing me here to just wind me up. One of the guards stayed put whilst the other opened the unlocked gate at the bottom of the steps and ushered me through. I followed behind as he stomped up the stairs. Once at the top he unlocked the brand new installed gate complete with unbent bars. I felt sad seeing this. It was as if history had been eradicated and the escape had never happened. I felt such futility.

I stared with suspicion as the guard glared at me whilst holding the gate open. I waited for an instruction but instead was pulled through, which caused me to fall over onto the floor. This really hurt but I held my breath trying not to shout in pain. I got up quickly and turned around. The guard just stood watching me with a nonchalant expression for a few seconds, then locked back up the gate and left.

Jesus Christ I am free! Back with the boys! With excitement I trotted towards the dormitory. I never thought I would leave solitary confinement so soon. I didn't think they would allow me back into the main prison. I thought I would just disappear like Dominic.

It didn't seem real I was back. I didn't care about the pain in my chest anymore. All I cared about was getting into my bed and seeing the lads. To feel the comfort of a mattress again and a sheet against my body. I couldn't believe I was getting excited about my piss stained, bedbug infested, bed. But anything was better than cold hard floor.

Then my spine shuddered as a feeling of dread washed over me. I froze and gulped down hard. Fuck what if they hate me. I was the one that organised the escape and it went tits up. What if they know about Danny? What if he's dead?

Come on Alan! Fuck what they think! You tried to get them out! If Danny is dead it wasn't my fault! I wanted to be first over the wall. With courage I headed into the brigada.

I entered the room to find the majority were sleeping. Only one Spanish boy was sat up and awake. He gasped as he looked in my direction. His tanned complexion drained from his face leaving a ghostly shade of green. I smiled back and was confused by his horror. What the fuck was wrong with him? It then dawned on me when I had a flash back to the night of the escape. He was obviously shitting himself because he and his mates grassed me up as the leader. He needn't have worried though. I never gave a moment's thought to the Spanish boys. In some ways it was a good thing. If they hadn't of pointed me out as the leader the guards would have badly beaten all the other European boys.

Despite not feeling anger towards the Spaniard, out of fun I did want to to make him worry. With a forced grin I walked confidently towards his bed. His eyes widened in fear as he sat up wriggling his feet under the sheet. When I got to the foot of his bed he clenched hard in both hands his sheet and stared at me without blinking. I put my finger to my lips and made a shush noise. After a few seconds I turned and headed off to my bed. I could hear from behind a sigh of relief as I walked on.

Quietly I tip toed though the throng of beds and found mine. It was a nice surprise to find my bed was empty and it hadn't been traded or occupied or moved. Well they must not hate me too much to keep my bed for me. I looked over to Danny's bed. That too was empty.

I looked back at my bed and let out a great sigh. To lie on something other than the floor was going to be heaven. Even though I was excited I still got into it carefully. Any sudden movements would have caused pain in my ribs and spoilt the moment. Firstly I sat down swung my legs across and then lay my upper body down. This sudden movement did cause pain which led to me letting out a groan but once my body was lying down it felt nice. This felt good.

'Mmmmmmm!' I said out loud without realising.

My moans of pleasure must have disturbed Joseph as I watched his face turn from a sleeping baby to a grizzly man. His lips pouted and his brow furrowed. After a few seconds he wriggled around, huffed and then opened his eyes looking in my direction. He swiftly shut his eyes and nestled his head back in the pillow. Then with a bolt of lightning he opened his eyes again.

'Alan! Oh my god! Alan!' he shouted.

'Hi Joseph,' I said trying not to laugh at his bewildered expression.

'Oh my god!'

'Shush you will wake the others man.'

But it was far too late to say that. No sooner had I uttered those words the whole room started stirring. Joseph quickly jumped to his feet. He shot out of his bed and sat on the side of my bed. He shook his head as he looked me up and down. I could see he wanted to ask a million questions but was struck dumb with shock. His eyes widened as if he needed to register I was physically here first.

Then to the left of me I could hear John next to me groaning and rubbing his eyes. When I turned and looked at him he too jumped back in shock. A few moments later he began to laugh uncontrollably.

'Well well well. The old bastard is back then.'

'Just about.'

Then the other seven Europeans woke up and surrounded my bed.

Before I could even worry about them hating me I was fired with question after question. Where had I been? What had the guards done to me? Had I eaten? Although exhausted I answered all their questions. After the last question everyone looked to the floor as if taking it in at where I had been and imagined what I had been through. In the silence I adjusted myself as my back was aching. I let out a gasp as I twisted my ribs.

'You okay Alan,' Joseph asked in concern.

'Yeah I am fine. Just a few aches. It's going to take a while to get used to a bed again.'

'What you had no bed?' said Joseph astounded

'Nope. In my cell I had fuck all.'

'Show us the damage them,' asked John.

'What do you mean?'

'I saw what the guards did to yous. Fucking sick whipping you with that chain man.'

'Okay well if you want to have a look.'

With that I sat up carefully. I tried to hold my ribs so they wouldn't cause pain. I didn't want to yell out with all the boys watching me. I took off my filthy T-Shirt and held out my arms. Each of my lads stared on in horror with open mouths.

'Fucking hell!' shouted John.

'Oh Alan,' said Joseph sympathetically.

I laughed and shook my head. I thought the bruises didn't look too bad now but I had seen them at their very worst. Only over half of my torso was now black. The colours were now more mottled with purple brown and yellow.

'Are your ribs broken?' said John.

'I think so.'

'How many?'

'Nearly all of them.'

'Haven't they taken you to the doctor or to the hospital?'

Joseph's comment made me instantly crack up with laughter. The involuntary movement hurt so much that I yelled loudly in pain. But although bittersweet it still felt nice to laugh. I hadn't laughed in such a while. Everyone else laughed too. Fucking doctor or hospital! I loved Joseph's naivety. He had been in the prison for long enough now to realise the guards wouldn't do things like that. Feeling embarrassed and annoyed he folded his arms and scowled.

'Look sorry Joseph. No they didn't.'

'Well Alan you will need them to be strapped up. If they are all broken they could pierce your lung.'

'Thanks! You really know how to cheer a guy up.'

Everyone fell about laughing again apart from Joseph.

'No Joseph is right we need to strap them up,' insisted John.

Without any agreement from me Joseph passed John a sheet. With a bit of struggle I watched on as they ripped it into pieces. The rest of the Europeans either went back to their beds or started to get dressed. I remained lying in bed. It felt such comfort.

Then again without any consent Joseph and John came over with the sheets. They both ordered me to sit up so they could start binding me. Once sat up Joseph looked at my torso as if deciding where was best to start. He also sucked in air with gritted teeth grimacing at the bruises.

'Come on Joseph don't be shy get winding round then. But remember this will be the one and only time you touch my body.'

With that Joseph started and bound it tight. After they had finished they were right I did feel better. It felt nice not to have to hold myself and have a bit of support. Bandaged up I laid back down on the bed.

Feeling extremely tired after weeks of hardly any sleep I let my eyes go heavy and started drifting. Before I went to sleep I felt a tap on my shoulder. I did not open my eyes but mumbled to communicate I was awake.

'Alan you stay here and rest. I will bring up your breakfast,' whispered Joseph.

'Cheers. Would really appreciate that,' I slurred.

I lay my head on the pillow and breathed out a big sigh. It was over now. I was back with my lads. For the first time in two weeks I felt relaxed and instantly fell to asleep. Thank god they were okay with me.

'Alan. Alan,' I heard Joseph shouting.

'What!' I groaned in a husky waking voice.

'Wake up Alan its two o'clock!'

I woke up and rubbed my eyes. My jangled brain tried to take in the fact it was two o'clock in the afternoon and that I had slept for about six hours straight. I stretched out my arms after a long sleep. I then cried out loud with pain. My stupid waking body forgot about my ribs.

'Sorry to wake you Alan but you have slept for a long time.'

'You have already missed breakfast I couldn't let you miss dinner as well. You need your strength.'

'Thanks Joseph.'

With that Joseph passed me my dinner and a bottle of beer. When I looked I couldn't' believe it. He had made me my favourite meal of cheese and toast. I could have kissed him. Despite being such a simple dish in here it felt like being shown caviar. With excitement my mouth started to water.

'God that looks fucking tasty.'

'Thought you'd be pleased.'

With that Joseph beamed a great smile and disappeared out the door. I remained in my bed munching on my cheese on toast. It was amazing. I tried to savour each bite but I was so hungry I shovelled it down like a pig.

I washed down the last of it with my bottle of beer. Great stuff!

After downing the beer I felt slightly giddy. I don't know whether it was the excitement of having nice food or my body reeling over the energy. But I didn't care; it felt nice to feel my body slightly out of control.

Feeling energised I headed to the patio. To see people again would be nice. To have freedom from the guards would be good too.

In the patio I looked up towards the sun closed my eyes and smiled. Today was a good day. My enjoyment was short lived though when in the air I sniffed a most putrid smell. I looked around to see if any of the Spanish were around but they weren't. I then sniffed in the air again. Then with a feeling of dread it dawned on me. The smell wasn't from anyone else, it was from me. Right I am not having that. It was alright being stinking when I was on my own in the shit pit, now I was with other people I wasn't going to be a stinker. With that I headed back to the cell for clean clothes and then to the showers. The showers felt wonderful despite the fact I could not clean properly as I decided to keep my bandages on. Then putting on clean clothes felt amazing too. I was like a new man. With my dirty clothes I headed straight to Franc and his brother. When I stepped in and said hello to Franc he nearly choked on his coffee. I laughed at his shocked expression.

With my dirty clothes I handed them over and flinched with embarrassment. Thankfully they did not say anything about how filthy they were. They nodded as if to say it was okay and put them to one side. Before I could leave I was interrogated by Franc about where I had been. Politely I answered each of their questions but made it obvious I wanted to leave fast.

The day went quick. I was busied by everyone coming up to me and asking me how I was and what had happened. At first I enjoyed the attention and people's company after being alone for so long but after a while it did start to get to me. I think it was all a bit too much too soon. After several rounds of questioning that day I made my excuses and went back to bed. I was left for a few hours until it was tea time. Joseph came up with some soup. Fair play he gave me all my comfort food, I thanked him and started tucking in. Then the other lads ambled in with their soups too.

Half way through the soup I put down the spoon. My stomach churned. Right, I had put off asking the question for too long now. I needed to ask about Danny. I looked to his bed and then to John and Joseph. John looked oblivious but Joseph avoided my gaze looking the other way. I think he saw me looking at Danny's bed and knew what I was going to ask.

'Joseph.'

'Yes Alan,' he said with a somber huff.

'Danny?'

'Oh Alan….. We don't know,' Joseph said in a depressive tone.

Just then I could see the rest of the lads ears had pricked up. I put down my soup and let out a big sigh.

'When we asked the guards they said he is alright though,' Joseph said trying to sound positive.

'I mean we also asked about you Alan.'

'And they said you were alright. And here you are.'

Everyone looked down or to the side thinking about Danny. I could read it on their faces they all feared the worst and believed he was dead. I mean if he was alive why hadn't they sent him back to the main prison like me?

When I looked at Joseph I could see although looking sad he did have a shred of hope Danny was okay. I was glad he had faith. I wish I could feel that too but I couldn't. I suppose he didn't see Danny being dragged by his hair across the floor. His face devoid of life and the amount of blood spilt. How can a man survive that! There was so much blood.

I decided not to tell him or the other lads about it. I wanted them to keep hope.

Why the hell did I think I could escape? It should have been me up on that wall and not Danny.

Despite not being in the mood to eat I forced the soup down my gullet. When I did everyone else slowly began chatting again. Then on my last mouthful John fell on his bed in hysterics.

'What the fuck is wrong with you?'

'I can't,' he managed to utter between bouts of great laughter.

'John you alright?'

'Your soup is gone,' he laughed again.

'You've fucking cracked up or what?'

'You've eaten it all,' he spluttered.

'So?'

He pointed at my soup whilst clutching his stomach in pain he was laughing so hard. The laughter then spilt out into the rest of the group. Despite the fact I didn't have a fucking clue what he was laughing about I was infected too and joined in laughing.

'Have you been smoking without me lads?'

'Oh Alan. I forgot to tell you,' said Joseph aghast and slightly embarrassed.

'What?' I said annoyed.

'Er….Well you know the black bits in your soup?'

'Yes.'

'They are chinches.'

'What the fuck are chinches?'

'Well………?' The boys roared with laughter after Joseph's reluctance to answer and my puzzled expression.

'Spit it out Joseph before I give you a dig.'

'They are bed bugs,' answered John.

'What!'

'You dirty fucking bastard!' I shouted over to Joseph.

All the lads were doubled up laughing around the room.

'Look Alan I didn't tell you because...' said Joseph apologetically.

'Just fucking shut up now. I don't want to talk to you.'

'But Alan I only did not tell as you were getting so thin. You wouldn't have eaten your food otherwise. And you always liked the soup.'

I remained silent and turned my head shaking it. Fucking bed bugs in my food. I have heard it all. I dread to ask what the other unidentified stuff was. Despite being the last to know about the fucking chinches I wasn't really that pissed off. It was nice to see the lads all laughing. I decided to play up to crowd more and pretended I was really horrified.

'I dread to fucking think was in that cheese and toast.'

'There was nothing. Look Alan I swear.'

'No that's it. I'm not touching another fucking thing you cook.'

'Alan if I had told you what they were you wouldn't have eaten it.'

'Too fucking right!'

'But you were losing so much weight.'

I couldn't keep up the pretence anymore and I too fell about laughing with the rest. Joseph face turned to relief as he punched me in the arm. He too then started laughing. To wind up the lads more I grabbed my bowl and started licking it clean.

'Mmmmmmmmmmmm chinches boys,' I said like a man possessed

Everyone again tittered.

After our hysterics we all decided to have a party that night and celebrate my return. In the hour left before lock up time everyone went round trying to buy as much alcohol as they could from the Spanish. I also went over to Palermo and sorted out an ounce of hash. I also bought a few bits and bobs from the economato.

That night I enjoyed myself getting drunk, stoned and being with the lads. I couldn't enjoy the night entirely as my eyes would every now again feel drawn to Danny's empty bed. I wish you were here pal.

I was the first to go to bed. The company and excitement of being with the lads was exhausting. Plus I wanted to spend as much time in my bed as possible. I closed my eyes but didn't sleep as the lads loud chatter kept me up. It was nice though listening to them. Eventually everyone did quieten down and go to bed. Despite the lack of noise I still couldn't drift off. Instead I looked through the barred window at the moon which was just under from being completely full. On cue old Wolfie didn't fail to disappoint and let out a big howl that echoed around the walls of the prison. His howl was so loud but yet comforting.

21 ALGECIRAS

The next day I awoke early. Despite only sleeping a few hours I felt refreshed. I had spent the majority of yesterday asleep so it wasn't a wonder I was awake. I didn't get out of bed though I was warm and comfy. Plus the guards hadn't opened us up yet. I looked at my watch and it was five minutes to seven. It wouldn't have been long now till they opened the gate.

Several minutes later I heard the guards clanking the gate and opening it. Right on fucking cue. Then I heard a set of footsteps coming towards the brigada. Wait that's not right. Why haven't they fucked off? Shocked I sat up. My ribs did not thank me for that. Looking at the dormitory door I watched on as a guard burst through. Loudly he shouted in Spanish walking to the centre of the room, he pointed on the floor and in the corners. What the fuck? I quickly retrieved my block of hash from under the pillow and put it in my gob. Please to god not another fucking drugs raid. Then the guard disappeared. What?

'Did you hear that?' said Joseph.

'Yes. I cannot believe it,' replied Gert a fellow French friend of Joseph's.

'What's going on?' I said not making much sense with a lump of hash in my gob.

'Quick Alan get your things.'

'Why?' I said as I spat out my lump.

'The guard just said we have fifteen minutes before we go.'

'Go fucking where?'

'Look Alan I don't know! Just get your things and shut up.'

With that I carefully got up and put my things in order. Then I remembered I had clothes with Franc and his brother. I quickly raced down to the laundry and retrieved them. Once I was back I put my fresh clothes in a pile and folded them. All the Europeans including me were packed and ready to go. I wondered if they were putting us all back into individual cells. Oh that would be nice. When I looked around I noticed the only people sat on their bed with belongings were us ten Europeans.

'Why isn't the Spanish packing?'

'They only said for the Europeans to pack.'

'Oh.'

After several minutes of silence we could hear the pounding footsteps of several guards coming up the stairs. Five guards poured into the room. Each barked at us in Spanish whilst pointing at the door. With that my lads stood up and left. I decided to hang to the back and take my cue from the lads who understood the orders the guards gave. I didn't want a dig in the ribs just because I didn't understand.

Altogether we marched down the steps and along the corridors to the Centro. What the fuck? We had passed all the cells. As far as I was concerned there were no more cells past the Centro. Oh I hope to god there is not a communal underground cell.

We were then beckoned into the Centro. Once in the office each of us had hand cuffs slapped on. We were then herded in a line and chained together by our legs.

'Hey lads we must be off for a trip,' I said jokingly.

All the lads laughed but also seemed nervous about what was happening and where we were being taken too.

All chained up the guards lead us outside. Waiting for us in the large space between the front of the prison and the large prison gates was the governor and two armed guards. I had never seen the governor before but I assumed it must have been him as all the guards stood to his attention. Plus he was the only one wearing a large array of badges and medals on his uniform. These were probably fucking chocolate medals and not actually from any service in the army. I couldn't see him actually doing any graft or fighting. He looked more like a coward to me. A bit like his prick of a son.

We were ordered to line up in front of the governor. It felt like were on an army inspection parade. The two armed guards stood proudly by his side with backs straight and chests plumped out. The governor strutted up and down past us with his arms behind his back whilst making sure he scowled at each one of us on the way. The numerous medals on his lavish army jacket swung back and fore as he walked. He also had black leather gloves on and a peaked hat despite it being absolutely boiling. He looked like a fucking Nazi! With his nose in the air he once more walked up and down until he spotted me. What a fucking prick! I thought his son was a cock! How dare he look down his nose at me!

In broken English he wittered on and on. I found it hard to understand exactly what he was saying but I basically got the gist. He was pretty pissed off and especially with me. Come on fucking get on with it. I am bored of this whole charade. I'd rather be beaten than be shouted at.

'Why you come to my prison?' the governor shouted staring me full in the face. From his venomous words I could feel a mist of spit spray over my face. I smiled as I was little taken aback. I could not believe he was asking me this question.

'Why?' he screeched in my face.

With that I couldn't hold my cool any longer.

'I didn't fucking want to come to your fucking prison!' I said loudly making sure I enunciated each word slowly so he could understand.

The governor look astounded at my comment and nodded to a guard behind who swiftly jabbed me in the back. The pain was immense. I longed to hold my ribs with my arms but I couldn't as they were bound by handcuffs. Instead I held my breath whilst holding my stomach in trying not to concentrate on the agonising pain. I could feel my leg chain being pulled as all my boys took a step forward. When I looked around I could see them all tensing as if ready for a fight. They were obviously reacting to my low blow.

'Alan fucking shut up,' growled John through gritted teeth.

The director carried on talking in broken English for a while. Again I understood very little. I only managed to pick up on the fact that he was saying the prison we were going to next was going to be a lot tougher on us and was more secure. I couldn't believe the tougher part. After what they did to Dominic, Danny and me. I didn't know what else they could do. I believed the secure part though. That wouldn't have taken much to improve upon. I doubted any other prison in the world gave keys to the prisoners let alone ones which led to the fucking roof.

Eventually the ear bashing came to an end and the director told the guards to take us away. We were then taken to a bus a few yards away accompanied by two armed guards. We were unlocked from our leg chains and encouraged to pile onto the bus. Once all in, one armed guard sat at the back of the bus whilst the other sat on a seat just behind the driver.

When the driver revved up the engine and slowly edged away on the dusty road I felt a glimmer of excitement at going to a new prison. I stared on through the window as the prison became smaller and smaller until it completely disappeared from view. Time for a change!

John angrily slapped his cuffed hands on my thigh in order to get my attention.

'What?'

'Alan I can't believe you shouted back,' he said half chuckling.

'I wasn't fucking having that. I didn't want to come to his fucking prison.'

'You're crazy! They beat you black and blue and you still won't keep your bastard mouth shut.'

I was glad I was away from Ceuta prison and the Spanish dormitory. I couldn't face seeing Danny's empty bed day in day out. Maybe the distance will help me forget. When I looked around at the lads they all were quiet and dejected. I tried to busy myself looking out the window as this might have been the last time in a while I could see the outside world again. About a quarter of an hour went by and still none of the boys talked.

'Hey lads,' I shouted looking in all directions making sure everyone was focusing their attention on me.

When I noticed I had all eyes on me I knelt up on my chair whilst also trying to steady myself so the bumps in the road didn't jolt me too much.

'Look lads I just want to say I am really sorry about this whole mess.'

'I mean if it wasn't for me nobody would have been beaten up and we wouldn't be going off to another prison. And well Danny wouldn't be………….'

'Look Alan shut up. We all decided to do it together,' said John impassioned.

Everyone in the group nodded and with gusto shouted yes.

'Thanks lads.'

'But…I just wanted you to know I am sorry and I hope the next prison is not as bad as Ceuta.'

'That would be fucking hard,' said John half laughing.

Before I could get too emotional the bus stopped. Everyone looked outside at where we were and appeared shocked. When I looked outside I was gobsmacked too. We had stopped at Ceuta Port. I mean I knew we were going to another prison but I didn't entertain the possibility we were going to a different country. Viva la Espana! I wonder what the prisons in Spain were going to be like. I hope to god they will be more fucking civilised!

Then the excitement dwindled as I looked across to offices at the port. This was where my nightmare had started. If I wasn't caught there I wouldn't be in the position I was now. Annoyed I looked in all directions keeping my eyes peeled for the customs officers who had uncovered my hash. I wanted to show them my appreciation by waving at them with my middle finger. Unfortunately they were nowhere to be seen. When I looked at some of the other boys they too appeared upset. Like me, the majority were caught here with their stash, so they too were probably reliving their moment of misfortune.

Looking back outside I realised that there was something strange about the port. I had passed through here so many times. What was it? After a few moments of brain strain it then dawned on me. The port was empty. There were no other vehicles, cars or people. For a port this was very weird. I had never been to a port where it had been completely empty.

Then a knock on the window jolted me. It was the customs officer trying to get the attention of the driver. The driver promptly opened his window and passed across documentation. After a brief chat between the two we were then waved on and driven onto the ferry. Again driving on the ferry was weird as we had no vehicles in front or behind. Even when we parked up on the lower deck there was no one else around to be seen. I then decided it was probably because they wanted to hide us away before the others passengers boarded. They possibly didn't want to advertise us bunch of dirty crims and worry the other passengers.

The bus parked up in a space that was furthest away from the exit. This probably meant we were to be the last off too. When the hand brake crunched the two armed guards quickly got to their feet and went to the front of the bus. We were then barked at to get off. As each one of us stepped onto the car park we were put into our leg chains again. When we were all off and chained up we were taken up a metal stair case onto a platform. After everyone had reached the top of the metal platform the guard pointed forward.

Great we were to spend our entire ferry journey looking at the frigging car park. We don't even get a view. Mind I suppose they couldn't trust us on the open deck. I would have been in two minds to jump off, leg chains or otherwise.

Looking across the platform I saw a door at the end. This probably led up to the upper deck.

As we were going to be on the ferry for a few hours standing I edged forward and beckoned the others to follow. I pointed at the railings in front and everyone nodded realising it would be a good idea to lean on them for a bit of comfort. We then all walked forward slowly in sync. Each one of us leaned on the metal rail and dangled our cuffed hands over the side.

After a few minutes I heard the revs of several engines. When I looked down I noticed cars and buses started to fill the empty space below. All the lads were quiet and just stared downwards watching the other passenger's board in their droves. I looked down trying to spot any women to gawp at. Unfortunately it was mostly men. Plus the girls I did see were either covered up or too far away to get a real good look at.

'I could really do with a fag,' grumbled John.

'Yeah me too.'

'Where do you think they are taking us?' asked Joseph.

'Don't know?' answered John.

'Well one things for certain boys it's not Ceuta!' I shouted

'Here here Al!' John yelled out excitedly.

Again everyone ceased chatting and just stared ahead at the passengers boarding the ferry. The majority of people didn't notice us and seemed more preoccupied with looking at their boarding tickets or carrying their cases. But the ones who did look our way always displayed the same horrified and frightened expression. If they were in a group and one noticed they would always point us out to the rest. I felt embarrassed at this. I felt like I was fucking monkey in a zoo. Mind we probably did look animalistic as we were quite a filthy bunch. Instead of like them fresh faced and relaxed after a nice holiday.

I grew bored of people staring at me so I looked to the ceiling. I also tried to look along the platform to the door to the upper deck. I pondered how I would escape if I didn't have leg chains on. Mind if I didn't have chains on escape was still a bit of a fantasy as the guards were armed. It probably wouldn't have ended well. Danny was a testament to that.

'Alan... Alan,' said John.

'Yeah.'

'Do you see those Dutch number plates?'

'What?'

'The Dutch number plate of that car pulling up there,' he whispered as he pointed in the distance.

After scanning the rows of cars, I eventually found the Dutch car that was struggling to park up.

'I can see it. What about it?'

'What's the betting they are like us?'

'What do you mean?' I said in hushed tones.

'Come on. You know. Smugglers.'

'Oh I see…...I suppose it's possible.'

'Well if they are John they have done well to get this far.'

With that we both watched on as they both slammed their doors shut. They both looked in their early twenties and had long curly hair. One went to the boot of the car whilst the driver locked up the doors.

'We have got to warn them.' I said.

'How?'

I looked back at the guards. They weren't watching and were busy talking. Right let's get these boys to notice us. I decided the only way to get their attention was to make a noise. So without warning I fell forward into the railing in front and pretended that I tripped. The noise from the clanging of my handcuffs ricocheted around the room. I looked behind at the guards. They looked on at me in suspicion. I put my hands in the air and pointed to my feet whilst shrugging. They shook their heads and eventually after a few moments went back to chatting.

When I looked down my plan had worked. The driver had noticed us and pointed upwards to show his mate. His mate then slammed down the boot of his car whilst holding on to a bulging travel bag and went to his side looking upwards at us.

With their full attention gained I shook my head at them. John noticed my head shaking and followed suit. Don't do it boys! Both boys jerked backwards and had their mouths open wide. We obviously had got through to them that we knew what they were up too. They then looked to each other and had an animated conversation. After a few moments they then went up to the metal steps to the right of us and disappeared.

'I wonder if they will listen to us Al?' said John.

'I wonder.'

On the whole the boys were quiet on the journey. It was as if everyone was deep in thought. Plus I had the feeling the boys didn't feel comfortable chatting whilst the guards were round. I personally didn't care if the guards were there or not but I was quiet as I was mesmerised by the Dutch car. When I intermittently looked over to John he too seemed preoccupied with the Dutch car.

The tannoy crackled as a man in a Spanish voice started to speak. The only word I understood was Algeciras. Then a few minutes later we saw people going back to their cars. Obviously the ferry was near to docking. Then another ten minutes later the tannoy crackled and words in Spanish were spoken again. After this everyone in their cars started revving their engines and went to leave off the ferry. The speed of the people leaving the ferry was slow but eventually holes did appear in the car park below. The holes got bigger and bigger as people slowly made their way in the queue off the port.

The guards behind looked at their watches and then down below. There were now only ten cars left. Nine of which were in a queue to get off. The only car left in the car park was the Dutch car.

'Hey John look.'

'I can't believe they didn't come back.'

'I know.'

'Well they might have left on foot with the hash.'

'I hope so because it is waste if it is.'

'Is it Al? I mean look at us man.'

'I suppose.'

Then once all the cars had left the car park, apart from the parked Dutch car that is, we were lead down the steps, unchained and put back on the bus.

We sped off and drove off the ferry and onto Spanish soil at Algeciras port. It was October 3rd 1978. I had never seen the port coming from this direction before. I was meant to have seen it on my last trip but that didn't happen. If only I had did what those fucking Dutch boys did. But then they were yellow bellies getting that far and running. Mind looking at us lot I wasn't surprised. We were enough to put anyone off. I wonder if they put the dope in their bags and went off on foot. I hope they did. They wouldn't have made good smugglers otherwise. You have to have balls to be a smuggler and be prepared to pay the ultimate price. Like the price I was paying and some of my fellow Europeans.

The whirring of the engine stopped as the driver pulled up beside a customs officer who signalled him over. The officer had a notebook in his hand as he looked on seriously at the driver, guards and then us lot. I couldn't believe it, only three months ago I was here and on my way to Tangier for the dope. In my head it felt like a lifetime ago. Just being in Ceuta for several months felt like an eternity. The amount of shit that had happened in such a short space of time.

My stomach groaned with hunger as it had no food to digest for over twelve hours. I can't believe the bastards at Ceuta didn't even allow us to grab some breakfast before we went. If they had told us what they had planned we could have gone to the economato at least. I hope to god the prison is nearby and not to the north of frigging Spain several hours away.

The engines started up again as the customs officer smiled and waved us on. The driver pulled off and nipped along the unusually quiet port roads. The other passengers from the ferry were nowhere to be seen. All around the bus were sporadic bangs of metal as the vibrations from the engine shook the frame. I tensed my stomach and pushed my back into the seat. With my cuffed hands I stiffened my shoulders and kept my arms rigid. I wanted to keep firm in order to restrict the movement of my body when we went over cracks in the road and potholes. I didn't want my partially healed ribs to snap again through a jolt. Looking through the window I prepared myself for the sharp corners and any uneven bits of road too. My attempts were in vain though as I was still flung around going over bends and bumps.

After twenty minutes or so going in around streets of Algeciras we stopped outside a big set of prison gates. I was grateful the journey was short and hoped we had made it in time for dinner.

At the large gates of Algeciras prison two armed prison officers instantly showed up and were keen to open them. I watched the two guards then with more eagerness close the gates once we were through. Wow the guards seemed on the ball here and not as half soaked as the ones in Ceuta. Plus from watching the other guards walking around I noticed they did so with purpose rather than arrogance. Oh fuck, it looks like they take the job seriously which means it going to be harder to plan an escape here.

When we were taken off the bus I looked in all directions to try and soak up the layout of the prison. Where would be the best place to run for an escape? I found it hard to concentrate looking around as I was pushed and shoved by the guards in the direction of the plain red bricking building which was to be my new home. I stopped to tie my pumps quickly so I could get a place towards the back of the line behind the rest of my lads. I wanted to hang back so I could stare at the perimeter walls for a bit longer.

At the big set of prison doors I drew in a big intake of breath as they opened them. I made sure I gulped in my last bit of clean outside air before I was yet again immersed in Spanish prison filth once again. We all wearily trotted inside tired and hungry from the long journey. I watched as the light faded fast as they shut the big doors behind us.

Inside we had a welcoming party of four guards and a head guard. The four guards quickly went around us and took off our hand cuffs. It felt nice to scratch my wrists again with freedom. Then one of the guards collected all the hand cuffs and headed off. The tall head guard stepped forward and smiled politely. He looked at the faces of each one of us as if he was trying to weigh us up.

'Hello and welcome to Algeciras,' he said politely.

Fuck me this head guard could speak English and pretty well too. It wasn't broken English like the Ceuta director. Maybe I could get through to this guy that us Europeans will not or shall not be treated like dogs.

'I will say nothing on why you are here. You all know why?' he said as if despairing at us being here. It sounded like he was pissed off that Ceuta washed their hands of us and dumped us with him.

'One thing to make clear is here there is none of this if you behave,' he said waving his palm signifying violence. I knew what it meant and so did the lads.

'Right who is Alan Jones?'

Another turn up for the books a register as well.

'Me,' I responded emphasising the point by raising my hand.

'Could you step over here please?'

I obeyed his command instantly overwhelmed by the fact he said please.

Once pulled to one side he looked back at my lads who were questioned by the other guards. He seemed very serious in demeanour as if he was very worried about something. After a few moments he looked back at me and smiled as if trying to convince himself everything was okay.

'Now Alan after what you did in Ceuta we are going to have to put you on your own in the punishment cells,' he said quietly.

When I turned around I could see the lads hadn't heard as they were looking in all directions or fidgeting. Then I saw guards ushering my lads towards the direction of the door.

'That's fine. But who will control the lads?' I said loudly whilst turning back around facing the head guard.

'What do you mean?'

'Well I am their leader. I normally control them.'

I turned around again to the boys. One of the guards could see Joseph held back and didn't make an attempt to walk to the door. The guard caught hold of Joseph's arm and gently tugged it. Joseph scowled back at the guard and shot a concerned look my way.

'What's wrong?' Joseph shouted as he kept pulling his arm away from the guard

'It's okay. Don't worry Joseph he is just putting me solitary for punishment.'

'What? Oh no... no... no.! If he goes down I am joining him.'

'Yeah and me!' shouted John.

After that all the lads chimed in saying they wanted to go in a punishment cell if we couldn't all be together. Despite the guards best efforts my lads would not leave the room and were causing fuss.

'Quiet!' shouted the head guard whilst looking to the floor and flailing out his long arms.

The room fell deathly silent and everyone stopped what they were doing, even the other guards let go of the prisoners they were man handling and looked on.

'Look men! I have told you if you behave there will be none of this,' he said shaking his fist.

'I don't care. If Alan goes down we all go down,' said Joseph defiantly.

'Look you won't be here long anyway. A few weeks at the most.'

The head guard shook his head and then put his finger to his lips whilst deep in thought. With a sigh he put one hand on his hip whilst rubbing his face in the palm of his other hand, as if out of annoyance.

'Right! If.....I let you be with the rest of your men will you promise me they will behave.'

'Yeah! Yeah! No problems. I will make sure of that.'

'That means no escapes, no riots, no fires and no fights.'

'Yes yes I can promise that.'

'Oh and you leave the Spanish alone too.'

'Sure, no problem,' I said smiling.

'You'd better,' he said still huffing.

'Guards take him to the cells with the rest of them.'

We all quite happily followed the guards along the corridors and off to a dormitory where they had room for us. It looked similar to the one in Ceuta, just a plain old room full of around fifty or sixty beds. Quickly each of us located a bed for us to lie on. I grabbed a bed nearest the wall in the middle of the room. I was glad of this location as it would give me time to hide hash if they were to do searches. After inspecting the bed I was surprised. There were hardly any stains and it didn't stink of piss. Feeling tired I hopped into bed like the rest of the lads and had a lay down.

Later that day we altogether in our large group explored the grounds of Algeciras prison. We were shocked at the differences compared to Los Rosales. The whole place was much cleaner and the food looked more like food. It didn't look like it had already being regurgitated once before. The guards too on the whole were more approachable.

After a few weeks we settled into the routine of the place. We also kept our promise as we never caused any trouble. Internally I was lying as I was always looking for a way out. I had my ideas but I kept them to myself. If we were to do another escape it would have to be a solid plan as I don't think the guys would rush into anything again. But I didn't want to stop trying. If we stopped now Danny would have fallen for nothing.

22 PUERTO SANTA MARIA

I was only in Algeciras for a few weeks with my lads until I was transferred again. In the middle of the night the guards stormed the dormitory and gave me ten minutes to collect my stuff together. I had only just fucking got to sleep when I was jabbed in the shoulder by a guard. Again the move was a complete surprise to me and I had not been given prior warning. Plus the guard only woke me up and not any of the other lads. I was to go it alone. Running around the room collecting my things caused everyone to wake up, including the Spanish prisoners.

After I packed my things together I just managed to shake all my European lad's hands and say a quick goodbye before I was plucked away in the night. I was kind of glad I hadn't been told in the day. I would rather a quick goodbye rather than hours of awkwardness. I did feel sad though. I wondered if I will ever get to see any of them again. Oh well a new prison here I go and new friends I shall meet. I suppose I had to think of prison like that of life, you enter it alone and you leave it alone.

Despite being told I was to be moved it was still a shock to the old system. I really thought if we kept our promise and stayed out of trouble they would keep us in Algeciras. But nope they went with the plan to move us, and now it looked like they also wanted to split us up, starting with me. I didn't foresee them splitting us up, but I suppose it was quite logical from the guards point to not trust us as a group again.

The next prison I was sent to was in Jerez around sixty miles away. It took over an hour to get to the prison, but it felt much longer as I was freezing and tired. My body temperature was already low after just being woken up but this was exacerbated by the cold outside air.

I only stayed in Jerez for a few days and then I was transferred again to Cadiz. Then again in Cadiz I only spent a few days there. God knows why they did this as it seemed pointless to stay in a prison for a few days. The amount of money wasted in travel expenses, for just me. The only possible reasons was they wanted to either disorientate me or because they only had spaces in specific prisons. If they wanted me to feel disorientated it worked. I didn't know whether I was coming or going. Maybe they didn't want me to feel settled so it made it more difficult for me to plan another escape as I wouldn't know when to make my move as the guards could burst in and get me at any time.

The next prison I was taken to was in Puerto Santa Maria. When I saw the sign I thought how lovely it sounded. However I had been fooled before by Los Rosales. That sounded nice too but it was no fucking bed of roses. From the outside Puerto Santa Maria prison also looked the most welcoming. When the gates opened you were confronted by a glorious blue, white and gold statue of the Virgin Mary. It was similar to the one in the Catholic Church at Ceuta but it was much more grand and larger in size. Oh I hope to god this was going to be my sanctuary.

Once inside my bubble was burst. Nope this was just another run of the mill Spanish prison. Inside as usual I was roughly shoved around from corridor to corridor by the guards until I was taken to my bed for the night. To top off the inhospitality I wasn't put in a dormitory or shared cells, I was placed instead in a punishment isolation cell set away from everyone else. There must have been an order sent from the guards at Ceuta to always keep me in a punishment cell. So not only did they not trust me to be with my lads. They did not trust me to be around anybody else. Great! Kept in isolation for god knows how many years.

I had to look on the bright side though the cell had a bed at least and it wouldn't be so bad having a room on my own. I didn't have any cell mates I had to be nice too or worry about. I could get to sleep much quicker knowing I was alone. I will miss the late night conversations I used to have with the lads though.

The following day at Puerto Santa Maria I wandered around and had a look out for people I could possibly befriend. Like with the other prisons it was largely a Spanish majority with a sprinkling of Europeans. I didn't really feel like mixing with people but I thought it would be best to find out how this prison was run and where I could get my hash and booze. If indeed I could.

The first person I was drawn too was a guy I heard speaking Spanish in a German sort of accent. He had golden brown hair and piercing blue eyes. He was speaking to a Spaniard who looked like he was trying to sell him something as he kept on pulling things out of his pocket and flashing them at the German. The German guy kept trying to walk away, shaking his head and hands showing he was not bothered. The Spaniard kept up walking with the German and tried a few more times in enticing him with his goods. Eventually the Spaniard withdrew and wandered around in search of another person to put on a hard sell too.

This guy looked good to talk too. He was German and spoke Spanish; I would also bet he could speak English too. Plus he also looked disgruntled so he would hopefully give up information easily as he looks like he doesn't care. I wouldn't need to barter with anything for information. I stalked behind him for a few yards to give him some space after the overpowering

Spaniard.

I think he sensed I was following him as he headed to a wall at the far side of the patio and stopped. He turned around and leant on the wall looking in my direction. I put on a big friendly smile and walked over. In his eyes were suspicion and in the muscles of his forearms I could see tension.

'Hi my name is Alan,' I said holding out my right hand.

'Hi Alan. I am Karl,' he replied in a huff as he begrudgingly shook my hand.

'Well only just came here last night.'

'Welcome to Puerto,' he responded in a monotone voice.

'What can you tell me about this prison?' I said enthusiastically.

'What can I say?' he said laughing as if through sarcasm.

'Only that this place is a cemetery?'

'A what?'

'A cemetery for the living.'

'Oh okay.'

I was stumped by his words. A cemetery for the living be Christ! Although quite bleak it was also quite poetic too. Before I could think of something to say back at the bleak German I heard shouts of my name across the patio. What the fuck! When I turned my gaze to the direction of the noise I could see two men running towards me. When they drew nearer I couldn't believe it. It was John and Joseph. Happy to see a friendly face I ran towards them without a seconds thought to saying goodbye to Karl.

'I thought I'd seen the last of you two.'

'Yeah didn't think I would see your hairy mug again,' John said.

'When did you arrive?'

'Only last night.'

'I see you met a new friend.'

'Hmmmm don't know about that.'

'I just asked him about this place.'

'What did he say?' asked Joseph excitedly.

'He said this place is a cemetery for the living.'

'Fucking hell what a depressing bastard,' John said whilst in fits of laughter.

After this we walked around the patio and caught up on what had happened to each one of us over the past few days. I couldn't believe it they were here. I had resigned myself to the fact I would be on my own from now on. I didn't entertain the possibility I would see a few of my closest mates again in the next few days. Mind fuck or what!

John and Joseph were upset when I told them I had been put in an isolation cell. Instantly on hearing this they looked into me moving in with them into the dormitory but it wasn't a possibility as there was no free bed.

I didn't really care anyway. I quite liked being alone rather than with scores of other men. Especially when I found that Karl the happy German was one of them in the dormitory. God I couldn't imagine waking up to his miserable face every morning. I would rather just a wall to stare at thank you very much.

That night, like the last three nights I found it hard to get to sleep. I would have thought the peace and quiet of having no-one around would have helped but it didn't. I think it was because I was on edge as to whether the guards could burst in at any time. The last three times I was asleep when they came to take me. It was a horrible feeling to be woken up and having to scrabble in the darkness for my things.

Trying to get comfy I rotated my pillow every few seconds. Each time I turned it I would achieve a moment of satisfaction from the coolness I felt on my face but this still did not ease me. My mind was wide awake. Out of frustration I punched my pillow a few times. I instantly regretted this as my ribs throbbed after such a powerful involuntarily movement. Oh fucking hell Alan let you mind go. I lay on my back and stared at the wall and desperately tried to achieve blankness.

Tomorrow I definitely need to acquire some alcohol and hash. I hope to god these will help knock me out for the night. I can't stand not being able to sleep and hated constantly worrying about the guards coming in.

I tried to think about something else but the only other thing on my mind was escape. This wasn't a healthy thought either as this too would keep the clogs working in my brain rather than relaxing them. Escape was always in the back of mind in the day. I would roam around looking for weaknesses or potential weaknesses in security, but for the last three days I saw none. I could only see obstacles to be faced and conscientious guards. The biggest hindrance of all was the raised platform around the perimeter of the prison which had armed guards patrolling on it 24 hours a day. In Ceuta they didn't have eyes from above and we still got fucking caught. Escape would be very difficult indeed.

I wanted so much to be free. Like the swallows tattooed on my hands I wished I could fly away from here out through my high cell window. In fantasy I closed my eyes imagining myself floating through the bars up into the sky. If only I could do this in reality and not just through my imagination.

Wait a minute that is fucking it! I had not explored the possibility of escape by looking outside my cell window. I could not see outside as the window was seven feet to eight feet high in the corner of my room. Even jumping on my bed using it as a trampoline did not gain me any view of the outside. I wonder if it was this high because it was so close to the perimeter fence. That would be great if it was. Plus maybe I will be able to see the guards patrolling around. I could document their patterns of patrol and see if they are really that conscientious throughout the night.

With excitement I hopped out of my bed and looked at how I would have to jump up the wall in order to grab the bars. My initial assessment was that this was going to be really fucking tricky. The main hindrance was the concrete window ledge, as it did not jut out at a straight angle instead it cascaded down at an obtuse angle. I would need to run up the wall, get on the steep ledge to run up that and pray that when I reached out with my hands I could grab the bars.

I put to the back of my mind the nagging doubts this was impossible and headed to the other side of the room pulling a sprinting position. On the count of two I ran full pelt across the room and up the wall and tried to climb up it using my hands. I only manage to climb up seven feet before my hands lost grip and I fell off and landed on my funny bone. I hated that sickening pain of landing on that part of your elbow. Well at least one thing it hurt more than my ribs, they must be on the road to healing. When I looked at my hands and feet they were covered in scratches and started to bruise. I decided then that I might need to wear shoes in order to have grip. I quickly retrieved my pumps from under the bed and was happy with the sufficient sole it had. It was unfortunate I did not have gloves but I was just going to have to harden them up to climb the wall.

That night I ran up the wall about forty times with a few breathers in between goes. I stopped around 4am as I was knackered. Plus my ribs started to ache. I was glad though they only ached and I didn't hear any cracks or crunches. When I got back into bed I must have fallen straight to sleep as I didn't even remember putting my head on the pillow.

The next day I felt so much better getting a few hours kip in. Plus planning an escape made me feel much more positive as I was doing something about my situation again and not worrying. Even if I don't manage to get up the wall tonight I know I will get a good night sleep from doing it. In the day I met up with John and Joseph. They did say I looked better today and asked why I was smiling more. I just told them I had a better night's sleep. I made sure I covered the bruising on my arms with my hands to avoid inviting more questions. I wasn't going to tell them of my plans.

I decided not to get any hash or alcohol as I need my full concentration and strength in running up the wall. I wouldn't need it anyway as I would probably sleep soundly again after the intense exercise.

Once I was shut in at seven pm I buzzed with excitement at forging a plan of escape. I did not straight away try to start running up the wall as I wanted the guards to be a few hours in their shift and hoped they would be less aware. Plus I wanted it to be a bit darker so there would less chance of me being seen. It felt like an eternity waiting for the sun to start to set, but eventually the light started to dim. With gusto then I ran up the wall and managed to make it half a foot off from grabbing onto the ledge of the window. I was happy about this as it was the highest I had climbed. My first attempt that night made me feel positive as it showed I had progressed from the night before. The next twenty times or so after were abysmal as I was falling short by a foot at least each time. The more and more I carried on the further I felt away from the window. Feeling tired and disheartened I decided to have a break. Maybe lying on my bed for a while would rejuvenate my energy.

I stared at the wall in anger. That fucking wall is not going to beat me. Neither was the guards going to control me and keep me in here. I want out. Come on Alan live the fucking dream.

After a brief rest and psyching myself up I could feel a rush of adrenalin and testosterone flood my body as I tensed my muscles. I was ready again to do battle. I stared up to the window above for several seconds and envisaged being successful. Then off I sped and went up and down the wall.

Thankfully on my tenth attempt after I managed to grab onto the bars with my right arm which caused the rest of my body to dangle down the slope. Feeling elated I sighed which caused me to lose my footing, but thankfully I steadied myself pushing down with my other arm. Digging my finger tips into the wall I carefully scuttled up with my feet towards the dusty window. Gritting my teeth I swung from my left shoulder out to grab the bars. I was just under an inch from grabbing it with the other hand. With my feet I shuffled up the slope a bit more. Again I swung my shoulder. This time it did work and I managed to grab hold of the bars with my left arm.

I breathed in deeply, panting at the exhaustion and strain in order to get up here, but at least I was there. Oh my god I ached and my legs, arms and hands all felt like they were ripped to bits. I tried to forget my pain and the crunchy feeling that had returned to my ribs.

With excitement I looked out of the window. This was a good fucking view. No wonder the window was high; from up here you could see the raised perimeter wall and even past the boundary wall to freedom. The perimeter wall was only about nineteen feet away if that and then the boundary wall I would say about fifty feet. It was worth all the pain. I breathed a sigh of relief and tried to forget that I would have to do this again several times over. The first few times would be to spy on the guard and the last time hopefully will be with wet sheets to bend the bars.

Through the tiredness and relief I relaxed my body whilst still clinging on to the bars. I allowed myself a few seconds to close my eyes and compose myself before looking out again. I couldn't believe it, I finally had made it. The hours and hours did pay off.

Then feeling ready I looked out to the left of me to see what else I could see. I was not prepared for what I saw. Staring back at me was a guard on the raised perimeter wall pointing a high powered rifle my way. I gasped in horror. He moved his head to the side of the rifle smiled and shook his head. He withdrew his hand off the trigger and pointed to the ground.

The bastard was laughing at me. He must have either heard or seen me trying over and over again. All that fucking effort for nothing.

With that I jumped off the window sill to the ground jarring my ankles on the steep decent down. Jesus Christ that hurt! I hobbled in pain over to the bed and got in laying in wait for my punishment. However the light of the morning came and there were no guards. Even when they came to let me out of my cell for exercise I was not asked about running up the wall. I found this very strange but a huge relief that I was not punished. I assumed at the very least they would have given me a light beating. Maybe the guard felt sorry for me? Or appreciated I made his presumably dull night of watch more interesting. Whatever the reason I felt really lucky.

Despite not being punished I knew I couldn't attempt an escape for a while. The guard probably informed the other guards of me running up the wall so they probably would take an even keener interest in my actions and movements from now on. I didn't give up hope altogether, in a few weeks time I would try again but only if I felt the dust had settled and the guards eased up watching me. The only problem now was how to occupy myself for two weeks in the night.

The only thing I could think that would stop me from jumping up the wall was by getting stoned and pissed. By being in a drunken and stoned stupor I wouldn't be able to do it physically or mentally.

Finding suppliers for hash and alcohol was quite tricky though as I couldn't speak Spanish and the dealers were obviously secretive about their trade. Unlike in Ceuta the guards here seemed more keener to keep prisoners in check. So to get stuff you needed to be in the know. John, Joseph and I did manage to find a dealer over the next few days. The dealer did not have much as getting the stuff in was hard. But I did manage to buy off him a little block of resin, but for an extortionate amount. From this I had a few joints in the night. This still wasn't enough to calm my brain. Maybe I could keep my mind occupied by getting a pack of cards or I could draw a chess table again on the floor.

On my fifth morning I was given another solution to my boredom in the nights. The guards on opening me up left me a present of a cell mate and it was none other than Enio.

It was the only thing positive that the guards woke me up for.

'Hi Alan,' said Enio.

'What the hell!' I said coughing.

My eyes struggled to open as I was still quite sleepy and all they wanted to do was close. With immense effort I raised my eyebrows and opened my eyes as wide as they would go.

'Hi Enio.'

'So what's new with you?'

Enio spoke in Italian and looked on at me confused.

My heart sank as I forgotten that he wasn't that conversed in English but it was still nice to see a friendly face. Plus he seemed better than he did in Ceuta, much more happier. The last time I saw him he was covered in bites and mourning Dominic.

'Er Alan I heard about errr what you say when you errr went.'

Realising the futility of responding I put my hands in the air and shook my head.

'When you ….. Joseph and Danny.'

My heart sank when it dawned on me he was talking about the escape.

'Yes like Dominic ….. you need trouble.'

'Yes like Dominic,' I said sadly.

'Alan err Dominic.'

'Yes.'

Enio looked to the corner of the room in thought as if trying to figure how to tell me something. He then scratched his head and looked forward.

'Dominic is,' he said smiling with thumbs up.

'He's okay?'

'Yes! Yes he is okay.'

'What! You have seen him.'

'Yes,' Enio said nodding emphatically.

'That's amazing.'

'Where now Dominic?' I said with my hands in the air looking around the room.

Enio shrugged and returned back to a disheartened look

'Alan you need to….er…..teach me English.'

'Yes…..I will certainly do that.'

I was glad Enio said to teach him English as I think it would have been a lot harder for me to learn Italian. I mean at least Enio had the heads up he did know a lot of words in English. I had nothing. He was also very good at Spanish too.

To start off my English 101 course I picked up a block of hash and put it in Enio's hands.

'Hashish,' I said.

'Hashish!' he repeated enthusiastically.

I think he knew the word in English anyway but I think he appreciated that I was teaching him the important stuff first. After a few phrases and pointing around the room at stuff I decided that I should learn Spanish too. When I asked Enio if he could teach me he seemed more than pleased to do so.

I had thought about learning Spanish, but the guards at Ceuta put me off. I did not want to learn the same language as them. Plus I wanted to make it difficult for them to talk to me. It was a sort of rebellion against their treatment. However now I was far away from Ceuta and the guards were much better. I was shooting myself in the foot really not learning the language. There would be so many benefits to be gained. For one when I bought a tin from the shop I would be able to read what the fuck was in it.

Over the week Enio and I made significant progress. We had the added advantage of trying out our new languages on John and Joseph. They were our testers to see if we had done right. Obviously John would converse with Enio in English and Joseph with me in Spanish. I think John and Joseph got a buzz out of it too. I mean doing anything different made the day go quicker. Even John started to learn Spanish too.

It felt great sharing with just Enio. I liked having his company. Of all the people they could put in me I was very grateful having him. It also felt nice to smoke with someone rather than do it on my own.

Sadly though the happy times of Enio and I couldn't continue as we were plucked away one morning to be moved. The only pleasure I got from the guards coming in was being able to understand the orders they barked. We were taken to the dormitory where John and Joseph were, so we had to be thankful it was not another prison. But still it wasn't a welcome move. I wondered if they did always plan to move me in here.

In the dormitory Enio and I were greeted with hostile stares. I had been in the dormitory before visiting John and Joseph but it felt different. I think it was because it was early morning and everyone was in bed. Usually we would go to the dormitory after midday when it was only ever a quarter full at most. So it was a shock to see all these men staring at me. My defence mechanism kicked in as I stared back and smiled. My smile was received with great confusion. I liked this! Maybe the usual response was to look at the floor and shuffle in but I didn't play that way. I wanted them to feel unease at why I was smiling. I wanted them to either think I did not care or was slightly mad.

In the corner of my eye I could see movement, when I turned and looked I could it was Joseph waving and beckoning us over. Instantly Enio and I darted over to them. In the beds next to him was John and Karl, the happy German.

The two free beds were both next to Karl. That figures! I wonder if he had bored them to death or they had killed themselves to escape his despair. I quickly dived onto to the bed the furthest away from Karl. There was no way I was being next to him absorbing any negative thoughts; I was battling with my own as it was. Enio hopped into the bed next to Karl without a care in the world. He mustn't have met Karl yet.

I left the dormitory as soon as I could. I didn't want to be in there a minute longer than I had to be. I would be stuck there all night so I wanted to experience as much freedom as I could.

In the day we did just what we normally did and walked around chatting. The first hour was spent talking about all being together in the dormitory. Joseph was well made up. I didn't have the heart to tell him I wasn't so keen. After we were used to the idea we would all be in the same room Enio took over the conversation. John, Joseph and I encouraged this as we three had not much to say as we had spent most of our time together and shared experiences of prison life. Enio hadn't and so brought a much needed breath of fresh air.

That night despite my reservations I did enjoy myself being in the dormitory. This was largely helped by lively conversation, drinking and smoking in a group. The atmosphere wasn't great though as I could not feel totally comfortable as the Spanish contingency were a lot more meaner in Puerto than I had experienced anywhere else. Nearly every day a fight would break out amongst the Spanish.

After speaking to Karl too I realised he had good reason to be a miserable sod. Unlike the rest of the Europeans I had met who were on smuggling charges, he was facing a sentence for armed robbery. So for a start he was looking at a hefty sentence. But his sentence was increased by the amount of bullets he had. For even single bullet they found they added a year. He was looking at over thirty years. Suddenly my twenty odd year sentence didn't look so bad.

Also in the dormitory was another British guy. I forget what his name was but he was a Londoner. As soon as we started talking in English he hopped over to see us. Not surprising as John and I were the only other British people here. We made him feel welcome and allowed him to have a joint or two and a few drinks. It felt strange talking to another Brit. It was also weird at how in our small group we British were the majority now in the European contingency.

When I asked the Londoner why he was here it was like I uncorked a reservoir as words gushed out of him. Poor fellow must have wanted to talk to someone for a while. From his verbal diarrhea I was shocked too to find he wasn't in prison for smuggling. Plus his crime was the most avoidable.

He moved from London to Marbella to run a bar and restaurant. He said business was great and he had wealthy British customers. He had a mix of British people who had moved to Marbella with British people who would come to him when they were on holiday. Although doing well he was still envious of the money his rich clients had. So to gain more riches for himself he would steal from his customers when they were in the restaurant. He would firstly make a fuss of them when they came in and then disappear to the kitchen making sure they saw him putting on an apron. Then he would nip out, rob them of money and valuable items before returning back to the restaurant and wishing his customers a good night. He had the perfect alibi from the victim of the crime. They would verify he had been there all night.

Robbing his customers became so second nature he couldn't even tell me how many he had done. I couldn't believe that. Becoming friends with people and then robbing them. I did admire however his genius of getting his victims to be his alibi's though.

He was also unclear about how he actually got caught but he did say he caught wind he was going to be arrested and tried to flee via a plane back to London. Unfortunately for him the police had put a message out to stop him boarding any flights from Spain.

After a solid half hour talking about him he did eventually ask me a few questions. I told him about my circumstances and that I was innocent. He did not laugh or disagree but I could tell he didn't believe me. I also told him about Ceuta and how I was beaten for trying to escape.

'I claimed I was innocent but eventually I had to own up,' he said disgruntled.

'Why? Too much evidence?'

'No they beat me and did sick things to me.'

'What the guards?'

'No not the guards. The police on my arrest.'

'What do you mean sick things?'

'It's fucking embarrassing to say.'

'Come on tell me?'

'Okay, okay,' he said leaning in as if to talk quiet so no one else would hear.

'Well one of the things they did to me was tie me up by my feet and dangle me over a bucket whilst they all pissed on me,' he whispered.

'Fucking hell that's disgusting!'

'I feel sick just thinking about it.'

'At my trial I told my lawyer to inform the judge about it.'

'Really?'

'Yeah I wanted my lawyer to plead the case they only got a confession as they used improper means.'

'Did they take it down as evidence?'

'Did they fuck?'

'Well I suppose you couldn't prove it.'

'Oh I could.'

'How?'

'Well one of the policeman who pissed on me was in court acting as a guard.'

'So?'

'Well I remembered he had a circumcised cock so I told the Judge.'

'Really!' I said trying not to laugh.

'The lawyer asked if this fact about the policeman could be verified by a doctor.'

'What happened?'

'Well the judge refused.'

'That's not fair.'

'My lawyer pushed one more time but the judge said even if he were to allow it there was no doctor in the building.'

After relaying the story he fell silent and so did I. Then without any goodbyes he went back to his bed. I think he was embarrassed about telling me and I didn't help by being quiet but I didn't know what to say back. I was too consumed thinking about how disgusting and degrading it must have been for him. It made the beatings I had seem in some way acceptable. I hope to god I don't have to endure that.

23 SEVILLE

On May 3rd 1979 I was sent to a prison in Seville. This was my fifth prison in ten months. I was getting used to the act of being ripped from my bed at night and being taken to another prison. A few of the prisoners I met referred to this process as catching the ghost train. Not a surprise as the other prisoners were not forewarned and the ones moved vanished into the night without a trace.

The journey from Ceuta to Algeciras must have been for special circumstances as we were shipped out in the day. Plus I suppose they couldn't do it at night because we needed to go by ferry and that would have cut into the time when the Ceuta guards liked to relax.

At first I did find it unsettling moving from prison to prison, but now I was getting used to it and even starting to enjoy it as the prisons, the food and the conditions were getting much better the more North I travelled. Another shock was John and Joseph came with me. I really thought we were to be split up.

In the early hours of the morning we were taken straight to a dormitory at Seville. This was strange too! Normally I would be put into a solitary confinement cell before being allowed to sleep with others. Or so I thought. The Spanish really did like to mind fuck.

The guards left us three in the dark to scrabble around and find three empty beds. This dormitory was much smaller than I was used too, but I think it still housed fifty men as the majority of beds were bunk beds. Well it made sense I suppose. They could cram more prisoners in with bunks.

Joseph was the first to find an empty bunk bed. He quickly on sight of it ran up and claimed the top bunk. John then claimed the bed underneath. I had to go in the lower bunk that was adjacent. I wanted go up top but there was already a prisoner up there. The prisoner on the top didn't even stir when I got into bed. I bet he will have a fucking shock when he sees my ugly mug in the morning.

The next day we all went exploring. I went off just for a tour, Joseph went off in search of the kitchens and John went in search of the bogs. After a full tour of the place nothing caught my attention. It was just like every other Spanish prison I had been too except with different colour paint on the walls.

Bored with looking around I headed to the patio to stretch my legs and to check out the other prisoners. The weather was perfect for walking in. The sun was out and the temperature was hot but interjected with a cool refreshing breeze. After several rotations I decided to stand near the wall and survey my fellow prisoners.

When I looked at the Spanish prisoners I was shocked. This was the first prison I had been too where the Spanish prisoners looked cleaner and more smartly dressed than the rest of the prison population. Including me! In every prison I had been to it was just the norm for the Spanish to look dirty and dressed practically in rags. Not these boys though. They really took pride in their appearance and held their heads high when they walked.

Their dress sense although clean and smart did also make me giggle as it looked more like fancy dress than normal everyday clothing. It was as if they had crossed the costume of a cow boy with that of a flamenco dancer. They wore tight black trousers with white ruffled shirts and bootlace ties. Fucking hell they must be hot in that gear. I might have bought clothes like that to wear for a laugh if the temperatures in Spain weren't so hot. But on a comfort level I will stick with my T-shirt and shorts.

After several hours just hanging around on my own in the patio my solitude was broken when John and Joseph came striding over.

'There you are!' said Joseph annoyed as if he had been looking for me for a while.

'Hi Al,' said John casually.

'Yeah just been having a stroll around the patio. I tell you what the Spanish look really weird in this place.'

'I know they look like funny flamenco dancers,' John said chuckling.

I laughed with him as we pointed as some of the Spanish and laughed.

'Shush you two. You will get us killed,' whispered Joseph.

'What do you mean?'

'Well the Spanish you are making fun of are gypsies.'

'Gypsies?'

'Yeah they are Gitano's.'

'What's that?'

'One of the major groups of gypsies of Spain.'

'So what?' said John with indifference.

'Well the Gitano's run this place.'

'So they are like the daddies of this place?' I questioned.

'Daddies? What do you mean?'

'The Gitano's are in charge.'

'Yes that is right! And you don't want to piss them off! They are very proud and passionate people. If you upset them in any way they will make you pay.'

'How do you know all this?'

'I went to ask about a kitchen job and they told me if I wanted one I had to speak to the Gitano's. So he filled me in on the history of the place.'

'He could have been winding you up Joe.'

'I don't think so. And for the last time my name is Joseph!' he hissed

'Best we don't piss them off John. We don't want to find out the hard way. Do we?' I said backing up Joseph.

'Yeah suppose your right. Why invite trouble when you don't have too.'

In this prison was also the first time I had seen a transvestite prisoner. In fact the first time I had ever seen a transvestite. I was gobsmacked. He was Spanish with long brown hair, big brown eyes and a pair of boobs. He also wore make up, a tight black top and a skirt. Fair play to the guy he did look like a pretty smart looking woman and when he walked past he did so with grace and femininity. For a few seconds I was mesmerised. She looked so real! I then shuddered back to reality thinking about his big hairy cock.

That night when we were locked up in the dormitory the main topic of conversation was about sex. I think the transvestite had made us all realise we missed women. We all sat on Joseph's bed on the top bunk and each reeled some of our choice experiences. Each time John and Joseph recited their encounters they would look out in the distance as if going back to that specific time. I did the same.

Towards the end of the room some of the Spanish gypsies had cleared some beds away for space on the floor to be able to play cards. I couldn't see what game they were playing but it looked like poker. In the middle of the circle was a pile of money and every now again we would hear the clinking noise of coins being thrown in.

One of the gypsies shouted and put his fingers to his lips making a shush noise. The room went deathly silent. I looked at John and Joseph who responding by raising their eyebrows. We all then looked back at the card game.

From feeling a little silly I had to hold my breath in order not to laugh at the serious faces the gypsies pulled whilst they rigidly held onto their cards. Looking at the money in the middle this game was for seriously high stakes.

'Look at all that money!' whispered John.

'I know!'

There were six men around in the circle. Four of the men obviously had bowed out of the game as they all leant back and did not plough any further money in. Although the four men had no vested interest they still all watched on intently. The two men who remained in the game were directly opposite each other and looked locked in battle. Then the moment arrived and both threw down their cards. The gypsy who won laughed and joyfully began scooping up his masses of money. The other gypsy looked at his cards scowled and then threw them down. He pointed at one of the cards already out and shouted. The other gypsy shook his head and continued laughing and started to count his piles of money.

A heated conversation in Spanish ensued. They both talked too fast for me to understand but I did manage to pick out the word cheat and liar. Before I could turn to Joseph to find out exactly what was said the argument intensified. Both men stood up nose to nose fists clenched challenging for a fight. The suspected cheater put his cash in his pocket, his hand in the air and turned around. The other man launched onto him. They scrapped around on the floor for several minutes. The cheater managed to break free and took several steps back from his attacker. He put his hands in the air and spoke a few words. He then pulled something metal from his pocket which glinted in the light as he held it out.

'Al he's got a fucking knife!' gasped Joseph.

His accuser did not back down from the weapon and instead created his own by smashing a bottle by its base on the floor. All the Spaniards around the two men moved away and retreated to their bunks.

The atmosphere grew tense as everyone watched them side step each other whilst lunging in making stabbing motions with their weapons. Each looked too afraid to make the first move. The cheater with the knife shook his head and withdrew his knife slightly. This gave the accuser the chance to run in and plunge the glass bottle to his chest. I couldn't tell if it had made contact as the cheater pushed him away. The accuser dived back in again and then they both started to really go for it. They plunged in and out with their weapons. Their white ruffled shirts became a bath of blood.

The cheater then ran towards the toilets whilst the accuser and a few other men followed. I could hear the groans as they continued to stab at each other. The rest of the room was split into gaspers and cheerers. John, Joseph and I did neither and just stared ahead bemused.

'Now do you believe me they are dangerous John,' Joseph said

'Aye I will give you that one kid.'

The commotion must have alerted the guards as they weren't long storming in. Four guards headed towards the toilets. The accuser was taken out first by two guards. He looked still in rage as he wriggled to get free from the guards. A few minutes later the cheater was carried out. His head wobbled like a rag doll as he was carried by two guards. The dormitory was in silence.

Shortly after, three other guards appeared at the door. They barked at us to face the wall. Despite the devastating situation I was pleased with myself that I understood his instructions in Spanish. Everyone in the room quickly jumped to their feet and headed to the wall nearest to them and spread their legs and feet apart. John, Joseph and I were right at the back of the room. One by one they asked the prisoners to move away from the wall and drop their weapons in the middle of the floor. I could not see the weapons as I was facing the wall but I could hear an almighty clang in the centre of the room each time a weapon was dropped. The noises seemed pretty constant too as each of the Spanish left.

It then came to Joseph's turn. Joseph turned around and started to speak Spanish. The guards seemed annoyed and kept shouting back at Joseph.

'What's wrong?' I asked.

'They want us to put down our weapons or there will be consequences.'

'But we don't have any?'

'I know.'

'Look I will tell again. And say about you and John.'

Before Joseph could open his mouth two guards approached and roughly searched both Joseph and myself. Then the guard who searched me also patted down John. We all then turned around with our arms in the air. The guards look bewildered and started muttering to each other.

'What are they saying Joseph?' I whispered

'They can't believe we don't have weapons.'

'Really?'

The guards then smiled nodded and pointed to the direction of the door. I had never seen guards smile sincerely before. Maybe they were impressed and respected the fact we did not carry weapons. But why should we? We knew not to mess with the Spanish and that they carried. We knew if we had an argument with a European it would normally get resolved with words. I would also like to think that if I got into a physical fight with any of my mates or Europeans it would be the old fashioned fair way with a set of fists. I mean where was the dignity to win a fight with weapons anyway.

When I left the room I couldn't take my eyes of the pile of weapons in the middle of the floor. There were loads. I knew they carried knives but I didn't imagine so many and some were huge in size. It must have been an art in itself to conceal such massive items.

We were all taken out into the yard. Everyone apart from John, Joseph and I were patted down again and questioned. After ten minutes or so the guards seemed happy and we were let back in the room. The pile of weapons was now gone.

That night everyone took a while to settle. One of the poker players cleaned up the blood and looked solemn. Probably thinking if his friend is going to make it as he was slashed pretty badly.

The next day I was knackered. Last night was so adrenalin filled it had taken it out of me. Plus I couldn't sleep worrying about whether a Gypsy would knife me in my bed. I knew it shouldn't really happen as I kept my nose clean but I still felt threatened. I mean one could have gone berserk and rampaged in the night.

I wandered round the patio and noticed gypsy's dotted around looking at the sky and seemingly pensive. What the fuck is going on now? When I looked around I also noticed some gypsies putting money into metal tins and then binding them with elastic bands or string. Then quickly the gypsies with metal tins stood in a line a metre or so from the back wall. One of the main gypsies's yelled out ready in Spanish and then counted to three. On three the gypsies all threw their metal tins up in the air.

Then the gypsies who had thrown the tins quickly and evenly dotted themselves around the patio. I decided to follow suit to see what the crack was. I waited in one spot looking at the wall whilst trying not to draw attention to myself just in case this was wrong. Several minutes went by but the gypsies did not take their eyes off the wall. Then all of sudden out of nowhere I could see a bombardment of missiles being thrown over the wall. I flinched as one of them nearly hit me and landed at my feet. The missile was a metal tin similar to the ones they threw over with the money in. As I looked around everyone was picking these tins up so I followed suit. I took my tin to the corner of the patio and opened it. Inside was a beautiful honey coloured block of hash. I will keep this thank you very much.

I wandered off to go back inside but before I could Joseph grabbed me.

'What have you got there Alan?'

'Nothing.'

'Al if it is a metal tin you need to tell me or you will be in deep trouble.'

'Look Joseph don't worry about it.'

'Did you pick up a package?'

'Why?'

'Look Alan you must give it to the owner.'

'What?'

'If you don't you will get stabbed.'

Reluctantly I withdrew the tin I was hiding behind my back and held it out towards Joseph.

'Look inside.'

When I looked inside I could see there was name. Feeling pissed off Joseph then instructed me that I should find the gypsy straight away so he doesn't suspect me of stealing it. As I wandered around I could see the tin owners marching around in search of their goods. I waited until there was just one guy looking around the patio frantically. Well that must be my man. To make sure in Spanish I asked him his name. He responded giving me the exact name in the tin. With reluctance I handed it over.

'Gracias! Gracias!' he wailed excitedly.

He looked around for the guards and then took out the ounce. He firstly examined it by twisting and turning it to look at it from different angles. He then put it in the palm of his hand and gently lowered it up and down as if to weigh it. I think he was checking to see if I had chipped any off I expect. He looked at me with one eyebrow raised. I responded with a smile and a nod and was ready to walk away. When I moved to turn my back he grabbed me by the arm and told me to wait. He then put the block in his mouth and bit off a bit of hash. He held his hand out with the hash with spittle on it smiling. I took the hash from him trying not to be disgusted at it being covered in saliva and nodded. Oh well free hash is free hash.

I went back to John and the boys to show them my offering. I didn't tell them he had bit it off though with his teeth. When I had a joint that night I let Joseph crumble the first bits in.

24 CORDOBA

I only spent a few weeks in the dormitory at Seville before I was moved on to yet another prison. John and Joseph were also awoken by the guards and were to accompany me on the midnight ghost train. This fucking flummoxed me again! I really had got it into my head they wanted to split us up. I thought they had made a mistake by sending us all to Seville, but it can't be as they have done it again. Maybe they thought having my buddies around would keep me occupied from thinking about escape?

Being pros now at being moved in a semi-conscious state, we all managed to gather our belongings together way before the fifteen minutes permitted. We even had chance to have a brief conversation about what we thought the next prison would be like and where it would be. Joseph also echoed my thoughts saying about how he was shocked at us being shipped together. John said a possible explanation could be we had trial dates close together.

Before I could ask John where he thought the trials would be held the guards entered the room. They made an awful racket stomping around with their heavy boots and jangling sets of hand cuffs. Simultaneously John, Joseph and I stood up holding our belonging in one hand whilst also putting our wrists together. The guards slapped on the heavy cuffs tight and pushed us towards the door.

When we got outside I was chilled to the bone. I really need to buy a jumper for these excursions. Jeans and a T-shirt just weren't sufficient enough for the chilly night air. Towards the back of the bus were all our belongings which were taken from prison to prison. My case was right on the bottom. John and I slung in our hand luggage on top. I then moved out of the way so Joseph could chuck his stuff in. Joseph threw his bag in but then took out a camera which was mixed in amongst the luggage. He hung the camera by a strap around his neck and started to make his way to stand with us. Before he could take a third step his cuffed arm was grabbed by the guard. The guard pointed at the camera and then back to the boot. Joseph shook his head and started rambling in Spanish whilst lifting his camera up every now and again. I concentrated hard to listen to the conversation but I was still a novice in learning Spanish and could not work out all what was said. I did manage to pick up a few words such as a no and a please but that was about it. The conversation quickened as it seemed to get a bit heated as spit flew everywhere. I had never seen Joseph playing fuck with the guards before, he really wanted his camera. He better have a bloody good reason because it was freezing.

Eventually the conversation ceased and we all boarded the bus. Joseph seemed well happy that he was allowed to keep his camera. I felt much better too having shelter from the outside air. The bus engine then revved up and away from Seville we went.

'Joseph, why the fuck have you got that camera around your neck?' said John

'Did you see where it was?'

'It was in the boot,' John said shrugging his shoulders. 'So what like?'

'Yes! On top of all our stuff. It could have fallen off and broke!'

'By the time we get out of here Joseph that camera will be ancient anyway!' John sniped back.

'Well there was another reason,' Joseph said in hushed tones.

'What?' I said quietly with interest.

Joseph looked all around to make sure the guards at the back and front weren't watching. He then opened the battery compartment. Then with another quick look around he brought out a 2" by 1" wrapped up rectangular block of hash and then hid it in between his legs.

'Now you see?' said Joseph smiling.

'Yes I will give you that one,' I said grinning at the sneaky bastard.

I was going to ask Joseph about how he was going to hide the hash if they did a pat down search in Cordoba but when I looked across I could see he had already thought about that as he was trying to shove it up his arse hole.

'Jesus!' I said in disgust.

I wish he would have warned me first as I didn't really want to see that. Although I looked away I could still hear him groaning from straining. John and I shouted at him to hurry up because we couldn't bear to listen. Mind I suppose it must be have been hard to shove something that big up your arse especially with handcuffs on. After witnessing this I decided I would never have any hash off Joseph ever again.

The next prison we were sent to was in Cordoba. Like with the other prisons I had been to across Spain they had high towers with turrets and armed guards patrolling. It was another prison where escape would be difficult.

Its funny people are always surprised when I say in prison I mainly thought about escape. A lot of people seem to think in prison the main thing on your mind would be sex. Well with me it wasn't. I did genuinely mainly think about escape. Plus a brash few always asked whether I wanked a lot in prison. Again they were surprised when I would say I very rarely did. To me this is not shocking. Being surrounded by hundreds of dirty sweaty men in cess pit conditions just didn't give me the horn to choke the old chicken.

The bus eventually stopped and we were taken inside the prison. We were escorted to individual cells that were side by side with each other. I was in the middle cell with John and Joseph either side of me. This was neat! Best of both worlds, in my own cell and near my lads!

Over the next few days Cordoba did seem to be the best prison to be in. The food actually looked edible and the guards seemed to be the most chilled out. We even had a canteen where all the prisoners could be seated at meal times. I almost felt civilised again. The British consulate too there was the most convincing in his role and surprisingly he wasn't British either but Spanish. Although he was Spanish his command of English was impeccable. He spoke English better than me. He also seemed a pretty nice guy and did actually seem to give a toss. The prisoner markets also were out of this world. I mean in every prison the Spanish would sell you anything and everything but in Cordoba it looked professional the way they would set out their products. All the goods would be sourced by their visitors and families. You could also order clothes made to measure. I found this a very handy service being quite short and slim. I did even test it out by ordering a pair of Taurus Jeans. I was amazed when they arrived as the quality was good and they were a snug fit.

Another difference between Cordoba and the other prisons I had been to was the presence of cats. They were fucking everywhere. They were allowed to roam around freely. I think they allowed it as a sort of free pest control in order to keep the rat population down. Being an animal lover I befriended one of the cats and had him in my room. I didn't name him as I didn't know how long I was going to be here for. It felt like if I had named him it would have made him my pet. I couldn't think of him as a pet if I was to have to leave again. I just thought of him as a welcomed visitor who I would stroke in order to gain comfort. John too had a cat which surprised me. I never saw him as an animal lover. Mind he probably liked the cat as it never fucking argued back with him. He always liked to be in the right. Joseph on the other hand thought John and I were fucking mental to have cats. He could not understand the attraction of having a pet. Every time he would catch me talking to my pussy he would laugh out loud. Apparently in France it was not common place to have a pet. In his home town he knew no-one who had a pet cat or dog. John and I put it down to a British thing as when we spoke to other prisoners they too thought we were bonkers. The only difference I found with Cordoba that I really didn't like was the wakeup call. When the guards would unlock the doors they would create a massive commotion with their truncheons and go on until the majority got up.

After a few weeks in a new prison I got bored as I usually did. I couldn't even distract myself with thinking about escape as no ideas came to mind, plus this prison seemed too tight on security. I did ask if I could work in the kitchens to busy myself but I was refused. I suppose having on my record attempting to blow up the kitchen in Ceuta didn't help. Joseph on the other hand managed to get a job in the kitchens, which made me envious. I had to look on the positive side though at least with Joseph in the kitchens we had bigger portions, better food and freebies from whatever Joseph could sneak out.

The nights became quite boring too. John, Joseph and I had pretty much talked about every fucking thing. God I can't imagine twenty more years of this! I hope to Christ the money I had shovelled in to the different consulates I saw was actually doing something. If it didn't each consulate would have to beware a hellish vendetta when I did come out.

The next morning I didn't get out of bed. I couldn't be arsed to move. I decided there was no point in getting up early I wasn't missing anything. Everyday the fucking same! Walking around and around in frigging circles. Plus my cat was sleeping on my feet and looked far too happy to be disturbed. The only motivation I had to get up was to feed my grumbling stomach. Maybe I will go back to bed after breakfast? Rubbing my eyes in tiredness I stared across my room to the floor where a tin of pears stood. I forgot about them. Maybe I didn't need to go to breakfast after all, I could eat them.

I looked back at my tom cat whose face looked like it was smiling, as he was curled up sleeping fast with the sun from the window shining down on him. Gently I moved my legs away and sat up. He stirred a little but soon went back to stillness and sleep. I stroked his head and he gave a little meow but remained with his eyes closed looking comfortable. If only I could be like an animal, happy with a bed, food and a roof over my head. The thorn of the human condition is to always want more. I continued stroking his head causing his purrs to grow louder and louder. Stroking him made me feel better. Maybe life wasn't that bad after all? Maybe I just need to change my mindset.

My quiet moment was broken when John barged open my door and stomped in. From the sudden noise the cat was scared out of its skin in fright and jumped off the bed and zoomed through the door.

'What's the crack Al?'

Despite being pissed off he disturbed my sleeping pussy I decided not to bother to say anything. He wouldn't have understood and just took the piss.

'Do you fancy coming out round the town with me?'

'Aye why not.'

I jumped off the bed and gauged the temperature of the outside air by putting my fingers through the cell window. The temperature did not feel warm enough for shorts so I grabbed my fitted Taurus jeans, t-shirt and flip flops. Not looking when putting my flip flops on I stubbed my toe on the tin of pears. I danced around the room holding my foot saying every swear word I could think of. John laughed at my pain. After a few seconds the pain died down and I put my naked foot into the flip flop again this time making sure I was well away from any object to stub it with.

'Have you got any booze left Alan?'

'Nah I drunk mine last night.'

'Joseph?'

'Nah he borrowed some off me last night.'

'Looks like we will have to get some more then.'

'Yeah it does.'

'I wish we could get the stronger stuff,' John whined

'Yeah me too.'

'Come on lets go shopping for beer tonight.'

'Coming,' I said in a silly voice as I walked through the door.

I was about to shut the door when I was jolted by a sudden flash of inspiration.

'That's it!'

'What the fuck! I didn't saying anything,' said John taken aback.

'Oh shut up John.'

'What's it?'

'Come back in my cell for a minute?'

'Why? You ain't turning queer are you?'

'Shut up!' I shouted. 'I have an idea.'

I opened the door and John came back in the room. Waiting for him to shut the door I picked up the pears.

'This John is our ticket to free alcohol.'

'Eh?.......... Pears?'

'Yes with tinned fruit we can make hooch'

'Fruit?'

'Yeah! Cider comes from apples doesn't it?'

'Aye I suppose.'

'Oh free booze Alan. That would be great!'

I had never seen John's eyes light up so much. I was definitely onto a winner

'Do you know how to make it?' John asked excitedly

'No.......But I suppose it can't be that hard.'

'Yeah anything is worth a try! I am game'

After Joseph had finished his breakfast shift in the kitchen I caught hold of him and told him of our plan to make hooch. Joseph seemed keen on the idea but he was not as excited as John and I. However he did have reservations when I told him the ingredients we needed had to come from the kitchen. He worried about being caught stealing the stuff and not being able to work in the kitchens again. He was right to worry as the stuff we needed could not simply be hid under a T-shirt as we needed an industrial size tin of fruit and piles of sugar and yeast. These would definitely be missed by the head chef who orders the food. To get round this problem I told him to offer money for the ingredients. Joseph seemed relieved about this and agreed to do as I asked.

That night Joseph imparted the wonderful news the head cook was on aboard and sure enough after a few days Joseph manage to quietly sneak the goods from the kitchens to the cells. When we had all the ingredients we had a brief chat about how best to make it. As none of us had a clue what to do we all agreed to fucking chuck everything in and hope for the best. We tipped a bit of the pear juice out first and then just dumped in the yeast and sugar mixing it as best as we could. I also bought a small hand towel from the prison market and covered the tin. I did this as I thought it might speed up the fermentation process and make it sweat more. Plus it would act a barrier to stop flies and mosquitoes from falling in.

Once the batch was made it was agreed I would keep the hooch in my room as it was my idea after all. However after only two days I could not stick the stuff under my bed a moment longer. The constant glugging and blooping noises from the fermentation process of the hooch really cooked my head. John instantly volunteered to take over and hide it in his room. Joseph and I looked at each other thinking whether John could be trusted. Nothing was said and both Joseph and I nodded in agreement John could do it. John instantly dived under the bed and hooked out the precious vat of hooch. I had never seen him look so excited before, he was like a big kid.

'Now John don't forget. We all decided to wait four weeks before we try it,' I said sternly like a father.

'Yeah! Yeah! I agree!' he said flippantly.

'Good!'

'Now make sure no-one sees you carrying that tin into your room.'

'God Alan you're like an old woman.'

That night we all congregated in John's room for our usual smoke and chat. We would normally hang out in my cell but the venue changed to John's room because of the hooch. We wanted to stay with our precious hooch as much as we could to protect it from being discovered by other prisoners or guards.

As the days passed the smell from the hooch grew and grew in its intensity. I thought the noises were bad but the smell was out of this world. It was like what I'd imagine a rotten egg would smell like if it had been trapped in a cat's anus for a year.

To keep the guards off the scent I told John to say it was the cats. I even made him keep my cat in his room to add weight to the story. Fair play to him every morning I would see him putting on a good act to the guards wafting his hand over his nose whilst saying 'gattlos' the Spanish word for cats. They must have bought it as they never questioned him further about the smell or even went to search his room.

Plus he listened to me about skimming the scum that formed on the towel in order to keep it pure, as each time I would inspect our brew it would be quiet clear. I bet he licked his fingers afterwards but I could forgive him for that. I probably would have done the same to have a little taste.

Halfway into making our hooch which was around two weeks I had a meeting with my consulate. I was glad of a visit seeing someone other than John and Joseph. Especially John as he constantly did my head in asking when the hooch was ready. I couldn't believe I had two weeks more to put up with his constant whinging.

With a spring in my step I whizzed off to the visiting room after being called by a guard. Once sat down in the chair across from my consulate I breathed a sigh of relief. Now I could have a nice chat with someone tidy. The usual happened we exchanged pleasantries and he asked me how I was coping. I told him I was fine and ploughed straight into asking about my trial and when and where it was to be. He skillfully as always avoided giving me direct answers but managed in his politician tone to make me feel things were underway. The only thing he did ever confirm was that money was being sent and received. It better fucking well had!

A silence ensued after I had exhausted all the questions I had for him. I took this as my cue to leave and moved my chair back from under the table ready to stand up. But before I went to turn around the consulate flapped his hand downwards as if to signal me to stay.

'Er Alan there is one more thing.'

'Oh yes. What's that?'

He cleared his throat as if out of nerves and looked at the table in front of him avoiding eye contact with me.

'We have had a request from your ex-wife?'

'What!' I said taken aback. 'What the hell does she want?'

'For you to sign these papers.'

Still avoiding my gaze and now looking very sheepish he shuffled around in his briefcase. Eventually he found the papers he was looking for and plonked them on the table with his right hand whilst rearranging his tie with his left.

'What are they?'

'They are adoption papers Alan,' he said holding them up to the glass window that separated us.

'What!'

'Yes your ex-wife Pauline has asked if you would agree in allowing her partner Jim to become the adoptive father of your sons Lee and Dale.'

I was completely stumped. I did not know how to react as I never saw this coming.

'No I can't sign them!' I said trying to hold back the tears.

'Look Alan,' said the consulate softly.

'Can I go now?' I said turning around to the guard and half standing.

'Look Alan let's talk about this.'

I shook my head and looked to the floor.

'Look,' he said clearing his throat. 'I will keep the papers on me for our next few visits just to give you time to think about it.'

I nodded at him as I couldn't speak. I was far too angry and embarrassed to utter any words. I quickly rushed to the door and barked at the guard in Spanish to let me out. Once free from the visiting room I blanked out everything around me and stormed straight to my cell.

I couldn't believe she wanted to delete me from my boy's lives just like that. Make it so I never existed. If it wasn't for me she wouldn't even have had them in the first place, they would still be rotting in care! I was the one who made her see she had to be a mother. The boys cannot forget me. I am their father.

I went back to bed and stared at the ceiling for a few hours just remembering my boys and the last time I saw them. Remembering the elation I felt when I took them out of care and the happiness and unconditional love they poured onto me. I wondered what they looked like now as it was well over a year since I last saw them. How could Pauline do this? I am their real father. Was I that bad?

I looked around the cell feeling helpless. I felt ashamed she no longer wanted me to be apart of the boys or her life. She wanted to cut me out like a tumour. The other thing that hurt was the way she had done it. I mean she could have written directly to me and sent me the adoption papers. Why did she have to make it so public? Because of her my consulate knew and presumably all the guards did too.

Before I could stew any longer there was a bang at the door.

'Piss off I am sleeping!'

'Alan!' shouted Joseph. 'You need to come quick.'

Annoyed I threw off my sheet, slipped my flip flops on and went to the door. Joseph looked nervous.

'I need your help with John.'

'Why what's wrong with him?'

'Just come and see.'

Annoyed but curious I followed him.

'Look,' he said gulping hard as he opened John's cell door.

When I looked I could see John singing and stumbling around the cell. I could not understand what he was singing as he was slurring very badly. He then stopped mid song and shone me a wicked grin.

'Oh hi Alan,' he said laughing like a girl and running towards me.

'Do you know mate…… you are my bestest bestest friend!'

'And Al I am not saying it cos were in here like…………… I do love you man………and I love Joseph even though he can act like a girl.'

'What!' said Joseph angrily.

'Yeah mate I love you for making this lovely lovely alcohol,' he said hugging me and overpowering me with the toxic fumes coming from his mouth.

'It smells and taste like shit though……..but it's great.'

'Get off me man,' I shouted whilst pushing him away.

Despite being paralytic he sensed I was not amused by his antics and released his grip from me. He walked backwards and put his hand tightly over his mouth trying not to smile like when a kid does something naughty.

'Oh Alan………. I have been bad haven't I? You did tell me four weeks.'

'Now John four weeks you said,' John said trying to put on a welsh accent but sounding more like a pissed up Asian person.

John then slipped over and fell on his arse making a loud thump. His eyes looked shocked but obviously he did not feel any pain as he broke down into tears laughing a few seconds later.

Joseph then burst out laughing as John started waggling his arms and legs in the air on his back. It looked like he was doing an impression of a bug that could not turn back over onto its legs. After looking at John and Joseph I was infected roaring with laughter too.

'I knew he wouldn't last four weeks,' said Joseph.

'Well at least we will know whether it's safe to drink if he makes it through the day,' I whispered to Joseph whilst still tittering.

Joseph managed to get a day off from his catering duties so he could help me babysit John and keep him away from trouble. Our main concern was to shield him away from starting any fights with the Spanish. He had a loose tongue at the best of times but with this much drink inside him we knew he could have been dangerous. We also tried to shepherd him away from the guard's gazes as we did not want them to ask questions about how John was so drunk early in the day. Thankfully though he was a happy drunk so it wasn't too hard a job

Despite being annoyed at first I was glad towards the end of the day John had broken his promise and had a drink. Babysitting him was a very welcome distraction after my serious chat with the consulate. I didn't want to deal with that yet.

It soon came to lock down time and John had survived the day so Joseph and I decided to follow suit and get plastered. John dived in the hooch with a cup and drank it straight away. He already had had enough

Dutch courage inside him to not bother about the stench or taste. When Joseph and I scooped in our cups we were a little more reserved. With worried expressions we both examined it by looking in our cups and having a sniff. It looked like dirty barley water and smelt foul.

'Ready Joseph?'

'Not really.'

'Come on! On a count of three. One, two and three.'

Holding my nose I took a mighty swig from the cup and tilted my head backwards. The sour taste that hit my tongue was worse than what I imagined. It tasted like bitter watery vomit. My gullet fought with me to swallow the liquid but tensing my neck I forced it down.

'That is gross,' said Joseph breathing in deeply as if trying to stop himself from being sick.

'Come on Joseph push through we need to get pissed to forget the taste.'

'I a....gree!' John said slurring whilst swaying from side to side.

'Is it me?' John asked whilst roughly elbowing me in the arm, causing me to drop some of my vomit water on my Taurus jeans.

'Watch it!'

'Sorry.... Sorry.... Sorry,' John said getting quieter with each word.

'But is it me.........or is the room moving?'

'It's you John.'

'It's me!' he said shouting whilst falling to the side and laughing hysterically.

Being envious of John's drunken stupor I took a deep breath and downed the rest of my drink. I wretched from the taste but kept my mouth shut and forced the hooch down. After the first drink it became easier and easier to swallow. My tongue was used to the taste and my mind just didn't care. I don't remember much of the night after the second drink. I don't even know how many drinks I had in total. The hooch must have been strong.

The next day I woke up at eleven, fully clothed and face down on top of my bed. All the evidence suggested I must have passed out and had a good night. My head felt warm and sweaty too. On further examination by touch I realised this was from my cat lying on my head and neck. It felt like I was wearing a Russian hat.

Groaning with a head ache I turned over and held my head in my hands. This spooked the cat and made him run scared under the bed. Rubbing my forehead I decided there were two ways I could get rid of my hang over. Firstly I could do it the sensible way and hydrate myself with coffee and water and have a spliff or two to take away the pain. Or I could try hair of the dog and just carry on drinking. Despite feeling sick I decided to do the latter. I still wanted to block all thoughts about the adoption and getting paralytic seemed a good way to do it.

I slowly got up and crawled under my bed. Carefully I hooked out the hooch and looked at it in disgust. I heaved as I scooped out a cup full of drink from the pear tin. Before I could take a swig there was a knock at the door. Quickly I pushed the tin and the cup under the bed and stood bolt upright.

'Hello… It's John can I come in?'

'Yes, yes, yes come in,' I said relieved

John could see I was flustered and smiled.

'What you up to?'

'I thought you were a guard.'

'And…'

'Well I was going to take a swig of the hooch.'

'But its morning?'

'Well you got pissed yesterday morning.'

'I suppose…Alright let's get pissed again.'

'What shall we drink too?' said John smiling.

'To distant family and friends.'

Throughout the day we made several trips back to our cell to top up on our alcohol levels. We must have looked a right site laughing and stumbling all over the place but nobody bothered us. The Spanish didn't care and the guards didn't question us. Everyone happily left us to bounce around the prison merrily drunk.

At tea time Joseph met up with us in the canteen after finishing his jobs in the kitchen. He was in hysterics when he saw us as he couldn't believe we had been drinking all day. I was the first to finish my tea that day as the constant drinking made me hungry. John wasn't close behind but Joseph was only half way through his. He was too busy laughing at us.

From constantly drinking all today I needed yet another pee. I left the table and wobbled towards the door. On my way out of the canteen I fell into a table of Spanish prisoners. I was a gnat's breath away from pissing myself from my spontaneous movement. The tallest and meanest looking of the group stood up with arms out ready for a fight. I said sorry and laughed. The guy looked confused at my behaviour and shook his head. Thankfully he sat down and allowed me to pass.

On my way waddling awkwardly to the toilets I saw two Spanish prisoners outside talking amicably. One of the men had a photo in his hand which he passed to the other. The man receiving the photo smiled. Being nosey I had a little look as I made my way to the toilets. My first instinct was that it would be a naked picture of a woman. Instead it was a picture of three children, which were probably his.

The picture made me think again about Lee and Dale. I had managed to not think about them all day and now this happens. My mood switched from happy to melancholy. Even drunk I could not block them out.

At the toilet I was lost in my own thoughts as I took a long piss. This was the first time I allowed myself to drift off in the toilets. Usually I was on constant guard for anyone looking like they wanted to jump me for money or sex. Thankfully despite my absentmindedness nothing happened and I was left unscathed and unbuggered.

Still in a bad mood I entered the canteen. I looked across at my table and could see John drunkenly prodding and goading Joseph. Joseph smiled and pushed John away. However John came back pushing harder.

I fucking hated it when John bullied Joseph. All the time I was telling him to leave him alone. I thought he had got over being a dick but now I could see he was doing it when my back was turned.

Each time I watched John prod Joseph in the distance my breathing quickened and my eyes widened. Tense I stomped over to our table. John didn't notice me at first and continued laughing and giving Joseph a dig in the arm.

'Get your fucking hands off him!' I shouted loudly.

'Calm down Alan. Me and Joseph were just messing.'

'No you are not. You are being a tosser!'

'Al its fine. Be quiet,' said Joseph in worried tones as he surveyed the canteen.

'Oh yeah and what you going to do about it old man?'

John grinned back at me and continued to jab at Joseph. Then when he started to laugh at me a veil of red mist engulfed my face. John had got on my very last nerve. I was already wound up about the adoption papers and the fact John did not wait four weeks for the alcohol. This was the final straw.

Not being able to contain my anger I leapt over the table and started punching lumps into him. John took a few seconds to hit back as he seemed surprised by my quick aggression. When he did he gave me a good right hook to the jaw. This stunned me but after a few seconds I went at him harder. Over and over we pushed and pulled, punched and elbowed. Being a little drunk I lost my footing and fell to the floor but I managed to grab onto John's T-shirt and pull him down on me. On the floor we wrestled. We both tried to pin each other down, but none of us succeeded as we both seemed just as equally determined and strong. Quickly John pushed me off and got to his feet again. I quickly jumped up too. Once I was up I became aware of the Spanish prisoners surrounding us and cheering. This was strange. I had never seen them doing this when they watched their own people fight. Mind the fights they were used to were normally with weapons and very short-lived.

Becoming tired we pushed and pulled more than we punched. Wanting to end it I squared up to John and seized my moment to put him in a headlock. Pulling him around I managed to hook my arm around his throat. As John struggled to pull my arm from his neck I concentrated on slowing my breathing. I had a brief look round and was shocked to see three guards at the other end of the canteen just watching us. Fucking hell they liked watching a good fight too. With my concentration distracted John elbowed me in the side and struggled free. We managed to exchange a few more punches before the guards inevitably thought enough was enough and came over to part us.

The guards dragged us quickly away to two isolation cells that were side by side with each other. They were nothing like the isolation cells in Ceuta but they were basic none the less. There were a few cells in this little block but the guards specifically chose to put us side by side. I couldn't believe it. I wanted to be as far away from that Liverpuddlian git as I could. It seemed they did it just to wind us up.

'You scouse fucker look what you've done,' I shouted to the wall.

'Me! You're the one who fucking threw the first punch you Welsh cock.'

'You shouldn't have being a shit to Joseph.'

'He needs to fucking toughen up!'

'You know Joseph is not like that.'

'Maybe he fucking should be. We're in prison not a pissing holiday camp.'

'You shouldn't have done it. End of.'

'You realise now the hooch will be gone,' I shouted

'What?'

'Think about it.'

'Eh.'

'They know we are drunk. So they will probably search our room and confiscate it.'

'Oh!'

'Yes!'

'No more fucking hooch!'

John went quiet. I waited for him to start up speaking again as I wanted to make sure it sank in about the hooch and his bullying.

'It was good that hooch wasn't it.'

'It would have been better if you had left it alone.'

'I tell you what Alan you have a good right hook on you.'

'Thanks,' I said whilst laughing. 'Not bad for an old man!'

In the morning the guards let us out of the cells. John and I shook hands and smiled at each other. The guards looked flabbergasted as they watched us walk past and chat like friends.

Despite being bruised and sore I was glad I had a fight with John. Hitting lumps out of somebody allowed me to release a lot of pent up anger. Plus I think John and I became closer friends for it. As I was a decade or so older, shorter and less stocky I think he always had the notion he could have me in a fight. But I showed him.

The only downside of the fight was the hooch was found and confiscated. I was surprised though Joseph wasn't punished. I mean surely they would have realised that from him working in the kitchens he would have got the stuff for us. But for some reason they didn't and he was still allowed to work.

The next day I had a visit from the consulate. He looked very surprised at my bruised right eye and cheekbone. I lied to him and said I fell over. He obviously didn't believe me but could see I wasn't willing to talk as he didn't question me further. As usual he went through the progress of the case and said vaguely about when the trial was.

At the end he also showed me the forms. He didn't say a word and neither did I. I just shook my head and left. I was still not ready to give him a decision.

After seeing the consulate I busied myself by washing my clothes. They needed cleaning anyway but I did it to try and keep my mind off things. Each time I scrubbed and wringed my pants, T-shirts and trousers I became more and more annoyed. I hated the fact we had to do this. In a British prison we had uniforms and people designated to do the laundry. Not fucking scrubbing our hands raw like this.

I hung up my washing to dry when John came in my room. He could see I was pissed off and probed as to why. I fobbed him off saying I was pissed off about the laundry. He seemed to buy it as he too began chiming in about how he thinks things should be done.

'You know John they should fucking have a prison uniform.'

'I mean what would they do if a prisoner came in here naked.'

'Why don't we ask?' said John.

'We could couldn't we?'

'No harm in trying.'

'Let's go now,' I said enthused.

With a sense of purpose we marched to the guard's office. In broken Spanish we asked the guards about the prison uniforms. They looked astonished at our request but did say they had some but we would not like them. John and I pushed and pushed and said we didn't care. We droned on in English and broken Spanish how we weren't prepared to put up with getting our clothes stinking. Whatever uniform they had we promised we would wear it.

After a timely debate the guard smiled and said he would see what he could do. John and I both felt great as we had won. We decided to give them four days until we would ask again about the uniforms. But after three days had passed we didn't need to as we had a message from the guards the uniform had arrived. They hadn't lied to us. Excitable we raced over and picked them up. The guard laughed as he passed the folded clothes over to us.

We both rushed back to our cells to try them on. Joseph waited in the corridor as he was curious to see how they would look.

'Oh my god!' I shouted.

'What? Come on Al show me what it looks like.'

With that I could hear John giggling loudly in his room.

'Come on guys show me.'

I opened the door first. Joseph gasped in shock and then broke down into uncontrollable hysterics. He pointed at my clothes but could not utter any words. The prison uniforms were horrendous. They were thick, itchy and about four sizes too big. Luckily I was supplied with rope to tie my trousers to my slim frame. They were a pale blue and looked like soldiers uniforms from the Second World War.

A few moments later John stepped out of his room. Joseph looked over and continued to laugh. I looked at John and could see how silly the uniform looked on him despite his fitting to his frame a lot better than mine.

'Oh my god Al what do we fucking look like.'

'Hey John think of it this way they are free clothes.'

'But we look like fucking clowns. We can't wear these out there man.'

I eventually convinced John to keep the uniform on and we headed to the patio to show off our new clothes. Every single prisoner that laid eyes on us laughed at us. Even the guards smirked and giggled as we walked by. To wind everyone up further every now and again I would pretend to flick off dust from my shoulders as if I was wearing an expensive suit. This would make the Spanish roar. Maybe the Spanish do have a sense of humour after all.

'Oh fucking hell Al we are the laughing stock of the prison.'

'Fuck em' John. Let them laugh. We are not doing any harm.'

'Hey Al your beard looks like it could do with a trim.'

'Oh no I am leaving it to grow.'

'Why?'

'Well I look like a fucking tramp in this so why not. Plus why the fuck should I trim and tidy it for? Who in here do I want to impress?'

'Well...I suppose…..' he said looking into the top corners of his eyes.

'No actually you are right. I think I will grow my beard too.'

After a few weeks we both had beards bushy enough to accommodate a small squirrel. The beards really set off the uniforms making us look more like tramps. I also was quite liberal with my personal hygiene too and didn't wash as often as I normally did. Again I applied the same logic as with the beard. Why did I need to be so clean, when there was no reason to look good in here? I could now identify with the Spanish and why they were scruff bags.

After another week passed we soon didn't get noticed anymore as it now became the norm that we looked like vagrants. No more were we laughed at, pointed at or stared at.

I even forgot about how stupid I looked when I went to see the consulate. I just walked in normally and sat down. It was only when he went a shade of green and did a double take I realised he hadn't seen my new look. To make him worry more I flashed him a big grin through my bushy beard.

'Er hi Alan….er…………you okay?'

'Yes I am fine,' I said settling down on the chair. 'Why do you ask?'

'It's just I notice your clothes.'

'Oh yes do you like it? It's the prison uniform they gave me.'

'I see.'

'Er well….. You don't have to wear it. I mean if you want I can go to the Red Cross and pick you up some clothes if you haven't got many.'

'Oh I have clothes.'

'Oh I see.'

'But I want to wear the prison uniform.'

'You want to wear the uniform,' he repeated.

The consulate shook his head and with a breath composed himself back to his usual self. He told me about the money and that my trial was going to be very soon but he couldn't tell me when or where it would be held. So it was just the same old news.

'Well Alan that's all I have to say, so I should get going. Are you sure now you don't want me to pick you up some clothes?'

'No its fine… but…'

'Yes?'

'Have you got the papers on you? As I think I am ready to sign.'

'Oh okay I will pop them across now.'

With that he left the room and handed them to the guards to give to me. He then went back to his side of the room and sat back down.

'On the third page you need to sign on the dotted line at the bottom.'

'Okay,' I said as I rifled through the pages.

'Now Alan are you sure about this? You can have more time.'

I nodded as I didn't want to answer. I was afraid I would back out, but I couldn't. This needed to be sorted. I quickly signed and threw the papers back at the guard.

It felt a long walk to the cell. I wanted to turn around and say I had changed my mind but I knew what was done was done. It was for the best. I mean I never have and probably never will be much of a father to them. Why should I deny them having a father? Jim was a good man to both Pauline and the kids. He was their true father as he had stayed with them far longer than I ever did and brought them up. In their short lives all I had done was served prison sentences and bugger off. Jim deserved the legal title of a father.

When I came back from my visit John had changed out of his uniform and had had his beard shaved. He didn't give the uniform back though as he said he liked to wear it in bed. This was the only time I enjoyed wearing it too as it kept you nice and warm from the chilly night air. Especially as there was no central heating or extra blankets we could have to keep us warm.

John tried to convince me to stop wearing my uniform but I couldn't be bothered. He even kept relentlessly teasing me about my beard and lack of hygiene but I just ignored him. I couldn't be arsed. It didn't matter how hard he ribbed me I just didn't give a fuck. I had just signed away my kids so his jibes were a walk in the park. Joseph also had a go to convince me to go back to wearing my normal clothes and shaving off my beard but I just ignored him too. The nagging did used to annoy me though so to steer away from it I would stay in my bed longer and would wander off on my own.

The next time I saw the consulate he tried to talk to me about the adoption papers but I said I didn't want to talk about it ever again. I told him what was done was done. He took the hint and waffled on instead about the progress being made on my case. I just allowed him talk on and on. I nodded and smiled when I thought it was appropriate but decided it was too much effort to ask a question. I didn't see the point.

Later that day an hour before lock down time I could hear raised Spanish voices and loud clanging. It sounded a right commotion as the shouting got louder and louder. One of the men sounded high pitched and quite distraught. John elbowed me and then ran towards the noise and commotion. Being nosey I followed and so did Joseph. When we arrived there were crowds and crowds of prisoners around the arguing Spics. There were also shrieks from above. When I looked up I could see why there was a panic, one of the Spanish prisoners had climbed up a very tall metal gate and was flailing around. He was so high he was level with the second floor of the building. His right arm was hugging around the gate whilst the other flapped around. A few prisoners at the bottom kept shouting things up to him.

'What the fuck is going on?' John asked.

'The man up there is saying he wants to jump to his death and his friends below are trying to stop him,' Joseph replied like a gossiping woman.

Several minutes later the guards arrived. They looked worried as they surrounded the gate and nervously jabbered with each other and shouted up to the guy.

After watching ten minutes of this I grew angry. I am normally a sympathetic guy but something in me just snapped. What a fucking attention seeker! If he wanted to die why not do it without all this fuss.

'Jump you bastard!' I shouted with venom not being able to keep my words in any longer.

'Go on fucking jump!'

'Alan shut up!' whispered Joseph.

'Why should I? The guy has made a dick of himself enough he might as well jump.'

'He probably will be happier dead!'

'Alan do you want to get stabbed by his mates. Shut up!' Joseph hissed.

Before I could shout more encouraging words the suicidal Spic was persuaded to get down. One of the guards or his mates must have finally gotten through to him. The guards then came in and shunted everyone back to their cells.

That night I went to bed early. I did not have a drink or a spliff. I just wanted to be alone with my thoughts. I was scared of how I shouted for the poor man to commit suicide and scared too as I began to contemplate it.

I did not get much sleep that night. I wrestled with my demons and didn't have my usual night tonic of drinks and spliffs to numb me. I awoke tired and early. Despite not feeling refreshed I did manage to feel hope for the first time in a while. I wasn't quite sure what I was hopeful for but I decided today not to just exist but actually do something positive. So the first thing I did was buy soap from the economato and have a nice long shower. Afterwards I put on some fresh clothes and decided to retire my uniform.

When John and Joseph clocked me in my normal clothes they did not say anything and just smiled. Even though they did not know why I was down they could see I had come through it. I also told them I wanted to get rid of my beard completely. I did not want to trim it anymore and keep it tidy. I fancied a clean shaven face and a fresh start. Plus I was curious as it was months since I had seen the rest of my face.

John took me to the Cordoba barber who he had had his beard shaved off with. When we arrived he had just finished with a customer. He had done a good job too as the man looked so fresh faced. The customer that left looked both happy and relieved as he felt his smooth skin and handed over some cash.

We asked for a shave and straight away he pointed to the chair. With glee I hopped in. I looked to the side and saw his tools. This consisted of a mug of tea, a tea towel and a cut throat razor. When I saw the razor I freaked out a bit but I remained rigid trying not to show this in my demeanour. The Spanish barber quickly went to work first by draping a tea towel around my face and then he started to rub tea into my beard trying to soak it into the skin. He then flicked open the razor and held my chin rigid. In the corner of my eye I could see John smirking. Although I didn't show it I could tell he knew I was shitting myself. I mean it was pretty natural to be shit scared when a prisoner who I had never met before held a cut throat razor to my neck. I mean I didn't know if he was a fan of Sweeny Todd and had a penchant for cutting throats. It was no wonder John was vague with the details when I questioned him about where he went. I smiled to myself imagining his face when he was in the chair.

Thankfully the barber was quick and I was left unscathed. He didn't even draw any blood or make a nick on my skin.

Feeling clean and fresh faced I felt ready again to battle with whatever the Spanish judicial system had in store for me. Bring it on! My fighting spirit was restored back to its natural order.

25 TO THE ROSES ONCE MORE

I was asked to pack my things in Cordoba at 7am in the morning. This was odd. The only prison I had left in the morning was Ceuta. Every other time I was taken in the night to another prison. This could only mean one of two things, either I was going back to Ceuta or they were taking me on a long journey that would take all day to another prison. I prayed for the latter.

When I arrived at Algeciras port my heart sank, it looked likely I was to go back to Ceuta. I entertained the possibility I may be taken to another prison in Morocco but I knew this was very unlikely. It was only logical I was to go to back to Ceuta and stand trial near to where I committed my crime. I had thought it all along that my trial was to be held there but always hoped otherwise, as I was never told anything so I could dream. I mean the Spanish prison authorities appeared to do what they wanted so it wasn't that farfetched to believe they could put me on trial elsewhere.

Time went swiftly on the ferry as I did not want it to end. I was dreading having to enter the stinking hole of Ceuta once again. It's seemed cruel to me to have a taste of the better prisons across Spain and then have to go back to that wretched place. I mean none of the prisons were a walk in the park or clean but Ceuta was by far the worst. Nowhere else had I experienced piss or bugs in my food. Nor were the beds as stained or guards as cruel.

After a bumpy short bus ride I sighed as my prediction came true and we arrived at the gates of Ceuta once again. Looking at the walls brought back images of the night of the escape. I had managed until now to forget about that night but seeing them up close again brought it all back. Oh god Danny! How could I have forgotten about you? I wonder if I will ever find out what happened so I can lay your ghost to rest.

Once off the bus my cuffs were taken off and I was shepherded to the entrance of the prison. Walking on the tiles towards the Centro door felt like déjà vu, however this time round I had no fear. I knew exactly what I was in for. I had seen and experienced the worst of Ceuta so nothing could scare me anymore.

The guards obviously remembered me as every one of them scowled as I walked past. I flashed them a big smile back, showing them I hadn't lost my nerve and I was going to play fuck. I contemplated on speaking to them in Spanish but I thought I would keep that as surprise. They will be more shocked when I do eventually speak back at them with vitriol in their native tongue.

I was taken from the Centro to my cell by the gingery blonde guard who had struck me in the bollocks after the escape. God I hated him. I think they were aware of my feelings towards him and teamed me up on purpose. It could have been worse though, the director's son could have escorted me. Now that would have been dangerous. I don't think I could have contained myself. I would have definitely gone to strangle that bastard.

Begrudgingly I walked with the gingery blond Spic past the familiar block of cells. After walking and walking I drifted off in a fantasy where I pulled out the baton from his belt and struck him to the floor. Then with glee I imagined striking him over and over in the ball sack.

The guard eventually stopped outside my allotted cell, smiled and pointed inside. I was surprised with a cell, I thought they would have put me in the dormitory and instructed the Spanish to keep watch. Then again when I was put in the dormitory the last time I did try and escape. Perhaps they didn't trust me in a large group as I might incite others to escape again.

Looking at the outside of the cell it felt familiar, I had definitely been in here before but it wasn't a cell that I had slept in. I didn't recognise anything about the inside of the cell, but the feeling of familiarity continued as I walked around inside. Whose was this cell? I looked outside the window for clues. Below I could see the inner prison wall. I then shuddered as I recognised the view from below. This wall was the only thing I could see outside my solitary punishment cell. Obviously that cell was below this one. I shuddered as I flashbacked to the two weeks I had spent there broken and battered. I bet the guards had specifically chosen this cell for me as a reminder to behave. But instead of quelling my ambitions of freedom it instead inspired me to make sure my plans of escape were more foolproof.

Wanting to forget about those dark days I looked back around the cell. It then clicked whose room this was. This was Cheno's old room. This was where he would winch down joint after joint, to provide me with much needed relief. When I looked around I tried to visualise how Cheno had it. It then came back to me slowly about his side table, cassette player and his cassettes. The room smelling of hashish and the floor covered in rubbish here and there.

The guard coughed as if to gain my attention. I turned around and could see him smiling smugly as he pointed to my two Moroccan cell mates. In Spanish he said enjoy your new friends. I pretended I did not understand and shot him a confused look. This made him laugh as he left the room.

This was strange. None of the guards had ever introduced me to my cell mates before. Normally I was just dumped. He was obviously trying to make a point, but what I don't know. I could only think he thought he was punishing me by putting me with the Moroccans. If this was true he was fucking thick as I liked the majority of the Moroccans I met. They were a clean bunch. Plus I could communicate with them as they spoke English. Unless there was something I was missing. Something bad about these two I didn't know about.

Disconcerted I shone a fake smile to my two new roommates. They both sat on the bottom bunk and looked on at me with concern and fear. They both looked very young, from appearance I would have said they were in their mid to late teens, but from their serious attitude they could have been much older.

I looked at the top bunk and then to the bottom bunk and could see there was stuff on it. It was obvious the single bed to the side was mine but I pointed to it anyway and then to me. The boys both nodded and carried on gawping at me without blinking.

I put my back to the boys and unloaded my stuff. It didn't take long as I didn't have much. I examined the bed and was quite pleased. It wasn't heavily stained or smelt too much of ammonia. I prodded the thin mattress which made the fragile metal spring squeak.

The room was deathly quiet and I could feel both the boy's eyes burning into the back of head. To ease the tension in the room I decided to make the first move and introduce myself.

'Hi boys. I am Alan.'

The boys looked at each other as if astonished by my friendly nature and nervously they both waved.

'Er. Hi..,., I am Enero,' said the taller one of the two wearing a black djellaba.

'I am Mohammad,' said his friend next to him wearing a white djellaba and half a smile.

Once I engaged eye contact Enero seemed threatened. Mohammad just looked nervous. Why the hell were they so frightened of me? They were like two mice. It then dawned on me they probably had a hard time being Moroccan in the Spanish part of the prison. Both the Spanish guards and Spanish prisoners were inherently racist towards the Moroccans. I mean they hated me and the other Europeans but with the Arabs they really cut loose with their tongues and fists.

I held out my hand for them to shake. Mohammad looked at Enero as if he wanted an instruction. Enero put his hands in the air and shrugged. Mohammad looked back at me with a smile and extended his hand. I further shocked him when I put my other hand on my heart. He repeated my action. Enero then plucked up the courage to shake my hand and he too touched his heart.

Introducing myself to Enero and Mohammad did break the ice as we engaged in a brief conversation but it still felt awkward as it was very clipped and drawn out. It seemed they still didn't trust me. I decided to leave them be and have a look around at the old place to see if it had changed much or if any of the regulars were still here.

After a brief look around I was disappointed there was nothing new to see. Plus I was further dismayed when I went to the patio as I saw none of my boys. There trials must have been before or after mine possibly. I wondered if they made it so we couldn't be together. Before I drifted off thinking about where they were I could hear shouts that breakfast was ready. With dread I lined up in the queue wondering what disgusting meal was to be set for us. It was fried ungutted fish and coffee. My favourite!

I decided to head back to the room and eat it. I may as well get to know my new cell mates as I had no old friends in here. Plus they may be able to point my way to a few Europeans they may have met. When I walked down the corridor I noted something was amiss. After a few seconds of confusion it dawned on me the smell of the corridor wasn't right. It didn't smell like stale piss, rubbish and sweat. Instead a spicy sweet home cooking smell hit my nose. I sniffed at my plate just in case it was the fish, but it definitely wasn't this. Like a cartoon character I felt my heels elevated and I floated towards the smell. Ahead I could see drifts of steam and smoke coming from my room. With excitement I ran into my cell to find the two Moroccan boys kneeling on the floor and cooking something using a metal tin which they had put on small blocks of charcoal. This reminded me of the Moroccan patio.

'What you up to?'

'We are making breakfast.'

'What is it?'

'Cous cous.'

'It looks amazing,' I said whilst grimacing at my fish.

I looked back at my food and at theirs. Theirs looked far more superior. I looked at mine and huffed and then with my spoon scooped the edible bits of my fish to one side and the guts to the other.

'You are right to cook your own food,' I said licking my lips at theirs.

They nodded acknowledging my words but were busy concentrating on stirring the cous cous.

'It looks better than what I have got.'

I looked at my food a bit more and mentally geared up myself to brave a bite. To gain a bit of courage I swigged a bit of coffee and then looked back at the Moroccans. My mouth watered considerably from there exotic creation.

The boys both looked at each other and whispered. They then turned to me.

'Would you like to try some?' said Mohammad with a tinge of

reluctance.

'Oh yes please,' I said excitedly.

'I would rather eat anything than this crap!'

I sat cross legged on the floor next to the boys and watched on as they stirred it around and around. Mohammad laughed as I stared at the food whilst licking my lips making loud orgasmic noises.

Once the food was cooked they both washed their hands in a bowl. Enero pointed at my hands and then to the water. I followed suit and washed my hands too. Mohammad then dished it up in one big bowl and plonked it in the middle of the floor. Both boys started to dive in with their fingers. Taken aback at the lack of cutlery I looked on. They both nodded and pointed to the food. Oh well when in Morocco! I dived in with my hands eating the food. I had to control myself and not eat too hastily as it was so delicious. The boys smiled in response to my appreciation of the food. It was one of the best meals I had had in months. It was also refreshing using just my hands as the dish was quite messy, I felt like an animal. After the breakfast I savoured the taste by sucking all my fingers. God I hope they cook for me all day.

The boys seemed much more relaxed with me after breakfast and we did manage to have an easy flowing conversation. I asked them about how they got their ingredients and charcoal in and was surprised to find it was brought in by their family, who made daily visits. It shocked me that the guards were fine with this. I thought they wouldn't want any prisoners to have access to nutritious food, but I suppose it was good for them to have a few less mouths to feed. Plus thinking about it there would have been uproar if the Moroccans did not have access to their own food as most were Muslims and would only eat food they know which has been prepared to honour Allah. The fact the food prepared in the European kitchen was not washed properly would have been forbidden for a start.

'Do you get any hashish in?'

'Oh no,' said Enero seriously. 'The guards search the food and packages so we wouldn't be able to get our families to bring that in.'

'Well boys there are ways and means.'

'We wouldn't want our families to get into trouble,' said Mohammad.

Despite Mohammad's reservations I brainstormed in my head ideas on how to smuggle in hashish with the food packages the boys families brought in. I looked at the ingredients and then at the charcoal.

'Can I just borrow a bit of charcoal?'

'Er…….. yes okay………….. I suppose,' he said as if intrigued.

With the charcoal I rolled it in my fingers and then across the floor. Both Enero and Mohammad watched on.

'Right got it!' I said clicking my fingers with excitement.

'Right boys, I know how we can make a lot of money with this stuff?'

'How?' said Mohammad.

'Who wants charcoal?' Enero said astonished.

'It's not the charcoal that will make you money. It's putting hash in the bags of charcoal that will make you the money.'

'But the guards search them,' argued Mohammad.

'Do they really?' I said grinning. 'I reckon they probably weigh them but don't really have a proper search.'

I waited for the boys to argue back but they just answered me with silence.

'I mean yeah sure they probably look on the top but I doubt they will tip them all out.'

'Plus that doesn't matter as we can disguise the hash by rolling it into a ball and rubbing them with charcoal dust.'

'I don't know,' said Enero.

'Come on! Even if they did tip them all out I very much doubt they will notice a couple of rolled up balls of hash.'

Enero and Mohammad looked at each other shocked and shrugged.

'Come on boys think of the money you could make for your families.'

'Well....' said Mohammad wavering.

'I am telling you. This is really easy money.'

'Look Alan we will think about,' Enero barked.

'You do that,' I said smirking. 'Also chat to your families and see what they say.'

After chatting with their families and being encouraged by me they finally agreed to smuggle in the hash. Although they were reluctant at first, I knew they would come round knowing how much money they could make. The boys didn't have much money and from what they had said about their families they seemed to be quite poor. For me making money wasn't the only perk. I did it so I could have a constant personal supply of hash. Also from selling the stuff would give me something to do in the days.

As I predicted the boys through their families managed to smuggle in the hash without it being detected by the guards. It was obvious when they first smuggled it in they were very nervous about the whole thing as they would be so tense coming back after their visit. They both let out a big sigh when they brought in the charcoal bags with hash in. It was if they hadn't allowed themselves to breathe throughout their visits. They did eventually get better and started to relax after several successful attempts of bringing the stuff in.

Our customers mainly comprised of the European prisoners. I found it easier to make deals with them as the majority spoke English. I did think about selling it to the Spanish to but feared I would get grassed up. There was also the possibility I would be targeted with violence by the Spanish drug dealers for encroaching on their patch. It just seemed an unwritten rule the Spanish sold to the Spanish and Moroccans to the Moroccans. The Europeans however were an untapped market as they did not have a European dealer of their own as Chino was long gone. Well that was until I came along. The only down side to just dealing with the Europeans was having such a small customer base as they were in the minority. However what the Europeans lacked in number they made up in wealth. The Moroccans and Spanish who liked a bit of hash would struggle to fund their habit whilst the majority of the Europeans had more money than sense. So I think I punched my own weight in the profits side.

I found it strange making money and not really caring. Outside of prison money was my main push in life. I wanted as much as I could to buy nice stuff and have properties. I even bought a car once because it matched my suit. In prison money was pretty useless. With it I could only get knock off goods, bits of extra food and alcohol. This didn't excite me at all. The only thing I wanted to buy was my freedom.

A large part of the profits I gave to Enero and Mohammad as they needed it more than me, especially their families. Enero and Mohammad were probably better off here in prison having a free roof over their head. I bet their families needed to beg or work their bollocks off in order to have shelter and food.

With the deals side I asked Enero and Mohammad if they wanted to get involved in selling or locating potential customers in the Moroccan patio, but both of them shied away from this and said they were happy for me to take on the role. I don't think they felt confident enough to act as a drug dealer, as you do need a certain edge to be able to make sure you get your money off your customers and keep others drug dealers off your patch. Even if they did try and tap the Moroccan market I doubted if they would have made much as it was probably teeming with dealers. They also couldn't help me with the Europeans as the guards would take them over to the Moroccan side in the day. I don't know whether they weren't allowed in the Spanish patio or it was just a case they preferred the Moroccan side. Maybe they or the guards feared reprisals by the Spanish quadrant.

The boys felt bad about me having to do all the work selling the hash. I didn't really mind as I felt comfortable selling it, plus it allowed me to make a few friends and contacts I otherwise might have not forged. But the boys could not accept me doing all the work with nothing in return so agreed that because of this they would cook all my meals and would do all the cleaning in the cell. This would do very nicely for me.

It felt a funny dynamic though. I would be busy wheeling and dealing all day whilst the two boys were either, scrubbing, sweeping or cooking. It was like I had two male platonic wives. If only I could get a woman in the prison for night duties.

From having a constant supply of hash and freshly cooked meals I decided Ceuta wasn't that bad after all. The only thing that could have improved things would have been if I had a few of my lads to hang out with in the night. Enero and Mohammad were great kids but too reserved and quiet for my liking. Plus they didn't drink due to their Muslim faith so I had no one to get rat arsed with in the nights. I missed the banter and rude stories from the boys. My liver was probably thankful though as I did drink less.

Being with Enero and Mohammad I always felt a little left out as they would sometimes converse in Arabic so I couldn't understand. I never got the impression they were talking about me but I did used to get awful curious as to what they were saying. I especially wanted to know what was going on in Enero's head as he could look like a right grumpy sod at times. I felt myself going in a deep depression just by looking at him.

After being in Ceuta for a few weeks one of the guards called me to the office one morning saying I had a letter. This gave me a buzz. I had letters before off family and friends but they were very few and far between so each time I was surprised. It was nice to hear about the outside world every now and again. It would give me hope and make me feel touched that people from home were still thinking of me.

With letter in hand, I went to get my morning coffee and then rushed to the patio to open it. I could see in the far corner one of my customers who I got particularly friendly with was reading a letter too, so I headed over to join him. He was French and his name was Jean Dominic Masuaro. As his full name was a bit of a mouthful I nicknamed him John Doe for short. He didn't seem to mind me shortening his name unlike Joseph. In fact I think he preferred his nickname. I did try and tell him that John Doe was the reference for an unknown dead guy in America but I don't think he understood.

'Got a letter?' said John Doe.

'Yeah,' I said sarcastically.

'Who from?'

'Don't know yet. I haven't opened it.'

Putting my coffee on the floor I held the letter out in front of me and studied the handwriting of the address. I didn't recognise it at all. It was definitely not anyone in my family and neither did it look like any of my friend's handwriting either. Intrigued I ripped it open and took out the folded letter. Holding the letter in my left hand I swooped down and picked up my coffee with my remaining right hand. I took a big swig and read the first line, as the words shocked me I swallowed my coffee the wrong way and choked. I couldn't believe it! At the top it read from the organisation for the welfare of British prisoners abroad.

'What the!' I shouted out loud before descending into laughter.

Welfare of British prisoners abroad indeed! Too fucking late now! I read on to see what help they could provide. After reading it twice I concluded that there was bugger all. Actually no sorry there was one thing they did want to offer me in order to aid my welfare and that was a pen pal. A fucking pen pal! What on earth is the use in that! A clean bed would be useful. Clean towels provided for washing would be nice. Improvement in the sanitation and modern washing facilities for clothes would be a help. Not a fucking pen pal. I couldn't believe it.

Whilst reading the letter a third time an uneasy feeling washed over me as if I was being watched. When I lifted my head up I felt relieved it was only John Doe. He looked at me with a worried expression, I must have been swearing louder than I thought when I was reading.

'You okay?'

'Oh yes, yes. I am fine.'

'It's just you don't seem happy.'

'Well it's not a letter I expected John.'

'Good news?'

'Well it's not good or bad really.'

'Who is it off?'

'The prison welfare association'

'The what?'

'Er they are people who want to look after me.'

'That's good isn't it?'

'Well they can't do much John,' I said smirking. 'The only thing they can give me is a pen pal.'

'Oh I see.'

I was going to have a rant about how the prison welfare association should actually be helping in regards to money, conditions and legal issues but decided it would be too hard to try and relay that to John. He did speak English but not fluently. I think I would have had to repeat everything I said which would have diluted my point. I wish John MacGloughlin was here he would be laughing his fucking tits off right now.

To change the conversation I asked him about his letter. He smiled and went a hint of red in the cheeks as he told me it was from his wife. Interested at his embarrassment I probed him on if it was of a romantic nature. His face went further red and he nodded with a cheeky smile.

'Well I have to write with romance Alan if I want her to wait for me.'

'Very true.'

'Have you got a wife?'

'I have two,' I said grinning.

'Two!' he said shocked.

'Yes but they are ex-wives,' I said laughing. 'I am afraid no one is waiting for me at home.'

John Doe looked embarrassed like he shouldn't have asked.

'So is your pen pal a man or a woman?' he said trying to change the subject.

'Oh I don't know.'

I quickly unfolded the letter again and scanned it for a name.

'It's a lady.'

'Oh.........' he said intrigued. 'Are you going to write to her?'

'Maybe.'

'Who knows write with romance and maybe she will wait for you.'

'Yeah maybe.'

'To help her fall for you. I would come up with a name?'

'A name for what?'

'Er I don't know how to say it but er........well with my wife I call her Mon Petit Poulet.'

'Mon pettie...............' I said trying to mimic what he said. 'What does that mean?'

'My little chicken,' he said quietly giggling in embarrassment.

'Ah John you romantic fool.'

From tensing my stomach in laughter caused it to groan loudly with hunger. I was glad as it reminded me to get back to my cell pronto for breakfast with the boys.

'Right John I am going to have to love you and leave you.'

'Love me and leave me?' he said looking concerned.

'Oh don't worry it's an expression in English to say goodbye.'

'Oh.............' he said still looking uneasy.

'Yes got to get breakfast.'

'Oh is breakfast being served already. I will come with you.'

'Oh I don't eat the stuff served in here,' I said forgetting he didn't know my arrangement with my cell mates.

'My boys Mohammad and Enero cook fresh food for me.'

'That must be nice.'

'Believe me it is.'

'Do you think they would cook for me?'

'I don't know they can be a bit thing.'

'Oh!' he said looking dejected.

'Look leave it with me I will see if I can sort something out.'

I rushed off towards the inside of the prison and towards my cell. On my way I bumped into Franc. I was shocked to see him but was glad there was a familiar face in Ceuta after all. I had a brief chat with him and found out he was still working in the laundry with his brother. I was glad to hear he was still washing clothes as I was sick to death of cleaning them myself. I couldn't believe I didn't check the laundry on my first day. I just assumed they would both be long gone now.

I managed to get back just in time as Enero was serving up grub in the one big bowl.

'Nearly missed out Alan,' Enero said laughing.

'Oh you know me Enero I like my food. No way I would miss this.'

Enero continued smiling as he spooned in the exotic rice mixture into the bowl. On the last few scoops he even started humming in happy tones. This was unusual behaviour for him. I had never seen Enero looking so happy. If we weren't in prison I would have thought he had just got laid. Mind it was possible I suppose, if he were gay.

Mohammad also looked confused about his happiness as when he could see Enero wasn't looking he furrowed his brow and shrugged his arms at me as if to say to me 'what gives?' I answered back with a similar confused expression. Although curious I didn't ask about his sudden change in mood. I was afraid by saying anything he would slip back to his moody self. I think Mohammad thought the same as he never uttered a word either.

After breakfast I asked the boys if John Doe could join in with our meals. Enero said he saw no problems with it but Mohammad asked if he could have a further think. I decided not to push the subject anymore and remained silent.

I think Enero felt uncomfortable and started to tidy up the dishes as if to disperse the silence. Mohammad went to help but Enero grabbed his hand and smiled. They had a few brief words in Arabic and then Mohammad nodded and left. Enero looked back at me and smiled.

'Well Enero much as I would love to help you I have a date with my lawyer.'

'I hope he can tell you when your trial is.'

'So do I!'

'Good luck and good bye,' I heard Enero shout when I left the room.

It felt strange going to the visiting room and seeing Malero again after so long. It made me feel like I had been in prison for a decade. Malero hadn't changed much in his looks or demeanour apart from the fact he didn't have his side kick Biggy attached to his hip. Poor poor Biggy slumming it on the mainland.

In the meeting was just Malero for some reason, I didn't get to see the new British consulate. Maybe they didn't trust me with his successor just in case I managed to inadvertently get him fired too from the Ceuta job. Maybe they just didn't replace him.

As per usual I asked till I was blue in the face for the date of my trial and as per usual I was told it would be soon, and to quote Malero 'imminent'. But exactly what imminent meant was anyone's guess. It could have meant the next day, the next week or the next month. I think the reason I wasn't told of dates was just in case I planned an escape. I suppose it was like when they were moving us, they would only give us fifteen minutes warning so all we could think about was getting our stuff together.

The only thing I could gauge my trial on was from asking other people when there's had been. From a handful of Europeans I discovered that their trials were between ten months and year after when they were caught. So my trial by that average was coming up soon as I was just shy of a year's service myself.

After seeing Malero I went for a walk around the patio. The sun was hot and there was a lively atmosphere. There was much clapping and singing. Everyone always seemed to be in a good mood after seeing their lawyers and consulates. It was as if they provided hope. It had the opposite effect on me now as I just felt disappointed. I felt there was more that could be done. I mean to wait a year for court was ridiculous.

Wanting to lighten my mood I decided to approach a group of Spanish prisoners who were selling various bits and bobs to see if they had anything interesting to buy. I thought a bit of retail therapy might give me a lift. As soon as I approached them I was ambushed by the traders. All sorts of weird and wonderful things were shoved under my nose from all directions. All around I could hear screams in Spanish to look this way and that way. Each one made flamboyant claims they had the most amazing things in the world for me to buy. After steadying myself from the dizzying crowd I was disappointed to see there was nothing I actually wanted. It was just the same usual crap.

With nothing catching my interest I looked for something cheap and small to buy so I could make a quick exit. I found that if you bought at least one item they would ease up a little and you had a fighting chance to break free from their tiring hard sells. If you didn't buy anything they would invade your personal space and jabber on frantically following you everywhere. I looked in all directions as if I was watching a pinball machine trying to find something that would at least be useful.

I know! I will look for matches. They were always good to have. I couldn't see any matches on show. I was just about to ask one seller selling tobacco if he had any when I came across a strange T-shirt with an unusual black and white Aztec design. It looked really different and out of the norm. Battering off the other sellers I went up to the Spaniard carrying the T-shirt. He practically threw it into my hands as he was excited to sell something. I held it to my torso and found it was a good size too and wouldn't be too big. Trying not to appear too enthusiastic I bartered with the Spaniard. We eventually settled on a price and I handed over the agreed amount of pesetas.

I folded my T-shirt and then rolled it up like a tube. With a deep breath I clamped my T-shirt under my arm and like a bull charged through the crowds. It was pretty easy to break free but I did have to bat a few of the more enthusiastic sellers with a dig in the elbow and a swat with the back of my hand. Once freed from the stifling Spanish salesmen I looked out for a few of the Europeans lads, I wanted to show off my new T-shirt. After scanning around I couldn't find any. Then the crowds of Spanish prisoners started to dwindle as they made a mass exodus inside of the prison. This was very strange for late morning as the patio was normally teaming with people. It was only busy at meal times, but dinner was hours away.

I walked over towards the entrance of the prison and joined the queue. From inside I could hear a muffled commotion. It sounded like a mix of panicked raised voices coming from both the guards and the prisoners. Excitedly I waded through the people inside the prison. If there was a riot going down I wanted to be involved. I wanted any excuse to knock out a few guards. The gingery blond bastard was mine.

When I got inside all I could see were hoards of Spanish and European prisoners just standing around gossiping whilst the smell of burning wood hung in the air. It couldn't be a riot as the men all around were too calm. Intrigued I grappled through the crowd to get to the front to see what was happening. Eventually I managed to scurry my way through. From the corridor of cells I could see a stream of black smoke. Before I could get my bearings I was pushed aside by a guard who quickly hurried past with a bag of tools. I then felt a cold hand grab onto my bicep. Shocked I turned to my left to find Mohammad looking very somber and pale.

'Are you okay?'

'It's Enero…' he said pointing in front of him.

'What?'

I looked back to the corridor where Mohammad was pointing.

'Fucking hell!' I screamed out loud when I could see our cell was on fire.

'Enero?' I asked in confusion. 'He is in there?'

Mohammad nodded in reply and breathed in loudly as if he was trying hard not to cry.

'Are you sure?' I said feeling my eyes lids widen in shock. 'You have looked for him everywhere.'

'Yes!' he said trying to choke back the tears.

'He's shut away in there.'

I turned back to the door and watched the guards struggle to get it open. Black thick smoke bellowed out from under the thin gap between the bottom of the door and the floor. Two of the guards tried to turn the handle with their naked hands but it was far too hot to touch. After a few seconds from the bag the guards took out a long pair of thick workman's gloves. Quickly the guard put them on and turned the handle. Not knowing what to do and wanting to help I rushed towards the cell. I was obstructed by two guards who told me to get back. I moved my head to the side to take a look inside the cell but the guards obstructed my view. Before I knew it I was frog marched by a guard to the patio. The other Europeans were herded up also and they joined me in the patio outside too.

I looked around for Mohammad to see if he was pushed in here amidst all the panic but after a look around I found he hadn't. I really wanted to know what happened and if he knew anything else.

Some of the European lads cornered me and asked me if I knew what was going down. I told them I didn't have a clue. Despite not knowing a thing the lads still interrogated me on what I did know about the Moroccans and how the fire could have been started. The only thing I could think of was that Enero was cooking and had an accidently knocked over the charcoal. Most of the boys accepted this as a plausible answer but seemed disappointed it was nothing more exciting. One of the boys did ask if I thought Enero did it to start a riot. I laughed at the suggestion and told them it wasn't in Enero's nature to do that, from the little I knew of him. The only strange factor though if it were an accident why was the door closed. This did not make sense at all.

Just after dinner time a few guards came outside and told everyone it was safe to go back in the prison. I joined the swarm of prisoners that headed inside to have a look at the remains of my cell. Before I could investigate two guards grabbed me and told me I was needed for questioning. Despite the fact I didn't provide any resistance they shoved me from corridor to corridor towards the director's office.

When I walked in the director greeted me sternly and beckoned me to sit, which I obeyed.

'What happened with Enereo?' I said in Spanish.

The director seemed shocked when I spoke to him Spanish

'I see you have started to learn Spanish. Well done Alan,' he said back to me in English.

'Yes, yes……. but what happened with Enero?' I said hesitantly this time in English

'We also want to know that too Alan.'

'Is he okay?'

'He has been taken to hospital. It does not look good.'

I looked to the floor as my mind raced with images of Enero being dead and badly burnt. I also thought of Danny's lifeless body being dragged by the guards. Everywhere I seemed to go there was death, especially in Ceuta.

'Alan!' shouted the director seemingly annoyed I wasn't looking at him.

'Tell me everything you know about the fire?'

I didn't feel up to talking as I was a bit in shock but I knew I had to as it would have looked suspicious. I needed to give my side of the story just in case they thought I was in some way involved. Although there was nothing to tell him really, as I didn't have a fucking clue as to what had happened behind our cell door.

'Well at about 8 o'clock Enero cooked me and Mohammad breakfast. Er Mohammad then left to the Moroccan patio and a few minutes later I left to see my lawyer. Then the next thing I knew there was a mass panic and the guards were putting out a fire in my cell. I didn't know Enero was inside until Mohammad came running up to tell me.'

'Do you think Mohammad was involved or told him to do it?'

'Oh no, no, no. As far as I was aware they were very good friends. Mohammad was always looking out for Enero.'

'Looking out?'

'Yeah he was always trying to get him to be happy as he could get down for time to time.'

'I mean it could have been an accident. He could have been cooking and caused a fire.'

'But why was the door closed?'

'Oh my god,' I blurted.

'What?'

'I think he may have done it on purpose!' I said quietly not wanting to say such a thing out loud.

'I think he wanted to kill himself.'

'It looks that way to us,' the director said coldly.

'But why do you think that Alan?'

'Well he was unusually happy this morning. I mean the happiest I have ever seen him……………..And he made a big point of saying goodbye to Mohammad and I. He must have been saying his last goodbye to us before……….'

'So you were aware he was down?'

'I knew he wasn't a happy man but I didn't see that happening. He never spoke about killing himself.'

'He never spoke about much……….. really…………….I can't believe he chose to burn himself to death.'

'Is there any more you can say?'

'No nothing sorry. There is nothing else.'

'Alan your story better be right. We will speak to Mohammad too. If anything doesn't match, you will be punished. Whether you were involved or not!'

'I don't care what you do,' I said defiantly in Spanish.

He looked stunned at my outburst.

'The only thing that matters is Enero. Punish me if you like I don't give a fuck.'

'Alan be careful what you say to me!' the director threatened.

'Look….. I honestly don't know what happened.'

The director nodded to me and then to the guard. My story seemed sufficient enough. Well it should be, it was the truth. The guard took the signal and went to grab me

'Alan this had better be the truth,' the director said pointing at me with a pen in his hand.

I looked him straight in the eye and nodded.

The guards took me back to the patio, as they did so John Doe, Franc and a few of the other Europeans rushed over. All I wanted to do was have a bit of time on my own but they surrounded me and hounded me for answers. I told them what happened in my interview but I could tell they yearned for more answers. Like if he was dead and if Mohammad was involved. They were shocked though at the suggestion of suicide. None of the boys could get over how someone could kill themselves in such a painful and horrific way. I found it hard to believe too.

After it sank in what had happened I started to think about more practical things like what belongings I had in the cell. Thankfully I hardly had anything. Most of my clothes were in the laundry with Franc, I had all my money and hashish on me, which was one blessing. The only thing I had in my room was a top, a pair of pumps and a pair of Y-fronts. It could have been worse. I could easily replace all these.

Just before lock down two guards came for me. They told me as my cell was burned so badly I was going to have to stay in the European brigada. I questioned the guard as to whether I heard him right as the only dormitories I knew about were the Spanish and the Moroccan ones. I thought I may have misinterpreted his Spanish. One of the guards looked at me as if I was an imbecile and said I had heard him correctly. I blindly followed them both trying to think where the brigada would be. I was shocked to find the room was above the Centro. I had never been up this corridor before and until now had never known it had existed. I thought I had been everywhere in Ceuta. The room was up a flight of steps. There was another flight of steps adjacent leading up to another room with a prison guard stood in a sentry position half way up. I had never seen a guard outside anyone's room before. God knows what prisoners were in there. I would love to meet them. The other odd thing about the guard was that he was Moroccan. I had only ever seen Spanish prison guards in Ceuta, and across Spain for that matter, but never a Moroccan.

The two guards opened the European brigada door. I was the first one in the room as they hadn't rallied up the prisoners for lock down in the night. Before I went in to settle myself down in my new surroundings the guards had a brief word with me. They told me I had to behave which meant no fights, no riots and no escapes. They also told me I was to be cappo meaning leader. This really fucking shocked me. Only this morning they thought I had been involved in murdering my cell mate through a fire and now they wanted me to lead a group of men. I agreed as I liked a challenge plus if there was any way I could get in favour with the guards I would take it. Maybe if I could gain there trust they would allow me freedoms which I could exploit in order to escape.

I had a look around and spotted an empty bed and dumped my stuff. The floor was covered in dust, dirt and unidentifiable bits. It was going to take a while getting used a dirty room again after being spoiled by the Moroccans. I suppose it wasn't the worst I had seen.

The bed was good though. It looked fairly clean and sturdy. In fact I would go as far to say it looked like the best bed I had come across, well in regards to Spanish prisons that is.

Although there were lights on the ceiling the room was quite dark as there was no natural light. It was devoid of windows. This was not surprising as the room was right at the front of the prison. From here I would imagine you could see the large prison gates and in the distance possibly part of Ceuta. This was a far too tempting view to have being a prisoner. Even the most timid would have been inspired to escape.

A few minutes later the rest of the Europeans entered the brigada. I had a warm welcome from Jean Doe, Franc, Franc's brother and Yan a Yugoslavian. On the whole the rest of the boys in the room were okay with me and actively walked up to me and said hello but there were a few who looked at me with suspicion. I don't know whether it was because I was the new boy in the room or the fact that the last cell I was in burned down and they were worried.

When we heard the guards had settled down for the night into drunken laughter we decided to have some fun ourselves and everyone reached for their blow and booze. I didn't have any booze on me as I hadn't had time to scout any out what with it being a busy day. So in return for some hash a few of the boys happily gave me a bottle or two each, which accumulated into a nice pile of drink for me.

When everyone congregated round I made an announcement about myself being the leader. Franc, Yan and John Doe nodded enthusiastically and voiced their happiness with this. The rest were not so sure and some even looked at me as if I was a turd in a buffet.

The unwelcoming few voiced their anger and questioned me as to why I should be the leader. I could see their point as physically I didn't look like a leader. I wasn't the tallest, fittest or the strongest man. Plus in attitude I wasn't like a usual daddy of a prison, as I wasn't particularly arrogant or openly aggressive. However when they asked me why the guards had chosen me they looked quite impressed with my answer, as I told them the guards chose me to keep me in check and not to plan another escape. They also asked me to tell them about the escapes which they seemed pretty impressed by, but they all fell silent when I told them about Danny and my two weeks in isolation. A few of the lads piped up saying they didn't believe my story but were soon silenced when Franc backed me up, as although not one of the eleven escapees he was at Ceuta at the time and knew what went down.

I was glad when the boys stopped asking about the escape and the fire. I had enough of questions. Today had been just one long interrogation. I was glad when the atmosphere turned back to a party one, where everyone was busy being intoxicated by hash and alcohol. I liked watching everyone falling around and having a laugh. Listening to others was a big welcome too as I now had a reprieve from being the centre of attention.

The boys also appeared to accept me as their leader as they didn't question further my authority. Instead they just continued to laugh and joke. That night I got to know all the Europeans quite well. God I missed this. Although these weren't my original lads they were all still good fun.

I also had an interesting conversation with Franc about the brigada itself. He told me that he only knew of the brigada a week after my departure. He asked around and none of the other boys knew about it too which led them to believe they had created it especially to keep the Europeans together. Also looking at the condition of the beds they also speculated it was the old sleeping quarters for the guards. It made sense as the Centro was just to the bottom of the steps and the beds were in too good a nick to have been let loose amongst the prisoners.

The next day when we were opened up from the brigada I looked over to the room next door. The Moroccan guard had now been replaced by a Spanish guard. I wondered when they had swapped duty. Did they have guards outside all night or were there only guards when we were allowed to roam the halls? What were they trying to hide?

I was going to ask John Doe and Franc about the room but I couldn't get a word in as John was going on about the fire. He also said how it was weird Enero had a Spanish name despite being Moroccan and the fact the literal definition of his name was January, which also started him wittering about the meaning of names and that it was probably due to him being born in that month. He seemed so animated and happy I let him prattle on despite not really giving a shit about what he was saying. I couldn't wait till it was old news. I had drawn a line under it and wished everyone else would too. It scared me thinking about his death, as I was quite close to losing it in Cordoba too. I decided to just concentrate thinking about myself now and not worry about anyone else.

When there was a break in the conversation I was about to ask about the room when again I was interrupted. This time it was by a guard who came running towards me and grabbed my arm. Stunned I watched as he pulled me to one side whilst breathing in deeply from running. I had never seen a flustered guard before. After steadying his breathing he then told me I had twenty minutes till my trial.

When the guard left I went into an excited panic. Finally the day had come! I thought about what I wanted to say and what I wanted to wear. Quickly I dived to the patio and took a very quick shower. I then hot footed it to the trusted Spanish prisoner with the key to the shack on the roof with my belongings. He was so slow opening up the lock which made me jig up and down as if I had a gallon of piss inside me. When he did finally open it I pushed him to one side roughly and headed for my suitcase. I quickly opened it up and carefully took out my folded pin stripe suit. Oh this was a nice suit. I hope to god this will give me good luck in court. I carefully put the folded suit under my arm and legged it to brigada. I quickly had a shave using the cold water from the sink and a blunt razor I had bought off a Spaniard. From rushing I gave myself a nick which started to ooze with blood. Also from being rough a red bobbled rash appeared a few seconds later all around my jaw line. I was annoyed at inflaming my skin and having a blotchy face but there was nothing I could do. With a small towel I quickly pressed it to my nick to stem the bleeding whilst also avoiding getting any blood on my crisp white shirt.

'Alan!' I heard John Doe shouting in the brigada.

'What John! I am trying to get ready!'

'The guard is here and............'

'Stall him I need a little more time.'

'But Alan!'

'For fuck sake!'

I removed the towel and the bleeding thankfully had now stopped.

I looked at my feet and realised I was wearing flip flops. The only other shoes I had were the pumps which were incinerated by Enero's fire. Fuck I can't wear these! I will look stupid! I might as well not bother wearing a suit if I have to go in these.

'Look John can you tell him I am not ready.'

'Alan there is no need to get ready.'

'Look John they can fuck off. I am not wearing flip flops with a suit.'

'Alan you don't understand.'

'Oh I do.'

I looked around the brigada and couldn't see the guard. Thinking he was waiting for me at the Centro I headed to the door.

'Alan!' John screamed.

'What!'

'The trial is not going ahead!'

'What!'

'That's what I was trying to tell you,' John bellowed in annoyed tones.

'The guard came up to say there is a delay.'

'Oh!' I said feeling deflated.

'Just like that it is off.'

'Yes.'

'Did he say when the next trial will be?'

John shook his head glumly.

I went to my bed and sat down as I slowly took off my tie and threw it down. John sat on my bed next to me looking concerned but not knowing what to say. He also put the bloody towel to my face as my nick started to bleed again. This was probably caused by my blood pressure rising through anger. Annoyed I snatched the towel off John and pressed it into the nick myself.

It took me while to calm down but I eventually did. I got dressed back in my prison clothes and neatly folded my suit and took it back to the room on the roof.

To stop myself from stewing I decided to take my mind off things by writing a few letters. One I wrote to my Mam and the other one I wrote for my female pen pal. To my mother I just told her what was going on. I didn't say anything about the trial as I didn't want her to be upset, but I did say I knew it would be soon. I also reassured her about the seven year diary she got me as in every letter since she had apologised about it. I told her not to worry and that I didn't take offence. In fact the diary was a bloody good one. It was a good size to carry around and had loads of pages in it. From it I amassed several names, addresses and phone numbers of the lads I met.

With the letter to my pen pal I sort advice from John Doe on how to be romantic and sauce it up. We had a laugh and a giggle on how to write passionately without being too rude.

That night when we were banged up all the lads heard about my trial and all seemed gutted for me. I was surprised at their empathy but then realised they were probably thinking about their own trials being delayed. My situation didn't encourage any hope in them of the Spanish justice system.

Although we had a few drinks and joints the night continued with depressing conversations. One of which was about having no hot water when shaving. I think this was inspired by the angry red rash on my jaw line. It was quite sore but nothing I couldn't handle.

Later that night the mood did lighten but it still did not feel like a party vibe as last night. I talked to John Doe for most of the night as he always seemed quite a happy sole. He always seemed to put me in a good mood. I allowed him to babble on about himself and listened in order distract me from my own thoughts. I found out John was a very clever and interesting man, who was also skilled electrician. He pointed to the electrics near the ceiling of the wall and tried explaining to me how it worked. What he said went completely over my head, but what I did gather was he was bright and knew a lot about electricity. When he finished droning on I asked him if he could heat up water with the wires. He said it was possible and a big grin came across my face. I told him that tomorrow we should have a go. He tried to dissuade me but I refused to take no as an answer.

The next morning when the guards opened us up, John was still in bed.

I could tell he wasn't sleeping and nudged him. With a sigh he opened his eyes and shone a pensive look and nodded. It was obvious he was nervous about messing about with the electrics, and wanted to delay doing it as much as possible. I managed to bring him round after chatting with him and massaging his ego to say he could do it.

First of all John looked at the box, rambled to himself and scrunched his eyebrows. Every time I asked him what he was thinking he shushed me. This annoyed me but I knew I would have to leave him figure out what to do and if this meant letting him think, this is what I needed to do. He was a man of science after all which meant he had to plan first and examine the risks. This was a totally alien way of thinking. I would rather dive into things and think of the consequences later.

The first problem we had to deal with was the height of the box as it was about 7ft high and out of reach to touch let alone poke around with. We tried putting a bed to the wall and stepping on that, but that was still too low. We also thought about bringing in furniture from outside to stand on but the guards would have probably grown suspicious carting a table around the prison. Then Franc had a brain wave and suggested he could lift up John to the electrics on his shoulders. John did not seem keen on this but relented as he could see Franc and I were keen to try it.

With a bit of a wobble Franc managed to lift John up so he was in line with the mains. John agreed that as long as Franc stayed steady he could take out the wires. The electricity mains looked so old. There wasn't even a cover for the wires which was great stuff for us as we didn't even need a screw driver to get to the wires.

After John had a look and was electrocuted a few times he seemed a bit more calmer. The electric shocks couldn't have been a high voltage as he wasn't shooting across the room. He just shook like he had Parkinson's and shouted in French a lot. Franc also received electric shocks and shook as he tried to hold John still against the wall, but it didn't seem to bother him as much as John, unless he was trying to look the big man. Each time they both rattled I fell to the floor weak with laughter.

John fiddled around and then unravelled two wires. I was shocked how long they were, they were so long they reached the floor. He carefully gave me the wires and told me not to touch them together. He then tapped Franc to lower him down.

Then at the end of each of the wires he attached a knife by holding them in place with elastic bands. Once the knives were secure he held the wires and carefully lowered them into a bowl of water. Again he made sure that the wires didn't cross. From several experiments and many electric shocks we worked out that after 20 minutes of the wires being in the water would make it warm enough to have a coffee and tea with. To make the water just warm enough for a shave or a wash would take just under ten minutes.

In the night we showed the rest of the boys we could now have hot water for warm drinks and washing. They gasped in shock when we told them. Not believing us they asked for a demonstration. John and Franc quickly hopped up and showed them how it was done. When John and Franc starting vibrating and making buzzing noises from their mouths, everyone fell about in fits of laughter, including me. Still to this day it brings a tear to my eye thinking about them.

When the water was ready everyone dipped their finger in, each one was shocked at how hot the water was. They couldn't believe how John had managed to do this without killing himself. I don't think John could believe it either.

After our demonstration the room seemed to buzz with excitement. Everyone was talking about the electricity and laughed whilst doing impressions of John and Franc vibrating. It was great to see them all looking positive.

Towards midnight we drifted off onto different subjects and split up into smaller groups of conversation. The buzz from before had died away and now everyone seemed calm and still. That was until our chatting was disturbed by the sound of guard's footsteps coming up the stairs. Quickly everyone seem to sober up as they jumped to their feet. Joints were immediately extinguished and booze and various drugs hidden around the room.

When the door opened everyone jumped to their beds and stayed still. From behind the door appeared two guards who looked rather sheepish.

This was odd. It obviously wasn't a raid as there would be more guards. Plus normally they wouldn't hesitate like this, they would be straight to work running around the room ripping into our beds and belongings. It also didn't seem to be a ghost run as for Ceuta it was the wrong time of day. Unless there were more Spanish run prisons in North Africa I didn't know about.

'Alan can you come over here?' ordered one of the guards in Spanish

Being very curious I hurried to the door and could see the two guards were each holding a Spanish looking prisoner. The guard then asked if we would have the men in our European brigada as there was no room anywhere else. I argued back saying there was no way I was having any Spanish prisoners. This was the European brigada and only non-Spanish prisoners would be welcome here. The only exception we would make would be for Arabs to come in.

The guard strangely listened to my points and argued that the boys were not Spanish as such but Basque. I argued on and on that I didn't believe them until I suddenly remembered in my drunken mind about an article I had read. The guard was right the Basque although they live in Spain do not class themselves as Spanish

The Basque are reported to being the oldest indigenous living group known in Europe. They live in North Central Spain and also in some areas of France. Their language, culture, customs, and land are all distinctly different from Spain and the rest of Europe. They also have their own newspaper, radio, and educational system. Although they consider themselves autonomous from Spain they do not have their own government or true independent status. It is because of this some of the Basque people formed an armed nationalist and separatist group Euskadi Ta Askatasuna (ETA) who have been involved in killing, bombing and kidnapping to get their point across.

'Oh I see they are Basque. I am a fan of ETA. Yes, yes they are welcome here.'

The guard looked angry at me mentioning ETA and welcoming them in as if they were part of that terrorist organisation. In no way do I condone ETA but I said it to wind up the guards. Although they didn't saying anything back I could tell I really hurt them by my comments, which gave me a nice fuzzy feeling inside. I smiled as I watched them skulk off.

I quickly introduced the boys to everyone and they pointed them to two free beds in the corner of the room. I was going to have a chat with them after they unpacked but they seemed quite content by themselves. Feeling tired I headed to bed too.

The next day when I left the cell I grabbed Franc as I remembered this time to ask him about the room next door. I was shocked when he told me it was the hospital ward for sick prisoners. I was also quite annoyed the way he said it in a very blasé attitude as if everyone knew. Stumped, I stood at the bottom of the steps to the ward with my mouth open whilst all the boys piled out towards the main prison.

A sodding hospital! What else is in this place that I don't know about? First the European brigada, now this! I needed to open up my eyes more. I wonder if there is a secret fucking library here too.

Intrigued I went over to have a chat with the Spanish guard. I was going to climb up to the steps when he put his hand out and came to meet me at the bottom.

'Hi I am Alan. I understand up there is the hospital.'

'Yes it is the medico.'

'The medico.'

'Yes a ward for sick prisoners.'

'Right I see.'

I thought about asking him why I wasn't sent there after my escape. I was injured pretty badly. It then dawned on me about Danny. I wondered if he was sent here that night. He might have known if he was dead or not.

'So you are English then?' the guard asked as if to break me from my reverie.

'Oh no, no. I am Welsh. I am from Wales which is in Britain.'

'Welsh!' he said excitedly. 'I have been to Wales.'

'Really?' I replied back in shock.

I couldn't believe it! I had never met anyone from Europe let alone North Africa who knew of Wales let alone who had been there. Constantly on my travels I had to explain to people about Wales and geographically where it was. This was very odd indeed.

'Yes I have friends who live in Cardiff.'

'What is your name?'

'Don Amadeo.'

Don wasn't his first name. Don is a Spanish word denoting title and status, a sort of a cross between sir and mister in English. Every guard introduced themselves as Don. I hardly called the guards Don. I would just say their name. I would only use Don when I wanted something.

'Don Amadeo can I ask about a friend of mine who might have been a patient up there?' I said pointing to the room upstairs.

'Yes, yes of course,' he said in unusual warm tones for a Spanish guard.

'Danny?'

'No............ We have not had a Danny.'

'You sure?'

'He is French.....Er his second name is Horman.'

'Oh Daniel Horman.'

'Yes Daniel.'

'Yes we have a Daniel Horman in the ward.'

'Still?'

'Yes he is up there now.'

I nearly fainted with shock. Not only was Danny alive he was still in Ceuta. This was amazing news! I couldn't believe the poor sod had been cooped upstairs all this time and none of us knew. I wish I had found out sooner I could have visited him.

'Er er can I see him,' I said excitedly waving my hands up and down like a puppet not knowing what to do with myself.

'Well I am not supposed to let any other prisoner up there unless of course they are sick.'

'Well is he okay?'

'He is well and slowly starting to walk again.'

'He can't walk!'

'Look Alan don't worry he is in good hands.'

'Oh please Don can I see him....Please!' I begged with overlapping my fingers in a prayer motion.

'I am not supposed to allow other prisoners up there.'

'Please Don he is my best friend and I haven't see him in a year.'

'Look,' he said looking around checking there was nobody else listening. 'Come back around two o'clock.'

'Thanks.'

'But Alan I will have to check with Danny first to see if he wants to see you.'

'Oh……… Okay.'

I walked to the patio with nervous excitement. I couldn't believe only a few doors separated me from my mate. It is strange to think that if my cell mate hadn't burned himself I may never have known. I wonder if I will get to hear about Enero. I couldn't see him being alive though, that room was too much filled with smoke and fire for anyone to survive.

To quell my excitement I busied myself chatting to people and looked on the Spanish market. Today one of the Spanish sellers had a lovely shiny silver Seko watch for sale. It was the nicest watch I had seen inside and outside of prison. Plus it was a very good price considering it was a branded watch. Straight away I snapped it up and then proceeded to show it off to all my European friends.

To further pass the time away I played chess with John Doe. John like Ernst was a very good chess player and like Ernst a person who I could never beat no matter how hard I racked my brain thinking of a strategy to win. Despite playing over a dozen games and not winning I still had a smile on my face. Today no one could bring me down. My good mate Danny was alive and that's all that mattered.

I couldn't wait till two o'clock and headed back to the Spanish guard half an hour earlier. Thankfully Don Amadeo didn't look to fussed and moved to one side and pointed to the room to signal I could go up.

I walked tentatively and slowly up the steps. I smiled with excitement at seeing him again. Then on the last few steps before the door I became nervous. It dawned on me he could hate me. I mean he has only now begun to walk. A year stuck in a hospital bed must be torture. I wonder if he blamed me for being crippled. After all it was my idea.

With a deep breath I opened the door and walked in. I had to find out how he was and what he thought of me even if it wasn't what I wanted to hear.

In the room were four beds, two on either side of the room. The two beds on the left were empty. In the bed nearest the door on the right contained a Spanish prisoner shaking and murmuring. It looked like he had a fever as his eyes looked wild as if he was hallucinating and his forehead was a bath a sweat. In the bed next to him was Danny. He still looked as handsome as ever with clumps of ruffled blond hair.

With a large gulp I edged slowly towards him. I felt courage to draw nearer when his smile grew wider and warmer. When I got to the bed I stared at him with guilt and sympathy. He smiled again. Losing my emotions I reached over and hugged him firmly. I was happy to receive a friendly slap on the back.

'Oh Danny all this time I thought you were dead,' I said withdrawing from a hug and sitting on his bed.

'Nope I have been here.'

'I am so sorry Danny,' I said looking at his bandages around his waist and leg.

'This is all my fault! Look at you!'

'Alan….. Alan……. calm down I have been fine,' he said almost giggling.

'I have a bad hip and leg but I am healing.'

'So where did you actually get shot?'

Danny started roaring with laughter.

'What's funny?'

'I didn't get shot.'

'But I heard gun shots……… and you fell off the wall?'

'No, no, no! They shot at me and I fell down.'

'Still that must have been quite a fall.'

'No I didn't fall off. I fell in a crack in the wall.'

'Oh.'

'The guard said it's only now you have started to walk.'

'Yeah I can walk a little…….but the doctor says I will always limp.'

'A limp!... Oh Danny I am so sorry mate!'

'Alan will you shut up. You are not to blame!'

'But!'

'Shut up Alan and tell me what happened to you and why it took so long to visit me.'

I wanted to tell him how sorry I was over and over but I could tell he didn't want my sympathy. So I did as he asked and brought him up to date with what I had been up to in the last year. I told him about being in the punishment cells for two weeks. I also made him laugh uncontrollably about John and I wearing uniforms and making hooch. My conversation flowed on and on. Danny was really appreciating this. I suppose he hadn't had contact with anyone for so long. Poor thing.

'That's a nice watch,' Danny said grabbing my arm and taking a closer look.

'Yeah bought it this morning.'

'Oh shit is that the time,' shouted Danny. 'I made you miss your tea.'

'It's alright I have some biscuits and stuff in my room.'

I was about to make an exit when I was startled by a door creaking open. It wasn't the door that I had gone through but a door I hadn't noticed in the corner of the room. Through the door arrived a nun carrying a tray of food.

I couldn't believe it. A fucking nun in prison! I stared at her for ages and was transfixed with her sweet face and big doleful brown eyes oozing with compassion. As I looked up and down her black smock I imagined what she was wearing underneath. I pictured a black lacy bra and knickers and then a silky camisole.

I gazed at her intently as she put down a tray of food at the bottom of the bed opposite. The sick Spic didn't even notice her as she hovered over him. Oh my god I would love to be him right now. She then put a cold compress on his forehead and mopped up the river of sweat that flowed. Oh please I want to get sick. I want to be that man. I want her bosom hanging over my face.

I felt a sharp tug on my left arm.

'What!'

'Alan close your mouth. Show some respect,' Danny whispered.

'Eh!'

'Alan stop looking at her like that.'

'I can't believe it she's a fucking nun,' I said still bemused by her presence.

'Yes they devote some of their time to looking after us.'

'You lucky bastard!' I whispered loudly. 'To think I thought you were dead and all this time you were being tended to by virgins.'

From my loud whisper the nun looked over to me with a disapproving glance.

'Shush Alan. You will get kicked out of here,' Danny said trying not to laugh.

'Sorry,' I said cheekily 'God it's been so long since I have seen a woman.'

'But Alan she is nun!'

'I don't care, she is still a woman underneath.'

With that Joseph smiled and grinned. When I turned around she was right beside me carrying a tray with two huge tomatoes on it which she gently rested on Joseph's knees.

'Gracias,' Danny said politely

The nun smiled wholeheartedly at Danny but when she looked at me she gave a disapproving look. I wonder if she could hear what I said. I wonder if she could be swayed from serving god and service me instead. I sighed as she disappeared back through the door.

'Hey Alan do you want to have a tomato seen as I made you miss your tea?'

'What?' I said still looking toward the closed door.

'Oi,' he shouted as he jabbed me in the arm.

'What?' I repeated again whilst turning around to face him.

'Have a tomato?'

'No, no it's okay I don't like tomatoes.'

'Come on I promise you will like them.'

'Danny I really don't like them.'

'Come on! Just try one.'

I really hated tomatoes. They are one of a very few foods I just wouldn't eat. However I felt I could not refuse Danny as he looked so happy and excited to see me and he was raving on and on about how good they were. So I agreed to take a bite. When I did I felt like I had a taste of heaven as they were so delicious and sweet. To add to their natural flavour they had been sprinkled with olive oil, sugar and salt, which really worked. The tomatoes were also huge. They must have been a sort of beef tomato as they were the size of a small grapefruit. This was and is the only tomato I have ever enjoyed in my life. Maybe it has something to do with the virginal touch or the fact I was fed so much shit in prison.

'Hey Danny the food of virgins taste good.'

'Shut up Alan,' said Danny laughing in disgust.

At around six o'clock Don Amadeo knocked on the door and said I should leave. I quickly hugged Danny and left. It was an hour from lock down time and I think he wanted me to go without being spotted by too many people. When I got to the bottom of the stairs I was about to leave to go the patio, when he stopped to ask me more about Cardiff. As we talked on and on it appeared he wasn't trying to make conversation but had aspirations to move there as he wanted to know everything about Wales and if I would agree to teach him Welsh. I agreed to tell him about Wales but informed him I couldn't teach him Welsh as I didn't know the language myself. He was both shocked and horrified at this. He couldn't get over how I had not been taught my own native language. This dented my national pride as he was right everyone in Wales should be taught Welsh. We should all know it. Plus I reckon in Britain it should be compulsory to be taught other languages. I felt stupid being the only one knowing one language. Everybody else could speak at least two.

A few weeks later I was called by the guard and told again I had only twenty minutes to get ready for trial. Again I zipped off to gather my stuff together but this time with less vigour as I knew it could get cancelled again. I decided not to wind myself up just in case I was to be disappointed. Again I had a shower, put my suit on and had a shave. This time though I was careful not to nick myself and I had warm water to soften my skin so I did not result in having a shaving rash.

In preparation I had already sorted out a pair of shoes. A Dutch guy said I could borrow his, as he said he had a nice pair of brown leather shoes near to my size. The only problem was I hadn't tried them on. I put my foot to the sole and thought they were big enough, but once I had them on it was different story. They were at least a size too small. I only just managed to squeeze them on my feet. Despite them being painful to wear when you looked down they did make me look the part.

When the boys came to the cells to wave me off they were very impressed with my get up. Nobody had ever seen anyone wearing a suit to court in Ceuta before.

I felt a million dollars when I walked through the prison accompanied with the guards, as all the Spanish were open mouthed at my smart appearance. I felt like I was a celebrity. Even the guards raised their eyebrows and nodded in approval when I walked through the Centro.

I was taken by car to the courthouse and escorted by two prison guards. It felt strange being in the outside world again and not being taken to yet another prison.

Once inside the courthouse I was surprised at how grand and clean it was. I hadn't seen a room so clean in a while. Another thing that surprised me was how professional and official everyone in the court looked. I don't know what I expected, but it wasn't this. The judge, Malero and the other lawyer were even wearing wigs.

When I walked past the judge and the other lawyer in handcuffs I did so confidently, quietly and with grace. I stuck my chest out and held my head up high whilst sporting a British stiff upper lip. I wanted to portray to the court a confident professional man and not that of a low life criminal. I wanted to try and instil in their heads I was a good decent man who could not be worthy of the crime that was bestowed.

Malero beckoned me to sit next to him. He pointed to a teenage boy who sat in the chair to the right and informed me this was my interpreter. I couldn't believe it. The boy looked like he had just come out of school. How could he be my interpreter? Plus he wasn't even dressed smartly. It was like as if he had been plucked off the streets. Which knowing Malero was probably the case.

Before I could get my bearings and look around, the court became animated and the judge started talking. I listened hard and stared at his lips trying to decipher his words. It was no good I didn't understand much, he spoke too quickly in Spanish. Then after his brief speech Malero began talking and then a while after the other lawyer spoke.

I nudged my interpreter and asked what he was saying as he hadn't said much. The young boy nodded and started to tell me what they were saying. However I didn't feel the interpreter was telling me everything, as for every thirty words that were said he would provide me with three words in English. As time drew on I grew more and more angry as I wanted to know everything that was been said and I whispered loudly for the boy to tell me. Malero shushed me for being too loud and then continued his speech.

I could feel my face becoming redder and redder with anger. I felt frustrated that I couldn't do anything. But I had to calm myself down.

Making a scene would just have made things worse. It was hard to keep my temper in check as I really wanted to know what was going down. This was my life they were talking about. I felt I had no control over the proceedings. The only thing keeping my mind off the worry was the pain in my feet from my crushed up toes.

When everyone stopped speaking and the judge went to leave the room, I jabbed at Malero's arm like an excited puppy.

'What's the damage?'

'The judge said eight years.'

'Eight years,' I said dumbfounded.

'But luckily for you I managed to persuade him to go down to seven years.'

'Seven years,' I said dejected.

'Yeah! Good isn't it!' He said smiling as if he had done me a massive favour.

I couldn't say anything back as I was disheartened. I would have been happier if my sentence was two years, seven seemed too much. I know I should have been grateful as I was originally looking at a twenty one year stretch. So he did manage to shave thirteen years off but that was in exchange of several thousands of pounds out of my bank account.

When I came back from the courthouse I felt numb. I didn't even feel my feet throbbing as I watched Ceuta zip past me in the car. Six more years to go!

Once I was taken through the Centro I took my shoes off straight away. I couldn't even bear to wear them just down the corridor to the brigada. With shoes in hand and just wearing socks I headed to my room and changed back into a t-shirt and shorts. I folded my suit and took it back to the room on the roof.

There was a mixed reaction from the boys. Some were made up for me that I didn't have to spend twenty one years whilst others thought six years was too long. Especially after all the money I pumped Malero's way.

For the rest of the afternoon I tried to stay out of everyone's way as I wanted time on my own to think and let it settle in that if I didn't escape I would be in prison for six more years. My solitude however was broken by a Basque boy that came over. I told him on the day's events but he seemed more preoccupied with my watch.

'You like my watch then,' I said smiling at his appreciation.

'It is a nice watch,' he said in a deep breath.

'It is,' I smiled.

'It used to be mine.'

'What?'

'Yeah one of the Spanish nicked it off me.'

'They did what!'

'Here have it back and I will get my money,' I said trying to loosen the strap.

'No, no, no Alan. It's fine. You keep it.'

'Wait here!'

Filled with rage I headed over to John Doe and Franc. I told them about the watch and how it had been stolen by one of the Spanish from one of the Basque boys. They both didn't seem too fussed and were confused at why I was so livid. I tried to tell them that by the Spanish nicking from the Basque boys was not just an insult to them but to all of us. Still they both shook their heads obviously not agreeing with me.

'Oh John, Franc just watch my back.'

'What?'

'I am going to have words.'

Seething with rage I headed towards the Spanish sellers and picked out the guy who sold me the watch. Grabbing the back of his collar I dragged him and shoved him to the boundary wall. In Spanish I asked him whose the watch was. He bullshitted it was given to him by a friend on a visit. It didn't matter how tightly I screwed his T-shirt more and more lies poured out, until I told him enough was enough. I told him the watch was from one of the Basque boys and told them not to mess with them as they were part of us Europeans. I argued with him to give me the money but then he jabbered on about how he had none. I shook the Spaniard and pushed him around a few more times. I then warned him to leave the Europeans and the two Basque boys alone. The frightened Spaniard nodded. I released my grip and watched as he scuttled off to hide amongst the other Spanish sellers.

After a few weeks I was moved on yet again. Like the last time I was plucked out of bed in the early morning and taken by ferry to the Spanish mainland. I went with a few other prisoners but none of my mates, they were mainly Spanish. Instead of taking me to Algeciras this time I was taken to a prison in Cadiz.

26 ROLLING STONE

I was very surprised when I was taken to a prison in Cadiz. I just automatically assumed once on the Spanish mainland I would be sent straight to Algeciras prison, like last time. Well I suppose that confirms it! Nothing could be predicted when in the Spanish prison system.

I would have loved to have known how they planned and decided where to put me and my fellow prisoners. I liked to imagine a prison director in full uniform, shuffling me around a map with a stick like a leader would in a war. But I very much doubted this as for one thing I don't think any of my moves were planned. When I was taken from a prison it always seemed an ad hoc affair as on arrival at a new prison the guards almost always seemed surprised. I just assumed it was because I was British they were taken aback, but maybe it was because they didn't expect me. Surely though someone in each prison would have had to be informed, even just to check there was enough room.

I only stayed in Cadiz a few days until I was shuffled on to Jerez. Jerez was quite a small prison; it was only several scores in population and mostly all European. I liked Jerez prison as the atmosphere felt very relaxed, not just with the prisoners but with the guards too. It also felt nice being part of the majority for a change. Without the presence of Spanish prisoners took away my worry of accidently upsetting anyone and being jabbed in the kidneys with a homemade knife or pointy stick filled with shit. Plus Cadiz didn't look as secure as the other prisons I had been too, so escape looked quite possible. Alas, I didn't get the opportunity to form an escape plan as I was moved on only after a few days. They must have known escape would have been far too tempting for me in Cadiz with my history.

Next I was sent to Seville for a few weeks and then again onto Cordoba. It was strange going to Seville and Cordoba twice round. It felt like déjà vu, as I had been there before but with something missing. I put this down to the lads not being there. I really missed them not being around. It was so much harder to try and keep upbeat without them.

In Cordoba I did meet a few Europeans to chat too but I didn't feel like I could get close to them. I don't know why as most of the lads seemed friendly enough, but I just couldn't stomach staying with them for too long. I think I found it hard as I knew in the next minute everything could change, I could be sent to a different wing of a prison or to a different prison. So I began to wonder what the point was of forming friendships.

I stayed in Cordoba for several months. It was the longest I had stayed in a prison for a while, so I again I naturally assumed it would be the prison I would serve out my sentence in. Wrong! I was glad though I didn't stay, which was a crazy thing to think really, as on paper Cordoba was a fantastic prison compared to the other dives I had been too. For one it was fairly hygienic. The guards actually treated prisoners like human beings. The consulate was actually sympathetic and the food looked edible. But, despite all this I couldn't settle and it was where I felt the most glum. I think Cordoba depressed me more than any other prison as it served as a reminder for when I lost my two boys. It was here I signed them away on the dotted line and it was here where I found it hardest to forget. The only way I could push it out of my mind was to think of Enero. If I kept on dwelling about my kids I could end up like him.

With relief I was plucked from my cell in Cordoba prison in the middle of the night. I was shocked to find my transport was via a bus. Normally I was taken in a car or by a small van that carried only a few prisoners at a time. I had never been on anything this big before. When I looked around I couldn't see anyone else being taken, but surely this couldn't have only being my ride. I then realised it wasn't as already onboard were several prisoners. They must have come from a different prison.

When I was pushed onto the bus by the guards and the doors shut, I was further shocked to find all the prisoners on the bus were Spanish and covered head to foot in black soot. Feeling self-conscious at being the only white boy I quickly walked down the middle of the bus towards the only empty seat. The smell of burnt wood and singed hair filled my nostrils. This took me back to being in Ceuta on my first day and that of when Dominic burnt down the place.

I tentatively sat down on the empty seat next to one of the Spanish prisoners. After a few seconds the engine revved up and off we went into the darkness on our magical mystery tour. I couldn't think where they were going to take me next. I hoped I would go back to Jerez, but I knew this wasn't likely. Jerez was small and appeared only to be a place where prisoners were held temporarily. But what did I know? I should have known better than to assume. The only thing I cared about was going back to Ceuta. I really really didn't want that!

The Spanish prisoner next to me didn't make any eye contact and seemed preoccupied with talking with his two mates in front. This was fine with me. In fact I pretty much welcomed Spanish prisoners treating me as if I wasn't there, it was far better than worrying about if they were going to attack me.

Trying not to create attention I shuffled around in my seat in order to get comfy. But it didn't matter how snug I made my bum and legs feel, this could not distract me from the burning pain from my wrists. I mean I was used to wearing handcuffs, but these buggers had been put on far too tight. I had to really squeeze my wrists together in order feel just a quarter of an inch space of relief.

Being distracted from looking at my reddening hands I was catapulted into the seat in front when the bus suddenly jolted forward. Luckily I managed to swerve and avoid hitting my nose and instead caught my elbow hard. The prisoner in front of me turned around in his chair and looked down. I had obviously hit the back of his chair with some force as he didn't look happy. I smiled and shrugged as if in attempt to say sorry but this didn't look sufficient as he continued to stare at my hands. When I looked across to the guy next to me he also seemed pre-occupied with my hands.

Oh fuck! So much for trying to being inconspicuous and trying not to piss anyone off! But come on, surely they would realise I banged into the back of him by accident.

I was then furthered disturbed when I looked at the hands of the man next to me. He was missing his handcuffs. Hearing jangling from above I looked up and could see he had hung them up on a rail going round the bus. In fact there were scores and scores of handcuffs jangling. Every Spanish fucker on this bus had a free pair of hands.

Great stuff! I had just pissed off a bus full of presumably armed Spaniards who had hands free to jab me as much as they liked. So I used the only defence available and said sorry in Spanish.

The man next to me then turned around and started shouting to other people on the bus. Oh fuck! Now he appeared to be getting everyone else involved. Surely they can't all fucking string me up. Now this is not fair. I looked ahead and behind at the armed guards in their metal cages. I hope to god they will be quick if I get stabbed.

I breathed a sigh of relief as several seconds went by where the three men didn't stare and continued talking to the others. Maybe I had been forgiven or forgotten about.

When I looked outside in the darkness I managed to pick out from the shallow beam of the bus lights a sharp corner up ahead. Quickly I pushed my hands in front to steady myself as we went around. I planted my feet firmly on the floor so as not to fall into the lap of my neighbour and tried not to push my hands too far in the front seat so he could feel it. I learnt my lesson the last time. Right now I needed to concentrate on the outside and not bump into anyone again. God I hope this journey doesn't go on for hours, as this may be hard to do.

The man next to me started shouting again and pointing at me. Oh fuck! I hadn't been forgiven. He stood up and beckoned to the prisoners in the opposite row. I looked up the isle and could there was something being passed from prisoner to prisoner and that the object was heading my way. I could see it was small and metal as it glinted when it caught the reflection of a street lamp. Here we go they have managed to scrabble together a knife. I sat on the edge of my seat waiting for the fashioned weapon to be handed back. I imagined in my head I would be ready to stand up and kick it out of his hands if he lunged at me.

The metal object was then handed to his neighbour by the prisoner in front who I had accidentally hit. He smiled at me which made me really uneasy. The fucking twat was going to enjoy his mate sticking a knife in me. I couldn't believe how a little situation could come to this.

With horror I looked at my neighbour with the metal object. He seemed confused at my reaction and held out his hand gently showing me the metal shiny object. I was shocked to find it was just like a skinny nail. What the hell is that? If that was their weapon I had no need to worry, as it didn't even look that sharp.

'Esposas! Esposas!' he said.

Not knowing what the fuck he was on about I shrugged. The Spaniard huffed and pointed at my hand cuffs.

'Oh..............hand cuffs,' I said nodding my head to my hands.

Before I knew it the man grabbed my hands. I struggled a bit until I saw him put his tool in the lock of the hand cuffs. Ferociously he wiggled the nail up and down, and then in a circular motion. It didn't look easy picking the lock as his face was deep in concentration, so much so he poked his tongue out and went slightly bogeyed. Eventually though I was freed.

Once the cuffs were off I hung them up on the metal mesh above. Now there was a complete set. To all the men on the bus I waved and then put my thumbs in the air and smiled. I was then taken aback when they all cheered and nodded. I showed the most appreciation to my liberator with a firm fond handshake. He smiled sheepishly at me and then continued chatting to the guy in front.

I sat back in my seat relieved. Well one thing I shouldn't judge a book by its cover. I would now not think about all Spanish prisoners being knife wielding horrible bastards.

Once I calmed down, I laughed to myself about the Spanish word for handcuffs, as although it was spelt esposas it sounded like spousers. I wondered if spouse was inspired by the Spanish word for handcuffs. You have to admit it is rather fitting.

What a fucking great bunch of lads. You could tell they were all genuine mates as they were continually laughing and chatting as if they had known each other for ages. I had never seen a bunch of Spanish prisoners who got on so well and actually had a genuine and close bond. Well they must have respected one another to be involved in the fire they started. It looked like they must have all owned up to the fire as it wasn't just one lad on the bus.

Unless they burnt down their dormitory and had to be moved.

Then just like with the metal tool something else was being passed around. Being nosey I got out my seat and looked in all directions to see what it was. It seemed several people were passing stuff around. For a while I could not see anything in view but sporadically I would hear something sounding like glass clinking together. The mystery was only solved when the clinking was heard under my seat and I watched on as my neighbour reached under and produced two bottles of beer.

Fucking hell these guys were class! Starting a fire, taking off their handcuffs and drinking beer. If they had a bit of blow too, I would have gladly being adopted into their group. By far these were the best bunch of Spanish prisoners I had ever met.

My neighbour looked at me perplexed whilst holding the two bottles of beer. I didn't say anything and looked on. He seemed like he was weighing up whether to give me a bottle. Thankfully he did, to which I said gracias very enthusiastically.

The first drink went down quickly. I asked for two more bottles as I had taste for the beer and the party atmosphere. I offered him money for it which he happily accepted. Well I didn't want to be cheeky. I tried to join in with the banter and conversation going around but I found it hard to keep up. Especially when I became more pissed, but I still enjoyed and laughed when everyone else did.

After a few hours the beer ran out. It was funny seeing the worry on the faces of a few of the boys around me as they looked at their empty bottles. Some even looked through the top of the bottle as if it was a telescope. It was as if they didn't believe it was empty. Then without warning one of the more vocal lads stood up and started shouting towards the guards. Not getting any attention he then stepped up his noise by banging repeatedly on the window. The armed guard in his metal cage at the front of the bus then stood up slowly and put his hand in the air. To my astonishment the Spanish prisoner began shouting and pointing to his empty bottle. I couldn't believe it he was showing the guard we had alcohol on board. The guard nodded and then sat back down on his seat. This seemed to please the loud prisoner as he too sat down.

About ten minutes later the bus made a stop at a petrol station which had a small shop to the side. The armed guard at the front of the bus came out of his compartment and then shouted something. With that everyone quickly grabbed the cuffs from above and put them on their wrists. What the fuck! My neighbour jabbed me with his elbow and encouraged me to do the same, which I did.

Then money was being sent by boys in all directions to the front. I asked my neighbour what it was for, to which he replied it was for the guards to get beer. Hastily with cuffed hands I rummaged in my pockets and pulled out a few pesetas. I quickly passed it to the guy in front who passed it on ahead. I was down with having a few more bottles.

Looking out the window I watched as the driver filled the petrol tank and the prison guard headed off into the shop. The other armed guard at the back of the bus remained in his caged compartment. I wished he'd had gone in the shop too, as this would have been a perfect opportunity to escape. I could of taken off my cuffs with the tool, broken down the door and ran off into the night. Okay albeit very drunk and in the middle of fuck knows, but these were trivial details to me. If he was in the shop I am sure I would have had a chance.

When the prison guard came back I was shocked to see how many bottles he got for us. I knew we had all given a huge amount of cash, but I still didn't expect for us to be allowed so much. What a great guy! I suppose it was beneficial for him to buy us booze. For one he probably took a handsome wedge of it and secondly we were kept sedated and out of trouble.

After a few more drunken hours my journey came to an end. I was gutted when the bus stopped, I didn't want the party to end. I was further saddened when I looked around and found I was the only one to get off the bus. I was again separated from a great bunch of lads.

The prison I was sent to next was right in the middle of Madrid. In my drunken state I managed to read the sign which said Carabanchel. It shocked me how far North we had travelled. Well I suppose I had done most prisons in the South, now it was time to travel further afield right into the heart of Spain. Hopefully Madrid being the capital city this prison should serve to be the most civilised. But hey we shall see.

I watched the bus pull away as I was dragged inside by two prison guards. I looked at them with annoyance as I hated being forcibly pushed anywhere, but both of them didn't look at me. Instead they looked around in jittery motions as if they were scared of something or someone. It felt very odd to see the guards so worried. What the hell were they afraid of?

Once inside I was taken to a circular area in the middle of the prison. All around were landings veering off like the spokes in a bicycle wheel. In the middle was a kind of platform with a guard standing on it. I stood at the bottom under the platform whilst a guard stood next to me.

This was very weird. Normally I was taken straight to a cell or a dormitory and dumped. Instead here I had to stand for ages, just waiting. I found it hard to stand being a little drunk and would continually stumble and sway. I also didn't feel very comfortable as my bladder felt fit to burst. I even asked the guard several times for a piss but he said I had to wait till I could be taken to my cell. What the fuck were we waiting for?

The guard hardly looked at me, and seemed conscious of what was happening in a landing to his right as he looked at it as if expecting a monster to break down the door. I was very tempted to tip toe away as he seemed very distracted, but I knew the guard above would spot me. Plus this place looked like a maze. It was highly unlikely I would be able find a door to the outside without being spotted.

Bored I concentrated on listening to the different sounds around the prison and was surprised at what I managed to pick out. Firstly from the roof I could hear a helicopter hovering nearby. I just thought that one had just flown ahead but I have since learnt that there was always a helicopter hovering every now and again over Carabanchel. This was because the prison held several terrorists. So as a matter of security one would fly above at all times.

Then I heard in a corridor to my right the sounds of screaming and shouting in Spanish. Amongst that I could also hear objects being banged on a hard surface and glass being smashed. It sounded like a riot was going down. Well from one bunch of crazy bastards to another. Just the right sort of people I wanted. Go on lads play fuck!

Then amongst the racket I was disturbed when I heard the sound of a horse's neigh. I doubted what I heard and leaned my ear further towards the direction of the corridor. Seconds later I could then hear a succession hard hooves being clattered on the floor. What the fuck were horses doing in the building! The sound of hooves was then drowned by horrific screaming. What the hell was going on!

Just under an hour later I was eventually taken to my cell. I was thankful I was in a cell on my own and that I had a toilet in my room. It was also nice that the toilet had a seat on it and was not just a hole in the floor.

I only stayed in the main prison at Carabanchel for a few days so I didn't get a chance to find out what had gone down. But I did find out later that horses were used in the prison by some guards when there was a riot. I also heard that the guards who rode the horses in times of riots were quite relentless in their pursuit to promote the peace that they would trample anything and anyone in their way. I even heard of casualties being inflicted on fellow prisoner officers who were caught up in the riot.

After Carabanchel I was taken to Burgos. This prison was the best so far in the way of food. But apart from that it was quite a boring prison. Nothing much went down here. Thankfully I was taken from there and then sent to El Dueso. El Dueso was in the nicest part of Spain I had been too and had the most things going on, including a prison DJ.

27 EL DUESO

After a tour of prisons from Morocco, Southern, Mid and Northern Spain I had finally come to an end. The prison in El Dueso was to be my last stop and where I was to serve out the rest of my sentence, which was give or take about five years now. I knew this as I was informed by my consulate a few days after my arrival here. This information completely bowled me over. I had never been told a fact before by a consulate. Plus it felt strange that I wouldn't be moved. No more midnight ghost trains.

El Dueso prison was situated in a very picturesque part of Spain. It was roughly between the two cities Santander and Bilbao, and a few hundred metres from the beach situated along the Bay of Biscay. From the prison we could see the sea but not the beach. Being so close to the sea meant there was a strong smell of salt and the air constantly felt damp and bracing. It was a blessed relief from some of the scorching hot cities I had stayed in. In the few moments the prison was quiet you could even hear the sea when the waves crashed into one another, especially when a storm was brewing.

I was glad that El Dueso was meant to be my last place before I was released. Incidentally it wasn't but at the time I really thought it was and so did the Spanish prison authorities. Well anyway I was glad because out of all the prisons I had been too; it was the liveliest and boasted the most facilities. It had a football field, a tennis court and a television room. There was even a prison DJ, who would blare out a weird mix of Spanish, British and American music from massive speakers positioned outside his cell pointing towards the courtyard. You could request songs to be played from his limited collection but this was in exchange for a small fee. He had his turn tables and record player in a little hut thing which also served as an economato.

The prison population was in the majority Spanish, with a few Basque and then a few Europeans. Yet again I was the minority, but I didn't give a fuck! I knew how to handle myself and had been fine so far keeping out of fights. Well with the Spanish prisoners anyway.

After a few days I did manage to locate two old friends, in the shape of Danny and an Italian acquaintance Pierro. Seeing Danny at El Dueso was fantastic and having Pierro was also a bonus.

It was funny seeing Danny again as I felt even more emotional than the last time. I don't know why but I struggled to hold back the tears. I think it got to me when I could see he had recovered and could walk around, albeit with a limp. Seeing him limp did upset me, but I didn't say anything. Danny wouldn't appreciate me being apologetic or feeling guilty. I just needed to suck it up, like he had to do.

It was nice to see Pierro, but I would have preferred to have seen one of the other boys as Pierro and I weren't that close. This was mainly because we never really got chance to talk properly as he always seemed to be moved on a few days or a few weeks after I arrived at a prison where he was.

When I spoke with Pierro he too picked up on the fact that he was moved shortly after I arrived and made a crack that I seemed to be walking in his shadow. This comment didn't sit well with me. I didn't walk in anyone's shadow. I went on my own road thank you very much!

I didn't react to his comment but stored it in my mind to build up a picture of Pierro. At that moment it was that he was a cocky prick. I put him straight away in the same category of John MacGloughlin. Here we go again! Another fucker who is going to wind me up and think he's the man! Oh well at least life won't be boring and John was a good egg in the end to be fair.

Despite reminding me of John, I will say Pierro did carry off his arrogance with a little more elegance and style. Even down to his swagger he seemed to ooze a coolness despite his over inflated confidence.

After a few weeks of hanging around with Pierro and Danny I soon settled into the routine of the prison. The first thing we would do in the morning was grab a coffee or an expresso from the economato. For prison standards the quality of both these drinks served were amazing. It was the must have drink for the morning. Plus it had medicinal benefits as it would wake me up, refresh me and also aided to cure my hangover if I went for it drinking the night before.

Then after a shot of caffeine we would have a walk around, maybe look at what was being sold by the Spanish prisoners on the markets. In the early evening we sometimes went to the television to see what was on. There was never much of a choice of programmes. All that seemed to be aired were films, usually of a pornographic nature and bull fighting. I didn't mind having a peek at the porn but the bull fighting I could not stand to watch. Why make such a fucking show out of killing an animal? My view is kill an animal humanely and then chop it up and put it into a burger. Don't play around with it especially with such cruel means.

Every now and again in the day I would join in with a game of football or play someone in tennis. Then in the night Danny, Pierro and myself would get stoned and drunk to some degree, depending on how much hash and alcohol we could get our hands on. On a Saturday in the day we would watch the tennis and football tournaments that were laid on between the prisoners. I never got involved as I could not compete with the amazingly athletic young Spaniards being only two years from forty. Also I never felt comfortable about competing as I never saw any Europeans getting involved. But most of the Europeans were too busy getting stoned to do any sports, like me.

Another activity that kept me occupied in the day was trying to befriend a cat. Like at Cordoba the prison was overrun with them, that and rabbits. However unlike Cordoba the cats were incredibly skittish. It didn't matter how hard I tried to coax them, none of them would come anywhere near me. This served as great hilarity to Danny and Pierro. They would be holding their stomachs in agony as they watched me on my fucking hands and knees puckering my lips and making squeaky noises. None of them could see the benefit of having a pet and thought I was soft or crazy in the head. But this was just the typical attitude of the other Europeans. Where was John when I needed him to back me up!

I was also caught by a few of the Spanish prisoners trying to give my food away to a pussy or two. I didn't care! Even if they stopped and stared I would still carry on talking to the cats in a soft and happy tone. I liked cats, fuck everyone else. As the Spaniards couldn't understand my behaviour too, they thought I was a little crazy.

Unaware I could speak and understand Spanish I would hear them telling each other they thought my head had gone. I liked this! Having a reputation of being a nutter would mean they would be very wary of me. Hopefully they would also think twice before picking a fight with me too.

After a few weeks I gave up on trying to win a cat over and instead focused my energies on walking around the vast prison to get exercise. I mean every day we walked around but I had never done a tour of the whole prison in one day as it was pretty big. So one Friday I coaxed Danny to walk all the way around. He agreed as he wanted to improve the mobility in his legs and hip. I asked Pierro to come, but he couldn't see the point in it and plus he said he had other stuff to do.

The walk was very slow and arduous as I had to constantly wait for Danny to catch up as he struggled with his hip. I didn't mind as it gave me a chance to case out the walls and security of the prison in order to escape. I was disappointed though as the security was tight. There was no chance of escaping with all the armed guards they had dotted in the turrets and around the prison grounds.

At least it was a nice day to have a walk. The sun was out and there wasn't a cloud in the sky, but despite being warm there was also a refreshing breeze coming from the direction of the sea.

In the distance I could hear the song, 'Fly like an eagle' by the Eagles being blasted out by the prison DJ. I had requested this song to be played continuously for an hour as background music for our walk.

After about a quarter of an hour Danny stopped and looked at me with sorrowful eyes. He breathed heavily as he let out a big huff. His eyebrows furrowed and several creases appeared on his forehead. He looked in discomfort. I was guessing his hip was giving him some jip.

A moment of silence dawned as I looked at him and him at me. I could tell he was about to ask if we could turn back. I didn't want that to happen, so I turned my back to him not knowing what to do.

I looked to the sky trying to think of something positive to say to inspire him to carry on when I saw a sea gull gliding around from side to side in the sky. It was a beautiful and awe inspiring sight, watching it blissfully be carried by the wind. Transfixed with the gull's splendour and lifted by the energy of the song I spontaneously began mimicking the actions of the bird. With arms stretched out I tilted my arms up and down whilst hovering around Danny. Danny stared at me with wide eyes looking perplexed. I carried on pretending to swoop up and down. I began to do it more energetically when I sang in tune with the lyrics of the song. The more I sang the louder I became. When there was a pause in the lyrics Danny burst out in hysterics and shook his head.

'What are you up to Alan?' he said whilst spluttering.

'Listen to the words Danny,' I said inspired. 'Fly like an eagle Danny.'

'What!' he said laughing nervously.

I stopped and pointed to the gull above.

'Look Danny at that bird,' I said softly. 'I want to be that bird. I want to be free like that.'

Danny smiled but still shone me a confused look.

'Come on Danny do it with me. Pretend you're a bird.'

'Alan?'

'Yes?'

'Fuck off!' he said laughing.

With that we both had a fit of giggles. Eventually we both composed ourselves and set off walking again. My daft actions had worked. For a few moments he rested his painful hip and forgot about this pain. I still to this day can't quite decide why I acted like a bird. I am not sure whether I did it to cheer up Danny or if it was a moment of madness. Maybe the Spanish were right to think I was going mad. Maybe I was.

On the walk around we talked and talked about our differing experiences, on the prisons we had both been too and the people we met. I noticed Danny didn't say much about Ceuta but was very excitable when talking about the other prisons he went to. This was not surprising as at Ceuta he must have spent the best part of a year cooped up in a hospital bed recovering. He probably didn't have much to say about that. I am just surprised he didn't go barmy. I would of. Staying in bed all that time and not being able to walk around and see people. That sounds like hell to me, especially in Ceuta prison. Even with virgins tending to my every whim.

On the walk Danny pointed out areas where we were forbidden to walk. These included the fields where they would grow vegetables and crops such as corn and near to a disused brick building. I could understand why the crops were out of bounds, but the dilapidated buildings next to the prison were a mystery. What the hell did they not want us to see? I mean yes they didn't want us nicking the crops they grew to feed us and other prisoners, but what was in that building.

Feeling mischievous I decided to trespass into the fields of crops. It would be worth my while as I could see there were cobs of sweet corn ready to be picked. They would be nice to have for supper. Plus I wanted to see if I could sneak across without the guards noticing me. I was taking a risk as the guards were armed and would shoot at me if I was noticed, but I didn't let this bother me. I had it in my head to do it now.

'Danny will you keep watch out for me?'

'Why what you going to do?'

'The corn over there looks ripe to pick.'

'But were not allowed to go near the corn field.'

'Danny!' I said astonished. 'How long have you known me for?'

'I don't know...... Why?'

'Look just signal me a thumbs up so I know when to run back after I get the corn.'

'You are crazy!'

When I could see no guards were facing our direction I quickly pelted it across to the field of corns. Before I could get there I had to sneak under a wooden fence. When I got close to the fence I was horrified to see several cats were nailed to it by their tails. Poor fucking things! No wonder they wouldn't come to me when I called them.

Quickly I dived over the fence and hid myself in the row of corns, whilst keeping as still as I could. I listened for a few seconds to see if I could hear any shouts or gun shots, but thankfully there was nothing. Relieved I quickly went to work looking for the biggest, ripest and nicest looking cobs. Then when I found the three that took my fancy I went back to the fence making sure no guards could see me, but also made sure Danny could see me. Then without warning Danny put his right arm in the air and gave me the thumb up. With adrenalin flowing and my heart pumping I quickly darted back over.

After a quick look around I decided all was well and carried on walking. It felt great I had gotten away with it. Maybe escape from here wasn't impossible after all.

In the late afternoon I brought out the three corns on the cob and grilled them on a homemade barbecue which was used by the prisoners to cook food outside. The barbecue was made out of bricks and had coals at the bottom with a few brown crusty metal grates that slotted in the bricks above the hot charcoal. On the barbecue already were several bits of meat, some of which looked like rabbit, some chicken and then there were some bits of meats which I couldn't classify in origin.

I lay my corns on the cob on the top shelf and as far away from the unknown meats. God knows what diseased animals they were cooking, but I didn't want to become ill from it.

When the corns were done I skewered them with the flimsy knife and fork cutlery we were handed out to eat with and gave a cob to Pierro and Danny. Pierro had the smallest one and I saved the biggest one for me. This seemed fair to me as I had after all done most of the hard work. Pierro was lucky I had even got him one.

When I took mine off from the barbecue Danny produced a packet of butter which he got from the economato. In turns we greased up our corns with butter. I blew on my corn a little to cool it down and then sunk in my hungry teeth. The sweetcorn tasted really sweet and delicious. In fact they were so good in flavour I even moaned so much the Spanish boys took the piss saying it sounded I was having an orgasm. There taunts didn't bother me. I just concentrated on enjoying my supper especially as it was so fresh and delicious. It was such a nice feeling eating something where I knew exactly where it came from and who had cooked it. I didn't have to worry about anyone else's grubby mitts being on it.

Whilst sloppily eating my corn lathered with butter a few of the Spanish asked if I had any more corns that they could buy off me. I shook my head whilst licking the butter dripping from the corner of my mouth. Undeterred they asked if I could get them some. I responded with a no and told them they could go to the corn fields themselves if they wanted. They look stunned and then began asking questions how I managed to get to the field without being caught. I don't know whether they disbelieved me or wanted a go themselves. I told them what I had done and they seemed very impressed. This felt strange to gain respect over nicking a few corns. Nonetheless I enjoyed the boys looking up to me and further showed off by telling them about the escape attempt in Ceuta.

I then changed the conversation by asking the lads if they had heard of anyone escaping from El Dueso. Most laughed and said it was impossible with the security. A few of the boys did say they had heard of people trying to leg it, but for their trouble they were shot at which resulted in mostly injuries, but there were also a few reported deaths. Despite the lads being pessimistic on the whole about escape, I did manage to acquire one story which inspired hope. Someone had heard of one successful escape from El Dueso where a guy rolled under a vehicle carrying food and hung on underneath when the vehicle left the grounds. I liked stories like these. I liked happy endings.

After the corn Danny, Pierro and I headed straight to my room in order to have a few drinks. The beers glided down with ease as they usually did. After a few hours cooped up in the cell I felt an urge to get out. I didn't want to feel cased in a moment longer. So I persuaded Danny and Pierro we should go to television room. It didn't take much coaxing at all. We all hoped tonight there was a film on.

Quietly we opened the door of the television room and all shuffled in. The room was quite dark and dingy. The only light came from the worn out battered looking television that was on. In front of the television were rows upon rows of chairs including one wooden beam.

Tonight only the few rows of seats were filled. I would say at most there were only twenty or so young Spanish men in the room. I had never seen it this quiet before. Taking advantage of the lack of people we all managed to grab a seat on the third row. The Spanish in front were so engrossed into watching the TV they didn't even turn round when we sat down.

The room fell silent and on the screen appeared the words 'Live Bull Fights from Barcelona' in big bold letters written in Spanish. It fucking had to be bull fighting tonight. I hated bull fighting. I hated the unnecessary torture of an animal. Why couldn't it be a film?

I did think about going back to my cell, but when I looked back at Danny and Pierro they seemed settled and interested. Plus I hadn't seen a bull fight before. Maybe I would think differently about the so called sport if I watched one. So with an open mind I decided to watch it.

After the credits flamenco music blared out whilst the camera man showed opening shots of the crowd laughing and cheering. Some were drinking and others eating. Mostly people were smiling and seemed to be in a carnival mood. Here and there you could hear people playing trumpets loudly and badly.

Then after a few minutes a dawn of silence descended and the people in the arena all looked towards the centre stage. Then a matador walked to the middle of the arena to the tune of a lone trumpet. After this the trumpet was sounded again and the matador was joined by six other men. Three were on horseback, whilst the other three stood to the side of him. This seemed odd to me. I only thought there was one matador, or murderer which incidentally is the Spanish definition. I didn't realise he had fucking staff. All those men to slay one fucking bull! Cowards!

The matador, the men on horses and the other men then went round the arena in a march. Every now again they would all salute looking towards the crowd. The camera man would then cut to a dignitary in the crowd who the men were saluting too. None of which I recognised, but from the chatter of my Spanish friends in front they obviously knew who they were.

Then the band playing the flamenco music really built up the tempo as the matador and his men paraded around once more. The matador was sporting high wasted black trousers and a brightly coloured ruffled short jacket known as a traje de luces suit of lights. The men then disappeared and the camera was pointed towards a pen where two bulls were being held. Why did they need the two? I always assumed it was the one animal per event.

Next, the band ceased playing and the crowds went quiet as the bull was released into the ring. The matador and his mates then walked up to the bull and teased him with capes that were magenta and gold in colour. The bull didn't seem bothered the first few times the cape was wafted over his face but as they did it more and more the bull did begin to charge a little towards them. The wafting of the capes went on for several minutes. Apparently this was done to test the ferocity of the bull. From the test it appeared this bull was quite placid. Eventually the men did manage to antagonise the bull into making an aggressive snort. This stirred up the Spanish lads in the TV room, as they began whistling, clapping and cheering.

Then the bull was allowed a few minutes of alone time in the ring. By this time it had calmed down and happily trotted around whilst staring at the crowd as if bewildered at what was going on. Then two men on horseback entered the ring. Each horse was protected by a thick cover, they were so thick they looked they had a thin mattress draped over them. This was there to protect them from the bull's horns from piercing into them. I have since learnt that before this protection was introduced many horses would die from being disemboweled.

Each of the men on horses held a sort of lance in one hand as they both slowly trotted around either sides of the ring. In the television room some of the Spanish boys began chanting 'Picador, Picador, Picador'. This was the title for the men on horseback involved in the bull fighting.

One of the picadors stopped his horse and shouted towards the bull to come and meet him. The bull responded and ambled over. When the bull saw the horse it seemed to become angry and began charging and knocking into the horse. The horse eyes looked nervous but it did manage to stay calm and reasonably still despite the continuous barrage of strong nudges. The picador steadied his lance until it was positioned near to a slab of muscle near the bull's neck. With a deep breath he then plunged in the lance which had big blade on the end. Then the other picador trotted over on his horse and did the same thing. Over and over both picadors picked and hacked at the bull's neck. The bull was stabbed so much the blood just seemed to gush out of its wound. You could see the neck muscles had been weakened by the blows as the bulls head began to hang low. This is apparently a sign of a successful picador if they can weaken a bull's neck like this.

In the next stage, which is known as the tercio de banderillas ("the third of flags"), the three other men who are known as the banderilleros entered the ring, each were carrying two razor sharp barbed sticks. All three men spread out into the arena and then one by one went in and stabbed the barbed sticks deep into the bull around the wounds caused by the picadors. The blood from the poor animal's neck continued to pump. The men then left and the camera showed a close up of the poor bull with six blades sticking into his neck and back. The camera then cut back to the banderilleros waving at the crowd. The Spanish lads in the television enthused by the crowd began clapping and cheering also.

For the final stage the matador entered the ring carrying a small red cape, known as a muleta in one hand and a sword in the other. This stage is known as the tercio de muerte ("the third of death"). I used to think the cape was coloured red to anger the bull, but I have since learned this can't be true as the bull is colourblind. The actual reason for using a red cape is to mask the bull's blood.

Over and over I watched as the matador wafted his cape around and around. I suppose it was impressive the way he did it, as he moved the material around with such elegance and grace, but I couldn't enjoy it. He was fucking torturing an innocent animal at the end of the day. Around and around he made the bull turn. You could see the bull getting out of breath and blood spraying from his large nostrils. Then the camera did a close up of the sword which the Matador held up. The blade glinted in the sun for a few moments before it was stained with blood as he plunged it hard in between the shoulder blades of the bull. The blade must have stabbed straight through its heart as it wasn't long before the poor beast fell to its knees.

When it was over I was horrified. I thought the idea of bull fighting was bad, but it was much worse than what I had imagined.

Shaking my head and with my mouth open I looked towards Pierro and Danny. They with their eyes shone a sympathetic glance but both shrugged as if they didn't understand why I was so appalled. Again they couldn't understand my love of animals and for not seeing them in pain. I mean I am not a vegetarian so I know animals are killed for me to eat. But I don't want to see one tortured before it is chopped up and put in my food. Yes kill animals for meat but do it humanely.

Danny and Pierro stood up and beckoned me to leave. I nodded in agreement and gladly got up from my chair. I couldn't watch any more of this. Slowly we all carefully negotiated the obstacle course that was the benches and row of chairs and made our way to the door. I then heard the Spanish boys sound angry and I couldn't help but look to the screen. To my delight the second bull was chasing the matador around the arena. The big powerful matador was reduced to looking like a little girl as he scampered around the arena as the bull charged. Go on bull you fucking get them. The matador left the arena without wafting his cape. It was obvious this bull was aggressive they didn't need to tickle his nose this time to prove it. It wasn't surprising the poor pull was pissed off. He had to stay in a cage and watch his poor mate be killed in front of him. He was probably after revenge.

'Hey boys I want to stay actually.'

'You sure Alan?' said Danny concerned. 'I know how you like your animals.'

'Yeah I might as well watch the whole thing.'

Danny squinted as if he was trying to work out why I wanted to stay. I ignored him and sat back down. Danny came over and sat next to me whilst Pierro said he had things to do and left.

With a smile I watched as the bull snorted and scratched the sand with his front leg. Come on bull fucking charge at the bastards.

After a few minutes the picadors came on for the first stage of cruelty. To my delight he charged straight into the horse that one of the picadors was riding and managed to knock him off. So happy at seeing the bull fight back I stood up and cheered, shouting over and over the Spanish word for bull.

The Spanish lads turned around slowly in horror as they had heard my shouts. Undeterred I carried on cheering the bull and ignored the stares by looking past them at the television screen. In the corner of my eye I could see the Spanish lads shrug and then turn back round

Danny sharply tugged the back of my T-shirt.

'What?' I said angered from having to avert my gaze from the screen.

'Alan what the hell are you doing?' said Danny very agitated.

'Cheering for the bull.'

'You can't do that!' said Danny gob smacked. 'It's their national sport. They will kill you!'

'Fuck em' Danny!'

I turned back to the screen and watched how eventually the picadors manage to get close and stab in their sharp lances around the neck of the angry bull. Each time the picadors stabbed the boys cheered and looked at me whilst smiling.

Throughout the rest of the fight, I cheered and the Spanish cheered. I carried on championing the bull whilst the lads predictably made noise when the bull drew blood. From outside it must have sounded like a football match. But in this unfair competition there was to only one victor. I knew that.

When the matador finally plunged in the fatal blow with his sword I kept quiet out of respect. The lads though erupted in a cataclysm of noise. I watched on as the bull fell to its knees. I will give it credit though, the bull did manage to proudly trot around before crashing to the floor. To the very end it fought it's oppressors.

Danny looked frightened when the Spanish started making their way through the row of chairs and benches. He was breathing deeply awaiting a fight. I tried to stay calm and stood my ground awaiting a backlash from the Spanish after cheering for the bull.

To my surprise only two men came over to us and the rest left the room. Each of the men that left either scowled or shone me a wicked smile. Feeling the tension Danny stood to his feet.

'Hey Alan isn't it?'

'Yes that is right.'

'The lads wondered if you would like to have a game of tennis tomorrow?'

'What?'

'Yeah we want to see that anger put to some good use.'

'Err……Tennis?'

'Yes midday tomorrow we want you to enter the competition.'

'Er okay…..Yes I suppose I can make it. I haven't anything else on.'

And just like that the boys left the room. I couldn't believe it. Danny and I were sure we would end up in a fight or at least an argument. None of us could have predicted a fucking tennis game. Still on edge we looked around each corner before walking just in case they planned to sneak up on us then attack. But thankfully nobody was lurking and we were free to go to our cells.

That night we drank, chatted and smoked up until five in the morning which was pretty late for us. Normally we would finish around two. But we had managed to stockpile a few beers and a block of hash so celebrated this fact. We hadn't got really pissed and stoned for a while.

The next morning I was shaken awake by Danny. Pissed off at being disturbed I launched out a fist to punch Danny, as I did it quite slow he could see it coming and swerved his arm way.

'Alan get up!'

'What! Why! Where's the fire!'

'You have to go and play with the Spanish.'

'What the fuck are you on about?'

'The tennis game remember?'

'Oh yeah …..the tennis game,' I said whilst holding the sides of my head which was pounding so much I thought my brain was going to fall out.

'Just give me five minutes more in bed,' I said nestling back under the sheet and nuzzling back into the pillow.

'No Alan you need to go now,' he said wrestling the pillow off me. 'You were very lucky they let you off with just playing a tennis game.'

Knowing he was right I slapped myself on the cheek and went for a shower. I felt slightly refreshed but decided I needed a few coffees if I was to wake up properly. With coffee in my hand and a throbbing headache I walked around the grounds. The piercing light from the sun felt like it was burning the outside layer of my eye ball. Trying to forget about my hangover I had a nosey at the people around. To my surprise I heard two men talking in Welsh accents.

With excitement I raced over to them to see if they were indeed Welsh and my ears weren't tricking me. After speaking to the two men I was indeed right. One was called Terry and he was from Newport. The other was called Andrew and he was from Pontypool. So not only were they Welsh they lived in the South like me. What a small world.

I talked to them for a while. They weren't the most interesting of people but it did lift my spirits hearing a familiar accent. It felt homely in some strange way listening to them both. When I was half way through a sentence I was interrupted by Danny storming towards me and shoving me to get a move on. Annoyed I brushed him off and told my new friends about the tennis match I was about to play. They both laughed and told me that I looked far too hung over to play and plus the lads who entered the championships were half my age. I fought back though saying that I might have a trick or two up my sleeve. I didn't but I said it just to get them thinking.

I also benefited from talking to my fellow Welsh men as one of them had a racquet to sell. With ten minutes to spare I rushed to their cell to inspect my new racquet. When Andrew showed it me I was surprised. It wasn't an old rickety thing, it was a brand new top of the range Donne racquet. After haggling over a price we eventually agreed on a set amount of pesetas and made a deal. Well with this racquet at least I will look the part.

When I got to the tennis courts I was shunted straight on by one of the organisers of the competition. With my sparkling new Donne racquet in hand I squinted from the sun and looked ahead at my opponent. I couldn't fucking believe it! It was the first fucking round and I had the Spanish champion who had won it the Saturday before. I looked at the Spanish quadrant of the crowd, and could see them all laughing at me and expecting me to fail. I then looked at Pierro and Danny. They raised their eyebrows and tried to express an encouraging smile but even they could not see any hope I would win.

Feeling pissed off as I was hung over and had to play tennis in the hot sun I squeezed the ball hard. I gritted my teeth and tensed my cheek muscles. This was all just to show me up and for what, because I stuck up for a bull. They were the bastards. They were the ones who should be punished for championing a sport where animals are tortured.

I bounced the ball in anger up and down testing the court. Looking at the Spanish crowd standing with heads up and arms folded made me seethe with rage. Why do they think they are so fucking macho? I mean what is so macho about hacking a bull to death?

Boiling over with so much resentment I struck the ball with all my might and watched it bounce fast on my side and then to my opponent's area and then out. I hit it so fast and with so much force the Spaniard didn't have chance to put a racquet too it. There was a silence and then the umpire shouted ace. I smiled. In the background I could hear Pierro and Danny shouting. On my second shot I did exactly the same. Again the Spanish champion could not return the ball. He looked worried. Maybe the Welsh older rookie could win after all. Sadly this was not to be. The Spanish champion from them on won every point. He played an outstanding game and beat me in straight sets. I shook his hand, as fair play he played well. He gave me an out and out thrashing. I wasn't happy about it though and I did regrettably throw a tantrum afterwards by throwing my racquet and making it skate across the floor for several yards. A group of Spanish boys picked it up. They looked in deep discussion and pointed to the racquet.

'Can I have my racquet back?' I asked.

'The racquet is not yours,' said one of the Spaniards

'Yes it fucking is. I bought it this morning.'

'No, look on the handle. I wrote my name on it. See.'

I snatched the racquet out of his hands and had a look. True enough there was a Spanish name on the racquet.

'Look I will pay for it if you want,' he said pitifully. 'I really like that racquet.'

'Here take the stupid thing. I am not really one for tennis,' I said slapping it in his hands.

I couldn't fucking believe I had been done over, especially as they were fellow Welsh man. Had they no camaraderie. Maybe it wasn't just the Spanish I had to be wary of.

I headed over to Pierro and Danny who were still stood to the side of the tennis pitch. When I met up with them the Spanish lad from the television room who organised the tennis game came over to me. To my surprise he was very flattering about my game and congratulated me on my two aces. He also went onto ask if I would play again next week. I flatly refused. Even without a hangover I doubted I could win a game against the super fit youngsters that entered the competition. The boy eventually relented and said I didn't have to play as long as I joined him and the lads that night for supper.

This was fucking weird. I couldn't think of any reason why they wanted to befriend me. I mean it was strange enough they offered me to play a tennis game after I took the piss out of bull fighting. What the fuck was in it for them?

Despite being dubious I accepted. I then went back to the cell for a few hours' kip to sleep off my hang over. The sleep felt good. Midafternoon I managed to locate Pierro and Danny outside and walked around with them. I wish I hadn't as they both took it in turns to take the piss out of my game. Pierro would run around pretending to throw my racquet and Danny was pulling jibs which apparently I did in the game. I let them carry on and laughed along with them. Bastards!

When it got to around six o'clock two of the Spanish lads called for me from my cell to join them for food. Danny stood up to come with me but I shook my head. He nodded and sat back down. Just in case this was a set up, I didn't want Danny involved. He had being through enough.

Nervously I walked alongside the two lads down the corridor to their room. It felt like agony as they were walking so slowly. Several yards away I could see outside the cell were at least ten Spanish lads. God knows how many were inside.

Tensing my arms I waded through the men and into the cell. One lad pointed to the bed for me to sit down and offered me a bottle for a few pesetas. I gladly agreed and looked around the room. Maybe they rewarded before they punished. After supping my bottle half full two men came in with platefuls of barbecued meat. Despite being slightly burnt it still looked good and smelt delicious.

I asked around what the meat was and where they got it from. They told me it was conejo which in Spanish meant rabbit. They said after my corn expedition they went to the field and caught one.

I was the first to be dished up the rabbit. I waited till everyone was given a dish of rabbit before I tucked in, not to be rude and to check if it was edible. Everyone else after me who had some meat wolfed it down without chewing. I inspected the meat just to make sure it didn't look like it had been tampered with or laced with anything. As far as I could tell it was okay. Tentatively I cut into the meat with my cutlery and raised a bite to my mouth. Quickly I pushed it in my mouth and chewed. Surprisingly the meat tasted good. It didn't taste like rabbit that I remembered from having at home. Mind I had never had rabbit barbecued before so that could of have accounted for the difference in taste.

When I finished my food another Spanish prisoner offered me another beer again for a small price which I didn't mind and gladly accepted. They had given me free food I couldn't expect free beer too. With a full belly and slowly on my way to becoming tipsy I enjoyed being with the Spanish. Maybe they weren't that different to us Europeans. They looked too like they were up for a party.

After my third bottle I decided to call it a night. I had enjoyed the food and company, but after a few hours I just wanted to lie on my bed, smoke hash and chat with my lads. Plus they probably were getting worried so I better show my face so they knew I was alright.

I said my goodbyes and headed up the corridor back to my room.

Before I got half way down the corridor one of the lads shouted in Spanish that the food I ate wasn't rabbit. Instead of it being conejo meaning rabbit, the meat was actually gato, which meant cat. Stunned I looked in horror back at the Spanish lad who told me. He smiled and then started laughing. So did the rest of the lads.

Shocked I carried on walking and went back to the cell. Pierro and Danny tried to act nonchalant but I could see they were happy I came back unscathed. However they could see I wasn't right as I walked with a stiff back. When I looked in the mirror I could also see I was sporting a white face.

'You okay Alan?' said Danny concerned. 'Did they touch you?'

'Oh no…. no…no…nothing like that.'

'You okay you look like you have seen a ghost?' said Pierro.

'Not really.'

'Why what's wrong?' asked Danny hesitantly.

'I have just eaten a fucking pussy cat.'

With that Danny and Pierro burst into tears laughing. I couldn't believe the fuckers. They knew how much I loved the animals and the buggers were laughing. But despite being quite upset I laughed too. I had to try and see the funny side. There was no point being resentful. I could go back and start a fight with the Spanish but that wouldn't achieve anything, apart getting stabbed. There seemed no point dying over a cat. I just hope they didn't torture the bugger beforehand.

The next day I kept away from everyone. I had enough of people laughing at me about eating a frigging cat and about my behaviour when I played tennis. Today I just wanted to keep a low profile, even away from Pierro and Danny. I spent most of my time casing out the dilapidated bricked building next to the prison. I looked at it from angles where I was permitted to go and couldn't work out what it was. It seemed odd to me why it was out of bounds and what it was used for. Never once in the day had I seen anyone go in there or out. That day I watched the guards and looked at my watch to see when the guards swapped over. I also looked for possible blind spots which would buy me time to have a quick run across for a look.

Before sleep that night I planned in my head how I was going to run across to the unknown bricked building.

28 HOUSE OF DEATH

'So fancy coming for a walk with me?' asked Danny.

'What?' I asked distracted.

'Do you want to go for a walk?'

'Nah I think I will just chill out in my cell a little longer.'

'Are you okay?'

'Yes I am fine. Just going to have a lazy day today.'

'You're up to something.'

'What?'

'You have that look in your eye Alan.'

'What do you mean?' I said laughing.

'The look that you are planning something.'

'I don't know what you mean,' I said grinning.

'Please Alan tell me you are not looking into escaping.'

'Don't worry I have already had a look and it is nigh on impossible.'

Danny shook his head and started laughing. I don't think it was the answer he was looking for, but at the same time he seemed relieved.

'You promise you won't try to escape.'

'I promise escape is not on my mind today.'

'Have a nice walk.'

When ten minutes had passed I quickly ran out into the patio with excitement and headed towards the mysterious bricked building. I looked around in all directions to check that Danny wasn't following me or that Pierro wasn't about. All was clear. I could happily get on with investigating without the fear of those two nosey bastards interfering.

Although I had been told the building was out of bounds by other prisoners I decided to put this to the test and walked over to it nonchalantly. As I did so a guard from the platform above shouted down when I got only yards near. It was true then. This building was forbidden.

I looked up towards the guard, put my thumbs up in the air and turned around. I walked back over to the main prison building and sat on the floor looking over.

'What where they hiding in there? What did it house? Solitary punishment cells maybe? But that didn't seem logical as the building was so much in view. Normally solitary cells are far away from the normal prison cells and prying eyes. I had enough experience in solitary across many prisons in different countries to know that. It had to be something else. But I couldn't think what?

I watched for over an hour at the building and the guard patrolling then to my surprise he went into the turret. He returned after a whole ten minutes with coffee and carried on keeping watch.

I quickly looked at my watch and noted the time as ten past one in the afternoon. This was good. Hopefully this was a regular break he took. I will have to check again tomorrow and see. I also paced around the patio and worked out possible blind spots so I could pick where I could run from to the building so the guard wouldn't see me. I worked out where one might be but couldn't be completely sure as I needed to see it from his viewpoint to see if it was obscured. There again I didn't have to worry too much as the midday sun was bright enough to make it difficult to see down anyway. I hoped to god all this effort was worth it. I could sense big trouble from doing this if I was caught. I hope there was something useful inside to make all this effort worth it.

'Alan!' shouted a panicked voice from a far.

I turned around and around until I could see Danny limping in the distance. I hurried over to see what was wrong.'

'Everything okay?'

'You have forgotten haven't you?'

'What do you mean?

'The consulate is here today. Come now or you will miss your chance.'

Danny was wrong about me forgetting about the consulate's visit. I had in fact remembered. I just couldn't be arsed seeing his fat smug face today. I didn't correct Danny though and just nodded. I knew if I said anything it would just invite questions as to why I didn't want to go and I couldn't be bothered to explain.

The main reason for my apathy was that I didn't see what use the consulate was to me anymore. I had been sentenced so legally he had nothing to instruct me on. I knew I had over five years to go and there was nothing more he could do to reduce that. I suppose I could have campaigned about having better facilities in the prison, but I knew from experience of doing this in other prisons nothing would be done. The consulate would just nod and pay lip service. But there again in El Dueso I didn't have too much to complain about.

I followed Danny towards the visiting rooms and waited in line with the rest of the European prisoners. Pierro must have been down early to see his consulate as he left only minutes after our arrival. Both Danny and I waved him to come over but he didn't. Instead he folded up a piece of paper and put it into his jeans pocket and walked very quickly in the opposite direction. He did smile and give a slight wave back but I sensed he didn't want to come over and explain the paper he had. The paper made me feel sad as it reminded me of the adoption papers. I knew Pierro didn't have kids but the secretive nature of the paper made me worry for him.

'Did you see Pierro?' said Danny annoyed.

'Yeah. He must have been down here pretty early to get first in the queue.'

'And did you see the way he ran off.'

'So,' I said pretending not to care. 'Maybe he needed a shit.'

'No he is up to something.'

'Today you think everyone is up to something.'

Danny smiled and said nothing back. Instead he looked at the floor as if he was pondering on what to ask the consulate.

I was just about to disappear into a reverie when I felt a light tap on the shoulder from behind. Shocked and on guard I turned around swiftly to find it was Andrew and Terry, the two fellow South Walians I had met the other day. I had a brief chat with them about the tennis racquet. They both denied it was stolen and swore they had bought it off someone fair and square. I wasn't wholly convinced as they both looked a little edgy, but I decided to let the matter drop. I couldn't be bothered creating a fuss over something so trivial. Looking at their shabby clothes and thin frames I could tell they needed the money more than me.

The line dwindled until it came to my turn. On my own I ambled into the meeting room ready to listen to the same old crap he would always spout. The consulate stood up and outreached his hand. He was the same as the rest of the other consulates I had met, tall, tanned, handsome and athletic in build. It was if they were being bred somewhere specifically for the job. The only one that looked vaguely different was the consulate in Cordoba, and that was only because he was Spanish. God I wish I could be a consulate, such an easy fucking job. I wouldn't mind tanning my arse in cheap exotic climbs in return for spending a few hours with crims.

'Hi Alan.'

'I was just reading your file.'

I couldn't believe it! I had a file! I had never once seen any paperwork being filled out about me from the day I was caught in Ceuta till now. Nor had I been required to sign or fill any documents. What the hell was in this file? Also why is he only reading it now? I had been here for over six months now. What made the lazy bastard want to familiarise himself with me now.

'Anything good in there?' I said smirking.

'Well I can see from your reports you have been quite unsettled.'

'Well it is hard to try and settle when you are moved from pillar to post.'

'You know this will be the last prison you stay at.'

'Yes you have told me that. But it is still hard to believe.'

'Do you miss home?'

'What?' I said a little taken aback.

'Do you miss your home and seeing your family?'

'There is only thing I miss and that is my freedom.'

'Well if you miss home,' he said as if not acknowledging what I had just said. 'We may be able to send you to a British prison.'

'A what?'

'Yes we are looking into to sending you to a British prison, even one possibly in South Wales so your family can come and see you.'

'Really?'

'Yes I have been talking with the Spanish and British authorities and we are looking into an agreement that you could be transported back.'

'Wouldn't that be good being closer to home?'

I didn't respond. It was such a shock announcement I at first didn't know how to react. I ran through what would could happen if I served the remaining years in Britain. At first ponder I wanted to jump at the chance as he was right I would be nearer home so my family and friends could visit and the conditions in the prison would be a hell of a lot better. But then the drawbacks started flooding my mind. In Britain I wouldn't be able to smoke hash and drink as freely and openly. I would also be put to work and won't be able to just doss around in the hot sun. Then there was the fact I might have two sentences for smuggling one in Morocco and one in the UK. I mean I didn't know this for certain but it would have definitely being on my record spending time in the UK for drugs. I didn't even bother to ask the consulate if it would count as two sentences as I knew he would have said no just to get me out of here so he would have one less Briton to worry about. What am I saying? I mean one less Briton for him to pretend to worry about.

'So Alan what do you think?'

'No. I would rather stay here.'

'What!' he said shocked.

'Don't you even want to consider it for our next visit? And understand it is still just an idea.'

'No. I have made my decision and it is here I want to stay.'

'But Alan………….. you will be close by to your family.'

'I'd rather them not see me at all than visit me in a prison.'

'At least think about it until our next meeting and I will see what I can do.'

'I won't change my mind so don't even bother looking into it.'

'I can't understand why Alan.'

'All I want is my freedom. Nothing else.'

'Well is there anything else you would like to discuss?' he said a little pissed off.

'Can I look at my file?' I said smiling at his annoyed expression.

The consulate pushed across the table the flimsy file made of card that was filled with tatty piece of papers. The papers looked like a series of reports that had been written about me. They were all written in Spanish so I couldn't really tell what they were on about. I had now mastered speaking in Spanish quite fluently but with my written Spanish I still had a lot to learn. But despite my lack of understanding I still had a look through. To my surprise I found I could get the gist of most of the reports. One report which caught my eye had the words altamente peligrosos which means highly dangerous and 10 hombres meaning 10 men. From these four words I worked out this must have been a report about the escape. I couldn't believe they had documented this. It also explained why in most prisons I would be sent to they put me in solitary. They probably did it to assess how dangerous I was.

It felt funny to be called highly dangerous. I had never shown any violence towards the guards and the only fight I had was with John and that was a scuffle. But I guess they had to put this in because of my escape. I suppose my homemade bomb could have possibly added to giving me this status too.

'Alan think about what I have said. I know you are saying no now but I still want to give you a chance.'

'I won't change my mind.'

As I came out the two Welshmen were about to go in, when I stopped them. I imparted the news about a transfer. Like me they were very shocked but also pleased. I then imparted my reservations about leaving. I told them that it was possible we would then have two records of drug smuggling but they didn't seem to care about that. They also weren't bothered when I said about not being able to drink and smoke. There again I don't think either of them had much money to be able to get a supply of drink and hash. I suppose without the money I would have probably reconsidered the transfer. Spanish prisons aren't much fun without currency. At least with money you can buy bits of decent food and pleasure drugs. But there again I would have found some way to earn money, such as drug dealing.

I watched as Andrew and Terry went into the visiting room with smiles. Just as they went in, the door to the French consulate's room whizzed open and Danny stepped through.

'Good timing Danny I had just finished with my consulate.'

On the way back I told Danny about my news. He was shocked. He couldn't believe I had been given the possible opportunity to go back and that I turned him down. I told him my reasons but he still couldn't get his head around it. Although he didn't say anything I could tell he was glad.

Danny, Pierro and I as we usually did congregated in my cell for a little drink and smoke. Tonight we weren't as lively. We all just stared in different directions quietly thinking. I was thinking about the red bricked building and my visit but I couldn't ascertain as to what Danny and Pierro had on their minds. Danny did probe Pierro about the piece of paper he put in his pocket after seeing his consulate. Pierro said it was a letter off his mother. I could tell Danny didn't believe him but he didn't question him any further. I followed suit. I knew we would find out sooner or later what it was about.

Despite the bottles of beer and several joints I couldn't get to sleep that night. I was wrestling with my decision to stay. My heart wanted to go back to Wales but my head was saying no. My quandary reminded me of when I refused parole in Shepton. However this time I wasn't thinking about what was best for my family. This time I was thinking about what was best for me. And anyways the consulate never gave any cast iron guarantees. It was all only a possibility.

Before I was able to fall unconscious the images of my friends, family, ex-wives and ex-girlfriends floated across my mind. Each person that came to mind made my chest twist in pain. I was yet again possibly denying myself to see them again for a few more years.

The next day Danny went for another walk. I didn't go with him and made the excuse I was going to talk to Andrew and Terry about transferring to Wales. This lie was fantastic as Danny was completely fooled by it. I mean why wouldn't he? I didn't have to tell Pierro as I hadn't seen him. Like me he had been elusive for the last few days.

Once a good few minutes went by I got up out of my pit and went over to the patio and watched the guard. I stood where I thought his blind spot would be and casually watched up. Then like yesterday he disappeared into the turret just after one o'clock. I was going to wait until the next day to have a look in the building, but I felt compelled to take action now. So quickly I ran over to the building and rolled down the grass embankment and towards the open entrance. I felt like Indiana Jones. I felt alive as my bloodstream was taken over with adrenalin.

I crouched down low outside and awaited noises of guards or gun shots. Thankfully there were none. It appeared I hadn't been seen. So feeling a little relieved my pulse rate calmed and the pounding in my heart eased.

After one quick look around outside I then on tip toes entered the building that had captured my imagination for months. Once inside I was quite disappointed. There was nothing of interest. It just looked like an abandoned building filled with crap. There were wooden chairs and tables. Just stuff that looked like it was on its last legs. This must have been where they dumped all the dilapidated prison equipment. What a disappointment!

I scouted around to see if there was anything small I could sneak back to the prison that could be of use or could be sold for a few bob, but nothing caught my eye. As I looked around I began to feel uneasy as if I wasn't alone. But this was odd as obviously I was, as it was deathly quiet. If the guards had seen me I would have known about it. It wasn't there style to hide in the dark.

The temperature in the room seemed to drop dramatically. Outside felt above twenty five degrees whilst inside it felt less than five. I could feel the hairs on the back of my neck stand up to attention and my body broke out in severe goose bumps. I rubbed my arms and continued to investigate.

Finding nothing of interest on the ground floor I decided to scale up some steps which were towards the back. I could see they led up to some sort of platform. Being dark inside with no lights on I couldn't see exactly what was up there.

I tentatively walked up the steps. Feeling exposed I kept darting my attention all around the room to check no one was looking. This place gave me the creeps.

Stepping off the last step onto the sort of platform I was first interested by the papers, files and grainy black and white pictures that littered the floor. I laughed to myself as this was just the sort of filing system the Spanish guards would have. I felt a tinge of sadness to see the pictures as they had just been strewn on the floor as if they were worth nothing and had been forgotten. Walking around the platform I felt even more uneasy. I thought downstairs was bad but here the atmosphere felt oppressive.

I picked up one of the grainy black and white pictures, which was attached to a piece of paper. It was of a Spanish man with dark menacing eyes and a thick beard. The paper attached looked like some sort of official certificate. At the top of the certificate were a few words typed in thick bold text. Underneath the heading were details about the man, his name and a date etc. The certificate had also being stamped. It looked an official government stamp. Why the hell were important looking documents just dumped up here?

In the middle of the room was some kind of wooden contraction with a chair. On closer inspection I could see on the chair it had several straps. There were two for the wrists, one for the waist and one for the legs. What the fuck was this? Some kind of torture device?

Behind the chair was a substantial wooden post in which there fixed a heavy screw. As I looked at the workings of this contraption I could see the heavy bolt was operated by a handle. This was then connected to a small star shaped blade which looked like an American sheriff badge. It looked like once you screwed and screwed it would run through the post and then through the back of the neck of victim who sat in the chair. Just under the screw was a rounded piece of metal. This looked like it went round the neck of whoever was to sit in the chair.

Then it dawned on me. This was a fucking garrote chair. I had read about such a device but never thought I would see one up close. Looking at it both sickened and thrilled me. I was in an execution room.

Looking at the bolt and the metal neck strap I imagined the pain of each victim that sat in the chair. I imagined a guard winding from behind and the nail sticking through their neck as the metal collar choked them. If they were lucky the nail would kill them instantly by severing their spinal column. However if they were unlucky and the nail didn't sever the spine straight away the metal strap around the neck would have eventually strangled them.

The room and its chair were covered in dust. It had obviously not been used for many years. The last execution in Spain was in 1977 and they abolished garroting in 1978. So as this was 1979 it was no wonder it hadn't been in use. Instead the building and this barbaric contraption just lay here forgotten, like the many pictures of the dead on the floor. Then again I couldn't be sad. Most of the men who sat there would have deserved it. I am sure even in Spain they would have saved garrotting for the very worst. Paedophiles, rapists and murderers hopefully.

After looking around a little more I decided there was nothing of use for me to keep or to sell and decided to go. My curiosity of the building had now been satisfied. I kept the picture of the man and certificate I had found on the floor and stuffed them in my pocket. I wanted to show Danny and Pierro as evidence for my trespassing.

With a deep breath I hung in the shadows of the entrance. After a count of five I went outside and hung close to the building. I could see the guard looking in the other direction. So I seized my opportunity and ran up the embankment and to the patio. Once on the fringes of the courtyard I stopped running and slowly shuffled around. I walked all the way to the back of the patio without turning around. Only when I got to the wall did I look back to the guard. Thankfully he was looking towards the sky whilst dangling his arms off the rail. He still had a cup of coffee in his right hand.

When I could see I had got away with it I let out a sigh of relief and breathed normally again. Well if I can get away with going into that building maybe escape wasn't impossible after all. All I needed to do was work out the guards patterns.

Feeling high after my discovery I shot around the prison in search for Danny and Pierro. I first went back to the cells but they weren't there. I also went to the television room but I couldn't see them there either. I eventually managed to locate them sitting down on the ground outside. It looked like they were enjoying the sun whilst watching the Spanish play a game of football. I didn't say anything and sat with them both. I watched on impressed at the youngster's talents on the pitch. It was a shame they were wasted here. If only they had led a straight life. They could have had a chance at playing football professionally. They reminded me of me. I could have had a future in sport. Who knows what level I could have played if I didn't break into those solicitors.

'So what did your friends say?' asked Danny.

'What do you mean?'

'About going home.'

'Oh I didn't end up talking to them.'

'What have you been up to?'

'Exploring.'

'What?'

'If you want to know where I have been have a look at this,' I said pulling out the picture and certificate.

Pierro snatched the photo and paper out of my hand and unfolded it. Danny craned his head and pushed in to have a look too. Pierro scanned the paper and then looked up. His face went white as he passed it over to Danny.

'This is a death certificate. How did you get this?' asked Pierro shocked.

'In the building where we are not allowed go.'

'What else was inside?'

'A garrote chair.'

'What!'

Danny started muttering in French after he had finished reading the paper. I think he was swearing. He seemed quite taken aback.

'Why the hell did you go in their Alan?' asked Danny annoyed. 'You could have been shot.'

'You worry too much Danny.'

'I have some crazy news myself to tell,' said Pierro looking to the floor a little sad.

'What have you been up to then?'

'I put in a request to go to Carabanchel prison.'

'What?' I said flummoxed. 'But why? I have been there and it's not that great.'

'Oh you have been in the prison part but you haven't been in the hospital bit.'

'What?' I said confused.

Pierro explained that he wasn't going to the normal prisoner cells at Carabanchel but instead he was going to the mental hospital that was housed there. Apparently it was completely sectioned off from the main prison. He was going there to work as a psychiatric nurse.

Now I had heard it all. Not only were the Spanish guards fucking lazy as to let prisoners run part of the prisons they also employed prisoners to look after sick mentalists. Pierro had had no training or experience but yet he was allowed to get the job. But what really stumped me was the fact he wanted to do it. I mean Pierro didn't normally do anything without getting anything out of it. I always thought he only hung around with me for the money.

When I asked him why he smiled and then told me that for every day he worked he would get a day off his sentence. From these words I was sold on the idea. I too wanted a day for a day. Carabanchel here I come!

'How do you apply? I want in.'

'Just ask for a transfer form from the guards and hand it into the director's office.'

We all sat down and carried on watching the football. Then when the first half was over Pierro left to go to the toilets.

Danny watched him disappear out of sight and then grabbed my wrist.

'What's wrong with you Danny? Get off!'

'Don't go Alan,' said Danny upset. 'Please don't go there.'

'Look if you're worried about being on your own come with us.'

'No way I wouldn't go there.'

'A day for a day Danny.'

'It's still not worth it.'

Danny began telling me about stories and things he had heard about the hospital from other prisoners who had been former patients. They told him they had been physically beaten and tortured. I didn't take much notice as I heard stories of beatings and torture in all the prisons I had been too. But he kept on insisting it was far worse than any prison. It was funny the more he tried to put me off the more Carabanchel inspired my interest. I wanted to see how despicable it was. I couldn't believe any prison could be worse than Ceuta.

Two days later Pierro disappeared and his room was empty. It was obvious he was taken to Carabanchel nut house via the ghost train the previous night. I am glad he told us he was going. At least I had chance to say goodbye. So it was true he was off. I just hope that he had got it right and he was nurse and not a patient.

Inspired by Pierro I went off to the office and asked for an application form. It took a while to get my point across but my persistence and Spanish paid off as they eventually handed me over a sheet of paper which I hoped was a transfer form.

I looked at the form and sighed. I couldn't understand much. So I had to enlist Danny's help. With great reluctance he did help me but made sure at every opportunity he would tell me how bad it was. I tried to make a joke and said that I was used to torture listening to him whine. He took it in good humour but still looked annoyed that I was pursuing Carabanchel as an idea.

With glee the next day I trotted over to the guard's office. I asked them if I could see the governor but they refused. Not taking no for an answer I begged and pleaded in my best Spanish. But they just looked at me with annoyance. They then kept asking me to leave but I carried on jabbering in Spanish trying to be as annoying as possible. My persistence did eventually pay off as I was eventfully allowed to go and see him but with escort from a guard. I didn't care I just wanted to hand my form personally to the director. I wanted to go to the top man as he was the one with authority. I also did it as I couldn't trust the guard to give it him. If I did it myself I would have definitely known he would have had it.

The guard knocked on the director's door. When a hello in Spanish could be heard he opened it and pushed me inside.

The director didn't look amused. On the table I could see a half cup of coffee and several biscuits. I think I had interrupted his breakfast.

He looked at me with stern brown eyes. I passed over my application form and shone a massive grin. He didn't smile back.

'Hi my name is Alan and I would like a transfer to Carabanchel,' I said in Spanish.

The director raised his eyebrow in surprise. I don't know whether my command of Spanish surprised him or the fact I was asking to work there.

He looked at the paper and then nodded. He then waved as if to shoo us both out of the room. The guard obediently opened the door and ushered me out of the room. From behind I could hear the crumpling of paper. When I looked back my application was scrunched up into a ball and then lobbed into a bin. The director looked up and smiled. Fucking bastard!

Annoyed I stomped all the way back through the prison and outside in the courtyard. Full of venom I whizzed around the prison looking for Danny. Once I found him I unleashed a procession of obscenities about the director. Danny was shocked and then began laughing as I became more impassioned and angry. I didn't find it funny but carried on shouting. When I eventually ran out of steam Danny tried to make me feel better by saying it was for the best. But this didn't soothe me. I was still determined to get transferred. I just had to find a way to get around the cunt of a director.

Then the next day it dawned on me. I could try and win over the director by getting the consulate to have a word. The only problem was twisting the consulate to do it. I mean he would pretend he would have a word but I needed to think of a way to make him sit up and listen. It took a few days but eventually I came up with what I thought was a good plan to convince the consulate.

When it was my turn to go through the doors of the visiting room to the consulate I smiled to myself. The consulate wouldn't know what has hit him today. With confidence I held in my hand a second application for Carabanchel.

'Hi Alan. So have you thought more about your transfer?'

'Yes I have and I would like a transfer to.'

'Oh that's brilliant I shall just find the relevant paperwork,' he said whilst rifling through his expensive looking briefcase.

'No I don't want to be transferred to Britain. I want a transfer to

Carabanchel.'

'What? But why would you want to go there?'

'I want to work in the hospital there.'

'What?'

'I think I would be good as a nurse and I would like to have days taken off my sentence.'

'Err..........well you will need to see the director.'

'I have but he just screwed up my application and put it in the bin.'

'The thing is Alan you are classed as dangerous so maybe they don't think it would be good to be in the hospital.'

'I am not violent. The only reason why they say I am dangerous is because of the escapes.'

'Yes but.'

'And anyway Carabanchel is tight with security. They have a helicopter above. That would be the perfect prison for me as I wouldn't be able to escape.'

'Look Alan my hands are tied. If the director doesn't think you should be transferred then there is nothing I could do.'

I was prepared for this answer and decided it was time to unleash my trump card. I told the consulate that I had written to my family that instructed them to go to the media if I died in prison. I told him that in the letter I wrote about the harsh treatment of guards, the lack of help from the consulates, that I feared being shot and that my death would be covered up. I then told him that if he didn't help me I would escape and would only stop running when I was shot by a guard. The consulate was shocked and looked at me with an open mouth.

'Alan you can't be serious.'

'Try me.'

'But you could get killed.'

'Yes and it would be your fault.'

'Look Alan I don't think I could do anything.'

'Fine,' I said as I stood up to leave.

'Alan!' shouted the consulate.

'Yes,' I said somberly.

'Look I will see what I can do.'

'You haven't got long.'

'Just give me a few days. Please don't do anything hasty.'

With that I handed over the rolled up application form to the consulate. He took it off me and looked again into my eyes as if to ascertain whether I would do what I said. He then unravelled it and pawed through it with diligence. I left the room trying not smile.

My trump card had worked. I had managed to convince him. But there again he could see from my file that I did have form for escaping and he knew I wasn't one to mince my words. The truth though was that I hadn't sent a letter to my family. I would have never have done that. I wouldn't want to frighten them if I didn't have too. I also didn't mean it when I said I would escape. That was a bluff too. Well at that moment.

Two days later I was called to the office. My plan had worked. The guards informed me the transfer had been accepted and I would leave soon. I couldn't believe it! I really must have put the shits up the consulate. Maybe consulates did have some use and influence after all.

With excitement I found Danny and told him. He wasn't as enthused but did pat me on the arm in a feeble bid to congratulate. From that day on I made sure I spent the majority of my time with Danny. I would never see him again so I wanted to make the most of it. I also tried to persuade him to come with me but he was having none of it.

A week later and my ghost train eventually arrived and whisked me away in the early hours to Carabanchel. On the way I began to have doubts of whether it was the right decision. I had been so consumed with planning on a way to be accepted I never gave too much thought about what I was doing. I mean I know working a day for a day would mean my sentence would be reduced but what if the place was miserable. I would rather be in El Dueso where I knew I could be happy for five years instead of a miserable place for two and half. But it was too late now. I had made my bed.

When I rocked up to the gates at Carabanchel in the early hours of the morning I saw the familiar sign and remembered the outlay of the building.

Lots of prisoners got out at the main building but only I was taken around the back. When the bus eventually stopped I was taken off by one guard. He then gently pushed me and pointed in the direction I should walk. This was strange normally I was pulled and ragged around. This guy was gentle. Maybe he fancied me.

Then he took me to an entrance whereby I was greeted by another guard. He promptly took off my cuffs and waved goodbye to the other guard. He then smiled and pointed in the direction I should walk.

Fucking hell gentleness and then smiles! Are the guards actually human beings in this place? Was I actually going mad? Surely I wasn't being shown respect.

The guard then took me down corridor after corridor. This place was like a maze of door and cells. It felt so claustrophobic. Echoing round the walls were strange noises, screams and maniacal laughter.

Eventually my tour was over and the guard took me to a corridor and then opened a cell. He then quietly said goodbye and left. How strange it was for him to be so polite.

I tentatively went in. In front I saw two single beds on either side of the small room. In one of the beds was a prisoner snoring. My early morning visit hadn't even woken my roommate. I tiptoed to the other bed and hopped in. I didn't want to wake him. I laughed to myself as I imagined the shock on his face in the morning

Then my laughter turned into fear as I realised my roommate may have been a nutter I had to care for. I hope to god he wasn't. Oh god what if he was violent? What if he stabs me in the middle of the night because I spooked him? I mean if he was crazy he was capable of anything. Feeling on edge I decided to keep myself awake. I didn't want to wind up dead. I needed to assess his violence and capabilities in the morning. I would also make sure he had no weapons and hide any objects that could be sharpened. What have I done by coming here?

29 ENTRY TO HELL

I did however fall asleep in the warmth of my bed and was awakened from my slumber by the sound of someone or something falling to the floor. Unnerved I bolted up right to see what was going on. At the other side of the cell I could see a man getting dressed. The bang must have been the noise of my roommate jumping off his bed. Whilst the man dressed he hummed a happy tune. Well if he is crazy, at least he sounds quite content at the moment, but time will tell I suppose.

Trying not to make any noise I shuffled off the bed and gently lowered both my feet to the floor. I wanted to observe a bit longer to see what I was dealing with before showing my presence. I couldn't see the man's face but from his complexion and the thick black hair on the backs of his legs and arms, I guessed he was Spanish.

From looking around the room he was quite a tidy and affluent one. I had never seen so much stuff in a prisoner's room before. He had a radio, loads of magazines, an array of toiletries and piles of clothes that looked brand new. My roommate seemed a very useful person to know.

I reached for my bag with my meagre belongings in it. Despite trying to being quiet I couldn't suppress the bag's crackling. The sound alerted my cell mate and he swiftly turned round.

'Good you're awake,' the man said in Spanish whilst grinning.

'Hi.'

'Well my name is Augustin,' he said whilst walking over and putting his hand out.

'Err.........I am Alan,' I said watching his hands very carefully.

I held my hand out but hesitated in shaking his. Augustin looked confused but took the initiative and grabbed my hand giving me a firm handshake.

'Right so you will be working under me,' he said playfully.

This comment didn't sit right. Was Augustin flirting with me? Nah I must haven't translated his Spanish incorrectly.

'Oh you're a nurse.'

'Course I am nurse.'

'Oh you didn't think I was a,' he said whilst laughing and putting his hand over his mouth.

'No……no…….. of course not,' I said trying to be nonchalant.

Feeling a great sense of relief I got back into bed. I decided to have a lie in till early afternoon. I was knackered after my midnight run and trying to keep awake.

'Right well you get yourself ready so you can come with me on rounds.'

'What now?'

'Yes now.'

'We start work at 7 am?'

'What?'

'Yes 7 am every morning.'

'Oh.'

Obeying his instructions I had a quick wash down in the sink and then got dressed. Augustin was still faffing around so I decided to lie on the bed a little longer.

What a time to start work. It never entered my head about working so early. Oh well I will just have to think a day for a day. No more going to bed really late at night then. I hope to god we finish our work early. Well at least the days will go quicker by doing stuff.

'Well I just have to go a minute. I need to get you a bata to wear.'

'A what?'

'I will show you.'

He went to the side of the room and picked up an apron. He then tied it around and did a twirl.

'Oh I see.'

Great as if I didn't feel emasculated enough working as a nurse, now I had to wear a fucking apron. Was there a matching garter with fucking tights too?

When he left the room I sighed and put my head in my hands. What the fuck had I done! I had left a perfectly nice prison with a great mate to come here and tend to crazies very early in the morning til the rest of the day. Plus Augustin seemed too much of a straight guy to have fun with. He didn't seem the type to while away the small hours drinking and smoking. But time would tell if this was true. Maybe I could corrupt him.

Augustin came back with the apron which I reluctantly put on.

'That looks good on you Alan,' said Augustin playfully.

'Oh shut up,' I said aggressively. His comment disturbed me as I couldn't tell whether he was actually paying a compliment or just taking the piss. I hoped it was the latter.

Augustin smiled and shook his head.

'Right lets show you around.'

On our corridor which Augustin called a ward were five cells in total, our cell and four other cells. In the four other cells were the crazy prisoners or patients as he referred to. The first thing we had to do as nurses was hand out the medication to everyone. Once we had sorted out whose was whose we would have to open up their cell and hand the tablets over. Each time we handed out the tablets I could see Augustin watching them like a hawk.

On the fourth prisoner we handed the medication as we did with the other three. I was about to leave the room when I could see Augustin wasn't budging. What is he doing? Curious I stood by the side of him and tried to see what was disturbing him.

'Open your mouth now!' Augustin shouted.

The prisoner shook his head and clamped his mouth shut folding his lips under.

'One last time! Open your mouth!' Augustin screeched.

With folded arms the patient turned his head to the side, ignoring Augustin's demands.

'Right!'

With vigour Austin stormed over and grabbed the patient's head and held the prisoners nose whilst tugging on his chin. After a tussle of a few seconds the patient eventually relented and opened his mouth showing a half dissolved white pill on his tongue.

'Now I am not going to ask you again,' he said sternly. 'Swallow!'

The prisoner tilted his head back and gulped hard. But just to double check Austin grabbed his head roughly and made him show all the sides of his mouth. Once happy the prisoner had indeed swallowed the pill, he then let go of the patient and slammed the door shut.

'Now Alan you can see why it is important we check they take their medication.'

'Yes I do.'

After the medication we then had to dish out the breakfasts. The breakfast came delivered to us via trays on a trolley. Augustin and I could pick out ours first and then dish out the rest. So with the first pick I made sure I had the one that looked the best and was biggest in quantity. But it didn't really matter as they all pretty much looked the same. For Spanish prison food it looked and smelt quite nice. It was also piping hot which was something I wasn't used to. It had been two years since I had had a hot meal. I was going to enjoy this. No more luke warm!

We quickly set to work handing out the food so we could retreat into our cell and have ours. As predicted it was sumptuous.

'So what do you think of the job so far?'

'Yeah alright,' I said mid chew.

'The food is nice!' I said enthusiastically.

'Yes it is alright I suppose.'

'Well once you get used to it, it's an easy routine.'

'Do you have any questions for me so far?' Augustin said fluttering his eyelashes.

'One thing I can't get over is that we open to let them out.'

'Why?'

'Well you would think the guards would do that?'

'No the guards don't do anything silly,' he said chuckling.

'But they're alright. They leave you too it,' Augustin said looking out in the distance.

'Plus another thing none of the patients seem well er… mad?'

'Oh they are, trust me. They just seem calm because of the drugs.'

'Oh right.'

'That's why it is important we make sure they take it.'

After a warm, tasty and filling breakfast we headed back outside. From each room we had to collect the trays. Augustin said we had to be vigilant that the same amount of trays went back on the trolley, as some of the patients had been known to use the trays in order self-harm. Fair play to Augustin it seemed he had this nursing job down to fine art.

The next job for the morning was we had to take two of the patients for their scheduled appointments with their doctor or psychiatrist. Today, two of the patients were penned down to see the psychiatrist.

So in our aprons we escorted our first patient out of the ward and through the many corridors of Carabanchel hospital. I vaguely remembered coming down here when I was dropped off in the night. Like last night behind the closed doors I passed I could hear laughing and screaming. My muscles tensed holding onto our patient. I was ready if he was about to do something or if any other patient was about to jump out and attack. But nothing untoward happened and our patient was very amicable. Looking in the patients eyes I could see what Augustin meant about the drugs. He must have been on a heavy dose as he seemed vacant. He made me feel queasy watching his pupils bobble around like the bars on a fruit machine.

Intermittently along the corridors we went past several prison guards. Each one smiled and gently nodded to us as we went by. This was weird. It was if they were showing respect. Despite working with crazy people I think the guard's behaviour was going to take the most time to get used too. But despite a few smiles and nods I still wouldn't trust any of the bastards. They were going to have to do a lot more than that to make me a friend.

Along the way we also met up with other nurses in aprons escorting their lunatics around. All would say hi and exchange pleasantries to Augustin and I. A few were obviously friends of Augustin as they would stop for a further chat; with some it was only brief. But whoever it was Augustin would always make a point of introducing me. I didn't like this as he made out I was his sidekick.

I was surprised at how long it took us to get to the psychiatrist office. This place was obviously quite big. There must be several hundred patients cooped up in here.

Finally when we got to the psychiatrists we deposited our patient inside. We weren't long as hardly much was said by the psychiatrist or the patient. Both seemed quite happy. Once we had the nod from the psychiatrist we escorted our patient back to the ward. We then repeated this process with another patient.

Shortly after this we then took all four of our patients and took them to the patio outside. I was shocked to find they were only allowed a half an hour to an hour outside. I was then even further shocked that the patients didn't seem to bother about not having exercise. You would have thought they would have cherished each moment in the fresh air and sunshine. But I suppose they were off their box on strong medication, so maybe they could escape in their minds.

I watched on as they all waddled around slowly with blank expressions or frozen smiles. They looked like zombies. Just husks of the people they once were and devoid of any sort of personality. I pitied them at first, but then thought it must be nice to be ignorant and not give a dam. Each one of them without a worry in the world and numb to all hurt.

After half an hour Augustin decided they had enough exercise and called for me to help him put them back into their cells. This was easy enough.

'Right Alan we would normally have a break now. However the doctors want to interview you.'

'Interview me?' I said confused. 'I thought I had the job.'

'It will be fine. Don't worry,' he said putting his arm around me and shunting his face uncomfortably close to mine. 'I have put in a good word.'

'Thanks,' I said pushing him away.

A shiver went down my spine at his overt friendliness. I had hugged Danny before but this did not feel the same. I rubbed my cheek roughly trying to numb my face that had been tickled by Augustin's breath.

I quickly left the ward and trudged onto the psychiatrists office trying to remember my way. Augustin had offered to take me, but I declined as I wanted a bit of space. I wanted to avoid another creepy hug. Was that just a Spanish thing or something gay? I needed to find out fast and put him straight if he liked the boys. I didn't really care if he was gay, I had a shared a room with Ernst and that was fine. But Ernst never flirted with me or made me feel so uneasy. Well I am just going to have to tell him I am not that sort of boy.

With a big smile I went in for my interview into the office where I had taken my two patients. I hope to god this was an interview and they weren't going to psychologically analyse me. If they did I very much doubted I would have passed. Then I would succumb to being another locked up, drugged up, dribbling mess. God could you imagine what Augustin would do if I was doped up! Come on Alan concentrate.

In the room was a psychologist, psychiatrist and a doctor. The doctor and psychiatrist were men and the psychologist was a female, a good looking one at that. I instantly tried to avoid her gaze. I knew if I stared I would have got distracted. I hated seeing unavailable women in prison; it only served to highlight what I was missing. God I missed sex. Oh well with a day for a day I will be soon be out of here and boy will I be on the pull.

The first question I was asked was whether I could speak Spanish by the Psychiatrist. This sounded straightforward but he was a little tricky the way he asked it, as he used Castellano as the word for Spanish. Castellano is the official Spanish word for Spanish but outside of Spain foreigners are more au fait with the word Español. So, to show my understanding I replied saying I could speak Spanish but I used the word Español. By doing this I wanted to show than not only did I know what Castellano meant but that I could also use other Spanish words that denote the same meaning. I think this worked as he nodded and smiled with his eyes at my answer.

The interview only lasted about ten or fifteen minutes and I was asked only a few questions. Which were all pretty easy to understand and easy to answer. All in all it was more of an informal chat rather than interview. I think they just wanted to gage my level of Spanish and if I was psychologically sound.

When I was told I could return back to my ward I felt quite optimistic. I did find it strange I wasn't asked about whether I had been a nurse before or whether I had worked with the mentally ill. You would think that would be quite important. Again that's the Spanish prison system for you.

In the afternoon after dinner we took our four patients back out in the yard for another half an hour. Again they walked around quite pitifully.

Watching them bored me so much that I wanted one of them to do something mental or strange. Come on crazies challenge me! But nothing happened.

The only thing that did entertain me was that fact one of them was the spitting image of Warren Mitchell as the character Alf Garnet. Like Alf Garnett he had a bald head, thick moustache, round black rimmed glasses and Groucho Marx eyebrows. Even in his mannerisms he was similar.

The more and more I watched him the more he made me laugh. I even laughed out loud which caught the attention of a passing guard. Disturbed by my laughter he stared at me and raised his eyebrows half an inch. Oh fuck! I shouldn't be laughing to myself in a place like this. Even if I did explain I don't think he would get it.

After the second break Augustin and I put the patients back in their rooms shutting the doors and locking them in.

'Right Alan it's our time now,' he said smiling with wet lips.

'What do you mean?' I said disconcerted.

'Well we have done our jobs. So we are free to do what we want now.'

'Oh good.'

'I just don't get it.'

'What Alan?'

'The fact the patients are only allowed a couple of hours out of their cells. It seems quite cruel.'

'Oh Alan don't worry. They all looked calm and happy.'

'Yes I suppose.'

'Come here Alan,' he beckoned flapping his index finger.

I went closer towards Austin but kept my personal space, I didn't want to feel his breath on me again.

'Now don't be scared Alan.'

'Stop messing about!' I shouted in annoyance at his jests. 'What's your point?'

Augustin screwed up his lips for a few moments as if was a little put out by my shouts, but with a little huff he soon regained his jaunty composure.

'Do you hear that?' he said putting his ear to the door.

'No,' I said sarcastically.

'Exactly,' he said looking smug. 'They are quiet therefore they are happy.'

'Fair enough.'

'Well I suggest you have a look around the place. I am going to have a chat with the doctors to see if you have the job.'

'Oh thanks Austin.'

'No problems,' he said smiling. 'I hope you are, as you are one of the nicest men I have had.'

'Thanks,' I said trying not to vomit into my mouth.

Thankfully he left the ward and trotted off to find the results of my interview.

Gees I couldn't take any more of his compliments, flirty comments and touching. He really made my skin crawl and stomach turn. Now I know what women mean when they describe a letch. I am going to have to say something. I know if I don't the anger will just well up and I may punch him hard in the face. But I couldn't do that. I wanted to wait till I had been accepted to work as a nurse first and have a few days under my belt before doing that. I mean he was technically my superior so I needed to try and keep him sweet. This was a tricky one. How do I say get your fucking queer mitts off me without upsetting him? Maybe I could get a transfer to a different ward.

To take my mind of Augustin and his unwanted affections I decided to rest my eyes and have a lie down. I couldn't fall asleep though. I tried but my mind raced with the day's events. I also thought of Danny and wondered what he was up to. I imagined him limping around the prison in the full heat of the sun. I hoped he was okay and that he wasn't too lonely.

But I could see him picking up new friends quite easily he was a great bloke to be around. I would certainly miss his company.

After lying down for an hour I had a nose outside the window. Craning my neck I could see a few little patios. Again most of the patios were very similar to mine. All the patios were empty. The patients must have been locked up whilst the nurses ambled around in their cells. I was going to miss my freedom of wandering outside.

After a few hours of blissful loneliness Augustin came back in the room. With a massive grin he burst in the room full of energy and informed me I had been accepted. He was like a coiled spring. It was obvious he was pleased and had been bursting to tell me the news. He then went in for a hug but I held out my arm ready for him this time and scowled. Despite rejecting his hug he didn't seem too bothered as he smiled and retreated to his bed. I also got into my bed.

Worried that Augustin might try a midnight rape I wrapped my sheets around tight and decided I needed to go to sleep after him. So in order to keep awake myself I talked to Augustin asking him question after question. Unfortunately Augustin loved the attention and willingly answered them all. It felt painful thinking of more questions and listening as I was ready to sleep.

Eventually he did have enough and said goodnight. Right come on Alan you're not out of the woods yet. You need to keep awake! In the quiet darkness I tried with all my might to keep my eyes open. Only when I could hear snoring I would close my eyes I repeated to myself over and over. Several minutes ticked by and I could hear no sounds. Come on Augustin snore you bastard! By now my eyelids felt twenty stone. But with determination I kept lifting them up each time they fell. I eventually lost the battle and must have lost consciousness as I didn't remember anything else after that.

The next morning I was awoken by a high pitched happy whistling. God that was piercing! Getting out of bed I checked my pants to see if they were still on. They were! I wiggled my bottom too. This felt normal. All was good!

Augustin turned round and smiled as he could hear my shuffling about. He then went back to the mirror and carried on shaving and whistled even louder.

'Augustin!' I shouted'
'What?'
'Do you have to?'
'Do I have to what?'

I couldn't remember the Spanish word for whistling so to convey my annoyance I mimicked his annoying whistling.

'Oh sorry!'

'No its okay. I am sorry. Just feeling tired with these early mornings.'

'No I am sorry. I shouldn't whistle when I know you are sleeping.'

'Look its fine.'

'Do you know Alan?' he said turning back round to look in the mirror to shave.

'You look like an angel when you are sleeping.'

What the! Never had I awakened so quickly before. That comment was not on! So shocked by it I couldn't do anything. I was speechless. All I could do was look at him in horror. But surely enough after a few moments I regained my composure and was ready to unleash a tirade of abuse.

'Now Augustin that's it!'

'Would you like to see my girlfriend today?' Augustin interrupted.

'Your what?' I screeched.

'Yes my girlfriend. I have a visit with my girlfriend today and just thought you might like to come.'

'Err………………err………………….yeah sure.'

'I am confused Augustin.'

'About what?' he asked with one eyebrow raised and hands on his hips.

'Never mind it doesn't matter.'

I just couldn't work him out. He tells me I look like a fucking angel but yet he has a girlfriend. Is he gay or what?

30 FATAL ATTRACTION

On morning rounds I didn't take much notice of what Augustin said or did. I merely just followed him around completely stumped about his revelation of a girlfriend. I was positive he was gay! I mean what straight bloke would say to another you look like an angel when you are sleeping. It can't be a Spanish thing. I had spent time with a few Spanish prisoners and I never got that impression. Unless……. the bastard wanted to frighten me? Well if it was an act I believed it. But me thinks he played the act too well. I suppose he could have been in the closet.

Pushing the trolley full of empty trays from breakfast I ran through my mind what sort woman Augustin would have attracted. I wondered if she would be a looker. I mean Augustin looked alright for a man I suppose, although he did have many feminine mannerisms. But would this matter to women? Maybe he was with a girl who was butch to compensate for his femininity. Well whatever she looked like or was like I envied him. At least he had a woman. Oh……. to have a female visitor that would be so nice. I hope to god he wasn't allowed conjugal rights too. Now that would really make me sick!

'Come along Alan you are being quite slow today,' Augustin said in soft tone as he minced down the corridor clutching on to Alf Garnet.

I didn't say anything back and just grunted, grabbing Alf by the other arm. I found it safer not to say anything as he seemed to twist the most innocent of words into something rude. And there was no way I was saying coming to him.

After we took Alf to see the doctors Augustin and I went for our break. I took the opportunity to tell him I wasn't happy with his affections. He laughed and shrugged it off. I hated this. He made me feel like I was imagining it. But I definitely wasn't! However not feeling comfortable talking about it I decided to change the subject.

'Augustin what is your girlfriend like then?'

'Oh she……..err…….she is a very nice girl.'

A very nice girl? This is something my Gran would say.

'And..' I said elongating the word to invite more description.

'And….' he said repeating the elongation.

'What else man? Like what colour hair has she got? Does she have a nice set of….' I said cupping my hand in front of my chest. 'Tits.'

Augustin shrunk his head in like a turtle and lowered his eyebrows in embarrassment. I stared at him smiling at his unease. I felt happy at making him feel awkward for a change. Now he knew how it felt.

'Err Alan well…..' he said flustered.

'There is no point in describing as you will see her soon enough.'

'Okay.'

What was so hard about describing her I wonder? Was she hideously ugly? Or maybe he could not describe her boobs as she wasn't a woman? But then that would beg the question as to why he called her a girlfriend. Unless………she was a transvestite. Yes! That would make more sense.

'Oh Alan I have to go and see the doctors. Would it be alright if you take Alf on your own see his visitors today?'

'Yeah no problems.'

'Alf?' he said laughing.

'I really need to see a picture of this Alf you talk about,' he said laughing.

'So when shall I take him?'

'Well…………' he said looking at his watch. 'His wife and her sister should be there soon I would take him now if I were you.'

'Okay.'

Augustin headed off out of the ward and I promptly went into Alf's room.

'Come on you have visitors!' I said enthusiastically, urging him to get up from lying on the bed.

Alf didn't say anything but just grunted and lifted his head up. Although he uttered no syllables you could tell by his tone he wasn't best impressed. He was such a funny belligerent bugger! He should be thankful he still had a wife and one who would visit him. Was I the only fucker in this prison who didn't have anyone?

'Come on off that bed. Your wife and sister-in-law are here.'

Alf responded by shaking his head and smiling. But he did obey and waddled to the door.

The journey to the visiting rooms was slow and arduous. It was obvious Alf was in no rush. I mean I knew he was miserable git, but Jesus. Was his wife that bad? Maybe it was the sister-in-law he didn't like.

When I got into the visitors room I shut the door behind and stood leaning against the back wall. Doing this made me feel like a screw. But I knew there was a difference. I actually gave a fuck.

After a few minutes two women entered the room and sat at the table looking through the glass at Alf. From the floor they picked up several brown packages tied up with string and plonked them on the table in front. Both women scowled. Alf turned around and smiled at me with his hands in the air. I smiled back. I wonder what the old bastard had done. He seemed too docile to do anything nasty.

'And how are you?' said one of the women with vitriol.

Alf didn't say anything and just shrugged.

'Good I am glad you aren't happy. I hope you rot in here for the rest of your life for what you have done.'

His wife then exploded into tears and cupped her face into her hands. Her sister comforted her by putting an arm around her shoulder.

'Death is too good for you!' his wife's sister spat.

Before the visit I had the intention of ignoring the conversation as I wanted to give my patient privacy. I had planned to bury myself in my own thoughts in order to block their words out, but I just couldn't switch my ears off. It also didn't help that the women were shouting so loud. Even if I had covered my ears I bet I still could have heard their shrieks. But despite my intentions, curiosity also got the better of me. What had Alf done to offend these women?

An icy cold silence descended, as the sister in law started unravelling the parcels. She nudged her sister with her elbow gently encouraging her to help her. Alf's wife promptly withdrew her head from her hands and looked forward. Her eyes were red and scratched from crying so much. Under her eyes were black semi circles, it was obvious she hadn't had a good night sleep in quite a while. Then with a big gulp she started helping her sister unravel the wrapping.

After a few seconds they crunched up all the brown paper and put it to one side. From the parcel they took out two scrumptious looking baguettes filled with slices of light meat which I think was chicken and four big cakes oozing with cream. The food looked absolutely delicious. I hadn't seen anything this tasty in years. I licked my lips in hunger despite stuffing my face with lunch only minutes ago.

'Look we got your favourites here!' said his wife seething with venom.

'Shame you won't be having any,' she added.

With that the sisters looked at each other and smiled. Then they started heartily tucking into the food. As they chewed they made orgasmic noises insinuating the food was good. They didn't have to do that though. From the other side of the room I could see it was tasty. It took all my might not to smash down the glass partition and grab the food for myself. Such cruel bastards! Why did I have to be tortured too?

'Look at what you are missing!' said his sister-in-law mid mouthful.

'You have lost your family and your freedom! And for what!' his wife said wiping crumbs from the side of her mouth.

After the baguettes they then both started munching on the cream cakes. Alf turned round to look at me. He smiled and shrugged again. I half smiled back conscious not to show too much sympathy and inflame his visitors.

Watching them eat made my mouth well up with saliva. If only he hadn't pissed them off, he could be having some of that too. And maybe I could with a bribe have persuaded them to bring food in. You fool Alf! Don't bite the hand that can feed.

When the food was finished the two women went back to staring. His sister in law then rubbed her hands together wiping off the crumbs.

'How could you!' his wife cried.

'As I told you woman! She wanted it!' he shouted back whilst crossing his arms.

'She wanted it? You sick bastard!' shouted his sister-in-law.

'But she was our daughter............our 14 year old daughter!'

Alf didn't respond.

'She didn't want it! I have spoken to her and she didn't want it! You are the sick one! Not her!' she screeched.

'You didn't see her eyes,' he growled. 'She was begging for sex!'

His wife gasped and put her hands over her mouth. Her eyes were wide with shock. Not surprising! How could a father say that about his own daughter?

Still in shock she started coughing and heaving at his sickening words. Alf responded to this with laughter.

'Come on let's go! We can't get through to him!' said her sister softly.

Alf without any remorse continued laughing and shook his head as if the women were being silly in their reactions.

They both turned their backs on him and headed to the door. They left the parcel wrapping littered with crumbs on the table. Before the wife left she wiped down her eyes and gave Alf one last icy cold stare.

'At least she is safe now!' She said whilst pointing. 'You will never ever see her again!' she croaked as her voice started cracking.

When the door closed Alf turned around as if nothing had happened and smiled.

'Shall we go?' he said grumpily.

'Err…….yes……..I will take you to your cell.'

After taking Alf back I was meant to let out the patients in the patio but I decided to have a little break before I did. Plus Augustin wasn't around, so I decided if he can shy off work so could I.

Normally when I had a break I would have a wander around the little bit of hospital I was allowed go through but today I fancied a bit of alone time in my cell. I think I needed a bit of time to get over the shock of Alf's visit and finding out what he did. Never would I have imagined Alf was capable of that. I mean being a paedophile was sick enough but raping your own daughter. That is just unthinkable. I wasn't the worst father after all. I mean how can you do that to your own flesh and blood? Jesus if Alf did that I wonder what the rest of the fucking loonies had done in here.

Lying on my bed I imagined what each of my children were up too. I envisaged them playing happily and laughing. I hope to god this was true. If I ever found they were mistreated especially sexually, there would be hell to pay. Please let them be safe.

The door burst open without warning and Augustin appeared.

'There you are!'

'What?'

'My girlfriend has arrived,' he said smiling. 'You coming?'

'Yes alright.'

'Well come along!' he said sarcastically. 'We don't want to keep her waiting.'

I picked myself up from the bed and headed off with Augustin to the visiting room again. God what was in store for me this time! I hope to god I don't find out what Augustin has done. I think its best I don't know. But I very much doubted he was in for rape, especially with women.

'So how did it go with Alf?'

'Yeah it was interesting.'

'You found out his crime then.'

'Yes Alf is one sick bastard.'

'And his wife and sister-in-law really shouted at him.'

'They always do.'

'They also ate food in front of him.'

'Yes they always do that as well,' he said chuckling.

'Why didn't you warn me?'

'And spoil the surprise,' he said with cheeky eyes.

At the end of the corridor I could just make out two nurses escorting a patient ahead. I squinted my eyes as I was sure one of the nurses looked familiar. Intrigued I lightly ran to catch up.

'Alan what are you doing the visiting room is just over here?' shouted Augustin.

'One minute!' I shouted back.

When I got closer to the three men, I could see the nurse that looked familiar was indeed someone I knew. It was Pierro.

'Pierro!' I shouted down the corridor.

'Eh……..What!' Pierro uttered looking in all directions as if confused.

'Over here!'

Eventually he spotted me and beckoned me over with a big inviting grin. I quickly ambled over to meet him.

'So you made it here too.'

'Yes,'

'Is Danny here?'

'Nah I couldn't persuade him.'

'That's a shame.'

'Oi Alan!' bellowed Augustin from behind. 'We are late for her as it is.'

'One minute!' I shouted back with one finger in the air emphasizing my point.

'Look Al I have to take this patient to a visit now.'

'Yeah I am going to a visit too.'

'You will have to come and visit me on my ward.'

'What ward are you on?'

'Agitado's.'

'The what?'

'Agitado's,' Pierro repeated.

The patient Pierro and the other nurse had hold of started to wriggle and get agitated. I could see in his eyes a wild energy. Never had I seen a patient look alive before. It was obvious he wasn't sedated with heavy medication.

'Look Alan I will have to go,' he said pushing the patients arm further and further up his back in order to restrain him.

'Alan!' shouted Augustin from behind.

'Yeah me too.'

'Well I will see you around! Don't forget Agitado's.'

Pierro and the other two men then disappeared around the corner. I turned around and casually ambled back towards Augustin. I felt so much better for seeing Pierro. I wasn't alone! Plus hopefully I could get a transfer away from my amorous friend.

I could see my tardiness in walking back infuriated Augustin as he had his hands on his hips and tapped his right foot over and over. To piss him off more I smiled and walked even slower.

'Come on! Come on!' Augustin shouted in impatience shooing me into the visiting room in front of him.

'Okay, okay Augustin. Just chill,' I said chuckling.

Once through the door I could see a line of tables and chairs. Only one of the tables was empty which had a woman sat on a table opposite side separated by a glass partition. Well he wasn't lying from the other side of the room it did look like a woman! I quickly scrabbled to the table and sat on the chair not taking my eyes off her, intrigued at what she saw in Augustin.

She wasn't amazing in the looks department but she wasn't ugly either. She looked Spanish with her long dark brown hair and tanned complexion, but there was nothing distinctive about her. Rather like what we call a plain Jane. But despite her nondescript features the more I looked at her the more I found her beautiful, although be it in an understated way. God the things I would like to do to her.

Augustin then sat down and started talking quietly to her and she responded affectionately with smiles, nods and a few words. He did most of the talking in the conversation but she didn't seem to mind. From reading her body language it looked like she hanged onto his every word. I wondered then if she was simple.

After a brief chat he eventually introduced me. I smiled at her and gave her a wave. Feeling flirty I also gave her a cheeky wink too and pursed my lips in a kiss. I think she felt flattered as she fluttered her eyelashes and turned her head to the side. The way she arched her neck looked so elegant. Also more importantly it was devoid of an Adam's apple, she was definitely a lady.

Then like before Augustin and his girlfriend descended back into a deep conversation. I decided not to join in as I could only understand half of what they said as they spoke quickly in Spanish. I didn't want to look foolish by saying the wrong thing. Mind even if I could have followed what they said I would have found it extremely difficult to interject as they both hardly paused for breath. They were like two gossiping old women.

In the beginning whilst they talked I pretended I knew what they were saying by smiling and nodding. I would flit my head back and fore each time one of them spoke. But after a while I found the pretence tiring and eventually drifted off in my own day dream.

My reverie was short-lived though as I was brought back into the room when I felt Augustin's hand stroke me on the shoulder. Disturbed at the way he touched me I snapped back my shoulder and scowled, tensing my fists. For a few seconds my back quivered with unease. This made Augustin smile and his girlfriend roar with laughter. What the fuck! Why would she find it funny that I flinched? Doesn't she care her bloke is touching up another bloke.

Confused I looked over to the girl but she just carried on tittering, putting her hand over her mouth as if she was trying to stop. Although embarrassed at her laughing at me I tried to pretend I didn't care by plastering on a fake smile. I also moved my chair further away from Augustin and folded my arms to show I didn't want to be touched again. But despite my distance and body language I still watched Augustin like a hawk, ready to move if he tried anything. I also listened carefully to their conversation as I didn't like the way she laughed at me. What was so funny?

Despite not having all the understanding of sentences said, I managed to extract a few words. With the words I swirled them around in my head and also looked at their body language trying to gather a meaning. The only thing that was obvious was that they were talking about me as every now again they would point and look over.

After a few minutes of connecting the words in my head their conversation became sickeningly clear. It seemed Augustin was only fucking telling his so called girlfriend I was his squeeze in prison. What the fuck was he playing at?

I am not having that! To show his friend or whoever the fuck she was I wasn't going to be playing along with this I pointed at Augustin and then me and whispered we were not together. Augustin smiled and nodded holding crossed fingers in the air.

'Oh no no!' I shouted out loud waving my hands in front of me.

'Me and him no way!'

She arched her eyebrow and looked at Augustin. Augustin nodded.

I was right he was saying I was his boyfriend. The bastard! In that moment I wanted to knock every tooth out of his head. But somehow I managed to keep a clear head and my fists down. A day for a day is not worth loosing over this gay tosser. Girlfriend indeed!

The only way I could see to get even and to show I wasn't gay was by flirting outrageously with his so called girlfriend. I started by making low guttural cave man growls and staring at her with sexed eyes. Tensing my body I grabbed the edge of the table with both hands, showing her I had to restrain myself from smashing through the glass and lunging at her. I think I convinced her of my intentions and sexual persuasion as she looked both scared and exhilarated.

I looked across to Augustin to see his reactions. I was pleased to find he was pouting. Good enough for you, you bastard! You get jealous! But it begs the question what was he jealous of. Was it because I was hitting on her? Or was he jealous because I wasn't hitting on him? It was possible it was both.

'Look I am going to go I have had enough,' I said annoyed.

Both Augustin and the girl looked to the floor in silence.

'Well I will leave you two 'lovers' to talk!' I said sarcastically.

I stomped to the door and slammed it shut. Feeling relieved to be away from Augustin I slumped on the wall and took a deep breath. A few yards away I could hear footsteps. Looking up I could see it was Pierro.

'You were a while. Who was visiting you?'

'Look it doesn't matter. But thank you for waiting for me.'

'You okay?'

'No. I am fucking not!'

'What's wrong?'

'I am sharing a cell with a fruit!'

'A fruit?'

'Augustin likes me!' I said quietly.

'Oh I see!' he said laughing.

'It's not funny Pierro. You have to help me.'

'Okay! Okay! Well as it happens there is a job going on my ward.'

'Really?'

'Yes.'

'Great when do I start?'

'Look I will have to talk to the guards and the doctors first.'

'How long will that take?'

'I don't know but leave it with me. I shall do it as quick as I can.'

For the rest of the day I didn't see Augustin very much. He was there to help me carry out the duties with the patients but straight after that he would bugger off, not telling me where he was going. In fact since the visit he hadn't uttered one word to me. This didn't bother me. I quite welcomed the silence. It meant I didn't have to suffer his inane chatter or flirting.

Over the next few days Augustin began to talk more and more. He wasn't his usual chatty happy self but I found him amicable enough. I think he learnt his lesson not to flirt with me and was now cautious of what to say and do. About fucking time too! Despite the change in Augustin I still wanted out of his ward. I craved to be with likeminded men. I was also running out of hash, I only had about a week's supply left and that was if I stretched it. I didn't bother asking Augustin as I had never seen him have a joint and he never asked to try any of my mine. I held out for Pierro, if anyone knew where to get hash he would.

After five days I still hadn't heard off Pierro. My block of resin was now just a little nub. Fed up of waiting I decided to hunt him down on my break and find out where this Agitados ward was. But just as I opened the door to the corridor Augustin yelled out my name from behind.

'What!' I said in annoyance

'Look sorry Alan. I know you have your break now but I need you to take Alf to the dentist.'

'Dentist?'

'Can't it wait?'

'No the dentist only comes once a week.'

'Why can't you take him?'

'I have to take a patient to the doctors.'

'Oh okay then,' I groaned.

With reluctance I turned back around and got Alf out of his cell. You could see he was in a great deal of pain as his face was pale and he held the side of his face whilst twisting his lips. If only your wife and sister-in-law could see this. They would relish his agony.

When I opened the door Alf couldn't move quickly enough out of the ward into the corridor. Fucking hell this was the fastest I had seen him move. He really wanted his rotting tooth out. All along the corridors he groaned in agony.

From asking directions off a few nurses and the guards I eventually located the dentist's room. I was surprised there wasn't a queue outside, there always one for the doctors and psychologists. I knocked on the door out of politeness, just in case he was seeing to another patient. But he wasn't as from behind the door I heard a shout in Spanish to come in.

Alf opened the door whilst cupping his mouth in the other hand.

'Hi.'

'Please shut the door.'

As I shut the door Alf hopped into the dentist chair. He promptly opened his mouth wide and held his head back into the headrest of the seat.

I watched and waited.

Without warning the dentist yanked Alf's chin downward. He then roughly pulled his cheeks back with his right index finger looking for the bad tooth. He then with dirty finger stuck it into Alf's mouth. He must have prodded the infected tooth as Alf gave out a gurgled yell.

'Right so that's the one is it!'

'Can you come over here?' the dentist asked.

'Er yes sure,'

I walked over to the dentist and stood beside Alf.

'Well get hold of him then?' The dentist said as if annoyed by my lack of experience.

'Okay?'

As instructed I went over and held Alf down by his shoulders. Alf looked up with scared eyes. Despite not the one in the chair with the bad tooth I was worried too. I hated dentists anyway but this guy really gave me the creeps. With his greying scraggly hair and dirty white coat he looked like an insane professor. Without the jacket I would have thought he was a patient as he seemed to ooze madness.

'No no no! One hand there,' he said putting my right hand on Alf's forehead head. 'And the other there!' he said moving it to his neck.

'Now just stay like that!' he said smiling.

The dentist then pushed down hard on Alf's chin and with the other grabbed a six inch thick glass hypodermic needle from the dirty table next to the chair. With force he stabbed it into Alf's tooth. Alf gurgled as he tried to yell. It took all my strength to keep his head straight as the dentist plunged in the liquid. Once the needle was empty he snatched it out from his mouth and chucked it to one side.

Thinking it was over I took my hands off Alf's forehead and neck. Alf sat up and held his mouth gently in his two hands. He rocked back and fore whilst whimpering in pain.

'What are you doing?' said the dentist sarcastically.

The dentist pushed Alf back down by his chest and pointed for me to constrain him again. I nodded and obeyed.

With a smile the dentist pulled out a pair of rusting metal pliers and clicked the handles together. I couldn't tell whether he was loosening them up or did it just to shit the patient up. But I did know one thing Alf was scared. As I held his neck I could feel him gulping over and over.

'Are you ready?' the dentist asked.

'Will it have worked by now?' I said pointing to the needle asking whether the tooth would have being numbed.

'Yes, yes. It will be fine,' he said flippantly.

'Come on then!'

I quickly assumed the position and Alf opened his mouth wide whilst keeping his head still.

The dentist then stuck the pliers in and began twisting and turning the tooth. Blood poured from down the side of Alf mouth as he carried on pulling and pulling. Alf let out high pitch groans and gurgled on the blood filling in his mouth. It was obvious the injection hadn't worked yet as Alf grimaced in agony. I knew it wouldn't have acted that quickly. Surely the dentist should have known this too. Unless he got off on giving pain. I looked away and tried to block out Alf's cries. I felt sick at how barbaric this was.

Eventually after tugging and tugging he pulled out the bloody tooth and plopped it in a metal container to the side.

'There we are! All done,' the dentist said smiling whilst handing tissue paper to Alf to mop up the blood.

Once back to the ward I went straight to sink and ferociously brushed my teeth. There was no way I wanted a fucking visit to that dentist. Mid brushing my teeth frantically Augustin rushed through the cell door. He looked like he was bursting to tell me something, but then he pointed at me laughing.

'You have been to the dentist haven't you?' he said laughing.

'Yes I have!' I said aggressively.

'Anyway what's wrong with you?'

'A guy called Pierro is here to see.'

'Pierro!' I said excitedly.

I mopped my mouth with a towel hanging up at the back of the door and then rushed out into the corridor. At the entrance to the ward was Pierro looking glum. Tentatively I walked towards him not taking my eyes from his face.

'Did you get me in?'

He looked at the floor shaking his head.

'Well?'

With a deep sigh he looked at me full in the face still looking saddened.

'Yes of course I did mate,' he blurted breaking out into a big smile.

Excited I hugged him tightly and gave him a big slap on the back.

'Well get your things.'

'Now?'

'You want to leave this ward don't you?'

I quickly spun round and headed to the cell. Augustin was stood outside the door with arms folded looking pissed off. I ignored him and went around the room collecting my things. It didn't take me long to put everything in a couple of bags.

On my way out Augustin grabbed the back of my T-shirt. I turned round and pushed down his arm.

'So this is goodbye then,' he said dramatically.

'Yes I am going to Agitado's with Pierro.'

'Agitado's!' he gasped.

'Yes. Why are you shocked?'

'Alan hurry up!' Pierro shouted from behind.

'Look I better go. Thanks for your help Augustin.'

I turned around and ran to the door.

'Good luck Alan! You will need it,' Augustin shouted. 'I will miss you very much.'

I didn't reply and shut the door to the ward. Pierro laughed as he made kissing noises.

'Stop it Pierro!' I said laughing.

'Well are you ready to join Agitado's'

'Yes!'

'It is the best ward, despite sometimes it being the most difficult.'

'What do you mean difficult?'

'I will explain when we are on our own.'

'Okay.'

After walking through corridors and corridors we eventually arrived to my new ward. Pierro held out the door and waved me in to go first. I nodded and walked into the ward.

'So what does Agitado's mean then? I haven't come across that word before.'

'Oh it means to be like agitated or aggravated.'

31 MEET THE AGITATED

When I entered Agitado's ward for the first time I was shocked at how big it was. It was over twice the size of the ward I was on with Augustin. Instead of five cells I was now on a ward with seventeen cells. It never dawned on me other wards were different sizes. I had just assumed every ward was the same. When I pointed this out to Pierro he informed me there were various sized wards throughout the hospital and that the size was based on a patient's violence. If a patient was deemed extremely violent they would have their own cell and be watched by two nurses all the time. If they were seen as harmless they would be put in a dormitory of around twenty prisoners, under the watch of two nurses.

On Agitado's ward they would aim to have four nurses. Each nurse had their own cell, which meant if the ward was full there was a possibility of having twelve patients to look after. But Pierro said although this was possible, he had never seen the ward that full. In fact the most he had seen at any one time was seven patients. Despite the possible low nurse to patient ratio Pierro warned that every patient that came to Agitado's should be considered violent and highly dangerous. This was because Agitado's was the first ward a patient would come to when entering the hospital, thus their psychoses and level of violence would be unknown. It was here they would be housed until the psychiatrists, psychologists and doctors had assessed them. Once they were diagnosed and medicated they would then be sent to an appropriate cell, ward or dormitory. Agitado's was only ever meant to be a short stay ward.

The patients who came here arrived via three different routes. Some were transferred here from other prisons after displaying extreme violence or bat shit crazy behaviour. Some were sent here straight from being sentenced, if the courts or the guards deemed it necessary. Then there were a significant number of men and young teenagers sent here straight from the Madrid streets only moments after being caught for their crime.

You also didn't have to be crazy to gain entry to Agitado's. Pierro warned various men and young teenagers were also brought here as punishment, either from the main Carabanchel prison or straight from outside. The punishment varied. Sometimes it was enough for the guards to see the men crack after being surrounded by mentally ill prisoners. But on other occasions they would also get heavy, especially if the prisoner was of Arabic origin. I knew the guards were inherently racist but I did not know they spoke their hatred with their fists too. Poor sods getting a beating for not being the right colour. I probed Pierro into what the guards actually did to hurt their victims, but he refused to tell me. Instead he said I would find out soon enough.

Pierro could see I was not happy about the beatings, but told me it happened whether we liked it or not. There was nothing we could to do to stop it. I knew that! It didn't matter if we had spoken up about it as no one would have done anything about it. It would still just be kept under wraps. Plus I bet if I even attempted to tell anyone, I would have received the same treatment. Or worse, I would have been sent back to another prison to do twice as much time. I just had to be thankful it wasn't me.

On the bright side Pierro said that it was because of the physical beatings the nurses in Agitado's were treated the best. If you do the job and keep your mouth shut you are awarded a hell of a lot more freedoms he said. Being an Agitado's nurse you were allowed access to almost everywhere in the hospital. This pleased me as I liked to roam around. I hated staying in the same place. We were also allowed to stay up as late as we wanted. But most importantly I found out the guards turned a blind eye to us smoking dope and drinking. Pierro said that we would never be raided for drugs as long as we just did our jobs.

On the first evening in Agitado's I found the first benefit of being there was having a cell all to myself. It felt great being on my own, especially without Augustin breathing down my neck. I could relax now! No more did I have to worry about him leering at me when I got changed or watching me when I was sleeping. I shuddered and felt quite queasy thinking about what he had said to me over the last few weeks. It was a good job I was taken out of his ward. I don't know how long I could have held back from giving him a good smack.

Feeling happy I danced around the room and tossed my carrier bag of stuff on the floor. I hopped over enthusiastically to the sink and toilet inspecting it for cleanliness. To my delight both were clean as a whistle. More importantly after running the tap and having a piss I found out they both worked! Not even a slight blockage in either! Great stuff!

In the middle of the room was a locker too. For once I had somewhere to put my stuff. It is surprising how a little bit of furniture makes you feel a little more civilised. It also felt strange as I had grown used to simply dumping my stuff on the floor.

On top of the locker was a draw that was lockable by key. This would come in very handy for storing my drugs and money. No more did I have to find places to hide the stuff. I was pleased with the locker too as inside it was quite spacious. It also housed a few shelves which helped you take advantage of the vast space.

From my carrier bag I pulled out my meagre set of belongings and set to work putting them around my room, trying to make it feel more homely and like it was mine. Firstly I put my soap on the shelf of the sink, my shoes under the bed and my block of weed in the locked draw. I left most of my clothes in the bag but folded my apron and put it in one of the shelves in the locker. Then with my hands on my hips I let a little sigh and enjoyed looking around. That's better! Home sweet home!

Feeling tired I headed over to the bed to have a lie down. I was careful to examine it first just in case the previous guest had left any nice surprises. But I needn't have worried there weren't many stains, it was fairly clean and didn't stink of ammonia. I also tested the sturdiness by pressing down on the mattress, and leaning in with all my weight. I was nicely surprised to find the mattress still had a bit of spring about it. Then for the ultimate test I whipped off my sandals and jumped on top. It felt good!

Although it was only eight o'clock at night I felt like I could drift off to sleep. I suppose the two weeks of disturbed sleep in Augustin's cell had caught up with me. Although my brain told me it was too early for sleep, I couldn't help but close my eyes. I felt so relaxed. I could feel my breathing slowing as my legs and arms sank into the bed. Tonight I was going to sleep for Wales!

'Alan!' shouted Pierro from outside the door.

'Uh……..What!' I shouted back a bit startled.

'Come on in my room for a party!'

'I might just have an early one tonight,' I shouted back.

With that the door burst open and Pierro stormed in.

'What you doing on the bed! Come on Alan! We have lots to catch up on! Plus you have to meet the other nurses.'

'Okay! Okay!' I shouted back a bit tetchy from being awoken.

I suppose I was going to have to get used to the late nights again of drinking and smoking again. Normally I would relish such opportunities but tonight from being tired it felt a bit of chore.

Pierro grabbed my arm and gently pushed me into his room. The party had already started as I could see bottles of beer dotted about and a thick heavy cannabis cloud hung high in the room. The smoke was being generated by one of the nurses who was slumped on the bed toking on a fairly large joint.

'This is Cellistino,' Pierro said pointing to the man on the bed.

'Cellistino meet Alan.'

'Hi Alan!' Cellistino said in Italian accent.

'Over there is Hans,' Pierro said pointing in the corner of the room at a serious looking man who also looked of European decent.

'Hi,' said Hans in a thick German accent.

Pierro sat next to Cellistino on the bed and beckoned for him to pass the joint and ashtray. I decided I wanted a bit too so I hopped on the bed ready in wait.

Whilst waiting for the joint I looked at Hans sat on the floor. On first impressions he both disturbed and intrigued me, but I couldn't put my finger on it as to why. All he was doing was sitting there.

Maybe it was his ice blue eyes that made me feel uneasy as they were piercingly cold and looked devoid of emotion. Maybe it was because he positioned himself away from everyone else and looked like a loner. Why did he want to hide from people? But then again he could have shied away because of the Cannabis smoke. I knew a few blokes who hadn't liked the smell of it.

Then all of a sudden Hans started jerking and twitching his body sporadically as if he was ill at ease with himself. They definitely weren't tics as when he caught me staring at him he stopped his sudden movement's dead. Connecting with his eyes I could tell all wasn't well with him mentally. If it wasn't for Pierro pointing him out as a nurse I would have assumed he was another patient.

Looking down to his clothes I could see he wore on his top half a white sort of jacket with buttons going up the front. It looked like he was wearing a doctor's coat. But looking at him you would not associate him as a doctor. An evil professor maybe but not a doctor. He reminded me a little of the dentist.

Out of nowhere I felt a sharp pain in my ribs. Clutching them in pain I turned round to find Pierro was digging his elbow into them trying to gain my attention. With a joint in one hand and the ash tray in another he held them out to me.

'Don't mind if I do,' I said smiling whilst retrieving his splendid gifts.

I inhaled three or so puffs and enjoyed the calming properties. I went from feeling relaxed to completely weightless. To entertain myself as I smoked I tried to blow smoke rings in the air. Both Pierro and Cellistino sniggered at my mouth movements whilst making seal noises. When I looked at Hans it was obvious he didn't find it funny as his face was expressionless.

'Hey Hans want some,' I said as I walked over to him.

'No thanks. I am okay.'

'You sure?'

Yes I am,' he said bluntly.

Both Pierro and Cellistino started laughing again. I looked back at them and smiled. As they began to titter more I found the laughing infectious and joined in. God I loved been stoned.

I handed back the joint and ashtray to Cellistino and sat back on the bed looking at the German again. He seemed to be in his own world. His face was mainly motionless, but every now and again he would grimace as if he had so much stress on his shoulders. Out of all of us he looked like the one who needed a joint the most.

'Hey Pierro where can I get a doctors coat like the one Hans is wearing.'

'What?' said Pierro not understanding.

'His white jacket. I want one,' I said pointing to Hans.

'Only I have a jacket like this,' said Hans abruptly.

'Oh.'

'Well where did you get it?'

'I found it,' he said smugly. 'I very much doubt you will find another.'

Before I could probe more about where he had found it a bell sounded in the corridor.

'What the fuck is that!' I shouted a bit startled by the sudden noise.

'The guards!' said Pierro taking one last toke of the joint before dabbing it out in the ashtray.

'What!'

'Yes it means they have brought someone in.'

I looked at my watch and it was eleven o'clock at night.

'It's a bit late.'

'They can bring them in at any time.'

'Oh.'

'Come on Alan we have a guest,' he smiled.

Pierro and Cellistino went straight to the door whilst Hans hung back and observed. I stood next to Hans and watched on too.

After a few moments the guard came into the corridor holding a Spanish looking man in his late twenties. The man didn't move and looked relatively calm. His eyes and pout told a different story though, as they both seethed with anger. The guards asked Pierro if it was okay to take him in by ourselves, to which he replied back confidentially with a yes. Then just as quickly as they came the guards left leaving Pierro and Cellistino holding our new patient.

The patient continued to be calm as he walked to his cell, but when Pierro opened the door it was a different story as the man completely freaked out. His eyes also displayed extreme terror.

From flailing and thrashing about the patient managed to slip his wrist from Pierro's grasp. Cellistino amidst the panic managed to keep hold of his other arm but had to duck every time he swung his free arm. Eventually Pierro snatched back the man's wrist again and gained back control. To help them I opened the door. Looking back at Hans I could see him putting his finger in the air as if he had had an idea and then trotted off down the corridor and rang the bell on the inside of our door.

Slowly with a lot of struggling they managed to drag the man on the bed. Pierro sat on the guy's chest whilst trying to stretch out the man's arm.

On the bed I could see straps on all four corners. Pierro eventually managed to straighten the man's arm out and caught hold of the strap. Celestino on the other hand was not having much luck. Every time he tried to straighten his left arm the man kept swinging his legs up in order to kick him.

'Alan help Celestino with the strap.'

'Err okay.'

As ordered I rushed over to the right side of the bed and held down the man's arm with one hand and with the other I pointed at the man's legs to Celestino. Celestino nodded and went to hold down his legs. With his legs and arms pinned down the man stopped fighting back for a few moments. Shocked I looked into the man's dark eyes. He looked shit scared.

'Alan strap his arm!'

'Err okay,' I said flabbergasted.

The man started swinging his shoulders back and fore again. He growled as he tried to wriggle free. To steady his arm I knelt on it like I saw Pierro do. Once restrained with my knee I managed to pull at the strap. It took me a few attempts of fumbling but I eventually I managed to strap his arm up. When I looked down the bed I could see Celestino had already done the leg restraints. Each one of us stood up with our hands around our waists panting a little from all the excitement. The man strapped in the bed continued to struggle and growl.

'He's a live one!' I said breathing deeply.

Celestino and Pierro both nodded and smiled.

Then the door burst open dramatically and the German appeared. In his hand I could see a syringe filled with liquid.

'Don't worry I have something that will make you sleep,' he said with a vicious scowl looking at the man in the bed.

With a big smile the German walked slowly over with authority and hovered over the strapped man. Pretending to be a doctor he flicked the syringe and squirted some in the air. He then put the needle to the man's face.

'I hope you enjoy my Molotov cocktail.'

The German's smile grew wider as he lifted the syringe up and then plunged it in his arm. He stuck it in with such venom and force I was sure it had stabbed into the poor man's humorous bone. The blood curdling scream the man gave out seem to suggest so. Then with just as much vigour he pushed in the liquid. I could her clicking as if the needle was scratching a hard surface, such as bone. Once the liquid was fully inserted he held the man's arm and yanked out the needle.

'There we are!' he said smiling whilst slapping the prick mark where he had just stabbed him. Within seconds the man fell unconscious.

'What the fuck was that!' I said disturbed.

'Just something to make him sleep,' Hans said whilst smirking.

'Look Alan it was obvious he was going to play us up all night. So it was best for everybody all around if he was asleep.'

'Look you can ask me to do most things but there is no way I will be sticking needles into anyone!'

'Look Alan it's okay you won't have too. Hans does not mind doing that,' said Pierro gently.

'Yes I don't mind,' the German said smirking.

'I can see that,' I said under my breath.

Celestino then started patting the unconscious man down as if he was searching for something. I watched as he starting probing into his trouser pockets.

'What's he doing now? Robbing the poor bastard!'

'No I am checking for drugs and weapons,' said Celestino coldly.

'What?'

'Yeah the police and guards don't do it so we have too,' said Pierro.

'Oh.'

I watched as Celestino produced from searching his pockets a block of resin, a bag of powder and two knives.

'Look,' said Celestino smiling.

'Yeah you don't what those being stuck in you now do you!' said Pierro smiling.

'I suppose.'

After putting to bed our new guest everyone decided to call it a night and go to bed. I think the adrenalin rush of struggling to strap him down had tired everyone out. Well everyone except for me! Tonight's excitement had awoken me. I could have done with a few more cans and joints to calm me.

That night whilst lying in bed I relived the night's events. I couldn't comprehend what as nurses we were allowed to do, especially as we were prisoners ourselves. I mean strapping people to beds and sticking them with needles containing god knows what. Surely these duties should have been left to the trained professionals? But alas it looked like the psychologists, psychiatrists and doctors were just as lazy as the guards. If it can be done by the prisoners why not let them do it.

But I had to be positive. I would just have to put up with the craziness for a couple of years and then I could be out of this place. A day for a day! Plus no one was really harmed tonight, so I had to be thankful for that.

The next day after awaking early I was washed, dressed and ready for a new day. I knocked up Pierro at half six. He opened the door in his pants with a tired expression on his face.

'A bit early Alan.'

'I know. I just wanted to run through what we have to do.'

'Okay come in,' he said rubbing his eyes.

Through yawns Pierro gave me a rundown of the day. I needn't have worried as it was similar to the schedule I was used to in the ward with Augustin. Get up at 7 am medicate the patients and then give them breakfast. Mid-morning take half of the patients to see the doctors, psychiatrists or psychologists and then the other half in the mid afternoon. Take the patients out for two hourly breaks. Hand out food at lunch and tea time. Find out if the patient has any visitors that day and fit it in the day's routine. The only thing that wasn't a set routine was the night time. Pierro said we just had to handle situations as best we could.

Several minutes past seven the breakfasts and medication arrived at the door. I stood back and watched Pierro, Hans and Celestino sorting everything out. Pierro could see I was shying away and with a wry smile beckoned me over with his finger.

'You haven't met Senen yet have you?'

'Senen?' I said shaking my head. 'Should I have? Is he a nurse?'

'Oh no Senen is one of the patients.'

'Here take these to him,' he said handing me over a cup of water and two pills, whilst pointing to one of the rooms.

'Oh okay,' I said intrigued.

Once outside the door I turned around to look at Pierro and the other two nurses. I was watching to see if they were smiling or sniggering as I feared they were playing a trick on me. But none of them looked up and instead went back to sorting out the tablets.

I turned my attention back to the door. Wanting to be courteous I knocked on the door and said hello. Putting my ear to the door I heard no reply from within.

Carefully I then opened the door to the cell. My shoulders tensed as if they were ready for a monster to jump out at me, but I needn't have worried, nothing did. As I edged myself further and further into the room my eyes and ears felt superhumanly alert for any noises or sudden movement. But the room and the inhabitant, wherever he was, seemed very calm. Where are you Senen?

Then after a few glances I eventually clasped eyes on him. I was disturbed to find him huddled in a fetal position bollock naked on the floor. His eyes looked ill at ease. Although he wasn't slim his bones stuck out. It was as if for his frame he should have been a lot bigger. I felt sick rise up from my stomach as he reminded of when I was in solitary confinement in Ceuta.

'What the fuck!'

'Look Senen it's okay. You are safe now. I will get you some clothes and a bed too.'

Senen looked back confused.

I ran to the door and shouted out for Pierro. Within seconds Pierro, Celestino and Hans arrived at the door. I ushered them all into the room.

'What's wrong Alan!' Pierro said startled.

'Look!' I said pointing at poor Senen shaking in the corner of the room with a disgruntled expression.

'What?' he said looking everywhere. 'What's wrong?'

'What to do mean what wrong?' I said angry. 'Look there at Senen! The poor guy is naked and without a bed!'

Pierro and Celistino started laughing. Hans didn't laugh but instead grabbed the tablets I had for Senen and went over to hand them to him.

'Why are you laughing?'

'Look Alan this is not punishment.'

'Yes it is!'

'No you don't understand Senen here likes not to wear clothes. We try and try to put them on him but he just rips them off. And when we give him a bed he does the same he just rips the mattress into little bits.'

'What?'

'Pierro then went to the corner of Senen's room and picked up some clothes that were torn.'

'Look! This is what he does,' he said lifting the clothes to my face.

'Maybe I could have a word with him.'

'You can try but I doubt it will help.'

'I can't see a man sleep on a cold floor.'

I watched as Celistino put the breakfast tray on the floor near to Senen. At first he put his nose up at it, but then after a few seconds he quickly snatched with his hand a few wedges of toast and gobbled it up like a starving animal. He reminded me of an angry goat.

We then handed out the rest of the medication and breakfast. Our new patient who we strapped to the bed didn't have any medication though. Obviously as he was only brought in late that night the doctors hadn't had a chance to see him yet to prescribe anything. But it didn't matter as he looked fairly calm when we all went in. I don't know whether he was still benefiting from the effects of the injection or whether he had just decided it was best he didn't struggle. He still looked very frightened, especially towards Hans.

Before Pierro took the straps off to give him his breakfast he asked if he was going to behave. Like a frightened child the man nodded frantically. Pierro also warned him that if he acted up again, we would strap him back up for two days with no food or water. The man nodded.

The day panned out like Pierro had said and I was right it was very similar to the schedule I was used to with Augustin. Well except with different patients and without a raging homosexual trying to get in my pants.

The only difference I noticed was when I took my breaks. Like Pierro had explained we could roam around the hospital a lot more freely than any of the other nurses. On each corridor we were waved through by the functionarios and allowed to pass. It seemed there was nowhere we didn't have access too. Before I was only allowed through a few corridors and then I had to state my business. Now I wasn't asked anything.

My best find of the day was a garden outside which had fig trees and flowers dotted around. It looked quite beautiful. It seemed a favourite to other prisoners too as it was teaming with people. I decided this would be where I would spend most of my free time on my breaks. I would also keep an eye out on the development of the figs as I bet when they were ripe they would taste delicious.

After tea and our last nurses break Pierro invited me, Hans and Cellistino back to his room for a drink and a smoke, like the night before. Everyone was up for it apart from Hans. He said he was too tired and went to bed. From last night he didn't seem one to party. The only thing I could see he enjoyed was fucking sticking needles into people. God knows what he was in for.

In Pierro's room we smoked and drank the night away. We all talked about the different prisons we had been to and what experiences we had. When it came to my turn I relieved the escape and trespassing into the garrote chamber. Although Pierro had heard them before he still listened intently and looked like he was enjoying them. Cellistino however looked stunned! He shook his head in disbelief several times. If it wasn't for Pierro backing me up constantly I doubted he would have accepted any of my stories as true.

Despite being prior friends with Pierro, I could tell Cellistino was far closer to him than I ever was. It was not surprising as they were both Italian. They were completely different in character but seemed to get along well. Pierro was the flamboyant, in your face and confident kind of guy whilst Cellistino was quiet, humble and hard working. Although Cellistino was far taller and stockier than Pierro and myself, in attitude he seemed a lot more gentle.

Just as I toked on my second joint the bell sounded. Startled I choked on the smoke that was at the back of my throat.

'Here we go lads,' said Pierro putting on his apron as he slapped my back.

I found it hard to catch my breath as I involuntarily coughed and spluttered. Holding my breath I put out the spliff and put the ashtray on the floor under the bed.

In the corridor I could hear the sound of stomping boots and raised voices. It sounded like the guards had carried this patient through. This was going to be fun. I tapped my chest and let out a few more coughs. Amidst my noises I could hear the sound of crashing doors and a man screaming.

I quickly opened the door and could see Hans disappearing through one of the cell doors. With speed I ran to the door and followed him in.

It was quite cramped in the cell as inside was me, three guards, Pierro, Hans and Cellistino. On the bed was a Spanish man in his late teens whimpering and sweating profusely. He lay on his side and had sheer terror written into his eyes.

'Pierro strap him up.'

'Yes of course,' said Pierro seriously.

'Alan can you come and help me.'

I nodded in agreement and went over to the right side of the bed. Before I could get to the straps the guard hung over him and poked his baton in his face.

'Move boy and you die.'

The boy made a high pitch squeak and went rigid. The guard then moved to the side and pointed to the strap for me to do it up. I nodded and started fumbling with the strap. The boy cooperated fully as Pierro and I strapped in his arms and legs. When we had both finished Pierro and I returned to the side of the room. The boy's bottom lip started trembling uncontrollably as the guard approached his right side again.

'Now any problems Pierro let me know!' he said looking into the boys eyes.

'See boy if you don't behave I will give you this,' he said squishing the boy's nose with his fist.

'Understand?'

The boy nodded

The guard then moved away from the boy but carried on looking into his eyes. After a few seconds he started laughing. When the guard looked back at the other guards they started laughing too. I and the other nurses remained quiet. Then without warning he swung his arm and launched his fist laden with thick gold rings towards the boy's chest. The boy whimpered and turned his head. The guard started laughing again. The guard never made contact with his chest as he stopped his fist just short. The boy looked up and could see the guard had only pretended. The boy then began to sob. After a few more tense seconds the guards eventually left. Before they left the corridor the guards told Pierro to keep him tied up all night.

We then went back to Pierro's room and tried to resume the party. Although I drank and smoked I didn't feel in a party mood. All I could think of was about the poor boy strapped to the bed and every now again I could hear him crying. Each time I did I stood up to go and see him, but Pierro told me to leave him. I think he knew I would have unstrapped him.

Later that night the bell went again. We all rushed out onto the corridor ready but the guards told us that they did not need our help and to stay in our cells. The biggest guard who was in charge introduced himself and strangely handed over his gold rings to hold. Before I went back into Pierro's room I watched as the three guards shoved the Moroccan looking prisoner into one of the cells.

'Alan get in here! You heard what the guards said.'

'Okay! Okay!' I shouted slamming the door behind me.

I was about to ask Pierro why the guard gave me his rings when I heard several bangs and screams. It was obvious then he had given them to me so he didn't have them scratched or dirtied with blood. I paced the room feeling helpless as I could hear the poor man yelp out in pain. Pierro could see I was getting more agitated and tried to drown out the screams by putting some music on. It did not make me feel better as when there was a quiet bit of music I could still hear the crashing, banging and screaming.

After ten minutes or so the door flung open and the three guards came in. Pierro quickly turned off his music.

I stood leaning on the wall and held out in my right hand the four rings he had given me.

He smiled as he went over to the sink and started washing off the blood from his hands. Once he finished he switched off the tap shook the drips and wiped the remaining moisture on his uniform.

'Thanks Alan for holding my rings,' he said as he snatched them from my hands.

I couldn't think of anything to say back and just nodded.

'Well good night gentleman! I think that is all for tonight!'

'Thanks,' said Pierro solemnly.

'Oh Pierro the man we brought in appears to have had a nasty accident. There is a bit of a mess on him so if you could clean him up.'

'Yes no problem,' Pierro said whilst looking at me.

When the guards left Pierro took out from his locker a few towels, bandages, flannels and ointments.

'What the fuck Pierro!'

'Alan either shut up or come and help me.'

In annoyance I grabbed the stuff out of Pierro's hands and stormed out of the room and stomped towards the cell where the poor young Moroccan had been beaten. When I opened the door I was shocked at the mess I couldn't believe what they had done to him.

32 BOTTOMS UP TO THE MOLOTOV COCKTAIL

The poor young Moroccan boy was sitting on the bed hunched over breathing heavily with pain written on every part of his body. He held his stomach with one hand whilst with the other tried to stem the blood from a deep cut on his arm. When I slammed the door and Pierro approached, he sat up with his back straight and tensed his fists

'Calm down!' I said in a soothing voice. 'We are here to help.'

To reassure him further I showed him the bandages in my bag to display our attentions.

The guy relaxed and hunched back over but continued to stare with hatred and mistrust.

Pierro crouched to the floor and tended to the man's feet. I watched what he was doing as I was unsure what to do. I had never done first aid before. Carefully Pierro wiped up all the blood from his toenails. Although he did it gently the man winced in pain. I was sickened to see that once all the blood was cleaned away the guy was missing several toenails. On the front of his feet were several bruises too, some in the shape of boot marks. It looked like the guards had stamped on them continuously.

'Alan!' Pierro shouted.

'Uh what!' I said waking after being mesmerised with the man's injured feet.

'Don't just stare. Clean him up.'

'Yes okay.'

I looked at the bruises and the cuts he had and decided the best place to start was stemming the blood from the deep gash on his arm. I fumbled around in the bag and brought out some tissue paper, antiseptic and some gauze. With the tissue paper I wiped up the blood and then dabbed on some antiseptic. But just as I had wiped up the blood more pumped out. I applied pressure with my thumb on the gash and then picked up the gauze. I continued to push in with my thumb in between wrapping it up with lengths of gauze. Once I had wrapped all the gauze around I tucked in the last bit of material so it would hold. At first the material soaked quickly with blood but after a few seconds the blood flow seemed to slow down.

Then I moved on to his hands. Like with his toes, several of his fingers were missing nails. It made me feel sick each time I wiped with wet tissue on the bloody underbelly of where the nail should have been. From shutting my fingers in the door and doing manual labour I knew what it was like to have pain from losing a nail. But to lose your nails by being repeatedly stamped on must of really fucking hurt, the thought of it made me feel sick.

Once we had patched up the poor man we put the bloody tissues in a bag and the remaining first aid equipment in another bag. Pierro went to the sink and filled a cup full of water. He held the cup to the man in one hand and after rifling through his pockets produced two circular white pills.

'Here, these are painkillers they will help with the pain.'

The man looked at Pierro in shock as if we are asking him to take poison. He then looked at me and shook his head.

'I promise you they are just painkillers.'

The man remained silent.

'Well it's your choice to take them or not. But you have five seconds to decide.'

The man looked at me again and I nodded. Then with a deep breath he snatched the tablets and downed the water straight away, as if he didn't want to contemplate what was in them. I hope to god they were just painkillers as the poor man had been through enough. But I couldn't see Pierro being cruel.

Before we reached the door, the man yelled out for us to stop. Both Pierro and I turned around.

'Thank you,' he said solemnly .

We both nodded appreciating his kind words and left.

I couldn't believe he was praising us. He should have hated us! We were apart of the system that hurt him. Although we didn't lay a finger on him we still both allowed it to happen.

Walking up the corridor I could hear whimpering from the room where the young Spanish lad was tied. I went to the door and put my ear to it.

'Hey shall we check on him. He doesn't sound good.'

'Look Alan he is tied up. He can't do any harm to himself.'

'Yes but listen to him.'

'Look Alan! Do what you think!' he said imperviously. 'I have had enough for tonight. I just want to get stoned.'

Not knowing what to do I stood there motionless and watched Pierro disappear into his cell. The young man's groans grew louder. I shook my head knowing that getting involved was the worst thing to do but I couldn't bear to hear him suffering.

When I opened the cell the man instantly stopped his whining. He widened his red watery eyes in horror and stared at me without blinking. He looked absolutely petrified. I walked across to stand by his bed, but with each step he scrabbled around moving his legs and arms in unnatural positions as if he was trying to get free.

'Calm down! It's okay I am not going to do anything,' I said lowering my hands up and down.

When I was a few inches from his bed my nose filled with the stench of shit. Taken aback I turned my face away covering my mouth and nose.

'I am sorry,' the man began sobbing. 'I couldn't help it.'

'Please don't hurt me,' he blubbered with spittle oozing out of the corner of his mouth.

I turned my face back to the man and withdrew my hands. I allowed the stench to hit my nostrils again and tried to get used it.

'It's okay,'

'I just............I just couldn't stop it,'

'Look relax I will clean you up,' I uttered trying to withhold my gag reflex.

'Thank you.'

'But you have to promise to be good or else I will get the guards.'

'Oh no don't do that...............I will be good.'

I unstrapped the man and wiped down the shit with the sheets as best I could. Once it was clean enough I turned the mattress over as it was wet. I then escorted the man to the shower room so he could wash himself down. Once clean I put him back in the straps.

He wasn't appreciative of me cleaning the bed or letting him have a shower not like the Moroccan was. He just looked too busy being consumed with worry. His forehead broke out in several lines and wrinkles. His chin also trembled uncontrollably and he blinked as if had developed a twitch.

I went back to Pierro's and joined him and Celestino with a beer and a few joints. I told them about the Spanish lad shitting himself. They both laughed and said they were glad I had attended to him. We all decided the poor boy must have shit himself through sheer fright. He must have heard the Moroccan having a good beating and was wondering when he was next. Despite the Moroccan copping it I decided the psychological torment with the boy on the bed was worst. He was waiting and waiting for something to happen. At least the Moroccan knew it was over.

Later that night we could hear the teenage Spanish boy crying again. I looked at Pierro and Celestino. They both didn't react to the noises and carried on playing cards.

'I take it no one is going to go and see him,'

'Go ahead if you want to Alan,' said Pierro smiling whilst putting a card down.

I looked at Celestino but Celestino didn't look back. He buried himself in the cards and purposely ignored me.

'Okay okay I will go.'

When I went into the room the boy had shit the bed again. Like before I cleaned it up, changed the bed and took him to the showers to wash it off. I turned the mattress back over to its original side which was still wet.

Obediently the man lay on the bed and held out his arms and legs to be strapped. When I did the last strap up on his leg I noticed the shaking in his chin had transcended to his whole body. He looked a complete wreck. If I had believed in the Molotov cocktails I would have got Hans to give him one just to provide him with some peace. But I didn't want that sadistic German to be let loose on him. He had suffered enough!

'Look calm down nothing is going to happen to you.'

'But I heard them.........I heard the man screaming next door.'

'Look the guards have finished for the night. Please don't worry.'

The man began to weep.

'Look I tell you what so you have more freedom to move I will untie one arm and one leg. Okay?'

'Yes...........Yes..............Okay.............I will like that,' he said whilst chattering his teeth.

As promised I undid one strap on his arm and one strap on his leg. I did opposite arms to leg so he couldn't get out of the straps completely. The young man seemed so fragile he looked like a contender to commit suicide, so I didn't want to free him completely so he would be a risk to himself. Plus if the guards or Pierro had got to him first in the morning I would have had a right bollocking for not following orders. I figured with half the straps on I wouldn't be told off as much.

The young man that night didn't make a further sound. I was glad he had settled. Either I had managed to reassure him or he had tired himself so much he went to sleep. Either way he was at peace.

That night I spoke to Pierro on why the man was so afraid even after I told him he had nothing to fear. Pierro told me that Carabanchel prison was ingrained into every young Spanish boy's mind as a place to fear. It was used as a sort of bogey man in order to scare them into being good as their mothers used to say 'if you don't behave we will send you to Carabanchel.' Although not many knew about the prison and especially about the hospital, stories did manage to seep out onto the streets of Madrid. But not surprisingly the Spanish public did not believe them and thought they were too outrageous to be true. If only they knew!

The next day I was glad to find the Spanish man hadn't shit himself. He also looked a lot calmer. He still seemed scared though but at a much lower level. He also thanked me for letting me free one of his legs and arms.

Later that day he was taken from the ward and so was the Moroccan. It felt strange that they were both gone so quickly. It seemed like what had happened hadn't. But I was sure similar instances would happen again to show I wasn't dreaming. I hoped they wouldn't but I knew they would.

After being in Agitado's for just under a week I was quite surprised at the high turn around. Patients were straight in and then shipped straight back out. I know Pierro told me it was a short stay ward, but I thought they would have been here for weeks rather than days. It then dawned on me that all the time I had seen people coming and going Senen was still here. Being curious I asked him the following morning as to Senen's story.

'Ah yes Senen he has been on this ward a while.'

'The doctors can't seem to agree where to put him.'

'Why?'

'Well he is not violent so some of the doctors think he should go in a dormitory.'

'But then the psychologist and psychiatrist think he should have his own cell and be looked at constantly as he is a danger to himself.'

'So he's with us until they decide.'

'Yes.'

After handing out medication and breakfast Pierro excitedly asked me to come and meet Ralph Romero. I was surprised to find although a non-patient Ralph wasn't a nurse either. He was in fact a secretary to the psychiatrists, psychologists and doctors. This place just got better and a better. A bloody prisoner in charge of all the medical records! But of course!

I was further disturbed to learn that it was Ralph who handed out the Molotov cocktails to Hans. He would even make up contents of the syringe. I didn't even bother asking whether he had any medical training or knew even what he was putting in there. I just decided to go with the flow and accept it.

Ralph seemed a nice guy on the whole, but at times he also appeared a bit of a smug git, as if he acted like he was far more superior to Pierro and I. I don't know why this was, but I assumed it was because he had direct contact with the doctors, and with the files and drugs. He probably felt the most powerful as he was possibly the most trusted out of all the prisoners.

'Ralph,' said Pierro in hushed tones looking around the corridor to see if anyone was watching.

'I have some stuff I want you to analyse.'

From under his apron and then under his jumper he produced a bag.

'In there is some powder and pills I want you to look at.'

Ralph quickly tucked it up his jumper.

'No problems,' said Ralph smiling.

'Nice meeting you Alan.'

'Bye,' shouted Pierro after him.

I turned around and headed down the corridor back to Agitado's.

'Alan don't go yet. There's someone I want you to see.'

'Who?'

Pierro didn't say anything back but stared intently at the female Psychologist's room.

'Well?'

'Shush,' he said listening to the muffled voices from behind the door.

After several minutes had passed a nurse and a patient left the office and headed down the corridor. Pierro said hello to the nurse and rudely barged inside. I tentatively followed him in.

'Come on quick before she has another patient,' he said with excited eyes.

'What?'

Like a sheep I followed him into the office. He seemed to glide in like a love sick puppy. Once the door shut Pierro shot to the desk and grabbed the side of the table with both arms.

'There she is Alan,' he said in amorous tones whilst laying on a thick Italian accent. 'This is the woman I love.'

The psychologist shook her head and smiled nervously. She also shone me a look as if to say 'is he for real'.

'You are so gorgeous. I wish you were my girl.'

'Now Pierro you shouldn't be saying things like that to me.'

'I can't help it. Every time I see you my heart pours with love.'

With a big breath she sighed and looked at me to stop his words of affection. I shrugged as I didn't know what to do. What the fuck was this saucy git playing at?

'Look Pierro I am very busy.'

'No one is ever too busy for love.'

'Well I am fine for love Pierro,' she said like a school mistress. 'As you well know I am married.'

'Oh yes,' he said disgruntled picking up a picture frame on her desk.

'How could I forget him,' he said pointing at the picture with disgust.

'Look Alan! Look at this man,' he said shoving it in my face.

I looked at the picture and could see it was a man in his late forties or fifties in full military uniform. I couldn't tell whether he was a senior prison guard or was apart of the Spanish army. He was balding and was quite chubby. Pierro on the looks department would beat him hands down.

'Look at you your gorgeous! And you're with him! He is so old.'

'Look at me I am fit and full of passion. You know you would have better time with me.'

Looking annoyed she snatched the picture back off him and put it neatly back on her desk.

'Pierro I am not going to ask again. Now go!' she said raising her eyebrows.

Pierro stared into her eyes lovingly and pushed his face further over the desk. Then there was a knock at the door. Pierro turned around and then back to her.

'Well ciao for now my beautiful. I will be waiting for you.'

The psychologist laughed and shook her head whilst folding her arms.

'Bye Pierro,' she said softly.

Afterwards I reprimanded Pierro about chatting her up. I couldn't believe he did that. And in front of me! I don't mind him jeopardising his own chances on getting out of here, but why the fuck did he have to drag me in with him. Pierro told me to relax and that he had been chatting her up for a while. He said if she hated it he would have been reported and taken away from Carabanchel by now. He also said he could see in her eyes she loved him and that if it wasn't for her husband she would be willing. Even though he was a big head and thought he was god's gift to women, I somehow found myself believing him. Her words did say no but I caught her smiling and fluttering her eyelashes a few times. Who knows?

At break time I went out to the large patio at the back hospital where the fig trees were. I wandered around in the pretty gardens, I also checked to see if the figs were ready to be picked, but they still weren't.

From ambling around I met up with Celistino. He was in a very chatty mood and seemed ecstatic to pour his verbal diarrhea onto me. Despite wanting some alone time I didn't grumble and just allowed him to get his conversation off his chest. Whilst distracted by his words I accidentally bumped into someone. When I looked up I could it was a patient as he wasn't wearing an apron. Despite looking a little narked he just shone me a cantankerous look and scuttled off. I laughed at the way he walked as it was in such a shifty and comedic manner. Not thinking anything of it I carried on walking. Celistino on the other hand look horrified and stood dead in his tracks.

'What?' I asked.

'You know who that was. Don't you?'

'Sorry no.'

'That's Manuel Delgado Villegas.'

'Who?'

'He is a serial killer.'

'Really!'

'Yes he is a very sick man. If you look carefully you can see the two nurses over there watching him.'

'How many people did he kill?'

'I am not really sure but someone told me fifty.'

'Wow,' I said looking at Manuel walking off in the distance. 'He doesn't look like someone who could kill.'

'Yes apparently in the papers they just kept finding more and more bodies.'

Manuel Delgado Villegas alleged 48 murders but was convicted for 8.

He killed seven of his victims between 1964 to 1971. The Spanish police reported that after he abducted his victims and killed them he practiced necrophilia

With that a couple of gentleman walked by. They were both German and very pleasant and asked us how are days were. Then just as quickly as they arrived they wandered off smiling as if they were taking a stroll on the beach on a summer's day. If we were actually on a beach they would have both appeared to be quite sane, but as we were in a nut house their overly happy nature greatly disturbed me. One of the men was in his late fifties whilst the other man was in twenties possibly early thirties. The younger man followed the older one as if he held him in high respect. Celistino also looked at them both with curious eyes.

'Who are they then?'

'Don't know,' said Celistino. 'They seem okay though, but you never know in this place. If you really want to know you should ask Ralph to give you their file.'

The rest of the day went quickly. Partly because I was busy with the patients and partly because I was dreading the night dawning. What poor fucking sods were the guards or crazy bunch, as I liked to refer to them as going to bring. The last few nights had been quiet so I knew we were overdue a visit by them.

That evening I was slow giving out tea to each of the patients. It was as if by being slow I could delay the night drawing in. I knew that wasn't possible but it was just how I felt.

The last person I gave out tea to was Senen. When I went in he must have been sleeping as he was curled up in a ball and looked at me with tired eyes. As he stretched he shivered rubbing his arms in a bid to gain warmth.

'Senen why don't you wear clothes you would be a lot fucking warmer,' I said putting the tray on the floor.

Senen didn't reply and folded his arms turning up his nose.

'If you wear clothes I will get you a bed to sleep on.'

Senen let out a light sarcastic laugh and shook his head.

'Wouldn't that be nice? A bed to sleep on instead of a cold hard floor.'

Senen carried on ignoring me. He also looked like he was trying to ignore the food but every now again I caught him looking at it as if was ravenously hungry. It was strange it was if he wanted me to believe he didn't want to eat. But every time I came back for the tray after leaving him it would be polished clean. Not surprising as he needed all the meat on his body being naked all the time and sleeping on the floor in the coldness of the nights.

'Look Senen do you want me to get a bed!' I said sternly being pissed off with ignorance.

Again Senen didn't say a word and just shrugged. Well this was good enough for me, at least he fucking responded.

'Okay then I will get you a bed.'

With his big sad doleful brown eyes he nodded. In that moment I felt like he listened to me. I was getting through. It then dawned on as to why he never spoke. Maybe he couldn't. Maybe he was mute or dumb. I mean I did hear him make noises and growls but no actual coherent words. Or possibly he had some kind of learning difficulty. That would go some way into explaining his strange behaviour and nakedness.

I left Senen to eat his food and went to have my own tea in my cell. I sat there thinking of who I could get a bed from. I had asked around but none of the other nurses knew of any spare. Half way through eating my paella it dawned on me where I could get a bed. How I could have been so stupid! There were plenty of empty cells in Agitado's and presumably with empty beds I could pinch one from there. Excitedly I shoveled down the rest of my tea and set to getting a bed and mattress for Senen. As I predicted in one of the empty room was a bed and mattress. Feeling elated I opened the door and dragged the bed with the mattress on top through the door and in the corridor. It was a struggle on my own moving the bed, not because it was heavy but because it was awkward getting it through the doors. After managing to heave it into the corridor I took a breather before carrying it across to Senen's room. Pierro and Cellistino caught me with the bed as they were putting their empty plates on the trolley. Pierro didn't say anything and just smiled.

'Want a hand Alan?' Pierro asked.

'Yes if you don't mind.'

Pierro lifted the other side of the bed whilst Celistino held Senen's door open. It was a hell of a lot easier shifting the bed having help. Putting the bed in made the room look a hell of a lot smaller, but a great deal more homely. Rubbing my hands together after a job well done I looked down at Senen. Senen however didn't look up. It looked like he was purposely ignoring me.

'Hey Senen are you going to look after your bed this time?' said Pierro jokily.

'Oi!' I said grabbing Senen's arm trying to gain his attention.

Senen looked up but stared right through me.

'Now Senen! Alan has gone to a lot of trouble!' Pierro shouted pointing his finger.

Senen still didn't utter a word and instead just smiled and nodded.

'Come on Alan let's just go and leave the miserable bastard to it!' Pierro said disgruntled as he left the cell. Celistino followed not long after, but I hung around in the doorway.

'Senen,' I said softly. 'I hope you enjoy having a bed tonight.'

Senen nodded at me and smiled again.

After shutting the door I felt good. Although he didn't say thank you I took his nod to mean he appreciated what I had done for him. Pierro called him all sorts that night but I didn't. I think I was getting through.

Later that night as I had predicted it wasn't a quiet one. The bell sounded which was shortly followed by the galloping footsteps of the crazy bunch. On tender hooks we all pelted out from Pierro's room after a few joints and beers to see what situation we had tonight.

In the guard's clutches they held a Spanish looking man who I would have said was in his thirties. He didn't look crazy, but as I knew appearances could be deceptive. Although not mentally disturbed he did look physically ill, as for a Spaniard his face was very pale and had a hint of greenness to it. Maybe it was fear that gave his face such a deathly pallor.

Tonight wasn't to be a night of torture physical or otherwise, as the guards left the man to us. Little did he know how lucky he was!

Pierro and I walked the man to his cell and all was calm, but that changed when we entered the cell. Feeling an old hand at restraining a new patient I sighed as I yanked and pulled him towards the bed. It didn't take long to lift him onto the bed. Instinctively I then grabbed the patients arm and caught hold of the straps on the bed. Pierro had hold of his other arm and was tying up the straps on his side whilst Celistino strapped in his feet. Hans stood slouched against the wall watching on. After several minutes Pierro, Celistino and I managed to strap him up completely.

'Now are you going to behave or do we have to give you a Molotov cocktail,' said Pierro.

The man started spitting and swearing in Spanish whilst equally awarding everyone a scowl.

'Fine by me,' said Pierro. 'Hans do the honours.'

With a smile Hans trotted off to get a concoction off Ralph.

'Is it me lads or has it been just one of those days,' said Pierro putting his hands on his hips.

Both Celistino and I nodded.

By the time Hans had come back the patient had calmed down. Pierro debated whether he should give it to him. Hans didn't listen to him and charged straight over with the needle.

'No no please you can't!' screamed the strapped up man.

Without hesitation he stabbed in the needle into his arm and plunged in the liquid. I watched as the man on the bed shook his head screaming and then slow drifted away until his head lollopped to the side.

'Right well he's done for the night.'

That night we all retreated back in Pierro's room for drinking and dope. I was surprised at Hans joining in and being sociable. He must have been happy as he got his chance to stab someone with a needle. It had been a few days since he had done that.

As I drank and toked the night away Celistino told me about the background of the two extra polite Germans who we saw earlier in the patio. He had been to see Ralph and had a look at their notes. From them he learned the two men were father and son. They had been put into the hospital after killing the wife and the daughter. The psychologists, psychiatrists and doctors seem to suggest it was done as some kind of ritual killing. It beggars belief what a man can do to another. In that moment I felt surrounded by evil. In the space of a month I had met a mass murderer, several killers and a rapist.

The next morning it was my turn to hand out breakfast to all the patients. I started by giving our very new guest a visit. Cheerfully I barged in and slapped the tray on the bed. I was shocked to see he didn't even flinch. He must have been still knocked out from the injection or sleeping fast.

'Breakfast time!' I shouted, but the man still didn't move.

When I looked closer I was shocked to find the man's lips were blue and drawn. His eyes also looked empty as he stared ahead. Shocked I waved my hand up and down over his eyes, but the man didn't blink or move. With my index and middle finger I gripped his wrist. I was horrified to find his skin was hard and very cold to touch.

'Oh shit!......Oh shit!.......Oh shit!' I danced around the room not knowing what to do.

33 SENEN

I look backed at the lifeless man strapped up and thought about how he could have died. My main suspicion was that the Molotov cocktail killed him. I mean I had seen Hans stick it into people many times without dying but I knew sooner or later it would have spelt trouble. Hans and Ralph were not men of medicine; they were just dicking around with things they didn't properly understand.

Plus the man was pretty insistent on not having a needle. Maybe he was trying to tell us he something. Like that he was allergic to certain drugs? Or that before coming in the hospital he had taken something and knew with the injection on top of it would make him overdose. He did look very pale, but I suppose he could have just been ill. If only the bastard German let him speak before sticking it in. Maybe this incident could have been prevented.

'Alan! Come on these breakfasts are getting cold!' I heard Pierro shouting from behind the door.

'Err Pierro,' I called out softly.

'What?' he said sharply as he poked his head round the door.

'We have a problem,' I said somberly whilst pointing to the tied up dead man.

Pierro walked over and stared at his face.

'Oh!' he said with his eyes wide and his mouth open.

A few minutes later Celistino and Hans walked in. They too gawped and stood looking at him motionless. Everyone including me seemed to shut down. It was as if we stared at him long enough he would disappear or be brought back to life again.

'Look Alan we don't want to upset the other patients...........so...........if you give out the rest of the breakfasts,' Pierro said as if was trying to gain control back from the situation.

'Hans now.......err....... have you given out all of the medication?'

Hans nodded.

'Good well you and Celistino...........err...........have breakfast.'

'Alan what are you still doing here get going.'

'Okay I am off.'

I stood motionless in the corridor with Senen's breakfast in hand when

Pierro grabbed my arm.

'Remember don't tell the patients anything.'

'I won't. It's okay.'

Pierro then slowly walked out of the corridor his shoulders hunched as if he had the weight of the world on them. I didn't envy him telling the doctors. How the fuck will he explain this?

Putting on a fake smile I opened Senen's door whilst trying to be careful not to spill any of his breakfast.

'Hi Senen!' I said cheerfully.

I was about to put the tray on the bed when I realised something was missing. Then looking at the bed I realised it was the mattress. Then as I scanned around the room I could see there was a hell of a mess.

'What the!' I shouted taken aback.

Like Pierro had warned the little fucker had ripped up the mattress and all the bedding was in tiny bits. Scattered around was foam, feathers and material. As per fucking always Senen was wrapped up in a ball lying on the floor like a fucking dog in the corner of the room.

'Why?' I asked as I slammed down the tray of breakfast on the floor.

Senen looked up and shone me his usual frown. He then raised his eyebrow and shrugged his shoulders at me like a bad tempered teenager. His belligerent shrug pissed me off. It felt worse than if he had stuck two fingers up.

'You little fucker!' I screamed launching full pelt at him in the corner.

Senen cowered putting his hands over his face and scrunching up his naked body.

Although still angry and only inches away I managed to stop myself from hitting him. I had a defining moment when I realised what I was about to do was wrong. If I gave him a dig I would be just as bad as the guards. Plus I shouldn't have felt pissed off. The only real person Senen was hurting was himself. Never again would I supply him with another bed or mattress.

After a few moments he unshielded his face and looked to see what I was doing.

'I give up!' I said trying to calm my breathing and reduce my anger levels.

'Look Senen if you want to sleep on the fucking floor! You sleep on the fucking floor!' I shouted pointing to the ground.

Shaking my head in disgust I walked out of the room not even giving him a second glance, whilst slamming the door with an almighty bang.

Later I gave out the rest of the breakfasts and then retreated to my cell. Although I didn't feel hungry after today's drama I shoveled the sad looking omelette on my flimsy fork and forced it in my mouth. The food was stone cold which didn't help my appetite.

After picking away at my meal I managed to eat over half and devour all the toast. I was going to need all my strength for whatever the guards had planned. I didn't much mind taking a beating but I really hoped I wouldn't have my day for a day taken off. But I knew that could be on the cards. And all because of that fucking German bastard! I wonder if they could add to my sentence for this?

Trying to forget about what was to happen I decided to put my tray of half eaten food on the trolley and bury myself in nursing duties. First on the agenda was collecting the empty trays. After collecting three patients' trays I put them on the trolley in the corridor. I was about to collect the rest when I was disturbed by the sound of footsteps behind the corridor door. The steps became louder and louder until the door opened and a disgruntled looking Pierro stepped through. Behind him followed a doctor and a guard carrying a kind of hospital trolley; obviously that was going to be used to take away the body.

Trying to ignore them I busied myself by stacking some of the loose trays but Pierro grabbed my shoulder and beckoned me to follow them into the room.

With a sigh I walked in. Pierro, Celistino, Hans, the guards and I all stood to the side of the room and watched on as the doctor examined the dead man. When I looked I could see the dead man's arms and legs were released from the straps on the bed. Obviously Hans or Celistino or both had done this. Either they did it to make it easier for the doctor or to hide the fact he was restrained? But I think the doctor knew about the practice as they were straps on all of the beds. Plus he would be able to see the marks on his wrists and ankles.

The doctor firstly grabbed the man's wrist as if to check for a pulse. He held the man's wrist for several seconds until he shouted out the time. I think he was calling a time of death. He then wrote it down on a pad of paper he had in his pocket. After putting the pad and pen back in his pocket he went about examining the man. He opened his mouth and had a look around. He then looked at his arms and checked them over. Then he looked at the legs. After a while I just looked to the floor trying to make myself day dream. Get the fucking stiff out already!

Eventually the doctor was satisfied and asked for two helpers to take the body to the morgue. Pierro and Celistino held their hands up and quickly went over to the bed. I watched as they struggled to lift him off the bed and onto the trolley.

After a bit of a struggle they got the man on the trolley securely and then covered him in a sheet. The doctor went out first and beckoned Pierro and Celistino. The guard followed closely behind, followed by me and then Hans. When the whole procession was out of the corridor and the door shut I gave a huge sigh. Hans though shone me a worried look and darted into his cell.

I felt very confused. Was this the end of it? Surely I was going to be interviewed. But if this was true I would have to think of what to say! But what could I say? The truth I suppose.

Trying not to think about it too much I busied myself in my nursing duties once again. First on the list was collecting the remaining breakfast trays. I only had two to collect. The one from the dead man's room and Senen's. I went into the dead man's room first and collected his full plate of breakfast and put it on the trolley. I looked at the bed and with a shiver and quickly left. Putting the full plate on the trolley made me feel sad. What a waste!

I then went into Senen's room. I was shocked to find he was standing in the doorway with a tray full of empty plates. Since I had been in Agitado's he had never done this. Normally when I went in he had his back turned, and the only time he would look at me was to show a grimace.

If he hadn't have ripped his bed up and pissed me off I would have praised him or shown some recognition. But instead I ignored him and snatched the trays off him. I then turned around and headed to the door.

'Alan!' said Senen softly.

I nearly dropped the tray in shock. I couldn't believe it! He actually said my name. This was the first time I had ever heard him speak. I mean he did grizzle and growl, but never had I heard a coherent word. So he wasn't deaf or dumb then! In response to him I turned around but I tried with my face not to look surprised.

'Yes Senen?'

'Did someone die last night?'

'Err............What?...........Why do you say that?'

'It's just I heard the doctor come in, and a trolley..................And the doctor said time of death.'

'Look someone has just been taken ill.'

'Somebody did die!' he said with wild excited eyes.

'Look Senen no!'

'Did he kill himself?'

'No he didn't.....I mean no one died.............' I said shaking my head. 'Just shut up Senen.'

I left Senen's room and quickly shut the door before he started asking anymore questions.

I put Senen's plates on the trolley. As usual each plate was clean as a whistle. He must have licked every crumb up like a dog.

Later that day Pierro, Celestino, Hans and I were all given times to be ready so we could be interviewed about what happened with the dead man. Hans was first up to provide an account, followed by Celestino, then me and then Pierro.

When it was my turn it wasn't so bad. They didn't ask many questions. All they wanted to know was what happened in my words. The only thing I could tell them was the truth. The guy came in and seemed agitated. Hans got an injection containing a sedative and gave it him. Then in the morning we found him dead.

On my way back to the corridor I bumped into Pierro. He looked really nervous.

'Hi Alan…So how did it go?'

'Alright……..I just told them what happened,'

'Oh……..ok.'

'Oh Alan can you do me a favour.'

'What?'

'Senen's Mum and Auntie will be here soon. Can you take him to his visit?'

'God!' I said pissed off. 'Do I have too?'

'What's wrong?'

'Oh he just pisses me off!'

'He's ripped up his mattress again hasn't he?'

'Yes!' I said with a sigh.

'What is his problem?'

'I don't fucking know and right now I don't care.'

'Look Alan if you want you can swap with Cellistino. He is taking another patient on a visit later on.'

'No, no! It's okay I will do it!'

Once back in Agitado's I went in to get Senen. Instead of lying in a ball naked he was hugging his knees and looking down at the floor.

'Come on Senen get dressed,' I ordered. 'Your Mam and Auntie are here.'

Senen growled and then struggled to lift his head as if it weighed thirty stone. He stared at me and pouted his lips. He was back to usual self again.

'Get fucking dressed! I am not going to ask you again.'

'Why should I?' he spat.

'You're going to see your mamma man. Isn't that good?'

'No!'

'I would love to see my Mam.'

'Well I don't fucking care!' he said shaking his head.

'Either you get dressed or I will get Celistino in here and we will dress you.'

'Go ahead,' he said folding his arms in defiance.

Under my breath I muttered a tirade of obscenities and went out into the corridor to get Celistino. When I told him he needed to help me dress Senen he didn't bat an eyelid. Obviously he had done this many times before. When we both went back in the cell I asked Senen again if he wanted to dress himself, but he just turned his head away.

Celestino and I threw our arms in the air and then began the difficult task of dressing. Never in my wildest fucking dreams would I have thought I'd be dressing a fully grown man! I mean I have clothed many a baby before but this, this was fucking ridiculous. Plus it didn't help that the bastard kept wriggling. I was glad though that Celistino put his Y-fronts on. I couldn't have beared to have brushed past his loose bollocks. But I suppose sooner or later I would have to do it and get it over with. Come on Alan remember a day for a day.

After ten stressful minutes or so Celistino and I marvelled at our achievement on putting clothes on Senen whilst we huffed and puffed. Senen scowled and pulled at the bottom of his t-shirt as if he were going to take it off.

'Don't you fucking dare Senen!' I snarled.

Like a little kid he brushed down his T-shirt and began folding his arms.

'Right you can go now Celestino I have it from here.'

I asked Senen several times to stand and follow me but he didn't. He remained crouched on the floor. Out of impatience I grabbed the scruff of his T-shirt and flung him to the door and practically pushed him all the way to the visiting room. Even when we got inside I had to plonk him on the chair. Why was he being such a knob!

I looked across and could see on the other table were two women. I could not tell which one was the Mother and which one was the Auntie, but both warmly smiled at Senen. Both looked very pleasant and dressed quite affluently. The younger woman handed me a package which felt like it had clothes in it.

'Hi Senen.........How are you?' said the younger woman.

He didn't answer and looked sideways at the wall. Not even his family could strike through to him. What the fuck was his problem?

'Well......' she continued looking at the woman next to her. 'We are all fine and ....err..................we are still looking into getting you out of here,' she said nodding.

'Don't!' he spat.

'Look Senen I know you are not well,' the other woman said whilst pointing her finger up and down. 'But don't shout at your mother.'

Senen breathed in deeply and shook his head.

'Look Senen don't worry,' his mother said softly. 'When you come home we will make you better. We will get you the right people.'

With that Senen launched out of the chair. I quickly responded by holding onto his shoulders, but it was okay he wasn't going to attack her he just stood and stared.

'Senen calm down,' I said in a low voice whilst looking into his dark brown hate filled eyes.

'If I come out of here I will kill you!' he said pointing at them both.

'Look son I know you don't mean it!' his Mum shrieked.

'I fucking do!'

I felt awkward as I watched his Mum swoon and her eyes flood with tears. His Auntie put her arm around her, but she too cried. What had his mother done to him that was so bad?

Then Senen struggled free from my grip and began ripping off his clothes. Shocked I picked up his clothes and tried to cover him but it was no use, as within seconds he was naked. His Auntie stood up and shepherded his mother out of the door. Before they left his mother mouthed that she loved him and left. She didn't look an ounce ashamed of his naked body. Obviously she was used to him exposing himself.

'What the fuck are you doing Senen?'

Senen ignored me with arms folded in the full splendour of his birthday suit.

'Well I ain't fucking taking you down the halls like that! Put these clothes on!' I said throwing the package at him.

Despite being an awkward shit I was thankful he heeded to my words as he began to put the clothes on. Once fully dressed I took him back. As we went through Agitado's main door we were passed by a miserable looking Hans who was being escorted out by two guards. I nodded at the guards and shoved Senen in the cell.

'Where's Hans going?' enquired Senen.

'Never mind about Hans what was all that about with your Mam?'

'What do you mean?'

'You stripped off and threatened to kill her.'

Senen went to the corner of the room and sat on the floor with his back to me. I waited a few seconds for him to speak, but I was only returned with silence.

'Fine have it your way!'

When I stormed out of the room Pierro and Cellistino were leaning against the wall outside and were looking in the direction of the main door.

'So when it is our turn to go,' I said.

'What do you mean?'

'Well Hans has been taken so I assumed we all would be.'

'Oh no we are fine! Hans has taken the blame for this as he was the one who gave the injection.'

'Well let's take a lesson from this. No more fucking injections!' I warned

Both Pierro and Celistino nodded in agreement.

On my afternoon break I wandered around outside in the big patio and walked under the fig trees trying to forget about the day's events. It had been a tough old day. Finding a stiff in the morning and having to contend with Senen. God knows what was going on in that young man's mind. I would never ever entertain the idea of stripping off in front of my mother like that!

Whilst walking around I saw Augustin in the distance. I was about to turn around and walk as far away as possible when I saw that he spotted me. He then started shouting my name in the distance. Oh god! I should have known if I wanted quiet time I should have gone in my own fucking cell. I put on an insincere smile and watched as he trotted towards me like an overexcited spaniel.

When he eventually reached me, he tried to give me a hug. I put my hand out and raised my eyebrow, trying to say 'fuck off' via my body language. Despite denying him an embrace he just turned his head to the side and grinned. Then he released a tirade of conversation onto me. Most of it I didn't particularly want to hear but there were a few nuggets of information in his gossiping that gave me some ideas. For one I didn't know he had weekend visits to see his 'girlfriend'. Apart from being a lucky bastard this was a very handy thing to know as I could ask to go shopping for me and bring stuff in such as clothes and magazines. Another thing that interested me was when he told me of his friend Antoine who had a predicament with his pet cat. Apparently when he had it he didn't know it was a she and that she was pregnant, until a few weeks later she starting panting and plopped out four kittens on his cell floor. He had managed to cope with them for a few months but now didn't think he could cope with all five of them permanently in his room. I told Augustin to help I would take one of the kittens, as I fancied having a pet. I tried to ask Augustin to show me his friend so I could go and pick one but he wouldn't tell who he was. He insisted on bringing the pussy to me personally. I think he just wanted an excuse to visit my ward.

After a while Augustin left to go back to his ward but I stayed outside for a bit longer. I approached some nurses that I didn't know just to have a chat as Augustin had reminded me it was useful to talk to people as you don't know what information you could gather. One conversation I had proved productive as I managed to find someone who was selling a radio with a tape player, a few tapes and two big speakers. I had been looking out for one of these for a while. Seizing the opportunity I went straight away to the nurse's ward and for a small fee took them off his hands.

When I got back to Agitado's I was like a kid at Christmas as I quickly went into my cell and wired it all up. To my delight the radio worked. I turned up the volume loud and blasted the music out. Feeling happy I danced around the room on my own bending my knees to the beat. Through the music I managed to just hear knocking on my door. I skipped over and opened it to find it was Pierro. He wasn't looking amused.

'Come on Alan were on afternoon break duty.'

'Do you like my radio?'

'Yes it sounds very loud. Very Good. Now let's take the nutters for their afternoon walk shall we.'

'Is it alright if I leave it on so we can hear the music in the patio.'

'Err…………..Yes………Why not! It will make the time go quickly.'

I went over to my new tape player and positioned the speakers on the window sill so the sound would be heard outside. Then I headed to the corridor and was about to open Senen's cell door, when Pierro stopped me by putting his hand on my shoulder.

'I would leave him,' he said.

'Why?'

'He has no clothes to wear and the guards won't allow him outside naked.'

'He's ripped all the clothes his mother brought in.'

Pierro nodded.

'But he needs to go out. He hasn't been out for days.'

'Look Alan it's his choice.'

'Look, let me speak to the guards and see if I can get some clothes for him.'

'How long is that going to take?'

'Look just give me 10 minutes to sort something. He has to have a break man.'

'I don't know why you bother with him.'

'Please.'

'You have 5 minutes,' he said huffing.

Quickly I ran through the main door to the guard's office. I told one of the guards I needed clothes for Senen. He shone me a look as if to say why bother like Pierro did. But fair play to him he did go off in search for something.

As I stood waiting I knew I was probably wasting my time. I knew Senen wouldn't thank me for it and would probably rip what I brought back into bits, but something inside told me I had to do it. He was a human being for god sake. He needed clothes, warmth and fresh air. I couldn't treat him like an animal and cage him up, although he seemed to encourage it. I was determined to break through to Senen and try and return his humanity back to him.

Several minutes ticked by until a guard returned with an item of clothing. I say clothing but it looked more like a gardening uniform, as they were green dungarees.

'That'll do,' I said trying not to laugh at them.

With the green dungarees in hand I ran back to the corridor. Pierro was waiting for me with his arms folded and leaning on the wall.

'I got him clothes,' I said holding them out

'What the hell are they?'

'I know they look pretty awful don't they.'

'Well put them on him then,' he said rolling his eyes.

I stormed into Senen's cell and tossed the dungarees across to him. He flinched when they hit him and then kicked them away.

'Put those on!'

'No!' he shouted back.

'God Senen you like a fucking old goat!'

'What!'

'You heard! A stubborn old moody goat.'

'Oh shut up.'

'I will if you put those on.'

To my surprise he put on the dungarees but for making him do it he stared at me with vitriol.

'Thank you Senen. Now let's go outside and listen to some music.'

I went back into the corridor to find Pierro and Celistino had herded the other four patients up. Pushing Senen out of the way I slammed his cell door. We then all trudged off to the small patio outside that was specifically allocated for Agitado's patients only. Once in the small yard we set free our patients to walk around and watched them from afar. In the corner watching us was a prison guard.

I was pleased that I could hear the music blaring out from my cell window. When I looked around I could see everyone bobbing up and down to the beat. Even Senen seemed to be swaying and appreciating the music.

'I think the patients like the music Alan,' said Pierro.

'Well anything to keep the fuckers calm.'

'Hey you know that powder and tablets I gave to Ralph.'

'Yeah.'

'Well it turns out the powder is coke and the tablets are amphetamine.'

'Oh right.'

'Do you want any?'

'Oh no dope is enough for me.'

'Fair enough I will go to the other nurses and see if I can sell it.'

'Oh and you know the guy who died,' Pierro gossiped.

'Yeah.'

'Turns out he was a drug dealer.'

'Alright.'

Before Pierro could continue Senen started shouting loudly. When I looked across I could see he was also jumping about like he was possessed. Celistino, Pierro and I looked at each other with worried glances. What the hell was he doing?

Then as we listened we could hear that what he was shouting was the words to the song being played on the radio. It was 'Bohemian Rhapsody' by Queen. Feeling relieved I started laughing and so did Celistino and Pierro. I had never seen Senen looking so lively in face and character.

The other patients then joined in with him and attempted singing the words whilst jumping up and down. Feeling happy to see a party vibe I joined in by singling loudly too. Pierro and Celistino soon followed. Even the guard in the corner started nodding and tapping his polished black shoes on the ground.

It felt a strange moment when I looked around. Everyone was dancing and in tune which each other. It was as if we were all connected despite our differences in our roles within the hospital, our religions and ethnic origins. For a few seconds everyone became equal and was as one.

But after the song faded in the background so did everyone's excitement. Senen went back to his usual cantankerous self. The guard looked on with serious eyes. The patients went back to their individual thoughts and Pierro, Celistino and I went back to our previous conversation.

Like Pierro said earlier the break did feel like it went by quicker by having music on in the background. We even overran by ten minutes as we didn't realise it was time to go back in. If it wasn't for the guard pointing it out it we could have gone on longer.

On the way back up I met up with Augustin. He was waiting outside the corridor clutching something under his apron.

'Quick take me to your room I have got it.'

'What?'

'The kitten,' he said looking around worried.

'Oh yeah come on in.'

I opened the door and then my cell door. I didn't go into my room as I didn't want any of the boys to get the wrong idea.

'Just put it in,' I said tetchily.

He put the kitten on the floor in the direction of my room and I shut the door quickly. Augustin looked upset that I hadn't offered him into my room.

'Hi Augustin!' said Pierro smiling.

'Hi.'

'So what you doing here?'

'Oh Alan wanted a kitten so I just dropped by to give him it,' he said smiling whilst looking shyly at the floor.

'Oh Alan you and those cats.'

'What?' I said loudly putting my hands in the air.

'Never mind!................Oh before I forget the guards have enlisted Pedro to help us now that Hans has gone.'

'Why has Hans gone?' asked Augustin.

'Oh he just got moved.'

'Really! Are you looking for a new nurse?' he said with super excitement.

'Well you heard Pierro we have Pedro now,' I quickly answered.

'Oh.'

'Yes..........but if we need you we will ask,' said Pierro with a wry smile.

'Yes do let me know.'

'Well Augustin I am afraid I am going to have to take Alan from you as I need him to give out the teas soon.'

'Oh yes. Well I need to get back to do that on my ward too.'

I breathed a sigh of relief as I watched him mince down the corridor and out of the ward.

'He likes you!' said Pierro tittering.

'Shut the fuck up!'

'You should thank me. I could have brought him on Agitado's.'

'If you did I would be gone.'

Today I was especially looking forward to tea, as I had paid some of the kitchen staff to bring in a leg of pork and cook it especially for me. I had been craving this for while and I had the appetite for a huge chunk of meat. I mean the food was nice in Carabanchel but it still didn't fill me.

When my tea came with the leg of pork I wasn't disappointed. It looked and smelt amazing. Feeling in a good mood and generous I gave some of the meat to Pierro, Celistino and the patients. Everyone warmly appreciated the offering apart from Senen and an Arab patient. Senen well was just Senen about it, he looked at me as if he didn't care less about it but he still took some. I knew though that despite acting like he didn't care that when I left him on his own he would have devoured it within seconds and would have loved it. But the behaviour of an Arab patient really shocked me. When I brought it out and asked him if he wanted any, he looked at it as if it was piece of shit on a stick. I couldn't believe how fucking ungrateful he was. He always seemed such a nice polite bloke, always thanking me for doing stuff.

Feeling pissed off I told Pierro and Celistino about it in the evening. Well I hadn't seen Pierro laugh so much in my life. He was holding his stomach as if it hurt to laugh so much. When I looked at Celistino he looked just as confused as I was. When he finally stopped he told me that reason the Arab was so rude was because he was Muslim and that pork was forbidden in the Islamic faith. Despite feeling a knob I fell about laughing too. No wonder he was so fucked off. He must have thought I was taking the piss by offering him that. I will have to say sorry to him in the morning for offending him. I hope he will see the funny side.

This incident got me thinking about Senen and his attitude. I wondered if I or Pierro or Celistino had upset him somehow and this was the reason for his insolence. I mean Senen was Spanish, maybe there was something we did or didn't do that was pissing him off. The nakedness could have be a protest to something. God knows what though.

Later that night I went into Senen's room and questioned him about his nakedness and attitude. I asked if it was something we did or it was something about the hospital that made him do it. But he didn't say anything back. He just shone a look as to say shut up and leave me alone. I continued to ask him questions over and over, but again to no avail. He wouldn't open up. Coming away from his room I felt more frustrated. I now had more questions rather than answers. I also took away his dungarees as I knew in the night he would just rip them up again. I decided to keep them in my room, until he needed to wear them again on visits or outside in the patio. If I had them at least I knew he had something to wear.

Over the next few days I continued my line of questioning with Senen but again he wasn't forthcoming. I think I would have had more information out of a brick fucking wall than him. I gave up on speaking to Senen and decided to broaden my line of questioning and asked Celistino and Pierro all they knew about him, but to my dismay they knew very little. The only additional information I could get out of them was that Senen came from a wealthy family. They said it was for this reason he was never reprimanded by the guards with their fists despite constantly damaging prison property i.e. beds, mattresses and flashing his bollocks off all over the place. This apparently used to piss them off greatly, but they weren't allowed to say anything about it.

I decided my only last hope of finding out about why Senen was like he was, was by looking at the notes by his doctor. Maybe there was something in them that would make me understand. So on one afternoon break I visited Ralph and asked if I could have a look. When I had a look I was stunned at what I read.

34 SCARED TO DEATH

'Look Alan not wanting to rush you but have you finished reading Senen's file?' asked Ralph impatiently.

I had finished reading several minutes ago but I couldn't take my eyes off one of the documents. My eyes were transfixed. Never had I read something so shocking.

'Yes,' I said clutching onto Senen's file. 'Yes I have.'

Ralph snatched the file out of my hands and put it back in the filing cabinet. He darted his eyes all around to see if anyone was watching us. When he could see we weren't spotted a relieved smile broke out onto his face.

'Did you find out what you wanted to know?'

'Er................sort of.'

This was a lie. His notes had created even more questions. I was still none the wiser as to why he acted the way he did. I did know one thing though. He was one fucked up individual.

I thanked Ralph and hurried back to Agitado's. I couldn't register what I had just read and decided to ignore it till the night. Maybe if I spoke to Pierro and Celistino later on I could make more sense of it. So until then I buried myself in my work. Work was always my defence mechanism when I didn't want to deal with something straight away.

I did manage to forget about it for several hours but when my nurse shift was over and I was tucking into my tea of Paella the contents of the file came flooding back to me. But unlike earlier I was now ready to unload. I was now ready to confide with Pierro and Celistino. I wonder how they will react when I tell them about the background of our longest serving patient.

I waited until we had settled down for the night in Pierro's room for a few drinks and smokes. Once everyone was relaxed and a quiet moment occurred I was about to open my mouth. But before I could get out my words the corridor bell pealed loudly. My plans had been scuppered.

We all ran into the corridor and awaited the arrival of the guards bringing out our latest guest for the night. After several seconds the door opened and two guards traipsed in. At our feet they dumped a very distressed looking man with olive brown skin and heavily bloodshot eyes. I had never seen someone's eyes looking so red before. It looked like he had either had chemicals thrown into them or that he had spent days on end crying.

The guards after a brief hello released the man into our care and left. This was weird as normally they would ask if we were alright to take him, but they didn't bother this time. Unless they were getting used to us and knew we could cope. Plus the man seemed quite calm, on first impressions, so maybe they didn't need to ask.

My gut instinct was correct as he went into the room quiet as a lamb. He didn't even freak out or question as to why there were straps on the bed. I mean we weren't going to strap him up, but just by the fact they were there used to shit up some of the patients, especially the sane ones.

We all watched the man for a few moments as he entered the room. Straight away he sat on the bed and just simply stared at the wall as if consumed with great sadness. Taken aback at how calm he was Pierro, Celistino and I all looked at each other. This was odd. We were more used to people shaking, shitting themselves or trying to fight with us. Never had we seen someone react like this. Either he didn't know anything about the hospital or he just simply didn't give a fuck. I would have hedged my bets it was the latter.

Being friendly Pierro sat on the bed next to him and had a brief chat with him in Spanish. When the man revealed he was Italian, Pierro quickly turned from speaking Spanish to his native tongue. This annoyed me on two counts. Firstly because I couldn't hear what was being said and secondly I felt left out being the only non-Italian in the room. Why couldn't I have a fellow Welshman in Agitado's? After a few minutes of chat, the calm man broke down in a flood of tears and started striking the bed with his fists.

Alarmed, I walked over and stood next to Pierro tensing my arms ready.

'Look Alan its fine. He is just upset.'

'You and Celistino go back in my room and enjoy a drink or two,' he said smiling. 'I will stay for a bit.'

After half an hour or so Pierro walked into his room to join Celistino and I. His brow furrowed as if he was burdened with much sadness. I turned off the music and patted the bed for him to sit down. He looked both Celistino and me in the eye and then gently took the lit joint in the ashtray and inhaled in deeply.

'What happened man?' I asked.

He looked up and with a sigh began to unload. He told us the guy was upset as his mother had just died and he wasn't allowed leave to go to the funeral. He was sent here to Carabanchel hospital as the guards in the prison he was in were worried he was suffering a mental breakdown. I could believe that, as the guy did look pretty distraught. What I found unbelievable was that the guards actually gave a fuck and sent him here.

'But he can't really expect that they would send him on a plane to Italy?' I said.

'He was prepared to pay for it,' said Pierro defiantly.

'But still he would have needed guards to go with him on the flight and to the funeral. How much would that cost? Even in Britain they wouldn't have allowed that.'

'So you would still feel the same way if your mother died?' said Pierro impassioned.

'Well......................I will be upset................I mean very upset..............but I know I wouldn't be able to go to the funeral................ I would just have to deal with it.'

Both Celistino and Pierro looked at me as if I had shat in their bed. After a few seconds of stony silence Pierro began to explain about how important the role of the mother was in Italian society. I mean in every culture the mother is important, but especially with the Italians he said, as they are held in very high esteem. They are considered not just an important part of the infrastructure of a family but they are also revered highly within the community too. The closest of bonds an Italian mother is said to have is with her son. A typical Italian mother is said to cater for her son's every whim, from washing his clothes to emotional support. I could see firsthand as both Pierro and Celistino welled up as they both spoke about their mothers. I mean I missed my Mam but they, seemed to pine for theirs as if they had lost a limb.

I decided to change the subject as the conversation was getting quite morbid, but the only thing I could think about was talking about Senen's file. As soon as I started talking I realised it was probably a mistake to change the subject with this as a) it was disturbing and b) it involved talking about Senen's mother.

'I went to see Ralph today.'

'Oh yeah?' responded Pierro

'I looked into Senen's files.'

'Did you find anything interesting?' asked Pierro.

'Well I was shocked to find he was studying to be a doctor.'

'A doctor?' blurted Celistino.

'Really?' said Pierro in disbelief.

'I was shocked too! I thought he was dumb as he didn't speak very much.'

'So why he is in here? What did he do?' said Pierro intrigued.

'He shot his father.'

'Oh...........Why did he do that?' said Pierro.

'I don't know how to say this.'

Both Celistino and Pierro edged in closer.

'I can't even bring myself to say it.'

'Come on Alan.'

'Well…………the……..psychologist…………….and psychiatrist……………………seem to think he did it.'

'Spit it out man!' shouted Pierro getting annoyed with my stammering.

'He did it as he wanted,' I said taking a deep breath. 'Sex with his mother.'

'His Mama?' said Celistino horrified.

I nodded. The room descended into silence for a few seconds. I felt dirty even saying such a thing.

'That is the most disgusting thing I have ever heard,' said Pierro. 'Don't tell me anymore.'

Celistino and Pierro looked very angry with what I had said. I mean I couldn't understand how Senen could think such a thing, but Celistino and Pierro couldn't even entertain it. They stared at the wall in silence as if trying to put themselves in a trance to forget what I had said.

Since writing this book I have since learned that the psychologist Sigmund Freud believed that every son possesses the desire to sleep with their mother and are jealous of their fathers for having her. The term he uses for these ideas is known as the Oedipus complex. Freud used the word Oedipus as it was the name of the Greek mythical character that killed his father, Laius and married his mother, Jocasta, but he did this all without knowing that they were his parents.

Freud suggests that the desires men have to sleep with their mothers stem from infancy and are largely unconscious. Being unconscious thoughts they only serve to influence our thoughts and behaviour without us knowing it. It is very rare as in Senen's case to actually fantasise about this in real life especially in adulthood.

Later that night we had an arrival of another guest. Again like the weeping Italian he did not act up or look scared out of his wits. He just seemed a very sweet polite boy. I say boy because he was only aged seventeen and had a baby face. His delicate and chubby features made him look several years younger too. From talking to him I found his name was Miguel, which is Michael in Spanish, and that he was sent here to be punished after several petty offences for stealing. This angered me. Miguel shouldn't have been sent here to be taught a lesson. This place was far too dangerous for someone so young in age and naïve in attitude. I could see I was going to have to teach him a thing or two to look after himself in order to survive the weirdos in this place.

That night Pierro, Celistino and I all went to bed pretty early. I think I had ruined the mood with arguing about the Italian guy and how he shouldn't have expected to be flown home. It also didn't help that I said Senen wanted to shag his own mother. Oh well hopefully after a night's sleep they will have forgotten about it in the morning and we could start again.

Before I had chance to strip to my pants and get into bed I was disturbed by a thud noise coming from the corridor. It sounded like something had struck a wall. Intrigued I opened my cell door and poked my head around the door to listen out for anymore sounds. Again a few seconds later I heard another thud. What the hell was going on? Then a few seconds later there were sounds of fast footsteps and then another bang.

I decided to investigate the noises further by opening the little hatch windows that looked into each cell. I looked in Senen's first because I knew he was bugger for breaking prison furniture and striking it against the wall, but when I looked in he was sleeping fast in the corner of his room. Next I looked into the youngsters' room. Again it was similar story, Miguel was in bed and all looked quiet.

Then I heard another thud. I could tell now it was coming from the Italian's room. I speedily ran over to his door and looked through the hatch. When I looked in I could see he was standing at one end of the room looking a little disorientated. Then all of sudden he ran full pelt into the wall opposite, using his head as a battering ram.

Shocked I quickly opened the door. On each side of the room I could see round football shape marks of blood on the walls on either side. What the hell?

Before I got my bearings the guy lined himself up again and I watched as he charged into the wall head first without stopping. Although shocked I hurried across and grabbed his shoulders to try and stop him from running back to the other wall. But as soon as I had caught hold of him his body went loose and he fell towards the floor. I managed to grab him but he fell like a sack of shit. With his body slipping from my grip I managed to gently lower him to the ground. He must have fallen unconscious as his whole body was limp. Looking at his forehead made me feel nauseous as it was stripped of skin and oozed with blood. How could anyone launch themselves head first into a wall over and over?

I yelled out loudly for Cellistino and Pierro. Within seconds they arrived into the room. They were equally as horrified at the marks on the walls and the mess on the guy's head. What a thing to have to do to get peace from his grief?

Pierro sounded the bell to get the attention of the guards. After a few minutes they arrived tense and ready for a fight, but when we showed them our unconscious Italian friend they relaxed their body and went grave in the face. I would go as far as to say they almost looked sympathetic.

The unconscious Italian was taken away to hospital as his injuries were far too severe for us to patch up. He was going to need a hell of a lot of stitches! And possibly an x-ray. He ran with so much force I wouldn't be surprised if he had broken bits off his skull. Cleaning the blood and skin off the walls made me heave as I imagined the pain he must have been in.

After a week I was expecting to see the Italian back on our ward, but we never did. Either he stayed in the hospital indefinitely or he found a way to cope and was transferred back to his prison. Whatever had happened to him I hoped he was alright.

Left on the ward was the seventeen year old Miguel, Senen and a couple of drug dealers aged in their thirties. All four of these patients seemed quite happy and on the whole behaved. This made the nursing duties easy and straightforward, but it also meant the days and nights felt longer. Even though I never wanted to encourage a commotion, I oddly still missed it.

To fill the void I passed the time by becoming friendly with Senen and the young teenage boy. With Senen I wanted to find out how he could have a bizarre view of his mother, and with Miguel I wanted to help him toughen up for when he would have to leave the ward and go onto another corridor.

When I spoke to Senen and mulled over his behaviour and the information in his file nothing seemed to add up. I mean why did Senen act aggressively towards his mother in the visit if he was supposed to have romantic feelings for her? Surely instead of threatening to kill her he would be threatening to shag her? Unless he was angry at the way he felt? Maybe he blamed her for being a temptress?

Although Senen did start speaking to me, it was only in one word answers and from me asking very benign questions. If I mentioned his mother, father or about why he likes to be naked he would just clam up. So getting nowhere with asking him direct questions I decided to change my approach. Maybe if I treated him like a friend and put him in relaxing surroundings he would feel able to talk.

To achieve this I allowed him in my room at night to listen to the radio and to the few tapes I owned, but I did insist that at all times in my room he was to wear his dungarees. There was no way I was having his naked bollocks rubbing against my sheets. No fucking way!

Pierro and Celistino thought I was fucking mad having him in my room, especially after finding out about his fascination with his mother. Since I had told them about it they both completely ignored Senen, not that this bothered him as they hardly spoke or interacted with him before. It was I on the whole who took him his food and trays away. I also seemed to be the one that was picked to take him on visits to see his doctors and his mother. It didn't bother me that they left him to me. In fact I relished it as Senen was the maddest fucking puzzle of a man I had ever met. I was determined to crack him or gain a better insight at least.

When he first came into my room he didn't really speak much. He just listened to the music and stroked my pussy. At first I was quite tense whenever he held my cat as I was scared about what he was going to do to it. I mean he had killed his father in cold blood so it wasn't beyond the realms of fantasy to believe he could pull the neck of my poor little kitten. But the kitten looked happy with him and after a while I trusted him with her.

The first proper conversation I had with Senen was incidentally about the cat. He had asked about what the cat's name was and I told him it was originally George because I thought it was boy. But when I met up with Augustin days later he told me with delight that George was actually a girl. Trust that perverted bastard to know!

When I told Senen this he smiled and gave out a laugh. I had never seen him looking happy before. It was really nice to see. He also commented on my charming name choice of Marrakesch when I found out she was girl. I called her this as her colouring reminded me of the sands in the Marrakech dessert in Morocco.

The cat seemed to be an invaluable tool to relax and get Senen to talk, as stroking her seem to soothe him. It seemed to make him forget his inner torments for a few seconds, and I would catch him smiling from time to time. Marrakech too also appreciated Senen's affection as she would close her eyes and purr loudly. But although he talked he still didn't really open up about himself. He would mostly ask me questions about myself and about the other patients.

The only thing he did manage to slip out to me was that he was deadly serious about killing his Mother and Auntie. He looked me straight in the eye and told me that if he was released he would have to do it. I asked him why but he couldn't give me a reason. He just said it was something he would have to do. Looking into his determined eyes I could see he meant it and that it wasn't just an empty threat.

Although Senen didn't really open up he did however seem to change dramatically in his behaviour and attitude after coming into my room. He didn't seem as angry anymore. He also after while started putting his dungarees on unprompted before the morning and afternoon break. Instead of the insolent grouch, he turned into an almost pleasant person. This difference in Senen was noted by the doctors, psychiatrists and psychologists too, as when I went in with Senen on his meetings they told him he was progressing well. Even the guards didn't seem to sneer as much when they looked at him. He was no longer seen as wretched animal, but now as another man.

With Miguel the seventeen year old boy, I didn't give him preferential treatment and allow him into my room like I did with Senen. This was because I didn't want Miguel getting used to going into a nurses room as I knew if he was sent to another ward he wouldn't have had this privilege. Well unless the nurse wanted to have sex with him.

So with Miguel I would talk to him in his room whenever I got the opportunity. I told him to project a confident demeanour at all times and try to avoid situations where he would be left on his own. I warned him that he needed to always be on guard to defend himself against burglary, violence and rape. But I think my words went in one ear and out the other. He would just look at me with his soft eyes and sweet smile and nod at my words. Even when I purposely pushed him about to provoke a reaction he still just shrank his head in and froze his body awaiting further punishment. It didn't matter how hard I tried to get him to stand up for himself, he just didn't seem able to.

A few days later the boy was sent from Agitado's and onto a ward with three other patients. I did try to ask the guards and the doctors to keep him with me till he was released but they didn't listen. They said he needed to be transferred. They didn't want Agitado's being clogged with people just because I classed them as vulnerable

The only thing I was glad to hear about when he left was that the ward he was sent on wasn't Augustin's. I dread to think what he would have done with such young male flesh.

But even the ward he was sent too wasn't safe. As a few days later I found out that on his first night in his new ward all three of the patients set upon him and took turns to rape him. Then due to the distress of this they found him dead after committing suicide by hanging himself the following morning.

When I heard the news I wasn't really shocked. I knew his gentle nature was going to be abused in some way. You could see it a mile off he wasn't safe. It angered me that it could have been prevented though. I had told the guards and the doctors he wouldn't last. I didn't think he would commit suicide or run into trouble so soon, but I had a bad feeling about it. The poor thing wasn't built to survive this place. If only I could have kept him. I would have made sure he was safe.

On the same day I found out about the boy I was also told to get Senen ready to be moved to another ward. Due to his change in behaviour the doctors decided it was time to put him in a permanent ward rather than in the limbo of Agitado's. I again begged with the doctors and the guards to leave Senen in my care but again like with Miguel they didn't give a shit. They knew fucking best! But I suppose with Senen it was different. Unlike Miguel he would fight back. I couldn't see him being a victim of rape or violence. For a scrawny runt he was quite strong.

When I told Senen first about the move he wasn't happy. He stomped around kicking the wall and refused point blank to get into his dungarees. Over and over I told him there was nothing I could do but instead he paced around and ignored me. Then in the corridor the bell sounded. Senen looked in the direction of the door and knew the guards had come for him.

To my surprise he voluntarily put on his dungarees and walked to the door.

'Good luck Senen!' I said putting my hand on his arm.

'Oh don't worry Alan I will be back,' he said grinning as if he was thinking up an evil plot.

'What do you mean?'

Senen didn't answer and instead turned his head to face me and beamed a great smile as the guard's frog marched him out of the corridor.

35 SYMPATHY FROM THE DEVIL

'I am glad Senen's gone,' said Pierro lying on his bed with a joint in one hand and a bottle in the other.

'Hey man be nice he was my friend.'

'Just think no more seeing his miserable face and having to dress the fucker.'

'I can't believe they have taken him to another ward,' I said ignoring Pierro's jibes.

'I know,' said Pierro. 'I feel sorry for the other patients.'

I scowled at Pierro. Although he was being jokey I wasn't appreciating his humour much. I know Senen was hard work and not the friendliest of people but he was still my friend. He should have respected that.

'Look Alan I know you liked him. But maybe it was good for him to go.'

'What do you mean?'

'Well he can settle in a ward and make new friends.'

'Senen make friends,' I laughed. 'The only person he has ever warmed up to was me and that was because I never gave up.'

'I am sure he will be alright.

Not feeling sociable that night I retired to my cell and left Pierro and Celistino to it. I still listened to music and drank and smoked but I just didn't want any company. I was mourning Miguel and the absence of Senen. Thinking about them both made me feel useless. It didn't matter what I did, I still couldn't control what happened to them. The evil in Carabanchel was going to lurk no matter what I did.

Lying on my bed I wondered what Senen was up too in the dormitory. I hoped he was happily snoring away in a deep slumber. But I knew this was probably not the case. He was livid about having to leave Agitado's so I knew he wasn't going to assimilate to the ward straight away. I also could predict he would play up in some way to protest about his transfer.

I really hope though that he would give his fellow patients and nurse a go. I mean it wasn't out of the realms of possibility that he would behave. He was after all surprisingly calm when he left, but knowing Senen I think this was just the calm before the storm. The fact that he was saying to me he was coming back, suggested he was planning something. But god knows what. I just hope the new nurse and the guards are prepared for the whirlwind that is Senen. I think some beds and furniture is going to be trashed tonight.

Although I knew Senen was much stronger physically and in character than Miguel I still feared about his safety. I couldn't bear it if after a few days I found out Senen was raped, hurt or killed. If that did happen I would be fucking onto those nurses and patients like flies on shit. No way would I let them get away with it. I think his mother would also have something to say about it too.

But I doubted anyone would harm Senen. I think he would be fit enough for most of the patients in here. Plus because of the way he acted everyone seemed to give him a wide berth, even the other crazy people. He reminded me of the Wolf Man in Ceuta in certain ways, as they were both solitary figures epitomising the word crazy. I knew though he was safe from being hurt by the guards as his respected family would have seen to that.

I wonder if in the forced company of others he would make friends. He was learning to interact with me, so I suppose he could start doing it with someone else. All I wanted for him was to be happy.

Halfway through the evening the corridor bell screamed out in the corridor. With a sigh I plodded out of my cell and into the corridor. What delights have the guards brought us this time?

Through the door arrived two guards and a young teenage boy. One of the guards had hold of the boy by the scruff of the neck. He looked like a naughty boy being taken to a school masters room rather than a patient sent to a psychiatric ward for mental prisoners.

The boy was short in build and quite wiry. He looked typically Spanish with his mop of brown hair, dark eyes and tanned skin. Although only young in his eyes I could see a confident mean streak in him. Unlike the seventeen year old this boy had a streetwise look about him.

'How old is he?' I asked the guards

'Fourteen,' replied the boy confidently whilst straightening his collar.

'Fourteen!' shouted Pierro. 'The boy is far too young to be here.'

'I am not a boy and my name's Pablo,' he shouted.

'Come on! You can't leave him here,' I pleaded.

The guards shrugged their shoulders and left. The age of the boy wasn't up for discussion apparently. Pierro, Celistino and I all turned around and stared at the young Pablo in amazement.

'What the fuck you all looking at!' he shouted.

After a few seconds of stunned silence, I laughed and so did Pierro and Celistino.

'So which cell is mine?' Pablo said flippantly as he looked around the corridor. The way he asked the question was as if he was in a hotel looking for his room, and not in a psych ward of a prison.

'You can have this cell,' I said opening up the cell opposite me.

Without any fear the boy waltzed straight in and sat on the bed. He first of all bounced his arse up and down checking the springiness and then looked towards the straps at the foot of the bed. He shuffled himself closer to one of the straps and studied it with grave concern.

'What are these for?' he said whilst clearing his throat.

'There for if you don't behave,' said Celistino in a spooky voice whilst raising his eyebrow.

'Oh,' smiled Pablo.

Celistino as part of the routine searched the boy. He didn't find any drugs but did find two knives in his possession. When Celistino took them off him Pablo became very abusive verbally. Celistino the big lump of a guy didn't say anything and just smiled. It was like watching a Yorkshire terrier snapping at the heels of a docile Shetland pony. I think the boy was aggressive as he felt frightened. The knives appeared to have given him a little confidence. Without them he was just a defenceless youngster.

'So what are you doing here?' I asked. Trying to rescue Celistino from the boy's jibes.

The boy confidently chatted about his several offences of burglary he was arrested for. When he described his crimes it seemed he was quite proud. He even at one point stood up and swaggered around the room as he spoke. Despite his small and skinny frame he walked around as if he was eight foot high and eight foot wide. Self-confidence oozed out of every pore.

Pierro soon became tired of the boys arrogance and interrupted the boy's jabbering. He warned Pablo to find a way out of Agitado's as being in the hospital wasn't safe. The boy knew of no way out and seemed offended by Pierro suggestion of vulnerability. I wanted to get the point across by telling him about Miguel who was raped by three men and then hung himself. But I decided not to say. If the boy had told the guards what I had said I may have been in trouble for snitching. Then I could have been taken from Agitado's ward or even worse from the hospital itself. I hadn't come this far and seen what I had seen just to be sent back to another prison to serve a longer sentence.

Although a little annoying I did admire the boy's energetic arrogance and confident attitude. I wondered where the hell this stemmed from. Maybe he was the hardest boy in school or a leader of a gang or something. But what I did know his aggressiveness in attitude wasn't enough in here. He needed also to have the physicality to fight off any attacks or advances by the paedophiles, killers, serial killers and rapists that dwelled here.

When we locked him up, Pierro invited me and Celistino in his room to discuss the boy. We all decided it wasn't right that the boy was here. Pierro said that first thing tomorrow he would speak to the guards and the doctors about getting him out. Or failing that we would urge them to keep him in

Agitado's. At least with us we will know he is safe. I didn't want any more blood on my hands. One death of an innocent was enough. Surely they will have to listen to us after Miguel's demise?

At around three in the morning my sleep was disturbed by the corridor bell ringing. This was a very late entrance for a patient. Usually they were brought to us around midnight, maybe 1am at the latest but this was very late indeed.

I rubbed my eyes and jumped out of bed. I was too tired to feel alarmed or worried. With my fingers I squeezed my eyelids and lifted them up in order to encourage my sleepy eyes to open. With a sigh I made my way out of my cell and onto the corridor. I was the first on the scene, followed by Pierro and then Celistino.

To my delight when the door opened I was greeted by a naked Senen and two guards who were either side of him. Senen was covered head to foot in soot and shone a devilish smile. The disgruntled guards trudged past Celistino, Pierro and I. I watched as they bundled him into his old cell, closing the door very quickly behind.

'What happened?' I said trying not to smile or giving them a 'told you so' look.

'He set fire to his bed in the dormitory,' he said thrusting Senen's singed dungarees in my hand.

'Oh.'

'Yes, so you are stuck with him again.'

I turned round to Pierro and Celistino. They both smiled and shrugged.

When the guards left I went into see Senen.

'What did you do?' I said trying not to laugh.

'Told you I would be back didn't I.'

'Night night Senen,' I said laughing whilst averting my gaze from his naked body.

When I went back to bed for the second time I felt more at ease. At least some sort of normality had returned. Senen was home. It was nice to see the miserable bugger back into his room.

The next day Pierro tried to reason with the guards and the doctors about releasing Pablo, but both refused. He was ordered by the police to be here so there was apparently nothing they could do. We even asked if failing that he could stay on our ward but the psychologists and psychiatrists said that they couldn't do that. Once he had been assessed he would be sent to a ward. Pierro did manage to get the female psychologist to promise to delay moving him by much flirting and begging. She also said that she would choose the ward carefully in terms of the patients and nurses. But I couldn't believe that. Without us by his side he was still a target. In the patios he could have been raped. I had even heard some of the guards had a tendency to homosexuality so even from them he wasn't safe.

After a week went by the female psychologist approached Pierro and told him she had done all she could to delay it but in the next few days he was planned to be moved. Pierro, Celistino and I then pleaded again with the guards.

To our surprise one of the guards did come to our rescue and suggested that the kid could be released if the burglary offences were apart of a fine. If we paid the fine he may be able to get released. The guard went off and rang up the courts to find out. To our sheer delight his offences were just because of a fine. And they had agreed that as long as it was paid the boy could be released. However the guard said there was a catch and I had to carry out a favour and work on another ward. Celistino and Pierro offered to help out too but the guards said the job only required one nurse and that the job started tomorrow. Although the guards wouldn't tell me what it entailed I didn't care. I was just happy that Pablo was going to be safe. Also despite working on another ward I was also allowed to stay in Agitado's in the nights.

After raiding our funds Pierro, Celistino and I put our money together the next morning and rang the bell for the guards. When the guards came we handed it over. One of the guards counted it and then nodded. With a shove Pierro pushed Pablo out of the corridor.

'Oi!' said Pablo angrily. 'Don't shove me!'

'Good bye Pablo!' said Pierro.

'And don't come back!' I said whilst pointing.

'Or else what?'

'You will have some of this,' I said shaking my fist whilst smiling.

'I could fight you old man,' he said with a cheeky smile

'Just go!' I said pointing to the door.

The guards smiled and then grabbed Pablo by the arm and took him down the corridor. We all watched as he walked off into the distance. Halfway down the corridor Pablo tried to turn his head but was stopped by the guards. We did hear him shout 'thanks' very loudly in the distance. It felt good to see him go.

An hour later the guards then came for me to show me the ward I was going to be working on. As we walked through the corridors I felt a little nervous and excited at what assignment they had planned for me. What sick things did I have to be privy to now?

To my surprise I wasn't taken to a ward but to a room that was right next to the guard's patio which they used for when they were on breaks. I had never been in this part of the hospital before.

In the room was a bed ridden frail looking man who I would have said was in his eighties. I could not translate exactly what the guards said he had but I did manage to understand it was something to do with the man's lungs and that his prognosis was terminal. I would have hazard a guess it was lung cancer.

The guards asked if I could look after the man who was named Manuel until he eventually passed away. They said that normally patients who were so ill were allowed to be taken home and convalesced by their family, but as he didn't have anyone he had to die here.

Although I knew it wasn't going to be a nice task, I was glad they asked me to do this rather than leave him just to suffer. I didn't mind keeping him comfortable until then. It would be nice to see someone die of natural causes in here for a change. This was how death was supposed to happen.

When the guard left I sat on the side of his bed and had a brief chat with him. He smiled and nodded but didn't say much. He looked both tired and drugged up to the hilt as his eyeballs bobbled around like peas in a soup. Every now again he would gasp for breath and press his hand down on his chest as if in a feeble attempt to stem the pain.

Looking at my watch I could see it was now time for dinner. I asked the guard out in the patio if I was to wait or to collect it myself. I found out it was the latter. So off I went and headed to kitchens for breakfast. I also went to Ralph to source painkillers as what he had been given seemed to have already worn off.

I gave the man the medication and then his dinner. For a bit of company I stood to the side of the room and ate mine too. However once I was finished he was only two mouthfuls in. Needing a smoke I left him to it and joined the guards in their patio. I only had normal cigarette to smoke as I didn't really like getting high in the day. That was more of a recreational thing in the night. Which was probably good in this instance as I know we were given leeway but smoking pot right under the guard's noses was probably a bit too much of taking the piss.

It felt strange standing outside with just the guards rather than with my fellow nurses and patients wandering around. It was like I didn't belong. But the guards themselves were quite pleasant enough. A few of them even spoke to me and smiled deeply as if they were appreciating what I was doing for Manuel. I would never have thought I would see compassion in a Spanish prison's guards eyes before. Maybe they were human after all.

Once I finished my smoke I went into collect the tray from Manuel, but I couldn't as he was still struggling to finish his breakfast. With very slow movements he put the fork to his mouth. Only just over a quarter of the food had gone on his plate.

Without asking I sat on the bed and took the plate and fork off him. I then scooped up some food with the fork and put it to his mouth. The man managed to croak a thank you and then opened his mouth so I could feed him. Intermittently through the feeding he would cough as if food was getting lodged in his oesophagus. To swish down the bits I would gently tip water in a cup down his throat.

Although only half the food was eaten he shook his head and put his hand up to signal he had enough. I didn't force him to have anymore as at least he had something. The man wriggled down the bed as if to get ready to drift onto into sleep. I lifted him up and then plumped his pillows in a bid to make him comfortable. I then pulled up the sheet to cover his chest He looked at me with watery eyes and smiled.

When I went back onto my ward everything felt speeded up. Time went so slow in the old man's room and everything was calm, but taking my patients to their visitors and out on their breaks seemed chaotic and a bit stressful.

I told Pierro and Celistino about the man. They seemed saddened he did not have family to dote on him and that his final resting place was to be here. Pierro even joked that he would absolutely abhor seeing my face before death. He would rather a pretty girl.

All day I found myself flitting back and fore to the old man. The guards didn't tell me to and I didn't have to as he spent most of time sleeping, but I just felt like I needed to be there. I just wanted to give him as much company as I could whether he was conscious or not. I mean as far as I knew no other bugger would visit him and he couldn't go anywhere as he was practically bedridden. I was the only person he saw, well me and the guards I suppose. I just didn't want him to feel so alone whilst dying.

When I took him down tea I also brought with me my radio. The man was over ore with gratitude when I put it on. Seeing his reaction I decided to leave it with him. I could busy myself with other things and live without music for a few weeks. The poor guy could do with something to take his mind off the pain.

That night when I had Senen in my room the roles seem to change. He was the chatty one and I was the one who was quiet and forlorn. Nursing Pedro had really taken it out of me, both physically and emotionally.

He started jabbering on at first about how he started the fire in the dormitory with a set of matches and described in detail the reactions of the guards when they found him. Then he told me about a few of the patients in the ward and then a bit about the nurse. I tried to be interested and follow his conversation, but my mind kept drifting off. I couldn't stop thinking about Manuel.

'So where have you been today?' asked Senen whilst he scratched Marrakech hard under the chin.

'Oh……..err…………I have been sent to care for another patient.'

'Who?'

'His name is Manuel and he is very very ill. He has only days or weeks left so they want me to care for him until he dies.'

'Oh,' he said taken aback. 'What is wrong with him?'

'It's his chest.'

'Oh,' he said looking ahead as if thinking of something very deep.

'Can you put some music on?' he said looking around for my radio.

'Sorry Senen I gave it to Manuel to listen to in the nights.'

'Oh….Must be nice to know your dying,' Senen said in jealous tones. 'I wish I was dead.'

'Senen! You don't mean that!' I said abhorred.

'Yes I do,' he said impassioned.

'You have loads to live for man. You are young! You have a kind mother who is trying to get you out of here.'

'But Alan if I get out of here I will kill her and my Auntie.'

'Stop it Senen! Why do you say such things! Grow up!'

'I will kill them!' he growled whilst stroking Marrakech hard on the back.

I took Marrakech off his lap and sat next to him plonking her on top of my lap. She went around in a circle a few times whilst kneading with her claws into my jeans. I could feel her sharp claws piercing my skin but I didn't pat her paws for her to retract them in, I just waited for her to rest.

'So how long has Manuel got?'

'I don't know Senen. But I hope for his sake it's not long.'

'I don't like to see anyone in pain and suffering.'

'I am suffering Alan,' said Senen quietly. 'I want to die.'

'Oh shut up! You are fine!'

'Can you take me back to my room?' he said coldly

'You don't want to stay with me a little longer and chat.'

'No I want to go back!' he said with arms folded.

When I went to see Manuel the next day he looked so much better than yesterday. He seemed more awake and happy with himself. I think the radio had bucked him up a bit. After taking his medication he clapped and sang along to a Spanish song blaring on the radio. He looked towards the ceiling as if he was remembering happy times in his past. He still didn't finish his food but he did manage to get down a few mouthfuls.

But despite the improvement on the second day in the subsequent days that followed, his health deteriorated and his skin became greyer. He became so weak I even had to help him onto his commode. I tried not to gag on the smell of his faeces, as Manuel seemed so embarrassed I had to help him. I didn't mind, plus I was getting used to clearing up another man's shit after working in Agitado's.

The pain Manuel was in seemed to get worse too, despite being given pills and pills by the doctor it didn't seem to help. He would writhe around in agony, groaning whilst rubbing his chest and guts. I decided to try and help by putting scrunched up bits of cannabis in his coffee and food. I didn't care if I was caught by the doctors, I just wanted to try and bring the poor man some peace.

On the fifth day of visiting him he was barely conscious, he drifted in and out from sleep to consciousness at the drop of a hat. Although he did not really respond to my presence I still put the radio on and spoke to him. Just in case somewhere deep down he could hear me. I wanted him to know he wasn't alone.

Watching his lungs I could see his breathing was getting much quicker and shallower. His time was coming. I was glad I didn't look into his notes at what he had done. I didn't want to prejudice my care. All I could think was that he was a human being and he needed my sympathy and care.

I was about to leave when he awoke suddenly coughing and groaning. He held his breath for a few seconds as if to take his mind off the pain. I held his hand and he looked at me with watery eyes. Then again he settled back down and went to sleep. I gently removed my hand and watched as his eyes rolled around.

As I anticipated the next day when I went to the old man's room he wasn't there. When I went out to the patio and spoke to a guard he had confirmed he had died sometime in the night and was now resting in the prison morgue. Although it was sad that he had died I couldn't help but feel relief for him. His pain and suffering was now over. He was now in the hands of God, if you believe such a thing.

When I went back to Agitado's the patients were in the corridor with Celistino and Pierro. They were taking everyone out on morning break. Pierro shone me a confused look as normally I would be away for hours looking after Pedro. After a few seconds when he saw my somber look it clicked Manuel had died. Celistino also caught on too.

Out in the patio I kept away from Celistino and Pierro and just stood next to a wall on my own. Senen came over and stood next to me.

'So he is dead?'

'Yes Senen.'

'Did you see him die?'

'No …………. He died in his sleep.'

'He had a peaceful death then.'

'Yes he did.'

'I can't wait for that Alan.'

'What?'

'I look forward to dying,' he said smiling.

'Oh Senen not this again.'

'I mean it,' he said grabbing my hand in desperation. 'I can't live like this anymore.'

'Look Senen you are a young and healthy man. You have many years. You can rebuild your life,' I said peeling his hands off mine.

With that he looked at me with anger and scowled. His body was rigid and stiff and he had a stare which seemed to burn straight though me.

'Alan you know I can't get out of here. And even if I do I will only kill again,' he said welling up with tears.

'Senen choose life.'

'I am dead Alan. I am just waiting for my body to go too.'

Before I could say anymore he walked off and looked to the floor. For all of the break he ignored me and just went into his own world.

After tea that day I was looking forward to a few minutes of alone time. Although Manuel's death was very much on the cards I was still saddened by it. But Agitado's didn't allow me any moments of quiet solitude as the corridor bell rang as soon as I went into my room. However I forgave the guards as the new visitor was a welcomed surprise. I never knew such a dear friend would darken my doors here, especially as a psychiatric patient.

36 BIG PROBLEMS!

Pierro was steering my familiar friend by the shoulders into one of the cells. Straight away I went over and chopped with my hand Pierro's grip.

'What the hell are you doing Alan?'

'I know this man. He is coming into my room for a chat and a smoke first.'

'But he is a patient.'

'Trust me Pierro he is fine.'

'Okay! Okay! Have it your way.'

I opened my cell and welcomed everyone in. Pierro, Celistino and my long lost friend. I kicked the box I used as a cat litter tray towards the end of the room. I really need to change it as it was starting to stink. For a little cat she could squeeze out some massive turds. Some I would even class as human size.

I straightened down the covers on the bed and picked up Marrakesh from the middle and put her nearer to my pillow so she wasn't obstructing anyone's way. She meowed at first in protest but soon settled. I pointed to my bed and everyone sat down apart from me.

'Well come on Alan who the fuck is this?' said Pierro.

'This is Enio.'

Enio shook both Celistino's and Pierro's hand warmly. When I looked at his face he didn't seem his usual self. He looked pale as if he had suffered a great trauma. Under his eyes were dark circles that looked like several days if not several weeks of having no sleep.

'Hey guys you will be pleased to know Enio is a fellow Italian too.'

'You didn't need to tell us. With a name like Enio we knew he was,' Pierro said laughing while giving him a friendly push in the arm.

Enio smiled but looked like he did it out of politeness rather than genuine feeling.

'So why the hell are you here man? This place is for crazy people.'

'Is that why your here?' said Enio with a smile.

'Very true!' piped in Pierro.

I laughed at his jibe. Getting my smoking materials from the drawer I sat down on my bed and preceded to role a fat juicy joint.

'So what's the story?' I asked.

'Hand me a bottle of beer and I will talk,' he sighed

Retrieving a bottle from under the bed I handed it across to him. He downed the bottle in one.

'Fucking hell you're thirsty,' I said whilst lighting my freshly rolled joint.

'Alan,' he said looking me square in the eye. 'Dominic's dead.'

'What?' I said taken aback coughing.

'They killed him Alan! They killed him!' he said putting his hands over his eyes as he snivelled.

For several minutes Enio was inconsolable with tears. Pierro and Cellistino looked uncomfortable. I waited patiently for him to regain his composure.

Taking in a big breath he eventually managed to stop himself from crying. After the tears he poured out the story surrounding Dominic's death. Although he spoke quickly in Spanish I understood every word and was shocked by it.

He told me the guards alleged Dominic died by committed suicide as they found him hanging in his cell. Enio however believes Dominic would never have done such a thing and that it was the guards who did it.

The guards said Dominic had done it as his father and mother had both recently died and he couldn't handle the grief. Enio said that this was not true. Although he was devastated about their deaths, Enio said he was still upbeat as he only had a few weeks to go till being released. This early release was partly due to the Spanish authorities reducing his sentence as both his mother and father had died.

Although he was being released early he still didn't show any mercy to the guards. In fact his campaign against their authority seemed to heighten. I mean when I knew him he was constantly being abusive, stirring up riots and damaging prison property. But Enio said after the death of his parents coupled with the fact he could not get leave to attend their funerals he became really riled up. Constantly he would play hell with the guards not caring about receiving a nasty beating at the end of each day. It was for this reason Enio believes the guard had enough and decided to take care of him. Whether it was a beating that got out of hand or they simply just hanged him he didn't know. But what he was certain of was that Dominic didn't kill himself. From what I knew of Dominic I would not have said it was in his nature to kill himself. And even if he did I couldn't see him doing it in the privacy of his own cell. He was sort of bloke to go out in a blaze of glory taking down as many guards as he could.

When Enio started asking questions and spreading suspicions to the other prisoners he was removed instantly and sent here. Enio was told that it was because they could see he was mentally unstable with grief. Enio however believes it was to get rid of him so as to not inflame any more tensions with the other prisoners. They wanted nobody else to take his claims seriously. So they sent him to a psychiatric hospital so his credibility would have come into question. Plus in the hospital it was very strict in regards to sending and receiving post. Even for me as a nurse everything I sent and received was scrutinised. I think the authorities did not want the outside world to know about the hospital and the goings on. It was a perfect place for keeping secrets.

Once he told me he let out a big sigh. It was as if he had been holding everything in until now. After he told his story he asked me about my life on Agitado's and was curious to know what I had been up too. I briefly gave an outline of what I did as a nurse here and about the pros and cons of the prison. He listened fascinated about what we did and were allowed to do. Although I told him about the drawbacks of the place he didn't seem to take that in. He just kept saying how lucky we were to smoke and drink freely without fear of raids. But I suppose as the saying goes the grass always looks greener.

At around 11 o'clock I could see Enio was flagging as he was sat on my bed slumped up against the wall constantly opening and closing his weary eyes.

'Time for bed?' I shouted.

'Yeah I think I need to get some sleep……….Take me to my cell then.'

I took him to a cell at the bottom of the corridor which I remembered had the nicest bed and a view out onto the patio. He would be both comfortable and have something to look out onto when he was alone in his room.

Straight away he dived on the bed and curled up into a fetal position. I was about to shut the door when Enio's shouted out my name.

'What?' I questioned.

'What the hell are these straps for?'

'Oh Enio you have a lot to learn about this place.'

'I will tell you in the morning,' I said nonchantly. 'Just get a good night's sleep.'

When I went back to my room Pierro, Celistino and I carried on our drinking and smoking session till just before midnight. When the witching hour struck we all decided to call it a night. But just as everyone departed from my room and I took my clothes off ready to hop into bed the fucking corridor bell sounded. Pissed off I put my still warm clothes back on and headed to the corridor. Cellistino and Pierro looked as equally displeased.

When the corridor door opened two guards appeared clutching onto a Spanish random. Pierro and I instinctively grabbed the guy by the arms and pulled him into the corridor. The guards informed us that the man was a drug dealer and quite violent. But that was nothing new. They explained how he had been caught with a large haul of drugs and wasn't happy on being found out. I could almost sympathise with the bastard.

The guards also asked if we needed their help, but we all declined. All three of us had bringing patients in down to a fine art. With a firm grip Pierro and I dragged the man down the corridor whilst Celistino opened the door of an empty cell. When the door closed and we moved him towards the bed the man started to wriggle. With a lot of fumbling we managed to pin him down to the bed with Pierro grabbing his left arm, me grabbing his right and Celistino holding onto his legs.

With a tight grip on his wrist with my left hand I reached out as I normally did for the strap at the top of the bed. But as the man jerked he managed to free his arm. With instant reactions I managed to grab his arm by the elbow. As I did this he began digging his nails into my face and scratched me over and over. Despite ripping my face to bits I managed to keep hold of his arm. Celistino then came over and pushed his wrist firm to the bed. I stepped out of the way and patted my face. I was covered in blood. When I looked over to Pierro he was white.

I watched as Celistino put on the last strap. He was now completely restrained.

'Fucking hell Alan you are covered in blood,' said Pierro as he pointed.

'I will be fine,' I said trying not to sound panicked.

When I went in my cell after, I too was shocked at the blood when I saw my reflection in my pocket mirror. However after dousing my face over and over with water I found it wasn't too bad. I did have plenty of scratches but none of them looked deep enough for stitches.

The next day we all agreed to teach the guy a lesson for gouging my face by leaving him strapped up till the following morning. He was to have no breakfast, dinner or tea. Not even a sip of fucking water. And as for toilet breaks, well he could just shit himself.

After leaving him for a day we all went in to have a chat with him. We warned him that if he tried to attack one of us again we would tie him to the bed again but this time we would leave him to the mercy of the guards. And as he well knew they had none. The guy nodded agreeing to behave but you could see a burning white hot hatred in his eyes. He also seemed to stare at me the most. Well he can stare all he wanted I was not going to be afraid of him. I didn't care if he thought he was a big bastard drug dealer he could bring it on.

As soon as I plonked down his tray of breakfast he attacked it like a ravenous dog. I felt bad in that moment. I had deprived a man of his freedom and rights to food and water. Was I just as bad as the guards? But he did need teaching a lesson. At least he didn't have to endure a Molotov cocktail.

After clearing up the breakfasts I noticed one of the spoons had gone missing. I had another look at all the trays and plates but it wasn't there. I also looked up and down the corridor to see if I had dropped it but I couldn't see anything.

When I took the patients on their morning break I found the spoon. It was in the possession of our newest patient the drug dealer who attacked me. With his back to the guards he was scraping the spoon on the floor. Intermittently he would stare at me with an evil scowl.

I had seen Spanish prisoners scraping cutlery on the floor in many prisons and knew they did it to create weapons. With the way he looked at me it was obvious he intended to stick the sharpened spoon into me. I walked past him to see how far he had got with the spoon. I had a crafty look so he wouldn't see me. From the quick glance I could see his weapon was quite benign and in the very early stages before becoming sharp and pointy. I could have said something to the guards in that instant I suppose but I decided to leave him for a few days with his spoon. At least it will keep him occupied.

After break I took my new drug dealer friend to the psychiatrist to be assessed. The psychiatrist asked me a few questions regarding the man's behaviour. One of the questions he asked was whether the patient had shown violence. I didn't answer and just pointed to my scratched face with a smile. The psychiatrist looked horrified.

'Did you do this?' the psychiatrist bellowed with anger.

The man was just about to open his mouth and say something when the psychiatrist launched over the table and slapped hard him across the face. I had never seen such a hard slap before. It shocked me that a highly trained professional psychiatrist could be reduced to such a thug.

The man looked frozen in shock as he touched his reddened cheek. I quickly ran over to the patient and held him down by his shoulders, just in case he tried to retaliate back. He did squirm a little but it was nothing I couldn't handle.

The psychiatrist then straightened his shirt and white coat and sat back down. As if nothing had happened he carried on questioning the man. I stood close to the side of the drug dealers chair just in case. Throughout the rest of the questioning the drug dealer shone an evil stare. I felt a little jealous as I thought he had only reserved that look for me. I wonder if he will create a new pointy spoon especially for the doctor.

That night the bell rang as it normally did but only one guard came up. He asked if one of us could go with him to retrieve the prisoner from the main doors. This was quite unusual as normally two or three guards would come up with the new patients. We had never been asked to collect them at the prison entrance before. I mean surely that was a bit of a security risk allowing us to be so close to the outside. Either they really had started to trust us or they needed my help. Maybe some of the guards were busy tending to a riot or hadn't turned up for night duty

Both Pierro and I volunteered, but the guards said there could only be one nurse. We argued amongst ourselves for a little bit until Pierro relented and said I could go.

I wanted to go and collect the patient for two reasons. One because to prove I was capable as I was little embarrassed with the incident with the drug dealer. Secondly I was curious to see the entrance of the prison and wanted to look at a possible means of escape.

Feeling excited I walked alongside the prison guard. As he was in charge of patrolling the entrance he was armed with a high powered rifle which was held around his body by a kind of sash. It was funny despite being a prisoner he never looked back at me with suspicious eyes. He simply walked beside me with his eyes forward. If I had a knife I could have so comfortably stabbed him in the back and relieved him of his gun.

After going through a few corridors we eventually came to the big prison entrance I vaguely remembered this when I was first dropped off. Just before the big doors and the large space for police vehicles there was a small flight of stairs. I was told to stay at the stop of the stairs whilst the guard stood ready on the second step down.

The guard still had his back turned to me and faced forward awaiting our new arrival. Several minutes ticked by. In that time I had planned an escape and visualised myself leaving the prison. Firstly I would stick a knife into the guard and render him unconscious or dead. Then I would take his uniform and his gun and attempt to walk out.

The guard in front started moving his head from side to side. I listened carefully and could hear the revving of an engine outside. Then without warning the large prison doors opened and quickly a police car parked in the large space in front of us. Then just as quickly as they were opened the big doors were shut again.

Once the van was stationary I could see it was bouncing from side to side, it was if it contained a severely pissed off lion. The police in front of the van on either side got out and slid open the van doors. They both went inside to retrieve the angry patient. The rocking of the van increased and whoever or whatever was inside was now really wound up. Minutes ticked by but no one materialised. The guard and I could only watch on as we heard much shouting and banging.

I could see the armed guard was a little nervous as he would crane his head in all directions to try and see what was going on. But it didn't matter how much he stretched his head he wouldn't be able to see. Giving up on trying to have a look he then shouted out to the police and asked if everything was alright but there was no answer. The only response he had was more banging, screaming and shouting.

I watched as the guard scratched his head as if in a quandary.

'Here! Here!' he shouted holding the gun in my direction whilst not looking at me.

Shocked I retrieved the gun and watched as he trotted down the steps towards the van. With the gun in my hands I froze in shock. I couldn't fucking believe it! All the escape attempts I had done over the years and here I was been handed a gun.

'Gracias!' I shouted down to the guard.

When the guard got to the bottom step I saw him freeze and whisper obscenities in Spanish. It was obvious he had realised what he had just done and with worried eyes turned round.

He quickly ran up the steps and held his hands out and asked for the gun back. It was funny to see his eyes so wide and scared. A bit shocked myself I looked down at the gun. Should I try and escape! Before I could contemplate further the gun was whipped out of my hands.

'Shush!' he said putting his finger to his mouth.

'No problems,' I said smiling trying not to laugh.

The man returned to his composed sentry position at the top of the stairs. By now the two policemen had got the patient out. I was gobsmacked by his size. He was over 6ft 5" and very stocky in frame. As I gawped at his cumbersome figure ambling up the stairs I thought to myself I should have let Pierro go.

On the way up the stairs he pushed and shoved the guards like they were rag dolls. I hung behind watching his actions still in ore of his immense presence. He seemed drunk as he swayed around unsteady on his feet and emanated overpowering fumes of alcohol.

Once the giant was up the stairs he was handed over to me and the guard. Summoning as much aggression as I could I nastily told the new patient through a variety of swear words in Spanish and dragged him with all of my force down the corridors. The armed guard also helped to push him along. When I got to Agitado's I was surprised at my strength of getting him there. He was vastly taller and bigger and considerably younger but I still managed to do it. It's amazing what a bit of adrenaline can achieve. Plus being drunk helped as he probably wouldn't have been able to coordinate his body enough to grab me.

In Agitado's I eased up a little as Pierro and Cellistino joined in with grabbing the man and proceeded to take him into a room. When inside he flopped on the bed. Pierro, Celistino and I held our stomachs and breathed in deeply after such a great exertion. Our new visitor also puffed hard, but it didn't look like he was tired. He looked scared and looked like he was breathing hard as he was hyperventilating.

After relaxing my breathing to a normal pace I realised looking in his eyes that the man wasn't to be feared. Despite trying to wrestle the policemen, the guards and me, I don't believe he wanted to hurt us. He looked more frightened than violent.

I slowly walked over to him. Pierro and Celistino whispered for me to get back but I ignored them and carried on. Although I was almost sure he was benign I was still a little hesitant as his massive frame was so imposing. Looking at his gorilla like hands I could just imagine with a few bops on the top of my head he could plant me in the ground like a fucking tent peg.

'Look it is okay,' I said in soothing tones. 'We are not going to hurt you.' I said putting my hands in the air.

The guy's frightened eyes turned into sorrow as he looked towards the floor.

'Why are you so upset?'

After a few seconds the man broke down into tears and sobbed like a child. Shocked I turned around to Pierro and Celistino. They both covered their mouths trying not to laugh. I was glad when I looked back at the man as he had his head in his hands. I had never seen them laugh at a patient before who was crying. But I think they did so because he was such a big lump. It seemed more out of place for him to show emotion. I also think it was a release as they were shitting themselves about how much damage the guy could have done.

When he composed himself he started explaining that he was from the Basque country and how he was from a wealthy and religious family. He said from an early age they were very strict with him and would readily hand out punishments. Now in his twenties he decided to rebel a bit against them by going out drinking and enjoying himself with friends. He tried to go out in secret but eventually his antics caught up with them. He promised to stop but just carried on again. But the thing that upset them the most was when they found he was cavorting with prostitutes. He explained that his parents only expected him to have relations with a girl if it meant a hand in marriage or children, not just for gratuitous sex. It was because of the prostitutes the parents decided to teach him a lesson by getting the courts to sentence him to prison. His parents had such a standing in Madrid and knew several legal people for this to be put in place.

Pierro, Celistino and I were astounded. We couldn't believe the poor sod had been put in this place for seeing prostitutes. It seemed such a heavy punishment. But I suppose to people who place great emphasis on religion and family this probably was horrendous to them. They also probably felt embarrassment as they were very well respected people in the community.

After a long chat the man seemed to calm down. He also started to have a laugh with us when we talked about sex and women. I found it funny that he had to frequent prostitutes to get sex as he was quite a good looking boy. Plus I bet a lot of women would have swooned at his tallness and stocky physique. However saying that he seemed a bit of a softie and I was betting a bit shy too. Maybe I should ask Pierro to give him a few tips as he was definitely a player.

The next few days were the happiest on Agitado's. Celistino and Pierro were great to work with and good fun in the nights. I also had the company of my old friend Enio and my new friend the Basque. They were both good boys to have a drink and a smoke with. The Basque also proved to be quite useful as a deterrent towards the other patients. I would tell the other patients that if they got out of line they would have to deal with me and then him. Not one of them misbehaved.

Senen was also the calmest I had ever seen him. Despite still being a bit of miserable git I could see him interacting more and more with me and the other patients. Each time I played music in the patio he still danced around as if it was a novelty. People kept complaining I was playing Queen far too often though, but I told them it was that or nothing. I did have other tapes but I liked to play Queen to get a reaction out of Senen. He would dance and sing to other songs, but it was mainly with Queen he would come alive.

The only patient I couldn't seem to win over was the drug dealer. There again I didn't really try with him. But if he wanted me to treat him favourably he was going to have to come to me. I already had one sulky belligerent git to contend with I wasn't having another bloody one. But he never came to me for help. He just kept himself to himself and carried on with the evil stares and sharpening his spoon.

After a week or so of lovingly scraping his spoon on the floor I could see he had made good progress. It was now pointy enough to do damage with. I decided now the time was right and told the guards. Instantly they went over and ripped the spoon out of his hands. They also roughed him up as a little punishment.

Afterwards I shone a smile at the drug dealer and he stared back with hate. He seemed so angry that he didn't get to try out his pointy stick.

After a few days the Basque left and so did the drug dealer. The Basque went back home and the drug dealer was sent to another ward. I was glad the Basque wasn't sent on as although in his mid-twenties and huge in frame I doubted he had the strength in character to be released with some of the disturbed freaks we had in here. With the drug dealer I couldn't give a shit. He could get raped and killed for all I cared.

When the Basque was moved I instantly went to ask the doctors about where Enio was to be sent. They said Enio was still deeply disturbed about his friend's death and they were looking at an appropriate ward to put him on. This worried me as I didn't think Enio should be put on a ward. He was a nice and rational guy. His psychosis I believed was a short term thing involving grief and anger. No way should he be permanently here.

I told Pierro to come with me to see the psychologist so as to enlist her help. Like a shot he came with. I do genuinely believe he wanted to help Enio but having a chance to flirt with her was a bonus too. I was surprised to find he was quite behaved with his words and actions. I was glad of this as she could take us more seriously without him slobbering all over her. I explained to her about Enio and about Dominic's death. I told them his psychosis was temporary and due to grief. To my surprise she agreed with me and said that she felt that with time he could leave the hospital. The only reason why they were keeping him in the hospital was because Enio himself said he wasn't ready. She said if he agrees he is ready then they could do more about moving him. I couldn't believe it. Why had he said he wanted to stay? Who in their right mind would want to stay here? Maybe he was fucking mad?

To find out if it was true I shot back to the corridor and went into Enio's room to ask. I found him dozing on the bed.

'Enio get up!'

'Gees Alan can't you knock.'

'Look Enio you don't get it do you. I am a nurse. You are a patient. I could come into your room at any time.'

'What are you on about?' he said rubbing his eyes whilst stretching his shoulders.

'I have just been to the psychologist and she has said to me you want to stay in the hospital.'

'Yeah that' right.'

'But Enio it is not safe here.'

'Well I have been having a good time so far.'

'Yes because you are with me.'

'If you go to another ward they won't be as nice as me.'

'I treat you like a friend. But they will treat you like a patient. You will only be allowed out for an hour a day and won't be given alcohol or cannabis in the nights.'

'You don't know that.'

'Yes I do.'

Enio looked to the floor in contemplation. I think it was finally sinking in what I had been telling him over the past few weeks. I hated shouted at him and telling him to leave but it was the only way.

'What about Senen? He is allowed to stay.'

'That is because he is completely nuts and he can't be trusted on another ward.'

'Enio you know I am right. Please get out of here.'

'Can you leave me to have a sleep please?' Enio said with no emotion.

'Okay man,' I said softly. 'Look Enio I would love you to stay you know I would.'

Enio turned over and closed his eyes. I couldn't say anymore and just left him to have a sleep. I told Pierro and Celistino that it was true what the psychologist said and that Enio wanted to stay. They were more shocked than me, but didn't seem to care as much. They just said I should respect his wishes. But there was no way I was doing that.

That night I invited Enio into my room. To my surprise he did come in for a few joints and drinks, but he wasn't his usual jovial self. I could tell what I said had weighed heavy on his mind. Despite being distracted he still managed to chatter along with Pierro, Celistino and I.

To liven the atmosphere I went over to my tape player and pawed through my cassettes for something to put on.

'Oh god please not fucking Queen again!' shouted Celistino.

'Nah Senen's not here so I don't have to put that on.'

'Alan before you put some music on I want to talk to you all.'

'Okay.'

'Look Alan I have decided to take your advice and tell the doctors I am ready to leave.'

'That's wonderful news! I will be sorry to see you go though.'

'I just wanted to say thank you for helping me,' he said whilst his eyes misted up.

He stood up and shook Celistino's hand and then Pierro's. He headed over to me and shook my hand too but we both reached in for a hug. I slapped him hard on the shoulder and then retreated back.

'I wish you could stay,' I said.

'I know,' he said choked up with tears. 'Right carry on with the music.'

A few days later Enio was collected by the guards and taken to another prison. They didn't tell me where, but I hoped it was El Dueso. That was the best prison I found to stay in. The only place I didn't want him to end up in was Cadiz but I couldn't see them doing that. I mean it would only stir up bad memories and he would probably want to kill the guards who he had thought killed Dominic.

It was hard to watch Enio leave Agitado's. He was such a great guy and friend. Someone who could boost you just by giving you a smile. I wished the guards hadn't warned me he was going and had just taken him. I hated goodbyes. I tried not to cry as I waved him off through the corridor.

Although I was sad I had to remember it was for the greater good. He could no longer stay in the hospital. He needed go to a normal prison where he could live life without being drugged up and surrounded by dangerous nutters.

The next lot of patients we seemed to get in didn't seem to be bothered about being befriended. They were quite happy to keep themselves to themselves. They just saw me as a nurse and not a friend. I didn't mind this as it became hard to get close to people only just to see them go. Plus it was also annoying to seeing them leaving and been left behind myself. I knew they were going to another prison or ward, but it still hit home how much I just wanted to be free.

When Christmas came round I was quite shocked. I had been in Carabanchel for well over a year. It hadn't seemed that long, but I suppose

I was constantly busied by my nursing duties and the night time visits from the guards. Christmas day was like any other day when in prison. Well except my Mam bless her would give me a few gifts in the post. They were always very much appreciated.

If it wasn't for my mother's gifts and watching people writing Christmas cards I wouldn't have known about it. I rarely looked at a calendar to see what day it was. I just didn't see the point counting down the days to my sentence. I knew roughly how much I had left and I was happy at that.

Unlike the other prisons Carabanchel did make a little bit of an effort to celebrate Christmas for the prisoners, as we would get more food than usual and we would get a pudding. Plus you would also get to visit the director and get a free glass of wine. Being cheeky I had two glasses. On the second time after queuing back up and seeing him, he looked perturbed. You could see he was trying to ascertain as if he had seen me before, but before he could decide I had already downed the glass. On the third time though he wasn't to be fooled and didn't even pour out a glass for me. He took it in good spirits though as he laughed when he pointed me to the door.

Just as quickly as Christmas dawned the New Year was upon us. It was 1982 which marked my fourth year in prison. Although the New Year is meant to be a time of new beginnings and reflecting on past events of the last year. I didn't see it this way. I just felt stuck. I didn't want to look back as I didn't want to think about the things I had seen and done. I didn't want to look forward as all I could see was more time in prison. A few days into January I did start to feel a little better. I slapped myself in the face over and over and told myself to pull it together. If I carried on getting depressed I knew I would crack up and I didn't want that, especially here. Any sign of psychosis or neurosis I would be marched straight down to the medical staff. Then I would probably be drugged up and put on a ward. Then my time out of here would be decided by the professionals. Which probably would have meant a far longer prison stay. It takes a lot to convince the professionals you are fit enough to leave the hospital let alone the prison. A large number of patients that were in here I knew would never ever get out despite serving out their sentence. Manuel Villegas Delguardo being one and he wasn't even sentenced. But he was a scum bag and serial killer nonetheless so he definitely deserved it in my eyes.

In comparison to my miserable self Pierro was full of joy around Christmas and New Year. He even joked about getting mistletoe and putting it over the psychologist's head. I don't know whether he did this or not but I wouldn't have put it past him.

I remember on one particular day in January his happiness really got to me as he danced around the corridor doing jazz hands and tapping his feet. A really jolly guy is something you don't really want when you're feeling down.

'Don't do that Pierro you look like a fruit?' I snapped

'I can't help it Alan I am so happy.'

'What's to be happy about?'

I have been given some excellent news.'

'What?'

'Guess?'

37 A TIME FOR GOODBYES

I shone Pierro a look of annoyance as I didn't want to play his guessing game.

'Come on Alan,' he said jabbing me with a playful punch in the arm. 'Guess!'

Although my heart wasn't in it I decided to play along and guess. I scratched my chin and tried to think of what could have made Pierro so happy. Looking into his excitable eyes I couldn't help but smile. His energy was becoming infectious.

'You have got a visitor.'

'No no it's better than that.'

'You got it on with the psychologist?'

'That would be good! But no it's not that.'

'Oh Pierro just tell me!'

'Okay okay,' he said still smiling. 'Well the reason I am so excited is because I am going.'

'What to another ward?'

'No!' he said laughing. 'Home stupid.'

'Wow. That is amazing,' I said genuinely pleased. 'When?'

'They haven't given me the exact date yet but it will be in the next few days or weeks I should imagine.'

'Oh man that is great news,' I said giving him a hug.

'I know! I worked it out to be months away.'

'I tell you what Alan coming to Agitado's was definitely the best thing I could have done. Just think if I didn't come here I could have been in prison twice as long.'

I looked to the floor a little glum. I was happy for Pierro to be going but I was also upset that I was staying. Pierro could sense this and put his arm on my shoulder.

'Look Alan you will be going soon. I can feel it. It won't be long.'

I nodded.

'I was only in Ceuta weeks before you.'

'I suppose.'

'Right I am off to tell Celistino.'

I watched as he skipped down the corridor excitedly humming a merry tune. It must have been an Italian number as I had never heard it before.

That morning Pierro's news provoked positivity into both Celistino and myself. We decided that night we were going to drink far more than we usually did to celebrate the occasion. I also asked the kitchen staff if they could bring in a large leg of pork. Normally I would give them a few days to get one in but today I asked if they could get any in by the night. They weren't confident they could bring it in but they said they will see what they can do.

This positivity poured onto the patients as well as they too seemed jovial. Well everyone apart from Senen. He was having a particularly bad day and hardly spoke to me. He also refused to put his dungarees on. I practically had to wrestle him to put them on so he could go in the patio. All those weeks and weeks of befriending him and making him feel like a person had gone through the window. He was like a brick wall again.

In the afternoon break I tried to cheer him up by putting on Bohemian Rhapsody, but even this song didn't turn anything in him. He just sat down on the floor playing with a couple of stones. Although he was ignoring everyone I did manage to catch him glimpsing at me when I put some washing out on a line in the yard and when I spoke to Pierro. I wondered then whether he was just doing it for attention.

At tea time I was happy to see that the cook had managed to bring in a big leg of pork. Feeling hungry I picked it up and chewed the meat straight off the bone like a ravenous animal. I then sliced off cuts and shared them out with Celistino, Pierro and the patients. I put the biggest slice on Senen's plate as I thought this might cheer him up.

When I went into Senen's room he was sat in the corner with his back to the door. His naked back used to turn me as you could see every nodule of his spine poking out. I walked over and put the tray of food behind him. I could see him sniffing in the air appreciating the smell of the food, but he wouldn't switch his gaze from the wall. What a sulky fucking bastard!

'Hey Senen I have brought you some pork.'

Senen breathed in deeply and folded his arms in defiance.

'What is wrong with you?' I bellowed with annoyance.

'You grumpy old goat!'

I waited a few moments but he still didn't turn round. In the end I decided to leave him to it. I didn't have time for his sulks. I needed to hand out the rest of the dinners and then have mine. I wasn't going to let my food get cold just because he was in a grouch.

Trying to forget Senen's miserable face I tucked into my dinner and extras of pork. I washed it all down with a bottle of beer. I didn't normally drink so early but I was in celebration mode for Pierro. Once I finished I quickly went round the patients collecting their empty plates of food.

Everyone polished off their teas and portions of pork. Well everyone apart from Senen. He had managed to finish off his tea but the big portion of pork was still in one piece and looked like it hadn't been touched. That really hurt! I had gone to great fucking lengths and expense to get that pork. I even gave him the biggest portion and this is what he does. The only way he could have upset me more was if he had took a shit on it.

'Not hungry,' I said sarcastically.

Senen didn't speak but shone me a scowl.

'I am sick of your fucking games Senen. Don't eat my pork see if I fucking care,' I said angry not realising how gay this sounded.

I put Senen to the back of mind for the night and celebrated with Celistino and Pierro. Although we drank and smoked every night, tonight we seemed to crank it up a notch. The bottles of beer were higher in volume and the joints were bigger and fuller. The music was louder and the laughs were aplenty.

It was a relatively quiet night on the corridor when we periodically checked as none of the patients acted up and we only had one new patient join the ward half way through the party. The new patient was pretty good in behaviour too as he wasn't violent and didn't cry. We just stuck him in his room as he seemed to settle down quite easily. I don't think we could have coped with a live wire with how pissed we were. But despite being rat arsed I did think we were quite professional with the new patient as we could have so easily laughed at his pair of tits and the dress he was wearing.

I mean the guy didn't even look funny as a woman. He pulled off looking feminine rather well, but I think as we were so drunk we just saw him as a man in a dress. He did however make me feel uneasy. In fact most transvestites in prison made me feel uncomfortable. It got me to thinking how easy it would be to accidentally pick one up from a club, especially with a little alcohol inside.

What I did find funny about him was his accent as he was Dutch because he came from Amsterdam. I had grown so used to hearing mainly Spanish, Moroccan and Italian voices, his sounded completely out of this world.

Despite his boobs, his feminine clothing and funny accent we all manage to keep our laughs at bay. Well until we all piled into Pierro's room, then the titters came flooding out. All in all it was a very good night.

The next morning I was punished for the debauchery of last night as I had the hang over from hell. It was one of those mornings where I instantly regretted how much I drank, ate and smoked. My stomach muscles were also tight from the laughter too. I felt better when I saw Pierro and Celistino though, they looked far worse.

Feeling so ill made the day feel like a lifetime. I didn't even utter a word to anyone as I was afraid the strain of talking would make me vomit. I was glad that everyone in the ward was contented. I couldn't have handled splitting a fight up between the patients. The only way I could have diffused it was by being sick on them.

Eventually the late evening dawned. As I put the last of the tea trays on the trolley I felt so relieved. Now I could sit in my room and relax. Pierro offered for me to come into his room but I wanted some space. I wanted some down time.

After a few hours I grew bored. My headache had finally gone and my stomach ceased gurgling. My stomach muscles were still tense but I could live with that.

Bored I paced the room and put my music on. I stroked Marrakech for a while, who was curled up my bed approaching sleep. She looked so happy and comfortable.

'If only I could be content like you babes.'

Hearing my voice she opened her right eyelid a little, but then closed it again into two tight little slits.

Bored I knocked on Senen's door. I decided to put my energies into finding out why he's been a particularly grumpy git of late. A few seconds later I opened up the hatch. When I looked through I could see he was sat on the floor naked with his legs scrunched up to his chest resting his head on his knees. I knew he knew I was looking at him. There was no way he wouldn't have heard me opening the hatch. He just didn't have the grace to give me eye contact. Bastard!

When I opened the cell and entered his room he still ignored me and carried on staring out the cell window. Part of me wanted to slam the door and leave him, but I decided I couldn't put up with insolence for much longer. I needed to find what I had done wrong. By refusing my pork it was obviously something I had done to upset him and it must have been quite a big misdemeanour as he never failed to eat his food.

'Senen you coming into my room?'

'Do I have too?'

'No but I thought you would like too,' I snapped.

Senen didn't answer and let out a big sigh.

'Are we friends or what?'

'Are we?' he snarled.

'What is that supposed to mean?'

He just stared at me for a few seconds and then buried his head in his hands. God he made me feel so angry. There were so many times I could have smacked him in the face. After all I have done for this sod and he questions my friendship. Being friends with him was worse than going out with a woman with PMT.

I found it funny to think that Senen was my patient and I could control his freedom, when he eats, when he drinks, when he has his medication etc, but despite all this I think I was the one who felt the most powerless. All I wanted for him was to be healthy and happy. Well as much as one can be in here.

'Come on Senen we are friends. Come to my room and tell me what's wrong,' I said warmly.

Senen popped his head up. I opened the door and pointed outside. To my surprise he stood up and walked over.

Once we were in the room I handed over his green dungarees. Thankfully he put them on and my bed was still free from the touch of another man's bollocks.

At first I started the conversation. I wittered on and on hoping that he would either join in or tell me to shut up. I didn't care which, I just wanted a reaction. I only concentrated on light hearted topics at first to see if I could influence a better mood and interaction. But I was to be disappointed as throughout the entire time I spoke he just stared ahead preoccupied with his thoughts. With pouty lips and a stony face he wasn't budging from his foul mood.

Not getting anywhere I decided to just come out and ask him what was wrong. I had tried the softly softly approach and that didn't work, so maybe if I tackled it straight on we could get to the root of the matter. Then later maybe I could be jovial with him.

Not knowing how to phrase my questions I paused for a few minutes and disappeared into my own internal dialogue. I pondered on how I could ask him what was wrong. I needed to make sure I did it correctly so I could provoke him and get him to open up. Senen was like a fucking hedge puzzle if you didn't start on the correct fucking path you will never ever solve where the end is. All you will do is trudge in the murky undergrowth and be just as lost as you were in the beginning. Fortunately I didn't have to be cunning as the silence was enough to encourage Senen to talk.

'Alan.'

'Yes.'

'When is Pierro going?'

'How did you know that?' I said astonished.

'I heard you two talking in the corridor the other day.'

'I was going to tell you but I didn't bother because you were in such a bad mood. I didn't think you would listen.'

'Really?' he said sarcastically whilst arching his dark eyebrow in disbelief.

'Yes,' I said angered. 'Why would I keep that from you?'

Senen didn't answer and just looked to the floor with his big sad brown eyes.

'Are you going to miss him?'

'No!'

'Hey don't be like that Senen I know you liked Pierro. He is a good guy.'

'I suppose.'

'But when you go I will miss you more,' he said whilst staring me straight in the eyes.

Senen's comment sent me into a stupor. I was a bit dazed that he said he would miss me. Never had he ever said anything nice to me. Let alone thanked me for any of my gifts or help, and now he was showing me he cared. But despite his words being warm it did make me feel uneasy as he said it in such a dead pan way. His eyes were also disturbing as they seem to change from dark brown to black. I had to turn away as my unease heightened the more I looked into his dark sad pools.

'Don't worry I won't be going for a while yet,' I said grabbing his shoulder.

'You will though Alan. You will.'

'Look Senen I don't know that.'

'Like Pierro said you should be gone within a few weeks of him.'

'Err……well………….you don't know that.'

'And I will be left behind.'

'There will be other nurses Senen. You won't be on your own.'

'They don't care!'

'Well they would if you were a little bit nicer to people.'

'What's the point?' he said throwing his hands in the hair.

'What can I do to make you feel better?'

'If you really want to help me………………..' he said smiling.

'Yes?'

'You can give me what Manuel has.'

'But he hasn't got anything…… He is dead.'

'That is what I want. I want to be dead.'

'We have talked about this. You are far too young and healthy to die. If you only eased up on yourself you could be released and do whatever you wanted.'

'Alan if I am released you know I will kill my mother and her sister.'

'No you won't.'

'Oh yes I fucking will. And then after killing them I will kill myself anyway.'

'I don't understand why?'

'You need to help kill me Alan. I know sooner or later my mother will have me out of here. If I died now no one else has to.'

'I will not kill you Senen.'

'Please! I need peace!' he begged whilst grabbing my wrists and falling into a flood of tears.

'I am sorry Senen I can't.'

Senen wiped the tears from his eyes and looked dead ahead.

'Look Senen we will have a word with the doctors. Let's see if they can help you see a way through this. I will help you as much as I can.'

'Talking! Talking! I don't need that,' he said laughing.

'There is only one way,' he said smiling.

'I can't!'

'You can stop the deaths of my Mama and Auntie. I know you don't want to see them dead too.'

I gulped hard. How could he be so cold about his family?

'If you were my friend Alan you would help find me a way to die,' he said clutching on to my wrist again.

'I can't,' I said knocking his hand off mine.

With that he left. I followed him out in the corridor and watched as he went in his room. He didn't even say goodbye. He just sat on the floor. I said goodnight and shut the door. I stood at the door for a few moments wondering whether I should go back in. From outside the door I could hear him muttering to himself. I decided to leave him be. He was wound up enough already.

In the morning I was shocked to find Senen was in a good mood. He was also very well behaved and didn't destroy any furniture and put on his dungarees without question. However when I brought him in my room for a few hours in the night he still asked me again to help him die. When I said no he didn't get upset and allowed me to talk about something else.

For the next few days he continued to ask the same thing when I had him in my room for a couple of hours in the night. He would indulge me in a bit of chit chat but then soon enough he would ask again. Each day the chit chat would become less and the begging to die would start up faster.

I was beginning to loathe bringing him in the nights as I knew he was going to ask the same thing, but I persisted as I wanted to try and get through that life was worth living for. The ironic thing was Senen seemed a lot happier despite asking of me such an awful thing. His improved behaviour and seemingly happier state of mind was commented on by everyone. Little did Pierro, Celistino, the psychologist, the psychiatrist and the doctors know he was telling me he wanted to kill himself and that his happiness was because he seemed to have a misconceived idea I would help him. I didn't tell the doctors, psychologists or psychiatrists about his expressed wish to die as I knew they would confront Senen about it. If they did then I doubted Senen would ever confide in me again. They did have an inkling, as in his notes he was marked up as high risk in hurting himself and was to be constantly watched.

In the courtyard one afternoon Pierro and Celistino were talking. They had been talking to the other nurses from the bigger patio. They were on about another a mysterious death on one of the wards. From the prison rumour mill it was said the guards had gone to town on him and he died from internal injuries. I could see Senen was listening to the conversation.

As I stared at him he looked down then stared back. With his finger he made a cutting mark across his neck. This sickened me. Even talking to my fellow nurses I couldn't escape the constant drumming noise of his suicidal thoughts.

That night I didn't bring Senen in for a chat. I had an excuse anyway as I was busied by the guards bringing us in another patient for us to look after. Although he was Spanish in origin he looked so pale and drained in colour. If it wasn't for his head lolling and his eyes rolling I would have assumed he was dead. I thought Senen was skinny but this guy was incredibly gaunt and thin. Even Pedro who had cancer had more meat on him.

This obviously wasn't his normal stature as I could see his clothes hanging off him. He looked like he had lost a lot of weight recently and fast. I did originally think cancer but it wouldn't have made sense to bring him here. It seemed a lot of effort for him to be brought here to die as the morgue was corridors away. They couldn't have wanted that surely.

They dragged the man to a spare room. I felt sickened by their aggression as they didn't need to be so forceful with him. You could see he was weak and would cause no threat. It was obvious this guy had seriously pissed them off as they snarled at him whilst dragging him along the corridor. Despite the man looking ill I could see in his eyes stubbornness. He reminded me a little of Senen.

I peered through the door as they threw him onto the bed. The frail man smiled as he stared blankly at the ceiling.

'Oi!' shouted the guard.

The man did not grant any eye contact and continue staring upwards. The guard became incensed by his ignorance and slapped the man hard across the face. The man turned his head with the slap but didn't react, despite the fact the thwack from the force sounded like it really would have stung.

'Alan,' shouted the guard to me.

'Yes!'

'Strap him to the bed.'

I obeyed the guard. It was only me in the room as Pierro and Celistino were busy comforting a distressed prisoner who had just come in so I had to do the straps myself. I didn't mind as I had the guards around and the guy seemed quite frail to put up any sort of a fight. The man was completely obedient and even held out his arms for me to strap him. It was as if he wanted to be tied up. Not for any kinky reason I don't think, but it was as if he was making a stand against something. Throughout strapping him he continually stared at the ceiling. He had an air of defiance about him. I would have loved to know what he was thinking. After putting on the final strap the guard beckoned me to the door.

'Alan this guy is refusing to eat.'

'Why?'

'Never mind why just tell me if he eats anything tomorrow.'

'Oh……..Okay.'

'Also try if you can to make him eat.'

'Is he is ill?'

'No………..he is just being a cock.'

Once the guards left I tried to speak to the thin patient but he would not cooperate, like with Senen he closed himself off. Looking back at it now and researching into Carabanchel prison this man could have been a Basque terrorist as they were prolific when it came to hunger strikes and protesting over incarceration and prison conditions. Whatever his reason I admired him. I doubted I could ever give up my food for any cause. Fair play

The next day and night the man didn't eat anything I gave him. He didn't even care that I released the strap for him to eat. I waited a while but he didn't even look at the food. I could see he was hungry though as he gulped hard and tried to screw up his nose so he couldn't smell the delicious scent. It was obvious his body craved it but his mind wouldn't give in.

I tried to coax the man by putting some food on a spoon and putting it to his lips, but he simply turned his head to the side. I wrestled with his head to try and keep it still so I could put the spoon to his lips. Then he looked me in the eyes and shouted no. He kept his free hand near the straps and continually asked for me to strap him back up. It was as if he didn't trust himself if he had one hand free.

I agreed to strap him but continued to try and get him to eat. I even prised open his mouth and managed to spoon in a bit of food. I smiled at him as I managed to get some in but the man stared back with vitriol and spat the mouthful towards the wall.

'No,' he shouted and went back to staring at the wall in rage.

'Please eat! I fear what the guards may do tonight if you don't.'

'I don't care!'

I decided enough was enough. It was obvious he wasn't budging from his protest. Whatever he was campaigning for he looked prepared to give up his life. But only time would tell now if he dies from hunger or via a beating with the guards. Either option was bleak but this didn't seem to worry the guy.

That night I brought Senen into my room. I wanted to take my mind off the skinny man and what the guards were going to do. It didn't work though as I found myself drifting off after speaking a few words. Senen could even see I wasn't myself as every time I drifted off in my own thoughts I would come back to find he was staring at me in bewilderment. This felt good for a change. He was wondering what I was thinking. Well good enough for the bastard. He has had me in knots trying to fathom his fucking mind out. Let him be puzzled for a change.

'I heard you talking in the yard,' said Senen

'What do you mean? What about?'

'Another death,' he smiled.

'Oh that.......Yes a patient had died.'

'The guards did it. Didn't they?'

'Well that is what they are saying.'

'When Pierro goes and you go. I will die that way.'

'Oh Senen stop please. I have had a rough day please don't talk about this nonsense.'

'No Alan I mean it. I will die. If you aren't going to help me. I will have to do it myself.'

'How?'

'I will get the guards to beat me up.'

'Senen the guards won't touch you.'

'Well if they won't I will just have to eat broken glass then.'

'Broken glass? You can't do that.'

'If it's the only way.'

'If you were a friend you would make it more peaceful.'

'Right that's it Senen I have had enough get out.'

'Why Alan? The truth too hard to take my friend'

With that I grabbed him by his dungaree strap and shoved him in his room. After slamming the door shut, I gently rubbed my temples as I could feel a headache coming on. God this job was fucking stressful!

I pushed open my door craving a lie down in the dark when the bell rang and the wild bunch marched into the corridor. A doctor also followed behind carrying a doctor's bag tubing and a jug of milky solution.

'Did he eat?' barked the head guard.

I paused a while. I didn't want to say yes as I didn't know what punishment lay in store for him. But I couldn't say no as he needed nourishment. After much deliberation I shook my head.

'Come with us then.'

Great not only had I condemned the poor man to punishment I also had the fucking privilege to watch. Normally I was told to go to my room and granted privacy from their torture. But no tonight I had front row tickets!

Once inside they vilified him. They asked him several times if he was going to be a good boy and eat. The man point blankly refused. Then the guards started warning him that if he didn't he would be force fed. Although looking shit scared now, the man continued to shake his head.

'Right that's it!' screamed the head guard.

The man on the bed shook with terror as the head guard leaned on the bed with one knee and hung over him. The patient turned his head pushing his right ear as far into the bed as possible whilst clamping his lips shut. He was breathing so quick I could practically see his lungs popping out of his sallow chest.

The guard on the bed then steadied himself and yanked the man's head so his face was facing forward. The prisoner eyes stared at the guard wildly in fright. When the guard grabbed his hair in his right hand and freed his left the patient closed his eyes. You could see he was expecting a punch to the face or some sort of strike. But no punches were thrown. Instead the guard pulled on his head so it tilted backwards. The doctor then approached carrying the tubing. The patient squirmed. The other guard then with both hands clamped his head whilst the doctor on the bed tried to find the end of the tubing. Then once with the end in sight he began shoving the hard plastic tubing up the patient's nose. I was shocked as I watched him force it down further and further. It squeaked as it rubbed on the inner gristle in his nose. As he continued forcing it down the patient gargled and screamed. I had to turn away as it looked so painful. It didn't help that the tubing was so thick. It didn't look like something they would use in a hospital. God knows where he had got that from.

The doctor strained as he continued to push and push the large tube down. Like a tap blood flowed freely from the man's nostrils. I was relieved when he had finished. Puffing and panting a little from the exertion the doctor took a minute to recover. The other guards just hovered over seemingly excited about the blood dribbling off the patient's chin. There was so much it collected in a sort of pool on his chest.

'Pass me the jug,' said the doctor.

The other guard gleefully picked up the large jug of milk from the floor and passed it across. With the jug in his hand he carefully took his knee off the bed whilst not allowing any of the milky solution to spill on the floor. He stretched in with his free hand and held the tube up.

'This is what you get for not eating,' screamed the head guard.

Then after a nod from the guard the doctor poured the solution in the tube in one swift movement. It went straight down in one right angular motion. I had never seen liquid disappear so fast in my life. The man gulped, gargled and spluttered as the solution had gone down. More blood pumped from the man's nose as he gasped for breath. Some blood also oozed from the corner of his mouth, along with some dribbles of milky solution. But the majority of the white liquid had gone down his throat. This wasn't surprising with how fast the guards poured it. He looked shocked and started coughing as if some of the liquid had gone down his wind pipe rather than his oesophagus. The guard let go of the tubing and watched as the patient struggled to breathe. As the patient moved his head back and fore the end of the tube in his nose leaked milky drops.

Once the patient stopped writhing the doctor with great force ripped

ALAN "DOGS" JONES by ANITA HUGHES

out the piping with a clenched fist. Despite yanking hard it took three attempts to pull it all out. More and more blood oozed from the patients nose. The patient continued to gasp for breath and cough up blood.

'Alan let us know if he doesn't eat tomorrow,' said one of the guards.

'Er.........okay.'

'We will just have to do the same again.'

'He will soon learn.'

I nodded. I couldn't speak. I was too shocked at what they had done. I know the man needed food but the way they did it was so barbaric. They could have put him on a drip. But maybe that was too much hassle. They didn't care about compassion after all, only quick solutions. It was probably a bonus that it inflicted misery. I knew the guards were mean but I couldn't believe the doctor's hand in all of this!

After collecting a medical kit from my room I went back to see the prisoner. He was now coughing less and was breathing more normally. He was no longer spluttering and gargling. Whilst I mopped up the blood he never looked at me once. He just looked at the wall saddened and disheartened. The only sound I could hear was his stomach bubbling with activity. It must have been excited to have had some sort of nourishment after days or possibly weeks without. The sound of the acid dissolving the solution sounded like a cross between an angry gremlin and daffy duck.

After I finished cleaning him up I tried to talk to him and comfort him but he shook his head and didn't speak back. He just stared ahead as if filled with sorrow. He looked defeated. He knew his protest was now over and the guards had won. Futility seemed to ebb from every part of him. He had lost the fight.

Over the next few days I was glad to see he ate food. Well he knew the consequences if he didn't. He didn't eat lots as there would be food left over each time I took a tray. His stomach and mind were probably getting used to eating again. After two days he was allowed to be unstrapped from the bed. I felt nervous for him when he made his first few steps as he looked like he was going to collapse. He didn't though; he cleverly used the wall to prop him up as he walked. In his eyes he looked dead though.

It was a slow process but I managed to get the man outside into the patio. I thought a bit of fresh air and interaction would make him happier. But all he did was lean against the wall and look sad. A few metres away Senen was propped up against the wall too. He too looked as equally miserable. They were like two depressed book ends. Both had lost their souls and fight to Carabanshel. I turned away from them as I couldn't look at them anymore. They were both drawing me into their morbid world. They may have given up but I hadn't. I wasn't going to be dragged to their depths of despair. But it was too late the two miserable bastards had got to me. I began to slip into a mood. I found it hard to get out of bed and I also felt lethargic completing my daily duties. I used to buzz around the hospital and do my jobs quickly but now they were becoming a struggle. Pierro and Celistino weren't in the best of spirits either. Celistino was upset that Pierro would be gone soon and Pierro was down as he had heard no more news about his release. You could see the wait was killing him as he went through the motions with me like a drone.

Then just as it was raining shit on me the next day Pierro brought me even sadder news. I can see him now racing down the corridor with something important to tell me.

'Alan! Alan!' he shouted.

'What's wrong?'

'I have some bad news.'

What's happened? I thought he might have been joking around and that he was coming to say goodbye before leaving, but if that were true he was a good actor as his eyes were filled sorrow. I took a deep breath in and prepared myself for the worst. From what I had seen in Carabanchel I was expecting rape, torture or death of an inmate who I liked.

'I am afraid you will have to give up Marrakech,' he said.

'What? Why?' I said shocked by his revelation.

Of all the things he could have said I had never expected this. What had my poor pussy done? She was the only thing that gave me comfort in such a wretched place.

'Look I don't know why but management have decided to get rid of the cats.'

'I don't care I am keeping her. I can hide her.'

'Look Al if they find her the guards will kill her and you can't keep her in your room forever. That's not fair.'

I knew what Pierro was saying made sense. It wasn't fair to imprison her. Plus she was a determined little thing, I knew one slip of concentration and she would be out of my cell. She then would be at the mercy of the guards, which is very worrying seeing as they didn't have any. I could see them easily breaking her poor neck or filling her with bullet holes. I couldn't have had that. She was my darling.

'I have heard they will start rounding the cats up in the next two days from Ralph.'

'Thanks for letting me know,' I said.

That day I locked Marrakech in the room. I also informed Antoine the breeder of my cat about the cat cull, as he had a few. He too looked equally perturbed.

For the next two days I petted Marrakech within an inch of her life. Hugging and stroking her as I prepared myself to say goodbye. I also made sure she had a good send off as I bought the finest fresh meat and fish from the staff in the kitchens. It was hard to look at her squinting with her eyes and turning up her cheeks as if she was smiling.

'Oh Marrakesh babes I shall miss you. I can't believe I have to say goodbye. But I can't keep you here forever my precious. Maybe it's for the best. Here is no place for a sweet animal like you. Just a wretched one like me!'

With that I put her in a box pierced with holes. Inside I put with her some scraps of pork to keep her satisfied. Trying not to look shifty I quickly ran from corridor to corridor with my pussy in a box. On my journey to Augustin's ward no guard's questioned the box. Even the guard outside Augustin's ward didn't bat an eyelid and simply let me into the corridor whilst he nodded respectfully at my white coat which I had pinched off Hans. When the door closed I found myself alone on the ward. I looked around at the five doors and reminisced. It seemed such a long time ago since I had been in here. Well in fact nearly over a year. Maybe it would have been better if I stayed. I doubted much torture, rape and death went on here. The only downside was deflecting Augustin's amorous ways of which I could have dealt with knowing what I know now about Agitado's. However it was too late now. I had my responsibilities. I had Senen to look after. With that my kitten gave out a cry. She must have finished her meat and now wanted freedom. Shush my little pet. You soon shall be free.

I knocked on Augustin's door. He opened it and was taken aback with shock. He mustn't have heard the guard letting me in. Then with a perverted gaze he looked me up and down. A big wide grin splayed across his face as he squeezed my arm. Feeling utterly repulsed I moved away my arm whilst also trying to keep the box steady.

'Is that a present for me?'

'No.'

'Oh.'

'Well sort of. I do need you to keep it for me.'

With that I put the box down and opened it. Tentatively Marrakesh poked her head out and looked all around the room. She looked nervous at her strange surroundings. She then looked at Augustin and back at me. After a few seconds she put her paw up on the edge of the box gently and sniffed the air.

'Look at her Augustin isn't she beautiful?'

'I suppose but I don't really like cats,' he said nonplussed.

'I don't really like animals at all,' he said with one hand on his hip and the other under his chin.

I scowled at him. I was upset that Augustin didn't look at her with adoring eyes as I did. I began to rethink whether it was the right thing to bring her to him. Although he was more educated than the majority of the Spanish I had met he still seemed to have cruel streak. Would he be like the boys in Santander and think nothing of plucking her fur and eating her like a common farm yard animal? I hope not for his sake.

'Look sorry Alan I can see she is pretty.'

'Good!' I barked.

'So why have you brought the cat to me?'

'I need you to take Marrakesh.'

'Why?'

'Because the guards are going to get rid of all the cats in the next few days.'

'And you want me to hide her?'

'No you fool I want you to take her home.'

'Home?'

'Yes. You have a weekend visit planned for tomorrow don't you?'

'Err...........yes,' he said with reluctance.

'Well I want you to take her out of the prison and give her to a good family.'

'Err........I don't know Alan.'

'Please Augustin take her. Give her to a good family,' I pleaded with my hands bound as if in prayer.

With that his eyes softened. He smiled as he watched the kitten lovingly rub her cheeks and forehead onto my legs.

'Okay Alan for you I will do it.'

With a sigh of relief I exhaled. 'Thank you Augustin!'

With that he patted the cat gently on her head. He looked unsure as he continued patting. Although it wasn't her favourite way to be stroked she looked up to Augustin adoringly, whilst intermittently closing her eyes. That's it Marrakesh work your magic.

'What was her name again?'

'Marrakesh.'

'Marra...Kesh.'

'Yes.'

'Now if I take Mar...ra....kesh can you do me a little favour Alan?'

'What?' I asked in dread fearing the answer.

'Can I borrow your cow boy boots?'

'What?'

'Yeah I noticed you had a pair of cowboy boots when you were with me. Remember I asked if I could wear them and you told me to fuck off.'

'Oh yeah.'

'So can I borrow them?'

'Yeah why not.'

Thank fuck for that! Never would I have assumed he would ask me a non-sexual favour. He wasn't such a pervert after all.

Once Marrakesh was sorted I was going to leave but Augustin asked me to stay and give me the low down on what was happening in Agitado's. I felt obliged to stay a little while as he was helping me out after all. I relayed a bit of information about the patients I was keeping. I told him about the hunger strike patient we had and the little scamp Pedro who we bought out from prison. I also told him about Senen. As I talked and talked I could see he was disinterested in all my stories. When I paused his eyes flashed with excitement and he touched my shoulder. I smacked away his hand hard.

'Ow! What did you do that for?'

'Remember my rule. No touching!'

'Sorry………I was just excited because I just remembered hearing you had a transsexual on your ward.'

'Er………..Yes we do.'

'Has he got breasts?' he said biting his lip.

'Yes he has,' I said feeling uncomfortable

'May I meet with him?' he said with excited eyes.

'I don't know.'

'What about tonight?'

'No! You need too look after my cat tonight.'

'Oh okay,' he said deflated.

'You do that and prove to me she has gone to a good family and I will think about letting you see our transsexual.'

'Thanks Alan! I will look after her don't you worry!'

'You better fucking had,' I snarled whilst prodding him hard in the shoulder with my fore finger.

'Ow! No need to be so rough.'

That night I felt so alone. I couldn't get to sleep and was awake in the early hours. It was surprising how much that cat had meant to me. I am even ashamed to admit that night I shed a few tears over losing her. But despite being sad I knew I had done the right thing. I just hoped for Augustin's sake she went to a nice family.

Without Marrakesh to stroke I felt left alone with my internal voice. No more could this be clouded by her gentle purring. I began to weep more as I thought about my year in Agitado's. The deaths I had seen. The force feeding. Senen's constant requests for suicide. It was all getting too much.

In my sadness it dawned on me why Senen was down. It was awful to see Marrakesh go which is the same as him watching nurse after nurse leaving him.

But I was sure though sooner or later his mother would get him out. But then was this the right thing? Senen over and over would tell me he would kill them and then himself if he was free. Even if they tried to stop him I knew he would do it somehow. He could be a very determined sole if he put his mind to it. Maybe if he killed himself it would be better. No more would he have to suffer the troubles of his mind or the conditions of Carabanchel.

The next day on break Celistino and Pierro kept asking if I was alright. I said I was fine and that I was upset about Marrakech, but this was only partially true. Senen came up to me and said sorry to me about Marrakech but then in the next breath he asked me again to help kill him. I just shut myself off. I busied myself by putting clothes on the washing line to dry. After an hour's break they should be bone dry in the heat of the Spanish sun. For the remainder of the break I stood with my back to Senen and talked to Pierro and Celistino.

When the hour was up I wander over and took down the line and put my clothes in the bag. When I looked up I could see Senen coming over.

'Oh Senen please don't. I have had enough.'

'Okay,' he said looking down and slightly embarrassed.

'Have you noticed I am wearing clothes today?'

I had been so preoccupied with my own thoughts I hadn't noticed he wasn't wearing dungarees but a pair of jeans and T-shirt his mother had brought in.

'Senen that's amazing!' I said patting him on the arm.

I carried on putting the clothes into the bag and headed up to Agitados. Senen followed closely behind.

After midday break Senen asked if he could come into my room for a few minutes. He said he wanted to apologise for continually asking me to die. I told him he could and welcomed the daft sod with open arms. It felt strange seeing him sitting on my bed in proper clothes and without Marrakesh on his lap. Although I was sad to see my cat go I was happy to see Senen looking normal and not in his ridiculous dungarees. I wondered how long this phase of wearing clothes would last.

Without Marrakesh to pat Senen seemed ill at ease with his hands. Despite looking fidgety he seemed quite happy with himself. As if he had achieved a sort of epiphany.

'So what is behind you wearing clothes and looking happy then?'

'I want a new beginning Alan.'

'A new beginning hey,' I said beaming. 'Finally you are learning to be happy.'

Senen didn't answer and instead just broadened his grin.

Although it was only for a few minutes it was the nicest chat I had ever had with him.

He also shocked me by giving me a big hug before I left him in his room. I asked him why he did it and he said he just wanted to make me feel better for Marrakesh. He also said he was grateful for what I had done for him.

Feeling elated I went on my break. I ate my food and then headed to the back patio. For half an hour or so I wandered around and chatted to a few nurses. I was glad the conversation was light as I didn't want my good mood to be ruined.

After my break was over I went straight to Senen's room as he had an appointment to see the psychiatrist. Feeling happy I whistled bohemian Rhapsody. I opened the hatch on the door and scanned around the room but I couldn't see where he was. He wasn't curled up in a ball naked in the corner like he usually was.

Confused I opened the door to find Senen dangling. Around his neck was the rope I used as a washing line which he had tied around a pipe that jutted out. I quickly went to him and put my fingers on his neck but I couldn't find a pulse. The touch of his body was cold and his lips were dark blue.

'Fucking hell Senen!' I shouted.

Pierro and Celistino must have heard my shouts as within seconds they were in Senen's room.

'Oh Alan!' exclaimed Pierro

Celistino just shook his head and look dumbfounded.

'I have to cut him down,' I said whilst a single tear rolled down my cheek.

I began loosening the rope around his neck, but Pierro stopped me by grabbing both of my hands and looked me in dead in the face.

'Alan we can't cut him down yet we have to wait for the doctors,' he said slowly.

'No………..No……….We have to cut him down.' I shouted.

'Alan I know he was your friend but he we have to leave him for the doctors to see.'

Feeling annoyed I ripped my hands from his grip and smashed my fist in the wall.

'Alan calm down and go and get the doctors. Then we can cut him down together.'

With that I choked down my emotion. I didn't want the doctors or guards to see I was upset. I didn't want them to get suspicious. It was my rope after all he had used to kill himself with. If only I wasn't so careless. Trying to compose myself I headed off in search of a doctor and a guard.

I found a doctor and a guard quickly and they came straight away when I explained what had happened. Unlike the other two deaths the doctors seemed more shocked about Senen. I think even to the medical staff, psychologists, psychiatrists and guards Senen was just part of the furniture. They all couldn't believe he had gone.

In the room two doctors examined him. I found it hard to look at Senen's body dangling so I looked at the floor. The doctors seemed to take forever looking at his body and then at the rope and the pipes. Coldly working out how he had done it. As they took more and more time I began to get angry. It was plain to fucking see what had happened. There was no need for all this meticulous investigation. I could feel my blood boiling.

Looking at his legs once more I gasped out loud with horror. His fucking feet were touching the floor. That must have meant he held his knees up in order to strangle himself. He died from asphyxiation. Fucking hell! That was proof enough of his sheer determination to die. I can't believe he held up his legs. Oh Senen you really wanted death badly didn't you!

Eventually the doctors signed the death certificate and nodded. They suspected no foul play. Senen was ready for his place in the morgue. Pierro and I then cut him down. I put him on the stretcher but I couldn't bear to look at his face. I wanted to remember him the way he was. Quickly I covered him with a sheet so I wasn't tempted to look.

When I wheeled Senen out of the corridor I looked back to see the guard pawing the rope. Oh god! He knows it's my washing line. They are probably going to blame me.

Trying not to think about that I pushed Senen on the trolley with Pierro down the corridors. The guards had emptied the corridors to make sure we had an easy path with no patients or nurses in our way. They always wanted as little people knowing when a death occurred. Not surprisingly as it was always unsettling hearing of a patient dying, for both the nurses and the patients.

Once in the morgue I helped Pierro lift Senen onto the slab. I went to leave the room but Pierro grabbed my wrist.

'Alan?'

'What!'

'Look at Senen's face?'

'I can't man.......... I just want to get back to work.'

'Please Alan.........you will be surprised,' he asked gently.

With that I went over to Senen's husk of a body trying to retain the flood of tears that I could feel welling behind my pupils. Tentatively I walked over. I put my hand to the side of the bed to steady myself and summoned the courage to look. Then taking a deep breath I gazed at his lifeless face. I couldn't believe my eyes. Pierro was right. Looking at him did make me feel better as splayed across his chops was a smile. He looked so happy and at peace. If he didn't have blue lips you could have mistaken him for sleeping and having a delightful dream. I stroked his hair and put my hand on his face.

'Goodbye Senen,' I said as lines of tears streamed down my face.

Pierro put his arm around my shoulders but I smacked it off. I didn't want fucking sympathy. It was Senen who needed the sympathy, well him and his poor family. I was partly to blame for his death. If I hadn't have left that flaming washing line out. Maybe subconsciously I knew what I was doing. But then again maybe it was for the best. Never had I seen him looking so at peace.

'Right lets go,' I said wanting to get back on with things.

'You sure you don't want more time with him,' said Pierro softly.

'No its okay,' I croaked.

When I got back to agitado's I had a quiet word with Pierro about the rope being my washing line, but the way he didn't react I could tell he had already figured it out. I asked Pierro if I should own up but he shook his head vehemently. After mulling on it for a few minutes we both decided to say we didn't know where the rope had come from. This was decided to be the best idea as pleading ignorance they could not question us any further. We managed to grab Celistino before we had our interviews and he agreed to say the same. But it wouldn't have mattered if we hadn't have told him as Celistino didn't cotton on it was my line. Although he could have remembered during the interview so maybe telling him beforehand was a good thing.

I was the first to be interviewed, which I was glad of. I wanted it over and done with. Despite being a bit nervous I found the actual interview was alright. It was very relaxed. I didn't feel like I was on trial. The only thing that did panic me was when they asked me where I thought the rope had come from. I just shrugged, but they asked me again and said could I hazard a guess. Being put on the spot I came up with a story saying that maybe he was passed the rope through his window as at the top of his window the glass was cracked and there was a hole. I said maybe a patient lowered it down from the corridor above and he managed to pull it through. The psychologist and the psychiatrist nodded and wrote down my account.

That night Pierro, Celistino and I were on pins. We didn't know who was going to take the fall for Senen's death? I had big odds that it was on me. I thought maybe one of guards would have spotted it was my washing line as I was forever putting it up and hanging my stuff on it at break times.

To our surprise no one had a reprise. Pierro, Celistino and I all lived to see another a day in Agitado's. The next day we were still on tenterhooks though as we still thought there was time enough for us to go. We did have an inkling though that if they were going to blame one of us they would have done it by now.

Several days later Pierro was asked to leave the corridor, but it wasn't for Senen's death. His time to be released from prison had come.

Celistino and I waited in the corridor whilst Pierro scooped all his belongings into a bag. Through the banging and crinkling of bags I could hear him singing in Italian at the top of his voice. It was nice to hear someone happy in the corridor again. For the past few days it had been deathly quiet.

I was startled when the doorbell rang. I don't know why this disturbed me as I should have been used to it, I had heard it many times. Plus I knew the guards were coming soon to collect Pierro. As predicted behind the door was Pierro's chaperones.

'Oi Pierro you bastard your escorts has arrived.'

'Coming!'

With that Pierro darted out carrying two large bags. He quickly dumped them on the floor and embraced Celistino and I with vigour. He looked at us with misty eyes and shone a massive smile.

'Well..........I guess this is goodbye.'

'Yes,' I said.

Feeling uncomfortable Pierro just turned and walked towards the guard at the corridor door. Both Celistino and I waved.

'Good luck!' shouted Celistino.

I started walking back down the corridor and then headed into my room. Celistino followed. I invited him in my room and we had chat about who was going to be the head cappo now. I volunteered myself and Celistino agreed. Despite Celistino looking the more opposing figure as he was taller and stockier I still seemed to exert more authority. I think it helped as I was a bit older than him and a lot more worldly. But Celistino didn't seem to mind me taking on the role. In fact he looked relieved. I don't think ordering people about was his thing.

When I went to bed that night after Pierro left I cried. I knew it was coming as I hadn't properly had a bang out of emotion with Senen. I felt consumed with frustration of losing Senen, Pierro and Marrakesh in just a few weeks. Like with anything in life it just seemed all or nothing. Well tonight I was experiencing the 'all'.

When I eventually stopped I came to an epiphany. I decided from now on I needed to be selfish and harden up. I had to forget Senen, Pierro and the cat and concentrate on myself. If I go down no one else will bring me back up. You enter this place alone you leave it alone. Such is life!

The next morning I felt quite good. I think it was because I had reached such rock bottom last night the only possible way was up. Despite feeling quite positive the day of nursing duties was quite hard as with Pierro gone we were one man down. We called on Pedro a trusted patient to help but it was not the same. We needed another pair of sane hands.

Knackered after the nursing shift I called in Celistino into my room to chat about who we would have as replacement. Celistino was quite useless as he couldn't think of anyone who he thought could handle the ward. I think it was only Pierro he hung around with. I racked my brain thinking on who I could enlist. Then after a few moments I uttered a sentence I thought I would never dream of saying.

'Augustin would cope on this ward,' I blurted.

I couldn't believe what I had just said. I felt uncomfortable in his company after a couple of weeks and now I was wanting him to join my ward.

'Yes I think we should ask him,' smiled Celistino.

'I will go and ask the gay bastard in the morning,' I said smacking my forehead in the palm of my hand.

That night as I thought about Augustin I strangely could only think of benefits of having him around Agitado's. Firstly he was a top class nurse. Secondly he had weekend visits so he could bring stuff in for me and Celistino. Thirdly I found I could trust him. The only drawback was that he fancied me, but this wouldn't have been much of a problem as we weren't sharing a room. I could now sleep soundly.

On my break the next day I slowly ambled over to Augustin's ward. I was still a bit dubious to ask him but he was the best option, well the only option really. I mean I knew a few of the nurses in Carabanchel but only from talking with them briefly. I wanted someone who I knew was good a nurse and someone who I could get along with. And despite being a knob I did get on with Augustin. Hopefully in this case it was better the devil you know as the saying goes.

When I went over to see him he looked so pleased to see me. But when he heard what I had to ask he was ecstatic. Watching him bouncing around and flapping his wrists made me squirm. It then dawned on me that by asking him to come on the corridor may have got him thinking I liked him. Oh well any touching and I will give him a swift punch.

I left him to pack up his room and headed back to Agitado's. In the corridor I passed one of the doctors who examined Senen's body. He shone me a cold look of suspicion. I smiled and nodded but he did not reciprocate. Did he know the rope was mine? Did he think I had hanged him? Well the guilt that weighed down inside I might as well had. I carried on walking and tried to convince myself I was wrong about the way he looked at me. I shouldn't admit or react to anything until it is presented to me. Don't crack up Alan! Stay focused.

When I got back to the corridor I took the transvestite patient out of his room to take him on his afternoon appointment with the doctor for a medical. I treated him like any other patient despite him looking like a girl and having a pair of tits. I found it is easier to keep a straight face when they actually looked like women. The dodgy looking transvestites though just made me laugh.

I went into the examination room with the two doctors. I stood at the door whilst the two doctors put him on an examination table and pulled the screens round. I could hear one of the doctors say to him to strip. Then a few seconds later both the doctors fell about laughing. They must have been laughing quite hard as I could see an elbow poke through the screen as one was probably bending over holding his stomach.

Intrigued I angled my ear to listen. From the bits I managed to pick up the man had disfigured genitalia and that when he was in Amsterdam he was half way through the operation to becoming a woman. I couldn't believe it! I had never heard of such a thing. They also pointed at his boobs and had a good old laugh at those too.

I started to feel sorry for the man. The poor sod shouldn't have been laughed at, especially by the doctors of all people. They are highly trained professionals. Where was there fucking decorum? I mean I know we are prisoners but they should have shown him some decency.

Eventually his humiliation was over and he was allowed to put his clothes on and leave. As he walked out the door he hung his head in shame. I patted him on the back and give a sympathetic smile. He looked up and nodded appreciating my empathetic body language.

On the way back to Agitado's he didn't say anything. Well in fact this wasn't uncommon. He was a very quiet boy, man, man/woman. Whatever he was he was quiet!

The day went quickly again. Both Celistino and I gave a sigh of relief packing up the tea trolley with empty places. Once it was done I started wheeling it down the corridor. Then the doorbell went. I halted the trolley and awaited our new arrival. Through the doors came a very smiley Augustin.

'Hi guys! Now where do you want me!' he shouted excitedly as he bounded down the corridor carrying bags and bags of possessions. His enthusiasm made me feel even more tired.

'That cell,' I said pointing to Pierro's old room.

I watched as he excitedly opened the door and skipped in. When the door shut I looked around to Celistino with worried eyes. He returned back a wry smile. Oh fuck what have I done!

That night Celistino came into my room for a few joints and drinks. Without invitation Augustin came in and joined us. I thought after a few hours he would have settled but he seemed to get worse with his verbal diarrhea and flapping arms. Even surrounded by the cloud of cannabis smoke he didn't chill. I offered him a joint to calm him down but he wouldn't have a puff.

'So what about my cat Augustin?' I said in stern tones.

'Oh yes Marrakesh,' said Augustin trying to impress me knowing her name. 'I have given her to a gorgeous family. She will be very much loved.'

'How can I take your word on that? I have seen you Spanish in a few prisons and you string them up and eat them.'

'I have just the thing to prove to you she is alright.'

I watched as he sprung up in the air from sitting on my bed and disappeared off into the corridor. I looked at Celistino and shook my head. Celistino thought it was hilarious watching Augustin swoon over me and hang on my every word.

A few seconds later the door swung back open and he minced back in carrying a bulging envelope.

'Here!' he said excitedly whilst holding out the envelope to me.

I looked at him with suspicion and then proceeded to have a look at the envelope contents. Inside were several pictures. When I looked at them closely I could see they were of Marrakesh with different members of a family and one was with Augustin holding her outside a farm house. In some of the pictures there was a man with a girl and a boy. Then in another a woman with the two children. I assumed the man and woman were father and mother and the children were well their children.

'She has gone to them?'

'Yes!' he said with his hands clasped together like he was going to kneel down and pray.

'Thanks,' I said trying not to choke whilst putting my hands on top of his clasped hands.

This made it all worth it. Despite being annoying and constantly looking at me with come to bed eyes I could live with him in Agitado's for what he had done for me. Knowing Marrakesh was safe did bring me some comfort in what was proving to be a very difficult month.

'Can I put on your cowboy boots now?' he said dancing excitedly on the spot.

'What?'

'You said I could borrow your cowboy boots.'

'Oh......yeah............' I said looking him dead in eyes after just remembering. 'Go on then. They are under the bed.'

With excitement he dropped to the floor and scampered around on his hands and knees. Being stoned Celistino and I found it hilarious watching him struggle. Augustin seemed to appreciate the joke too as I could hear him laughing. Eventually he came back out and with speed he put my boots on. Then like a model he pranced around the room. Celistino and I sank into more laughter.

I even had tears in my eyes I was laughing so much. As I continued watching him prance around I realised I had made a good decision in picking Augustin. He did bring energy and fun into a room. This was the tonic I needed after so much doom and gloom.

Feeling comfortable now with Augustin I began talking about my day. Without thinking about it I blabbed about the transvestite being in the middle of a sex operation. Augustin eyes lit up. This was just the type of thing he loved to hear. As I started I knew I had to finish, but I could read Augustin's mind. He wanted to see him. I mean he wanted to see him when he was just a tranny, but being a boy who was now nearly a girl I could see this was right up his street. He could have the best of both worlds, well if he was truly a bisexual.

Only minutes after telling the story Augustin suddenly had to go to bed. I followed him out and watched him go into his room. Augustin hung by the door and pointed me to go back in my room but I stood firm and said I would wait. He then sighed and went in his room. I went back in my room and stood near the door listening. After a few minutes I heard Augustin's door open and then a few footsteps. Quickly I opened my door and caught Augustin in the act of going into the transsexual's cell. He looked at me with an embarrassed smile.

'You jealous Alan?'

I put my head in my hands. Only fucking Augustin could come up with that. He was the pervert for wanting to have a look at the patient's bits and then possibly wanting to shag him/her. But despite this he made me feel like I should be the one who should be ashamed.

'Look Augustin do what you want but if I hear screaming it stops!' I said pointing whilst staring sternly.

'Okay,' said Augustin sheepishly.

I propped the door open and listened out for a commotion but there was none. The man didn't scream or thrash about so I assumed it was consensual. I was glad as that was something I wouldn't want to break up. Give me a fight any day and not two men playing hide the sausage. Then after ten minutes or so I heard the squeaking of springs. Straight away I kicked my door shut and put some music on.

The next morning the he/she seemed okay. In fact he was glowing and was whistling a tune. This made me feel so sick I couldn't finish my breakfast. God the thought of them two together? Why couldn't I have not known about their rendezvous?

In fact after that night our he/she became a bit of whore. As the skinny guy who was a firm supporter of the new forces in the wild bunch gang used to take him out of the corridor in the middle of the night. I didn't clock this the first night. I just thought he was been taken to another prison or being released. Only when he came back did I become aware something was amiss. I theorised he must have taken him to his sleeping quarters for a good seeing too. But if this was true then a few of the other guards must have known too. Maybe they also had a go! The mind fucking boggles! But I didn't care as long as he/she was alright and he/she did seem fine and quite happy enough.

After a week I managed to get back into a routine again with the nursing duties. Augustin was largely to help for this. He made everything so easy and he more than pulled his weight with the patients. Then the night came and everything was blown out of the water again. I had told myself time and fucking time again not to settle, but I couldn't get myself out of this habit.

For the night shift brought a new set of guards. I didn't mind as they seemed younger, keener and more professional. I couldn't see any of this bunch wanting to shag our he/she or abuse Moroccans. The leader of the guard group came over and shook my hand. This was a good start.

'Hi! You must be Alan,' he said deadpan like a superhero.

I nodded. I was a little taken back by his knowledge. He has done his homework. I could see things were going to change around here.

'There has been a change guards.'

'I can see,' I said trying not to sound sarcastic.

'Well the first thing we want to do is search the cells.'

Yeah sure well the patients are in there, there and there,' I said whilst pointing to various cells. 'The rest are empty.'

'We will search all the cells thank you.'

'What?' I said stunned. 'Even ours?'

Celistino and Augustin must have heard me talking and came out of their cells and into the corridor.

I explained to them about the new guards and that they were going to search each room.

Once I finished explaining I watched as they went from room to room. Whilst I watched I wondered why Don Raphael the head guard of the wild bunch didn't warn me of a change of guards. Plus I was a bit unnerved as to why they were searching our rooms. I felt a bit vulnerable. I thought we were respected in the jobs we do and now we were being searched. I shook my head. I suppose we were still prisoners at the end of the day despite our roles.

When they went into my room I followed the guards in. I didn't care they were going in as I didn't have anything to hide. They can look and look if they wanted, I didn't give a fuck! But I did want to make sure they didn't nick anything or break any of my stuff.

I watched as the new Don opened my door to my prison issue cupboards. He pawed through the weapons and the drugs. He looked at me stunned as he put them on the table. I looked on confused as to why he was so shocked. It didn't dawn on me he thought they were mine.

'What are these?'

'There from the prisoners. When they come in I search them for drugs and weapons so they can't hurt themselves.'

He nodded. I think he believed me but he put them in a bag and took them away looking at me gravely. Something wasn't right here. If they were to be the new guards why weren't they friendly with me? Why were they so cold?

Later that day I had a visit from the old head guard Don Raphael.

'Hi,' I said warmly to Don Raphael.

'Err Alan I have some bad news.'

38 THE PALESTINIAN AND THE JEW

Don Raphael looked greatly upset. He looked to the floor in shame. It felt weird to see him down normally he was bounding around like the big I am. What happened to his cocky attitude?

'What's the bad news?'

'Well you are going to have to leave agitado's.'

'Why?'

'They are not happy with the drugs and weapons they found in your draw.'

'But you know they weren't mine,' I said shocked. 'You know they are things I take off the prisoners. You know that!'

'Look Alan I know that.'

'I wish I knew what they were planning and I could have warned you.'

'The change of guards was out of my hands,' he said rubbing his sweaty forehead whilst looking troubled.

'I am afraid you haven't got long. You will have to pack your things now.'

'Oh okay.'

'I am really sorry.'

With that I packed my things. I left Don Raphael standing in the corridor whilst a couple of the other guards from the crazy bunch took me away from the hospital though the many corridors of wards and then into the main prison. I was glad I didn't have chance to say goodbye to Augustin or Celistino. I hate goodbyes. I couldn't have imagined how inconsolable Augustin would have been. But there again he wouldn't have been too unhappy. He had his he/she. His needs were now being met.

In the main prison I was put into a regular cell again with no one to care for. To a place where I didn't know anyone again. Well at least I didn't have to pass Senen's old cell. I could revive myself from that misery at least.

My new cell was three to a room. It contained a bunk bed and then had a bed to the side. The normal set up in the majority of prisons I had been to. As the door slammed shut I looked at my two cell mates with a wide smile but inside my heart sank again. I just wanted to leave Spain. I had had enough. As I sat on my bed both the men looked on.

Things rushed in my mind about whether I would be allowed to leave here. Would having those weapons and drugs in my room make them increase my sentence? Did the doctors believe me about Senen? I was so tired and emotionally exhausted. I couldn't take anymore. Carabanchel please just let me go!

To take my mind off things I spoke to my two roommates. One was from Palestine whilst the other was from Israel. I know it sounds like the start of a joke but I swear it was true.

As they told me this I laughed. I couldn't believe it a Palestinian and a Jew in the same cell. I asked them how that went down. When they looked at each other I could tell they hated one another, but despite this they did seem to have some kind of camaraderie. They explained that in Carabanchel they had decided it would be best to treat each other as the same. However once back to their original countries they would think nothing of shooting one another if they met again on the battle field. Fucking madness! It had the feeling like the Christmas football event that happened in the war. I never would have thought Carabanchel could have brought two opposing nations together.

I bet that the guards knew exactly what they were doing when they put these guys together. I reckon they wanted to see them both turn on one another. However luckily for these guys they didn't do that. They just simply got on. Good for them.

Days passed and there was no talk of a reprisal. But still no talk of my release either. The not knowing was killing me but I couldn't very well ask whether the sharp pointy things and drugs they had found in my draw had decreased my chances. It would be best to leave it and not stir up any more trouble for myself.

As I was out in the courtyard trying to mind my own business a guard grunted to me to come with him to the office. Was this it? Were they now going to tell me my sentence was longer? Were they going to investigate me about Senen?

Through corridor after corridor my heart raced and adrenalin pumped. What was I going to say?

With that the door flung open. Inside were two smartly dressed men. Even before they spoke I knew they were detectives. Shit! This was serious. I sat down awaiting my questions and my trial. When they introduced themselves they were from Interpol. This flummoxed me. What the fuck were they doing getting involved in this? Surely they would want to make this a Spanish matter. Listening to them talk they sounded like they were from Denmark.

What was going on? Then after the introductions one of the detectives slapped down a picture. Confused I picked it up. In the picture was Troy's car outside a hotel in Oslo. That is where I used to go. I recognised the place. Oh shit I realised in that instant they must have got Troy and Mort.

This was very confusing. However if they were nicked why the fuck were they talking to me about it. Not wanting to give anything anyway I pointed and shook my head. I looked at the picture more pretending I didn't have a clue. I figured if I had put it straight down this would have shown pure guilt. So I studied it as if I was deliberating whilst screwing my lips and then shook my head. I then placed the picture face up on the table

'We have found Mort and Troy.'

'We know you worked together.'

'What?' I said perplexed. 'Who is Mort and Troy?'

'Your partners.'

'Partners.'

'Yes in smuggling drugs?'

'As I have said over and over I am innocent!'

The two detectives smiled.

'Do you recognise the place and car sir?'

'No sorry I don't.'

With that they seemed annoyed. It wasn't the right response and they left. As I went to my cell I felt sick. My head was whizzing around. Just as I thought I knew what was going down everything fucking changes and something new was round the corner. Interpol what the fuck!

I was glad to see the month of February arrive. In January I had seen and lost so much. I wanted a fresh month and start. It proved to be a good month as on the very first day of it one of the guards hinted that I was to be released soon. I couldn't believe it! I daren't believe it. Even after Senen's death, the guards finding weapons and drugs and not helping Interpol they still wanted to release me. I hope to god the guard was right.

The guard proved to be right as only three days later on the 4th of February at 8.30pm at night I was released onto the streets of Madrid. It was a strange feeling to leave as I had been cooped up for so long. I was a little unnerved at being able to wander so freely. After walking for a few minutes down unknown streets I managed to spot a taxi driver in the distance and hailed him over. Once he saw me he raced over with glee and wound down the window. I asked him in my fluent Spanish to take me to a hotel nearest the British Embassy. It was too late to go there now but I wanted to be near so I was ready to go there in the morning. I needed to see the consulate as he had my passport which I needed to get out of the country and money which I had put by for a ticket home.

I felt embarrassed when I pulled up and walked out to the hotel. Everyone around on the city streets looked so clean and was dressed smart. I on the other hand wore jeans, a T-shirt and prison filth. I felt wretched. Putting the embarrassment to the back of my mind I went in and booked a room. I didn't engage in eye contact with the hotelier as I didn't want to see him looking at me like an animal. When he handed the keys over I snatched them off and went in search of my room. Walking through corridor after corridor made it feel like I was in prison again, which strangely calmed me. It took a while of wandering around to find my room. I didn't want to ask any of the hotel staff or residents for directions, I was too embarrassed about dishevelled state. After much searching I eventually found my room. Once inside I threw my suitcase down and headed straight to the shower. It felt like the nicest shower I had had in years. It was clean and I was alone. Two things I had really missed over the last three and half years. I also took advantage of the free soap and shampoo at my disposal. It felt nice to smell slightly of perfume.

I went off to bed but I couldn't sleep. It was still not over as I needed to get my passport and then go. With my mind on overdrive I couldn't shut off, everything was so quiet. With that I hit the hotel bar. I had a mixture of coffees and cognac. My thinking was that the coffee would keep me awake so I don't sleep in tomorrow and the alcohol was to settle myself.

It did the trick as I managed to sleep a few hours but still awoke early. I danced to the consulates and made an appointment. This was prompt and all felt good. However when he gave me my passport he said I couldn't leave yet as I needed to get a visa. Technically as I had been in the prison system for just over three and half years I had outstayed my welcome in the country. So I need to get a visa in order to legally be on Spanish soil before leaving it. For Christ sake! He stamped in my passport something to say I had two days grace to leave the country but he warned I needed to go to the local police station to fill in paperwork and to get a visa. At the police station I spent the best part of a day there as everything seemed to take forever. Then once I eventually finished at the police station I was told to go back to the consulate again. What the fuck! Due to it being late I had to go to the consulates the next day.

I felt in my waters something was up. This can't be what happens! What are they stalling me for? Once back to the consulate the next day he drove me personally to get my tickets and my visa. He also made sure I was in the taxi on my way to the airport. What the fuck was going on why was I getting so much special treatment? But when I boarded the plane I didn't give another thought to the consulate or to Spain. I just carried on looking forward.

I took a plane to Heathrow as I wanted to spend a few days in London. I wanted to knock on a few ex-girlfriend doors and see if they were single and up for stuff. Oh god sex! Sweet pleasurable sex! I hope to god one of them is a willing.

When I walked through the plane door and down the steps I couldn't help but beam a great smile. I had finally made it back to Britain. Not long now till I was on British soil. As I headed into the airport there were several people lining up waiting for people coming off the plane. Some had bits of cardboard with names on whilst others just looked on.

In the crowd I could see two men who looked like detectives, as they were wearing suits and faces of distrust. The third guy who stood with them looked out of place as he was much younger and wore more relaxed clothes of army fatigues. All three looked straight at me. I looked behind hoping they were a welcoming committee for someone else but there was no one behind. With that I tried to walk past but one of the suits grabbed me.

The guy in the fatigues shunted the suited guy's arm away and pulled out his badge and introduced himself. The fatigues guy was from the London drugs squad. The other two suits were detectives from Pontypridd and Cardiff. In that instant I knew they didn't want me. Like Interpol in Madrid I knew they were going to hound me about Mort and Troy. The guy from Pontypridd asked me for my passport. I obliged and held it out. But he ripped it out of my hands and showed it around. They all pointed to my name. I was the one they were looking for. With that they followed me into the airport and took me to an office.

The guy in fatigues put his arm round me and whispered in my ear.

'You haven't got anything really to say to me have you?'

I smiled and said 'No.'

It seemed he had clocked me. He knew I had just been released from prison for drug smuggling and had thus far kept Troy and Mort out of it, so why was I going to risk all that and speak to them now. He seemed to be very astute and understood perfectly my predicament.

The guy from Pontypridd put my passport in his pocket. This pissed me off greatly.

'Can I have my passport back please?' I asked sternly.

'Not until you answer our questions.'

'On that passport it says it is the property of her majesty the Queen,' I shouted.

'So!'

'Well so it should be respected and kept safe.'

'Don't worry it is safe with me,' he snarled.

With that the detective in fatigues whipped the passport out of the detective's pocket and gave me back my passport. You could see he wanted to lamp him one but this was obviously a big career mistake seen as he was a higher ranking officer.

'Well I am going to go now Alan,' the guy in fatigues said.

'I will leave you with these two,' he whispered in my ears.

The two remaining suits kept asking me question after question but I said I didn't have a clue what they were on about and I had been in prison for the last few years. When they eventually gave up on questioning me they insisted on giving me a ride home. I decided not to take them to any of my London haunts as I didn't want them to get any information on Troy and

Mort. So I decided to go back with them to the valleys. It was a big trek to Wales from London. But despite having a free taxi ride home it was tainted by the fact I had to endure more endless questions.

Never again have I been back to prison and never again do I want to go, especially to ones in North Africa or Spain. It took a long while after prison to settle down into normal life. At first I tried to forget about it by not talking about what had happened. I denied many interviews regarding my story. Then after reoccurring nightmares night after night I drank myself to sleep to try and forget. For many months alcohol was my new friend. It allowed me to get used to my new found freedom.

It is only now after writing this book several decades on have I finally put to bed all the things that had happened to me. I also have to thank Susan my long standing partner for helping me to stop drowning my sorrows and to live life again. Without her and the girls I dread to think where I would have ended up.

Despite running away in my formative years I now feel at peace living in the valleys. I can now appreciate its beauty and the sleepiness of the people around. No more do I feel I need to run away. I have had enough excitement for one lifetime. Although, even if I did have hindsight I probably would do it all again! But I would have aimed not to get caught.

For more on Alan, please come visit us at…

WWW.ALANDOGSJONES.COM